THE WORLD IN
1973

The Associated Press lost through death in 1973 one of its most distinguished professionals, Relman "Pat" Morin, who won two Pulitzer Prizes in a 40-year reporting career with The Associated Press in all parts of the world. His professional skills were admired by his colleagues as much as they valued his friendship.

THE WORLD IN
1973

History as we lived it...

by the
Writers,
Photographers,
Artists and Editors
of The Associated Press

CONTENTS

Foreword

The year 1973 can best be described as a year of controversy and confusion. The news had to be assessed with particular care and handled with the special objectivity which is a characteristic of The Associated Press staff in its efforts to give a balanced account of world events.

The year was marked by the end of the controversial war in Vietnam which had seen four Associated Press men killed and 17 wounded, and it saw the development of Watergate, the resignation of Vice President Agnew, another war explode in the Middle East, an energy crisis and some of the most rapid inflation in U.S. History.

All of this required not only clear, concise and unbiased reporting, but also taxing work on the part of Associated Press specialists in many fields.

The World in 1973 attempts to summarize in an equally clear manner all that has happened.

Wes Gallagher

Wes Gallagher
President and General Manager

January 1, 1974

January

With the graves of Arlington National Cemetery stretching out in the distance, a Washington newspaper lay against an unmarked headstone proclaiming the cease-fire

After 25 Years Of War
A Cease-Fire In Vietnam

But few people were optimistic enough to believe
That the strife had really ended

THE ATMOSPHERE in the gilt ballroom of the former Majestic hotel in Paris was cold and gloomy as the historic moment arrived for the signing of the Vietnam peace treaty. Hostility crackled between the North Vietnamese and Viet Cong delegations on the one hand and Saigon's foreign minister Tran Van Lam on the other.

For all the ballyhoo surrounding the conclusion of the peace accords on Jan. 27, few were optimistic enough to believe that 25 years of war, 12 of them with the United States as a participant, had really ended. The hatreds were too deep and the fundamental issues of the struggle largely unresolved.

Foreign diplomats said they believed the best the treaty did was to give the United States an honorable way out of the conflict that had been the most divisive foreign war in this nation's history. It ended for the most part a massive military commitment by Washington. It had cost the country some $150 billion and more than 45,000 lives.

Secretary of State William P. Rogers signed his name 62 times to the various documents and protocols on behalf of the United States. Its longest war was finally terminated. The war had so divided the nation internally that many Americans were eager only to see the conflict buried.

The final document negotiated after the U.S. Air Force and Navy launched history's heaviest bombing campaign in the Christmas season of 1972 was at best a vague and ambiguous compromise. Presidential adviser Henry A. Kissinger, who negotiated the peace for the United States, said that who achieved what "depended on the relative satisfaction and therefore the relative dissatisfaction of all the parties concerned."

Entitled the Agreement on Ending the War and Restoring Peace in Vietnam, the document gave everyone something, but far less than any of the four parties had once trumpeted as minimum goals in the war. The United States agreed to quit Vietnam within 60 days with no guarantee that its South Vietnamese ally would survive. North Vietnam agreed to free more than 500 U.S. POWs and abandoned its once strident demands that South Vietnam's President Nguyen Van Thieu and "his clique" quit the government entirely and that members of the Viet Cong be given as a price for peace a major say in running the South. It seemed clear that both Saigon and the Viet Cong in the end were forced to make major concessions by their two more muscular allies.

President Nixon promised that he would seek several billion dollars to help rebuild war ravaged sections of Indochina, including North Vietnam. At least one aim of this magnanimous gesture appeared to be an attempt to burnish America's image in the world community where it had suffered some serious reverses in the final years of the war.

The flood of international criticism alternately baffled and infuriated Washington. Charges of U.S. brutality never seemed to be tempered by reports of Communist atrocities. Bombing of the North excited passions in Europe and elsewhere because civilians were often involved. The fact that the Communists had executed nearly 3,000 persons in the city of Hue alone during a brief occupation lost its impact somehow, even though most of the victims were women and children, and many were buried alive in mass graves. With the war's end even some of those abroad who had been firm friends of the United States said this country had forfeited its long-held moral leadership role in the West, possibly forever. The administration went to great pains to prove that with the Vietnam conflict over, its concern for Europe was again the top priority at the State Department and the Pentagon.

In Asia, the shock waves caused by the war and the shape of the peace treaty were perhaps more profound, particularly after Nixon's move toward friendly relations with Mainland China. Many leaders spoke privately and publicly of the need to depend less on U.S. commitments that might never be fulfilled in a crisis and to make the best diplomatic peace possible with Peking.

The pact called for an International Commission of Control and Supervision of some 1,160 members including Canadians, Indonesians, Hungarians and Poles. Canada was a member of the old International Control Commission set up under the 1964 peace accords between France and the Communists. Her experience and sense of frustration growing out of membership on that largely ineffective body led Ottawa to say it would pull out of the peace keeping role if events repeated themselves, as many forecast. Canadians emphasized they were part of a supervisory force and not a group with either the muscle or mandate to force the warring parties to halt their fighting.

Critics also were quick to point to a provision setting up a National Council of Reconciliation and Concord. The council was to be manned by the men of Saigon and the Viet Cong together with "neutralists" who would form the swing group. Such a concept was tried in Laos where it broke down decisively. In the end the Communists recognized only what they called the "true neutralists" who had broken with Neutralist Premier Souvanna Phouma and openly backed the Communist Pathet Lao.

Elections, too, were promised. But Saigon sources said there appeared to be serious doubt that either President Thieu or the Viet Cong would ever permit them to be held on an open basis. The 1964 Geneva Accord which ended the French Indochina War also promised elections. But the late President Ngo Dinh Diem refused to hold them. Washington supported Diem on the point.

A seemingly insoluble problem with the accords was determining who held what in Vietnam in terms of territory and what should be done about the vast areas where neither side exerted full control—the so-called contested areas. The government said it held areas with 90 per cent of the population. The Communists shouted that this was a lie. The problem was serious enough that renewed fighting, some within a few miles of Saigon, broke out almost immediately as the two warring parties abandoned what the United States hoped would be a fairly firm cease-fire and a turn to political struggle. Indeed within weeks the war resumed with vigor over much of the country; hardly a hopeful harbinger for the future.

After World War II, the United States moved into the international sphere and decisively set its feet on a path opposed to Communism. The feeling grew in many quarters that American might would prevail in any situation, and that the nation's policies not only were right but morally immune from challenge. It was in this mood that the country entered the Vietnam War and that Congress voted almost unanimous backing of President Johnson's Vietnam policies after the Gulf of Tonkin incident in 1964. Subtly the mood changed over the years until the war left the nation bitterly divided over Vietnam. The war is considered responsible for President Nixon's international doctrine that in the future the United States will help only those countries who prove themselves willing and able to muster their full national resources in their own defense. While bombing and naval support was kept as a possible U.S. response, the President appeared to promise the nation no more Vietnam style conflicts.

There were many in Congress, including hawks turned doves, that saw the Vietnam War as a watershed in U.S. international relations. These men, including Sen. William Fulbright, said the American effort to play world policeman was forever ended. The Arkansas Democrat, chairman of the Senate Foreign Relations Committee, led repeated unsuccessful attempts to force President Nixon to end the war that drained America of so much blood and treasure.

Backers of the President said Nixon had won the peace by applying force against the Communists, answering them in their own language. Supporters said Nixon realized that the growing American peace movement was weakening not only his mandate at home but his bargaining strength in Paris. In pursuing what he called an honorable peace in Vietnam, Nixon only repeated public and private sentiments of past administrations that he was not prepared to be the first American President to lose a war. But the peace pact made it clear the U.S. military had failed to win the conflict.

For many Americans, Vietnam will never be any more vivid than newspaper headlines and film clips on television. Less than 2 million American servicemen had combat assignments in Vietnam and for them the terror of the conflict could not fade from their dreams and daytime reveries at the mere stroke of a pen, not even with 62 strokes of a pen. The war was more a frequent series of relatively small battles in unnamed hunks of jungles, mountains and forests. There were many obscure offensives and counter offensives and a slow draining of blood for the most part rather than the climactic battles which typified World War Two. The biggest offensives that resulted

With the Arc de Triomphe in the background, Henry Kissinger and North Vietnam negotiator Le Duc Tho shook hands after their marathon discussions in Paris

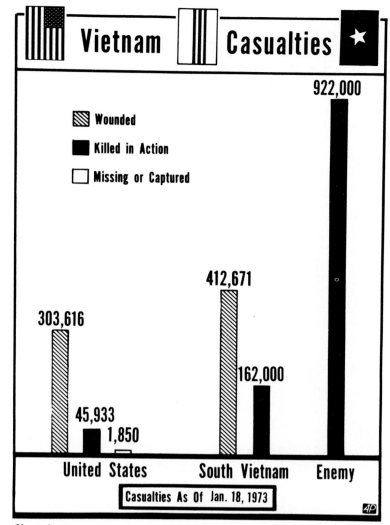

Vietnam | Casualties

- **▨ Wounded**
- **■ Killed in Action**
- **☐ Missing or Captured**

922,000

412,671

303,616

162,000

45,933

1,850

| United States | South Vietnam | Enemy |

Casualties As Of Jan. 18, 1973

Chart listing casualties sustained by three sides in the war as of Jan. 18, 1973.

in truly heavy fighting almost inevitably were launched by the enemy, which said something about the course of the war. It was the final enemy offensive—and President Nixon's decision to resume after four years wholesale bombing in the North—that probably did more than anything to bring the peace. In a "go for broke" Easter offensive last year the Communists suffered perhaps their heaviest casualties of the war and made only minimal gains. The offensive's failure, the return of American war planes to the North and pressure from Hanoi's major backers, the Soviet Union and China, broke the four-year stalemate in Paris. Hanoi had long gambled on winning the war by breaking Washington's spirit to continue. Despite mounting dissent in America and an ever growing number of doves on Capitol Hill, Nixon held firm for a peace he could interpret as acceptable, although this was short of his earlier aim of absolute security for the Saigon government.

The American phase of the quarter-century war in Indochina began in a small way. Limited American aid began reaching the French in Indochina late in that phase of the war. In fact Paris implored President Dwight D. Eisenhower to launch 7th Fleet bombers to break the siege of Dien Bien Phu, the final French military disaster in 1954. Washington ultimately refused.

After the French collapse, Eisenhower ordered an aid program set in motion to bolster Premier Ngo Dinh Diem. In October the South declared itself a republic and Diem became president.

In 1956 Eisenhower sent 350 military men to Saigon which was under far more serious pressure from religious sects and a pirate army than from the Communists.

In May of 1960, the number of U.S. military advisers was increased to 685. By year's end the total was 900. The U.S. role was much bigger now. American prestige was clearly being put on the line in the world. That fact troubled only a small segment of the American population that was caught up with the change of administrations in Washington.

In 1961 the number of American servicemen increased to 3,200. A year later the figure was 11,300 and by the time of John F. Kennedy's death in 1963, the figure is 16,732 including hundreds Kennedy described as this nation's top antiguerrilla fighters. History has yet to make a determination whether Kennedy's proportionately rapid buildup sent America past a milestone that was a point of no return or whether he contemplated keeping the U.S. role small enough that he could extricate the U.S. fighting men with a minimal loss of prestige.

In November of 1963, Vietnamese military leaders with at least tacit support from the U.S. Embassy launched a successful coup against Diem who was killed together with his brother and counselor Ngo Dinh Nu. Catholic Diem, his family and his lieutenants had by this time thoroughly alienated the Buddhist majority in Vietnam and bonzes or priests set the stage for the coup with riots and self-immolations. Some in the United States were beginning to question whether America could or should prop up a regime that was so unresponsive and unpopular. Subsequent coups and political struggles that erupted as the generals scrambled for power failed to find a truly popular government, a situation that remained to the day the peace treaty was signed.

While the power struggle occupied the generals in Saigon, the Communists made stunning gains in the countryside, at one point virtually cutting the country in two and destroying Saigon's battalions one by one in a meat grinder offensive. The feared collapse of Saigon's government led President Johnson to send in the first U.S. ground combat units. Johnson acted under the Gulf of Tonkin resolution passed by Congress the previous year after a clash between U.S. destroyers and North Vietnamese naval craft. There were quick U.S. air strikes against North Vietnam for the first time in the war.

In 1965 regular air strikes were begun against the North despite studies which said such bombing would have no decisive impact on the outcome of the war. A steady American buildup continued through the year and was not to peak until 1968 when more than 550,000 American servicemen were in Vietnam with another 35,000 serving on bomber bases in Thailand or aboard 7th Fleet ships patroling and launching air strikes from just off the Vietnamese coastline.

In 1966, political turmoil surrounding the political takeover in the South by Gen. Nguyen Cao Ky overshadowed war developments. Both Washington and Hanoi continued reinforcing their armies in the South. U.S. troop strength at year's end: 389,000. American combat deaths: 6,644.

By 1967 the war was again center stage. U.S. war planes now had authority to range over all of North Vietnam although dozens of targets were declared off limits. Hawks said they were legitimate to hit on purely military grounds, but the White House was said to fear world reaction to an all-out bombing offensive. On the ground, where once battalion size battles were the rule, regimental attacks had become common.

Tet is the most sacred of Vietnamese holidays. Technically the Buddhist New Year's Day, it also embodies rituals found on Christmas, Easter and other holidays in the West. The Communists chose 1968's Tet for their most massive attack of the war—to that point. Most major cities in the South were attacked during a cease-fire period proclaimed by both sides. Enemy commandos fought their way inside the U.S. embassy compound in Saigon, and enemy troops were not driven from the city for weeks. Two North Vietnamese divisions sur-

Right, a Vietnamese war widow cried as the bell in a Buddhist pagoda in Saigon rang in the cease-fire. Opposite page, a North Vietnamese colonel extended his hand to a South Vietnamese security guard but the latter refused to accept it

A group of American Air Force pilots and crewmen celebrated the cease-fire by tossing an airman into a trailerful of ice water

rounded a regiment of U.S. Marines and a government ranger battalion at Khe Sanh combat base just south of the Demilitarized Zone. Gen. William C. Westmoreland, the U.S. commander in Vietnam, staved off disaster at the cost of heavy U.S. casualties—some 3,000 at Khe Sanh alone. But he so severely punished the enemy side in the first push that two weaker offensives later in the year collapsed quickly. The war died down to what the U.S. command considered manageable proportions.

In Washington, the Tet offensive weakened U.S. morale from top to bottom. It was a major influence in a decision by Johnson to retire from politics and to stop bombing the North in return for the beginning of peace talks in Paris. In four years the formal talks produced nothing but polemics and propaganda.

By 1971 Washington announced that Saigon's forces had rebuilt themselves to the point they could go it alone. President Nixon decided to step up withdrawal of U.S. troops. But he also ordered U.S. forces to accompany South Vietnamese troops into Cambodia to smash previously untouched enemy border sanctuaries used to launch attacks into the South. Huge quantities of war materiel were seized. A later attack by an all-Vietnamese force into Laos, however, resulted in a near disaster as many of Saigon's best troops were routed.

By 1971 Henry A. Kissinger, the U.S. Presidential envoy, and Hanoi envoys were deep in secret negotiations on ending the war. U.S. troop pullouts in the South continued and by the end of the year only 139,000 U.S. fighting men were still in Vietnam. Thieu was reelected president in a one-man race that stirred anger both in Vietnam and the United States.

The biggest and most sophisticated enemy offensive of the war was launched at Easter time in 1972. Its failure to achieve significant gains coupled with Saigon's inability to recapture wide areas particularly south of the DMZ set the stage for the final round of secret talks between Washington and Hanoi in Paris. U.S. bombing of the North, the most intensive of the war, was halted when Kissinger returned to the United States declaring "Peace is at hand." The pronouncement turned out to be premature and the talks broke down. The United States then unleashed the mightiest aerial offensive in history over the Hanoi and Haiphong areas, and talks were resumed in January 1973. Citing progress in the sessions, Nixon again halted the bombing together with the mining of North Vietnamese ports and the shelling of the enemy's coast.

The final signing in the chilly atmosphere of the ballroom preceded by only a few hours the beginning of what was supposed to be a permanent cease-fire throughout Vietnam. The foreign ministers at the Paris conference toasted "peace and friendship" with champagne after the ceremony. But renewed upsurges of fighting proved that strokes of pens on elaborately formal documents could not dampen quickly the passions and bloodshed of a quarter century.

13

President Nixon, with his wife holding the Bible, took the oath from Chief Justice Warren Burger

President Nixon Spoke of "A New Era of Peace in the World" at His Inauguration

Richard Milhous Nixon's second inauguration wore, for the most part, the look of the first. Again he stood coatless and bareheaded in a raw winter wind beneath cheerless gray clouds. Again he placed his left hand on two family Bibles, each opened, as before, to Isaiah's adjuration to beat swords into plowshares. Again he spoke of peace, but therein lay a difference.

Four years earlier when Nixon became President, he had dwelt upon aspiration rather than accomplishment, of dedication in a time of war and turmoil "to the cause of peace among nations." This time, on a dreary Jan. 20, 1973, his words had the welcome ring of greater immediacy: "America's longest and most difficult war comes to an end."

He could not offer, on Inauguration Day, any of the particulars to prove that such a moment had, indeed, finally arrived, The nation, would have to wait a bit more for that, assured nonetheless by the President's hint that only the formalities remained.

The President, never referred directly to Vietnam or Indochina as he spoke now of the "the threshold of a new era of peace in the world." More than 20,000 Americans had died and more than $65 billion had been drained in Southeast Asia since the promise of Nixon's first campaign to get the United States out "with honor."

As Nixon took anew the 35-word presidential oath, around him were gathered most of the Capital's dignitaries and all of the pageantry that the government could muster. More than 50,000 invited guests streamed in from out of town to participate in the event. Another 200,000 public spectators lined the parade route from the Congress to the White House. A presidential inauguration is the grandest of all federal ceremonies, and Nixon's handpicked Inaugural Committee had seen to it that this one which cost $4 million was the grandest and biggest of all.

Aside from the pomp, Nixon could claim the hour as one of personal triumph. He had failed, to be sure in his hopes of undoing the Democratic majority in Congress, but his landslide

Antiwar protesters tried to haul down the flag near the Washington Monument on Inauguration Day

Domestically, too, he said, a citizen victimized by the "condescending policies of paternalism . . . can be expected to act responsibly only if he has responsibility."

"From this day forward," Nixon went on, "let each of us make a commitment in his own heart: to bear his responsibility, to do his part, to live his ideals—so that together, we can see the dawn of a new age of progress for America . . ."

Again, the President avoided all specifics, postponing until his budget message his formula for overhauling the federal bureaucracy and pruning away the "old policies that have failed." But even as he promised that the government would "learn to take less from people," he said it would "act boldly and lead boldly."

With that, the 60-year-old chief executive stepped down from the Corinthian-columned inaugural platform—fashioned at a cost of $410,000 to resemble the marble and limestone of the Capitol behind it—and went to lunch with congressional leaders before beginning the joyful, if somewhat anxious, ride down the Avenue of the Presidents.

Then came the most discordant moment of the inauguration. Despite elaborate security precautions—only invited guests were allowed onto the Capitol grounds for the swearing-in—a handful of dissidents broke through the crowds along Pennsylvania Ave., and they hurled insults and threw eggs and fruit at the President, but Nixon remained standing for the length of the ride, his head and shoulders and outstretched arms protruding well above the bubbletop of his limousine. All of the missiles proved poorly aimed, and Nixon gave no sign he had taken notice.

Not far away, at the Lincoln and Washington monuments, a far larger and more orderly group, about 25,000 strong stood vigil in protest against Nixon's war policies, particularly the December 1972 bombing of North Vietnam. That issue, coupled with the charge that the chief executive was usurping more and more congressional prerogatives, had also prompted nearly a hundred congressmen to boycott the inaugural ceremony, many of them attended instead a Leonard Bernstein-conducted "Mass in Time of War" at the National Cathedral the previous night.

But the four days of inaugural affairs, put together, in the main, by the same cadre which orchestrated the President's campaign, were hardly lacking in box-office appeal. Frank Sinatra broke his retirement, sang "Fly Me to the Moon," Bob Hope came armed with a fresh bag of one-liners, including the observation that this was "the time when Richard I becomes Richard II." Dr. Henry A. Kissinger, the President's globe-girdling foreign policy adviser, showed up at the JFK Center with Nancy Maginnes on his arm, thereby assuring another flurry of society page stories. A crush of autograph hounds brought on Kissinger's most quotable inaugural remark: "Where is everybody?"

With the President remaining at his winter compound in Key Biscayne, Fla., until inauguration eve, his wife and daughters, Tricia and Julie, joined by Mamie Eisenhower and Edward Cox, Tricia's husband—led the way through the early round of events. First on the agenda was a Thursday evening reception for Vice President Spiro T. Agnew at the Smithsonian an estimated 12,000 persons paid $10 each and waited up to two hours in line for a handshake with the No. 2 man. That turned out to be the bargain of all inaugural festivities; tickets to other events ranged up to $500. Such prices coupled with the Inaugural Committee's sales of medals and license plates and other paraphernalia, covered much of the cost.

Agnew said he would remember the inaugural for the frenzy

victory over Sen. George McGovern 75 days earlier had embossed his name on a select list of only 12 other men who had more than once been elected President of the United States.

Few could recall having seen Nixon in better spirits as he beamed and waved and danced his way through a day and night that would end, finally, back at the White House over a 3 a.m. plate of scrambled eggs.

Inaugurations, however, are most remembered for what the President has to say. And Nixon turned some memorable phrases. In one reminiscent of John F. Kennedy's inaugural speech 12 years earlier, Nixon declared: "Let each of us ask—not just what will government do for me, but what can I do for myself?"

Rarely in his first four years as President had Nixon stressed the self-reliance theme with such emphasis.

On the international front, said Nixon, "The time has passed when America will make every other nation's conflict our own, or make every other nation's future our responsibility, or presume to tell the people of other nations how to manage their own affairs."

it produced at his Shoreham Hotel living quarters, where he and his wife Judy had gathered all four children, one daughter's husband and another's fiancee for the duration.

"They were running through the apartment, borrowing things from each other and from my wife," Agnew said. "They were missing one of this or one of that . . . It was one disaster after another."

The Nixons, meanwhile, were more organized about it all, although the First Lady got unsettled for a while Jan. 19 as she was mobbed by admirers at a heritage show in the Corcoran Gallery of Art. But that night she was in a radiant mood as she walked back into the Kennedy Center—where she and Julie had attended a "Salute to the States" the night before. This time the entire family, including the President and Mrs. Eisenhower, showed up. There, the Nixons hopped between three concerts, Tricia drawing oohs with a dress that featured a fluffy feather cape, and Mrs. Nixon exclaiming after a round of rock music: "Wasn't that fun!" Mamie Eisenhower appeared the most pensive, particurlarly when she prayerfully clasped her palms while listening to the Roger Wagner Chorale sing "America the Beautiful." The President smiled all along, applauding each performance with enthusiasm even though he was unable to get the beat right when the audience was invited to keep time to "This Land is Your Land."

The next day, of course, there came the strains of the Marine Band playing "Hail to the Chief" and the earsplitting thud of cannon firing 21 salutes as Richard Nixon renewed his oath to "preserve, protect and defend" the Constitution and then made his triumphant return to the White House. Behind him came the inaugural parade, with bands and floats representing every state, including one unit from nearby Fairfax County, Va., featuring 1,776 members—in observance of the "Spirit of '76" theme set by the President.

That night, the President and Mrs. Nixon kept their promise to look in on each of five balls in their honor. Guy Lombardo and Lionel Hampton and the Serendipity Singers and some 21 other groups kept up a steady variety of music even if all of the sites were so crowded (total attendance: 30,000) that there really was little room to dance. Room or not, the tuxedoed President took his wife—glittering in a longsleeve turquoise gown—arm in arm and shoe-horned their way onto each floor, asking the bandleaders for "something in four-four time, for Four More Years" and then exulting: "Here we go!" He also entertained the frolicking Republicans with lighthearted banter about both his private and political lives, noting at one point that this was his fourth inauguration, the first two as vice president, but the first at which he dared to dance, for which he confessed little skill.

At a special Youth Ball for 18-to-30-year-olds at the Sheraton Park, the President told the girls that "If any of you would like to cut in, please do." In 10 minutes, by his account, he danced with 10 different partners. The family got to the last of the five balls, at the Museum of History and Technology, at 1 a.m., where he again joshed with patrons (who had paid up to $1,000 for an eight-seat box) and then took Pat for one last whirl to the beat of Ray Bloch's band. The song, naturally, was "Some Enchanted Evening."

A few hours later, the President arose for the crowning event of the weekend, a special Sunday worship service at the White House. There, the music of the Mormon Tabernacle Choir came in solemn contrast to the gaiety of the night before, and a weary, but still smiling Richard Nixon heard his favorite clergymen pray for the nation's unfulfilled dreams.

"Mr. President," said the Rev. Billy Graham, "I speak for the overwhelming majority of the American people when I say 'God bless you, and God bless America.'"

Nixon dancing at one of his five inaugural balls

An armored Marine helicopter hovered over the hotel as sharpshooters tried to draw a bead on the sniper

Gunfire from a New Orleans Hotel Roof Killed Seven

THE MURDEROUS ATTACK came as unexpectedly as lightning from a sunny sky. Bullets killed six men and a woman and wounded 16 other persons in downtown New Orleans. It ended when police gunners riding a Marine helicopter cut down a sniper on a hotel roof.

The gunfight paralyzed the heart of New Orleans for 24 hours and when the shooting was over it left a question which haunted police. Was there only one sniper?

"I am not going to say definitely there was only one, but the evidence is overwhelming that there was only one," Police Supt. Clarence Giarrusso reported after an exhaustive investigation of the bloody day at the 17-story Downtown Howard Johnson's Motor Lodge.

The dead sniper was Mark James Robert Essex, a thin 23-year-old Negro from Emporia, Kan., who was discharged from the Navy in 1971 for "character and behavior disorders." Essex had wound up in New Orleans drawing $49 a week from a federal antipoverty program as a vending machine repairman trainee.

He left expressions of racial hatred scrawled on his apartment walls. "My destiny lies in the bloody death of racist pigs," he wrote, with a can of spray paint.

The people who were killed would hardly be called "racist pigs." One of them, Deputy Police Supt. Louis Sirgo, once told a police fraternity that poverty breeds crime and that the status of American blacks was "the greatest sin of American society. . ."

Sirgo was one of three policemen slain by bullets presumably fired from Essex's .44-caliber magnum rifle. The others were patrolmen Phil Coleman, killed by a shot from the eighth floor of the hotel, and Paul Persigo, cut down by a shot from the 16th floor.

The first victims were Dr. Robert V. Steagall Jr., 28 of Roanoke, Va., and his bride of seven months, Elizabeth, 25. They had arrived at the hotel on a second honeymoon. Police said the next victim was Frank Schneider, an assistant hotel manager who had hurried to the 11th floor to check a report rumor that somebody was running around up there with a gun. Man-

17

Essex when he was serving in the Navy

ager Walter Collins, who went to the 10th floor to investigate the same report, was shot in a hallway and died 19 days later.

After these random killings, most of the sniper fire concentrated on police who swarmed around the hotel, located little more than a block from City Hall. Fires broke out all over the upper floors and some of them smouldered for hours. Firemen who tried to get to them were shot at. One of them, Lt. Tim Ursin, was wounded while climbing a ladder. Fire trucks equipped with long booms were moved in to hose the building with high streams of water.

Some guests at the 300-room hotel were trapped by the bewildering violence and fires but most of them fled down stairs or elevators to huddle in the lobby. Those who couldn't get out locked their doors and took refuge on balconies outside their rooms.

"We were out on the balcony because our room was filled with smoke," said Raymond Strecker, 21, of Philadelphia, Pa. "The hose from the firemen's snorkle was making a tremendous noise and there was a lot of shouting. Apparently what happened was the sniper kicked in the door of our room. He fired two shots low, right through the window. We had been sitting up a few minutes before; if we had still been sitting there when he fired he would have hit us."

A painstaking police reconstruction of the action said it all started about 11 a.m., Jan. 7. Essex—pursued by police—drove a stolen car into the Downtown Howard Johnson's parking garage, abandoned it on the fourth level and darted into the stairwell. The hotel has two emergency stairways, roof to sidewalk, one at each end of the rectangular structure. At each floor level a door opens from the inside only. After futile attempts to get in at the eighth and ninth floors, Essex ran on up to the top floor. How he got in that door isn't known. But as soon as he got in, he began setting fires, using ripped up pages of telephone books and sheets as kindling.

Police said Steagall apparently came upon Essex as he was setting fires and tried to stop him. In the struggle the physician was shot in the chest. The report said his wife, cradling her dying husband in her arms, "was executed by Essex." She was shot in the back of the head, the rifle muzzle just inches from her hair. A black, red and green "black liberation" flag was found beside the bodies.

Scrambling floor to floor, blasting open locked doors with bullets and setting fires, the police account continued, Essex killed the two hotel executives and Patrolman Coleman. The report said he made one attempt to escape, returning to the parking garage level where he left the car—only to find police there. He fired one hurried shot at them through the glass pane of a door, then raced back up the stairs.

Deputy Supt. Sirgo led a party of police up the stairwell to search for snipers and to try to rescue two officers trapped inside an elevator which stalled at the 18th floor when fire disrupted electric power. He was shot in the back and killed by a gunner above him when he reached an elbow landing between the 15th and 16th floors.

The two policemen in the elevator later wiggled out an opening in the top of it and slid down the greasy cables.

Essex went on up the stairs to the roof.

From the top floor to the roof the stairs were narrow, with three elbow turns. A structure about the size of a small room squatted on the roof above the stairwell. It opened onto the roof and, like the roof, it was made of reinforced concrete. It looked like a fortress bunker. There Essex stopped running. Police couldn't get at him from below with bullets or tear gas.

It was about 1 p.m., two hours after Essex had wheeled his stolen car into the Downtown Howard Johnson's garage.

Seven persons were dead or dying; the hotel was afire at scattered points on five floors; a 50-block area around it had been cordoned off by police due to the danger of ricocheting bullets, and nobody had any idea how many snipers were involved.

After checking out each floor, room by room, police began a frustrating waiting game.

Bullhorns were brought in to amplify pleas that the sniper or snipers surrender. The only reply was jeers and bullets.

Police sharpshooters were placed in buildings overlooking the hotel roof. They caught glimpses of their quarry inside his concrete fortress but never got a clear shot.

Supt. Giarrusso, a one-time Marine, finally called on the Marines for help. They sent a helicopter, a big "Chinook," with rotors fore and aft and a Vietnam veteran, Lt. Col. C. H. Pitman, to fly it. The chopper, which carried no guns, was to serve police as a makeshift gunship. It landed on a parking lot behind City Hall. Half a dozen police gunners, armed with AR15 automatic rifles, climbed aboard and the helicopter took off on its first pass over the hotel.

It was bad weather for it. Misting rain. The visibility ceiling had dropped to the 30th floor level and tops of the taller buildings around the city disappeared into the clouds. Dusk was falling.

An AR15 rips out a clip of small but high velocity bullets at machinegun speed. Col. Pitman held the chopper over the hotel roof and the police gunners concentrated a withering fire into the concrete structure, hoping ricochets would hit the two or three snipers believed to be inside.

The same pattern was followed on other strafing passes as dusk deepened to night. The big Marine helicopter would clatter out of the night to hover in drizzling rain, 50 feet above the hotel roof. Searchlights glared down from the chopper and the police gunners, firing their weapons until they were hot, systematically shot away chunks of concrete from the stairwell shelter.

On the eighth strafing pass over the roof, a man darted out of the concrete shelter to get a better shot at the helicopter.

"He popped out and aimed that big rifle and the guys in the chopper ripped him up," a police observer said.

The man, later identified as Essex, got off one quick shot, putting a neat hole through the helicopter just below one rotor engine. A hurried burst from the chopper's gunners struck inside the doorway into the concrete structure just as Essex whirled to dart back inside. Tracers smashing off the concrete threw a spray of phosphorous sparks. The sniper cut to his right and began to run, zig-zagging like an infantryman. Hundreds of bullets hit him. Even after the helicopter slanted away, police on surrounding buildings kept firing at the figure sprawled on the roof. Little chips of concrete jumped all around him. After a minute or so, the gunfire dwindled and died away. It was 8:50 p.m.

After that, the helicopter made more strafing passes over the hotel. Col. Pitman said the chopper received return fire. Crewmen, who went over every inch of the craft with flashlights after each flight, found new bullet holes. A sharpshooter in one of the buildings took several shots at what observers said was a shadowy figure wiggling across the roof next to a ledge.

However, in the light of the day the only figure visible on the roof was the body left over from the night before. The chopper made a test pass, hanging low over the roof. It drew no fire.

At about 2 p.m. with live national television looking on, police came cautiously up a ventilator opening onto the roof and stormed into the concrete structure. It was empty. They shot open the doors into the boiler house and the top of the elevator shaft—with a couple of men receiving superficial wounds from ricochets in the process. Those structures were empty, too.

What police did find on the roof was Essex and his .44 magnum rifle, its barrel bent and the wooden stock shattered by bullets. Eighteen .44 magnum cartridge casings ejected by the semiautomatic rifle were in the concrete structure over the stairwell. A total of 83 of the fat, powerful bullets were found in the hotel—51 of them fired and flipped out by the rifle, the others apparently dropped in reloading during Essex's frenzied scramblings. A jacket identified as belonging to Essex was found on the eighth floor. It was reversible, dark blue on one side and beige on the other.

The investigation of the sniping failed to turn up any confirmation of numerous reports that more than one sniper was in the hotel. The report said evidence, including spent bullet casings, proved that Essex was the sniper who hid in the darkness near police headquarters on New Year's Eve and fired the shot that killed a black police cadet, Alfred Harrell, as he stood silhouetted in a bright doorway. Another shot wounded Lt. Horace Perez.

Giarrusso said Essex also was the gunner who shot Patrolman Edwin Hosli in the back when he went to investigate a burglary alarm at a warehouse near police headquarters a few minutes after Harrell was killed. Hosli died in a hospital March 5.

Police could compile only a sketchy picture of Essex's movements after Hosli was shot. He fled, leaving traces of blood, having cut himself on broken glass during the break-in. He apparently never went back to his apartment but exactly where he stayed is another nagging question. At one point, he took refuge in a church in a black neighborhood. Police, summoned

Patrolman Paul Persigo leaned against a police car as he tried to spot the sniper. Minutes later the sniper killed Persigo

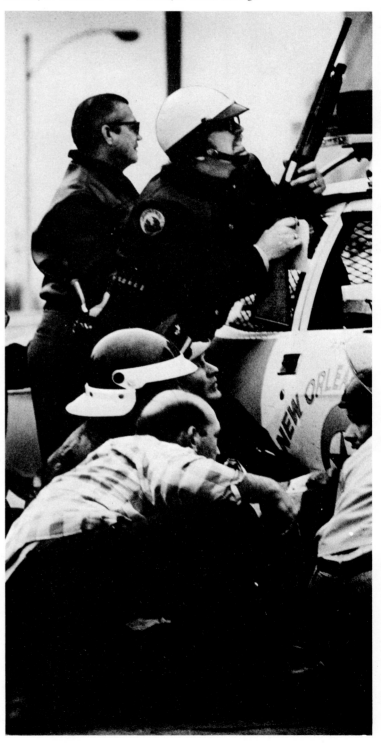

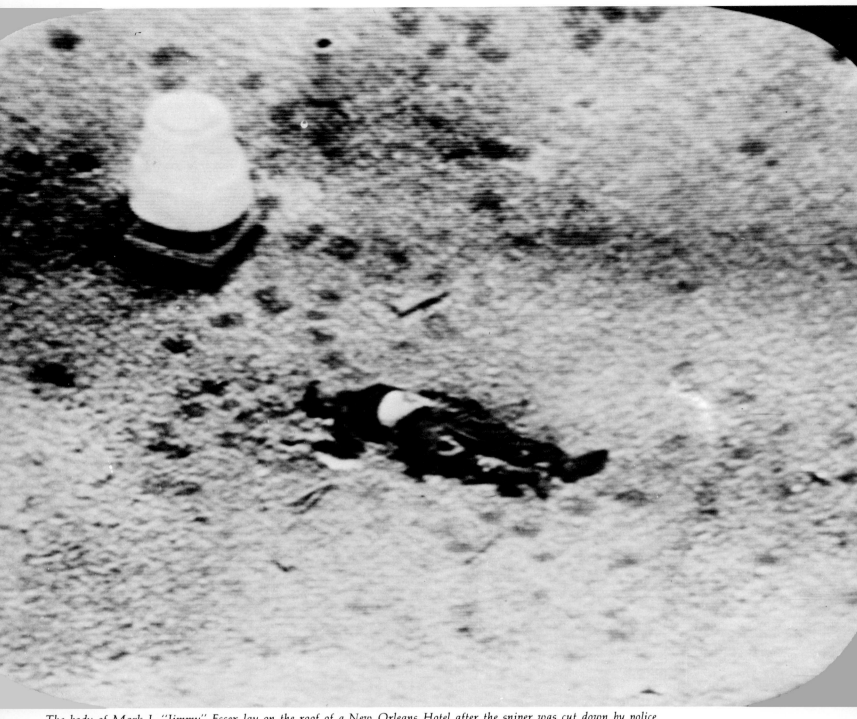

The body of Mark J. "Jimmy" Essex lay on the roof of a New Orleans Hotel after the sniper was cut down by police

to roust an intruder, found blood stains, a sack of .38-caliber cartridges and a letter addressed to the minister apologizing for the break-in. It was in Essex's handwriting.

From Jan. 3 to Jan. 7—the day of the sniper—Essex's movements could not be traced.

The police report said Essex had bought a razor and some blades at a small grocery in the neighborhood Jan. 2. He re-entered the grocery store on Sunday, Jan. 7, at 10:15 a.m., rifle in hand. He ordered the grocer, "You come here," shot him, and ran.

Police refused to discuss why Essex shot the grocer.

Essex trotted a couple of blocks, commandeered a car at gunpoint, the report said, and drove away. Police said they spotted the stolen auto a few minutes later, pursued it a short distance, lost sight of it at an intersection.

At 10:40 a.m., 25 minutes after the grocer was wounded, the stolen car was in a hit-and-run collision at another intersection. The other driver copied down the license number as Essex sped away.

Mayor Moon Landrieu described the sniping attack as "an insane criminal against the entire community." In Emporia, Essex's mother didn't agree. She said her son's terrorist attack was "a clear signal for white America to get off the seat of its pants and do something."

Lyndon Baines Johnson

President Johnson after making a TV address from the White House in 1968

Aug. 27, 1908–Jan. 22, 1973

A BRIGHT WINTER SUN beamed down on President John F. Kennedy as his motorcade moved through obviously friendly crowds on downtown Dallas streets. Then three shots rang out from a mail order rifle.

Kennedy slumped forward and in a following car a Secret Service agent threw his body in protection over that of Vice President Lyndon Baines Johnson.

Kennedy was dead and Johnson was the 36th president of the United States. The date was Nov. 22, 1963.

The assassin's bullets changed the 6-foot-3, slow-talking Texan from a highly successful career in the legislative branch to the chief executive's lonely pedestal.

For five years Johnson tried to bring peace abroad and prosperity with safety on the streets at home.

He was responsible for more civil rights legislation than any president since Abraham Lincoln, yet the riots in the ghettoes were a major problem of his administration. He sponsored and won passage of massive aid to education but college students demonstrated frequently against him.

Johnson's dreams of a "Great Society" were darkened most

Vice President Johnson with Kennedy and former Presidents Dwight D. Eisenhower and Harry S Truman after funeral for Sam Rayburn

Johnson sworn in as president aboard the presidential plane at Dallas after John F. Kennedy was assassinated

by the antiwar militants who blamed him for escalating the war in Vietnam—a war he had inherited from Presidents Kennedy and Dwight D. Eisenhower.

Finally, the man who had come to Washington as a congressmen's secretary in 1931 left in 1969 as a former president. He did not choose to run for a second term, although he won his first full term in 1964 by a landslide.

In retirement, on the banks of his beloved Pedernales River in Central Texas, Johnson spent most of his time writing his memoirs, building a memorial library to hold his presidential papers and mementoes, in making a National Historic Site of his birthplace and boyhood home and playing with his grandchildren. Illnesses became more frequent, particularly chest pains.

Johnson lay down for his usual afternoon nap on Jan. 22, 1973. Shortly afterwards nearby Secret Service agents got an emergency call. In a few minutes the 64-year-old former president was dead of a massive heart attack.

The day after Johnson's death, President Nixon announced that a cease-fire agreement had been reached for South Vietnam.

Johnson was born Aug. 27, 1908, in a frame house near Stonewall, Tex. the son of Samuel Ealy and Rebekah Baines Johnson. There is a story, that the former president liked to tell, that his father, an ex-Texas legislator, on seeing his new-born son predicted accurately: "He'll be a United States Senator some day." His mother remained one of Lyndon Johnson's driving forces throughout his life.

When Johnson finished high school at his boyhood home of Johnson City, named for his grandfather, 50 miles west of the state capital in Austin, he felt an urge to travel. He walked and hitchhiked to California. However, homesickness brought him back home in seven months, working as a laborer on highway projects in Central Texas.

He went to a state teachers college at nearby San Marcos, where he was editor of the college paper and got a certificate to teach in public schools in 1930. He taught for two years at a little country school in Cotulla and as debate coach in a Houston high school.

In 1932, came the step that started Johnson on his road to the presidency. He went to Washington as secretary of Rep. Richard Kleberg, part owner of the famous King Ranch who represented a vast South Texas district. In 1934 Johnson married Claudia Alta (Lady Bird) Taylor. A nurse said she was "pretty as a lady bird," and the name stuck.

Once in Washington, Johnson became a protege of Speaker Sam Rayburn who ruled the House longer than any other speaker. He learned quickly and made an impression on President Franklin D. Roosevelt. In 1935, Johnson was named director of the National Youth Administration for Texas.

Another opportunity came in 1937 with the death of Rep. James Buchanan, D-Tex, representing Johnson's hometown district. Johnson ran and was elected with the blessings of FDR. Lady Bird borrowed $10,000 from her father to finance the campaign.

In 1941 he tried to advance to the U.S. Senate but was defeated by former Texas Gov. W. Lee O'Daniel. Johnson spent a brief tour in the Navy then returned to the House. On an inspection tour in the southwest Pacific, Johnson was in a Navy plane attacked by Japanese air raiders. He received a Silver Star and proudly wore the ribbon in his coat lapel the rest of his life.

Johnson tried again for the Senate in 1948 and following a long controversial vote count was declared the winner over

Johnson at his Texas ranch shortly after his retirement from political life

Johnson rounding up a yearling at his ranch in 1964

23

former Texas Gov. Coke Stevenson Sr. by a margin of 87 votes out of one million cast. The race won him the nickname "Landslide Johnson."

By 1951 Johnson had collected enough political acumen to be chosen Democratic whip and when the Democrats took control of the Senate in 1954 he was made majority leader.

It was as majority leader and chief spokesman for the nation's Democrats during Eisenhower's administration, that the "Johnson treatment" became such a powerful political weapon in Congress. Even Johnson's critics admitted that his personal charm, his commanding bearing, his shrewd timing and sure political senses as a legislative persuader and compromiser amounted to a touch of genius at times.

But the 18-hour days took a toll. In 1955 he suffered his first major heart attack. "About as bad as a man can have and still live," Johnson said afterwards. The 47-year-old majority leader cut his weight from 220 to 180 pounds and eventually returned to work at full speed.

Johnson told friends that one of his proudest victories as majority leader came in 1956 when he overcame President Eisenhower's forces by a two-vote margin to put coverage of disabled persons into the Social Security system. His most memorable success was in 1957 when he piloted through the Senate the first civil rights bill in more than 80 years. Another triumph came in 1959 in the 49–46 defeat of Eisenhower's rejection of Lewis L. Strauss to be secretary of commerce.

Johnson's ambitions turned toward the presidency.

He was a favorite son candidate from Texas at the 1956 National Democratic Convention but soon swung the 56 Texas delegates votes to Adlai Stevenson, who lost a second time to Eisenhower.

In 1960, a much better financed and organized Johnson-for-president campaign was made with John B. Connally, later to become Texas governor and U.S. Secretary of Treasury, heading the national organization. Johnson's bid at the 1960 convention in Los Angeles failed when he trailed 809–409 on the first ballot vote. Then, despite protests from some of his conservative-minded Texas friends, including Rayburn, Johnson accepted Kennedy's invitation to become the vice presidential nominee. Johnson was credited with helping the Democratic ticket carry the South.

As vice president, Johnson served as Kennedy's emmisary overseas, making trips to Southeast Asia and West Berlin in 1961, to the Middle East in 1962 and to Scandinavia in 1963. He also was head of the National Aeronautics and Space Council, a member of the National Security Council and attended cabinet meetings.

Then in November, 1963, Kennedy and Johnson made a two-day political trip to Texas, largely to settle controversies between backers of Johnson and Connally and those of Kennedy.

The Johnsons were to entertain the Kennedys at the LBJ Ranch, 65 miles west of Austin, the night of Nov. 22, but the ranch party never took place.

As the Kennedy motorcade, with Johnson in the third car, completed a morning visit of downtown Dallas, the president was felled by three rifle shots that were fired from a warehouse building.

Johnson took the oath of office from Federal Dist. Judge Sarah T. Hughes in a ceremony aboard the presidential plane at the Dallas airport.

"All I have I would have given gladly not to be standing here today," Johnson told Congress five days later. He reminded them of Kennedy's resolve to "Let us begin." Johnson

Johnson stirred up a controversy when he posed for picture holding his pet beagle by the ears in 1964

said: "Today, in this moment of new resolve, I would say to all fellow Americans, let us continue."

Johnson said he intended to pursue Kennedy's legislative program and went to work immediately. Within 12 weeks the House passed the 1964 Civil Rights Act and the Senate passed the tax cut asked by Kennedy. Johnson signed the completed Civil Rights Act July 2, substantially the same bill Kennedy had wanted.

On May 22, in a talk to the University of Michigan graduates, he first proposed the "Great Society," in which big cities would be revitalized, natural resources protected and educational opportunities guaranteed for all. The "Great Society" remained his great ambition and dream throughout his life.

Aug. 5, 1964, also became a date in Johnson's career that would follow him forever. In a speech to the nation he said there had been two attacks on U.S. destroyers by North Vietnamese patrol boats in the Gulf of Tonkin. He asked, and received promptly, from Congress a resolution of full support "for all necessary action" he might need to protect U.S. forces in Southeast Asia. This resolution became the basis for all military buildup and operations in South Vietnam during Johnson's administration and even afterwards.

Johnson won election to his own four-year term Nov. 3, 1964, by the greatest vote majority ever—61 per cent of the popular vote with Sen. Barry Goldwater, R-Ariz., carrying only six states. His political sweep gave the Democratic party its largest majorities in Congress since 1936.

Johnson told Congress in 1965, when asking for powerful new voting rights legislation:

"I want to be the President who helped to end hatred among the people of all races and all regions and all parties.

"I want to be the president who helped to end war among the brothers of the earth."

But the nation was divided, frustrated and angry over the Vietnam war, troubled by racial strife and caught by inflation.

On Feb. 7, 1965, U.S. planes were ordered into action over North Vietnam after a North Vietnamese attack on a U.S. base. Escalation on both sides continued and the first regular U.S. troops were sent to South Vietnam.

In April, Johnson offered to take part in "unconditional discussions." He said: "Our objective is the independence of South Vietnam and its freedom. We will do everything necessary to reach that objective." Although 17 countries agreed to peace talks, Red China and North Vietnam declined.

On April 28, Johnson ordered 400 Marines into Santo Domingo to protect Americans caught in the Dominican Republican governmental upheaval. Some stayed as long as 17 months.

Meanwhile, Johnson finally got Congresss to approve another Kennedy aim, placing medical care for the elderly under Social Security. The Medicare bill was signed July 20, 1965.

The voting rights act was signed Aug. 5.

On Christmas, 1965, there was a 30-hour cease-fire followed by a "peace offensive," led by Pope Paul VI. It failed after two weeks of negotiations. Hanoi, Peking and Moscow denounced the efforts as a smoke screen for further escalation of the war.

In his State of the Union message, Johnson repeated that the nation should honor its commitments to South Vietnam. The President asked for almost $13 billion more to continue the war.

On Feb. 6, 1966, Johnson met with Premier Nguyen Cao Ky of South Vietnam and the two signed the "Declaration of Honolulu" pledging that each would continue their firm war stand.

American military strategy took another step June 26 when Johnson ordered U.S. jets to bomb oil depots at Hanoi and Haiphong.

Johnson made a 17-day, seven-nation tour in October, 1966, meeting with heads of all governments involved in the Vietnam fighting. He also made a surprise visit to U.S. soldiers at Cam Ranh Bay, just 50 miles from the combat Zone in South Vietnam.

The war in Southeast Asia remained dominant throughout 1967 but rioting in Negro slums became a major concern. It was the longest, hottest summer of all for Johnson. Rioting lasted for three days, July 12–14, in Newark and 27 died. The president had to send paratroopers to Detroit July 24 after 36 died in riots.

On June 23, 1967, Johnson met with Soviet Premier Alexei N. Kosygin in Glassboro, N.J., following the Israeli-Arab war. Then on Aug. 24 the United States and the Soviet Union agreed on a draft treaty to prevent further spread of nuclear weapons.

Johnson made another peace move Sept. 29 in San Antonio when he said the United States was prepared to "stop all aerial and naval bombardment" of North Vietnam if this would lead to prompt productive discussions. Hanoi rejected the proposal.

By November, 1967, there were 469,000 Americans in South Vietnam.

Johnson announced in a nationwide televised speech March 31, 1968, that "I shall not seek and I will not accept the nomination of my party as your president." He said he wanted to devote full time for the remainder of his term to ending the Vietnam War without the distractions of campaigning.

Coupled with his re-election statement was an announcement that he had ordered an end to the bombing of North Vietnam and called for peace talks. The Hanoi government said it was willing to negotiate, but it took eight months of bickering before the peace talks began.

On Jan. 20, 1969, Johnson handed over the presidency to Richard M. Nixon, and retired to his ranch in Texas.

Johnson spent his years of retirement close to the LBJ Ranch, west of Austin. Public appearances were rare.

Much of Johnson's time after retirement was spent on preparation of his written memoirs, "The Vantage Point," published in 1971.

In his broadcast memoirs, a series of TV interviews with commentator Walter Cronkite, Johnson said that he did not regret turning down a try at a second term at the Presidency. He added "there's some disappointment that the results I hoped would flow from it—namely peace in the world—have not yet come; but I'm still hopeful."

On Jan. 22, 1973, the 64-year-old former president drank a glass of cold milk and lay down for his usual afternoon nap. About 4:50 p.m. EST Johnson called the ranch switchboard and asked for his Secret Service agents. The agents appeared about two minutes later, from their quarters about 100 yards from the ranch house, with a resuscitator. Johnson was on his back by his bed, apparently dead. He was rushed the 80 miles to San Antonio where a doctor officially declared him dead.

Doctors said Johnson had suffered during his last months from both a painful intestinal inflammation and angina pectoris or sharp chest pains. Open heart surgery had been discussed, but Dr. Michael DeBakey, the heart surgeon in conjunction with three other physicians, decided that the former president's condition was too uncertain for cardiac surgery to be risked.

A few days after the funeral, Mrs. Johnson revealed that the former president died knowing that a cease-fire agreement had been reached for South Vietnam. She said her husband had been personally informed by President Nixon of the cease-fire on Jan. 19 and was in the process of preparing a statement. Nixon told the nation of the cease-fire on Jan. 23, the day after Johnson's death.

MIAMI DOWNED WASHINGTON 14-7 TO WIN SUPER BOWL VII

The heaviest pressure should have weighed on Coach Don Shula and his Miami Dolphins, winners of 16 straight games in a perfect season and three-point favorites to walk off with pro football's biggest prize. But it was George Allen, coach of the Washington Redskins, who was edgy.

"There are too many distractions," the intense, dark-haired Allen said three days before the game. "I'm having a hard time getting through to the guys. Miami has been through this before, we haven't."

Nerves, expectedly, were wearing thin. Since August—five months earlier—the beefy behemoths and the skillful touchdown artisans of the National Football League had been hammering away at each other, tearing up knee cartilages and title hopes with equal disdain. For months, millions of fans had scrounged for seating space in the big arenas and scores of millions of others had sat transfixed in front of their television screens watching the unfolding drama on zebra-striped 100-yard fields.

Now the ultimate had been reached. It was Super Bowl VII. The place was the Los Angeles Coliseum. The date was January 14. The antagonists were the champions of the National Conference, the Washington Redskins, and the winners of the American Conference, the Miami Dolphins.

Interest found its way into the White House. President Richard M. Nixon, a football player himself in his college days and the nation's No. 1 fan, wasn't averse to taking sides. "I always root for the home team," the President said, "and my home team now is Washington." Nixon entertained the Redskins in the East Room at the White House and even sneaked Allen secret plays.

The contrast in the attitudes and techniques of the rival coaches was quite marked, and the teams appeared to reflect the dispositions of their leaders. The Redskins were called "The Over the Hill Gang." Operating on the theory that "the future is now," Allen wheeled and dealed, patched and padded until he came up with a team which he regarded as capable of holding its own in the tough NFL. Many of the players were trade-ins. Some were castoffs. Most were mature veterans, weary of looking over their shoulders at fuzz-faced giants pressing from the sidelines. As pro teams go, they were a unique group, stirred to a schoolboy enthusiasm by Allen. It was a whoop and holler team.

Not so the Dolphins, honed into a confident, precision machine by Shula, a firm disciplinarian but a man of deep feeling and compassion. "We never let an error go unchallenged, " Shula said. "Uncorrected errors will multiply." Once asked if, in the interest of maintaining team morale, it might be wise to overlook a small flaw, Shula asked tartly, "What is a small flaw?"

Yet it was the stocky, jut-jawed Shula who was relaxed and coldly confident before the game and Allen who acted as if he was ready to jump out of his skin. Allen enforced strict curfews and training procedures. Shula was loose and jocular throughout the week leading to the game and his high good humor appeared to be translated to his team.

However, there was nothing in the form charts to presage anything but a close, hard-fought contest. The Redskins had handed the Dolphins their last defeat—in an exhibition game—and had twice beaten the Dallas Cowboy team that whipped the Dolphins in the Super Bowl the year before. In the playoffs, the Redskins, led by quarterback Billy Kilmer and hard-running Larry Brown, had beaten Green Bay 16-3 and Dallas 26-3, both impressive victories. The Dolphins, meanwhile, had edged Cleveland 20-14 and squeezed past Pittsburgh 21-17. The Dolphins' hopes seemed to lie largely in the rushing punch of their two 1,000-yard ball carriers, Larry Csonka and Mercury Morris, and their vaunted "No Name Defense," so-called because the defensive unit lacked big name stars although no one questioned its muscle.

When the two teams took the field, the sky was cloudless and the San Gabriel Mountains formed a backdrop to the colorful pre-game ceremonies in which the Apollo 17 Astronauts led the 81,800 fans in the Pledge of Allegiance, mortar rockets shook the stands and 1,000 pigeons soared overhead. Before the half, a California haze had settled over the Coliseum and the flashily clad athletes were barely perceptible.

It wasn't until kickoff that the identity of the Miami quarterback was known. Shula elected to go with Bob Griese, who had been sidelined for 11 games, and not Earl Morrall, the substitute who had led the Dolphins masterfully during that span.

No one got a chance to second guess the Miami one-man brain trust. Near the end of the first period, Griese directed the Dolphins on a 63-yard march to the first score. Jim Kiick picked up 11 yards in two carries. Griese rifled a pass to Paul Warfield for 18 yards. Kiick and Csonka banged to the Redskins' 28. Griese faded back, shot a pass to Howard Twilley on the five and Twilley scampered across for the score.

Midway of the second period, Griese hit Warfield with a 47-yard pass for an apparent second touchdown but the play was nullified by a penalty. Moments later, however, Nick Buoniconti, one of the No-Name boys, plucked off a Bill Kilmer pass at the Miami 41 and returned it to the Washington 27. Kiick and Csonka went to work again and, aided by a 19-yard pass from Griese to Jim Mandich, drove to a second score, Kiick going the last two yards in two punches.

Garo Yepremian, Miami's balding little place-kick specialist, made good his second conversion and the Dolphins led 14-0. It was the same Yepremian who kept the game from settling into an exercise of complete boredom. With the Redskins throttled by Miami's strong defensive play, the two teams just shoved each other around until 2:07 was left on the clock.

At that point, Yepremian came in to try for a 42-yard field goal only to have the ball bobbled. Yepremian picked up the loose ball and attempted to throw it. Washington defensive back Mike Bass grabbed the floating ball and ran 49 yards for a Redskin score. The game ended with Kilmer futilely attempting to penetrate the Dolphins' concrete defense. The game ended 14-7. The Dolphins had their 17th straight.

Griese had a great day, completing his first six passes. Csonka was the game's leading rusher with 112 yards. But the laurel wreaths were reserved for the defense—safety Jake Scott, who intercepted two passes and became the game's Most Valuable Player; tackle Manny Fernandez, who made 11 unassisted tackles, and Buoniconti, whose pass steal set up the second score.

The Dolphins, in characteristic college style, carried Shula to the dressing room on their shoulders. "This is the greatest moment of my coaching life," the Miami coach said. "We have gone unbeaten and won the big one. Nobody else has done that. Let the record speak for itself."

Miami's Larry Csonka racing through the Washington line

George Foreman walked to a neutral corner after sending Joe Frazier to the canvas

MUSLIM HEADQUARTERS WAS SCENE OF MULTIPLE MURDER

The three-story stone and brick house sitting on a tree-shaded corner in an area where many of Washington's wealthiest black families live served as the headquarters for a Muslim religious sect. It was purchased in 1971 for $78,000 by Kareem Abdul-Jabbar, 7-foot-2 Milwaukee Bucks pro basketball star.

Adul-Jabbar, formerly known as Lew Alcindor, was not in the house the afternoon of Jan. 18. But nine persons, five of them children, were when a group of black men invaded the house. When the men left shortly after entering, all of the children and two of the four adults were dead. The other two were wounded.

Police called the slayings a "systematic execution." They identified the dead as Bibi Khaalis, a 1-year-old girl; Abdullah Khaalis, a 3-year-old boy; Khadyja Khaalis, a 1-year-old girl; Abdul Tasibur Khaalis, a 2-week-old boy; Rahman Uddein Khaalis, an 11-year-old boy; Daud Khaalis, a 26-year-old man, and Abdul Nur, a 26-year-old man. They said the first four were drowned and the last three shot. Wounded were two women, Bibi Khaalis, 26, and Almina Khaalis.

Reasons for the worst mass murder in Washington history were not clear but one theory held that it resulted from a feud between two branches of Islamic adherents in the United States. One branch was led by Elijah Muhammad and the other stemmed from a breakaway faction begun by Malcolm X.

A spokesman for the Black Muslims contended that "the nation of Islam, under the guidance of the Hon. Elijah Muhammad, does not tolerate such acts. We are peaceful and taught to attack only when our peace is broken."

But a few days after the slaughter, Hamaas Abdul Khaalis, leader of an orthodox Moslem sect whose daughter, Amina, was wounded in the raid, blamed the Black Muslims for the slaying. He said the killings were in retaliation for letters he sent to the ministers of Elijah Muhammad which, he said, "exposed Elijah." He said his daughter told him that the man who wounded her said, "You should have expected this. Your father should not have written those letters."

GEORGE FOREMAN BEAT JOE FRAZIER FOR HEAVYWEIGHT CROWN

Joe Frazier climbed into a ring at Kingston, Jamaica, the night of Jan. 22 to defend the world heavyweight championship against George Foreman in what Frazier said would be his last fight until a multimillion-dollar rematch with Muhammad Ali.

At 1:35 of the second round the fight was stopped with a bleeding Frazier reeling, the victim of six knockdowns that stunned a crowd of 36,000 at the outdoor National Stadium and a worldwide television audience. The shock was not just that Foreman won but that he dominated Frazier, a solid favorite to retain the title.

Critics of Foreman had contended that although the 1968 Olympic champion was unbeaten in 37 pro fights and had scored 34 knockouts he had not fought enough world-class opponents to be able to handle the wilting pressure applied by a devastating puncher like Frazier.

But midway through the first round Foreman hurt Frazier with a right-hand punch to the body and a short time later sent the defending champion down with a right which landed just above Frazier's nose. Frazier got up almost immediately, as he did after each knockdown.

Late in the round a series of rights and a left hook to the head sent Frazier down again and left him badly dazed. Then he was knocked down for a third time as the bell sounded. The count continued, according to the rules, and reached three before Frazier climbed up and wobbled to his corner.

Frazier opened the second round with a left hook to Foreman's head. It was a last gasp, as the 6-foot-3 Foreman, who weighed 217½, smashed Frazier, 214, to the floor three more times. After rising from the last knockdown Fra-

zier reeled, his hands at his sides, blood gushing from a three-stitch cut in his lower lip. Referee Arthur Mecante of New York stared for a moment and then signaled the end.

The Sunshine Showdown, the biggest sports event in Jamaica's history, was over and a 24-year-old Job Corps trainee was the heavyweight champion of the world.

"God told me I would win," Foreman, a native of Houston who lives in Hayward, Calif., told sports writers after being carried from the ring by fans.

Both fighters scoffed at the theory that Foreman had beaten a fighter who had given too much of himself in pounding out a grueling 15-round decision over Ali on March 8, 1971 *(The World in 1971, 46.)*

"You think I was in there with a little girl," Foreman said the next day. "This man beat everybody. He went right down the line of heavyweights. He beat up on his sparring partners. He was 100 per cent fit."

Frazier said simply, "No excuses. I just got clipped."

The loss was Frazier's first in 30 fights since he turned pro after winning the Olympic heavyweight title in 1964. It was the first time two Olympic heavyweight champions fought for the world heavyweight championship.

Frazier's purse of a guaranteed $850,000 against an option of 42½ per cent of all income was the second biggest of his career, behind the $2.5 million he received for fighting Ali.

The new champion got his biggest purse, $375,000 or 20 per cent of all revenue, and found himself on the threshold of purses several times greater.

PLANE CRASH CLAIMED 176 LIVES

Boring in through fog for a landing at Nigeria's Kano Airport, the chartered Boeing 707 jetliner carried 209 persons, most of them Nigerian Moslems returning home from a pilgrimage to Mecca. As the big plane skimmed down to the runway for a landing, it suddenly crashed, then burst into flames.

Police, firemen and soldiers sped to the airport to help with rescue operations. As they worked thousands of Nigerians ringed the airfield, many wailing and shouting with grief. When the rescue operation was completed it was determined that 176 persons died in the crash while another 33 survived. The death toll equalled the worst air disaster ever involving a single plane, the crash Oct. 13, 1972, of a Soviet airliner near Moscow *(The World in 1972).*

When it crashed the four-engine plane had flown about 2,100 miles from Jidda, near Mecca, in Saudi Arabia. Mecca is the Moslems' holiest place.

BLAZING SHOOTOUT IN BROOKLYN

At 4:46 p.m. Jan. 21, a chilly, sunlit Sunday, four young black gunmen clad in camouflage uniforms, one critically wounded, abandoned their armed refuge in a bullet-riddled store in a Brooklyn slum and surrendered to police.

Their decision ended a 47-hour siege that began with an attempted robbery of the sporting goods shop. Their long holdout was marked by gunfire and the fatal shooting of a policeman.

The first break in the two-day action came four hours before the actual surrender, when nine hostages who had been held at gunpoint escaped to the roof of the three-story building by a hidden stairway unknown to the gunmen.

From then until they decided to give up, it was only a matter of waiting for the young desperadoes—who earlier had vowed in a phrase borrowed from the Moslem faith they professed to have "victory and paradise" and to "go out in a hail of bullets"—to see the futility of their stand. A force of 200 armed police backed by a tank-like armored vehicle covered them as they emerged.

"The cheapest thing we had was time," Deputy Police Commissioner Benjamin Ward said afterward, commenting on the police decision not to storm the store.

The episode began Jan. 19 when four young blacks dressed in military garb and brandishing pistols walked into John & Al Sports store in Brooklyn and announced a stickup.

Twelve customers and employes were herded by the gunmen to the rear of the store, as one employe quietly pressed a silent burglar alarm to summon police. One of the hostages was Jerry Riccio, 36, co-owner, who would lead the dramatic escape two days later. When police pulled up in front of the store the store's other owner, Samuel Rosenblum, 56, appeared at a side door with the gunmen directly behind him. "Don't shoot! Don't shoot!" shouted Rosenblum.

Within seconds, gunfire erupted. Rosenblum fled down the street and the bandits retreated into the store. In the exchange of shots, Patrolman Jose Adorno was hit in the arm and one of the gunmen in the stomach.

Hundreds of police reinforcements sped to the scene. Patrolmen took up positions behind idling radio cars and sharpshooters armed with sniper-scope rifles stationed themselves on rooftops, at windows and on elevated train tracks overlooking the store. At the height of the siege, as many as 500 policemen were on hand.

Inside the store, meanwhile, the three able-bodied gunmen found the sporting goods store provided them with an arsenal of shotguns, high-powered hunting rifles and vast quantities of ammunition.

At 6:10 p.m. another round of heavy firing broke out, and Patrolman Stephen Gilroy, 29, crouched behind a pillar of the elevated train tracks, fell mortally wounded in the head. Another patrolman, Frank Carpentier, was wounded in the leg.

For the next five hours the gunmen blasted away from inside the store, but the police held their fire under orders from their commanders.

The police brass commandeered the office of an insurance agency a few doors away from the sporting goods shop to use as an operations center. Police Commissioner Patrick V. Murphy took charge, aided by Chief Inspector Michael Codd, the department's top officer, and Donald Cawley, chief of field operations.

Police crouched behind a patrol car as they besieged a Brooklyn sporting goods store where gunmen held a group of hostages

At 8 p.m. that first night one of the hostages, Judy Malavet, 20, was released and told police one of the gunmen was "lying on the floor spitting up blood." A few hours later, another hostage, Michael Zayas, 21, was freed to bring word that the gunmen wanted food, medical supplies and a doctor.

At 9:30 p.m. tension heightened again as a tank-like police armored personnel carrier rumbled through the street, first picking up six policemen pinned down by the heavy gunfire and then rescuing 15 patrons trapped in a tavern across the street from the besieged store.

Abruptly, a police bullhorn ordered: "Come out with your hands up. If you don't, the tank is coming in on you."

The reply from the store was more gunfire, and the armored vehicle pulled back. The night wore away, broken only by the repeated pleas over the police bullhorn for the gunmen to surrender.

One of the ignored pleas came from a black clergyman. Another came from a black Muslim minister who spent five minutes inside the store with the gunmen after being brought to the door in the personnel carrier.

"This is the end, this is glory—we'll go out in a hail of bullets," the Muslim minister said the gunmen told him.

As dawn broke Jan. 20, four shots rang out from the store, the first gunfire in more than six hours. The situation remained deadlocked.

Then, at 5:15 p.m., a third hostage, Domingo Pillot, 36, was freed, and Dr. Thomas Matthew, a black neurosurgeon, went into the store to treat the wounded gunman. Matthew brought word that the gunmen were members of a Muslim sect and that they were prepared to kill the hostages.

Two hours later, Matthew returned to the store to further aid the wounded man. When he emerged, Matthew brought a letter from the gunmen which expressed the trapped men's adherence to the Muslim faith and their belief that "we have nothing to lose and victory and paradise to gain . . . our actions are an expres-

sion of our opposition to oppression. Our demand is that justice be meted out to all, and the only way of judging is by what Allah has revealed."

By daybreak Sunday, police had reopened telephone communication with the store. Over the line, police and relatives of the gunmen sought to talk them out of their position.

At 12:57 p.m., to the surprise of everyone—including the police—the nine remaining hostages appeared on the roof of the three-story building. Led by Riccio, while the gunmen were distracted by a police detail moving around in the basement of an adjoining building, the hostages had smashed a plasterboard wall, climbed a concealed flight of stairs and emerged through a skylight onto the roof.

At 4:21 p.m., a police official said the gunmen had indicated in a series of last-minute telephone conversations a willingness to give up. Minutes later, a police detail hurled a stretcher through the store's shattered front window, the first hint surrender was near. Less than a half hour later the three uninjured gunmen walked out of the battered shop into the January sunlight, one with his hands on his head and two carrying their wounded comrade on the stretcher. They placed the stretcher on the pavement, and the three unhurt men were quickly handcuffed by detectives.

The three able-bodied prisoners were taken to a police station and booked on a variety of charges, including murder and attempted robbery. They were held without bail. The wounded man was booked at a hospital, where he underwent surgery for his stomach wound.

All four men identified themselves to police by Muslim names, assumed when they converted to Islam. They were were said to be members of the Sunni Muslims, an orthodox sect. They were identified as Salih Ali Agdullah, 25, also known as Sellas Richardson; Shulab Abdulah Rahemm, 23, also known as Carry Earl Robinson; Dawud A. Ar-Raahman, 22, and Abdulah Almussudug, 22, also known as John Sullivan.

THE DAY THE POPE MET
THE CARPENTER'S DAUGHTER

"Listen, what's going on around here," Israel's premier, Golda Meir, exclaimed to an aide as they prepared to go to the Vatican. "Me, the daugher of Moshe Meibovitz, the carpenter, going to meet the Pope of the Catholics?"

"Just a minute, Golda," replied the aide, "Carpentry is a very respected profession around here."

So on Jan. 15, the carpenter's daughter had an historic audience with Paul VI; the first Vatican meeting between a head of the Roman Catholic Church and a head of the Israeli government.

It soon became apparent that the encounter between the two noted figures had not been an entirely happy one.

A Vatican communique issued after the meeting observed that the Pontiff had remained firm on his stand on the Middle East, the plight of Palestine refugees and holy places in Jerusalem.

The communique also said that the Vatican had warm relations with the Arab World and was concerned about "weak and defenseless" Palestinians who had been made homeless when Israel became a nation in 1948. Some experts viewed this as a "diplomatic slap in the face."

At a news conference called in the wake of the audience, Mrs. Meir had a few comments of her own. She declared that the subject of an international Jerusalem never came up, although a Vatican spokesman said it had. She added that Israel had no intention of administering religious places in Jerusalem.

Later, Mrs. Meir told the Israeli newspaper Maariv that the talk had not been entirely comfortable; in fact that it had been marred by moments of tension.

"I didn't like the opening at all," Mrs. Meir was quoted as saying. "The Pope said to me at the outset that he found it hard to understand how the Jewish people which should be merciful, behaves so fiercely in its own country."

Israeli Premier Golda Meir shaking hands with Pope Paul VI

"I can't stand it when we are talked to like that," Mrs. Meir reportedly said.

"I've had previous experiences of this sort, and I won't give in to anyone who begins a conversation in this way. Oh no.

"So I said to the Pope: "Your holiness . . . do you know what my earliest memory is? A pogrom in Kiev. When we were merciful and when we had no homeland and when we were weak we were led to the gas chambers."

There were positive aspects to the audience as well. Mrs. Meir recalled that the Pontiff had stated explicitly "that it is necessary to continue the dialogue between the church and Israel."

"This I unhesitatingly call an historic moment," she said.

CORONA FOUND GUILTY OF 25 SLAYINGS OF TRANSIENTS

The grisly story of mass murder which began in a dusty Yuba City, Calif., prune orchard in the spring of 1971 came to a dramatic, tearful climax on Jan. 18, 1973, in a hushed courtroom in Fairfield, Calif.

Twenty-five times, Superior Court Judge Richard E. Patton read the verdict of the jury of 10 men and two women: ". . . we find the defendant, Juan Vallejo Corona, guilty of murder in the first degree."

Jurors deliberated one week before finding Corona guilty of the hacking slayings of 25 drifters and transients whose bodies were found in May and June of 1971 *(The World in 1971, 197)* in makeshift orchard graves 100 miles northeast of San Francisco along Northern California's Feather River. In the greatest mass murder case ever brought to trial in the United States, Corona was convicted entirely on circumstantial evidence—blood stains, a tire track, unexplained comings and goings by the defendant, and a list, in Corona's handwriting, of the names of murder victims.

The 38-year-old Mexican national, who maintained his innocence throughout, sat silently through the 28-minute process of reading, affirming and recording each of the 25 guilty verdicts.

In the spectators' section of the crowded courtroom, Corona's wife, Gloria, and his four daughters sat with about a dozen other family members.

A single tear rolled down Mrs. Corona's face about the time the 15th verdict was read. She wiped it away, but it was followed by more tears.

The four-month trial had been dominated by defense attorney Richard Hawk's allegations of inconsistencies, mistakes and omissions by the prosecution.

But the verdict was not the end of the case. Juror Naomi Underwood, who had been the last holdout for acquittal, later told reporters she still had "reasonable doubt" that Corona was guilty. The 63-year-old widow also described a conversation she had with sheriff's matron Georgia Wallis the night before she changed her vote. She said the matron promised to tell her things to "ease her conscience" about convicting Corona and had said the defendant was "faking" heart attacks he had reportedly suffered since his arrest to avoid testifying.

Hawk demanded a new trial charging "jury tampering" by the matron. Patton denied the motion after a day of confusing and contradictory testimony from the two women. Several hundred Mexican-Americans demonstrated outside the courthouse, demanding a new trial with some Spanish-surnamed jurors.

It was a bizarre end to a bizarre trial. Jail sentences for contempt of court were slapped on three of the four attorneys in the case. The defense rested without calling a single witness. The judge publicly reprimanded the prosecution for botching evidence.

Bodies of victims had been misnumbered, evidence was lost and crucial pieces of evidence were mishandled, the prosecution admitted. But the prosecution's case totaled 2.3 million words of testimony from 116 witnesses and nearly 1,000 pieces of evidence—including bank deposit slips and meat market receipts bearing Corona's name found in graves.

On Feb. 5, 1973, some 621 days after his arrest, Patton sentenced Corona to serve 25 consecutive life terms in state prison—the maximum possible.

Patton specified the sentences "be served consecutively, and not concurrently." But a spokesman for the state parole board said California law recognizes no term longer than life. An inmate serving a life term is eligible for parole after seven years, but state officials said it was "unlikely" Corona would be freed that soon.

MARCOS SIGNED NEW CHARTER

After having declared martial law in The Philippines more than three months earlier, Ferdinand E. Marcos then assumed the powers of president, prime minister, legislature, and military commander-in-chief by signing into law a new constitution which allowed him to rule by decree for an indefinite period.

The new pact signed, Marcos, 55, announced the dismissal of the vice president and members of Congress and the suspension of the interim National Assembly. He added that martial law—imposed Sept. 22, 1972—would continue indefinitely but promised to work hard to restore normalcy in the country.

Marcos claimed his authority to ratify the new charter came during earlier voting in citizens' assemblies held across the land at which Filipinos were asked to raise their hands to signal approval of the president's martial law policies.

At a news conference Jan. 20, Marcos said he was not a dictator and the Filipino people would not stand for one. "Anytime the people want to change leadership they are free to do so," he said. "And if the people no longer want me to continue as president, I will step down voluntarily."

He added that his major tasks were to eliminate threats to the nation in the form of Communist insurgents, Moslem dissidents, rightist conspirators, and growing criminality. There had been bloody clashes reported between leftists and government troops and in the southern provinces Moslem rebels and government forces had exchanged gunfire on many occasions.

W. C. FIELDS WAS REMEMBERED

They celebrated a birthday in Philadelphia Jan. 29 by insulting children and kicking dogs.

Which would have pleased the man the citizens had gathered to honor since one of the many mouth-watering sayings attributed to the legendary W. C. Fields was, "Anyone who hates children and dogs can't be all bad."

Fields, who died in 1946, would have been 93 the night his fellow Philadelphians gathered at Temple University to pay him homage. They had a dog kicking contest in which contestants vied to see who could kick a stuffed toy dog the farthest. There was a Fields monologue competition in which the contestants, a woman among them, tried to imitate Fields' unique gestures and delivery.

There was an olive pitching contest in which they tried to zing olives into a martini glass from eight feet off. And there was the child-insulting contest in which the entrants got one minute to browbeat the kid. One insulter, in the Fields manner, sidled up to the youngster and remarked: "This must be the dog kicking contest. Where's the kid."

Robert I. Alotta, master of ceremonies, said the gathering was intended "to improve the city's image by commemorating one of her noted citizens."

FOR THE RECORD

DEAD. Michael James Brody Jr., the heir who offered to give away his fortune. Police said Brody shot and killed himself Jan. 27 at a home in Ashoken, N.Y. Brody, 24, drew attention in 1970 when he wrote hundreds of checks that never cleared the bank and attracted hundreds of people seeking money to his home. Brody, whose fortune came from his grandfather, John F. Jelke, the so-called "oleomargarine king," once claimed his money extended into the billions. But a lawyer who had probated the inheritance said it was $1 million, evenly divided between Brody and his sister.

SOLD. The New York Yankees baseball team, by Columbia Broadcasting System Jan. 3. CBS said it was selling the club for $10 million to a 12-man syndicate headed by Michael Burke, president of the team, and George M. Steinbrenner III of Cleveland, Ohio. The price was $3.2 million less than CBS paid for the franchise in 1964, the last year the Yankees won the American League pennant.

MARRIED. Jane Fonda, 35, and Tom Hayden, 33, in a ceremony Jan. 19 that included the singing of Vietnamese songs and the dancing of Irish jigs. The ceremony for the Oscar-winning actress and Hayden, a defendant in the Chicago 7 conspiracy trial (The World in 1972,) was attended by some 100 persons, including the actress' father, Henry Fonda.

RECALLED. 3.7 million 1971 and 1972 cars, by General Motors Corp. on Jan. 22. The autos were the firm's full-size Chevrolet, Pontiac, Buick and Oldsmobile models. GM said a shield would be installed at the car bottom to keep gravel from getting into the steering mechanism which could jam the steering. The auto firm said the condition could become a problem only if a car was "driven over loose gravel, on extremely rutted roads at speeds which caused the car to pitch excessively."

Sen. John C. Stennis, D-Miss., was shot Jan. 30 on the sidewalk in front of his Washington, D.C. home in an apparent robbery attempt. He recovered after surgery and a long period under medical care

February

For the POWs Release Meant A Surge Of Joy and Then The Problem of Adjustment

Some faced family problems after the long absence;
Most had to get used to a different world

THE WEASEL, as the commandant of the Hanoi Hilton prison camp was called by American POWs, stared impassively down on the ranks of gaunt Army, Air Force and Navy men one day in January. Peace, he said, had been signed two days earlier in Paris. The doors of the Hilton, where some downed fliers had spent almost eight years, would open. The Americans would go home at last, their role as pawns in the Vietnam War over.

Maj. Norman McDaniel of Greensboro, N.C., remembered no shouts of joy, no backslapping among the Americans. Many were too numb. Others feared Communist cameras were recording the event and their emotions would be used by the enemy propaganda machine.

The Weasel was deeply hated by the Americans. It was he who ordered the tortures, meted out beatings for minor breaches in camp discipline, provided a diet that cost many men a third of the weight they entered captivity with. The Weasel, and some of the more brutal guards, were also responsible for the deaths of POWs, for the failure to provide medical treatment to injured fliers. Some had broken limbs that had not been set.

McDaniel and other POWs recall that as the speech went on, it was the Weasel who seemed most excited about the war's end. And that night some men even felt a bit of compassion for their jailer. For the Weasel probably had been at the business of war for a quarter century. Perhaps he, too, had a family he wanted to be with, secure in the knowledge that there would be no more bombings.

Even the trip to the Hanoi's Gia Lam Airport was restrained as the busloads of POWs gradually were turned over to American delegations for the long flight home. But when the droop winged Air Force medical evacuation transports roared down the runway and broke ground, pandemonium broke out. The shoot downs, as the airmen called themselves, launched into an emotional binge that lasted for weeks and months.

It was a release of emotion that caught up virtually all of America. Hawks, doves and those indifferent toward the war joined in an outpouring of joy that some of the ex-prisoners said they found odd considering how deeply divided the nation had been over America's longest war.

Not since the return of the first astronauts from the moon had the nation rejoiced so at the return of men who had dared all for their country. Television station switchboards were flooded with calls of praise as the planes brought the POWs home. "Corny," said one POW later of the repeated references in planeside speeches to love of God and country. "Corny, but by God that's the way we felt. If Nixon hadn't hung in there tough, resumed the bombing, we might all still be there. And God, well, he was a personal friend for months and years, even for men who thought they had lost Him."

Behind the ramrod straight appearance of the POWs as they went on public display was the knowledge, reinforced by officers assigned to each planeload of the ex-POWs, that he was representing the faith and pride of the nation in and for itself. Privately, later, some men hedged. But if some felt there had been too much made of their homecoming, a fierce patriotism remained long after the welcoming ceremonies for most. "If they hadn't believed so fervently in their country and its cause, how do you suppose they could have hung on for all those months and years," a Pentagon officer involved in the return of the POWs said privately.

Through news accounts, the nation quickly got a glimpse of the ex-POWs' lives in enemy hands. But men sitting in neatly-pressed uniforms somehow could not convey the full meaning of the despair, the loneliness, the hardship and the fear of captivity. Like war itself, those who have not experienced it must live largely in ignorance of life in combat.

In all there were 562 POWs on the enemy's list. But there were 1,300 men still listed as missing in action as the American phase of the war ended in Vietnam. Some might turn up later, especially those who might have been held in Cambodia where the war went on. But the Pentagon said that these men probably were almost all dead. How they died probably will never be known, just as their bodies might never be recovered and returned to their native land for burial. Undoubtedly many were killed in aerial or ground battles. Equally certain, many died in captivity from diseases that often were not treated, the poor diet, torture and broken spirits.

Army Maj. Floyd H. Kushner, a physician who was a POW for 5½ years, said after his return: "Ten good men died in my arms, and I'm damned mad about that. It was all the result of maltreatment in South Vietnam" where he was initially held

Above, Navy Cmdr. Brian D. Woods, first American POW to set foot on United States soil after the Vietnam cease-fire. Top right, Mrs. Sue Flesher jumped into the arms of husband Maj. Hubert K. Flesher. Bottom right, Sgt. Don A. MacPhail of looked dubiously at the long hair of his brother Scott, 19. Below, as his wife held a banana split, Navy Capt. Harry T. Jenkins, a POW for seven years, ate it with gusto

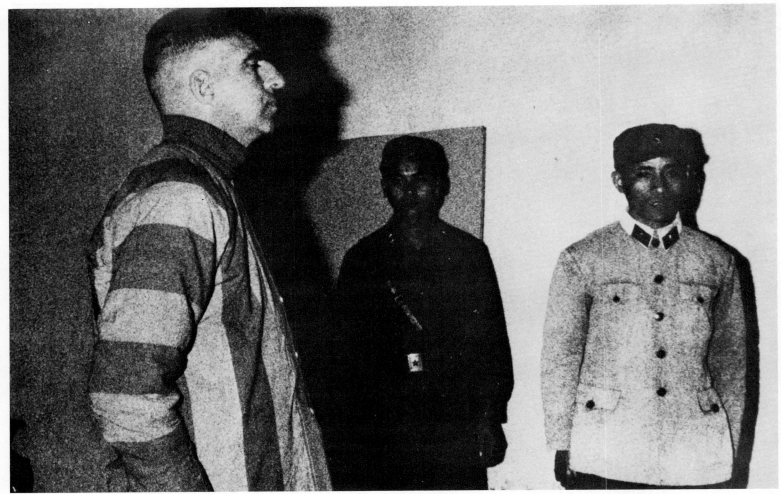

In this photo from Japan's NDN news service Navy Cmdr. Richard A. Stratton stood at attention in prison garb at a March 6, 1967 news conference

prisoner by the Viet Cong. "Our mortality rate in South Vietnam was 45 per cent. I guess there was a parallel with Japanese treatment during World War II."

The joys of homecoming were tempered for many, especially the old-timers in the prison camps. Parents had died as had brothers and sisters. Many men found they had been divorced. Others learned their wives were involved in affairs with other men. Some had had children out of the affairs. Women's liberation which burst on the American scene at the end of the decade had changed many wives who had waged their own battles with loneliness while trying to be both mother and father to their children. The joyous kisses when the men touched down at U.S. Air Force bases for reunion with their families gave way in many cases to long nights of argument over how the family affairs now would be run.

The Pentagon in anticipating the POWs return had tried to provide protective shielding for the men until they could become accustomed to life in America as it is now lived. But the re-entry process had begun years before in the Hilton and other prison camps. Recent shoot downs were grilled by the hour by men hungry for news of home. When the POWs arrived in America wide lapels, ties, and clothes colorful enough to be considered gaudy by mid 1960 standards showed up in many men's wardrobes. They were also aware of if not totally prepared for the sexual revolution in America and the fact that perhaps some of their sons and daughters might be living in communes. The drug problem, and the possibility of their children's involvement with it, also was anticipated long before the Weasel's speech.

Less well publicized were other Pentagon preparations. Some men would require months, perhaps years of care to restore their health. Some doubtlessly would require intensive psychiatric treatment. The possibility of a disproportionately high rate of alcoholism also has been taken into account. The years of captivity cannot be shed from the mind as easily as the striped prison garb from the body.

Many of the captives, especially those lost early in the air war over North Vietnam, spent months and even years in solitary confinement. Some men stood it well, some badly. Some broke down and died. Men composed long letters to their wives that they could never send. At first no letters were permitted in or out of the Hilton and other camps. Finally in the North the men were permitted one letter a month, all the words they could write on six lines of narrow tablet paper. Near the end of their ordeal, the lineage was jumped to seven. In the South many men were unable to send or receive any letters at all.

God became a very personal friend to many of the prisoners, even men who had left behind their religious traditions over the years. The Weasel for some reason appeared highly suspicious of the Bible and allowed men use of it only on special religious holidays. Maj. McDaniel and others memorized as much of the Book as possible during those periods and later wrote down what they remembered when they were allowed pencil and paper. The bootlegged Bible grew to impressive proportions and finally was smuggled back to the United States.

Boredom and a feeling that the war might go on forever

Cmdr. Stratton after his release held out his arms to show scars which he said were caused by beatings and torture

U.S. Navy Capt. Jeremiah Denton demonstrating torture techniques "The cuffs and shackles"

were harder enemies of the POWs than the guards who dealt out torture and beatings. The Communist Command continually referred to the fliers in the North as war criminals and swore to try men who did not show a so-called proper attitude in camp. Many men pretended such attitudes as long as it did not hurt any of their comrades. Some made radio broadcasts calling for the war's end. Some recanted after their release, saying they were forced to make the broadcasts. Some said the statements reflected their true feelings. The war, and especially the way the Pentagon was fighting it, resulted in many heated arguments. Although the prisoners maintained reasonably tight discipline over themselves as the best way to preserve their sanity and physical well being, some chose to go their own way. One senior U.S. officer said after his release he would do everything in his power to bring to justice some 20 POWs who he said had openly curried favor with the enemy in return for better treatment and more privileges.

Treatment of POWs in the South at the hands of the Viet Cong generally was far rougher than that in the North.

Maj. Kushner, who was transferred from a VC prison camp to one in Hanoi, said: "I was damn glad to get to North Vietnam, to get to a jail. I thought it was splendid there." Capt. George Wanat Jr. told of being chained in a cage for five months. As further punishment the VC had taken away his mosquito netting. "I'd kill those bastards if I ever saw them again."

Some of the guards at the Hanoi Hilton bordered on the friendly. One told a POW that the food the prisoners were getting there was superior to what regular army soliders were

receiving and that the latter were angry about the situation.

Some, particularly those in the antiwar movement, were taken aback at the POW's strong defense of their government and President for America's role in the war. There were suggestions of Pentagon brainwashing and the like. But in interviews many POWs said the big debate over the war was whether it was being pursued vigorously enough, not whether it was right. Most of the men in the Hilton were military career men, trained to accept war and peace decisions from their superiors without question. Many were not bitter about having such huge chunks torn from their lives.

"We knew that flying pay and combat pay were for taking chances. If you don't turn in your wings, then you know your life is at stake every time you get into a cockpit," said one captain.

Some men saw a deeper significance to their ordeal than their own personal lives and what had happened to them. One told a news conference in Washington that he hoped the homecoming of the POWs would help the country heal the wounds caused by the fighting between hawks and doves. Certainly the men who survived presented moving testimony to the endurance of the human spirit in adversity.

There was some bitterness among Vietnam veterans, thousands of whom had suffered permanent disability in the war. There were no letters from the President to these men, no keys to the city, no bands. And years after their return there were too few jobs. Some in the Veterans Administration saw the contrast in the enormous outpouring for the POWs and the nation's relatively ho-hum attitude to returning vets as a new wedge separating the young ex-servicemen from the mainstream of the national life. Many veterans' hospitals have virtually segregated wards to keep the young ex-GIs away from the vets of older wars who are openly contemptuous of the younger men's long hair and penchant for way out life styles.

But at last peace brought them all home. But hundreds of American pilots were still involved in massive air raids in Cambodia where they risked being shot down and becoming new pawns in an Indochina War that for all the legal documents signed in Paris in January refused to go away.

International money dealers came to grips with another day of crisis in Frankfurt, Germany

World's Monetary System Came Down Like a House of Cards

ON MARCH 12, 1973, after five years of partial collapses and patchwork repairs, the world's monetary system finally came down like a house of cards.

The system, set up at Bretton Woods, N.H., in 1944, before the end of World War II, had ensured an unprecedented three decades of postwar recovery and economic growth around the globe. Its twin pillars were the American dollar and gold, and it fell when the erosion of international confidence undermined the once-mighty dollar.

Its end left the world on the threshold of a new monetary era, with a sense of trepidation and uncertainty, amid fears of a return to the chaotic exchange rates, shrinking world trade and global depression of the 1930s.

The end came at emergency meetings in Brussels and Paris in which the countries of Western Europe cut their currencies loose from the American dollar, just as Washington had previously cut the dollar loose from gold. The European decision, West German Finance Minister Helmut Schmidt declared, marked "the end of the Bretton Woods era." The world was now adrift in a sea of floating exchange rates with no common anchor.

What led up to it was the biggest dollar-dumping operation in history. For more than a week in February the world's big-time foreign currency operators had stacked up billion dollar bets against the U.S. dollar—mostly with the West German Central Bank. On Monday Feb. 12, 1973, they suddenly cashed in.

At 10:30 p.m. in Washington—after a day in which foreign exchanges were shut tight around the globe—U.S. Secretary of the Treasury George P. Shultz announced the dollar would be devalued 10 per cent against gold. Those who had bet against the greenback were an estimated $500 million ahead on the announcement.

For the average American it meant he was an immediate loser. Foreign vacations, imported Volkswagens, French wines and other things from abroad all would cost him more. For the United States it meant—hopefully—more sales of cheaper American goods abroad, and the end of a chronic deficit in its accounts with the rest of the world. But that would take time.

For the battered U.S. currency it was the second devaluation in a little more than a year—and within three weeks it would be in trouble yet again. Only 14 months before, on Dec. 18, 1971, the U.S. had agreed with other major economic powers at a meeting at the Smithsonian Institution in Washington to cut the dollar's value by 7.89 per cent (*The World in 1971, 230*). This agreement had been hailed at the time by President Nixon, whose administration favored devaluation, as "the most significant monetary agreement in the history of the world." It cut the official value of the shrinking greenback to $38 per Troy ounce of gold, and then the Feb. 12 devaluation clipped it further to $42.44 an ounce—by then a merely theoretical price since Nixon had declared the dollar totally inconvertible into gold on Aug. 15, 1971.

For 38 years before this turmoil the dollar had held rock-steady at $35 an ounce, and for 27 of those years it had been the gold-backed standard against which all other currencies were measured. As a prominent American foreign exchange brokerage house commented, the first half of the 20th century saw the rise of the U.S. dollar, the second half "sees its decline and may yet see its fall."

The United States emerged from the depressed 1930s and World War II in 1945 as the richest and most powerful nation on earth. Most of the world's gold was buried in its vaults at Fort Knox. The United States was the great creditor of the globe, financing the recovery of war-torn Europe, dispensing foreign aid to undeveloped countries, maintaining troops abroad to defend its allies against Communist expansion.

Its currency, under the 1944 Bretton Woods agreement, was declared freely convertible into gold—so that other nations were guaranteed an ounce of the precious metal for every greenback they wanted to trade in at any time. Their own currencies were pegged to the dollar at fixed parity rates. In a world ravaged by war and hungry for dollars, American corporations made the most of their opportunities to export capital and establish themselves in foreign lands. By the early 1950's all this was beginning to show up in chronic U.S. balance of payments deficits. The United States was living beyond its means in the world.

In 1971 another danger signal flashed. The United States suffered a deficit in its foreign trade balance—its first in the 20th Century. The balance of payments that year (including capital movements, foreign military expenditures and other fund transfers as well as foreign trading) showed a deficit of $30.5 billion, nearly three times the record deficit of 1970.

Domestic problems also played a part in the drain of dollar funds abroad. The Federal Reserve—the U.S. central banking system—imposed interest rate limitations on savings and time deposits in American commercial banks, mainly to protect savings banks and savings and loans associations from their competition. Owners of funds in the United States were thus tempted to send their money abroad to countries where they could earn higher interest rates than at home. The outflow fed a large and growing pool of expatriate dollars, the so-called Eurodollar market, which grew by the billions year after year. In 1963 President John F. Kennedy attempted to cut off the outflow by means of the Interest Equalization Tax, which levied a percentage charge on dollars invested abroad. No matter what was done to stop it, however, the pile of dollars overseas kept on growing. By March 1973, according to a government estimate, foreign central banks were holding $70 to $80 billion in American currency while private owners abroad held another $20 billion.

This enormous hoard of $90 billion to $100 billion abroad was "a source of concern to the government," Under Secretary of the Treasury Paul Volcker told Congress March 7. The only way to get it back home, he pointed out, was by achieving a balance of payments surplus so that more dollars flowed into the country than flowed out. By this time the Bretton Woods system was coming apart piece by piece. Washington, its gold stock dwindling to $10 billion, was no longer able to honor its 1944 commitment to redeem paper dollars for gold to all comers, since it would have been swamped by the nearly $100 billion in foreign hands.

The U.S. Government backed out of this obligation by stages. In 1968 Washington announced it could no longer supply gold to hold the price down at $35 an ounce on the world's free markets, where private buyers then pushed the price as high as $42.60 that year. Washington then made a gentleman's agreement with other nations, whose central banks agreed not to push their claims against the American gold stock.

Finally, on Aug. 15, 1971, the gold window was slammed shut: Nixon announced dollars no longer were convertible into gold for anyone, not even foreign central banks. The twin pillars of the world monetary system thus were separated and each now stood alone. The outcome was predictable from previous examples of unbacked paper currencies in the history of the world: gold went up and the paper dollar went down. Cut loose from its rigid price control (the U.S. Government guarantee to sell gold at $35 an ounce), the precious metal rose constantly on the world's free markets, hitting a peak of $95 on Feb. 23, 1973. The dollar—with nothing to back it now but Washington's restraint in printing more bills—sank steadily as foreign confidence in the greenback declined and the foreign deficit mounted.

On Dec. 18, 1971, the dollar buckled under the pressure and was devalued 7.89 per cent by agreement with other nations at the Smithsonian conference. The devaluation was designed to reverse America's foreign trade deficit by making its exports cheaper on world markets and foreign imports dearer on the United States market. The immediate effect was the reverse. The 1972 trade balance was $6.8 billion in the red, nearly three times the 1971 deficit of $2.7 billion. The reasons were not far to seek. In some cases foreign trade barriers made any increase at all in United States exports impossible, no matter what the devaluation. As New York's Morgan Guaranty Trust Co. pointed out, the European Economic Community (EEC) nations kept out American farm goods by applying variable duty barriers "which are fixed at whatever height is needed to prevent farm imports rising above levels EEC officials find acceptable" to protect their own farmers. Against such barriers, no dollar devaluation could ever increase American farm exports, which totaled about $9 billion yearly, including $2.5 billion to the EEC.

Only international negotiations to dismantle trade barriers could solve this aspect of the dollar problem, and no really basic discussion of the question was scheduled until September 1973 at a meeting of the United States and other major non-Communist nations participating in the General Agreement on Tariffs and Trade (GATT), at a conference planned for Geneva, Switzerland. Some exports, furthermore, required time to benefit from currency devaluation because foreign buyers plan far ahead on large items such as airplanes, computers or industrial machinery. And some of these items are not particularly sensitive to price changes anyway. There also was the unfortunate fact that the same volume of imports cost more in devalued dollars than they did before, while the same volume of American exports brought in less foreign currency than previously. The net result of all this was that U.S. exports did increase 14 per cent in 1972, but imports rose even more, by 22 per cent, and the nation was even deeper in the red.

The United States thus did not have time to get through the perverse effects of the 1971 devaluation when it was hit again

Bank of Tokyo clerk stood in front of a board bearing foreign exchange quotes

The second dollar devaluation crisis itself finally was triggered by events abroad. On Jan. 21, 1973, the Italian Government, plagued by a flight of capital from the country, imposed a two-tier system for the lira, with a free market exchange rate for capital transactions. Speculators then took funds out of Italy, changed into dollars and sold the dollars for Swiss francs. The Swiss Central Bank bought up about $200 million but then decided to give up supporting the dollar with its purchases, and on Jan. 23 it allowed the Swiss franc to float. Dollar owners then wondered whether the American currency would be supported by other European central banks, and the storm broke. As dollar holders around the world tried to dump the greenbacks they no longer had any faith in, foreign central banks found themselves obliged to buy up $9 billion in the last days of January and the first nine days of February 1973. West Germany alone took in $6 billion, Japan $1.5 billion.

Even under the disintegrating Bretton Woods agreement, the U.S. government was not obliged to support the value of its own currency against others. Washington did not do so, and in fact positively desired devaluation. As Hendrik S. Houthakker, one-time member of President Nixon's Council of Economic Advisers, explained: American policy, "first formulated by a Republican pre-election task force in 1968 . . . was aimed at forcing a depreciation of our overvalued dollar. At that time there was no possibility of devaluing the dollar unilaterally, since several other countries had made clear they would devalue by an equal amount, thus nullifying our move. These countries therefore had to be persuaded by a continuing accumulation of inconvertible dollar balances. It was not an easy policy to carry through; for one thing it could not be publicly explained and therefore was widely misunderstood. It put a considerable strain on the international monetary system, and even so results were slow in coming.

The results had now come. As the crisis deepened, Washington dispatched Volcker on a 30,000 mile secret mission to inquire whether other nations would now accept another de-

Arthur Burns, left, chairman of the Federal Reserve Board, and Herbert Stein, chairman of the Council of Economic Advisers, heard the dollar had been devalued.

by the 1973 devaluation, which in turn could be expected to have similar perverse effects before the positive results came through. One prominent bank economist estimated consequently that 1973 would hand the United States another foreign trade deficit of about $5 billion and that the country, gripped by a self-perpetuating crisis, would not get into the black with the rest of the world until 1975.

Meanwhile other nations found themselves obligated by the Smithsonian agreement to buy up dollars—inconvertible now into gold—whenever the United States had a balance of payments deficit. One of the dollar's major problems was the huge trade deficit with Japan. In 1972 Japan exported about $9 billion worth of goods to the United States and imported only $5 billion worth of American products, gaining a surplus of $4 billion—despite the Smithsonian devaluation. By the end of 1972 it was becoming increasingly evident the U.S. would be running a balance of payments deficit for the foreseeable future, that little progress was being made on monetary reform or international trade negotiations which would stanch the outflow of dollars, and the run on American currency then began in earnest.

valuation. The position of the foreign central banks being untenable any further, the reaction was favorable. On Feb. 12, the dollar was formally devalued for the second time.

Who were the owners of such vast funds that they could bring down the currency of the world's mightiest nation twice in 14 months no matter what the central banks of other nations did to prop it up? According to Volcker, "the speculative potential of the enormous dollar holdings of the Arab oil-producing countries probably was a factor." Finance officials of Kuwait, Saudi Arabia, Iraq and Libya revealed they had taken steps to avoid losses from the dollar devaluation. Libya alone had $2.8 billion in foreign exchange in its official reserves, and Saudi Arabia $2.3 billion, as 1973 began.

The Middle East oil nations were acquiring wealth at such a rate from their petroleum exports that one New York bank estimated they might pile up $100 billion in reserves by 1985. In early 1973 the reserves of the entire world were only about $150 billion. A New York financial magazine warned that by 1980 the stability of the dollar, the pound sterling or the yen could depend on "the whim of the Saud family" in Saudi Arabia, whose oil income would pile up to $30 billion by then.

For U.S. labor leaders the major villains in the dollar's decline were the U.S. multinational companies. Andrew Biemiller of the AFL-CIO told Congress in March that through their foreign exchange speculations these companies "put profits ahead of patriotism, selling their country's currency to make swift profits for themselves."

The Department of Commerce estimated in December 1972 that 300 American multinational companies alone were selling goods outside the nation to the tune of $100 billion a year. This enormous and growing income was a major factor in foreign exchange markets as company executives decided whether to make use of their funds in one country, transfer them to another, or bring some of them home. A Tariff Commission study concluded, in fact, that multinational corporations controlled such enormous sums of money that they could cause a currency crisis no matter what any of the world's central banks did to prevent it. Also, according to one American banker's estimate, about $30 billion to $50 billion held by foreign central banks were in excess of what they needed for their transactions and to maintain liquidity. These mobile billions also exposed the dollar to huge short-term speculative movements whenever confidence waned in the American currency.

By this time, after two devaluations of the world's major trading currency, confidence in all paper currencies was fading, and the great flight into gold speeded up.

Only 11 days after its second formal devaluation, the dollar plunged to its new floor level in half an hour of panic selling as European foreign exchanges opened, and the price of gold soared to a record $95 an ounce. In Paris, a gold market official said everyone was buying gold, Arab oil nations, Americans, Frenchmen, "anyone who feels the dollar's present gold value is unrealistic." In two weeks they had driven the gold price up $27 an ounce, from $68 at the time of the devaluation.

As the renewed speculative attack mounted in Europe, Nixon assured the world "there will not be another devaluation." Asserting that the dollar was "a good bet in world markets", the President admitted, however, that "we can do nothing" to bring the speculators under control. "All we can do," he said, "is keep our dollar as sound as we can, our economy as sound as we can."

Meanwhile the U.S. Labor Department was reporting that American wholesale prices were rising at an annual rate of 13.2 per cent in January after a 19 per cent annual rate in December

1972, the sharpest monthly increase in 22 years. Even Herbert Stein, chairman of the President's Council of Economic Advisers, was forced to admit the rate of increase was "inconsistent with the nation's anti-inflationary goals."

On March 1, West German Chancellor Willy Brandt and British Prime Minister Edward Heath met in Bonn and let it be known that one of the main subjects discussed was "monetary cooperation." Interpreted as a hint of a possible joint float of European currencies against the dollar, this added more fuel to the speculative fire. That same day a new monetary crisis swept across European financial centers. European central banks bought up about $3.5 billion to support the value of the currency as a flood of dollars was dumped on the market. The main target was West Germany, whose mark was considered a prime candidate for upward revaluation. The German Central Bank was forced to mop up about $2.7 billion to maintain the mark at its agreed parity of 2.8350 per dollar. The Dutch Central Bank bought $600 million after taking in $150 million Feb. 28, the French and Belgian Central Banks absorbed more than $100 million each. By this time German Central Bank officials were convinced that purely monetary measures of revaluation or devaluation were no longer sufficient to deal with the recurrent crises, and closed down the official exchange.

Since the beginning of 1973 the West German Central Bank had taken in about $7.7 billion it had no desire for, and which furthermore were fuelling inflation in Germany as the Bonn government issued new marks to pay for the incoming greenbacks. By March 9, with foreign exchange operations paralyzed around the globe since the beginning of the month, there was a new sense of urgency in the air. In Paris, French Finance Minister Valery Giscard d'Estaing warned an emergency meeting of the non-Communist world's 14 major nations that the Western world's entire monetary system could collapse unless they took immediate concerted action to combat the speculative wave against the Dollar. Attending the meeting were the nine European Common Market countries, the U.S., Japan, Canada, Sweden and Switzerland. Also represented was Indonesia, whose delegate was chairman of the Committee of Twenty, a larger United Nations group studying long-range monetary reform.

At the same time in Washington, Arthur Burns, chairman of the Federal Reserve Bank, was telling Congress the monetary crisis was no longer "a problem we can fiddle with for years. I want to do the job now in three months." Burns warned that "confidence in paper currencies has greatly declined. Not long ago the dollar was the great sign of safety and stability and strength around the world. Two devaluations in 14 months have shaken confidence and people are looking for harbors of safety" by buying gold, strong currencies like the Swiss Franc and German Mark, or commodities.

"We also have sophisticated financial people," Burns added, "riding on the backs of these scared people."

On March 12, West Germany, France, Belgium, Luxembourg and the Netherlands agreed at a Common Market meeting in Brussels to undertake a joint float, in which they would all stop supporting the value of the dollar. They would support each other's currencies so as to permit a maximum fluctuation of 2.25 per cent between them. Italy, Britain and Ireland allowed their currencies to float independently. West Germany also agreed to a 3 per cent revaluation of the mark. The Canadian dollar and the Japanese yen also were floating.

As Schmidt, the German Finance Minister pointed out, both main features of the Bretton Woods system were now discarded: firstly, a system of fixed parities, and secondly reliance on the U.S. dollar as chief reserve currency in international dealings.

Emphasizing the change, the German mark was revalued not in terms of the dollar but in terms of Special Drawing Rights (SDR's) issued by the International Monetary Fund (IMF). The German authorities made clear they intended to give SDR's the role of reserve unit instead of the dollar in a new monetary system. Agreement thus reached, official foreign exchanges reopened around the world March 19, and the dollar began its first days as a floating currency—on an upbeat, and in quiet trading. Calm had returned to the money markets, at least for the time being.

At the end of March the U.N. Committee of Twenty met in Washington to discuss the long-range establishment of a new world monetary structure. The group decided the world's currencies could continue to float for the present, but in the future should be tied down to "stable but adjustable par values." The details of a fundamental reform of the system were left to the annual meeting of the IMF scheduled for September in Nairobi, Kenya. However, the group declared that in the restructured system the role of reserve national currencies like the dollar should be reduced. The committee stated that the international SDR should become the principal reserve asset.

Since 1969 the IMF had been creating SDR's (also known familiarly as "paper gold") to settle debts between nations.

They were not convertible into gold, and were in fact book-keeping entries, based fundamentally on mutual trust between nations, a factor which some critics noted has not been a particularly reliable item in the ledgers of human history. In the first three years of their existence, the Fund had issued $9.3 billion worth of SDR's. Compared with world monetary reserves of all kinds totaling $150 billion in 1973, they had a long way to go to fill the shoes of the dollar and metallic gold.

As regards gold, the Group of Twenty avoided any mention of its use in the future monetary system. The U.S. and other countries favored a gradual phasing out of the precious metal. Other nations, mainly in Europe, wanted gold retained as a monetary asset. Private speculators noted that in all the debate and monetary turmoil of previous months no central bank in the world was selling any of its gold reserves. Drawing their own conclusions, private buyers continued to bid the gold price up toward the $100 an ounce mark in the free market.

On this point—the desirability of holding gold—there seemed to be at least tacit agreement in private and official circles. In the long run of history, paper currencies such as the dollar had come and gone, but gold had been the world's ultimate store of value for centuries. It was also possible to issue additional SDR's at will, critics noted, but nobody had yet managed to run gold off a printing press.

American tourists tried to sell their dollars at a Tokyo bank

Smoke billowed from the shattered Staten Island gas tank

A Hissing Sound,
A Ring of Fire
And 40 Men Died

Victims Perished in the Explosion
Of A Giant Gas Tank on Staten Island

THE GIANT TANK rose in a massive gray mound on Staten Island's western shore. Almost primitive in shape and sheer bulk but with an ultramodern tangle of pipes snaking to the top on one side, it stood dominant amid acres of marshland tank depots storing fuel to bring light, heat and motion to the millions across New York Harbor, 10 miles to the east.

It was one of the first of a new design for storing liquefied natural gas at 260 degrees below zero. Its owner, Texas Eastern Transmission Co., said it was a safe way to meet the rising demands of a fuel-short Northeast. Its unseen concrete walls were banked to the top in a squat cone of gravel and cinder. Its lid—starting six stories up and wide as a football field—was a concrete dome rising another 40 feet at the center.

It was empty of gas Feb. 10 when 40 construction men climbed inside for another afternoon of repair and mainte-

nance work. But something went wrong that bitter cold Saturday.

Someone outside heard a cry: "Fire, fire, fire."

There was a hissing sound, then a ring of fire at the narrow lip where the dome capped the gray mound. The dome lifted from the lip and shattered inward on itself. Then it fell and smothered the flaming bottom—and 40 men—with concrete chunks the size of a house.

"I heard the sound," a welder in a nearby shed recalled. "I don't know what kind of sound it was. But I knew what it meant. It was smoking. I ran." A worker just inside the top of the dome told of a "hissing sound in the hole, like air blowing the smoke out. I started to run out of the tank and got half way down the side and she blew."

The squat cone, now gaping open at the top, belched impenetrable acrid chemical smoke. For hours it was impossible to tell whether there was hope for the 40 men—or even how many there were.

Fire truck after fire truck arrived, their men mounting the windswept rim to pour water blindly through the smoke from four stations as they tried to make out the dim outlines of disaster in the pit. Weeping families gathered at a police station 10 miles away. Officials compiled a list of the missing by counting the workmen outside the tank and then subtracting—or by noting whose cars were still parked unclaimed outside the tank.

It would be nearly nightfall before firemen could see from above what had happened in the tank—and it would be daybreak before the fire was out. Then it would take 12 days around the clock to jackhammer through the steel and concrete that had fallen to retrieve the last of the shrunken, charred bodies at the bottom.

At one point in those first hours a huge crane was rigged with a rescue basket and firemen were lowered with oxygen masks through the smoke. "It was like a science fiction novel, or Dante's 'Inferno'," fireman Edward Cooper said. The firemen spotted a magazine on the tank floor that had curiously escaped being burned. But they saw no sign of life. One workman stood on the tank's rim, crossed himself, and quietly wept. "My buddies are down there," he said.

By night the firefighting continued under searchlights as the dense smoke cleared and firemen could finally aim for the still-glowing crevices. The temperature hovered near 10 degrees, and a marrow-chilling wind blew in from the harbor. By the time the fire was out, firemen estimated the rubble on the bottom of the tank was packed in ice three to four feet thick.

At 1 a.m. that first night, firemen descending by crane found the first four bodies—blackened beyond recognition, their stumps of arms pitifully upraised as if to shield them from the heat. Medical examiners later found they had died quickly of suffocation. The first of 40 numbered pine boxes were lowered into the tank, then raised again to be shipped to a morgue by truck. The ritual would be repeated day after day until the last body was out Feb. 21.

Through the night, with no sign of hope, men who had worked with the victims—and their families—talked in hushed, numbed tones about camaraderie on the job, about the victims' sons and daughters, about brothers still trapped inside.

A few talked of a "lack of safety measures" by the construction contractor for whom most of the men worked. But others disagreed—John Mafaro for one. His kid brother, he said, had taken the job with a gut feeling there was "no danger at all." Bill Williams, the welder who heard the ominous sound and ran, said: "The thing was safe or I never would have gone into it or on top of it." "Texas Eastern went overboard on safety," said crane operator Robert Garraputa. "They are fanatical about safety. If there was a hint of a gas leak, nobody went inside."

When a funeral mass was celebrated for the workers Feb. 15, nearly 1,000 people, including New York City Mayor John V. Lindsay, attended. Some came in work clothes, some carried hard hats. Terence Cardinal Cooke, Roman Catholic Archbishop of New York, was celebrant.

The scale of death, the scale of fire, the scale of rescue and grief, it seemed, had proved the equals of the hugh tank itself—and of the controversy that followed.

The tank, believed to be the largest of its type at the time, had been built for a subsidiary of Texas Eastern in the late 1960s to help meet burgeoning fuel demand.

Natural gas could be liquefied at the site after shipment via overland pipeline, or it could be delivered in liquid form from tankers anchored nearby. The idea, a company spokesman said, would be to store enough gas over the warm months so the company could meet peak winter demand by converting the liquid back to gaseous form.

The tank was opened in 1970, but it was shut down and purged of gas two years later after its insulation lining developed leaks. The workmen were sealing that thin liner—which covered two feet of polyurethane foam insulation on the inside of the tank—when the explosion occurred. Later, fire officials would come to the preliminary conclusion that the combination of materials might have played a part in the explosion, and that a pocket of gas trapped in the foam insulation might have fueled it. The foam, they said, was what had burned so fiercely. But whatever the immediate cause, the explosion intensified a debate already under way in the city about whether huge fuel tanks should be built.

Only the day before the explosion, the City Council heard arguments from safety-conscious Staten Islanders against construction by Texas Eastern of four naptha storage tanks in the same 213-acre area a half-mile from residential housing. Dr. James A. Say, a mechanical engineering professor from the Massachusetts Institute of Technology, warned that a spill of liquefied natural gas or naptha could destroy an area a mile in diameter.

Two days later, as the first bodies were being lifted out of the tank, Mayor Lindsay declared: "It's obvious the future of these things will have to be examined." And within a month, City Council acted to prevent future construction by prohibiting the Board of Standards and Appeals from granting the kind of variance that had been granted in 1967 to Texas Eastern. The normal limit of size is 500,000 gallons.

To many on Staten Island, though, that action was not enough. It would not halt construction already under way at the island's southern end of two still-larger liquefied natural gas tanks for Distrigas Corp. An organization calling itself BLAST (Bring Legal Action to Stop the Tanks) held a memorial motorcade for the dead workmen Feb. 20, and on April 5 some 1,200 high school students staged a five-mile march to protest the Distrigas construction. Their signs read: "Tanks, No Thanks," and "Stop the Tanks Before They Stop Us." They and their parents argued safety was more important than fuel needs, and that the tanks could be built in less populated areas elsewhere.

But the other side of the argument—the pressure for more fuel and what it meant economically—had force of its own. The two Distrigas tanks, each with a 900,000 barrel capacity, were designed specifically to hold liquefied natural gas to be imported in special ships from vast deposits being developed in Algeria. Those deposits could not be wished away, and their developing potential for U.S. markets built momentum even as the students were preparing their demonstration. On March 31, Chemical Construction Corp. of New York signed a long-sought contract with an Algerian government gas firm. Chemico, according to the agreement, would build a $35 million facility in Algeria to produce one billion cubic feet of liquid gas daily when completed in four years. Over-all, the project was expected to cost American interests $2 billion—with the expectation that the operation could supply 10 per cent of the gas used on the East Coast. Liquefaction for tanker transport was the logical way to bring it across the Atlantic.

The balance that had to be found—between assurance of safety and meeting rising fuel demand—was not unlike the balance sought when the tank that exploded was first built, or when it was closed down after the leaks were found. The tank itself was a new design. The explosion's force had been directed upward and not outward. The dome's collapse had served to muffle the explosion. The tank's walls remained intact in their cone-shaped sheathing. If nobody had been inside, the way it was built might have served to minimize catastrophe, not compound it.

But there was irony. The tank had been built to be full, not empty with men working inside. When the unforeseen happened, disaster followed.

Several workers said there had been substantial safety precautions during the repair work. Identification of bodies was hampered, for example, because workers had to dress alike in static-free overalls and shoes, and they had to remove all metal from their bodies.

Three of those who perished were, in fact, safety inspectors for Texas Eastern.

What, then, had happened?

On the first day a company spokesman said it was inexplicable. Four investigations were immediately launched—by the company, by city fire and municipal service agencies and by the federal Labor Department—whose chief, Labor Secretary Peter Brennan, visited the site while the fire was still burning.

Gradually, in the aftermath, explanations were offered.

Retired engineer Walter Fleischer Jr., who had helped install gas feed pipes, said pockets of gas could have been preserved for months in the insulation after seeping through the Mylar lining leaks that were being repaired. All pipes into the tank were checked and found sealed, and the company said it had begun repair only after purging the tank of gas for months. Yet in the month after the holocaust, fire officials suspended cleanup work twice when they found traces of gas still present.

And Fire Chief John T. O'Hagan came to the conclusion that gas trapped in the insulation did, indeed, fuel the explosion. He said that just what had set it off was still undetermined more than a week after the fire.

But O'Hagan also disclosed that the polyurethane used in the tank—which had burned fiercely once set afire—was not the type originally approved by the fire department. It was, he said, slightly more flammable. Texas Eastern had gotten his department's approval to substitute for the original insulation when it turned out not to be readily available, he said.

At the time of substitution, O'Hagan said, it didn't appear that it mattered. "If there was a fire in the tank full of gas, the fire-spread rate of the insulation wouldn't make much difference."

"Nobody," he said, "foresaw a situation where men would be working inside."

Coffins were lowered into the huge tank

Britain's Princess Anne rode a mule during a three-day February safari in Ethiopia

DEATH AT A FISH FRY

The door to Glen McCauley's barbershop in Eagle Grove, Iowa, was locked. A sign in the window read: "Back Soon."

But McCauley didn't return. He was one of 13 persons who perished Feb. 2 when a violent explosion leveled three brick business buildings in this north-central Iowa farming community of 4,500 persons.

For the next two nights and days, volunteer teams used industrial cranes to sift through the burning debris for bodies. No one in the buildings survived the blast, and one body was never found. The force of the explosion broke hundreds of windows in the business section.

A number of the victims were customers of the Chatter Box cafe who, like McCauley, had gone there for their regular Friday night "fish fry."

Three of the bodies were found still sitting in a booth in the cafe. A Red Cross nurse, Barbara Eckoff of Des Moines, said most of the bodies were in sitting positions with their hands over their heads.

Among the victims was Donald Blue, 42, son of former Iowa Gov. Robert Blue. Another was Mrs. Viola Helgevold, 66, who lived alone in an apartment above the cafe. Her two sons watched from a building across the street as her body was the first removed from the burning rubble. Volunteer fireman Woodrow Loux, 58, suffered a fatal heart attack at the scene.

Phil Jorgensen of Cedar Falls turned down a second cup of coffee in the Chatter Box and it may have saved his life. Jorgensen said he'd gone into the cafe for supper. "I smelled gas when I walked by the kitchen," he said. "I told the woman there was a gas smell. She said an oven hadn't lit. Later, she said it was fixed."

But the gas smell persisted, Jorgensen said. "I got kind of edgy then. The waitress offered me another cup of coffee, but I thought I had better get out of the restaurant." He mentioned the gas odor to a waitress, who told him: "There's something wrong here. I hope the place doesn't blow up."

"Three or four minutes later, she was dead," Jorgensen said.

POWER FAILURE HIT NEW YORK

"Look," a disgruntled New Yorker grumbled, "I just spent $8 on a flashlight and batteries so my wife and I can see—and Con Ed turns the lights on."

The lights he referred to had just gone back on after being off for 2½ hours Feb. 19 in a blackout apparently caused by a fire in a Consolidated Edison Co. transformer. The power failure affected almost a million people in Brooklyn and parts of Staten Island—with lights out, elevators stalled, traffic signals not working, and subway trains slowed. It was the second major power failure to hit the Brooklyn area in seven months (*The World in 1972, 138*).

As a result of the failure, hospitals in the affected area switched to emergency generators; schools released students early, and many residents went to work directing traffic tied up by nonworking traffic lights.

Remarked one 17-year-old guiding traffic at a busy intersection: "My mother always tells me that I never do anything right, but there haven't been any accidents yet so I guess she's wrong."

Eleven persons died in Alameda, Calif., when a U.S. Navy Jet fighter crashed into an apartment building. Firemen fought for hours to stop the blaze

87-YEAR-OLD-GETS HONORABLE DISCHARGE

Shortly after the turn of the century, Dorsie W. Willis and 168 other black soldiers were discharged without honor from the U.S. Army for failing to volunteer information on a 10-minute Texas shooting spree in which one man was killed.

Although later evidence indicated the troopers—members of what was then called D company, First Battalion, 25th Infantry (Colored)—knew nothing to volunteer about "The Brownsville Incident," the official record of the 1906 case was not corrected until the fall of 1972. By then all of the former soldiers were dead, except for Willis.

In a ceremony at his Minneapolis church on his birthday Feb. 11, Willis, 87, was honorably discharged from the Army. Maj. Gen. DeWitt Smith Jr. told the congregation, "I stand here today before the friends of Dorsie Willis to make absolutely and officially clear what has been true and clear in the minds of those who have known Mr. Willis. That is, that he rendered honest, faithful and entirely honorable service to his country while in the uniform of the U.S. Army."

Willis, who spent 59 of the years after leaving the Army shining shoes in a Minneapolis barbershop, was presented his honorable discharge certificate—backdated to Nov. 25, 1906—an American flag, and copies of his amended service record to present to relatives.

"I think," Willis said after the ceremony, "I'll just keep that flag to put on my coffin."

This 150-year-old windmill still being used to produce flour stands in the shadow of a modern generating station in Nottingham, England

ANTI-HIJACK PACT SIGNED

After 101 attempted aerial hijackings to Cuba over the years, of which 84 were successful, the island nation apparently got fed up with its role as the ultimate landing field for air pirates.

Following the 100th and 101st incidents late in 1972 *(The World in 1972, p. 31)*, Havana said it wanted to negotiate an agreement aimed at curbing hijacks with the United States. "The Cuban government," it said, "affirms that it has absolutely no interest, nor does it desire in any way, that Cuban territory be used as a refuge by persons responsible for common criminal acts that occur in any part of the United States territory."

Although the United States and Cuba had not had diplomatic relations since 1961, the negotiations got under way with the Swiss Embassy, which represents U.S. interests in Cuba, doing the negotiating in Havana. Talks on the pact began Nov. 25, 1972, and on Feb. 15, 1973, Secretary of State William P. Rogers signed the accord for the United States in Washington and Foreign Minister Raul Roa Garcia did the same for Cuba in Havana.

The accord, called *"Memorandum of understanding on Hijacking of aircraft and vessels and other offenses,"* called on both countries to either extradite or punish with "the most severe penalty" anyone who "seizes, removes, appropriates or diverts from its normal route or activities an aircraft or vessel" of one nation and takes it to the other.

Said Rogers of the pact—which went into effect immediately—"There will be no safe haven for hijackers in Cuba or the United States."

FRANK COSTELLO, ONCE CALLED "PRIME MINISTER OF THE UNDERWORLD," DIED

For years he was known to Americans as the "prime minister of the underworld," the boss of a multimillion dollar slot machine racket who managed to sidestep repeated attempts to deport him to his native Italy.

But when Frank Costello died Feb. 18 of a heart attack at the age of 82 he had become a conservative figure who had spent the last nine years of his life in seemingly respectable security.

Costello not only managed to avoid deportation. He survived an attempt to kill him in 1957 because the gunman's aim was poor. But things didn't always go the way Costello wished. He achieved unwanted fame in 1951 when he was summoned before the Senate Crime Investigation Committee headed by Sen. Estes Kefauver and asked some searching questions about his activities. His voice rasping from throat surgery undergone years earlier, Costello told the senators that he had once been a bootlegger and a bookmaker but that he had become respectable.

Chafing under the sudden glare of publicity, Costello demanded that the television cameras be kept away from his face. So for millions of fascinated TV viewers, there was only the gravel voice and the arresting spectacle of his hands, neatly manicured and forever fidgeting on the table before him.

The hearing led to an 18-month prison sentence for contempt of the Senate after Costello strode out of one session pleading a sore throat. In 1954, Costello received another sentence, five years for income tax evasion. The verdict rocked him. As he left the courtroom he lit a cigarette with trembling hands and seemed on the verge of tears. But the next day he was more philosophical. Said he, "What's the use of worrying? That's the way it goes."

In addition to his five-year sentence, Costello was fined $30,000. He eventually was released from prison, pending an appeal. In May 1957, while out on bond, Costello was shot from behind as he entered his New York apartment house. The bullet creased his scalp, and Costello insisted that it must have been a case of mistaken identity.

What reportedly hurt Costello most of all was loss of citizenship. It was revoked by a federal district court after he had been returned to prison in 1958 to serve out his tax evasion sentence. The court ruled that Costello had obtained citizenship under false pretenses by concealing his record as a Prohibition era racketeer.

But deportation was something else. For 14 years the government tried vainly to expel him from the United States, but Costello, who had left Italy in 1895 when he was four years old, felt that New York was his home. He fought to stay in the city and he won his deportation case in the Supreme Court in 1961. The court held 6–2 that he could not be deported for crimes committed while he was a naturalized citizen, even though that citizenship had later been revoked. Commented Costello: "This is the greatest victory of my life."

The man who had been powerful enough to summon the nation's top mobsters to a "peace conference" following the 1929 St. Valentine's Day massacre in Chicago last hit the front pages in 1964—for a vagrancy arrest. Costello was picked up while lunching at an expensive midtown restaurant with a Broadway bookie.

"What are your means of support?" demanded the arresting officer.

"I'm retired," replied the natty, bespectacled Costello.

The charge was quickly dropped at the station house.

FOR THE RECORD

NAMED. Thirty new cardinals by Pope Paul VI on Feb. 30. The appointments included three Americans and broadened the senate of the Roman Catholic Church and made it younger. The Americans named to the Sacred College of Cardinals were Archbishops Humberto S. Medeiros, 57, of Boston; Timothy J. Manning, 63, of Los Angeles, and Luis Aponte Martinez, 50, of San Juan—Puerto Rico's first native-born cardinal.

DEAD. Twenty-one students, most of them children, attending evening music classes at a four-story high school in Paris when fire broke out Feb. 6. The blaze destroyed the school within less than an hour. Witnesses said the flames shot up the entire height of the building in minutes. Corridors and passageways were choked with black, billowing smoke. About 50 students were evacuated soon after the fire began.

KILLED. Seven young persons ranging in age from 9 to 18. On Feb. 6, when a freight train slashed into the rear of their school bus as it crossed the railroad tracks at Littlefield, Tex. Sixteen other children and the bus driver were hospitalized. Police Chief James Cox said the train was traveling at more than 50 miles an hour and "the impact alone killed the kids." Cox added, "This is the biggest tragedy that ever hit this town."

FIRE. On a crowded Boston commuter train Feb. 6. One person died and almost 90 were hospitalized when the fire broke out aboard the train and sent black smoke through a subway tunnel. Scores of riders were led choking and gasping through the smoky tunnel after the fire struck one car of the four-car subway. Others affected by the smoke were carried out on stretchers and in wheelchairs.

Frank Costello stepped from a police van in 1961 on a contempt charge booking procedure

Above, the body of Marshal Philippe Petain, the French World War I military hero who collaborated with the Nazis in World War II, was stolen from its grave on the Ile d'Yeu in February. It later was recovered. Here Petain is shown in 1949 while serving a life sentence for treason. Below, fifteen inches of snow blanked the Dixie area in February. Here an Air National Guard helicopter sits by the side of the road after flying food and supplies to stranded motorists in central Georgia

Skipjack Oystering Off Maryland

Below left, skipjack crews raising sail as they set out for a day of oyster dredging. Below right, the skipjack and the men who sail her set out as the first rays of the morning sun glinted over Chesapeake Bay. Left, a ghostly galleon, sleek and graceful

An Airliner Was Shot Down And Hostages Were Slain as Terror Hit the Middle East

Israeli soldier looks at wreckage of Libyan airliner

CORPSES LITTERED the Sinai Desert and three dead diplomats sprawled in a blood-spattered embassy cellar. A world becoming inured to sudden death in the Middle East was shocked anew by the savage slaughter of innocents in the "no war, no peace" stalemate.

The incidents occurred nine days and 1,000 miles apart, in the gritty, searing sandstorms known as "haboubs" that stretch nerves and tempers in late February and March. The victims were uninvolved in the Arab-Israeli conflict. Both sides were to blame.

First was the downing of a Libyan airliner by Israeli jets.

It was early afternoon on February 21. A haboub obscured Cairo Airport and Libyan Airlines Flight 114 was lost. The three-jet Boeing 727 had taken off from Tripoli and made a brief stop in Benghazi before heading for the Egyptian capital into the teeth of the sandstorm.

It carried 104 passengers—all Arabs except for one American, one Pole and one German—and a crew of nine, including five French nationals on loan from Air France. Passengers taking advantage of Libyan Airlines' advertised "24-carat standards of comfort, efficiency and punctuality" included Egyptian television star "Mama Salwa" Hijazi and the 26-year-old sister of the Libyan ambassador in London.

Pilot Jacques Bourges was flying blind, but he was not particularly worried. Cairo traffic control had watched Flight 114 as it approached the sprawling city from the west and gave him permission to descend and prepare for a landing on runway 23.

At 1:50 p.m. Cairo control was surprised to see Bourges veer off eastward toward the Suez Canal and the Israeli-occupied Sinai Desert. Radio contact was lost momentarily and French steward Jean-Pierre Burdiat later recalled: "It was my understanding the compass was not working."

Five minutes later Israeli radar spotted the track of an unidentified aircraft at an altitude of 15,000 feet. It had not been a normal day for Israeli forces in the Sinai. Early that morning Israeli commandos had attacked Palestinian guerrilla bases in northern Lebanon and the Israelis were on the alert for retaliation from any quarter.

The Israelis quickly scrambled a flight of Phantom interceptors, who had no trouble locating the green-colored Libyan airliner above the sand haze several miles east of Suez.

Bourges looked out of the port window and saw the jets, mistaking them for Soviet-built MIGs of the Egyptian Air Force. He had re-established radio contact with Cairo, and messaged ground controllers: "We are being followed by four MIGs." Then he went aft to see how the passengers were doing.

Feisel Mohammed-Sharaya, an Egyptian waiter flying to Cairo to meet his fiancee, saw the jets as Bourges was walking down the aisle and asked him: "What's happening?"

"Don't be afraid," the captain replied. "They are ours."

"I thought it was a joke," said Sharaya. "An Egyptian plane with Israeli markings?"

Two Phantoms closed in on the Boeing as it flew deeper into Israeli territory and the interceptor pilots used hand signals and waggled their wings to signify "follow me and land." One of the Israeli pilots said he was "close enough to see the pilot's face."

The Libyan airliner continued to flow over one of Israel's most sensitive military areas, within sight of a sprawling air base at Bir Gafgafa, about 50 miles east of the Suez Canal. At about this time Bourges realized his mistake.

He radioed Cairo: "I guess we have serious trouble with the headings and the compass." He lowered his wheels as if to land, then veered westward on a heading back to Egypt.

Bourges' Libyan copilot, El Mahadi el Kidifa, said the captain "decided to land but at the last moment he changed his mind." At this point the Israeli jets opened fire.

One of the Israeli pilots later recalled: "We had orders to bring him to an air base. With my thumb I pointed back to Bir Gafgafa. Then I turned back . . . but he kept going straight. I came close and fired a burst of cannon fire under his nose."

The Israeli closed in again and loosed another cannon shot "parallel to the plane" so Bourges could see it. The Boeing retracted its wheels and picked up speed, continuing toward Egypt.

The Israeli pilot said he and his wingman "fired more warning shots into his right wingtip, not to disable him but to show him we meant business." As the Boeing neared the canal without any effort to land the Israelis aimed for a spot where the wing joins the fuselage "to cause more serious damage."

"I saw a red flame and black smoke come out of the wing and I assume we hit fuel," the Israeli pilot continued. Steward Burdiat, however, said he heard two Israeli shots and one of the shells pierced the rear of the fuselage.

"We are now shot," Bourges calmly told Cairo. "We are shot by a fighter. We are shot by a fighter."

These words, recorded on tape in Cairo, were the last from the flight. The Boeing crashed and exploded in the Sinai Desert. Of the 113 persons on board, 106 were killed outright. Two, including steward Burdiat, died in hospital. Four passengers and the Libyan copilot survived.

The survivors were treated in Israeli hospitals. The bodies were turned over to the Egyptians in plain, wooden coffins.

Israeli Premier Golda Meir expressed her government's "deep sorrow" at the loss of life and "regrets that the pilot did not heed the repeated warnings which were given him in accordance with international procedures."

Arab governments screamed for vengeance against the "Jew-

A survivor of the downed Libyan plane

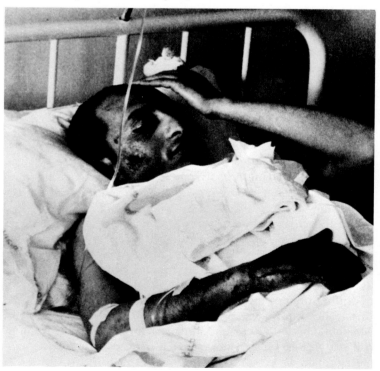

ish murderers." The Arab regimes also hooted at Israel's proposal for a "hot line" between Tel Aviv and Cairo to prevent future tragedies.

The crash cast a shadow on Golda Meir's visit to Washington later that month and dashed hopes for any interim settlement concerning reopening of the Suez Canal and a possible Israeli withdrawal from the Sinai. Israel maintained it was an honest mistake, that it thought the airliner had hostile intentions. Defense Minister Moshe Dayan claimed: "I have no feelings of guilt." But in the world's eyes Israel had become the villain.

Not for long.

One week after the crash, six young Palestinians traveling on Jordanian passports arrived at the dusty airport terminal in Khartoum, capital of the Sudan. Members of the extremist Black September Organization, they had obtained Sudanese visas in Beirut and were met by representatives of the Palestine Liberation Organization and Al Fatah.

In Khartoum, the six met their leader Rizik Kass, a Voice of Palestine broadcaster for Omdurman Radio, and an eighth Black September accomplice who would take part in one of the bloodiest acts of terrorism ever suffered by a diplomatic community.

The target was a diplomatic reception at the Saudi Arabian Embassy. The victims: Two Americans who had played a major role in the restoration of diplomatic relations between Washington and the Sudan, and an Egyptian-born Belgian diplomat who had recently become engaged to be married.

As the dean of Khartoum's diplomatic corps, Saudi Ambassador Abdullah Al Malhouk hosted the reception to honor U.S. Charge d'Affaires G. Curtis Moore, who was leaving for reassignment in Washington, and newly-arrived U.S. Ambassador Cleo A. Noel, who had previously worked on the Sudan desk in Washington.

It was a stag affair, ending at 7 p.m. March 1. There was almost no security provided by Sudanese police, who were all in position at the presidential palace for an official dinner later that evening for Ethiopian Emperor Haile Selassie.

The Saudi party was nearing its end when Noel said goodbye and strolled toward the embassy gate together with the Dutch charge d'affaires. As Noel's car began to pull out of its parking place to pick him up, Belgian Charge d'Affaires Guy Eid pushed in front of the Dutch diplomat and said he wanted to discuss something with Noel.

A white land rover with diplomatic license plates, which had been parked at a street corner for the entire 90-minute reception, raced up and rammed the side of the American ambassador's car. Four men leaped out with AK47 rifles and fired at the feet of the diplomats.

Eid went down, wounded in the foot. Noel was grabbed by one of the commandos. The Dutch diplomat ran away, followed by two Sudanese policemen who had been guarding the embassy gate. Four more Black September guerrillas appeared brandishing arms.

The French ambassador coolly strolled to the garden wall at the rear of the embassy and climbed over to freedom. The ambassador from the Cameroons ducked behind a hedge in the garden and hid there for 30 minutes before escaping over the wall.

Within minutes the embassy was in the hands of eight guerrillas. They allowed several more diplomats to leave but kept Malhouk, his wife and children, Jordanian Charge d'Affaires Adli Al Nasser, Noel, Moore and Eid. The two Americans and the Egyptian were tightly bound.

Top left, Charge d'Affaires G. Curtis Moore; his wife, Sara Anne; Mrs. Cleo Noel, and U.S. Ambassador Cleo A. Noel, Jr. posed for this picture only seven hours before the two men were captured and then executed. Bottom left, two terrorists on the balcony of the Saudi Arabian Embassy at Khartoum. Above, the bodies of Noel and Moore were returned to the United States

Sometime in the first hour, a brave woman neighbor of the Malhouks walked into the building, told startled guerrillas "You can't keep these children here," and walked out with the youngsters. The guerrillas offered to free Mrs. Malhouk, but she elected to stay with her husband.

Outside the embassy, the escapees contacted police. Sudan's vice president, a dignified, tough career soldier, Maj. Gen. Mohammed Baghir, immediately took charge, deploying hundreds of police, troops and several armored cars around the residential area. They were ordered not to approach, not to alarm the guerrillas in any way. Baghir contacted the guerrillas by telephone. They agreed to let a Sudanese army doctor enter the building, but warned that the hostages would be killed at the first move by security forces outside.

The doctor found Noel unharmed, tied to a chair. Eid was also tied to a chair, bleeding from his foot wound. Moore was tied up, lying on the floor, and his face was badly battered as if kicked or hit with rifle butts. The Saudi and Jordanian diplomats were not tied.

He also reported that the room was rigged with demolition charges and the terrorists told him they would "blow up the building" if Sudanese troops made any hostile move. After treating Moore and Eid, the doctor was given a list of Black September demands aimed at four governments.

In exchange for the lives of the hostages, it sought the release of Palestinian guerrilla leader Abu Daoud and 16 other commandos imprisoned in Jordan, members of the Baader Meinhoff terrorist group imprisoned in West Germany, women guerrillas held by Israel, and Sirhan Bishara Sirhan, the convicted assassin of U.S. Sen. Robert F. Kennedy.

The inclusion of Germany in the terrorists' demands indicated they had hoped to capture the West German ambassador at the Khartoum reception. He had been a guest, but had gone home early.

Rizik Kass, who also identified himself by the guerrilla code name of Abu Salam, told the departing doctor to tell Mrs. Noel: "Your husband is all right. We mean him no harm. Our cause is just."

Lengthy negotiations, mostly by telephone, dragged on through the night of Thursday, March 1, and all day Friday. The guerrillas set a 7 p.m. Friday deadline for their demands to be met, later extending it to 8 p.m. It soon became apparent that they did not expect the United States, Germany and Israel to grant their demands—but they continued to insist on the release of the commandos held in Jordan.

King Hussein, personally contacted in Rabat, Morocco, where he had stopped on his way home from a visit to the United States, rejected the demand. "No capitulation" was his reply.

In Washington, President Nixon dispatched State Department troubleshooter William Macomber to Khartoum, but announced: "We will not bow to international blackmail." The Saudi ambassador later reported that this had a sharp impact on the commandos, who heard a broadcast of the Nixon speech.

Inside the embassy, the commandos had loosened the bonds of the three western diplomats, allowing them to eat, drink tea and smoke cigarettes. The five hostages and Mrs. Malhouk were kept in an upstairs room.

The guerrillas had also set up a powerful radio transmitter in the embassy and were in contact with an undisclosed headquarters somewhere outside the Sudan. Wearing ski masks, they periodically appeared on the embassy balconies to shout threats and new demands to Sudanese negotiators in the street below.

A variety of proposals were offered to the Black Septembrists, including the offer of an escape flight to Algeria, Egypt or Libya. At one point the guerrillas asked for a plane to take them to the United States with two high-ranking Sudanese hostages. The U.S. Embassy in Khartoum rejected this demand, and an embassy spokesman later revealed the details of what he called "a gruesome plot to kill the hostages in the United States."

"Three Sudanese ministers volunteered to be hostages," the spokesman reported. "What they did not know was that the guerrillas intended to land the aircraft at a major American airport, line the diplomatic hostages on the tarmac, make sure the television cameras were rolling and kill them all on the spot. Then they planned to use the Sudanese ministers as hostages to negotiate their escape from the United States."

The embassy officer did not reveal how the plot was uncovered and there was never any independent confirmation of this. In fact, it was unclear whether the guerrillas had intended to kill the diplomats from the start, or whether they had received orders to do so after they had seized the Saudi Embassy.

American officials had hoped to buy time for the hostages by delaying the arrival of Macomber after the 8 p.m. Friday deadline. Through Baghir, they told the guerrillas Macomber was arriving Friday night when in fact he had disembarked from a U.S. Air Force C141 jet in Cairo and planned to overnight there before coming to Khartoum on Saturday.

The plan didn't work.

At 6 p.m. Friday the U.S. Embassy received a telephone call from Noel.

"Is there any news?" he asked.

"Are we being overheard?" replied a U.S. Embassy officer.

"Yes," said Noel.

"A high-ranking American official is due to arrive tonight," said the embassy officer.

"That will be too late," were Noel's last words before the telephone connection was cut off.

Shortly thereafter, a howling sandstorm enveloped Khartoum. Sudanese troops and armored cars closed in on the Saudi Embassy.

Eyewitnesses said later it wasn't an attack but a "natural movement, a desire to keep the building in sight as visibility decreased." They conceded it "might have looked like an attack to the guerrillas."

At about 8:30 p.m. the commandos received a radio message from their mysterious headquarters. It contained the words "Cold River"—the name of a Palestinian refugee camp in northern Lebanon that was raided by Israeli commandos in February—and it turned out to be a coded death sentence.

The Sudanese Embassy in Beirut later disclosed that it had received a similar message from an anonymous caller who asked that it be transmitted to the commandos in Khartoum. This gave rise to the suspicion that Black September was headquartered in the Lebanese capital.

The Saudi and Jordanian hostages noticed a radical change in the guerrillas' mood after they received the message. Some looked scared. There were arguments in another room, loud shouting, angry looks at the American hostages.

Guerrilla leader Abu Salam emerged shaken from a conference with his companions and told the Western diplomats they would be executed as "enemies of the Palestinian cause." Malhouk pleaded with the guerrillas to wait for Macomber's arrival.

"No," said Abu Salam. "We know the American answer. We heard it from Nixon. Secondly, we have received our final orders."

The two Americans spent their last 25 minutes writing wills and letters to their families. Malhouk said they were "very brave and calm. They kept themselves composed."

Eid, however, broke down and was unable to write anything on the paper placed in front of him.

The commandos then took the two Americans and the Belgian to the basement. Abu Salam told his men they would all "have the honor of taking part in the shooting," and exhorted them to repeatedly pump bullets into the three men.

The Jordanian turned his face away as they walked down the stairs.

At 9:06 p.m., a small group of spectators huddling together for protection against the wind-blown sand outside the embassy heard several bursts of automatic weapons fire.

Within a half hour the Saudi Arabian undersecretary of foreign affairs, Fadil el Odeid, telephoned the U.S. Embassy to relay word from the guerrillas of what they had done.

Secretary of State William P. Rogers escorted the widows of the two slain U.S. diplomats after services at Arlington National Cemetery

Tears glistening in his eyes, a grim embassy spokesman told foreign newsmen: "Our people are dead."

The siege continued through Saturday. The guerrillas refused to give up the bodies of the dead, they refused to free their Saudi and Jordanian hostages until Jordan released Abu Daoud and other imprisoned Palestinians.

Baghir was pessimistic: "They are prepared to die," he reported after one fruitless negotiating session. "They are making no promises, only demands. You cannot negotiate with people like that." Sudanese troops prepared to storm the Saudi Embassy.

Late Saturday night, Malhouk relayed a final surrender offer to the guerrillas. Armored cars moved into position for a salvo of fire against the Saudi Embassy, and Baghir announced a dawn deadline for the guerrillas' capitulation. At midnight a guerrilla with a bullhorn asked for a telephone call from Baghir. The surrender was arranged for 6 a.m. Sunday.

The siege ended quietly, 60 hours after it began. The sandstorm had dissipated and most of the Sudanese who maintained a vigil around the embassy had gone home to sleep when the Black Septembrists emerged, flashing victory signs with their fingers. They were whisked away to an army jail.

Sudanese policemen who entered the embassy cellar found large pools of blood, bullet chips in the walls, spent cartridge cases on the floor and a shattered wristwatch belonging to Noel. The bodies, badly decomposed and so torn up by bullet bursts that they were virtually unrecognizable, were carried out in blankets and taken to a city morgue.

The next day flag-draped caskets of the two Americans, ac-companied by their wives and children, were flown to Washington aboard a special presidential jet. Eid's body was flown to Cairo, his birthplace, accompanied by his weeping fiancee.

The world reacted with outrage. American officials hastened to praise Baghir and Sudan's handling of the siege while pressing for swift and heavy punishment of those responsible. A note from Washington indicated that any leniency by the Sudanese would "aggravate the horror and revulsion created by this incident."

President Nixon appealed for "a firm stand against the menace of international terrorism."

Sudan's President Gaafar Numeiry termed the killings "outrageous" and high-ranking Sudanese government officials privately assured the Americans that the eight Palestinians would "never leave Khartoum alive." There is only one penalty for murder in the Sudan—death.

But it soon became apparent that Numeiry faced a delicate dilemma—whether to treat his captives as common murderers or political prisoners.

While not wishing to anger the United States, which reestablished diplomatic relations with the Sudan in July 1972 and in 1973 contributed $30 million in foreign aid, Numeiry was equally reluctant to lose his standing in the Arab world as a supporter of the Palestinian cause.

Sudan is populated by Moslem Arabs in the north and black Christians in the south. They were celebrating the first anniversary of a shaky peace when the diplomats were killed—a peace which could have been jeopardized by hasty execution of the Moslem-supported Palestinians.

An example of Japanese art

Japanese Art Lovers Are Collecting Western Paintings In A Big Way

Modigliani was among the many Western artists who interested Japanese buyers

Y ON-JU-ROKU-MAN-EN, YON-JU-ROKU-MAN-EN," the auctioneer chanted. In Japanese that meant 460,000 yen, and the auctioneer was singing back bids which dealers were shouting from a straw-mat floor as customers signaled with hand gestures. The chanter urged higher bids.

The scene was Japan's first public art auction held in 1969 amid the surroundings of a lovely Japanese garden and tea drinkers seated on straw mats. The auction was sponsored by Christie's, the famous London auction house, at the Tokyo Art Club. But it was unlike anything an European art patron would have recognized.

"A great success," Christie's Ivan S. Chance said, summing up what he called an experiment which yielded bids totaling $1.89 million and firm sales of $1.11 million.

The highest price was $141,666 for Amadeo Modigliani's Impressionist *Portrait of Young Farmer.* Charles Francois Daubigny's *Landscape with Farmer and Cattle,* drew $24,583, and Andre Derain's *Nude Bust,* $30,000.

Since 1971 the affluent Japanese have been hustling throughout the world, purchasing land, hotels and golf courses, winning bids for race horses and buying jewels. With the nation's national purse bulging with $250 billion in Gross National Product (GNP) and $18.4 billion in foreign exchange reserves in the spring of 1973, their appetite was insatiable.

The Japanese are noted art lovers, having produced great wood print artists such as Hokusai (1760–1849), Utamaro (1754–1806) and Sharaku (about 1790); painters Sesshu (1420–1506) and Tessai (1836–1924), and School of Paris artist Leonard Tsuguji Foujita (1886–1968). Until recent years, however, most Japanese could only admire art in museums and galleries. Now they have developed a strong flair for collecting them, many figuring Western paintings would be an attractive form of investment in a time of international monetary crises. Said one owner of a gallery on the Ginza, ". . . due to the instability of international currency and as a means to protect themselves from inflation they are buying works of art as security. . . ."

But the Christie auction in Tokyo four years ago marked what generally is described as the start of Japanese connoisseurs—dealers and collectors alike, both seasoned and amateur—and a new breed known as the "ote gasho" (large art business houses) making a run for works of art and seeking out art auctions in London, New York and Paris.

Major art dealers and department stores—among the principal purveyors of art in Japan—have men stationed in Europe and the United States whose sole job is to gather information on the art market. Some keep in contact by Telex while expert buyers are later dispatched to attend auctions or to try and negotiate directly with galleries, owners or artists.

The purchase of Henri (Le Douanier) Rousseau's *Monkeys in the Jungle* for a whopping $2 million from New York's Metropolitan Museum of Art not so long ago stunned art lovers and collectors alike. Another headline maker was a Japanese outbidding Americans and Europeans for Pierre Auguste Renoir's *Portrait of Madame Mithouard*. The Renoir was auctioned by Christie's in London in March 1973 for $370,000. In fact, the Japanese took 47 per cent of the total sales in that auction.

Many art dealers and critics in Tokyo admit the behavior of the affluent Japanese leaves much to be desired. "You go to a major auction abroad," said Susumu Yamamoto, director of the Fuji TV Gallery, "and you'll find a group of Japanese bidding against each other only to shoot the price up to a ridiculous high for which seasoned Western art patrons wouldn't pay half what the Japanese bid."

A higher standard of living, westernization of Japanese homes despite a growing housing shortage, and mushrooming high-rise buildings set off Japan's art boom.

For the past two or three years it has become a sort of keeping up with the Satos or Watanabes for the white-collar worker to own works of art. With his twice-a-year bonuses, he easily can afford spending about $750 for a Western painting to give him an air of being the man of the world. Some buy on the installment plan since credit is now a fashionable postwar institution.

In the past it was the custom for the alcove of the living room, the inner sanctum of the Japanese home, to be decorated with a traditional "kakejuku" hanging scroll, or a work of calligraphy.

Changes in the style of homes and mode of living emphasized displaying on walls western canvases, usually a good Barbizon School landscape by Renoir, Cezanne or Monet, or the works of the Ecole de Paris artists such as Modigiliani, Derain,

Maurice de Vlaminck, Henri Matisse, Maurice Utrillo and Raoul Dufy.

The skyscraper boom also spurred demands for Western art. At least one gallery is opened with every new high-rise building and firms occupying offices display a portrait, landscape, still life or nude on the walls of the reception room, conference room or the boss's office.

Today there are 324 art galleries and art shops in and around Tokyo, a far cry from 1951 when there were only 58. Annual sales jumped to $76.9 million in 1972 from less than $10 million.

In a country where booms come and go, artists and critics say the art vogue may taper off and be replaced by another. Anticipating such a possibility, they have urged the government to do something to keep up the interest.

Until 1971 the government had been appropriating $277,000 annually for national museums, said to be the smallest appropriation among the advanced nations.

"The amount is piddling," an official at the Ueno National Museum in Tokyo commented. "We can't even maintain our galleries properly, let alone buy a major work by a Western painter."

The government, apparently aware of the situation, for the first time provided the Ueno in 1972 with $446,000 to buy an oil painting by Spanish master Lucientes de Goya *Gruppo De Cabesas*. The previous high government purchase was a canvas by Camille Corot for $182,000.

Government authorities have had to be cautious in buying Western art, having once been taken in by three paintings purchased in 1963 and 1964 by the National Museum of Western Arts from an art dealer in Paris for $73,800. In 1967 their authenticity was questioned in Japanese Parliament, resulting in a probe that continued for three years. The three oils turned out

It looked like a snake-dance but it really was Japanese art lovers lined up some years ago to view French art at the Tokyo National Museum

to be forgeries. They were declared fakes and removed by embarrassed officials from the display chamber of the museum.

The Japanese came too late for Vincent Van Goghs and Paul Gaugins. Most of them were in museums. But there still were plenty of others around—Monets, Cezannes, Renoirs, Matisses and Rouaults. Joan Miro and Pablo Picasso sell well in Tokyo.

Between World War I and World War II, Kojiro Matsukata, a wealthy industrialist, bought many Western canvases and other objets d'art in London and Paris. Matsukata's collection totaled 309 paintings and 62 sculptures, worth an estimated $3 million in the 1930s. After the war they were held in custody by France and later returned to Japan. Today they are housed in the Museum of Western Art in Tokyo.

Another prewar wealthy businessman, Magosaburo Ohara, assembled a fine collection that makes up the Ohara Museum of Western Art in Kuraskiki.

Newcomer collectors include Kiichiro Okano, director of the Suruga Bank in Shizuoka. Okano is an avid collector of French painter Bernard Buffet. Okano collected more than 100 Buffets, in 10 years. He won't disclose what his collection cost but he says, "If I miss a Buffet I feel like an angler who's let a big one escape."

Masami Ogawa is another newcomer. Ogawa quit an executive post in 1972 to head the art department of an import firm, because, he said "I've always been fond of art and even dreamed of becoming an artist." He has concentrated on Georges Rouault and in less than a year managed to collect 11 Rouaults.

The Japanese art market is open not only to world-famed masters but also to up-and-coming Western painters.

Once it was Americans but now the Japanese are snapping up works of little-known French artists. It is difficult to tell if the Japanese pursuit of French art has equalled the craze of Americans for such works a decade ago. But some art shops in Paris aim for the Japanese market by hanging invitations in windows and by hiring Japanese-speaking clerks.

"The Japanese seek only paintings that look like potential traveler's checks . . . and they're gullible if told what they buy could be a mint," said Kiyoyubki Tamenaga, a gallery owner who assembles an exhibit once a year for showing in Japan. "The Americans have matured over the years. They've acquired a taste for art." Tamenaga said he believed the Japanese needed at least 10 more years before they become selective.

Speculative or selective, the Japanese art boom does not show signs of diminishing. Books on art, both quality and quantity, along with reproductions, enjoy a boundless market.

Exhibitions of young foreign painters are held from time to time, usually under the sponsorship of department stores. A modern Ecole de Paris exhibition attracted attention by selling exhibited works on the spot at reasonable prices and on the installment plan. Another department store opened a modern European art mart right next to bargain counters for golf clubs, fashion ware and daily necessities. One supermarket chain sells paintings alongside foodstuffs. One of the principal money-earners for department stores in 1972–1973 was paintings.

The interest in art, however, was not confined to Western canvases and sculptures alone. There has been an active movement to "rediscover and revaluate" traditional Japanese art which was neglected in the haste to copy and catch up with the West.

Museums, both public and private, are eager to collect such art objects as woodcut prints by Hokusai and Sharaku, which were sold for a song when Japan opened its doors to the outside world more than a century ago.

An example of Japanese art

Auctions dealing with "Netsuke"—tiny ivory, jade or wooden ornaments—swords and ceramics are among art works which fall under the hammer following Japanese bids.

Prompted by publicity and news reports that paintings can survive inflation and make good investments, money has poured into the picture market from all sorts of sources, among them provincial millionaires who have made a fortune selling their land.

One newly-rich landowner was said to have sent a large sum of money to an art dealer and asked him to send whatever painting he thought appropriate. "I leave the choice with you," he was reported to have said. Such paintings are being treated like stock certificates, and stock journals often feature articles by so-called experts on how to invest in art works.

The boom has given rise to many amateur art dealers, some of whom don't even have an office. They simply move around the country like caravans.

Outside of Japan, Japanese art dealers prowl the art centers of New York, Paris and London to buy or arrange showings of French, American and Western art in Tokyo, Osaka and Kyoto.

What Does the Future Hold for 22 Million People of the Third China?

For hundreds of years overseas Chinese had helped build everybody's country but their own. Suddenly, with the emergence of their ancestral homeland from 20 years of isolation, 22 million Chinese expatriates were faced with sometimes bewildering questions of who they were and where they were going.

The Chinese call the persons of this third China the "Huachiao," the sojourners. They are the descendants of impoverished thousands who fled China's southeast coast for greener paddies abroad, largely in Southeast Asia. Original immigrants came as traders, or as contract laborers in what the region's local peoples, who never thought much more of the Chinese than the Chinese did of them, dubbed "the pig trade."

While still considering China their home, they settled into their own colonies abroad where hard work, thrift, and a strong sense of loyalty to their Chinese heritage bound them together and kept them separate from local natives. Regular visits to homes in China were an important part of the lives of the Huachiao before World War II and the establishment of the People's Republic of China in 1949. But these two events strengthened pressures—already growing—to keep the Huachiao abroad. And as China emerged from two decades of relative isolation, it became clear how greatly their position had been changed.

In 1973, just over a million of the Huachiao represented what most of the world outside Asia sees of China and its varied culture.

Chinese food? A collection of Chinese dishes based on what the Huachiao brought with them from Kwangtung and Fukien provinces, often modified beyond recognition to suit local tastes. The same Cantonese dish that is served in New York with sweet sauce comes from the kitchen smothered in garlic and hot peppers in Malawi.

Chinese culture? Dragons and lions in the streets on Lunar New Year, drums, gongs and as many firecrackers as local laws permit. Or performances of Cantonese opera that go on about as long as you would expect the opera performances of a 4,000-year-old nation to go on.

Chinese people? Depending on where you lived, they were the laundryman, the restaurant staff, the fellow who could loan the money to buy a few more cattle, or the one who shipped the rhinoceros horn to Hong Kong.

The stereotypes were limited and unfair, compounds of misunderstanding and prejudice in the Huachiao's host countries and of the ways the Huachiao themselves were forced to adapt to their adopted homelands. These images often shocked non-Huachiao Chinese when they first ran into them outside Asia.

The story is told of a distinguished Chinese diplomat who mistakenly showed up at the wrong room of a New York hotel for an appointment in the 1950s. The woman occupant of the room opened the door, took one look at him, and tossed out a waiting bag of washing. "Madam," the diplomat is said to have replied while firmly returning the dirty clothes, "All laundrymen may be Chinese, but I assure you not all Chinese are laundrymen."

Had the woman lived a while in Asia she would not have made the same mistake, though then she might have taken him for the owner of the hotel. The 21 million Huachiao living in the great Asian belt from Sumatra to Seoul were for several hundred years the most important economic power in the region outside of European colonialism. And now that the colonies have gone, one long time observer said, the Huachiao are "the glue that holds Southeast Asia together."

When the European colonists and traders first showed up in Asia they needed a class of middlemen who knew the area, but had no particular attachment to the nations in which they

A modern apartment building towering over Chinatown in Singapore

lived. Chinese traders who had worked the region for generations were the perfect solution, and the two were efficient partners throughout most of the colonial era.

And when World War II and the waves of nationalism that swept Asia in its wake pulled down the colonies, it was the Huachiao who were left in economic control, often to the chagrin of the new nations' nationalistic leaders. The richer Huachiao ran whole national economies and dominated intra-regional trade. From narcotics to noodles, if it moved in Asia it was likely the Huachiao were moving most of it.

British-controlled Hong Kong was rivaling Greece as a world shipping center, thanks largely to a Huachiao named Y. K. Pao, who claimed recent purchases made his personal fleet the largest in the world with 13 million tons of cargo-carrying capacity.

In Thailand, a Huachiao with the partly Thai name of Chin Sophonpanich was president and major stockholder of Asia's largest commercial bank outside Japan. It was the Bangkok Bank, and the Thai government was a junior partner.

Beginning in Laos and spreading through a dozen other Asian cities, a tight network of Huachiao from Fukien Province run the Asian connection, running the region's drug trade for profits that can only be guessed.

The Huachiao's importance had long been illustrated in Indonesia, where they provided financing and advice to the generals who run state corporations originally set up to drive the Huachiao out of business. One Indonesian Huachiao described it as a "polite robbery system"—the Indonesians called it the "Alibaba network." The word came from "Ali," a name common among Moslem Indonesians, and from "baba," a Chinese word for father. When the state corporations were set up, they confiscated extensive Huachiao holdings, but then the generals found the Huachiao were the only ones who could run the corporations at a profit. Gradually the tables turned back to what they had been.

"The Chinese are like the grass," observed one Singaporean. "It's trampled, burned, without water . . . but when the rains come, it's back again, stronger."

Though the Huachiao as a group were the major economic fact of life in Southeast Asia outside of Japan, the majority were not rich and often suffered grinding poverty. Many outside Asia were in Chinatowns, a word that might conjure up pleasant images of sizzling pork and bamboo shoots. But all too frequently the districts were also scenes of ghetto poverty as bad as that endured by any minority, though often enlivened by a conscious determination to keep Chinese ways alive in a foreign land.

As difficult as this was, in many ways the condition of poor Huachiao was even more difficult in Asia than outside it. For they were less able to insulate themselves from the dislike of local natives, an emotion that could range from simple discrimination to outright rage. While the Huachiao felt they had earned their place in their host countries, native nationals frequently asked what right they had to dominate so much of the wealth. The question rose in pitch according to the nationalism of the country and the time.

Devices used against the Huachiao ranged from legal harassment to outright robbery. Referring to one area of Malaysia, a long time foreign resident remarked that, "Their idea of capital acquisition there is to stick up a Chinese shop." Hundreds were killed in 1969 riots that broke out between Malaya's six million Malays and four million Huachiao, and a Chinese-dominated guerrilla movement kept tensions simmering through 1972.

A communist-sponsored coup attempt in Indonesia in 1965

Street merchants in Singapore

led to one of the most severe anti-Chinese pogroms in Southeast Asian history. Tens of thousands of suspected Communists —whom Indonesians frequently identified as Huachiao—were slaughtered. Now Huachiao schools are closed and public use of the Chinese language is banned. The Philippines deported more than 48,000 Huachiao to Taiwan between 1960 and 1972, usually on criminal charges disputed by the Huachiao themselves.

The stresses and upheavals of war shook the almost total control that Huachiao used to exercise over the economy of Vietnam. American aid to Vietnamese enabled them to develop their own business class, and burnings and lootings by Vietnamese destroyed much Huachiao property. A friend attempting to intercede for a Vietnamese Huachiao in a legal case was once told by a sympathetic government official, "I'm sorry. If he were Vietnamese there would be no problem. But for a Chinese. . . ."

Thailand was the region's classic example of Huachiao acceptance and assimilation, perhaps because its lack of a colonial experience meant the Huachiao were never in the position of being intermediaries between Western rulers and native Thais.

Huachiao assimilation was so widespread that Thais had a common joke: "A Thai hates all Chinese except his own father."

As government pressure and popular emotions forced poor and middle-class Huachiao to ease their traditional separation from their native neighbors, the demands of modern commerce pushed in the same direction for the wealthy, those who traditionally provided the money for the preservation of the old customs.

In the day of credit analysis, regulation of business and international corporations with intelligence and communications networks that put most governments to shame, there wasn't much room for business done with a telephone call and a handshake based on family honor. When wrong guesses on a stock market could lose millions in an afternoon, there was no place in the board room for that extra cousin who couldn't seem to make it elsewhere.

Moreover, the difficulties and uncertainties of emigrating back to China, or the alternative of a life in Taiwan, an island few Huachiao consider home, gave them few alternatives to trying as best they were able to get along where they were. And despite anti-Chinese discrimination there were signs of increasing acceptance of the Huachiao. Philippine President Ferdinand Marcos is part Chinese, as are ranking members of the Thai and other governments.

But even the pressures for, and the signs of, assimilation, did not mean they were giving up their sense of being Chinese. In many ways the pressures for assimilation raised racial consciousness, particularly among the young. China's emergence as a world power, while it in effect denied many Huachiao access to their homeland, also rekindled a new pride in being Chinese.

"I'm not Communist, but I'm glad China has the bomb and that Nixon is being forced to deal with Peking," said one Huachiao in New York. "Nobody's pushing China around any more."

Anything that smacked of China—movies, dance troupes, ping-pong teams—drew stand-up crowds almost anywhere in Southeast Asia.

Every year thousands of college-age Huachiao were migrating to universities in Hong Kong, Singapore, Taiwan, or, for a few, China.

Rising racial awareness in the United States rubbed off on young Chinese there, who were taking increasing interest in their history and place in the world as a people.

Often young Huachiao were more zealous than their parents, studying Chinese classical music, literature and the martial arts.

Both the Communist government of the People's Republic on the China mainland and the anti-Communist Republic of China on Taiwan had employed this interest to vie for the support of the Huachiao in their host countries abroad. China traditionally claimed responsibility for the Huachiao as her nationals, even to the point of sending Imperial inspectors of education to overseas Chinese schools in Southeast Asia in the 19th century. And it was Huachiao money and support that backed the 1911 revolution that overthrew the Ching Dynasty and led to the creation of both Chinese governments.

Each government still obtained some financial support from the Huachiao, though the Nationalists were more direct about soliciting it. Some 20 per cent of all foreign investments in Taiwan were from overseas Chinese, who also sent an estimated $200 million to relatives and friends in China last year.

Many Huachiao intellectuals asked themselves which would be stronger in the end—pressures for assimilation or increased interest by the Huachiao themselves in their culture.

Both Chinese governments were making it clear they would be just as happy if most Huachiao made their homes abroad. Some 75 per cent of all Huachiao had been born outside of China by 1972.

In addition, the non-Chinese world was exerting a powerful pull on the overseas communities. What some characterized as a Huachiao identity crisis deepened as modernization in China and Taiwan led to the shedding in both of old customs— customs still preserved overseas by the Huachiao as the basis of their culture, and frequently unchanged since the first immigrants performed them generations ago.

A major question was what the Huachiao would find to replace their increasingly outmoded imitation of a Chinese culture long gone. A Singapore woman summed up her dilemma: "Culturally, I'm Chinese. Socially, I'm Singaporean. Intellectually, I am international."

In many ways it wasn't a question of whether traditional or anti-traditional forces were stronger. The context of both was changing, and both could be strengthened without either overwhelming the other. A Huachiao could study both computer design and Taichi boxing, and a Chinatown could build new temples after the subways were installed.

It was increasingly a question of whether the term "Huachiao" itself any longer had meaning. The sojourners, the temporary residents. But were the Huachiao any longer temporary residents of their adopted lands?

In most places, no matter what they thought of themselves or their place in society, the Chinese outside China weren't thinking about going back. Three and one-half decades of war, revolution and international upheaval had thrust a permanent new minority on dozens of nations across the world.

A letter writer drafted a message to a relative in China for an illiterate customer in Singapore

Ice Cutting— An Old Winter Tradition

Top left, as they have for three generations, residents of Miller's Mills in Herkimer County, N.Y., cut chunks of ice from the community pond for storage. Bottom left, blocs of ice were stored in a barn for making homemade ice cream in the summer. Below, Dick Cook, 73, began cutting ice at the age of four. Right, a third generation ice cutter waiting to take his turn with the saw

IRELAND'S FIANNA FAIL OUSTED FROM POWER AFTER 16 YEARS

For 16 years, the Fianna Fail (Soldiers of Destiny) had held political power in Ireland. Then, on Feb. 28, the party and its prime minister, Jack Lynch, was tumbled from its position of power.

Winner of a close election was Liam Cosgrave's left-of-center coalition made up of the Fine Gael, or Irish party, and the Labor party. The coalition was able to loosen Fianna Fail's grip on power when Fine Gael, led by 52-year-old Cosgrave, won 54 seats in the Dail and Labor took 19. This gave the coalition a slim majority since Fianna Fail won 69 seats and independents took the other two.

The victors captured the voters' eye with a 14-point program that promised widespread improvements in social services, eventual abolition of local real estate taxes, and immediate elimination of food taxes and death duties.

Cosgrave, whose father was the first president of the Irish Free State 51 years earlier, took over as Ireland's prime minister March 14 to officially end Fianna Fail's long reign.

TWO SPANISH JETLINERS COLLIDED OVER FRANCE KILLING 68 ABOARD ONE PLANE

The weather was clear and fine March 5 as two London-bound Spanish jetliners winged their way across western France. Suddenly, a passenger on one of the ships recalled, there was "an enormous bang and a flash" then "we dropped and dropped."

The planes, flying during an air controllers strike, had collided. One exploded and crashed. All 68 aboard died. The other, with 117 aboard, made a safe emergency landing with a damaged wing. One passenger remarked that he knew there had been a collision when he looked out the wind and saw "half the wing was missing."

French officials attributed the collision to pilot error or misinterpretation. The planes, said French Transport Minister Robert Galley, "were on converging patterns and, almost against the orders they received, they arrived at the same place at the same time."

The striking civil air controllers' union issued a statement which said the Defense Ministry, which had been supervising air traffic during the walkout, bore "full and total responsibility" for all consequences of the stoppage.

Russian gymnast Olga Korbut posed with her "Female Athlete of the Year" award in New York's Madison Square Garden. Olga rocketed to fame at the 1972 Olympic games in Munich

UNITED STATES CAST A RARE VETO ON PANAMA CANAL ISSUE

It was no secret why Panama had invited the U.N. Security Council to hold an unprecedented meeting on its soil. The Panamanians wanted to put international pressure on the United States to agree to a new treaty governing the U.S.-run Canal Zone.

But when the resolution calling on Washington to conclude the proposed pact "without delay" went before the 15-nation council, the United States killed it with a veto; the third it had cast in United Nations history.

U.S. Ambassador John Scali who had become Washington's top U.N. delegate only two months earlier said his delegation had cast the veto with regret since there was much the United States and Panama agreed on regarding the need for a change in the old pact which had been in existence since 1903. But Scali made clear why the United States had vetoed the draft.

It was not "appropriate or helpful," Scali said, for the United Nations to get involved in an issue between Washington and Panama. Britain which registered the long abstention, expressed agreement with Washington that the canal question was a bilateral matter between the United States and Panama.

But thirteen of the 15 council members clearly felt otherwise. The resolution they supported

noted that the United Nations had the mission of entering into international situations "which might lead to a breach of the peace."

The resolution said the proposed Canal Zone treaty should "guarantee full respect for Panama's effective sovereignty over all its territory."

The old pact gave the United States perpetual jurisdictional rights over the 500-square-mile Canal Zone and control of canal operations. This had long been an explosive issue in Panama.

Panamanian foreign minister indicated that despite the blocking veto, he felt Panama has succeeded in winning the moral backing of many nations. The 13–1 vote seemed to support this.

AFTER 20 YEARS, RED CHINA FREED CIA AGENT JOHN DOWNEY

On Nov. 29, 1952, during the Korean War, young John Downey boarded a plane in Seoul en route to Tokyo. The plane never got there. After a futile air search, U.S. authorities said the plane must have strayed off course and been shot down over North Korea. Downey, described as a civilian employe of the Army, was presumed lost.

In 1953, the missing man's mother, Mary Downey received his death certificate from the Defense Department. The case of John Downey appeared closed. But the following year Peking Radio announced that Downey had been convicted of espionage. Described at his trial as the "arch criminal of all U.S. prisoners," Downey was sentenced to life imprisonment.

The U.S. State Department denounced Peking for keeping Downey's imprisonment secret. American authorities also branded as "trumped up" Peking's insistence that Downey was an agent for the Central Intelligence Agency.

Following the Cold War ethics of the spy trade, the United States stuck to its story that Downey was a civilian employe of the military. The Chinese kept Downey prisoner, but after many appeals, Mary Downey was permitted to visit her son five times. Then in December 1971, as relations between Washington and Peking improved, the Chinese commuted Downey's sentence from life to five more years or until December 1976.

The case took a new twist in 1973 when President Nixon suddenly admitted at a news conference that Downey had indeed been a CIA operative. Then in March, 75-year-old Mary Downey suffered a stroke. Connecticut Gov. Thomas Meskill, a boyhood friend of Downey, phoned the news to the White House. After an appeal from Nixon to Premier Cho En-lai, Peking announced that Downey would be released to go to his mother's bedside half a world away.

On March 12, Downey, the last known POW of the Korean War and now 42-years-old, walked across the Lo Wu border bridge to Hong Kong and freedom.

A day later his plane landed in Connecticut where it was met by a group of dignitaries led by his friend, Gov. Meskill.

After a reunion with his mother and brother, William Downey, the released POW held a news conference. Downey said he had been subjected to intensive questioning by his Communist captors and told them "about every bit of information I had." But he brushed aside a suggestion that any information he had given might have had lasting importance. He called it "ancient history."

Downey declined to disclose what his mission had been before the fateful plane ride, but a former assistant director of the CIA said the agent had been on a mission of supplying Nationalist Chinese teams inside the mainland.

SIR NOEL COWARD, A CELEBRITY'S CELEBRITY, DIED AT AGE 73

To several generations of playgoers, Sir Noel Coward represented the quintessence of British sophistication. He was a major spokesman for the dazzling years between two World Wars, when chic, smart-talking, young and beautiful

Former CIA agent John Downey was released by the Chinese after more than 20 years imprisonment

people delighted in shocking their Victorian elders.

His characters were often amoral. They used mildly profane language and dared talk about sex at a time when sex was a taboo topic. As a result, Coward's plays sometimes ran afoul of the censors and usually made a lot of money.

But there was another side to this urbane theater jack-of-all-trades who died March 26 of a heart attack at the age of 73. Coward's sophistication was tinged with a glowing patriotic sentiment that emerged in *Cavalcade*, a salute to the average Englishman, and *In Which We Serve*, a tribute to the courageous British warship crews of World War II. That film was regarded as an important contribution to Britain's morale in its dark hour.

During his 63 years in the theater, Coward wrote 27 comedies, dramas and musicals for the stage which brought him fame and fortune. He also was known for his music, including such memorable melodies as *Someday I'll Find You, Mad Dogs and Englishmen*, and *I'll See You Again*. The fact that he only played the piano by ear did not deter Coward from providing both the words and music to 281 songs.

As man of many talents, Coward often acted in, directed and produced his own plays and films.

Some critics complained that Coward's plays were brittle and shallow. They cited the glittering comedy *Private Lives* which contained such lines as "Certain women should be struck regularly, like gongs." But most students of the theater felt Coward's plays and films had insight and possessed an enduring quality even though some of them seemed to have been spun from gossamer. His *Brief Encounter* is regarded as one of the finest movies on the subject of romantic love. Another enduring favorite was *Blithe Spirit*, Coward's biggest hit of World War II.

After World War II, Coward's fortunes declined. He reportedly lost a great deal of his own money on a musical *Pacific 1860* and plays such as *Quadrille*. Critics began to conclude that Coward and his works had become outdated.

In 1950, plagued by a declining income and mounting taxes, Coward left England to take up residence in Switzerland and Jamaica. Then came a surprising turn. In the last years of his life, there was a sudden and enormous revival of

interest in Coward's works both in England and the United States.

In December 1961, in celebration of his 70th birthday, Coward's songs were played endlessly over the radio, and his plays were revived in theaters all over England. A few weeks later, he was invited to Buckingham Palace where Queen Elizabeth II dubbed him a knight of the realm.

Coward observed his knightly role with a word of advice for the new school of "kitchen sink" playwright. Said he, "Consider the public. Treat it with tact and courtesy. It will accept much from you, if you are clever enough to win it to your side."

Playwright-actor Noel Coward leaving his hotel for Buckingham Palace when he was knighted

BERMUDA'S GOVERNOR GUNNED DOWN WHILE STROLLING IN HIS GARDEN

On the evening of March 10, Sir Richard Christopher Sharples, the courtly, 57-year-old governor of Bermuda gave a party for a small group of guests in his 17th century hilltop mansion facing the sea.

The air was balmy and after the last guest left, Sir Richard and his aide, Capt. Hugh Sayers, 26, set out on their ritual night stroll through the fragrant gardens with the governor's gangling Great Dane, Horsa loping at their heels.

Shortly before midnight, a police guard heard the crackle of gunfire. Running toward the sound of the fusillade, the guard found Sir Richard, Sayers and the dog laying dead beside a pink hibiscus hedge.

The killings came just six months after Bermuda's police commissioner, George Duckett was slain and his 17-year-old daughter wounded under eerily similar circumstances. That outburst of violence had horrified the inhabitants of the orderly little British crown colony 570 miles off North Carolina's coast.

With the murder of Sir Richard and his aide, Scotland Yard dispatched two top men from its murder squad. Both had been investigating the Duckett slaying without being able to find a motive.

There seemed little reason for anyone to murder the affable governor who had proved to be informal compared to his predecessors, shunning the official uniform as much as possible and the pomp that went with the office. In an interview shortly after he took over the post in October 1972, Sir Richard said he wanted to change the image of the British governor in Bermuda. In a statement read to a news conference after his death, Sir Richard's widow said her husband had been sympathetic to the idea of independence for Bermuda. She declared that a "terrible mistake" had been made, if his murderer thought otherwise.

Sir Richard was accorded more pomp in death than he had tolerated during his life. After the funeral service, the governor and his aide were given a 17-gun salute and buried side by side in the graveyard of St. Peter's Church, the oldest Anglican church in the Western Hemisphere.

FOR THE RECORD

SENTENCED. Mrs. Clifford Irving, 37, the "Helga R. Hughes" in the $650,000 Howard Hughes autobiography hoax *(The World in 1972, 102)*. Mrs. Irving was given a two-year prison sentence March 8 by the Zurich, Switzerland, Superior Court on charges of multiple fraud and forgery. Mrs. Irving, a Swiss national, pleaded guilty to all counts.

ELECTED. Mrs. Hale Boggs, in a special election March 20 to succeed her husband as a Democratic Representative of Louisiana. Boggs was house majority leader when he vanished Oct. 16, 1972 *(The World in 1972, 224)* while on a plane flying from Anchorage, Alaska, to Juneau. Her win made Mrs. Boggs the first woman ever elected to Congress from Louisiana.

Bermuda's British governor, Sir Richard Sharples, and his aide, Capt. Hugh Sayers, who were both shot and killed after a dinner party

The newly-built ski-jump at Obersdorf, Bavaria, scene of World Ski Jump championships

April

Watergate I:

A Political "Caper" That
Proved One Of The Biggest
Scandals In American History

Breaking and entering is hardly a crime to be lightly dismissed, all the more so if it is perpetrated at the national headquarters of a major political party in the course of a presidential election campaign.

When the Democratic headquarters in Washington, D.C., was broken into during the 1972 campaign, however, it seemed such a pointless political adventure bungled in such comic opera fashion that the electorate passed it off as a mere dido. The papers called it "The Watergate Caper,"and the relatively few citizens who the polls said were aware that it happened at all seemed generally to pass it off with a wink.

It happened in mid-June, 1972, while President Richard M. Nixon, the obvious Republican candidate for re-election, was taking the sun on Grand Cay in the Bahamas. He could afford to relax. Not only was he enjoying a high point in popularity as president, but the California presidential primary of June 6 [see *The World in 1972,* 96] had all but certified that his Democratic opponent in November would be Sen. George McGovern of South Dakota. Nixon strategists had long considered McGovern to be the weakest among a half dozen potential

opponents. Sen. Edmund Muskie of Maine, a formidable foe as Democratic vice-presidential candidate against the Nixon-Agnew ticket in 1968, seemed in June to be out of the running. Muskie had been a clear front-runner among his Democratic rivals in the political winter book, but when the primary campaign heated up in the spring his candidacy faded. Among his other problems were some bizarre and unexplained setbacks. They appeared on the surface to be the result of sloppy staff work and planning although Muskie suspected more sinister causes. Meanwhile, McGovern's fortunes, to the regular Democrats' dismay and the Republicans' delight, steadily improved.

In the wee hours of June 17, 1972, at the posh Watergate overlooking the Potomac, a complex of apartments, offices and boutiques, a young security guard made his rounds. Frank Wills noticed that the latches on two basement doors had been taped open. He took the tape off and closed the doors. On his next round, at 1:52 a.m., the tapes were back on. Wills called the police.

Inside the offices of the Democratic National Committee on

Former White House aide E. Howard Hunt Jr., who pleaded guilty to six charges, talking with newsmen after being released on bond.

Watergate conspirator G. Gordon Liddy got 6 to 20 years for his part in the conspiracy, plus 18 months for refusing to talk to a grand jury.

the sixth floor three District of Columbia police officers, wearing plain clothes, surprised five men. The five were wearing blue rubber surgical gloves and were carrying burglar tools, cameras, electronic eavesdropping equipment, walkie-talkies—and more than $5,000 in consecutively numbered $100 bills.

All five gave false names but the police soon learned their true identities. One was James Walter McCord Jr., a 20-year veteran of the Central Intelligence Agency and at the time of his arrest "security chief" for the Committee for the Re-election of the President—CRP, or, as the democrats called it, "CREEP." The committee was a group set up apart from the Republican National Committee, staffed by White House aides and financed by its own fund raisers. Arrested with McCord were Bernard L. Barker, a former Havana police agent; Frank Sturgis, a soldier of fortune; Eugenio Martinez, an operative once hired by the CIA; and Virgilio R. Gonzales, a Miami, Fla., locksmith.

The five had rented two rooms in the Watergate, a search of which turned up some papers which led to the arrest of two others: Everette Howard Hunt Jr. and George Gordon Liddy. Hunt, like McCord, was a former CIA agent who, more recently, had served as a White House consultant. Liddy was a former FBI agent. He, too, had lately been a White House consultant and left that job to become general counsel to the Finance Committee for the Re-election of the President.

But it was no caper. It developed 10 months later into one of the most serious scandals ever to rock the American ship of state. The president of the American Bar Association called it "a domestic crisis of unparalleled proportions." As revelation followed ugly revelation, the scandal scarred the Presidential office as it besieged the man. The word itself, Watergate, came to represent the very antithesis of one of President Nixon's most frequently invoked concepts, honor. Watergate stood for allegations of moral and legal rottenness at the highest levels of government, allegations involving obstruction of justice, subornation of perjury, political payoffs and influence peddling, destruction of evidence, subversion of the electoral process through espionage and sabotage and character assassination through counterfeited documents, not to mention, of course, burglary and invasion of privacy. By the time the cherry blossoms bloomed in Washington more than a dozen of the President's closest aides were dismissed or had resigned under fire; two former cabinet officers were indicted; and in congressional cloakrooms a word all but unheard for a century was uttered openly: impeachment.

Just after the break-in, Sen. McGovern referred again and again in his campaign speeches to "burglars caught in the dead of night with their rubber gloves and cameras and bugs" but the electorate seemed only to yawn. Other allegations of Republican misdeeds dug up by newsmen—mainly involving questionable fund-raising tactics and the granting of official favors in exchange for large contributions—fell on equally deaf ears. Nor did the resignation of John N. Mitchell as President Nixon's campaign manager seem to hold much significance. Mitchell had resigned as Attorney General to run the campaign, then quit on July 1 at the insistence, he said, of his voluble wife, Martha. She said she wanted to get out of town, "away from all these dirty tricks."

Even the disclosure that the Watergate raid was financed with funds donated to the CRP failed to arouse the public. Ronald Ziegler, the President's press secretary, dismissed the raid as "a third rate burglary attempt" which the President knew nothing about and most certainly "would not get involved in."

The Democrats, plainly hoping to make political hay before the election by finding out in court who ordered the raid, filed a civil suit against the CRP. The CRP sued back, charging the Democrats with using its lawsuit to abuse the courts. All of which, to a bemused electorate, smacked of election-year politics as usual, nothing to get upset about.

Besides, the President seemed to be anxious to get to the bottom of the matter himself. Attorney General Richard G. Kleindienst, on Aug. 28, promised that the Justice Department's investigation would be "the most extensive, thorough and comprehensive investigation since the (one conducted following the) assassination of President Kennedy." The following day, at a news conference, Nixon himself atttempted to lay the Watergate matter to rest with these words:

"Within our own staff, under my direction, counsel to the President, Mr. [John] Dean, has conducted a complete investigation of all leads which might involve any present members of the White House staff or anybody in the government. I can say categorically that his investigation indicates that no one in the White House staff, no one in this Administration, presently employed, was involved in this very bizarre incident."

Politically speaking, at least, that seemed to do the trick. A Gallup poll taken a few days later indicated that "only a small percentage of the electorate believe corruption in government to be one of the nation's top problems." As if to certify that no part of the "bizarre incident" involved higher-ups, John Mitchell, testifying four days later in the Democrats' civil suit, said he had no advance knowledge of the bugging raid.

If the public was satisfied the press was not.

Throughout the remainder of the campaign and beyond, investigative reporters, citing confidential sources, dug up enough evidence to indicate that the Watergate "caper" was but the tip of a very large and very ugly iceberg. They reported, for example, that Liddy and Hunt were also inside the Watergate the night the five others were arrested. And they identified an eighth person, Alfred C. Baldwin III, a former FBI agent, who allegedly delivered sets of eavesdropping logs to the re-election committee before the June 17 raid—indicating that there must have been a previous break-in to plant the bugs. That was only the beginning. On Oct. 10, the Washington Post reported that Nixon's re-election apparatus included a massive effort to sabotage the Democratic campaign beginning with the primaries. Later reports identified a former Treasury Department lawyer, Donald H. Segretti, who had been hired by the President's appointments secretary, Dwight L. Chapin, to conduct the sabotage campaign, and had been paid for his work by the President's personal lawyer, Herbert W. Kalmbach. In late October, news stories said that Jeb Stuart Magruder, a re-election committee official, had authorized the expenditures for the Watergate bugging, and that no less a White House personage than Harry Robbins Haldeman, the President's chief of staff, was one of the officials authorized to approve payments from a secret campaign fund for espionage and sabotage.

Haldeman, 46, was the man who saw the President most often. He worked at a desk 32 paces down a gold carpeted hallway from the Oval Office and determined who and what should be admitted therein. He even sat in on Nixon's "private" meetings with others and took notes. Sharing Haldeman's level of White House authority was John Daniel Ehrlichman, 48, whose job was to screen for the President every proposal or piece of advice on domestic issues. Because of their jobs, their Teutonic names, their zealotry on behalf of "the boss" and their icy dispositions, they were accused of building a "Berlin

Wall" around the President. Any suggestion that either of that lofty twosome could be involved in what the President, on October 5, had referred to as "this kind of reprehensible activity" apparently seemed too far-fetched for the voters to believe. They returned Nixon to office in one of the greatest landslides of all time.

The trial of the "Watergate Seven" opened in Federal District Court in Washington on Jan. 8, 1973. Presiding was Chief U.S. District Judge John J. Sirica, a trim, 69-year-old son of an Italian immigrant who had worked his way through Georgetown Law School and developed a reputation for rock-honest traditionalism and tough sagacity. President Dwight D. Eisenhower named him to the federal bench in 1957.

The special quality that Sirica brought to the Watergate trial, however, was a willingness to prod and probe witnesses on his own. The reason was that five of the seven—all except McCord and Liddy—pleaded guilty rather than testify to all they knew about the incident, and that didn't satisfy the judge. "The function of a trial judge is to search for the truth," he said to defense attorneys. He frequently took over the questioning, and once snapped at defendant Bernard Barker: "I'm sorry, but I don't believe you."

For all the trial did not bring out, it at least disclosed these tantalizing facts:

—Magruder, who was deputy director of the CRP, had ordered Liddy to set up a political intelligence operation.

—Liddy had received $199,000 for the operation, and John Mitchell, through the CRP's finance chairman Maurice Stans (who was Nixon's former secretary of commerce), had confirmed Magruder's authority to make the payment.

—The Democratic headquarters had been broken into and bugged a fortnight before the June 17 raid, and Hunt had hired a student for $175 a week to infiltrate the Washington campaign offices of Muskie and McGovern and provide typed intelligence reports.

On Jan. 30, Liddy and McCord were convicted of all charges. It was clear, however, that much more remained to be disclosed. The Senate on Feb. 7 voted to set up a committee to investigate what was now being called "The Watergate Affair," or "The Watergate Matter," terms which clearly included all the related skulduggery apart from the specific break-in, even as "Teapot Dome" became a blanket term for the widespread corruption of the Harding administration. What appalled many political commentators about the Watergate Affair was that, unlike all past scandals, it was not the result of private greed or lust or any of the more common sins of the flesh. At least at this stage there was no evidence that it was. It seemed instead to reflect a cynicism by which seekers after power felt willing to justify their ends by any means. Commentators spoke of an "atmosphere" within the White House, a vaguely defined aura of arrogance which could nourish a belief among some in high places that they were above the law. A deeper irony was that the misdeeds apparently were done solely to re-elect the candidate who took the hard line on "law and order," who had criticized society's "permissiveness" and had referred to "softheaded judges" who could not be counted on to apply justice evenhandedly.

He could not have been talking about Judge John J. Sirica. When sentencing time came, March 23, the angry judge unloaded a $40,000 fine and a 6-to-20-year sentence on G. Gordon Liddy, who had not pleaded guilty but had been especially close-mouthed during the trial and appeared to have been the ringleader of the break-in gang. Then he handed out provisional maximum sentences to the others—with the hint that the

sentences might be reduced for anyone willing to come clean before a grand jury or testify before the Senate committee investigating Watergate. Unknown to the public, one defendant already had shown such willingness. In a letter to Judge Sirica dated March 19, James McCord said that higher-ups had indeed been involved in the Watergate plot, that perjury had been committed at the trial and that the defendants had been pressured to plead guilty and keep silent in order to cover the tracks of others.

The combination of McCord's willingness to spill the beans, Sirica's jolting severity, and a relentless corps of reporters who had been attacked but never silenced, finally broke the dam. There followed an orgy of finger-pointing and whistle-blowing by one after another official of the CRP and the White House, each spreading, or threatening to spread, the blame. Their revelations—some made before a grand jury called by Sirica to restudy the case, others made in private sessions of the Senate committee—tended to give credence to allegations that had appeared in the press over 10 months—and denied with regularity, and increasing acerbity, by the White House.

The first to sing was Jeb Stuart Magruder, the 38-year-old deputy director of the CRP. He told federal prosecutors that John Mitchell, while still Attorney General, had cleared the Watergate bugging plans in advance and was at least aware of a subsequent effort to pay off members of the burglary gang to plead guilty and shut up. The accusation forced Mitchell to retreat from an earlier position in which he had repeatedly insisted he knew absolutely nothing about the bugging plans; he now said, yes, he had heard such a plan discussed but dismissed the idea as foolish and never could find out who it was who kept bringing it up. Magruder also named John Wesley Dean III, counsel to the President, as one involved in the cover-up of the crime.

The cover-up, not surprisingly, came into larger importance than the break-in itself, involving as it did the more serious act of trying to subvert the judicial system in an effort to conceal wrongdoing by ones sworn to uphold the law. Moreover, each new overturned rock indicated that the break-in was only a small part of an over-all ugliness designed to give Nixon an unfair, and illegal, advantage in his re-election drive, a campaign of espionage and sabotage financed with secret campaign funds contributed in cash by anonymous donors and used as well to buy the Watergate defendants' silence.

Other evidence of White House involvement in efforts to cover up the crime emerged in the Senate judiciary committee. There, senators reviewing the nomination of L. Patrick Gray to become permanent director of the FBI, took the opportunity to find out what Gray knew about Watergate. As acting FBI director (since the death of J. Edgar Hoover; see The World in 1972, 87) Gray had directed the FBI investigation of the crime—the investigation that Attorney General Kleindeinst had promised would be as thorough as that of the 1963 Warren Commission. With striking candor, Gray told the senators that he had sent reports of his investigation to the White House, that his agents had questioned White House staffers only in the presence of John Dean, that Dean had probably misled his agents on at least one occasion, and that he had turned over the Watergate wiretappers' telephone transcripts to Dean. Gray's biggest bombshell, however, was his confirmation that Herbert W. Kalmbach, the President's private lawyer, had told FBI agents that he had paid up to $40,000 to Donald H. Segretti—the man the press had revealed as the leader of a campaign to sabotage Democratic candidates—and that he had done so at the request of Dwight L. Chapin, the President's appointments secretary.

Martha Mitchell surrounded by newsmen as she arrived at her lawyer's office in New York

Pressure on the President to confront the issue openly increased steadily. From his own party, respected members such as Sen. Barry Goldwater of Arizona, Sen. Hugh Scott of Pennsylvania, the senate minority leader, and George Bush, the Republican national chairman, urged him to get to the bottom of the scandal and be done with it. It was no secret that many Republican leaders resented the more prominent members of the White House staff, none of whom had political backgrounds.

On April 17, President Nixon decided, in effect, to take the offensive. Appearing before a hurriedly summoned gathering of the White House press corps he announced that "major developments" had come to light in the Watergate matter—as a result of a new investigation that he himself had conducted. He did not say what the major developments were but he did make a major concession. He said that all members of the White House staff would, after all, appear before the Senate committee and testify under oath, subject to only modest restrictions. This was a reversal. Previously the President had invoked the rule of "executive privilege" on all White House aides, past and present, and his attorney general had expanded the claim to include all members of the executive branch of government—a claim that boggled most legal minds in the country. The President also said he would immediately suspend any member of the executive branch who was indicted, and would fire anyone who was convicted. His announcement took only three minutes. When he finished, he refused to answer questions. Press secretary Ziegler, when asked to explain the string of White House denials, brushed questioners aside with the comment that all previous White House statements on the matter were "inoperative."

There was no way, however, to snatch the fat from the fire by declaring the past inoperative. In the weeks that followed the blows to the Nixon administration fell with trip-hammer speed and the scandal called Watergate spread to include these disclosures:

—Acting FBI Director Gray revealed that he had burned some files which had been retrieved from the office of one of the original Watergate gang, E. Howard Hunt—at the wish, or so he thought, of top White House adviser Ehrlichman. The papers were said to include forged diplomatic cables, which Hunt said he had faked at the thinly-veiled request of White House aide Charles W. Colson. They purported to show that President John F. Kennedy had ordered the assassinations of South Vietnamest President Diem and his brother in 1963—presumably to be used to discredit the Kennedy name in case Sen. Edward Kennedy became a presidential candidate in 1972. According to Gray, Ehrlichman had suggested to Dean that Dean toss the papers in the Potomac River. Instead, Gray said, Dean, at a meeting in Ehrlichman's office 11 days after the Watergate break-in, gave the folders to Gray with the remark, "Thoese papers should never see the light of day." Accordingly, Gray said, he burned them without reading them. And when that fact became known, Gray resigned.

—Magruder, revealed to have been lying when he testified at the trial that he had had no advance knowledge of the Watergate break-in, resigned from his job at the Commerce Department, a post that had been given him when his usefulness at the CRP came to an end.

—Former Attorney General Mitchell and former Commerce Secretary Maurice H. Stans (who was finance chairman for the CRP) were hailed before a federal grand jury in New York

71

inquiring into the activities of a New Jersey financier, Robert L. Vesco. Vesco had been accused in a Securities and Exchange Commission suit of milking $224 million from his own firm, Investors Overseas Services, Ltd. While under SEC investigation he donated $200,000 to the CRP after a conversation with Mitchell and Stans. The money was ultimately returned to Vesco, but the grand jury still wanted to know what the financier thought he might be buying with his donation.

—A number of "funds" were discovered to have existed in various private offices during the election campaign: one, of about $1 million, in the office of Stans, all in cash, which was tapped to finance the Watergate break-in; another, of about $350,000, said to have been kept in the office of Haldeman ostensibly to be used for "polling;" a third, of $500,000 from undisclosed contributors, in the office of Nixon's lawyer, Kalmbach.

—A shocking revelation, however, came to light during the trial of Daniel Ellsberg for espionage, conspiracy and theft in connection with the purloining of the Pentagon Papers (see *The World in 1971, 182; The World in 1972, 260*). Trial Judge William Matthew Byrne was handed a note from the Justice Department disclosing that two of the Watergate gang, Liddy and Hunt, had broken into the office of Ellsburg's psychiatrist on Sept. 3, 1971. The judge called for an investigation—and revealed the additional bombshell that during the course of the trial Ehrlichman had approached him, the trial judge, with an offer to become FBI Director. Byrne's investigation revealed that Liddy and Hunt were members of a White House parapolice unit called "the plumbers" set up to plug leaks of information. Result: the judge tossed the Ellsberg case out of court, because of the government's mishandling of the prosecution.

—A grand jury in Orlando, Fla., indicted Donald Segretti for dirty tricks against Democrats in the Florida presidential primary. Other dirty tricks came to light as well: a rigged poll designed to show the public widely in favor of President Nixon's decision to mine Haiphong Harbor in May of 1972; a half-page ad in the New York Times reportedly written and paid for by the CRP but bearing names of 10 persons who had no apparent connection with the committee.

As the morass called Watergate deepened and the shouts of outrage mounted in Congress and on editorial pages throughout the land, the President could no longer postpone decisive action in the matter. The issue, had reached such crisis pitch, in fact, that Rep. John Moss of California suggested a preliminary House inquiry into whether grounds for impeachment existed—a move set down by leaders of both parties as "premature."

At his Camp David retreat in Maryland's Catoctin Mountains, Nixon labored over a speech until past dusk of April 30, then flew back to Washington. Looking wan and nervous, he appeared before television cameras at his desk in the Oval Room. Behind him, clearly visible, were a bust of Abraham Lincoln and a photograph of his family. His voice was unsteady.

He began with a familiar assertion: that he was appalled by the Watergate break-in the previous June. But during the nine months that followed, he said, he had believed the reports he had been getting that none of his men was involved. Only in March, he said, had he come to realize "that there had been an effort to conceal the facts both from the public—from you—and from me."

Then he turned to the big announcement made earlier in the day. He had accepted the resignations of Haldeman and Ehr-

President Nixon addressing the nation on the Watergate affair

lichman, his two top assistants, and of Attorney General Kleindienst. He regretted having to do so, he said, calling the former "two of the finest public servants it has been my privilege to know," and the latter "my personal friend for 20 years." He also bade a curt farewell to his White House counsel: "John Dean has also resigned."

He said he accepted "responsibility" for the whole affair, as the one at the top must, but he excused himself of any of the blame. He said that he had, for the first time in 27 years of politics, delegated management of his campaign to others and was thus befouled by "people whose zeal exceeded their judgment." He said that both parties in the past had done shady things and that Watergate "may have been a response by one side to the excesses or expected excesses of the other side," a remark that his Democratic critics found particularly gratuitous.

The talk lasted 24 minutes. When the television cameras were turned off, the President blinked back tears and was heard to mutter, "It wasn't easy." Walking back to his living quarters he stopped unexpectedly in the press office. Reporters weren't even aware he was there until his voice brought them to attention. "We have had our differences in the past," he said, "and I hope you give me hell every time you think I'm wrong."

In the days that followed, a long list of others joined his senior command structure in tendering resignations: Gordon Strachan, once one of Segretti's contacts in the White House, quit as general counsel to the U.S. Information Agency; Egil Krogh, who had admitted he had approved the raid on Ellsberg's doctor's office, resigned as undersecretary of transportation; David Young, who had assisted Krogh, left his staff job in the National Security Council; numerous other lesser officials left too, many of them persons whose names had become familiar to most citizens only because of the Watergate disclosures.

For Richard Nixon, it was apparent that the hell was just beginning.

Pablo Picasso: A Great Talent

The famous artist painting an urn in a workshop on the French Riviera in 1948

"Painting," Pablo Picasso once said, "is my hobby. When I am finished painting, I paint again for relaxation."

And paint he did. During the long creative years of his life, Picasso produced at such a furious pace that no one really knew how many paintings he had made, although one estimate put it at more than 6,000 pictures. In 1969 alone, when he was 88, the artist produced 165 paintings and 45 drawings. Possessed of a prodigious talent that drove him from his youth, he painted some of his pictures in hours. Others, however, took weeks to complete. And when he wasn't painting he created in other areas—water colors, pastels, gouaches, pencil and ink drawings, aquatints, etchings, lithographs, sculpture, ceramics, mosaics and murals.

Asked once to explain this constantly erupting energy, Picasso replied, "Everyone is the age he has decided on, and I have decided to remain 30." He couldn't, of course, and on April 8 Picasso died at age 91 in one of the 35 rooms in his hilltop villa of Notre Dame de Vie at Mougins, France. At his passing, American artist Robert Motherwell said, Picasso was "the last artist in this century who will dominate the scene, who will have been a real king during his lifetime. Now it will become a republic. . . ."

There were those, of course, who disputed his kingship. For Picasso in addition to being one of the most praised artists of his time also was among the most damned. When critics referred to him it was in superlatives, either as the greatest contemporary painter or as the least effective. But one point they did agree on: Picasso was the best-known artist of his time.

"Whatever else he was," wrote John Canaday of the New York Times, "Picasso was the most potent single force in the art of the 20th century. To think of Picasso as dead is next to impossible. Two generations ago he was already, with Matisse, the most commanding presence in art for an avant-garde that at that time was still small and was still opposed by the academic legions.

"But for a generation Picasso has been the established symbol not only of the revolution of modern art, but also of its conquest of the intellectuals, the collectors, the schools, and the last academic fortresses—the museums. The conquest is so complete that there are schoolchildren who know Picasso's name but have never heard of Giotto's. There are college students who can tell you more about the cubist revolution than the Russian Revolution. Picasso turned the avant-garde into a mass audience."

Picasso, in old age a short, squat man with broad shoulders, muscular arms, and a near bald head, was born Oct. 25, 1881, in Malaga, Spain, and baptized Pablo Diego Jose Francisco de Paula Neopmuceno Paria de los Remedios de la Santisima Trinidad Ruiz Picasso. The son of an art teacher, he showed talent for painting and sculpture at an early age, painting his first oil, a picture of a bull ring, when he was nine. After attending art schools in Barcelona and Madrid, Picasso moved to Paris in 1904. Extremely poor, he shared a garret with Max Jacob, a poet. Since there was only one bed, Picasso slept in it during the day while Jacob worked and then did his own work at night. The habit was to last throughout his life, when, rising

at 10 or 11 in the morning, he would spend a few hours with friends and family and then go to work at 3 or 4 in the afternoon and often keep at it for 12 hours or more.

While a young artist, Picasso developed what was to become known as his "blue period," a time when all of his paintings, such as *La Mort D'Arlequin,* had variations of the color blue in them. This period, which ended about 1904, established him as an artist, and Picasso then moved into his "rose period" in which hues of that color dominated his pictures. The period ran from 1904 to 1906. Among the best-known "blue period" pictures were *The Two Sisters* and *The Woman with the Jackdaw.* It was during this time that he also executed his famous etching of a hungry couple at an almost empty table, *The Frugal Repast.* Examples of Picasso's "rose period" are *The Woman with a Fan, Youth Wearing a Frilled Collar, The Harlequin's Family,* and *Riding Horses to Water.*

There has been speculation that Picasso's use of blue was to mirror the poverty of that time while the change to rose signaled a change for the better in his fortunes. Whatever the significance, there was no doubt that Picasso's financial fortunes were on the rise and would continue to do so dramatically. Leo and Gertrude Stein and Ambroise Vollard, a Paris dealer, were known to have secured Picassos' for $30 in 1906 and 1907 but they probably were the last to do so.

His *Acrobats,* for example, sold for $3,000 in 1914 and the prices of his work kept rising. In 1965, he charged London's

Tate Gallery $168,000 for *Les Trois Danseuses*, a painting he had executed in 1925. And in 1973 the National Gallery of Art in Washington reportedly paid $1.1 million for *Nude Woman*. The sum paid for the oil, which was executed in 1910, was believed to represent the highest price ever paid for a Picasso work.

In his later years, collectors felt $35,000 was not too much to pay for a current painting. With his pictures hanging in the world's finest museums and reproductions of his work hanging in countless homes around the world, Picasso—who said once that "there is no such thing as a bad Picasso. Some are less good than others"—was extremely popular and many years earned more than $1 million. He was able to command high prices by driving hard bargains with his dealers while keeping the bulk of his work off the market, releasing for sale some 40 paintings a year out of perhaps hundreds.

He was in such demand that it got to where he could get money merely by drawing a few lines on a piece of paper and signing it. It also got so that faking Picasso work became a small industry. The story goes that a friend once bought Picasso a picture to have it authenticated and Picasso proclaimed the picture was a fake. When the friend told Picasso he had seen the master paint the picture Picasso replied, "I can paint false Picassos just as well as anybody."

The paintings he did not sell he kept stored away. Near the end of his life he gave 800 to 900 of his early works to a Barcelona museum. And after his death it was announced that Picasso, who left no will, had gifted France with his collection of works by other great modern painters such as Matisse, Degas, Van Gogh, Cezanne and Renoir.

Following his blue and rose periods, Picasso suddenly turned from his semi-classical, post-Impressionist style and erupted onto canvas with an entirely new technique—cubism. The birth of cubism was marked in 1907 with his oil called *Young Ladies of Avignon*, an abstract, distorted angular painting of five girls.

"When we painted as we did," Picasso said, "we had no intention of creating cubism, but only of expressing what was inside us. Cubism is neither a seed nor a fetus, but an art which is primarily concerned with form, and once a form has been created, then it exists and goes on living its own life."

A restless rebel of art, a radical and innovator, Picasso was a man of many styles—neoclassicist, cubist, surrealist, modernist.

"For me," Picasso said, "a picture is neither an end nor an achievement but rather a lucky chance and art experience. I try to represent what I have found, not what I am seeking. I do not seek—I find." And, on another occassion, he said, "Everything I do is only one step on a long road. It is a preliminary process that may be achieved much later. Therefore, my works must be seen in relation to one another, keeping in mind what I have already done and what I will do."

Amazingly prolific, Picasso painted thoughts and feelings in the hope they would pass on to those who looked at his work. There were many who caught, or thought they caught, what he was trying to say. But there were others who didn't get the idea and found his works just meaningless collections of daubs.

Asked once, "What is art?" he replied, "What is not?" Then backed up what he had said by grabbing a bicycle seat and a pair of handlebars and combining them to make a bull's head.

"Whatever the source of the emotion that drives me to create," he said, "I want to give it a form that has some connection with the visible world, even if it is only to wage war on that world. Otherwise a painting is just an old grab bag for everyone to reach into and pull out what he himself has put in. I want my paintings to be able to defend themselves, to resist the invader, just as though there were razor blades on all surfaces so no one could touch them without cutting his hands. A painting isn't a market basket or a woman's handbag full of combs, hairpins, lipstick, old love letters and keys to the garage.

". . . I don't want there to be three or four thousand possibilities of interpreting my canvas. I want there to be only one and in that one to some extent the possibility of reorganizing nature, even distorted nature, which is, after all, a kind of struggle between my interior life and the external world as it exists for most people . . . I don't try to express nature, rather . . . to work like nature. And I want that internal surge —my creative dynamism—to propose itself to the viewer in the form of traditional painting violated."

Picasso was pure artist, of course, but there also were other sides to him. In politics he was a member of the French Communist Party, and in 1950 the U.S. State Department refused to let him and a European "peace delegation" visit America to present a petition to Congress calling for immediate reduction in war budgets and military forces and the prohibition of atomic weapons.

Picasso had shown little interest in politics until civil war broke out in his native Spain in 1936. He sided with the Republican forces against those of Gen. Francisco Franco, whose armies eventually won.

One of his most famous paintings came from this violent period. It is *Guernica*. Painted in 1937, the 11¼ foot high by 25½ foot long picture depicts the slaughter of unarmed civilians by fascist planes. Called by some the most famous painting of the 20th century, *Guernica* is based on the bombing of the Basque town of that name by German airmen provided to Franco by Adolf Hitler. The town, of no military importance, was bombed to test the effect of explosive and incendiary bombs on civilians. The canvas is in New York's Museum of Modern Art, which has the world's largest public collection of Picasso's work.

Friends of the artist said he had come to admire the Reds who served in Spain's republican army, but it was not until

Picasso's powerful painting "Guernica" depicted the Spanish Civil War

1944 that he formally joined the party. He became a Communist, he said, "because the Communists are the bravest in France, in the Soviet Union, as they are in my own country, Spain."

The Dove, a Picasso lithograph, was used as a symbol for a Moscow-sponsored "peace movement" and it later came to be a peace symbol. The picture brought him a Communist award but during Joseph Stalin's rule in Russia the display of Picasso's paintings was prohibited. This puzzled Picasso, who, after being attacked by a Russian art critic, queried, "I don't try to advise the Russians on economics. Why should they tell me how to paint?"

After Stalin's death, however, the Soviet marked Picasso's 75th birthday by exhibiting a number of his pictures and ceramics to the Russian public.

Another of Picasso's sides was his relationship with women. Always as he worked there seemed to be a woman beside him. Some served as models for his controversial paintings. First there was Fernande Olivier, with whom he lived from 1904 to 1907. Then came Marcelle Humber, from 1907 to 1918. While doing the scenery and costumes for a ballet, Picasso met and married ballerina Olga Kokhlova. She bore him a son, Paul. They had been separated 20 years at the time of her death in 1955.

After the separation, Picasso lived with Marie-Therese Walter, who bore him a daughter, Maya. She was followed by Dora Maar, who in turn was followed by Francoise Gilot. Mme. Gilot was with Picasso from 1946 to 1953 and they had two children, Claude and Paloma. She later wrote a book, "Life with Picasso," which the artist tried unsuccessfully to have banned in France.

In 1961, Picasso married Jacqueline Roque. He was 79. She was 35. The Paris-born divorcee added her daughter to the family that Picasso enjoyed so much.

"I love life and I love children," Picasso said on his 80th birthday. "I want to have them around me all the time. It is they who keep me young."

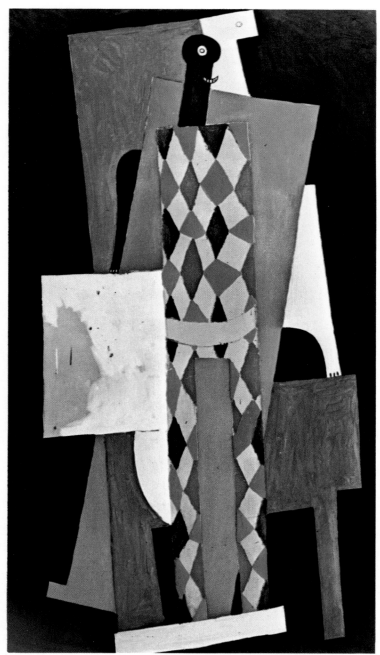

"Harlequin" painted in 1915

"Les Desmoiselles d'Avignon" painted in 1907

Once Again the Mississippi River Broke Loose and Went On a Destructive Rampage

The sun broke through in West Alton, Mo., as waters of the Mississippi and Missouri began to recede

IN THE SPRING of 1973, the Mississippi River did much more than just keep rolling along. Penned by dozens of dams and miles of levees, bloated by record rains and melting snows, the mighty Mississippi broke loose again; a relentless force periodically rising from its banks to scorn man's many attempts to tame it.

The mighty waterway, dubbed "Father of Waters," by Indians and recalled in melody with gentle affection as "Old Man River," went on its worst rampage in the 200 years or so that records have been kept of its long, meandering path and its sudden savage upheavals.

From March to May, the Mississippi plunged south through Iowa and Illinois, past Missouri, Arkansas and Tennessee, over much of Mississippi and Louisiana to the Gulf of Mexico.

At its worst, the Mississippi climbed from its lush banks and created a moving lake 10 miles wide and 40 feet deep. It carried the debris and pollution of dozens of towns where it crested and topped levees and spilled it over the vast farmlands which hug its banks.

The Mississippi flooded 13 million acres in seven states and chased 30,000 persons from their homes. It caused more than $400 million in damages and thousands of planters from Illinois to Louisiana were faced with a complete crop loss for the year.

Four separate crests flowed down the Mississippi with record heights at many places. It reached 43.5 feet at St. Louis on April 28, covering for the first time since 1785 a high water mark scratched on a huge rock by obscure French trappers.

At Thebes, Ill., a hamlet of 450 persons living under and around a small bluff overlooking the river, Herb Prater watched the muddy waters lap over the main street.

"I've been watching 'em since 1912 and this is the grand-daddy of 'em all," he said. "I recall the flood of 1912. It was bad. We was poor and living in boxcars along the railroad tracks . . . and we had to get out. But it's never come up this far."

The river's flood bank was 100 yards above the tracks. From the red brick courthouse built on the bluff in 1848, the Mississippi looked like an ugly brown lagoon spreading for miles across to Cape Girardeaux, Mo. Lofty poplars and cottonwoods peeped above the stained surface like yard shrubs.

At Cairo, Ill., about 25 miles south of Thebes, the Mississippi is joined by its biggest tributary, the Ohio, and continues south toward the rich cotton delta of Mississippi and Louisiana.

The floods came early and stayed late in the backwaters of the Yazoo in Mississippi and the Red and Black in Louisiana.

"The water just kept crawling," said Cliff Burr, 60, who has a 200-acre farm near Vicksburg, Miss. "I bulldozed a levee around the house. They kept saying the water wouldn't go no higher. It kept crawling. I fought it, but it was a lot of wasted sweat."

Soaked in five feet of water for two months, Burr's once comfortable home was a muddy wreck when the water drained.

At St. Charles, Mo., just above the confluence of the Mississippi and the Missouri rivers, a triangle of land separating the two rushing streams, was almost completely inundated.

Walter Rooney and his brother, Raymond, lived with their families near Dardenne Creek, a tiny inlet a few miles from the Mississippi.

"The water started to come about the first of April," said Walter Rooney, a lean man with a salt-speckled crew cut. He moved his family from their mobile home to his sister's house on the high side of the creek. The night of April 25, that house was flooded.

Rooney's wife said, "We lost everything except some clothes . . . all the letters and grade school pictures and graduation photographs . . . just everything."

Ray Rooney rented a house on the creek. "The water first came up in February. We moved to the second floor and it came within two inches of there. Then it went down and I had no idea it would ever get that high again. But it did."

For many river-dwelling residents from Hannibal, Mo., to New Orleans, that was an old story. The river crested twice, three times and sometimes four times in many communities.

"We just get it licked and here it comes again," said the mayor of Ste. Genevieve, Mo., the oldest settlement west of the Mississippi. Ste. Genevieve's business section is located nearly two miles from the river and thousands of sand bags were brought in to stem the rising water. The residents kept pumping and digging and waiting and praying. The makeshift levee held all through March and April.

On the final day of April the crest which had reached 43.5 at St. Louis, drifted 55 miles downstream and topped the sandbags at Ste. Genevieve.

The churning river which drains 28 states from the Alleghenies to the Rockies, from Montana to Virginia and New Mexico to New York, created vest pocket disaster areas along many of its tributaries where the waters backed up. And many of its tributaries were flooding on their own. The Illinois River spilled over Grafton, Ill., where it joins the Mississippi and where the Mississippi was boiling past the town at the rate of 13.5 million gallons a second.

There was flooding as far west as Denver, Colo., where the Platte River left its banks. And high waters left over from extraordinary, steady, heavy spring rains had swelled the Wabash, the Cumberland, the Platte, the Cheyenne, the Canadian and the Arkansas rivers, all of which ultimately join the Mississippi.

Louisiana wild life agents pulled this deer to safety from the waters of the Morganza Floodway that had to be opened to ease pressure on a dam of the Mississippi River

In dozens of communities there were families like the Rooneys who sought refuge at hastily established disaster centers; most of them in church basements or fraternal society halls.

In these areas, the federal government's disaster teams sent officials from the Red Cross, the Small Business Administration, the Department of Housing and Urban Renewal, the Internal Revenue Service and the Social Security Administration to lend aid to the homeless.

In Ste. Genevieve, Mo., a major problem was getting the flood victims to apply. Mayor Erv Wiener said, "I've had to go out on the streets and tell the people to come and apply for help. They deserve it. They've paid their taxes. But they're just a bunch of proud old Dutchmen."

In many of the communities, there was nothing but praise for the teen-agers who worked hour after hour packing sandbags and stacking around schools and churches and grocery stores.

The Corps of Engineers which directed the three-month long fight against the Mississippi reported that 13 million sandbags were stacked in the hardest hit states. It cost the Corps an estimated $48 million to fight the floods and there were more than 2,000 Corps employees working extended hours from March to May. In addition, 400 members of a reinforced Army engineer company were used.

"Those engineers built a bridge at West Alton in 25 minutes," said a Corps official in St. Louis.

The Corps counted final flood damage at $409 million with $166 million of the losses in agriculture. But without 2,220 miles of floodwalls and levees, the Corps said losses would have been much worse. Maj. Gen. Charles C. Noble of Vicksburg, Miss., head of flood control from Hannibal to the Gulf, said, "It would have been a catastrophe. Lives lost, damages would have gone to $8 billion." There were 24 deaths attributed to the flooding compared with more than 200 in the devastating 1927 flood which spilled over 17 million acres.

A glimpse at state-by-state flood effects:

—Illinois counted 550,000 acres flooded, including 45,000 acres of destroyed winter wheat. Total farm damages mounted to $35 million. Kaskaskia Island in the Mississippi across from Ste. Genevieve, Mo., was inundated by 17 feet of water.

—Missouri was among the hardest hit states with damages estimated at $134 million. Experts said 18 per cent of the tillable ground was knocked out of production by floodwaters. At Hannibal, there was four feet of water in the lobby of the Mark Twain Hotel. An 11-mile system of floodwalls, pumps and levees saved St. Louis.

—Tennessee had two heavy periods of rain in November and December and by March the Mississippi swelled a width of three miles near Memphis. For the first time since the Memphis Cotton Carnival started in 1931, the landing of the Royal Barge was canceled because the river banks were crumbling.

—Arkansas' Gov. Dale Bumpers said the 1973 spring floods were the most damaging natural disaster in the state's history. Two million farm acres were flooded and damages were estimated at $38 million. Hundreds of farmers were prevented from planting their usual cotton crop.

—Mississippi's farm losses alone were counted at nearly $100 million and other losses figures at $30 million. Only 10 per cent of the state's wealthy cotton crop had been planted by mid-May, long after the normal season.

—Louisiana farm and livestock losses were estimated at $66 million which, in turn, would cost the state's economy about $204.5 million. Some of the best land in the state was covered by 20 feet of water. An estimated 2,000 head of cattle drowned and 100,000 were stranded, moved or sold under duress. Hundreds of oil and gas wells were forced out of production. The Bonnet Carre spillway above New Orleans diverted floodwaters to Lake Pontchartrain and was credited with saving New Orleans from a disastrous flood.

Despite its enormous damage to agriculture, the Mississippi's 1973 flooding was not unexpected. "There was no drama, no emergency rescues," said a Coast Guard commander. "Everyone knew the water was coming." In St. Louis, the Corps of Engineers noted in December that the Mississippi was far above normal levels and planned for mid-February a flood fight control exercise.

Residents crossed a pontoon bridge constructed by the Army Corps of Engineers to the north side of St. Mary's, Mo., cut in half by rampaging waters of the Mississippi River

Floods swept So. St. Louis, Mo., inundating homes and leaving families without shelter

"We knew we would have a flood fight on our hands," said one Corps official, "but we never believed it would last as long as it did."

The Mississippi officially went out of its banks March 11 at St. Louis when it climbed past the 30-foot flood stage level. It remained out of its banks a total of 77 days and nearly three weeks longer than the 58-day record established in the monumental flood of 1844.

The Corps in St. Louis was justly proud of the 39 federally constructed levees in its district, only one failed; at Kaskaskia Island.

Kaskaskia, the first capital of Illinois, is a 10,000-acre plot of rich farmland where 100 families reside. Kaskaskia was separated from Illinois in 1901 when the Mississippi carved a channel between the town and the state. Kaskasia residents now are connected with St. Mary's, Mo., by a four-mile bridge. They began fighting the flood in early March. The Coast Guard began hauling grain and feed for chickens and cattle and finally, in April, helped evacuate both animals and people.

On April 27, after three nights of strong buffeting from river waves swelled by unusual southwesterly winds, the levee broke through. In a matter of hours the Mississippi covered the island and began climbing past the porches and first floor windows of the houses. Barns were tipped over and the water eventually reached 17 feet, covering nearly everything but rooftops. About six families had returned by July but most of the residents went back only occasionally to salvage what few possessions survived the flooding.

Louis Bauman, 71, and his wife, Verna, have lived in government housing in nearby Chester, Ill., since their two-story frame house was swamped. "I don't know if we'll move back," Bauman said a few months after the flooding. His wife differed, "We'd be silly not to come back here if they build up the levee again. We've lived here all our lives. You can't move just like that . . ."

Agriculture Department experts doubted many farmers along the Mississippi would be forced to quit their land.

But there were many farmers facing a bleak year.

Melvin Evans of Taylor, Mo., across the Mississippi from Quincy, Ill., said, "We'll have to have a miracle to get any crops planted this year . . ." Evans figured he would lose $35,000 in 1973.

Mississippi farmer Cliff Burr looked miserably at the fields which he would be unable to plant. "Ain't no need of me even thinking about it," he said.

James Picou, 48, of Kaskaskia, couldn't afford to wait a year without a crop. "I'll have to change my mode of living, go get a job somewhere, that's all. Our family's been farming Kaskaskia Island since 1848 when my grandfather came upstream from New Orleans. It may be all over."

Not only the smaller farmers suffered from the rampaging Mississippi. W. T. McMillan farms 1,400 acres near Jonesville, La., where the deep backwaters covered all but treetops. The water still was high in late June and McMillan figured it would be the middle of July before crops could be planted.

"It'll be too late," said McMillan who figured to lose $60,000 in 1973.

By May 27, the Mississippi was back in its banks at St. Louis. Downstream, the clean-up still went on and the farmers gingerly stepped on the soggy land throughout June and July.

The government shipped in mobile homes on hastily laid concrete pads to give housing to those who lost theirs to the Mississippi, the rushing, muddy ribbon of waterway that Mark Twain accurately called, "not a commonplace river."

With meat markets ordered to post prices, one butcher in Grand Island, Neb., decided to tell all

For Seven Days American Housewives Shunned Meat But Prices Remained High

FOR SEVEN DAYS, housewives across the nation, aroused by rocketing meat prices, boycotted their butchers and bulldozed their husbands into following suit.

The effect of the boycott launched April 1, seemed dramatic on the face of it, as a number of prominent political figures swung into line. U.S. Treasury Secretary George Shultz, New York's Mayor John Lindsay and the governors of at least 10 states announced that they would eat no meat during the seven days.

But the actual impact of the boycott was limited, to say the least. Some national food chains announced a token drop in meat prices, but for the most part prices stayed right where they were. The farmers brought fewer cows and hogs to the market and warned that they could hold back several months more, if need be. Meat packers also cut their output, so that the butchers who insisted that they had nothing to do with the soaring prices, bore the brunt of the hardship.

The housewive's revolt had been building for months. In scores of communities they had been parading, picketing and distributing pamphlets. Some had cut down their purchases of meat, while others pledged meatless Tuesdays and Thursdays.

But meat prices kept rising and with each ring of the butcher's cash register, the pressure mounted; pressure that was being felt by political leaders and by the White House itself.

Finally President Nixon acted. On March 29, only two months after he had loosened wage and price controls in Phase III of his economic program, Nixon appeared on nationwide television and announced that ceilings were being clamped on the prices of beef, pork and lamb.

"The major weak spot in our fight against inflation is in the area of meat," said the President. He vowed the ceiling would be maintained "as long as is necessary to do the job."

The presidential move was quickly challenged by the housewives who questioned whether a ceiling would work. They called for a rollback of prices as well.

Some scoffed at the President's imposition of price ceilings. "He thinks he's done something, when all he's done is recognize what we've been telling him," said Yvonne Mosca, who was organizing the boycott in Mount Vernon, N.Y. "A ceiling on veal at $4 a pound does not help me a bit in the marketplace."

Mayor Lindsay issued a statement directing that no meat be sold in any of New York City's institutions on Thursday of the boycott week. He also took a potshot at the Administration.

"To put a ceiling on prices at the highest level in our history is not a sufficient remedy in the current crisis," said the Lindsay statement.

The farmers weren't happy with the ceilings either. Deven Woodland, vice president of the National Farmers' Organization (NFO) said, "The farmer is at the bottom of the totem pole as usual, and will wind up with whatever is left after all other segments of the monopolistic food industry grab off big margins and assure themselves of a good profit."

On Sunday, April 1, the boycott began. From one end of the nation to the other, consumers rallied to the cause. Sarah Daniels of New York, whose husband and two children were described by her as beefsteak eaters, said the family would spend the week consuming lots of scrambled eggs, potato pancakes and vegetables.

For thousands of other families, Sunday dinner meant things like macaroni, tuna fish and vegetable casseroles.

In San Antonio, Tex., Mrs. Charles Weaver, wife of an engineer for a computer company, said she had been cutting down on meat for some time.

"We're using a lot of fish," she said. "We dropped coffee when it went up and we can do without beef."

Some consumers said they would not actually buy any meat during the week of the boycott, but admitted that they had bought in advance, on sale, and stocked up their freezers.

"Most of the meat this week will come from my freezer," said Ruth Francis of Philadelphia. "I don't plan to go out and buy any meat. One of our meals will be ground meat and some time during the week I'll serve creamed chicken, and one night I plan tuna casseroles . . . Saturday we usually have pizza."

The trend against meat eating was felt elsewhere, including military bases. At Ft. Knox, Clifford Wilson, chief of the services division and the man responsible for supplying meat to the 89 mess halls on the post, said the cost of feeding a soldier three meals a day had risen so high that he was trying to serve more chicken in place of red meat. But, Wilson added, "There are no meatless days."

At West Virginia's Kanawha County Jail, Maj. Howard Parks of the sheriff's department, said most of the jail's $55,000 budget for meat had been used up, and the prisoners were being fed more chicken and fish in place of beef and pork. But the housewives apparently couldn't take credit for the switch in the jailhouse diet.

"We aren't doing this as a matter of following someone else's boycott," said Parks, "But we're now paying 99 cents a pound for hamburger—wholesale."

The boycott produced some interesting spinoffs, especially for the vegetarians who had long been treated with tolerant amusement by most meat eaters.

"I'm glad meat's high," said Lynne Morvant, owner of a health food restaurant in New Orleans. "It's a vegetarian's market now."

"Meat's dangerous anyway," said Miss Morvant, as she offered an interviewer a soyburger. "Meat is not easy to digest, has uric acid and is shot full of harmful hormones and antibiotics."

Some people did switch to vegetables but others went on a cheaper meat diet—horsemeat.

In Westbrook, Conn., Kent Carlson had been operating a small meat market for three years. Finally the spiraling price of beef got to him and he decided to do something about it. Carlson contacted a wholesale meat packing firm in Connecticut and ordered about 6,000 pounds of horsemeat. Carlson was given the go-ahead to open a horsemeat market, provided he sold no beef at the same time. Within one day, he sold 2,000 pounds of horsemeat.

One reason for the popularity of Carlson's wares: a horsemeat sirloin was offered for 85 cents a pound compared to the $1.79 he had been charging for beef sirloin a week earlier.

The western White House where President Nixon was playing host to South Vietnam's President Nguyen Van Thieu, apparently did not take part in the boycott. The main course listed for a dinner for Thieu at the Nixons' seaside villa was roast prime tenderloin of beef.

There were protests against the boycott. In Rochester, Minn., more than 90 persons, most of them farmers and their families, bought out the entire stock of the Red Owl Store on the second day of the boycott, spending $1,483.25.

Mrs. Robert Love of Rural Harmony was the first through the checkout counter and paid a bill of $153.17 for her grocery cart filled with hams, roasts and other meats.

"I just want to say meat and food prices are very reasonable," she said. Mrs. Love disclosed that she and her husband farm 1,000 acres.

By Tuesday, the meat industry had begun to feel the pinch. Wholesalers reported layoffs, and supermarkets said sales were declining.

"It's beginning to look like they mean business," said one New York store manager.

An Associated Press survey showed that the man in the middle—the wholesaler—had been the hardest hit.

In Los Angeles, Robert Miller, head of Union Packing Co., said some retailers had stopped all beef orders. J. J. Rodriguez, head of Meat Cutters' Local 563 of Los Angeles said 350 union members had been laid off. In Philadelphia, union leaders said about 300 meat cutters had been idled and several hundred were working shorter hours.

Dugdale Packing Co. of St. Joseph, Mo., said it was cutting down its production of dressed beef for an indefinite period. The move affected about 300 employes. Leroy A. Hughes, principal officer of the company, said the firm had been caught between farmers who "are being tough and holding firm to the prices they want" and buyers who "are being tough and holding firm to what they will pay, in addition to the government's price ceilings on these dressed beef prices."

Elsewhere it was the same story. Don Richards, manager of the meat counter at a supermarket in Portland, Maine, said meat purchases were off 60 per cent. And an operator of a market in Kalamazoo, Mich., said he had only 10 customers in five hours on Monday. As a result, he closed down the retail meat counter and said it would remain shut until Friday.

A note of desperation began to creep into the complaints. "It's like my meat has some disease," said a meat counter man in Glen Cove, N.Y. "Nobody'll even touch it."

There were attempts to fight the boycott. In Vermont, farmers announced a counter-demonstration, a roast beef dinner for a meeting at Bridport.

"If the meat boycott were to force the prices down for the farmer, it would mean that more farmers would go out of business and in the end consumer price would be much higher than it is now," said Mrs. Paul Blair, of the NFO.

The boycott dealt a blow to many New York steak houses. houses.

"People are jumping away from the beef and going into fish and eggs—a great, great percentage," said Joe Weber, assistant general manager of Gallagher's Steak House in Manhattan. Pointing to row upon row of aging 18-pound slabs of prime steak, Weber said his chef had removed only three of the slabs on Wednesday morning, in contrast to the normal 25.

At the Cattleman, manager Fritz Alfred said business was down to 50 per cent—"and the people who come eat fish, not meat."

At the Pen and Pencil it was a different story. John C. Bruno Jr. said business was unchanged, except that he had sold a few more steaks than normal. Bruno said his clientele of mostly men apparently were eating what they could not get at home.

For some restaurants it proved a lucrative week. John Elden, manager of the Oyster Bar in New York's Grand Central Terminal, said fish and shellfish stew orders had risen 25 per cent.

The boycott even had repercussions at United Nations Headquarters. At a reception given by the Netherlands delegation, an American guest staunchly refused to eat a tiny meat canape. A West German diplomat said he and his family had not bought any meat during the boycott.

A Chinese delegate said he was amazed not so much by

Nemo, the disgusted lion at Jungle Habitat in West Milford, N.J., did not appreciate nibbling fish in place of red meat

Mrs. Jan Alfaro of Logan, Utah, temporary chairman of the Consumer Congress (right) predicting that the meat boycott would continue unless Congress rolled back prices to January level

the boycott but at how much meat Americans ate in the first place in contrast to the representatives of Peking. "Our problem at the mission is finding the right Chinese vegetables on the New York market," he said.

From Livermore, Calif., came a word of advice for the protesting housewife from an expert. Instead of engaging in boycotts, said Mrs. Margie Thompson who had been in the butcher business for 30 years, women should learn how to cut meat themselves and retrieve choice cuts from less savory ones.

A round steak selling for $1.49 a pound in Livermore, if properly cut, yielded top and Swiss steaks which sold for from 20 cents to 60 cents more in stores, said Mrs. Thompson. She added that housewives could save "at least 40 cents a pound" by cutting steaks and stew pieces off a prime rib roast.

Mrs. Thompson spoke from the heart. She had been laid off at the supermarket where she was working as a meat wrapper because women were not buying meat.

Some experts began to question the effectiveness of the boycott.

"It may make a lot of people feel better because they are doing something," said Dr. A. James Miegs, economist at New York's Argus Research Corp. "But to have significant impact on the price of beef, you would have to bring about pretty fundamental changes in American buying habits—and I don't believe that's likely to happen."

At week's end, a survey showed that supermarket sales of beef, lamb and pork were down and butchers had reported heavy layoffs. But farmers had kept their cattle from the market and prices remained just about the same.

"The impact of the meat boycott on retail prices was anything but sensational," said Nathan Herschberg of the New York Market Information Service. "It seems strange that a

drop in consumption of the magnitude reported—20 per cent to 80 per cent—should have had so little effect on prices." Along the Eastern Seaboard, market analysts reported quality cuts such as porterhouse steak and rib lamb chops had dropped about 10 cents a pound, but that otherwise prices were unchanged.

Herschberg said it would be a mistake to conclude from all this that the nation's housewives who had promoted the ban had achieved nothing. The boycott, he said, had probably "kept live animal prices from getting further out of bounds."

The boycott had another effect. It brought protests from both the butchers and the farmers that they were not the villains in the drama.

In a bid to convince housewives that they were not the bad guys, the meat cutter's union began handing out pamphlets titled "Lady, Please Don't Blame Your Butcher."

Patrick E. Gorman, secretary-treasurer of the Amalgamated Meat Cutters and Butcher Workmen AFL-CIO estimated that up to 75,000 union members had been laid off or put on forced vacations because of the boycott.

"The victims are the meat cutters and clerks who lost their jobs while the supermarkets continue to operate," said Gorman. "The ladies have a right to complain, but it's idiotic to blame us."

In turn, the farmers presented their side. Members of the NFO claimed they were being unfairly blamed for the soaring prices. They noted that other food items had gone up as well and said they were faced with rising production costs. The farmers told a story of flooded fields, skyrocketing farm expenses and concern that overproduction could send agricultural prices tumbling.

It became apparent there was no clear villain. Economic specialists noted that conditions for the sharp rise in food prices had been set up in 1971 when the Administration cut farm production in an effort to improve depressed farm income.

The economists said no one could have foreseen that the United States would make a deal to sell grain to the Soviet Union in July 1972 and that Russian traders would quietly buy up massive supplies of American wheat and feed grains. This was followed by a severe winter that interfered with harvests and cut beef production. The unusually wet weather prevented farmers from harvesting all their corn and soybeans, major ingredients in feed for cattle and hogs.

American housewives could draw some consolation from a report by the U.N. Food and Agricultural Organization (FAO) that a series of bad harvests in many parts of the world—caused mainly by severe droughts, in contrast to the rains that had drenched America—had caused acute food shortages. FAO experts said meat shortages were plaguing many areas in Western Europe and the Soviet Union.

The experts said meat prices were soaring everywhere, not only because of insufficient supplies, but also as a result of inflationary pressures and speculation.

Meanwhile, the boycott leaders, their anger unspent despite a meatless week, gathered in a Congressional conference room in Washington and echoed demands they had been making before the meat ban. They called anew for two meatless days a week and demanded a rollback in food prices. But they were unable to agree on how far to roll back.

Rep. Benjamin S. Rosenthal, Democrat of Queens, N.Y., gave a terse summation of his views on the meat ban. He declared the boycott had been "senseless" to many of his constituents.

"The prices were so high they couldn't buy meat anyway," said Rosenthal.

VIOLENCE IN A TRANQUIL KINGDOM

Throughout its history, the kingdom of Sikkim—a 2,744-square mile valley sharing frontiers with India and China—has been known for its many varieties of birds, butterflies, wild flowers and rare orchids. Even more rare in the tranquil kingdom is violence.

But on April 4 the ruler of Sikkim appealed to India for help in putting down unprecedented political turmoil in the usually placid Indian protectorate. The appeal came after about a week of protests against alleged rigging of elections and political mismanagement by the chogyal, or king, Palden Thondup Namgyal. The chogyal is considered a god by most of the 200,000 Sikkimese, and the demonstrators—who clashed with police and soldiers—demanded only that he become answerable to the people in the administration of the kingdom.

Indian troops moved in and went about guarding the Sikkim capital of Gangtok as well as the palace and its occupants, including the chogyal and his American-born wife, Hope Cooke, a former New York debutante. Demonstrators numbering 10,000 to 15,000 had surrounded the palace and vowed to prevent its occupants from leaving and others from entering.

India took over the government of the small Himalayan state April 12, the first time it had done so since a 1950 treaty made the kingdom a protectorate under New Delhi which became responsible for Sikkim's defense, foreign relations and communications.

The agitation ended April 13 when the cho-

Demonstrators burning a photograph of Sikkim's royal couple in Gangtok

gyal announced an agreement in which he said he had come to "a very close and confident understanding" with India. Leaders of the Joint Action Council, which had led the protests, said the agreement "guaranteed such of the democratic rights as we desired." After a "victory celebration," the thousands of demonstrators dispersed from Gangtok.

Bob Shawkey, left, and Whitney Witt, who both played the opening game in Yankee Stadium a half century earlier, planted kisses on Babe Ruth's widow as old timers joined in marking the stadium's 50th birthday on April 9

LAST FREEDOM FLIGHT FROM CUBA BROUGHT 84 REFUGEES

When Eastern Airlines flight 8894 touched down at Miami, Fla., at 11:55 a.m. April 4 it was more than just another plane arrival. It was the last in a series of flights that began Dec. 1, 1965 *(The World in 1965, 191)* to ferry more than 260,500 Freedom Flight refugees from Fidel Castro's Cuba.

Cuban authorities said before this final series of flights began that only 850 refugees remained. With the arrival of flight 8894 the last of those 850 had arrived.

There were 84 persons aboard the final flight. Many were old. Some walked with canes. Others had to be helped down the stairs. Some seemed dazed as they reached American soil and were hurried off to waiting buses. A few had tears in their eyes, and only a handful smiled. Just three children were aboard, one of them a handicapped boy who was placed in a wheelchair.

The last of the refugees to step off the last flight was Mrs. Caridad Caballero, 69. As she sat quietly in her black shawl, waiting to move on to join a daughter in New York, she said, "I am very happy. Very happy."

Mrs. Mionela M. Ferrer screamed at the fence outside Cuban Freedom House in Miami as she realized that her husband was not among the last refugees to leave Cuba

Wrecked railroad cars smouldered after a train loaded with 250-pound bombs exploded in suburban Sacramento

THOUSANDS FLED HOMES WHEN MUNITIONS TRAIN EXPLODED

Richard J. Dashnau, his wife, and their two sons and daughter were standing in their backyard watching a boxcar burn in a railroad yard near their Sacramento, Calif., suburban area when suddenly a mushroom-shaped cloud spurted from the blazing car.

The family ran to the garage to escape falling debris, but, Dashnau recalled, "the garage was collapsing and I looked to my left and the house was a shambles. Then I heard the detonation and I knew it was ammunition, and we just flat got out."

The burning car in the Roseville yard that April 28 was loaded with 250 pound bombs as were 20 other cars in the 103 car freight train. The more than 7,000 bombs were on their way from the U.S. Navy munitions depot at Hawthorne, Nev., to Port Chicago on San Francisco Bay when fire broke out on the train.

The exploding bombs spewed flames, shrapnel and debris over a square mile area, turning the rail yard into a nightmarish scene of flaming boxcars. It was, said Sacramento County Sheriff Duane Lowe, "a mass of craters and twisted debris that looks like a hydrogen bomb might have been dropped in the middle of it."

The recurring blasts broke windows and tore garage doors off their hinges as far as five miles away and citizens reported feeling and hearing the explosions as far as 40 miles away. There were no deaths, but at least 52 persons were injured and thousands of persons were evacuated from an area that stretched for a three mile radius around the yard until the danger was over.

The State Office of Emergency Services estimated personal property damage—including 400 homes damaged and about 10 destroyed—at $2 million. A spokesman estimated damage to railroad property would "run into the millions."

Family Life in the Animal World

Right, baby polar bear "Paddiwack" following in his mother's footsteps during his first public appearance at the London Zoo. Below, "Patty Cake" clutching her mother's arm as she is taken for her first outing at New York's Central Park Zoo. Below center, letting sleeping lions lie is a good rule to follow, but this cub at the Louisville Zoo threw caution to the winds as he wallowed in Dad's mane. Below right, day-old camel reaching up to touch her mother at the San Diego Zoo.

NATURAL GAS ERUPTIONS TURN COMMUNITY INTO GHOST TOWN

At first it didn't seem serious, just one of those little incidents that break up the quiet life in a small town.

A motorist called the sheriff's office in April to say a hole suddenly had appeared beside a state road in the northwestern lower Michigan town of Williamsburg and water was bubbling out. That wasn't too unusual in a north woods area dotted with deep artesian wells.

But shortly after Grand Traverse County Sheriff Richard Weiler reached the scene, it did become serious. Natural gas began bubbling out of the hole.

"We were lucky," the sheriff admitted later. "We didn't find out about this by having somebody's house blown up."

That eruption, along Michigan 72, signaled the beginning of weeks of problems for the 250 or so residents of Williamsburg. It was followed by hundreds of other eruptions in yards, basements and fields that eventually caused the evacuation of more than 80 families.

Investigators from the state's Department of Natural Resources (DNR) quickly found what they considered the cause for the sudden outburst of natural gas blowholes.

They said a natural gas well being drilled three and a half miles from Williamsburg by Amoco Production Co., a subsidiary of Standard Oil Co. of Indiana, apparently was causing the trouble.

DNR geologists said the well was down to 6,200 feet, tapping a huge underground natural reservoir. Then came an accident and the well shaft was broken. That allowed underground gas—at pressures of 3,300 pounds per square inch—to escape into a layer of porous limestone.

The DNR said the company attempted to contain the escaping gas, but that required special equipment. Meanwhile, as one state official put it, "that gas was being pumped into the ground at high pressure. It had to come out somewhere."

That somewhere was Williamsburg and while drilling teams attempted to plug the well, gas companies brought in teams of "sniffers" with gas-detecting devices sensitive enough to record one part per million of natural gas.

The recording devices only go up to 1,000 parts per million. When natural gas becomes that concentrated, it's explosive, the experts say.

Williamsburg was deserted quickly. Newsmen gingerly walking through the village thought they were in a ghost town.

Buildings were deserted. Doors and windows gaped open, to prevent the accumulation of gas. Clothes, abandoned when it came time to flee, flapped on a clothesline.

Several neatly trimmed front lawns featured ugly mud basins as much as 10 feet across and more than five feet deep. Geologists said most were caused when the high-pressure gas pushed to the surface all underground water and mud in the area.

A steady hiss, as if someone had left the gas on, could be heard from several holes.

That was one of the ironic twists of the whole affair. Although the village sits atop a gigantic field of natural gas, there was no natural gas pipeline or service to Williamsburg. Residents had to rely on bottled gas, oil or electric heat.

The evacuated families fled to the homes of friends and relatives. Later, the local American Red Cross chapter arranged emergency housing.

"It's frightening to be awakened in the middle of the night and told you have just an hour to collect some belongings and flee the possibility of an explosion," one resident said.

"It was fun and games at first, but later we got to thinking about it and realized it was serious," said Mrs. Charles Johnson.

"It was terrible. We didn't have time to pack. I remember thinking, 'what should I take?' It was awful to leave behind things like pictures of my children and know I might never get back."

After a few days, the novelty of the situation wore thin. "My husband went to work with dirty socks today," Mrs. Johnson said. "We don't know what we're going to do. I'm just thinking about today and forgetting about tomorrow."

"At first we told them they'd be gone a week," Sheriff Weiler said. "Then we started talking about two weeks. Now I hear it could be months."

Amoco eventually succeeded in plugging the well, while continuing to issue denials its operation caused the problem. Gas concentrations in the deserted village started dropping.

Even then, the problem wasn't solved.

"The situation was about what we expected," a state official said. "As one blowhole subsided, others broke out. It was like a bottle of ginger ale. You take the top off and the bubbles keep coming out for a long time."

Meanwhile, the legal complications promised to be enormous.

Operators of a motel on Acme Creek filed a lawsuit against Amoco, claiming underground water was polluting the creek and the lake it feeds which runs into Grand Traverse Bay. County commissioners asked a drilling ban until they could be assured it was safe.

Environmentalists claimed the DNR was too lenient in its attitude toward well drillers.

Unless the state adopted more rigorous standards from the oil companies, said prize-winning wildlife biologist Ford Kellum, similar eruptions elsewhere were inevitable.

Drillers should be required to put metal casings in all well shafts sunk, he said. Casings are required only for producing wells, he said.

"Most companies get by as cheaply as they can," he said. "If they don't get caught or are forced into it by public pressure, they won't."

Oil company sources said requiring casings on all wells, even dry ones, would up the cost of each well 25 to 30 per cent.

The state did act to require casings on all wells digging into the porous sandstone layer which lies beneath most of Michigan's Lower Peninsula.

But that did nothing to help Williamburg's residents.

Six weeks after the first gas eruptions, more than 50 families were still waiting to go home. Most returned home by early summer but about 15 families waited far longer for dangerously high gas levels to subside.

Immediately after the evacuations, a state official warned, "it could be months" before Williamsburg and its residents returned to normal.

He was right.

Mace Brown, one of the F.B.I.'s 10 most wanted, lay mortally wounded April 18 as two policemen took cover behind a car outside the Chase Manhattan Bank in Harlem while two other bandits held more than three dozen hostages. Two hours later, the two gunmen surrendered.

William Ray Bonner was booked in connection with the mass killings

MASS KILLINGS MADE EASTER A NIGHTMARE IN LOS ANGELES

It was a peaceful Easter Sunday in South Central Los Angeles. William Ray Bonner, a 25-year-old unemployed gas station attendant, was at home with his parents. The time: 2 p.m.

Less than three hours later, Bonner would be in custody, wounded in a gun battle with police. Behind him, at eight different locations, lay 16 victims, most critically wounded if not already dead. Ultimately he would be charged with seven counts of murder, nine of assault and three of kidnap. His fiancee, a friend and a 12 year-old girl were among those killed. So was the private security guard who stopped Bonner's getaway, felled not by the gunman but by police.

The Bonners were visited by a former neighbor, Otha Levitt, 53, who wished to make a telephone call while the two teen-agers who lived with her waited outside in the car. Carolyn Cleveland, 17, and Anthony Thomas, 16, would later tell authorities they heard arguing, saw Bonner run outside. He shot them both with a pistol, then returned to the house. The wounded teen-agers heard another shot and, despite their serious injuries, headed for the house. Bonner, now carrying a 20-gauge shotgun, rushed by them, got in their car and drove off. Inside, Mrs. Levitt lay dead. The time: 2:14 p.m.

Later, detectives would theorize that Bonner was upset because his fiancee, Dianne Lore Andrea, 22, had intervened when he was arguing with another man, Vernon Thompson. But at the moment they weren't even aware of what was taking place. Bonner drove to a gas station where he took money, and shot and killed 12-year-old Arlene Wells and critically wounded her 18-year-old sister, Vicky. Station owner A. C. Wallace was working when he heard the gunfire.

"I hid behind a gas pump," he recalled later, "and looked around. He was shooting point blank at two girls. I just tried to stay out of his way, even when the ladies were screaming for help. One of them ran into the station's service area and was gunned down as she got there. There was nothing we could do. I never heard him say a thing. He just started firing point blank like he was gone crazy." The time: 2:43 p.m.

Two minutes later Bonner was at another gas station, one where he had worked and become friends with Raleigh "Butch" Henderson, 33. Another attendant, James Morrow, 35, who would later recall that Bonner had "worked as well as anybody else here" before quitting and had been close with Henderson, witnessed the incident.

"He walked in and asked for Butch. Butch turned around and he just started shooting." Then, Morrow said, as he looked on in horror, Bonner turned to him, pointed at Henderson's body and said, "Do you know if anyone wants some of that?"

"For a moment my mind just left me," Morrow would recall. "I didn't know what to think. It was something I couldn't understand. There had been no argument, no talking, just those shots." The attendant said Bonner asked for a .38-caliber gun, was told the station didn't have one and left.

Bonner drove to the house belonging to the parents of Vernon Thompson, with whom authorities said he had some type of argument. He went inside and shot Thompson's parents and brother. The father, Javie Thompson, 57, was killed by a shotgun blast in the stomach and his wife and 15-year-old son were seriously wounded. The time: 2:50 p.m.

The gunman's next stop was a liquor store where he shot and wounded two employes. Fifteen minutes had elapsed. He drove to another liquor store, killed the owner and wounded a customer. Now it had been an hour since his argument with Mrs. Levitt. Thirteen people had been shot, five fatally.

Bonner then drove to his fiancee's home, burst in and killed Miss Andrea with a bullet in the neck. The time: 3:40.

By now a police bulletin was out for Bonner and two officers in a patrol car encountered him in an alley about 10 minutes after he had left Miss Andrea's home. The policemen said Bonner tried to block the alley, then took aim with his shotgun and fired. Nothing happened. He was out of ammunition. As he began to flee, the officers fired four shots. All missed.

Bonner's flight was halted a few minutes later when he crashed into another car stopped at a traffic light. He ran to the other car, pointed a pistol at Mary Felton and got in. "Drive," he told her. With Mrs. Felton, 45, were her daughters Elizabeth, 12, and Karen, 10.

This scene had been witnessed by Versell Bennett, 58, a private security guard who was driving by. Bennett drove ahead one block, then used his car to block Bonner's escape. Bennett fired at Bonner as Mrs. Felton grabbed her daughters and pushed them to the floor. The pursuing police car was quickly on the scene and, with other units it had summoned, surrounded Bonner.

More than 30 shots were fired in the ensuing gun battle. After being hit several times, in the legs and abdomen, Bonner finally was captured. The time: 4:40 p.m. Mrs. Felton had received a minor flesh wound and Bennett, caught

in the crossfire, had been hit in the head by a police bullet. He died several days later, and a deputy district attorney said Bonner would be held responsible because he had instigated the fight which led to the death.

At the hospital bedside arraignment four days later, the Bonner family attorney, Herman A. English, told reporters he had known Bonner for 10 years and considered him a "kind, easygoing, cooperative person, a very submissive man."

The U.S. Court of Appeals overturned on April 18 the 1967 court martial of Howard B. Levy, an army doctor who refused to give medical training to combat troops on their way to Vietnam.

FOR THE RECORD

MARRIED. Bernadette Devlin, a member of the British Parliament who has championed the cause of the Roman Catholics in Northern Ireland, and Michael McAlaskey, a schoolmaster, on April 23. The marriage was the first for both Miss Devlin, 26, and McAlaskey, 24.

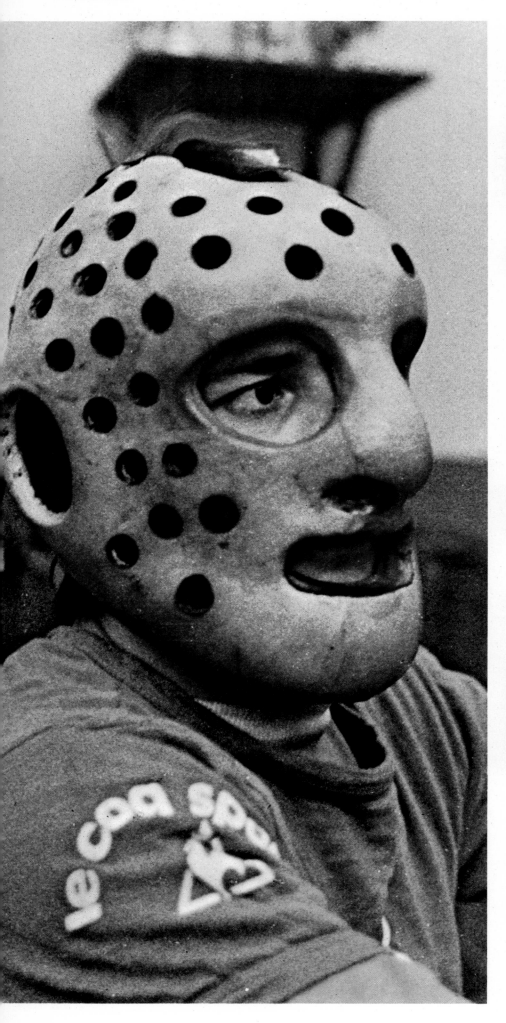

Above, a man who had been threatening to jump from a fire escape was finally dissuaded by police and a priest when his foot slipped and he plummeted three stories. But he was caught in a police net and escaped injury. Left, Swiss Boxer Walter Blaser wearing a "Frankenstein" protective mask during a training session in Paris.

May

Government agents searched all cars on road leading to the Pine Ridge reservation

For 71 Days, Indian Militants Held Wounded Knee, Defying Washington

U.S. marshals and FBI agents ringed the historic site where 146 Sioux were slain by U.S. troops in 1890

FOR A FEW BRIEF HOURS it looked like victory for the American Indian Movement, some 200 of whose members and followers had taken control of the historic hamlet of Wounded Knee in South Dakota. Eleven days after the men of AIM had made their move, the Justice Department unexpectedly removed its cordon of FBI agents and U.S. marshals.

In Washington, the Justice Department said the roadblocks had been lifted because many of the government's objectives had been accomplished. "This is the proper step at this point in moving toward a peaceful resolution," a federal spokesman said.

The Indians began a drumbeating celebration as the roadblocks were removed. Said Dennis Banks, a Minnesota Chippewa and leader of the takeover, "We have won a moral victory."

That victory was to be short-lived.

The following morning, Sunday, March 11, four men carrying sidearms and credentials as postal inspectors entered the village. Heavily armed Indian sentries disarmed the federal agents and held them for several hours in a museum that had been converted to a jail.

Although the 300 FBI agents and marshals had removed the net of seven blockades from around the village, surveillance continued as scores of Indians and white sympathizers joined the invaders to celebrate.

The village had been free only 24 hours when two militants in a van approached two FBI agents sitting in a car about five miles from Wounded Knee. Gunshots were exchanged and FBI agent Curtis Fitzgerald of Chicago was wounded in the arm. The two militants were also wounded. Both sides claimed the other had shot first.

It was not the first bloodshed of the occupation. The first person injured was an insurgent who was shot in the foot when his firearm accidently discharged a few hours after the takeover. But Fitzgerald was the first officer wounded and the relaxed atmosphere turned to tension.

The shooting and declarations by the Indians that they were claiming the village as their own as a sovereign nation at war with the United States dashed hopes that the confrontation was over.

By Monday the blockades were in place again. Over the next two months, sporadic gunfire exchanges resulted in six more persons wounded and the deaths of two insurgents.

The confrontation was not to end until May 8, or 71 days

Two Indians scanned the country-side following the setting up of block-ades on roads leading to Wounded Knee by federal agents

after the AIM forces had driven into the village and had taken 11 persons hostage. They ransacked the trading post, pilfering an estimated $150,000 in food, clothes, guns and Indian relics. Later the trading post was burned to the ground, churches desecrated, trailer houses and homes where the white traders lived looted and vandalized.

The insurgents had taken the village by force in the name of the Oglala Sioux, a nation of Indians that had been driven into South Dakota by the Minnesota Chippewas more than a century earlier.

Wounded Knee is a village set in the apex of two dry streambeds about 15 miles northeast of Pine Ridge on the largest Indian reservation in the state. It covers about four square miles, but the focal point of the 71-day demonstration was a 40-acre site on which the 150-foot long trading post and several housing units were owned and occupied by the family of Clive Gildersleave, a clan that is part Indian, but considered all-white by the militants.

The Pine Ridge enrolled reservation is home to 11,000 of the 13,000 enrolled members of the Oglala Sioux Tribe. The tribe and 1.5 million acres of reservation land is administered by the Bureau of Indian Affairs and an elected 18-member council presided over by Richard Wilson, a 39-year-old plumber turned politician.

It was toward the Bureau of Indian Affairs and Wilson that the militants directed the protest.

AIM leaders acknowledged that Wounded Knee had been selected for occupation because of its historical significance. They said they felt it would attract attention nationally and abroad. In fact, only hours after the armed takeover, TV newsmen were invited in and escorted past federal roadblocks.

Within hours of the invasion, AIM leaders Banks, 41, Clyde Bellecourt, 41, another Minnesota Chippewa, Carter Camp, 39, a Ponka from Oklahoma and Russell Means, 35, the only Oglala Sioux among the movement chiefs, said they would not evacuate the village until Wilson and the BIA had been dealt with.

The AIM leaders demanded that Wilson be ousted and that the tribal constitution be invalidated and new elections held. They also asked that Congress investigate the BIA and that an audit be held of both the tribal council and BIA finances. They asked that Sen. Edward Kennedy, D-Mass., chairman of the Interior and Insular Affairs Committee, and Sen. J. W. Fulbright, D-Ark., chairman of the Foreign Relations Committee, meet with them and agree to the investigations of the BIA and Indian treaties.

Kennedy and Fulbright declined the invitation, but South Dakota's two Democratic senators, George McGovern and James Abourezk, joined Justice Department officials in a parlay with the AIM leaders within two days of that takeover.

While McGovern and Abourezk were meeting with the militants, a house in Pine Ridge caught fire, causing serious burns to a woman. The house was owned by Aaron DeSersa, public relations director for AIM, and the injured woman was his wife. The Indians broke off the meeting, claiming tribal leaders had fire-bombed the house.

McGovern and Abourezk said they would not intervene for the militants so long as they remained in the village by armed force. The militants said they would not leave until their demands were met.

The pattern for the first major confrontation between the U.S. government and the Plains Indians in 83 years was set. The site was by the militants' design because the last major bloodletting in the Plains Wars of the late 19th Century was also at Wounded Knee.

The American Indian Movement was born on a sultry night in July 1968 in Minneapolis. Within months the leaders had attracted attention by protesting at the Minneapolis office of the Bureau of Indian Affairs (BIA) and demonstrating against what they termed a "double-standard of justice" in western South Dakota after a white rancher had been freed after admittedly shooting an unarmed Indian. In 1971 Banks and Means led the takeover of the Naval Air Station in Minneapolis, claiming it belonged to the Indians and should be given to them.

In 1972, the AIM leaders were in Gordon, Neb., less than 40 miles from Wounded Knee, demonstrating against the handling of the death of Raymond Yellow Thunder, an Indian. Yellow Thunder had been found dead in a car several hours after he was allegedly beaten by a group of whites. The whites were later tried and convicted of manslaughter after the militants led hundreds of area Indians in protest against the manslaughter charge. AIM sought a murder charge.

AIM celebrated its achievement in Gordon by going to Wounded Knee and taking the museum from the white traders. It left within a day, however, but the action served notice to the Gildersleeve family that the eyes of the militants were on the historic hamlet.

AIM's most ambitious effort was to come in the fall of 1972 with the "Trail of Broken Treaties" caravan to Washington, D.C., to protest what it termed the U.S. government violation of 371 Indian treaties. The Indians stormed the BIA headquarters, occupying it for several days. The government estimated damage to the BIA at $1.5 million and finally provided $666,000 in expenses before the demonstrators removed themselves.

The stabbing death of a young Indian in the western South Dakota village of Buffalo Gap set in motion a series of events that culminated in the siege of Wounded Knee. Wesley Bad Heart Bull, 21, was stabbed in a street outside a bar in the early hours of Jan. 1, 1973. The alleged assailant, Darld Schmitz, 29, a gasoline station operator from Custer was charged with manslaughter.

Indian leaders insisted on negotiating in a classical tepee

A preliminary hearing was set for Feb. 6 in Custer, a community of about 2,000 persons in the southern Black Hills National Forest. Russell Means called the manslaughter charge "another example of cowboy justice" and called for Indians to converge on Custer the day of the hearing.

About 150 Indians met in Custer that day and after prosecutors refused to change the charge from manslaughter to murder, the militants attempted to storm the court house. It turned into a rock-throwing, club wielding melee in which two buildings were set afire, several persons were injured and more than a score arrested.

Trouble was brewing in the southern Black Hills and the government moved U.S. marshals and FBI agents into the area. The South Dakota Highway Patrol was dispersed through the Black Hills as rumors of more demonstrations by the Indian militants continued.

On Feb. 20, the AIM leaders met with the traditional chiefs of the Pine Ridge reservation, men like Frank Fools Crow and Ben Black Elk. "They asked us to come to the reservation and help them," said Camp. "Between Wilson and the BIA, the ordinary Indian didn't have a chance."

Feb. 27 dawned bright, clear and warm for a winter day in

South Dakota. The temperature was in the 50s as the warm winds of the Black Hills drifted across the Pine Ridge reservation, which nestles next to the Nebraska line in the foothills of the pine-covered Mountain range.

Pine Ridge is an Indian agency town of about 2,500. Legal aid attorney Gary Thomas and Means were together part of that day, driving the dusty streets, discussing the ramifications of the incident three weeks earlier at Custer and the problems of being a reservation barrister.

"Means and I had driven to a store to buy a newspaper," Thomas recalled. "He went into the store and came out with the paper. An elderly lady came up to the passenger window, carrying a stack of probate papers and told Russell she needed some help with them. A guy came out of the store and walked up to my side of the car. I asked him what he wanted and he turned and walked into the store.

"He came out with four other men. Two came to my side of the car. I rolled up the window. They joined the other three on Russell's side, pushed the old lady out of the way and one of them started slugging Russell through the open window. I started the car and drove away. They had hit him in the mouth a couple of times."

Thomas said he drove Means to a house and returned downtown. "I was going to report it to the FBI, but I ran into a marshal and told him about it. I told the marshal I thought there was a potentially dangerous situation. He told me to go to tribal court and sign a complaint. I did, the men were arrested, but they were released shortly and my complaint was tossed in the waste basket. I was told I hadn't filled it out right, that I hadn't used the word 'threatened.' "

The word went out around the vast reservation that afternoon that the traditional chiefs, the rebel Pine Ridge Civil Rights organization and AIM were having a meeting that night at Calico Hall, a meeting hall on the outskirts of Pine Ridge. The subject, according to Camp, was to be the form the protest against the tribal leaders and the BIA was to take.

One of the options, an occupation at Wounded Knee.

"Our people came from all over the reservation," Camp said. "There must have been 200 at the hall when we announced it was too dangerous to meet here. We told them we would drive to Porcupine." Porcupine is a village much like Wounded Knee, about eight miles to the northeast of the historic hamlet. To reach Porcupine traveling from Pine Ridge, one drives past Wounded Knee.

"There must have been 40 cars," Camp said. "They didn't know it, but they were heading for Wounded Knee. The security force that I led was in the first two cars. We dropped sentries off at the junction and the rest of us went into Wounded Knee and secured the trading post. The sentries detoured the caravan into the village and it was ours."

The Rev. Paul Manhart, pastor of Sacred Heart Roman Catholic Church, was confronted by several young Indians in the church. They tied his hands and ushered him into the choir loft where he spent the night. The next morning he was taken to the Gildersleeve house.

Agnes Gildersleeve, 68, and her husband, Clive, 73, heard the caravan drive up. They also heard the gunshots as street lights exploded and watched as the militants vandalized the trading post. "They hauled stuff out of there all night," she said. "We didn't sleep a wink."

The BIA called for help and the U.S. marshals and FBI immediately set up a cordon, arresting about 30 persons who attempted to leave the village that night with food, clothing and relics. The seal around the village did not keep newsmen out, however, as some 15 were led into Wounded Knee about daybreak by DeSersa, who had remained in Pine Ridge.

Mrs. Gildersleeve said she was told by one of the insurgents that she and others were political prisoners. Means called them "prisoners of war", but later denied they had been held captive. Within 48 hours the 11 hostages, ranging in age from 12-year-old Adrienne Fritz to her grandfather, 80-year-old Wilbur Riegert, were told they were free to leave Wounded Knee. For a week they refused, but finally conceded they weren't welcome in their own homes and left voluntarily.

The militants set to work fortifying the village, digging bunkers around the Catholic church on the hill, blocking roads with burned-out vehicles. The government officers set up their blockades about a mile from the Indian bunkers, working 12-hour shifts and trying unsuccessfully to keep reinforcements out of the village and the insurgents from leaving.

In addition to the more than 200 insurgents in the village, another 300 permanent residents remained in their homes.

Members of AIM who held the village

Many of the residents voiced their support of the occupation force.

There were several telephone lines into Wounded Knee when the invaders captured the village. Within 24 hours there was one, a main circuit to the trading post with an extension in the Fritz trailer home, which had been turned into a command post for the AIM leaders and a press room for the newsmen. "Russell tore the other telephones out in order to maintain better control of what was going out," said a young Indian in the command post Friday evening. An hour later a mysterious explosion at a transformer seven miles away silenced the single telephone. Service was out for three days.

The two most pressing problems were communications and food. The first was solved when the Justice Department brought in their social service arm, the Community Relations Service, to serve as a courier between the federal officials in Pine Ridge and the AIM leaders in Wounded Knee. The food problem was resolved when the insurgents herded nine head of cattle from a nearby range—cattle owned by a white rancher—and butchered them.

The National Council of Churches entered the picture on Saturday, March 3. The Rev. James Armstrong, Bishop of the Methodist Churches in South Dakota and North Dakota, said the clergymen had a proposal that would be acceptable to both the government and the Indian occupation force. It included withdrawal of federal officers, purchase of the trading post area by the American Indian Movement and agreement that arrests would be made by grand jury indictment only. The Indians accepted the plan. The government ignored it.

Tribal President Wilson warned that if peace talks broke down he would lead a force of nearly 1,000 reservation Indians into Wounded Knee on Monday, March 5. Asked what his followers were doing in the interim, Wilson replied: "They're shining their rifles."

A teepee was erected in the demilitarized zone on Sunday morning by spiritual leader Leonard Crow Dog. The teepee was to play an important role in the Indian occupation as the Indians refused to negotiate in any other dwelling during most of the next two months.

For weeks the rhetoric flowed, cease-fires were agreed upon and then broken, nightly fire-fights between officers and Indians continued. Indian religious rites were conducted daily as the insurgents prayed to Mother Earth for guidance.

Meanwhile, a grand jury was convened in Sioux Falls, S.D., to hear evidence in the takeover.

In mid-March Means proposed that President Nixon appoint a special emmissary from the Sioux people to negotiate a settlement. The government had submitted an earlier proposal which included a provision that AIM leaders meet at a neutral site in eastern South Dakota. AIM said it amounted to total surrender.

There were three "settlement" announcements from government sources during March. All were erroneous. A second federal officer was shot on March 26. Lloyd Grimm, 56, a marshal from Omaha, Neb., was shot in the chest as he manned a roadblock. The wound resulted in paralysis from the waist down.

There were scores of arrests as federal officers stopped sympathizers and adventurers en route to the western South Dakota village. A pilot from Grand Rapids, Mich., was charged in connection with an airdrop into the village. Two other flyers escaped. A federal court judge stepped in and forced the government to permit adequate food and medical supplies through the cordon.

A blizzard swept across the northern Plains. The temperature dropped to 30 degrees below zero, and travel was impossible for two days.

Following five days of talks, an agreement was reached in early April. It provided for a group of the reservation's traditional chiefs and Means to meet with Presidential adviser Leonard Garment in Washington to establish a Presidential Treaty Commission. It also provided that the Indians would disarm when the meeting began, that there would be no mass arrests and that government investigators would conduct civil rights hearings on the reservation within three weeks.

The group flew to Washington, but the meeting never occurred. Means said there was a difference of opinion on when his telephone call ordering disarmament was to be made. The government said it would not meet with the Indians and their attorneys until Means agreed to make the call.

An Indian youth emerged from a sweat lodge during a heavy snow storm

The first death was recorded on April 26 when Frank Clearwater, 47, succumbed from wounds suffered a week earlier. Clearwater, originally identified as an Indian from North Carolina, was later identified by the government as a Caucasian from Apache, Calif.

Two days later the second death occurred. Lawrence LaMonte, 29, an enrolled member of the Oglala Sioux tribe, was killed in another gunfire exchange. LaMonte's death ended the heavy gunfire and negotiations resumed.

By the time the May 8 settlement was reached, the physical appearance of the village had changed dramatically. The trading post had burned to the ground, several houses had been destroyed by fire and the BIA estimated it would take more than $200,000 to restore the dwellings that remained to a liveable condition.

The insurgents had endured the cold and snow of a South Dakota winter, sleeping on floors in churches and houses warmed only by clothes that had accumulated in the churches, gifts of Indian missions. They had subsisted for weeks on one meal each day, respiratory ailments had spread among them. The 5,000 gallons of gasoline in an underground tank which they used indiscriminately for fire bombs and fuel for their cars and pickups was long gone.

Half of the AIM leadership had left the village, Means on a free pass to attend the meetings in Washington that never came off, Clyde Bellecourt on his own. Bellecourt turned himself in at Rapid City and was freed on $50,000 bond.

AIM couldn't wait to get out. The final agreement, almost identical to that of April 5 which had failed, called for the insurgents to lay down their arms on May 9. Banks and Camp asked that the evacuation be a day earlier. The government agreed. But when the marshals moved in Banks was gone. He had slipped past the federal outposts the previous night and didn't surrender for more than a month.

The AIM leadership had split during the siege. Banks and Means had left the village one night to rally support at the nearby Rosebud reservation. When they returned, they had to overcome the leaders of the Oglala Sioux Civil Rights Organization—specifically Pedro Bisonnette, a young reservation Indian who had closed ranks with AIM just before the takeover. They accomplished the task by the same method the village had been taken—by force.

The AIM leaders were in jail, finally released on bonds ranging from $50,000 to $105,000. Churches, for the most part, raised the money to free Banks, Means, Bellecourt, Camp and Stan Holder, who had emerged as the security chief with tight control over the men who held the guns.

On Feb. 27 the militants had entered the village carrying small caliber rifles and shotguns. They confiscated a few deer rifles when they took over the trading post. As the weeks progressed, infiltrators brought in automatic weapons and ammunition. The first time an automatic rifle was spotted was two weeks after the takeover when the Rev. Ralph Abernathy, civil rights leader and president of the Southern Christian Leadership Conference, met with the insurgents. One of the sentries was carrying an AK-47, a Communist-made weapon apparently smuggled into the United States from Southeast Asia. When the marshals and FBI agents walked in on May 8 only 60 persons remained and the only weapon was a rusted shotgun.

The agreement called for a meeting between White House officials and the reservation chiefs later in the month.

AIM did not get the BIA investigation, the probe into activities of the tribal council, nor the treaties commission. But Sen.

Government armoured personnel carriers kept watch on the village of Wounded Knee

Abourezk conducted extensive hearings on the takeover and alleged civil rights violations on the reservation.

The 400 permanent residents of Wounded Knee returned to their homes shortly after the occupation ended. Warnings from federal officers that the village might be mined proved foundless. The marshals had also warned that the invaders had tanks and heavy machine guns the day after the takeover.

The grand jury in Sioux Falls adjourned late in May after returning indictments against 119 persons involved in the takeover. The indictments included charges of conspiracy to riot, assaulting federal officers, interstate transportation of weapons to be used in a civil disorder, burglary, larceny, impeding federal officers.

The AIM leaders were free on bond by early summer, the village restored to liveability and Richard Wilson was still the elected tribal president.

The Rev. Paul Manhart returned to his mission church a few days after the occupation ended. On the eve of Independence Day, Father Manhart awoke to discover the Sacred Heart Roman Catholic Church afire. It burned to its foundation, the scars of the filled-in trenches around it still visible.

Ellsberg Case Collapsed After Wiretap Disclosure Involving White House

IT WAS MAY 11, 1973, and for Daniel Ellsberg and Anthony Russo it was the last day of nearly two years in legal limbo. Their trial, initiated because of spilled government secrets, had disintegrated in explosive fallout from another case involving secrets—the Watergate Affair.

Now, the heavy brown doors of Los Angeles federal courtroom number nine burst open to a flow of exuberant defense workers, reporters and smiling defendants.

"Dismissed! Dismissed! Dismissed!" shouted a woman running toward crowds waiting outside.

Moving silently past the jubilant throng, three government prosecutors stepped into an elevator and someone asked, "Will you try this case again?" The tallest of the three muttered, "It's dead" as the doors slid shut.

*   *   *   *

In the beginning, before Watergate was mentioned, the Pentagon Papers case was on the surface a simple confrontation.

Daniel Ellsberg, 41, a slender graying scholar once close to the heart of power in Washington, stunned the country by flaunting in public secrets he had discovered in guarded government documents. The secrets were considered special, for they concerned the most volatile issue of the day—the Vietnam War. The release of the Pentagon Papers in newspapers, exposing unrevealed motivations and tactics of those who ran the war, scraped sore spots in Washington and set off instant reaction.

The Justice Department rebuffed by the Supreme Court in its attempt to stop publication of the top secret war study, brought criminal charges against Ellsberg who had acknowledged leaking the documents to news media. He said he had hoped his action might help end the war. "I am prepared for all consequences," he declared.

Within months, the indictment had been expanded to include another former government researcher, Anthony J. Russo, 35, and the charges became more grave, centering around the accusation of espionage with accompanying counts of conspiracy and theft.

It was the first time in the nation's history that Americans had been accused of espionage for releasing information to newspapers in their own country.

The government, though never claiming that Ellsberg and Russo had intended to harm the United States, stood fast on the contention that they had committed a crime. The government did not specifically charge the men with releasing the documents to news media; they charged them only with copying the documents.

Ellsberg and Russo, who had signed pledges to keep government secrets, insisted that the Pentagon study of the war was wrongfully classified and should have been released to the American public long ago. "If we are traitors," declared Russo, "then the American people are the enemy."

In pre-trial months the issues seemed clear, and the case was seen by many as a legal testing ground for First Amendment rights of free speech, government powers of secrecy and U.S. involvement in the war. But by the time it ended, the only thing clear was that nothing in the Pentagon Papers case had been predictable since it was launched in June 1971.

The war that spawned the case ended before the trial; the issues raised remained unresolved; and the aims of the trial were overshadowed by wiretaps, withheld documents, and ultimately by revelations of Watergate and White House involvement in the case.

In a startling turnaround the trial had become, as one Ellsberg attorney put it, "a case of what the government had done to us, not what we did to the government."

When the Pentagon Papers trial got under way in January with opening arguments to the jury, there was little drama.

The defendants had publicly confessed that they copied the Pentagon study of the war, and the main issue was whether that constituted a crime or not.

This was not even the first trial for Ellsberg and Russo. Another jury had been chosen the previous summer and dismissed in November in a mistrial caused by a four-month delay while the defense sought to unlock contents of a secret government wiretap.

On Jan. 17, the trial prosecutor, slight dark-haired David Nissen arose and told jurors that his would not be a "TV-script type of case." No last-minute bits of evidence pulled out of a hat. No surprise witnesses. Instead, he promised "a calm unemotional presentation of the facts." He declared, "There will be no appeals to the passions and prejudices of anyone."

The Vietnam War, said Nissen, was "irrelevant to the charges" and the government would not mention it. As he spoke, some 20 Vietnam Veterans Against the War, many in khaki fatigue uniforms and one in a wheel chair, watched from front row spectator seats. They had come to court with the defense team.

Ellsberg's chief attorney, gray-haired Leonard Boudin, a veteran civil rights attorney informed jurors the defense would mention the war a great deal. The case, he said, "is about a war which in the view of all defendants and many other people had origins and reasons that nobody could understand and that were concealed from the American people."

Boudin announced plans to attack the classification of documents as "not a lawful government function," and said Ellsberg would contend it was "not only his right, but his duty as an American citizen and former government official to give this information to the Congress of the United States."

Government testimony began but was less than a day old when the first of many secrets began to spill. A Defense Department official, brought in for the routine task of identifying the Pentagon Papers, revealed during cross-examination that the government had done several secret studies of the

Left, Daniel Ellsberg answering questions from newsmen outside the Federal Building in Los Angeles. Above, Anthony J. Russo after a court appearance during the trial.

Papers—studies which had been kept from the judge and defendants. Testimony stopped while U.S. Dist. Court Judge Matt Byrne launched a "trial within a trial" probing the case of the missing documents. Jurors were sent home.

The studies, Byrne concluded, could be helpful in proving the defendants innocent, and the government had violated a court order by withholding them. In time, he decided to punish the government by dropping two of the 15 counts on which Ellsberg and Russo were indicted. And the 37 newly discovered studies were given to the defense.

The government case proceeded. Only ten witnesses were called in four weeks of testimony and only two of the ten addressed the trial's key issue, whether Ellsberg and Russo risked national security by copying the Papers.

The two star witnesses, Army generals whose rank was played down by their appearance in gray suits, said that the release of the secret study in 1969—the year it was copied—could have harmed U.S. national defense.

The point was hypothetical. The Papers had not been released until 1971. The bulk of the government's case would hinge on a thesis of "what if this had happened."

Both Lt. Gen. William DePuy and Brig. Gen. Paul F. Gorman conceded some points to the defense during probing cross-examination. Yes, they said, Gen. William Westmoreland had included many of the secrets of the Pentagon study in a report he wrote which was published by the government and put on sale for $6 a copy.

The balance of the government presentation was dominated by detail—introduction of Ellsberg's and Russo's work records at the Rand Corp. "think tank" where Ellsberg gained access to the papers, testimony by former colleagues about security rules, the brief appearance of the two men's former girl friends who gave no personal information and claimed poor memories on many points.

Then, the prosecution rested. A juror would say later, "I was shocked when the government said they were resting their case. I couldn't believe it. They only had 10 witnesses and two of them were obviously friends of Ellsberg, and one of them besides that couldn't remember anything."

Months later it would seem clear that the prosecutor's long-range strategy had been to save the heaviest witnesses for rebuttal, a plan which was overtaken by outside events and finally abandoned.

The defense case opened on Feb. 27 with attorney Leonard Weinglass delivering a delayed opening statement in behalf of Russo. Weinglass adopted a restrained tone. "The defense will present evidence," he told jurors, "not to prove that a crime has been committed which you should excuse because you agree with the motives. Our case rather will be that no crime occurred."

No sooner had defense testimony begun than another bitter dispute arose over an alleged government attempt to hide the identity of a CIA employe who wanted to testify in favor of the defense. When the witness Samuel A. Adams finally appeared, he told jurors there had been "a definite attempt by the government to keep me from testifying in this court."

Jurors were kept in the dark about disputes that raged outside their presence, but they could hardly miss the animosity between government and defense attorneys, an open hostility that went beyond the expected differences of legal opinion.

The thrust of the lengthy defense case was to summon current and former powers in government to speak out against the government's case. The most glamorous of the witnesses were the emissaries from President John F. Kennedy's "New Frontier."

McGeorge Bundy, Theodore Sorensen, Arthur Schlesinger and John Kenneth Galbraith mingled their testimony with nostalgic reminiscences of the Kennedy years. All four said that the data in the Pentagon Papers was useless by the time Ellsberg and Russo copied it in 1969.

"I came here," Sorensen told reporters, "because I felt justice should be done. My basic feeling is that no one should go to prison for releasing these documents to the American public."

The defense witness list also included an adviser to Henry Kissinger, a retired Canadian diplomat, former Defense Department and State Department officials and representatives of more radical views; antiwar activists Tom Hayden, Noam Chomsky and Howard Zinn. The defense case lasted twice as long as the government presentation with nearly three times as many witnesses.

Perhaps most fascinating to jurors was the testimony of Ellsberg and Russo themselves. The jury, hearing the defendants speak for the first time in four months of trial, was confronted with Russo bursting into tears as he recalled the songs of a North Vietnamese prisoner.

They heard Ellsberg emotionally describe his dissillusionment as a government adviser in Vietnam, losing faith as he stood among the burning huts of a South Vietnamese village destroyed by its own army. When jurors left the room during a recess, Ellsberg sat down at the counsel table and sobbed.

Both men portrayed themselves as loyal government servants dismayed by what they saw during official missions to Vietnam. Both admitted copying the Papers, though Russo said he barely knew what they contained when he helped Ellsberg with the task. Ellsberg said he hoped release of the Papers would give Congress "the self-confidence to end the war."

Then the prosecutor, in cross-examination, sprung one small surprise by asking Ellsberg whether he thought the United States had committed "war crimes" in Vietnam.

Appearing stunned, Ellsberg thought for a moment, then said, "I'm not a lawyer, Mr. Nissen. But as I read the law, I believe there were illegal actions, some of which, I regret to say, I participated in myself, without asking myself what they were."

He suggested that the question of violations be examined by an international lawyer, but when the defense sought to introduce one as its last witness, the judge ruled the matter irrelevant. The witness did not testify and the defense abruptly rested its case.

The end of the trial seemed in sight, and testimony might have ended then but for the government's fateful decision to put on a lengthy rebuttal. The prosecutor began calling more witnesses on April 20.

Testimony was tedious and slow, as low-key as the original case. Thus, it was noteworthy that on April 25 the government case suddenly changed style.

Departing from the mood of determined blandness, Nissen startled the participants by calling to the witness stand one of the top ranking military men close to President Richard Nixon. Beribboned and glittering with medals, Gen. Alexander M. Haig, then vice chief of staff of the U.S. Army, arrived in full uniform to give testimony.

Within weeks, Haig would be named a special advisor to the President, replacing two men pushed from office by the Watergate scandal, John D. Ehrlichman and H. R. Haldeman.

And, within one day, the trial judge would be confronted with news sent from Washington that would shake the trial's course and turn it into an event which became known as "Watergate West."

*   *   *   *

April 26 was a day of anger for familiar reasons. The trial was halted again by discovery that the government had failed to turn over documents relevant to questioning of witnesses. An irritated Judge Byrne recessed court early, scolded the government and demanded that the missing papers be flown in from Washington. But court was not over for the day after all.

In late afternoon, Byrne summoned attorneys and defendants to return. Visibly disturbed, he revealed that the government had secretly given him some information he felt he could not keep secret. Saying no more, he sealed the data in an envelope and gave the government overnight to decide its next move.

By morning, Prosecutor Nissen still opposed revealing the secret to the defense or the public. But the judge gave him no choice. Opening the envelope, Byrne stunned the courtroom by reading the explosive news in a memo from the Watergate prosecutor.

*   *   *   *

U.S. District Court Judge Matt Byrne dismissed all espionage, theft, and conspiracy charges against Ellsberg and Russo.

"United States Government Memorandum: From Earl J. Silbert, Principal Assistant, United States Attorney. To: Honorable Henry E. Petersen, Assistant Attorney General, Department of Justice. April 16, 1973.

"This is to inform you that on Sunday, April 15, 1973, I received information that at a date unspecified, Gordon Liddy and Howard Hunt burglarized the offices of a psychiatrist of Daniel Ellsberg to obtain the psychiatrist's files relating to Ellsberg. The source of the information did not know whether the files had any material information or whether any of the information or even the fact of the burglary had been communicated to anyone associated with the prosecution."

*　*　*　*

There were muffled gasps in the courtroom. An ashen-faced Ellsberg asked for a recess, rushed past reporters and commented bitterly, "I wish as a citizen that I felt surprised at this. I hear words around here like astonishing, surprising. I wonder where these people have been the last few weeks."

As the scandal grew, it involved a Presidential adviser, White House aides and even the judge himself.

Prodded by a "leaked" story in newspapers, the 42-year-old Byrne, a youthful jurist with an unblemished record for fairness, announced that he had met with Presidential Adviser John D. Ehrlichman at the Western White House in early April, was approached about becoming director of the FBI and was introduced to the President. Byrne said he told Ehrlichman he couldn't consider the offer until the Pentagon Papers trial was over. But the judge later revealed that he had gone to a second meeting with Ehrlichman within the same week. He said he refused again to discuss the FBI job.

Dr. Lewis Field, Ellsberg's psychiatrist, opening door of his Beverly Hills office.

The judge's startling announcement from the bench was followed almost immediately by his release of an FBI report on an interview with Ehrlichman. In the document, Ehrlichman said that it was he who hired Liddy and Hunt to investigate the Pentagon Papers case directly out of the White House. And eventually, he said, he found out that they had broken into Ellsberg's psychiatrist's office. Ehrlichman said he told the men "not to do this again," but took no other action.

The defense attorneys reacted swiftly.

"We would, were we to use blunt language, characterize this as an attempt to offer a bribe to the court," the attorneys said in a motion for dismissal. "An attempt made in the virtual presence of the President of the United States . . ."

The judge refused to dismiss the case on those grounds. The meetings with Ehrlichman had not prejudiced him, he ruled.

But that was only the first of many dismissal motions hurriedly filed in the wake of mounting details involving the White House in the plan to get Ellsberg's psychiatric records.

The developments piled up:

—Ehrlichman disclosed to the FBI that because of the President's "interest" in plugging leaks of classified information, Ehrlichman had formed a special investigative unit which would become known as "the plumbers squad." He said the unit was headed by his two aides, Egil Krogh and David Young, and utilized the services of Hunt and Liddy. It was the plumbers who planned and executed the break-in.

"There was information available that Ellsberg had emotional and moral problems and Liddy and Hunt sought to determine full facts relating to these conduct traits," said the FBI report on Ehrlichman's story. Ehrlichman said he knew that Hunt was "endeavoring to prepare a psychological profile relating to Ellsberg."

Ellsberg, seeking to understand why the White House wanted psychological data on him, surmised there was a connection to the Watergate political espionage plans for the 1972 presidential election. "It appears," he said, "that they wanted to smear me and then connect my name with the Democratic presidential candidate."

—Dr. Lewis Fielding, the Beverly Hills psychiatrist whose office was ransacked, revealed that Spanish-speaking cleaning people in his building had spotted the intruders, some of whom appeared to be Cuban. Ellsberg's attorneys immediately linked this to an earlier report that Cubans had been hired to attack Ellsberg at a political rally in 1972. The plan to beat up Ellsberg and call him a "traitor" reportedly failed.

—Chief U.S. Dist. Court Judge John J. Sirica announced in Washington he was releasing secret grand jury testimony of E. Howard Hunt to Judge Byrne. Byrne, receiving the testimony, moved swiftly to make its secret content public.

—The release of Hunt's testimony revealed a mind-boggling cloak and dagger story of the plan for what he called the "Ellsberg bag job." He told of meetings in "safe houses" to pick up disguises and secret cameras provided by the Central Intelligence Agency. He spoke of the recruitment of the Cubans including a Watergate conspirator. And Hunt gave the first possible explanation of the reason the break-in scheme was devised.

"At that time, as I understood it," he said, "there was some concern in the White House about the appropriateness of seeing the prosecution actually take place in regard to Dr. Ellsberg and his associates, and I shared that concern, my own feeling being that he would probably become a martyr . . ." He said the psychiatric profile was needed for a study of Ellsberg's "prosecutability."

—Hunt, who said he operated on orders from Krogh, contended that no information on Ellsberg was found in Fielding's office. This was reported to Krogh, he said, and the Cubans were told to get out of town.

—Hunt's testimony involved numerous persons as well as the CIA and the FBI. A congressional committee immediately began investigating the CIA role. Hunt credited the FBI with providing the White House with weekly reports on the Ellsberg case.

—Following release of Hunt's testimony, Krogh resigned from his job as undersecretary of Transportation. He had previously been an aide to Ehrlichman.

Krogh then filed a sworn affadavit with Judge Byrne in which he took responsibility for approving the break-in. He also said that Ehrlichman had approved the use of "covert activities" in the effort to prepare a psychiatric profile of Ellsberg.

—Another chunk of Hunt's grand jury testimony, released by Byrne in Los Angeles, revealed Hunt's claim that former presidential counsel Charles W. Colson told him to forge State Department Cablegrams. This was done, he said, in an effort to show that President John F. Kennedy's administration arranged the assassination of South Vietnamese President Ngo Dinh Diem in 1963. Once the forged cables were ready, Hunt said, a reporter was invited to view them. Colson denied the story, but the reporter, William Lambert, recalled being shown the cables.

—An inventory list of items from Hunt's safe given to the FBI by former White House counsel John W. Dean III showed that Hunt kept weapons, camouflaged microphones and information on Ellsberg in his office adjacent to the White House.

—Judge Byrne released sworn affidavits by several CIA agents confirming that the agency provided paraphernalia to Hunt and saying the help was authorized by former CIA Deputy Director Gen. Robert E. Cushman, now commandant of the U.S. Marine Corps. The agents said Cushman stopped the aid in August 1971 days before the burglary, because of growing suspicions that Hunt was involving the agency in "domestic clandestine operations."

—Four Justice Department officials filed sworn affidavits saying they knew nothing of the burglary until April 16, but they didn't explain why the judge wasn't notified until April 26.

With the White House-related developments finally engulfing the trial, the government abruptly rested its rebuttal case without calling many of its planned witnesses. Jurors, who had been kept in the dark about the Watergate involvements, were sent home and told to shield themselves from news reports in the case. Then, Byrne took up the problem of what to do about the trial's future course.

Byrne, obviously angry at the government for its slow pace in providing information to him, ordered more data and mulled his decision. He was about to rule on the morning of May 10 when the sudden delivery of another document wrecked any anticipated efforts to save the trial from sinking.

Attorney Weinglass quipped, "This case has been dead for 10 days, and every morning the judge has been putting a Band-Aid on it."

In a memo to the judge, acting FBI Director William Ruckelshaus disclosed his discovery that Ellsberg's telephone conversations had been overheard on government wiretaps as early as 1969—two years before he was indicted. The tap was believed to have been on the phone of an Ellsberg associate Dr. Morton Halperin, then an employe of the National Security Council.

The records of the wiretaps, said Ruckelshaus, had mysteriously vanished.

The revelation stunned Byrne who had ordered the government more than a year before to disclose all wiretaps relating to the trial. He demanded a search for the logs and records of the conversations, declaring "I want them now."

While awaiting the results, Byrne made one more disclosure. Colson, in an FBI interview, had revealed that Ehrlichman and Dean instructed him to remain silent about the Ellsberg burglary saying it was "a national security matter and not to be discussed with anyone."

*   *   *   *

Judge Byrne's courtroom was filled to capacity on the morning of May 11—spectators, defendants' families and friends frozen in tense silence. The wiretap records had not been found, and the judge wearily ceased his efforts to press the government for swift action. Instead, he ordered attorneys to begin their arguments for and against dismissal of all charges or, in the alternative, a mistrial.

It was the defense attorneys who arose to plead that the judge should not dismiss charges merely because of a wiretap. Fearing the issues of the trial and the questions of government misconduct would be brushed aside in favor of the wiretap technicality, Boudin and Weinglass accused the government of disclosing the wiretap purposely to end the trial and the judge's probe into matters that placed the government in "a very uncomfortable situation."

Hours later, when the judge spelled the end to the lengthy trial, it was not merely the wiretap he cited but a series of actions he said constituted extraordinary government misconduct.

"Commencing on April 26, the government has made an extraordinary series of disclosures regarding the conduct of several governmental agencies regarding the defendants in this case," said Byrne. ". . . Much information has been developed, but new information has produced new questions, and there remain more questions than answers.

"The disclosures made by the government demonstrate that governmental agencies have taken an unprecedented series of actions with respect to these defendants. After the original indictment, at a time when the government's rights to investigate the defendants are narrowly circumscribed, White House officials established a special unit to investigate one of the defendants in this case . . . We have been given only a glimpse of what this special unit did regarding this case, but what we know is more than disquieting."

Noting that government officials had hidden the existence of the special unit and that Silbert's memorandum itself was concealed for 10 days, Byrne further chastised the prosecution for its trial-long record of withholding documents.

"These recent events compound the record already pervaded by incidents threatening the defendants' right to a speedy and fair trial," he said.

He cited the wiretap disclosure and the missing records as one other violation and expressed doubts that the questions left open by that incident would be answered.

"A continuation of the government's investigation is no solution with reference to this case," said Byrne. ". . . No investigation is likely to provide satisfactory answers where improper government conduct has been shielded so long from public view . . ."

". . . The conduct of the government," said Byrne, "has

Ellsberg and his wife, Patrica, elated after all charges were dismissed

placed the case in such a posture that it precludes the fair dispassionage resolution of these issues by a jury.

". . . I have concluded that a mistrial alone would not be fair. Under all circumstances, I believe that the defendants should not have to run the risk . . . that they might be tried again before a different jury.

"The totality of the circumstances of this case," said the judge, ". . . offend 'a sense of justice.' The bizarre events incurably infected the prosecution of this case.

". . . I have decided to declare a mistrial and grant the motion to dismiss."

*   *   *   *

Freed into the bright California sunshine outside the courthouse where friends and strangers waited to touch them, to applaud them, Ellsberg and Russo tempered their rejoicing with an attack on those who had brought them to trial.

"We feel this case should have never been brought," said Ellsberg. "We feel we didn't need vindication for telling the truth to the American people. Tony and I did something right in our lives."

Russo said he believed the revelations of the trial's last weeks proved that "our country has been run by criminals."

Both men threatened to file suit against the President. "The President has led a conspiracy to deprive us of our civil liberties," said Ellsberg. "We will bring suit against all the conspirators, of which President Nixon appears to be the ringleader."

As the men walked away from the courthouse with their

wives, a woman spectator ran up, embraced Mrs. Ellsberg and declared, "Thank God!"

"Thank God indeed," Mrs. Ellsberg replied.

*   *   *   *

But the dismissal was not the end of the case. Within days, Ruckelshaus announced that the Ellsberg wiretap records had been found—in the safe in Ehrlichman's White House office. Within weeks, a Los Angeles County grand jury began investigating the burglary of the psychiatrist's office. Russo began efforts to start a presidential impeachment movement, and Ellsberg appeared before a Senate committee in Washington to talk about the issue that had spawned the trial—secrecy in government.

Though Ellsberg's name was likely to remain in the news for months to come, the issues he sought to challenge were likely to remain unresolved. One of the jurors who said she would have acquitted the defendants—the majority said they would have voted acquittal—summed up the effect of the dismissal weeks later.

"I was very glad that the defendants were freed," said Phyllis Ortman. "But I was so upset that those issues were left unresolved. Afterward, I kept thinking we're going to have to go through another whole Vietnam and another Pentagon Papers before issues like this can be resolved, before there'll be a case on record where people can divulge information that the American people have a need to know."

Troops, Tanks and Planes Helped Mark Israel's 25th Anniversary as a Nation

TEL AVIV was sweltering in the onset of a long, hot and deadly summer. Crowds shouted in the streets outside the city's art museum where a rotund immigrant from Poland unfolded a hastily-typed proclamation and declared "the establishment of a Jewish State in the Land of Israel." The declaration of independence was only 979 words long, but it was the biggest event in modern Jewish history and it changed the snarling face of the Middle East. Troops of seven Arab armies were poised on the undefined borders to annihilate the crudely armed and outnumbered Jewish settlers. The date was May 14, 1948, and the leader who announced the rebirth of the ancient homeland was David Ben-Gurion—farmer, fund-raiser, political fighter and Israel's first premier.

On May 7, 1973 (Israel celebrates its independence by the changing Jewish calendar) the aged and wizened Ben-Gurion sat in a grandstand in Jerusalem watching the most muscular birthday party ever held in the land of the Bible. Four hundred warplanes bellowed out the message of Israel's 25th anniversary with blue and white vapor trails. Two thousand parading troops and 160 tanks and artillery guns signalled an anniversary warning to Israel's Arab neighbors that the Jewish state had reached adulthood and was a permanent part of the Middle East. The massive parade of jets and guns, with a touch of glamor from the girl soldiers, was an awesome contrast to Israel's first victory parade in 1949 when weapons were carried on muleback and the Signal Corps showed off its carrier pi-

Below left, Israeli tanks rolled past a reviewing stand in Jerusalem. On the rostrum were Prime Minister Golda Meir, Defense Minister Moshe Dayan and Chief of Staff Lt. Gen. David Elazar. Below right, French-built transport planes flew above the military parade marking Israel's 25th anniversary celebration.

geons. But Ben-Gurion and other veteran Zionist settlers of the early days watched the procession in pride tinged with sorrow. Pride in the country's attainments, sorrow that the parade was in a way an admission of failure. For the need to display such military might showed that Israel had failed in its first quarter century to reach its major goal: peace with the Arabs.

Still, Ben-Gurion and the pioneers had more than ample reason for pride. In 25 years, the New Jersey-sized corner of Palestine that was once empty desert and swamp had built itself into the most advanced country in the Middle East, rivaling the industralized nations of the West. With a population of just 3.1 million—about the same as Mexico City—Israel had seven universities, two internationally-renowned science institutes, and what the United Nations called the highest agricultural growth rate in the world. The tiny country had given a home to 1,545,000 immigrants. Its growing industries were exporting instant coffee to Korea, soap to Thailand and Uzi submachine guns to the U.S. Secret Service. Israelis were running aid programs for other, older countries. The Israeli Philharmonic Orchestra was exporting classical music, and Israeli doctors were in the front rank of world medical research.

Summing up the achievements in his book "The Israelis," author Amos Elon writes: "In one short lifetime, a nation, spirited and cohesive, had developed out of a horde of frightened refugees, the outcasts of Europe, survivors of concentration camps and primitive, half-literate masses from the shoddy souks (bazaars) of the Near East and North Africa . . . in one short lifetime, big cities, theaters, orchestras, ballet troups, had sprouted in a confusion rarely found in much larger nations. Zoos, ports and airfields, industries, superhighways, traffic jams, great universities . . ."

Without the oil or resources of its Arab neighbors, how did Israel surpass them? David Horowitz, former governor of the Bank of Israel, said the answer was "a capable and determined population with a broad base of well-educated and energetic people," plus money—mostly money donated by Jews in America and other countries, and huge reparations payments from West Germany. West Germany had given some $16 billion to Jewish victims of the Nazis and much of it had gone to Israel—where many a driver of a new car carried a concentration camp tattoo. From the United States had come $9.2 billion, most of it from Israeli Bond sales and private donations.

Yet at 25, Israel was not only menaced from without by the Arabs, but troubled from within by problems of politics, religion, discrimination, absorbing Soviet immigrants, combatting inflation and growing discontent, and universal troubles such as crime and pollution. And many Israelis such as Miss Donia Rosen, a 42-year-old survivor of Nazi terror in Poland, worried that "Israel is losing its sense of values and joining the rat race of the West." Many younger Israelis such as newspaper reporter Avishai Amir, born the same year as the state, thought growing materialism was inevitable because "people want to live good lives. We are sick of living in tension. But Israel is a success . . . do you think the Jews who founded Zionism would have dared to dream that Jewish doctors would someday perform kidney transplants in a Jewish hospital in a Jewish state?"

A complex of new high-rise apartment buildings stood behind the ancient Monastery of the Cross in Jerusalem.

Israeli grandparents can remember when no Jews spoke Hebrew, when they feared to venture from their villages in Europe, when they waited for the next wave of soldiers or rioters to start the next pogrom, looting, burning, killing Jews. Newcomer Ya'acov Kirschen of New York, a cartoonist who lampoons Israel's faults, contends "Sure, many things are wrong. But the fact is that the Hebrew language has been restored to everyday use, the Jewish people are being ingathered as the Bible said, and cities like Tel Aviv are thriving. It's all amazing. Twenty-five years ago, who would have bet on this happening?"

Twenty-five years ago, many outsiders would not have bet that Israel would survive, let alone prosper. The land was Palestine, a battlefield for countless centuries, divided between Arabs and Jews, seething with hatred and ruled by Britain. When Britain threw up its hands and pulled out of Palestine and the Jewish state emerged, it had no real government, no civil service, no official army. It was bankrupt. Thousands of homeless and derelict Jews were arriving on the Mediterranean seashore. Bent on wiping out the state before it was 24 hours old, Arab troops invaded from Egypt, Jordan, Syria, Lebanon, Iraq and Saudi Arabia, reinforced by Palestinians.

"I was an artillery officer in the fight for Jerusalem," said Dr. Reuven Berger. "We had one gun—a cannon with wooden wheels left over from the Spanish Civil War." Israelis said that in 1948 they had only 3,000 regular soldiers, 14,000 undertrained recruits (some Nazi survivors went straight from the immigrant ships into battle) four cannons and no tanks. All their weapons had been smuggled through a British blockade. But the people who had been shoved into the fiery furnace by Nebuchadnezzar in Old Testament times, and again by Hitler centuries later, trained more troops, brought in planes and arms, and beat off the invaders.

Seven years later in the Suez crisis of 1956, an organized Israeli army routed Egypt, and Israel was established as a military power. And in just six days in 1967, as the Arab world again tried to drive the Jews into the sea, the Israelis stopped the combined armies of Jordan and Soviet-supplied Egypt and Syria, taking 26,000 square miles of Arab land in the process.

"We never underestimate our enemies," said Lt. Gen. David Elazar, Israel's Chief of Staff. "But I do not believe the Egyptians have the faintest chance of winning a battle. Indeed, today's battlefield is not the Middle East, but faraway points such as Europe or Bangkok, where Palestinian terrorists have killed Israeli sportsmen at the Munich Olympics, hijacked airliners, taken hostages."

Some of the victims, such as two American diplomats and a Belgian murdered in Khartoum, were not even Israelis. An underground war between Israeli and Arab secret agents flared in Europe, and more than a dozen were killed, all in mysterious circumstances. Israel vowed to hit Arab guerrillas wherever possible (a month before Independence Day, Israeli commandos mounted a midnight raid right inside the Lebanese capital of Beirut) and battles flared regularly along the frontiers of Syria and Lebanon. Since the American-sponsored cease-fire of 1970, the frontier fights had been the only open warfare in the Middle East.

"The root of the problem," said Premier Golda Meir, a 75-year-old grandmother, "is that our Arab neighbors have not reconciled themselves to our existence . . . We say that we are ready to negotiate. They demand that first we give them everything on a plate, a golden plate." The Arabs, prevented by pride, refused to bargain unless Israel surrendered everything it won in the 1967 war. The main thrust of Israel as it began another quarter century was not fighting, but seeking peace and security and solving its internal troubles.

106

One domestic difficulty was the mixture of Israeli politics, a combination of socialism, Marxism, free enterprise, religion and nostalgia. It was so complex that the 120-member Knesset (parliament) was split into 15 factions. So delicate was the balance that when Premier Meir asked to retire to family life on a kibbutz collective farm, no acceptable candidate could be found to replace her, and Mrs. Meir stayed on. Many young Israelis complained that Mrs. Meir and her ministers were too old, all of European background, and unable to meet the challenges of today.

Religion hampered both politics and the private life of Israelis. Orthodox Jews, whose National Religious Party was essential to the government, held control over Israel's mainly unreligious population. No buses or trains were permitted to run from sundown Friday to Saturday, the Jewish Sabbath. Private cars were stoned in the Mea Shearim quarter of Jerusalem, where a medical autopsy could start a riot. Friday night movies were banned. So was pork, although it was sold everywhere in disguise as "white steak." Civil marriage was illegal, and critics contended that 40,000 Israelis were unable to marry because of restrictions by the rabbis. Zealots had tried to burn down the home of Chief Rabbi Shlomo Goren, complaining that the paratrooping former army chaplain was too liberal. Many Sabras—native-born Israelis, named after the country's prickly cactus plant—argued that, "I do not have to be religious to be a Jew. Being an Israeli is enough." They chafed at the restrictions, but the orthodox insisted that without their influence, Israel would cease to be a Jewish state.

Social problems were a bigger issue. In 25 years, the Jewish population had swollen from the original 650,000 to almost 3 million, mostly through immigration. First came the European survivors of Hiltler, then waves of backward and primitive Jews from the Middle East and North Africa. The clusters of tents where they began their new lives vanished long ago, and food rationing to feed the newcomers was no longer necessary, but many of the Oriental Israelis failed to integrate fully into the modern state. They made up about 65 per cent of the population, but they complained of discrimination. Young protesters and conservative elders argued that the Jews of Western descent (who conceived and built the state) monopolized the good jobs, made the most money, dominated the government and the armed forces. The Easterners lived in overcrowded conditions, got less education and as "second class Jews" did the poorly paid work. Even Mrs. Meir agreed the Ashkenazic Jews of Western descent were more privileged than the Sephardic Orientals, and "dangerous strains have appeared in the inner fabric of Israeli society." But she and most Israelis denied deliberate discrimination existed, and said the solution lay in education. Mrs. Meir pledged money and effort for integration, and for the first time in 1973 the government budgeted more on social services than the $1.46 billion allotted to defense. Israelis hoped this would also halt a disturbing growth of crime, prostitution and drugs.

Moscow's unexplained decision in 1971 to let Jews leave the Soviet Union provided Israel with a blessing and a challenge. Once the communist gates were open, Soviet Jews began arriving by airlift at the rate of 2,500 a month, a Godsend for immigrant-hungry Israel which needed people to settle its empty areas. By May 1973, about 50,000 Russians had arrived and were busily becoming Israelis, studying the language and working at everything from unloading ships to computer programming. The newcomers included scientists, musicians and teachers who enriched the country, but many had to be trained for their new lives. Even doctors and dentists were sent back to school before they could practice on Israeli patients. And the Russians had to be housed. Within hours of getting off the big El Al Airlines planes, every newcomer either was sent to an absorption center to learn Hebrew or moved straight into an

The shells of armored vehicles used during Israel's war for survival in 1948 lined the highway leading to Jerusalem as a memorial to those who died in the conflict.

empty apartment, equipped with food and furniture. Young Israelis resented such red carpet treatment, protesting that they were born in Israel and served in the army, but could not find or afford a place to live. Almost all Israeli housing is for sale, not rent, and raising $25,000 or more for a small Tel Aviv apartment involves heavy sacrifice and pressure.

Housing was not the only expensive thing in Israel. Taxation is about the world's highest (mainly to pay the colossal defense bills) and despite U.S. prices, a man was lucky to take home $250 a month. It didn't go far. Hamburger, the cheapest meat, cost $2.40 a pound, instant coffee was $4.50 to $6.50 a pound, a small European car cost at least $6,000 and the license and insurance for a year was another $500. Inflation was racing far faster than in the United States—the cost of living jumped 26 per cent between January 1972 and May 1973. This, too, caused resentment, and labor union problems were growing severe. Even some rabbis—in the marriage registry office—went on strike in 1973.

Despite labor problems, Israel's economic growth rate averaged more than 10 per cent a year and the export of goods and services in 1971 was $1.5 billion, a gain of 11 per cent in a year. The gains brought losses, however, such as pollution. The Israelis had made the desert bloom—more than 130 million trees had been planted, and apartments, factories and universities stood where once there was only sand—but the Biblical Sea of Galilee was contaminated. Every river in the country, including the Jordan, was polluted. Almost all the kibbutz communal farms that helped build the Jewish state now boasted factories as well as fields, but the water around Tel Aviv was becoming unsafe to drink and fish were dying from mercury poisoning.

Some Israelis, including Mrs. Meir and her pioneering generation, feared the Zionist idealism which created Israel was dying too, or at least fading. Many a Jerusalemite today was more interested in a new TV set or acquiring a thoroughbred dog than in intellectual improvement or frugality and back-breaking work. To many young Sabras (and Sabras numbered 47.2 per cent of the population) the old ideas were unfashionable. Even the magic word "Zionism" (building a Jewish state) had become slang for "empty talk."

"Sometimes I say to myself 'This is no longer your world.

This is not your generation'," Mrs. Meir has confided. The Sabras had proved their patriotism in the 1967 war and many times since, but they wanted change. The most extreme example of youthful dissent was the discovery last December of six young Sabras in a Syrian spy ring, the first Israeli Jews ever arrested for plotting sabotage against the homeland. All were given long jail terms. It was a rare development and it hardly reflected the spirit of young Israelis, but it jolted the country.

"Here and there, mostly among the youth, a guilt feeling is developing," said Mrs. Meir, examining Israel's rights in the Middle East. "A feeling that here in our land we have robbed and dispossessed . . . to the best of my knowledge, this is a distortion."

She was referring to the most basic problem of all—the 700,000 Arabs who fled their homes when Israel took over the land in 1948, many of them to live the lives of refugees, and the one million Arabs under Israeli occupation in the war-captured zones of 1967. Israel flatly refused to let the Arab refugees return, insisting it was up to the Arab world to solve their plight. These refugees became the Palestinians who spawned the guerrilla movements and terrorist bands such as the killers of the Black September. Under Israeli guidance, the million occupied Arabs were enjoying a prosperity they never knew before, and the occupation, after some initial abuses, had become a sort of cordial coexistence. About 60,000 Arabs from West Jordan and the Gaza Strip commuted to work on Israeli pay scales inside Israel, but they resented Jewish domination and they posed a problem that was both moral and practical. Morally, most Israelis didn't want to rule as masters over an alien population. Practically, they worried about how to get along without the Arab labor if the occupied zones were relinquished under a peace agreement. And if the zones were kept as a permanent part of Israel, Arabs would be 45 per cent of the population by 1980. Mrs. Meir said, "I don't want to wake up every morning and ask who had babies last night and how many? Are we Jews still in the majority?" Israel built 42 Jewish settlements in the occupied zones—"farmer-plating the borders," it has been called—a clear indication that it intended to keep a lot of Arab land in any peace pact. Just what territory Israel was prepared to give back would depend on negotiations, a problem for the coming quarter century.

Twenty-five years of progress in the state of Israel were seen as a modern car passed a horse-drawn cart in Tel Aviv

TUSKEGEE STUDY CONDEMNED BY BIRACIAL CITIZENS PANEL

For 40 years in poor, backwoods Macon County, Ala., doctors of the United States Public Health Service conducted an experiment in which black men suffering from syphilis were allowed to become crippled or to die so the course of the disease could be studied.

The men did not know they were being used as human guinea pigs.

They were not told the nature of their disease or the damage the disease could do.

They were given no treatment for syphilis and, in some cases, were prevented from seeking help on their own.

It appears that more than 100 men may have died in the experiment as a direct result of untreated syphilis. Countless others suffered the crippling side effects of the disease: central nervous system damage, bone deterioration, heart disease and insanity.

The story of the experiment, which became known as The Tuskegee Study, was kept within medical circles for 40 years until it was disclosed by The Associated Press in July 1972.

The Department of Health, Education and Welfare, its own officials apparently unaware of the experiment, launched an immediate investigation, appointing a biracial citizens panel whose personnel came from diverse fields: medical, the clergy, legal, labor, civil rights and academic.

In May 1973, after months of study, the panel made its final report which included these findings:

—That The Tuskegee Study was ethically unjustifiable.

—That the participants were unjustly denied syphilis treatment.

—That the participants never were asked for and never gave their informed consent to take part.

—That the study was conducted sloppily and provided little, if any, useful data.

—That major steps must be taken immediately to fully protect the rights and health of human participants in research projects.

The Tuskegee Study had its genesis in 1929 when the Public Health Service began a demonstration study of venereal diseases in six southern states. Macon County, Ala., was found to have the highest incidence of syphilis with some 35 per cent of the people tested showing signs of the disease. By 1932, the Public Health Service had begun a major effort to eradicate venereal disease.

How the federal doctors moved from what was supposed to be a treatment program to a program of deliberate non-treatment probably never will be known. PHS records indicate there never was a protocol—the proposal, design and justification for an experiment—written for The Tuskegee Study.

What is known is what survivors of The Tuskegee Study can recall and what medical personnel who had a role in the experiment can explain.

Participants say they were recruited in their churches on Sunday mornings and told that federal doctors were coming to Tuskegee. They were told that if they came to a local hospital on a specific day the following week, the doctors would examine them and give them free medicine.

When the people of Tuskegee showed up they were examined and many probably were treated, but several hundred were set aside, and without their knowledge, relegated to the syphilis experiment.

J. W. Williams was an intern at the John A. Andrew Hospital in Tuskegee when the experiment began and was loaned to the PHS doctors to help in the screening.

"The people who came in were not told what was being done," Dr. Williams said in an interview. "We told them we wanted to test them. They were not told, so far as I know, what they were being treated for or what they were not being treated for. We didn't tell them we were looking for syphilis. I don't think they would have known what that was."

Another doctor, Reginald G. James, who works now for the Social Security Administration, was in the Tuskegee area during the early years of the study—sent there to help fight venereal disease. His aide was a Public Health Service nurse, Eunice Rivers, who also was assigned to PHS to keep track of Tuskegee Study participants.

"I was distraught and disturbed whenever one of the patients in the study group appeared," Dr. James told the AP. "I was advised that the patient was not to be treated. Whenever I insisted on treating such a patient, he never showed up again. They were being advised they shouldn't take treatment or they would be dropped from the study.

"At that time, certain benefits were proffered the patients such as treatment for other ailments, payment of burial expenses, and a $50 cash benefit. To receive these benefits, the patient had to remain in the study.

"It was my task to find, diagnose and treat venereal diseases in Macon County, using a mobile clinic to travel into remote areas. When we found one of the men from The Tuskegee Study, she (Nurse Rivers) would say, 'He's under study and not to be treated.'"

One of the survivors of The Tuskegee Study, Charlie Pollard, said that on one occasion during the study, a bus picked up local residents to take them to a Jackson hospital for syphilis tests and for treatment for anyone found to be infected. When he tried to get on the bus, Pollard said, he was told that his name was on a list of people forbidden to go, and he was left behind.

Another experiment subject who somehow got on the bus and into the hospital was discovered before he could get any treatment. The subject was then removed from the hospital and sent home.

Over the years, doctors conducting the experiment wrote periodic reports about their findings. Among the more startling disclosures:

In 1936, after The Tuskegee Study had been in operation for only four years, the doctors said they had concluded that withholding syphilis treatment could endanger life and health and that even inadequate treatment did a lot of good. Yet instead of ending the study and treating the participants, The Tuskegee Study went on.

The doctors said in a 1953 report that some of the black men who took part in the experiment were led to believe they had joined a popular type of social club. The report also clearly describes the doctors' feelings that the men were so ignorant that they had to be rewarded and punished like children to get them and keep them in the program.

Among the rewards was the opportunity to ride in a big chauffered car with a government seal on it for all their friends to see. Among the punishments was a threat to withdraw a promise of government-sponsored free burial. Generally, the report said, the men did as they were told.

Olympic swimming champion Mark Spitz with his bride, the former Susan Weiner of Los Angeles after their May wedding in Beverly Hills.

THOMAS BRADLEY ELECTED AS LOS ANGELES' FIRST BLACK MAYOR

In 1963, Thomas Bradley ran for the Los Angeles City Council. He became the first black elected to that 15-member body. In 1973, Bradley ran for mayor of Los Angeles, the nation's third largest city. On May 29, the 55-year-old ex-cop became the city's first black mayor defeating incumbent mayor Sam Yorty, 63, with more than 56 per cent of the vote.

During the bitter name calling campaign with racial overtones, Bradley had said he wanted to show that Los Angeles had matured in the four years since Yorty capitalized on the race issue to beat him in the final days of their 1969 campaign. When asked if he thought the city of nearly three million residents was ready for a black mayor, Bradley replied, "I think this city is ready for a mayor who has the ability, who has the kinds of programs which will deal with the issues in this city."

Bradley, who defeated Yorty by nearly 100,000 votes, said he saw his victory as an inspiration to young people who had lost faith in the American political system. He said that he felt the system could not be changed by working from the outside. "I've been trying to say to them that I lived in the system, I believed in it, I thought it would work."

Earlier in May, a drive by Black Panther cofounder Bobby Seale to oust incumbent John Reading as mayor of Oakland, California's fifth largest city, failed.

Tom Bradley taking oath as mayor of Los Angeles

Reading, 55, had held the part-time, non-partisan mayor's job since 1966, the year Seale and Huey Newton cofounded the Panther party. Despite the loss, Seale, 36, said, "It's good either way it goes. Whether we win or lose, something has happened in this town that has never happened before in the history of this country."

The Twin towers of the World Trade Center in New York soared 1,350 feet into the air following completion of seven years work.

UNITED STATES AND CHINA MOVED TOWARD FULL DIPLOMATIC TIES

The breakthrough came one year after President Nixon's historic visit to Communist China. In a communique released simultaneously in Washington and Peking, the two powers announced that they would set up "liaison offices" in each other's capitals, a move that in effect ended their long estrangement.

Presidential advisor Henry A. Kissinger who had hammered out the details in Peking described the agreement as an important step toward normalization between the two regimes. In fact the action amounted in everything but name to the establishment of diplomatic relations.

The results of Kissinger's mission—his fifth visit to the Chinese capital—demonstrated the desire of both China and the United States to move much faster than most people had expected. The two powers had progressed from the tensions of two decades toward a normalization of relations.

Kissinger said his talks with Chairman Mao Tse-tung and Premier Chou En-lai had covered four major areas:
—"The desirability of normalization of relations.
—"The desirability of reducing the danger of military conflict.
—"The affirmation by both sides that neither would seek hegemony in the Pacific area.
—"And each of them opposed the attempt of anyone else to achieve it, and that the relations between China and the United States would never be directed against any third country."

It was apparent that Peking was making a big concession in agreeing to exchange official liaison offices with Washington. Observers felt that a major reason was China's rivalry with Moscow.

The Nixon administration which wanted to avoid offending either of the two Communist giants kept mum about this aspect of the surprise speed in normalization of relations with Peking.

The agreement between Washington and Peking represented a full turn of the wheel in the history of American attitudes toward Red China over three decades. The first such U.S. mission set up in July 1944 in Yenan, Mao Tse-tung's cave city capital was officially known as the U.S. Army Observer Group.

Ostensibly the objectives of the 1944 mission had been purely military but it conceivably could have led to establishment of American relations with the Peoples Republic when Mao took power in October 1949. But the ensuing five years led to an implacable hostility between Washington and Mao's regime.

As the new rapport with Peking burgeoned, the Nixon administration turned to an old pro to carry the ball. Nixon told newsmen that as his new emissary to China he had called on David K. E. Bruce, 75-year-old diplomat and statesman for five presidents. "We call him out of retirement," said Nixon "because I thought it was very important to appoint a man of great stature to this position."

On May 14, Bruce made the journey to Peking and paid his respects at the Chinese foreign office. Observers noted that in a welcome greeting, Deputy Foreign Minister Chiao Kuan-hua addressed Bruce as "Minister Ambassador" even though the American mission did not have embassy status.

ANOTHER BRITISH SEX SCANDAL ERUPTED

Ten years had passed since John Profumo admitted having an affair with party girl Christine Keeler and then resigned as Britain's Minister of State for War causing headlines that rocked the Tory regime of Prime Minister Harold Macmillan.

This time, the cast of characters seemed even more intriguing. It included two lords, Soho vice kings, shapely call girls, two-way mirrors and picture snapping pimps.

In May, a police investigation turned up evidence that Lord Lambton, a 50-year-old millionaire who had been in the House of Commons for 22 years, had been detected fraternizing with a couple of call girls.

The woman who touched off the sex scandal was identified as Norma Levy, slim, dark-haired daughter of an Irish cattle dealer with a taste for champagne, fast cars and mink coats.

The case might have stopped there, but Lambton held the non-cabinet post of Undersecretary of the Royal Air Force which meant that he could have access to secret information.

The day after police talked to him, Lambton sent a letter to Prime Minister Edward Heath resigning his air force post. The following day he issued a statement saying that he had had a "casual acquaintance with a call girl and two of her friends" and that "her husband had taken some secret photographs which he had sold to the newspapers."

Twenty-four hours after Lord Lambton's admissions, a more prominent figure became enmeshed in the burgeoning scandal. Earl Jellico, government leader in the House of Lords and a personal friend of Heath, admitted that he had had "some casual affairs" with prostitutes. Jellico, holder of the ancient title of Lord Privy Seal and a senior member of Heath's cabinet had full access to top government papers.

Both Lambton and Jellico denied that their links with call girls had involved lawbreaking, blackmail or security leaks. But Jellico, son of a World War I naval hero, conceded in a resignation statement that his actions had been a "grave embarrassment" to Heath's administration.

Acting swiftly to avoid any suggestion of a cover-up, Heath told a hushed House of Commons that there would be an independent inquiry into security implications of the scandal.

Many Britons expressed sympathy for the two lords and commended them for owning up to their misdeeds publicly.

It was also recalled that ever since the Duke of Wellington, victor of Waterloo and later prime minister, had told the top London call girl of his day to "publish and be damned", Britain's lords had provided an avid public with some of its spicier sex scandals. They recalled Lord Byron's romance with Lady Caroline Lamb whose husband became prime minister and another prime minister, Lord Palmerston, whose affairs reportedly included the Countess of Jersey and Princess Lieven, wife of the Russian ambassador.

U.S. CONSUL RECOUNTED HIS KIDNAPING ORDEAL

"There was no bodily torture, but the mental torture was really something. I thought to myself—'How do I know they don't have a gun pointed at my head?' When they got ready to release me I didn't know if they were going to let me out of the car or throw me out and put a bullet in my head.

"Kidnaping is one of the most horrible things that can happen to a person."

The words were those of Terrance G. Leonhardy, spoken shortly after the U.S. consul general had been released in Guadalajara, Mexico, by the terrorists who had kidnaped him May 4 and held him for 76 hours until the Mexican government released 30 prisoners and arranged a ransom of $80,000.

Leonhardy, who had been with the U.S. diplomatic service for 31 years, came to Guadalajara from El Salvador in 1972. He was kidnaped as he was driving home alone, transferred from his car to another, blindfolded and held until the kidnapers' demands were met.

"I was two blocks from home in my car when they stopped me," he said. He said the kidnapers took him to an unknown destination. "I was blindfolded all the time except one brief instance when they wanted to write some notes. They kept saying they were going to let me go. But you know how that is. I had ups and downs. I wasn't very hungry, but they did offer me food, and I did eat some rudimentary stuff that kept me going. I lost four pounds. It was a pretty rough situation for me."

Leonhardy's kidnap was the latest in a wave of political abductions in Latin America that began more than four years earlier in Brazil (The World in 1969, 194). He was taken by armed men who said they were members of the Revolutionary Armed Forces of the People. At first they asked only the freedom of the 30 prisoners and their transport to Cuba. But when the Mexican government met this demand, the kidnapers then asked for the $80,000.

London subway riders read details of a sex scandal that caused the resignations of two government ministers.

A PROMINENT DEMOCRAT
JOINED RANKS OF GOP

After supporting the Democratic party all of his life, John B. Connally, 56-year-old friend and adviser to three presidents, formally switched his allegiance to the Republicans May 2 because he felt his original party had "moved so far left it has left the majority of Americans who occupy the great middle ground of political thought in this country."

Added the former Texas governor who had served 18 months as President Nixon's treasury secretary, "I think the instrument of the future of this country in the political sense is the . . . Republican party because, frankly, it has moved from the right . . . and now occupies the broad middle ground where most Americans are and want to be."

A protege of President Lyndon B. Johnson, Connally served as secretary of the Navy under President John F. Kennedy. He was Texas governor when Kennedy was slain in Dallas, and was wounded while riding with Kennedy in the presidential car.

AN ENGLISH-BORN PROTESTANT
BECAME IRELAND'S PRESIDENT

When the final election returns were posted in the Republic of Ireland May 31, the results they gave were somewhat surprising. They showed that Erskine Childers, an English-born Protes-

tant, had been elected president of the overwhelmingly Roman Catholic country.

By defeating Thomas O'Higgins for the post, Childers was able to succeed Eamon de Valera as president, a largely ceremonial and nonpolitical job which consists of receiving heads of state and other dignitaries, signing legislation and accepting and confirming resignations and appointments of the government.

Childers was the candidate of Fianna Fail, the party founded by De Valera. Fianna Fail had lost control of the government in elections three months earlier. O'Higgins was the candidate of the government coalition of Fine Gael and Labor.

Childers was the second Protestant to be elected president of a 95 per cent Catholic country. The first president as well as first Protestant was Dr. Douglas Hyde.

H. RAP BROWN CONVICTED IN
NEW YORK CITY BAR ROBBERY

Patrons at New York City's Red Carpet Lounge were enjoying themselves the night of Oct. 16, 1971, when four gunmen stalked into the bar. The bandit quartet forced the 30 persons in the lounge to lie on the floor, robbed them, and emptied the cash register.

Then they fled into the street; to be met by arriving police cars. Shots were exchanged. One of the gunmen, although wounded, managed to escape but later was captured while hiding on

the roof of a building near the lounge. He was identified as H. Rap Brown, 29.

Brown came to national attention during the racially-troubled year of 1967. That was when he took over the leadership of the Student Nonviolent Coordinating Committee.

Later that year, he was charged with inciting to riot after a speech he gave in Cambridge, Md., was followed by rioting and burning (The World in 1967, 142). But Brown disappeared shortly before the case was scheduled to come to trial. He managed to remain in hiding until his capture after the Red Carpet lounge holdup.

On March 29, 1973, Brown was convicted for his role in the holdup of the bar and a gun battle with police. On May 9 he was sentenced to 5 to 15 years in prison.

FOR THE RECORD

SIGNED. An economic cooperation pact, by Leonid I. Brezhnev and West German Chancellor Willy Brandt. The May 19 pact gave a framework for multimillion dollar future deals, such as an exchange of Soviet natural gas for German pipe and joint ventures building Soviet factories. The two leaders also agreed to encourage cooperation in the chemical industry, the peaceful uses of atomic energy and the exploitation of the Soviet Union's mineral wealth, especially crude oil.

Thousands of Italian construction workers staged a demonstration for better working conditions in a Rome square

June

President Nixon and Party Leader Leonid I. Brezhnev clasped hands aboard the presidential plane en route to the Western White House.

Brezhnev Exuded Good Will During His Visit with Nixon

*But some Americans nervously recalled the
Russian proverb "beware the friendly bear"*

MORE THAN ANYTHING ELSE, it seemed, the reigning chief of Soviet Communism wanted to impress upon his American hosts in the citadel of capitalism that things in the world had changed radically.

Into a United States made gloomily introspective by the burgeoning Watergate scandal breezed Leonid Ilyich Brezhnev, general secretary of the Soviet Communist party. Throughout a mid-June week of summitry and ceremony with President Richard Milhous Nixon in Washington, Camp David and San Clemente, he exuded an exuberant bonhomie, and if the visi-

tor's words and attitude were a reliable barometer, the ice-storms of the cold war had passed into history.

Once again, as in the first Nixon-Brezhnev summit a year before in Moscow, the incredible unfolded before the eyes of bemused Americans. Here was Brezhnev working hard to project the image of friendly cousin from the old country, mildly clowning now and again, mixing happily and easily with Congressmen, movie stars, highly conservative capitalists and assorted politicians. To all of them he gave the insistent Kremlin message of "peaceful coexistence." Here, on one oc-

114

casion, was the Number One man of the Kremlin, determinedly amiable and intensely earnest, jawboning an aggregation of the elite among U.S. industrialists for 90 minutes about the golden dawn of a new day of bountiful business.

The summit week saw nine major agreements signed: on avoiding nuclear conflict, on principles of nuclear arms limitation and on transport, oceanography, agriculture, income tax, airlines, culture and commerce. But it was the tone of the summit that was remarkable. The note was hopeful almost to a point of creating an atmosphere of euphoria.

When it was all over, Brezhnev taped 47 minutes for television as a farewell to the Americans. He spoke in a soft baritone that sounded almost like a contented purr. His gestures were few and modest, his expression the soul of earnest goodwill, his appearance that of an indulgent uncle talking to favorite nieces and nephews. This was the image of the new Brezhnev, the image of the quiet-spoken peacemaker, of the man who had labored tirelessly to bring the cold war to an end.

"Mankind has outgrown the rigid 'cold war' armor which it was forced to wear," the bushy-browed, 66-year-old Communist chief would tell American viewers, beaming benignly over his spectacles. "It wants to breathe freely and peacefully."

Brezhnev's powerful 200-pound frame seemed symbolic of the Russian Bear as he frolicked, a bit clumsily and self-consciously at times, among his erstwhile foes in the lairs of capitalism. Americans who remembered the Russian proverb, "Beware the friendly bear," would wonder about this apparent declaration of an end to the cold war. Was it really over? How much of mankind, wanting to "breathe freely," could really do so in that part of the world dominated by Brezhnev's Soviet system?

There was still lots of room for reservations and skepticism

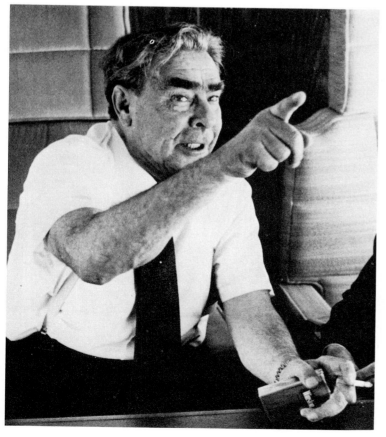

Brezhnev getting a point across with aides aboard the U.S. presidential jet "The Spirit of '76"

about where all this developing new relationship between the two superpowers might lead. Among the main worriers were those who weren't represented at the summit: Europeans, Chinese, people of the so-called "third world." For them, some nagging questions remained. Were the two superpowers between them going to decide everyone else's future? Might the Americans and Russians collaborate to the exclusion of others and seek to impose their own sort of peace?

One thing was certain: Change indeed was at hand. Much of it could be traced back to policies of the bald, squat peasant who surprised Kremlin-watchers in 1953 by rising to pre-eminence among Stalin's heirs. Nikita S. Khrushchev had been the innovator. Brezhnev had been his pupil and protege and then his successor after participating in the 1964 plot that tumbled Khrushchev from the pinnacle of power. Now Brezhnev was following his mentor's example by journeying to the "enemy" heartland.

For Americans who had seen Khrushchev in action in the first visit of a Soviet leader to the United States, the Brezhnev performance was a pale substitute. As in Brezhnev's case, the primary aim of Khrushchev's summitry had been trade.

Khrushchev had come in 1959, in his own words, with "pure heart and good intentions." Brezhnev arrived 14 years later for the announced purpose of shelving the cold war. Khrushchev's spectacular tour across the nation had been punctuated by his loud and lusty vulgarity and his irrepressible, peasant-like clowning. Brezhnev saw nothing of the United States save Washington, Camp David and the Western White House at San Clemente, Calif., and throughout it all remained the picture of polite propriety. He clowned, but only mildly, as if anxious to confer an air of informality upon the momentous doings.

However, there could be little doubt of Brezhnev's confidence. The new Brezhnev seemed to have made himself enormously strong in his position at home. Behind him was a special meeting of his party central committee that had, in April, given unanimous approval to his foreign policy, the policy on which he had staked his leadership.

For several years Brezhnev had been the subject of a remarkable propaganda buildup as outstanding leader, soldier-patriot turned politician, blazer of new paths, friend and benefactor of all the Soviet people. Then, two months before his new venture into summitry, his central committee enlarged the ruling Politburo to 16 members, adding three who could be regarded as Brezhnev men. One of these was the able and durable foreign minister, Andrei A. Gromyko, who would accompany his chief to the summit in the United States.

By his own account, the root of Brezhnev's policy lay in the 1969 international meeting of Communist leaders from 75 countries in Moscow. Billed as the "anti-imperialist" conference, it voiced approval of a developing Soviet peace offensive. This was further elaborated in March, 1971 at the 24th Congress of the Soviet Communist party. There Brezhnev made a marathon speech laying down both foreign and domestic policy lines. A Congress resolution directed the party to "carry forward into practice the principle of peaceful coexistence, to extend mutually advantageous relations with capitalist countries."

Thereafter, even up to the eve of his departure for the United States, Brezhnev repeatedly referred to the 1969 and 1971 meetings as major steps in a battle against "imperialist forces." The April central committee meeting applauded "positive changes" brought about by the program, but added there still was need for "constant vigilance and preparedness to give a rebuff to any manifestations by aggressive, reactionary circles of imperialism." To Moscow, Washington is the bastion of "imperialism."

There could be little doubt about what was topmost on the Brezhnev agenda as he took off for the United States to return the Nixon visit of May, 1972. The Soviet Union, a mighty military power, had achieved rough strategic parity with the United States. Nuclear war was unthinkable, yet confrontation remained a clear and uncomfortable possibility, especially in such hot-spot areas as the Middle East. Brezhnev had to worry about China and its developing nuclear potential, and he would want tranquility in the West while keeping an eye on Peking. But most of all, his agenda had to do with trade.

The Soviet consumer sector had been badly neglected for a half century of Communist party power. Clearly the regime had been feeling pressures from below reflecting impatience with the idea that a nation as big and rich and powerful as the U.S.S.R. had so shabby a domestic economy in comparison with those of both Eastern and Western Europe.

Already Brezhnev had registered some striking profit from the new look of Moscow-Washington relations. In an atmosphere of receding political war, the Soviet Union found a quick and cheap way out of an agricultural crisis in 1972, through enormous purchases of U.S. grains, deals that would arouse bitter American controversy and charges that granaries were depleted at the expense of the U.S. consumer.

Brezhnev had prospects of big deals with American capitalists to help exploit Soviet natural riches. There were hopes of access to the sort of western technologies that could speed considerably the development of the Soviet consumer sector. There were hopes of profitable collaboration in many fields: environment, space, air travel, oceanography and others. And Brezhnev hoped for yet more. He was insistent on a claim to most-favored-nation status from the Americans that would insure the Soviet Union treatment on a par with that of America's best trading partners.

Clearly, it was no time for Brezhnev to do or say anything that might upset so promising an applecart. Ordinarily, a spectacle like the Watergate scandal would have made perfect propaganda ammunition for Moscow, but the Kremlin passed it up. Brezhnev himself was all sympathy. After all, he retorted when asked about it, "it's not an earthquake."

Just before his departure for the United States, Brezhnev held an unprecedented mass interview with U.S. correspondents in Moscow. Asked sharp questions about Watergate, he pleaded innocence of any thought that he might profit from a weakened Nixon position.

"The thought has never entered my head as to whether or not President Nixon has lost any influence or gained any influence as a result of Watergate," said Brezhnev indignantly. "And I am not therefore going to the United States in the hope or with the intention of bringing any pressure to bear on the President in connection with what is purely a domestic affair."

It would be "quite indecent and quite unsuitable," thus, to comment on Watergate, said Brezhnev. The Soviet leader added that he had deep respect for Nixon "based on the fact that the President chose to take a realistic and constructive approach to the problem of improving relations between our two countries."

The Soviet press long had used the word "realistic" in that context. The burden of what was being said in the orbit about the new stage of East-West relations was that the United States and the West, noting the growing military might of the U.S.S.R., had been "forced" to adopt a realistic approach.

To Americans, however, Brezhnev stressed trade. He even suggested that this quest reflected Soviet generosity.

"Would it be a bad thing if the Soviet Union would agree to share part of its wealth with the United States?" he asked at that news conference. "Naturally, we would not be doing it simply free of charge, just as American businessmen would never do anything free of charge."

The Russians are not famous for giving things away. They badly wanted trade, just as they badly wanted the capital, technology and knowhow for getting their great wealth of natural riches out of the ground.

Brezhnev flew to the United States on Saturday, June 16, his arrival a far cry from the scene 14 years earlier with the coming of Krushchev. This time there were no ceremonies, at Brezhnev's own request. He had tended to get sick on long air trips and would need time to rest up. Thus, he was whisked quickly from Andrews Air Force Base to Camp David, the presidential retreat in the Maryland hills, 30 miles away by helicopter. There he talked with Henry A. Kissinger, the President's ace national security adviser, and he conferred with his own staff, including Ambassador Anatoly F. Dobrynin and Foreign Minister Gromyko.

The official Brezhnev state visit began Monday, June 18, on the White House lawn amid the usual scenes of pomp and pageantry reserved for chiefs of state. Technically Brezhnev wasn't entitled to all that. He was neither head of state nor chief of government. But he was boss, by virtue of his control of the Communist party which, in turn runs everything else in the Soviet Union.

In a speech of welcome, the President noted that the world, including the Soviet people, watched the proceedings on television with hope "because the people of the world know that if the leaders of the two most powerful nations of the world can work together . . . the chance for a world of peace is infinitely increased."

Brezhnev, responding, referred to the 1972 Moscow summit and went on: "During the past year a good beginning has been made . . . and now we regard our visit to the United States and forthcoming meetings with you as an expression of our common determination to make a new contribution to what was jointly initiated."

When the ceremonies were over that morning, Brezhnev put his arm around the President and in a burst of enthusiasm announced: "We are moving forward." The hefty Communist acted up for the cameras, grinning widely, waving his arms, clasping hands above his head in a gesture of triumph. "Make one more for history," he shouted at the laboring photographers. To the President he volunteered a prediction: "by the end of the week you'll be speaking Russian and I'll be speaking English."

That night the visitor was feted at a gala White House dinner where he exchanged toasts with his host. To Nixon's comment that "in a nuclear age there is no alternative to a policy of peace," the Soviet leader responded: "What is needed also is to overcome the inertia of the cold war and its after-effects in international affairs and in the minds of men."

The two leaders began talking business in the Oval Office Tuesday afternoon. Agreements that had been the result of a year of painstaking negotiations were ready for their discussion and approval.

That evening, Brezhnev boarded the presidential yacht, Sequoia, for a sail on the Potomac, and thereafter was flown back to Camp David by helicopter where on Wednesday he would have a full day of negotiations.

Above, Soviet leader Brezhnev seemed to be comparing his champagne glass with President Nixon's. Below, Brezhnev and Nixon received plaques commemorating the Skylab space operation from astronauts Pete Conrad (left) and Joseph P. Kerwin

Brezhnev seemed never to lose sight of his primary goal: increased trade. On Friday, June 22, Salesman Brezhnev met for an hour and a half with leading American capitalists and read them a friendly lecture on the mercantile history of Russia—all about how the old merchants carried their goods to the East and West and came home with assorted goodies in return for furs and other natural resources. He led up gradually to the clincher: The cold was was fading fast away and a new day of commerce already glowed on the horizon.

"The cold war did put a brake on the development of human relations, of normal human relations, between nations," he went on. "And I ask you gentlemen as I ask myself, was that a good period? Did it serve the interests of the peoples? And my answer to that is no, no, no and again no".

Now, he said, things had changed and it was possible for him, "the representative of our socialist country, the country of Lenin," to meet with U.S. business executives. He was reasonable-sounding, friendly, frank.

A "super-salesman," commented one industrialist.

But there was a shadow on his efforts. The question of the right of emigration for Soviet Jews haunted the Brezhnev mission and threatened, in fact, to interfere with Congressional approval of Soviet deals. He tried industriously to convince Americans that there was no such thing as a "Jewish question" in the U.S.S.R., but the question kept popping up in spite of him and he was the target of a determined drive for some sort of pledge on the issue. Patently, the whole thing irritated him immensely. He claimed the issue had been dragged into the picture "artificially."

In spite of that, Brezhnev could probably reckon that he had accomplished a good deal for Soviet policy in his venture into the unfamiliar world of the capitalists, and his farewell to Americans reflected a large measure of satisfaction with the results. He taped 47 television minutes to be broadcast to the U.S. public after his departure, reading it with a display of masterly showmanship. Again he made it plain that his heart belonged to the trade aspects of his trip.

"The truth is," he told the Americans, "that broader and deeper economic cooperation in general and the long-term and large scale deals which are now either being negotiated or have already been successfully concluded by Soviet organizations and American firms, are bound to yield real and tangible benefits for both sides. . . . Both the Soviet leadership and, as I see it, the United States government, attach particular importance to the fact that the development of long-term economic cooperation will also have very beneficial political consequences. It will consolidate the present trend, consolidate the trend of better Soviet-American relations generally."

Throughout the whole visit Brezhnev had consistently dominated the scene at social gatherings, determinedly and conspicuously projecting an image of enthusiastic well-wisher. Ever-conscious of the cameras, he acted up for them frequently. On one social occasion he pretended to hide his face from the cameras by holding up a little cocktail napkin. In the process he slopped champagne over his jacket. On another occasion he pretended to race Nixon in a signing ceremony. He mugged and mimed now and then, but always in a modest way, nothing at all like the style of the boasting, quarrelsome, blustery Khrushchev.

On the final day while waiting to leave the Western White House, Brezhnev gave one of his stellar performances. A fan of western movies, he had just received two Colt .45 six-shooters and a cowboy hat, and he mimed a "High Noon" shootout for the assemblage of notables. Then, spotting western star Chuck Connors near the helicopter pad, Brezhnev lumbered over to him and threw his arms around him. The big, husky movie cowboy lifted the leader of Soviet communism off his feet with a mighty bearhug as the two laughed delightedly and the President smiled benevolently.

And so, on Sunday, June 24, Brezhnev left San Clemente on the first leg of his journey home. The summit had come to an end with the signing of the joint communique applauding the results of the meeting. The President pictured himself as "very pleased with the range of issues discussed, with the wide scope of agreements reached in all fields, with the excellent atmosphere that pervaded all the talks, with the emphasis on concrete accomplishments." Brezhnev saw the summit as a "happy moment."

More summits were in prospect. The Soviet leader invited the American back to Russia and indicated the trip could come in "six to eight months." The President accepted. This could mean that Brezhnev in turn would have to make yet another return visit to Washington.

These, in brief, were the nine agreements signed during the summit:

NUCLEAR WAR—The two sides pledged themselves to avoid confrontations that could provoke nuclear conflict.

NUCLEAR ARMS AND ENERGY: The two defined principles for more negotiations on nuclear arms limitation and on negotiations for cooperative use of atomic energy for peaceful purposes.

TRANSPORT—Pledged cooperation to solve land, air and sea transport problems.

AIR TRAVEL—Added U.S. and Soviet stops for passenger services of Aeroflot and Pan American airlines.

CULTURE—Expanded scientific, cultural, technological and educational contacts and exchanges.

COMMERCE—Established a Soviet-American Chamber of Commerce and arrangements for his physical facilities.

INCOME TAX—Agreed to reduce income taxes on citizens of one country living in the other to avoid excessive tax burdens.

AGRICULTURE—Planned trade, research, development, production and processing cooperation.

OCEANOGRAPHY—Agreed on cooperative study of the world's oceans.

The major agreements on nuclear war and nuclear arms were couched in rather vague terms suggesting little more than good intentions, but the fact that such intentions were put on paper and signed was in itself important. The agreement on avoidance of nuclear conflict, for example, could inhibit a Soviet military move to cancel China's growing nuclear potential. It might also have an effect of taking some of the heat out of the chronic Middle East crisis.

Nations involved in long-term trade agreements might be less likely to risk confrontations, and the Russians already had entered into major deals with the United States and others in the West. One that could have important impact, long-term, on a developing energy problem in the United States was a $10 billion package deal with Dr. Armand Hammer, chairman of Occidental Petroleum Corp., for exploitation of Soviet natural gas. It would require generous credits for the Russians and there was sentiment in influential Washington circles to require the Russians to meet pre-conditions. Another deal between Dr. Hammer and Moscow envisions construction of a large fertilizer complex, with prospective U.S. loans running into hundreds of millions. It had explicit White House endorsement. A good many other deals were in the talking stage.

While Europe welcomed a look of eased relations, a good deal of doubt lingered. There had been periods of detente before when Soviet leaders had seem amiable, and those detentes had faded in the heat of new crisis. Also, there was a widespread feeling that doing business with the vast Soviet bureaucracy would be tricky and difficult.

Brezhnev left for home by way of France, stopping off in Paris for talks with President Georges Pompidou, and the stop in itself signified awareness on both sides of such doubts.

"Is it conceivable that the United States and the Soviet Union could make decisions about Europe without consulting it, especially in matters of defense and security?" asked the French newspaper Le Figaro, and there was similar comment in West Germany.

Detente, Le Figaro went on, "must not be used by the U.S.S.R as a means of lulling Europe's legitimate distrust into a false sense of security; detente must not be bought by the United States at the exorbitant price of renouncing the role of protector of Europe which it assumed for 25 years to Europe's benefit."

Although Washington had been trying to ease European worries along such lines, there remained a large measure of concern that the new U.S.-Soviet relationship would lead eventually to a U.S. military withdrawal from Europe which would leave the Soviet Union in a dominating position with its enormous conventional military strength.

Whatever the Soviet intent might have been, Moscow's press created around Brezhnev an aura of triumph, treating him like a hero on his return from the land of capitalism. The enormous amount of press coverage and its enthusiastic tone suggested an intention of presenting Brezhnev's summitry as the biggest thing since the Bolshevik revolution.

Brezhnev was greeted by actress Jill St. John in San Clemente as the President looked on

Astronauts Set Flight Record Aboard First American Space Station

But the $2.6 billion space project was in grave danger when heat shield ripped away from the station

SUNLIGHT GLINTED off the windmill-shaped object looming larger in the window of the Apollo spaceship.

"Tallyho! Skylab!" exclaimed commander Charles Conrad Jr. as he maneuvered to give his crewmates, Dr. Joseph P. Kerwin and Paul J. Weitz, a closer look at America's first space station.

Until a few days before, the Conrad crew had doubts it ever would see the orbiting station. But here they were, 275 miles above the earth, ready for the first salvage mission in the young history of manned space flight.

The adventure began May 14 when a powerful Saturn 5 rocket roared away from Cape Kennedy, Fla., boosting into orbit the unmanned Skylab, as large as a three-bedroom house. It would not end until June 22.

Barely 63 seconds into the flight, ground controllers knew the project was in trouble. Radio signals indicated a combination meteoroid and heat shield had ripped away from the station, exposing it to the searing rays of the sun.

The shield in flying off also tore away one of the workshop's twin electricity-producing power panels and jammed the other against the side of the vehicle. That drastically reduced the power available.

The launching of Conrad, Kerwin and Weitz, scheduled the

Below left, the Skylab I space station boosted by a modified Saturn V rocket lifted off from the Kennedy Center Complex. Below right, Skylab commander Charles "Peter" Conrad took a bath in the orbital workshop

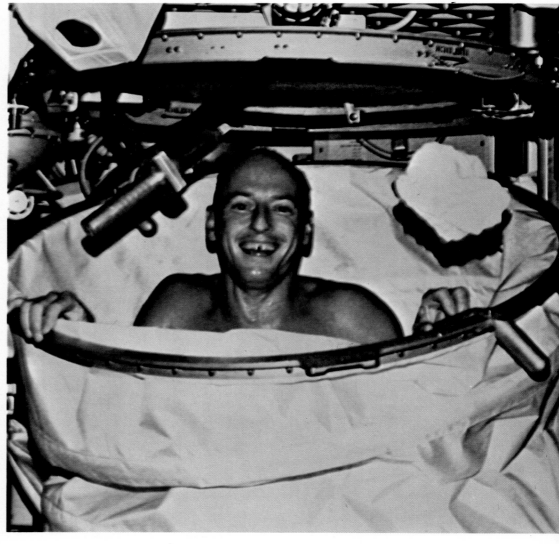

next day, was postponed five days, then another five days, while NASA engineers and controllers struggled to find some way of saving the $2.6 billion project.

First priority went to cooling down the laboratory, where temperatures inside soared to 125 degrees, too hot for the astronauts to live in for a long period.

Experts decided that by erecting some sort of giant fabric sun shade over the exposed area of the laboratory, the astronauts might be able to lower the temperature.

The effort required the skills and ingenuity of several specialists, from pipefitters to seamstresses, to space physicists and chemists who evaluated the effect of solar radiation on the thin, aluminized Mylar and nylon sheet used to construct the various canopies.

Because the exact situation on the station was not known, three different sun shades were developed: an umbrella-like device that could be deployed from inside the station; a "window shade" that could be unrolled on tubes during a space walk, and a sail-like device that could be positioned by a crewman leaning out the open hatch of the Apollo ferry ship.

For freeing the solar panel, various cutting and prying tools were devised.

As each potential solution was developed, the astronauts practiced it in a 1.4-million-gallon water tank at NASA's Marshall Space Flight Center, Huntsville, Ala. The tank contained fullscale models of Skylab and Apollo and the water provided some sensation of working in space weightlessness.

As the work progressed, the situation aboard Skylab became desperate. Food and medicine began to spoil from the heat, and deteriorating foam insulation began to fill the cabin with poison gas.

Mission Control in Houston, Tex., had to constantly maneuver the lab to keep some areas from getting too hot and others from getting too cold on the shadow side of the vehicle.

The feverish preparations continued until just four hours before the launching of the astronauts when the last gear was packed aboard the Apollo.

At 9 a.m. May 25, the rescue mission began with the liftoff of the Skylab 1 astronauts from Cape Kennedy atop a Saturn 1B rocket. They were hoping to complete a full 28-day mission.

"We're on our way," Conrad shouted as they shot into orbit and began a series of maneuvers to track down the 85-ton laboratory. Six hours later they moved in on their target and inspected the damage.

They confirmed one solar panel was gone and the other was deployed a few inches, hung up by a one-inch wide, two-foot-long piece of aluminum, a remnant of the meteoroid shield.

"I think we can take care of it," Conrad said of the aluminum strip.

While Mission Control considered the report, the astronauts docked to one end of the 118-foot-long laboratory and ate dinner in their Apollo cabin. The control center then gave them the go-ahead to try to free the panel.

Space station photographed by the Skylab astronauts from their command module

Conrad undocked and maneuvered the command ship to within 10 feet of the panel. Wearing a bulky space suit, Weitz opened the hatch and, with Kerwin hanging on to his legs, he leaned out and attempted to jerk the stuck panel loose with a long-handled tool resembling a boat hook.

After an hour of pushing, shoving and tugging, Weitz conceded he couldn't break the aluminum strip.

"We ain't going to do it with the tools we've got" he observed.

Another disappointment followed. Apollo's docking mechanism, which had worked the first time, suddenly balked and the astronauts were unable to re-dock with the Skylab.

Determined to avoid aborting the mission, the astronauts suited up again, depressurized the cabin, removed the docking device and repaired it. After two hours they linked up successfully and went to sleep.

In the morning, they removed connecting hatches and transferred for the first time into the sweltering laboratory. There, the first order of business was to jury-rig the umbrella-like sun shade which ground engineers settled on as the first choice of shadowing the workshop from solar heat.

The astronauts shoved the folded "parasol" through a small scientific airlock module with a telescopic pole, then opened it into a 22-by-24-foot sheet.

"We got a good deployment of the sail," Conrad reported.

Almost immediately, instruments in Mission Control noted a slow drop in temperature in the workshop cabin. Within days it fell from 125 degrees into the 70s.

That problem solved, the space men began the task of putting their space station in working order.

They unpacked supplies and set up scientific instruments. Kerwin, the first physician to fly in space, organized his medical laboratory.

Then they were ready for the main job of the mission, conducting medical, earth resources and solar astronomy experiments. They aimed a giant array of telescopes at the sun and pointed photosensors at the earth. And Kerwin supervised the drawing of blood, the monitoring of bodily functions and medical workouts on bicycle and other devices.

In brief telecasts, Conrad, Kerwin and Weitz showed off the impressive spaciousness of their 12,000-cubic-foot home as they romped around the cylindrical cabin, sliding around lockers and through hatches as if they had lived in weightlessness all their lives.

But because of the power shortage, the astronauts had to curtail many of the experiments. When two of 18 batteries failed, the situation became more critical.

Conrad suggested that they think again about freeing the stuck solar panel.

"I think we have the tools to cut that strip or pry it loose," the commander said, and recommended a space walk to give it a try.

After evaluation and testing on the ground, Mission Control said okay. And on June 7, the 13th day of the journey, Conrad and Kerwin opened an airlock hatch and stepped outside for the daring and difficult task.

After they assembled five sections of tubing into a 25-foot extension pole and attached to it a two-foot cutting tool similar to pruning shears, they uncoiled the 60-foot umbilical cords that provided them with oxygen and a communications link to the control center. They made their way through a maze of trusses on Skylab's telescope mount to a point within pole's reach of the jammed solar wing.

One difficulty was immediately apparent. "My feet keep flying away. It's not a handhold I need, it's a foothold," Kerwin shouted.

But they managed to secure the cutter end of the pole near the wing and Conrad moved hand over hand along the rail. He clamped the cutter over the aluminum strip that held the panel down and hooked one end of a piece of rope to the panel. The other end was secured to a strut on the telescope mount 25 feet away.

Conrad moved back, and Kerwin tried to sever the strip by maneuvering a lanyard to operate the cutter from a safe distance. The commander told later what happened.

"He hauled in on the cutters as hard as he could and nothing happened," Conrad said. "So I said 'let me go out the pole and look.' I got about two-thirds of the way out the pole and, bango, it decided to let go all by itself. So, whango, the thing flew up, along with me, the pole and the tether."

With the strip broken, he said the spacewalkers then provided the muscle to erect the panel. Both men tugged on the rope, with Conrad pulling it over his shoulder and Kerwin jerking from his position near the open hatch.

"We had quite a wild ride when we broke the damper restraint," Conrad reported. "I was facing away, heaving with all of my might. Joe was heaving with all his might, too. It let go and both of us took off. When we came down from our whipperdills (tumbles), why the wing was all shifted and deployed."

Once the wing beam was out, three sheets of solar cells began extending from the edge of the beam. However, hydraulic fluid in the spring mechanism had stiffened in the extreme cold of the Skylab shadow, and the sheets only partially came out.

Mission Control shifted the station's position to put them in sunlight and within five hours they were fully deployed.

Immediately, the sheets caught the heat of the sun and converted it to energy to charge eight batteries which until then had been inoperative. It added 3,000 volts of electricity to the laboratory supply, nearly double the amount previously available.

"Wowee! Super-duper," Conrad exclaimed.

"No more cold showers," Weitz commented.

"Hot dogs instead of cold dogs," Kerwin quipped.

On the ground the astronauts became known as the "fix anything guys."

With almost full power restored, the crew settled into a daily routine of experiments. On the 21st day, Weitz was at the solar telescope console when a massive flare erupted on the sun, spewing radiation into space.

He quickly trained his instruments on the explosion and captured the first photographs ever taken of a flare from above the earth's obscuring atmosphere.

Science is eager to learn about flares, because they influence, weather, communications and other events on earth. Study of the photographs might also help unlock the secret of thermonuclear fusion, which is the source of the sun's energy. This could aid in the search for an unlimited and pollution-free power source on earth.

The astronauts also focused sensing instruments on various areas of the earth to determine whether scientists can realize their hopes of mapping and studying earth resources.

Their expectations were ambitious: that these high-flying instruments can detect leaf blight and other crops diseases; map runoff waters, forests, population growth, the geography of inaccessible areas; discover new sources of petroleum and other minerals and increase knowledge of weather patterns on a global scale.

Astronauts Dr. Joseph P. Kerwin, Paul J. Weitz and Conrad as they held a news conference in space

The spacemen also conducted metal-processing experiments as a first step toward using the unique weightlessness and vacuum of space to manufacture such things as superstrong metals, perfectly round ball bearings, precision optical lenses and pure medical vaccines.

On the 24th day, Conrad, Kerwin and Weitz became history's longest-flying space travelers, surpassing the single mission mark of 23 days, 18 hours, 22 minutes set in 1971 by three Russian cosmonauts.

Two days later, Conrad and Weitz took another space walk to retrieve film from the solar telescopes. While outside, Mission Control asked them to do one more repair job.

They were called on to try an attempt to fix a battery regulator by tapping on it with a hammer.

Conrad wielded the hammer and successfully loosened a stuck relay in the regulator.

"It worked, gentlemen. You've done it again," radioed capsule communicator Rusty Schweickart.

The astronauts spent the final two days packing the Apollo ferry ship with film, tapes and other experiment results to be brought home. They also cleaned up the laboratory for the Skylab 2 crew, scheduled to visit it for 56 days later in the year.

On June 22, they boarded the Apollo and cast off for the trip home. "Bye, bye, Skylab," Conrad said as they pulled away.

Five hours later, they blazed back through the atmosphere and made a pinpoint landing in the Pacific Ocean within view of hundreds of white-clad sailors on the deck of the recovery carrier USS Ticonderoga.

"We're all in good shape. Everything's okay," Conrad radioed from inside the bobbing spacecraft at the end of the 28-day, 11-million-mile voyage.

Doctors were not certain what condition the astronauts would be in after their record exposure to weightlessness. So instead of picking them up by helicopter as on previous missions, the carrier steamed alongside and hoisted the Apollo on deck with a crane.

Medics stood by with stretchers in case the spacemen had trouble walking. But physician Kerwin reported they were okay, and all three emerged smiling and waving through the hatch.

Nevertheless, all three showed some effects of the long flight as they walked unsteadily to a mobile medical laboratory 60 feet away.

Doctors later reported that all three experienced dizziness, lightheadedness and nausea, with Kerwin suffering more than the others.

But by the time the carrier steamed into San Diego, Calif., harbor two days later, all three spacemen were in excellent shape, having quickly readapted to earth's gravity.

Before returning to their homes in Houston, Conrad, Kerwin and Weitz helicoptered to San Clemente, Calif., for a meeting with President Nixon and Soviet leader Leonid I. Brezhnev at the Western White House.

Brezhnev congratulated the astronauts and told them their flight was a great achievement for science for peaceful purposes.

As experts began the months'-long task of sorting out the mountains of data, space officials praised the accomplishments of the astronauts in saving the Skylab station and conducting nearly a 100 per cent mission.

Said Dr. Christopher C. Kraft Jr., director of the Johnson Space Center in Houston: "I think Skylab, even if nothing had happened to it in the terms of its problems, would have shown that man is very important to carrying out complicated scientific and engineering experiments in space."

Center, Self-appointed President George Papadopoulos cast his ballot in Athens referendum on whether to confirm him in office; At left, Deputy Premier Stylianos Patakos cast his ballot, and, at right, former Premier Panayiotis Canellopoulos received ballots at Athens polling center

Exiled Constantine Was Ousted as Greece's King and the Nation Declared a Republic

IT WAS SATURDAY the first of June. A day filled with rumors—rumors that usually circulate quickly among talkative Greeks at Athens' sidewalk cafes. Gossip was that an important decision had been reached by the army-backed government at an early morning cabinet session.

As the clock struck one, the martial music on the radio suddenly stopped and the familiar raspy voice of Greek regime strongman George Papadopoulos came over the state-controlled station:

"People of Greece . . . the young king had applied himself to activities abroad directed against the national government, disclosing an unforgivable immaturity for an adult. He had allied himself with adventurers, fellow travelers, saboteurs and even murderers." The former army colonel asserted that King Constantine "fell from the throne by himself. . . ."

Thus, Papadopoulos announced the end of the monarchy, proclaimed himself temporary president of the new republic

King Constantine of the Hellenes, in happier times, saluted during a memorial service in Athens in 1966

and pledged nationwide general elections by the end of 1974. He said that if they voted for him in a referendum as the republic's first president for a single seven-year term and for amendments to the present constitution ratifying his government's decision abolishing the monarchy, then complete individual freedoms would be restored. There was little doubt as to the outcome of the referendum.

When Papadopoulos brought down Damocles' sword, King Constantine was lingering in self-chosen exile in Rome, plotting his eventual return to the throne.

Abolishing the monarchy was perhaps the most drastic act the army-supported government had taken since it seized power April 21, 1967 (The World in 1967, 150), and suspended democracy. The monarchy's end came after 142 years of destructive conflicts, political controversy, exile and even a taste of republicanism. It died bloodlessly and unceremoniously.

In Rome, the 33-year-old king was caught by surprise. He was taking a stroll when he heard the news. He immediately sought help from friends to confirm what he had been told.

Once official confirmation was in hand, Constantine retreated to his Roman villa to prepare his next step and huddled in conference with his family. Then he denounced Papadopoulos' decision dethroning him as "an illegal act by an illegal government. If the regime fails to freely permit the people to choose its form of government, then I shall be compelled to

King Constantine and his daughter, Princess Alexia, under a Christmas tree at the royal exile villa in Rome

regard myself as the sole possessor of legality. I shall fight with all my strength as a soldier. I will have on my side the people of Greece and the armed forces."

Later, Constantine described the Athens government as a "harsh dictatorship" and added: "I have said that I will return to Greece, and I will return. . . ." He called on allied countries to withhold recognition of the new Greek republic. But the United States said it would recognize it, and other countries followed suit.

Constantine's statements created little stir when they were heard later the same day over short wave foreign stations beamed to Greece. The lack of interest gave the Athens regime added confidence in its bid to seek ratification of its decision making Greece a republic.

Constantine no longer commanded very much affection from his Greek subjects. He had been absent for six years and had lost considerable stature when his December 1967 counter coup (The World in 1967, 259) failed to get off the ground.

Superstitious Greeks feared from the time he ascended the throne that the rule of King Constantine II would be ill-fated. Although he was only the second Constantine of his dynasty, he was the 13th Constantine since the days of the Byzantine emperors. And Greeks agree that 13 is an unlucky number.

Constantine was born during World War II and when less than a year old was taken into exile. He returned at age eight to a Greece raked by a Communist uprising. But with the end of the civil war it appeared his luck had changed. He became popular with his people and was rumored to have dated a Greek movie actress, of even greater popularity. With several accidents behind him in sport cars, Constantine took up karate, gained a black belt and then represented his country to win a gold medal in sailing at the 1960 Rome Olympics.

Quickly developing a reputation as a playboy prince, Constantine had responsibility thrust upon him when he ascended the throne in March 1964 on the death of his father King Paul. Six months later, after a whirlwind royal romance, he pleased the people by marrying beautiful 18-year-old Danish princess, Anne Marie, a distant cousin.

Constantine's wedding to the shy, youngest child of King Frederick and Queen Ingrid, was hailed as the beginning of a new modern era for the Greek royal court. Scores of reigning and deposed members of European royalty and heads of state attended the three-day festivities in Athens.

It was a fairy tale royal wedding right down to the young couple riding in a gilded carriage pulled through the streets of Athens by white horses. Constantine and Anne-Marie were acclaimed by more than a million persons that day in September, unaware that the monarchy's time was measured.

Constantine's problems began almost before he had a chance to settle into his throne and assume the responsibility of ruling the 8.7 million Greeks. Fifteen months later he was involved in his first political struggle when he ousted popular liberal Premier George Papandreou whom he accused of attempting to purge the army of right wing elements.

In a dramatic exchange of letters, both men set the stage for the political crises and the army takeover that were to follow. Relying heavily on the advice of his constitutional advisers, Constantine fired Papandreou despite his overwhelming parliamentary majority. Both the center and the left turned against Constantine for entering politics and he alienated the right by trying to form a cabinet of moderates and deserters from Papandreou's party. At that stage, the familiar cry by opponents to the throne echoed across the land: "Who rules, the king or the people?"

The country was plunged into political turmoil, nightly rioting and street demonstrations. Constantine stuck to his decisions, but it appeared that every move turned against him.

The king was unseated with ample warning. The regime which had ruled by force since 1967 leaked its intentions immediately after a group of royalist navy officers failed on May 23 in their attempt to dislodge Papadopoulos. Constantine rejected charges from Athens that he had helped plot the navy rebellion.

Newspapers friendly to the regime called for am early decision on the monarchy's future. Seizing the opportunity by using the abortive navy rebellion as a pretext, Papadopoulos took the momentous step sooner than Greeks had expected and another king joined the ranks of the unemployed.

In order to ward off any unexpected resistance, the army was placed in a state of readiness. But it was an unnecessary move, since Greeks were bewildered and there was no evidence of overt opposition in the aftermath of Papadopoulos' proclamation.

Most Greeks took the decision calmly. Only loud murmurs of conversation were heard at the scores of sidewalk cafes that dot the sun drenched city of Athens on the edge of the Saronic Gulf. Some noon-day drinkers downing ouzos at cafes on Consitiution Square at the foot of the closed parliament building, scurried to buy extra newspaper editions announcing another chapter in Greece's turbulent past. Others turned on their transistor radios to hear further developments.

Constantine had lived in Rome ever since he fled Greece Dec. 14, 1967, with his family, following his inept day-long abortive royal counter coup against the ruling army junta. His move was the culmination of built-up frustrations and the will to regain the reigns of power.

When the army seized power in his name in 1967, Constantine was not aware of it until an elite unit of infantrymen knocked on the door of his country residence early in the morning. Constantine played along with the ruling junta and left the impression he actually was signing decrees being issued in his name. When he decided to move, it turned out to be another tragedy of errors that led to self-imposed exile in Rome.

The royal family's exile was quiet with virtually no significant incidents to speak of until Constantine's ouster.

Constantine was, technically speaking, not in exile but absent from his throne. When he fled the country, the government appointed a general to act as regent. In 1972, Premier Papadopoulos fired the regent and took the post himself.

The royal couple lived in virtual retirement with their three children, Princess Alexia, 7, and Prince Paul, 6, who was born 10 days after the army coup and Nicholas, 3, born in Rome.

At first, the royal couple shared a villa with Queen Mother Frederika and her daughter, Princess Irene, but later lived separately in the face of charges from Greece that Frederika had induced her son to carry out the abortive December coup against the Athens regime, the queen mother and Princess Irene moved to their own villa. But the rumors and charges continued that Frederika had plotted the coup along with royalist army generals.

Constantine, however, remained loyal to his mother, a headstrong former German princess who became queen of Greece when she married King Paul.

Constantine ignored the charges and openly sought his mother's advice whenever he could.

Constantine continued to receive his $580,000 annual stipend during his exile in Rome. Part of it, however, was retained for the upkeep of the royal homes in Greece. It was delivered monthly by special messenger to the Greek Embassy.

Life in Rome for an exiled monarch was not considered too harsh. The daily major problem Constantine was confronted with was what to do with his endless free time. He was often seen at horse shows in Rome's Villa Borghese park each spring, hunted in the north, sailed in the Mediterranean with his visiting brother-in-law, Juan Carlos of Spain. To break the monotony, Constantine played golf at Rome's aristocratic Acquasanta Club. He also loved to read and pored over books and papers at home. Occasionally, he flew to London to attend classes in political science at Cambridge.

In Rome, Constantine avoided Greek ex-politicians seeking audiences and was often seen sitting alone at the bar of a hotel, deep in thought, fingering a drink. When he dined out with his wife, Constantine usually chose restaurants more noted for their food than their fame. The royal couple also attended tennis matches, opera and Sunday services at the Greek Orthodox cathedral.

The government moved quickly to erase all vestiges of the monarchy. Within hours after the birth of the new republic, photographs of the royal couple were removed from all ministries and official offices. The bulky crown, symbol of the constitutional monarchy, that adorned entrances to government buildings also was taken down. Constantine's annual stipend was cut off and a special announcement disclosed that royal property in Greece would be expropriated.

As a final touch, Greeks went to the polls July 29 and endorsed the decisions made to abolish the monarchy and install Papadopoulos as president of the new republic. The government, hailing the balloting as a vote of confidence, said the people had given their assent to a series of constitutional changes which would insure the rule of Papadopoulos for eight more years.

Constantine with his attractive wife, Queen Anne Marie, after his dethronement

TRAGIC SAGA OF THE SEA LINK

On the morning of Sunday, June 17, the mini-sub Sea Link with four oceanographers aboard submerged beneath the waters off the Florida Keys. Its mission: to observe fish life around the hull of a World War II destroyer the Navy had scuttled in 60 fathoms.

The Sea Link had been designed for utility rather than beauty. Her bubble-shaped forward compartment constructed of transparent acrylic plastic provided submerged scientists with unparalleled visibility. And her sausage-like after section was made of lightweight aluminium permitting a far heavier payload than similar vessels made of steel.

The grotesque-looking underwater explorer was the creation of Edwin A. Link millionaire designer of the Link Trainer for aircraft pilots. Sharing the after compartment of the Sea Link was Link's 31-year-old son, Clayton, and Florida diver Al Stover, 51. In the bubble up front were two oceanographers, Archibald (Jock) Menzies, 30, and Robert Meek, 27.

One hour after the mission had begun, the Sea Link's six electric motors, probably with the help of underwater current in the Gulf Stream propelled the 23-foot craft into the grip of rusting cable, cargo nets and electronic gear that hung from the superstructure of the aged destroyer.

The distress call from the trapped craft set off a desperate rescue effort that lasted for more than 30 hours.

From the outset it was clear that Link and Stover were in great danger. They would need protection from the cold that would penetrate the aluminum fuselage of their after compartment much more quickly than it would the thicker less heat-conductive acrylic bubble of the forward chamber.

The mother ship above with Link Senior aboard dispatched distress calls. Capt. Thomas W. Cuddy, commander of a Key West submarine squadron was summoned. And the crew of the submarine-rescue ship USS Tringa was called back from weekend liberty. The navy's roving Diving Bell was airlifted from San Diego, and New Orleans shipped along emergency supplies of oxygen and helium tanks. Another to respond was the A.B. Wood II, a civilian oceanographic ship anchored at Port Everglades, Fla.

At first those directing the rescue operation considered the possibility of young Link and Stover pressurizing their cabin to the 200-pound per square inch level that existed outside the submarine and attempt a free swimming ascent using breathing equipment. But because of the 40-degree temperature of the water, at that depth, this procedure was deemed too dangerous.

Since it was Sunday, it took nearly three hours to round up the crew of the Tringa and for the ship to get underway. Then the shifting flow of the Gulf Stream impeded progress in getting the Tringa into position over the trapped sub.

The first divers did not get into the water until 12 hours after the first distress call for help. And then darkness and the swift current prevented them from doing much good.

Later the A.B. Wood II appeared on the scene and after several tries, guided a grappling hook attached to a cable against the hull of the little sub with the aid of an underwater television camera. Fifteen minutes later the Sea Link rose to the surface and her forward compartment was opened.

Menzies and Meek whose forward compartment was better insulated than the rear were taken off and pronounced in good shape. The aft cabin was depressurized the following day. Both Link and Stover were found dead.

The ill-fated research mini-submarine Sea-Link

SOVIET SUPERSONIC AIRLINER CRASHED AT FRENCH AIR SHOW

"You would have thought we were in hell," a survivor said sadly as he looked at the wreckage of some dozen homes in the French village of Goussainville where one of the Soviet Union's new TU144 supersonic airliners had crashed.

The big plane fell from the sky and made a fiery plunge into the village June 3 while going through its paces at the Paris aviation show at Le Bourget Airport. The four engine TU144 can fly at 1,550 miles an hour but was at subsonic speed for its demonstration on the last day of the show.

The plane had just made a low pass before the 300,000 persons crowding the airport, then pulled into a steep climb and leveled out just below the clouds. Suddenly, it tipped over and dived out of control toward the ground. A piece of the huge delta wing ripped off, then an engine, and finally the plane broke up an instant before it hit Goussainville. All six members of the plane crew died. Eight persons on the ground were killed and 28 others were injured. Most of the dead were children who were in their homes or playing in their gardens when the plane came screaming down out of the sky.

Some aviation experts who saw the crash speculated that the pilot may have overestimated the plane's ability to go into a steep climb under the circumstances. The plane was flying at less than the speed of sound and the undercarriage was extended. Experts said the pilot, reacting to a stall, may have turned on full power, and the abrupt influx of fuel may have caused an explosion.

The Soviets claimed a major victory when they put an earlier version of the TU144 in the air on Dec. 31, 1968—ahead of the British-French supersonic Concorde which first flew in 1969. American attempts to develop a supersonic transport died in 1971 when Congress cut off funds (The World in 1971, 152.)

THE MARATHON HIJACK

It began when two masked gunmen took over an airliner with 89 persons aboard as it winged its way on a domestic flight from Cali to Medellin, Colombia. By the time it ended it had become the longest aerial highjacking on record.

After taking over the plane May 30, the gunmen demanded $200,000 and freedom for 140 "political prisoners." They said if the demands were not met the four-engine Electra turboprop and its passengers would be blown up. Then they ordered the pilot to fly the plane to the Caribbean island of Aruba.

Eighteen passengers—women and children—were allowed to leave the plane at Aruba. But as the hours wore on other passengers were allowed off and a number escaped by jumping from the rear emergency exit.

Bargaining over the demands went on as the plane sat under a blazing sun, but then the hijackers ordered the plane to take off for Lima, Peru. Although the hijackers left with nothing, they did not carry out their threat to blow up the craft.

The flight to Lima was shortlived. The plane developed engine trouble and it returned to Aruba May 31 and the bargaining began again. More passengers were released or escaped—leaving 28 aboard—before the gunmen once again ordered the big ship to take off—this time for El Salvador. But as it droned through the sky, the gunmen changed their minds and the plane did not land at El Salvador. Instead it returned to Aruba for the third time.

On June 1, the airlines conceded to the ransom demands but bargained the hijackers down to $50,000. The plane took off once again and stopped at Guayaquil, Ecuador; Lima, Peru; Mendoza and Resistencia, Argentina; and Asuncion, Paraguay, before coming to the end of its long journey at Buenos Aires, Argentina, June 2.

As the plane door opened and the pilot got out he told the waiting police the two hijackers had gotten off in Resistencia. They "ordered me to fly to Resistencia and threatened to kill the stewardess if I refused," Capt. Hugo Molina said. "In Resistencia, they fled in a pickup truck provided by the local police. I don't know where they went."

It was the longest hijacking recorded—some 15,000 miles. And the near 65 hours the plane was under terrorist control surpassed the record 44 hour hijack of a Brazilian airliner to Cuba in 1970.

WORLD'S OLDEST HEAD OF STATE STEPPED DOWN AFTER 57 YEARS OF PUBLIC SERVICE

Thousands of Dubliners cheered as the gates of the presidential mansion in Phoenix Park swung open and the Rolls Royce bearing the venerable figure inched through the throng.

They were cheering 90-year-old Eamon De Valera, the world's oldest head of state, passing into retirement on June 24 after 57 years in the service of Ireland.

Winding up his second term as Ireland's president, De Valera who had been nearly blind for years, said he and his wife Sinead would retire to a nursing home in the southern part of Dublin.

De Valera said his parting words at a ceremony at Boland's bakery where it had all begun 57 years earlier. It was De Valera's stirring command of an Irish Republican Army battalion quartered in Boland's brick sheds during the uprising of Easter, 1916, that put him at the head of his people. De Valera was the last commander to surrender and the only one to escape execution.

The old man's speech was brief and in the Gaelic tongue he loved. It was nearly inaudible because he would not bend to use the microphone.

"I was once afraid I would not live to see Ireland united," said De Valera. "I now think I will see it. I have always been loyal to the country and the Irish language."

Erskine H. Childers, the man who was to succeed De Valera as head of state, was the son of a protege of the aged leader. The father, also Erskine Childers, had been executed by the Free State government in the civil war of the 1920s.

The huge, varied crowd of Dubliners had massed in Phoenix Park before the presidential residence for hours before the aged leader appeared. There were middle aged party workers and young people whose fathers had fought with "Dev". There were delegations from the 26 counties, singing and holding banners aloft.

And along the route of the presidential limousine stood an honor guard of aged veterans of the uprising and the civil war.

The crowd represented the great span of De Valera's life—the uprising, the civil war between those who accepted the British treaty that led to partition of the six northern counties from the South and those who resisted, his long period in power that shaped the Irish nation and the 14 years of presidency that made him largely a figurehead.

As the Rolls Royce picked up speed and swept through the park, a small, wrinkled woman in tweeds gave a farewell wave and took her husband's arm.

"That was Dev," she said.

Secretariat, with jockey Ron Turcotte up, thundered down the stretch at Belmont Park moments before winning the Belmont Stakes and the Triple Crown

TWO SHIPS COLLIDED AND TEN PERISHED IN A SEA OF FIRE

The bustling stretch of water in New York Harbor known as the Narrows is rarely without heavy seagoing traffic, and the early morning hours of Saturday, June 2, were no exception. As the Belgian-registered tanker Esso Brussels, loaded with nine million gallons of crude oil, rode at anchor off Staten Island's Stapleton Anchorage, the American bulk container ship Sea Witch approached, on her way with cargo for Norfolk, Va.

Just south was the famed Verrazano Bridge, carrying traffic on a graceful suspension span between the Brooklyn shore and Staten Island. It was a clear night. Suddenly, the container ship veered off course, and, in the confines of the heavily-trafficked straits, there was no margin for failure. Crewmen frantically sounded distress signals on the cargo ship. Capt. William Patterson—who within hours would be dead of a heart attack—let out a cry heard by one crew member as: "That damned steering gear again!" And then, the crash. The container ship sliced into the tanker amidships. In an instant, oil poured onto the water and ignited, setting the night sky ablaze.

The ships, coupled in an embrace of death, tore loose from the tanker's mooring and drifted south toward the Atlantic—for a few frightful minutes passing under the great suspension bridge, closing it to traffic and searing its roadbed. Meanwhile, on the water, frantic crewmen dove for their lives.

"The fire was all around," said one mariner on the Sea Witch, Bravely Outlaw. "I kept going under water because I didn't want to get a mouthful of fire." A signalman named Van Steenbergen on the Brussels said: "there was no panic. There was no time to panic." And Joseph Degreve, a cook on the tanker, put it this way: "The flames were all around the lifeboat. I thought: 'I will die.' "

Crewman after crewman told of great slicks of fire on the water, of diving under them, of thinking about death—and then of seeing the tugboats and fireboats that tore through sheets of flame to rescue them.

"We began to shout, 'hi ho! hi ho!' " Outlaw said. "The fire was between us and the tug. Then they went right through the fire to get us."

On the 699-foot tanker, owned by the Exxon Corp., the collision ruptured two of 11 storage tanks, spewing thousands of barrels of flaming oil onto the water.

And the Sea Witch, owned by American Export-Isbrantsen Lines, was even less fortunate. Her flammable cargo burned fiercely—even longer than the tanker's—and by later in the day firemen feared she would capsize so they briefly stopped pouring water and let her burn.

It was not the first trouble for the Sea Witch, as later testimony before a Coast Guard board of inquiry confirmed. Built in 1968, she had run aground in Ambrose Channel in New York Harbor after engine failure June 16, 1969. Her engine room had flooded off Staten Island Oct. 17, 1970, causing $1.2 million damage. And she ran around again in Felixstowe, England, Aug. 12, 1971, experiencing steering trouble on the next trip across the Atlantic.

And on the fatal night, Lt. Cdr. George F. Ireland of the Coast Guard would testify, the crucial breakdown was simple. A $20 universal joint failed. A month later, the count was 10 dead, six still missing, and 63 rescued.

Smoke and flames rose into the darkness as two ships collided in New York Harbor

FOR 19 MONTHS CADET WAS SUBJECTED TO THE SILENCE

The Silence. In an Army memorandum it is defined as "a traditional and unwritten proviso" of the Honor System designed to deal with a West Point cadet convicted of an honor violation, but who does not resign and cannot be discharged because of insufficient legal proof.

The penalty of total social ostracism rarely is imposed since most cadets, faced with the prospect, choose to resign.

James J. Pelosi chose not to resign. Pelosi, then 20, held the highest peer rating in his 100 man company when he was convicted in November 1971 by the senior Honor Committee of finishing an answer on a quiz after the examiner had given the order to stop. Pelosi denied the charge, backed his claim with witnesses and an officer board was convened. But the case later was dismissed after it was learned a high-ranking officer had urged board members to "expedite" their deliberations.

That, however, did not end it for Pelosi. The Honor Committee, supported by a cadet referendum, imposed the Silence on the young cadet and for most of the next 19 months he roomed by himself and ate alone at a 10-man table in the cadet mess hall. Almost none of the 3,800 cadets talked to him except on official business.

But, said Pelosi, "I was determined to make it through. The Silence is . . . supposed to be a punishment that's too hard to bear. I showed them it wasn't so."

On June 6, 1973, he received his commission, graduating with a ranking of 452 among 939.

"It was the one day I had looked forward to since the first day of Silence," Pelosi said.

Cadet James J. Pelosi who endured the silent treatment

SECOND LONGEST ECLIPSE KNOWN TO MAN DARKENED AFRICA ON JUNE 30

It was a bright afternoon in sub-Sahara Africa. And then, suddenly, it was dark night.

"The great fire has gone out," an African tribal chief told his people as they fled frightened into their huts. Outside Nairobi, Kenya's capital, a man called to his wife, "The sun has gone out!" Nervously, she asked, "Will it come up again?"

It did. Seven minutes and four seconds after the moon had blotted it out in a total eclipse June 30. The natives who had hidden in their huts rejoiced in its return with song. The animals of the jungle who had curled up to sleep awoke again.

The eclipse, one of history's longest, also was seen in southern India, where the Hindu religion considered the phenomenon the worst form of bad luck. Orthodox Hindus washed their houses with water after the eclipse because legend maintained it polluted everything. Pregnant women were warned that unless they lay quietly while the sun was gone their children might be born with split lips, blindness and mental retardation.

But the phenomena also was watched by scientists from around the world. A French delegation camped on the desert at Atar in Mauritania as did a Soviet group. There was an American scientific camp at Chinguetti in Mauritania. And another group of scientists sped along with the eclipse in the British-French supersonic Concorde jet to observe the phenomena for as long as possible. In addition, an American Aerobee rocket was launched to film the eclipse at an altitude of 100 miles.

In Kenya, more than 100 scientists assembled on the shore of Lake Rudolf to gather in a crop of data. Many of the 21 American experiments involved measuring the sun's corona or gaseous atmosphere, which is visible only during a total eclipse.

The eclipse was the second longest known to man. One in 1955 was four seconds longer. It would be another 100 years before another of this length came along. The eclipse began at dawn in Brazil and stretched in a 9,300 mile of totality across the Atlantic Ocean, then across sub-Sahara Africa to the Indian Ocean. All Africa, except for the extreme southern tip, experienced varying degrees of partiality.

TERRORIST KILLED AMERICAN MILITARY ADVISER IN IRAN

Since early 1970 the 11,000 American businessmen and technicians in Iran had been targets of a leftist terrorist campaign against the pro-American regime of Shah Mohammed Reza Pahlevi. Although the terrorists had wounded an Air Force general and damaged two American buildings with bombs they had not killed an American since their campaign began.

Then, on June 2, Lt. Col. Lewis Hawkins, 42, a U.S. military adviser, left his home in Tehran and walked to a nearby street corner to be picked up by his driver. As he did so, a motorcycle sped up, a terrorist shot Hawkins in the head and killed him, and then sped off on the bike.

Hawkins was one of some 500 American military advisers and personnel assigned to work with the Iranian armed forces. A spokesman said Hawkins worked as a finance adviser and field controller and denied local reports that the slain man was a defense intelligence agent.

FOR THE RECORD

DISSOLVED. The Uruguayan Congress, by President Juan Maria Bordaberry on June 27. Bordaberry said constitutional rule was falling apart and subversion threatened the nation. The military and the government had been fighting the leftist Tupamaro guerillas since 1968 in the country of 2.8 million. The suspension wiped out constitutional government for the first time in 40 years and it was the first time Congress had been locked since 1933.

NAMED. Adm. Luis Carrero Blanco, as premier of Spain, on June 9. Carrero was sworn in at El Pardo Palace, where Gen. Francisco Franco has resided in his 33 years of autocratic rule since his victory in the Spanish Civil War. Carrero is the first man besides Franco to head the Spanish government since the Franco regime began. Political sources said Carrero's elevation meant a reduced work load for the 80-year-old Franco, who remained chief of state and the effective ruler of Spain.

FIRE IN NEW ORLEANS' FRENCH QUARTER CLAIMED 29 LIVES

The Upstairs, a second story bar in New Orleans' French Quarter, was a popular place on Sundays. It offered all the food and beer you could drink for $2.

As many as 60 persons reportedly were jammed into the small bar on Sunday June 24 when, as one later recalled, "I looked up and the door was on fire. The place just went up. Everyone panicked and started running for the windows. I jumped to the window in the left corner, opened it, swung out, grabbed a pipe, and slid down."

He was one of those lucky enough to escape the flaming room. By the time the blaze was extinguished, 29 of those who had been in the room were dead and at least 15 were injured. Bodies lay piled under a burned piano and jammed against three windows. One man's body was kneeling beside a window, with one foot outside. At another window, an arm dangled outside with a six-inch piece of unburned green sports coat around the wrist.

A passerby recalled that, "There was just a bit of smoke, then all of a sudden flames just shot out all of the windows. People started jumping out and flames were shooting 20 feet high. One man was hanging out a window and screaming . . . We knew there had to be at least two dead because they were yelling and screaming behind the window and they never came out."

Adm. Luis Blanco named president of Spain by Gen. Francisco Franco

July

"Out of Gas" signs appeared at service stations throughout the nation

Limits on Gasoline Brought the Energy Crisis Closer to Home

Shuttered service stations spread
fears that vacationing motorists
might become stranded

In the beautiful Berkshire Mountains, along the Massachusetts Turnpike, the hand-lettered signs on the pumps at the service station read, "Limit 10 gals."

In the publication *Physics Today*, one of the articles was titled "Laser-induced thermonuclear fusion," and it spoke of "focused laser pulses in the gigawatt range" as a way of creating "energy-producing reactions."

The word "energy" was what both these things were all about. And the word energy came coupled with another word, such as "crisis" and "gap." Closed service stations and limits on gasoline for travelers brought the energy situation to virtually everyone's attention. The talk about fusion power might be the ultimate answer to the problem, but it was a long way off.

For years, until about the mid-1960s, just about everybody went along on the assumption that there would be ever-increasing supplies of energy at ever-decreasing costs. The magnitude of this error could be quickly appreciated by summer vacationers in 1973 being warned they might be stranded, unable to buy gasoline for their automobiles during their trips, and by these same vacationers reading in their newspapers about possible shortages of home heating oil during the winter ahead.

With complacency gone, the difficult facts of the energy situation became apparent. These facts reflected the complexity of this highly industrialized society, its overwhelming dependence on energy and the fragility of this complex web.

One thing stood out for the average person: Americans would most likely have to change the way they work and play. Perhaps no longer would one person ride alone to work in a big gas-eating station wagon. We might all ride buses and trains more. Building standards would probably be changed to conserve precious energy used in heating, air conditioning and lighting. In times of shortages of energy, hallways in large office buildings would be dimly lit and the air conditioning cut back, making life a little more uncomfortable. Indeed, these cutbacks were already common in such places as New York City, where power shortages might some day even dim the lights along old Broadway.

The United States was what the experts called "energy intensive." The nation had only 6 per cent of the world's population, but used fully a third of the energy produced in the world. At the heart of this situation was oil. It would be hard to overemphasize the importance of oil. With demand up, domestic oilfield production was declining. Worldwide demand also was increasing, and J. K. Jamieson, chairman of Exxon U.S.A., described things this way:

"The present and future demand for oil is on a truly massive scale. To replace the amount of oil the world is consuming, the industry would have to find about 20 billion barrels of oil every year—the equivalent of two fields the size of Alaska's Prudhoe Bay. By 1980, the required amount could be 30 billion barrels a year."

But the catch was that the discovery of oil had remained fairly constant in recent years, as Jamieson noted, adding: "Even if demand growth is moderated—as I believe it must be—we need to face the fact that the world's conventional oil resources will not indefinitely support increases in production."

Thus, the nation, and the world, was left with a two-fold answer:

1. Energy must be conserved.
2. Other forms of energy must be developed.

Before looking at these avenues, it must be noted that part of the blame for all this trouble lay with both government and industry. (The Federal Trade Commission charged that a number of big U.S. oil companies combined to monopolize petroleum in large areas of the country. The industry denied the charges and a long court seige seemed assured.) In a major new study by researchers for the American Association for the Advancement of Science, it was pointed out that restrictions on imports of foreign oil meant that the country faced shortages of heating oil and gasoline despite a surplus of crude oil on the world market. The study also noted that a number of government agencies were charged with actually promoting energy consumption in a time of shortage.

The AAAS study went on to comment:

"A more cynical view lays the fault for this country's present difficulties to the economic greed of the oil industry and its political allies. This view may be overstated, but it is clear that the economic self-interest of the oil companies does not always coincide with that of the consumer or that of the nation as a whole. Oil import quotas, for example, have had the effect of guaranteeing the oil industry a minimum price for its product and of hastening the day when domestic reserves will be gone."

Many individuals believed that the gasoline shortage was created by the major oil companies in an effort to drive prices and their profits up and to force independents out of business. Again, the industry vigorously denied the charges.

And as just one more complicating factor in the over-all picture, there was the strong public concern for the environment. Environmentalists challenged the construction of nuclear power plants on safety and pollution. The environmentalists had the legal right to intervene in public hearings and they did, sometimes slowing the licensing process—a valid move from their point of view but not from the power industry's vantage point.

The environmentalists would continue to challenge the power producers on pollution, such as the use of high sulphur content coal and oil, and would argue that growth in general could not go unchallenged, and they were ready to oppose the idea of drilling for oil in the waters off the east coast of the United States and Canada. Nobody wanted a power plant in their back yard or oil rigs off their beach. But we needed the power. As S. David Freeman, a leading energy expert said, "Where do we put the skunk works?"

In historical terms this energy crisis had come fast upon us. Just 100 years earlier wood still was the source of 75 per cent of the nation's energy. It was the Industrial Revolution that signaled the Energy Age. By 1973, about 75 per cent of our energy was supplied by oil and gas. And the demand grew and grew.

One answer was conservation of energy, and while the potential savings might not sound like much, they could in fact be enormous. David Freeman, of the Ford Foundation and formerly director of the energy policy staff in the White House, made these suggestions:

"Energy demands could be scaled down if two-ton automobiles which are less than 10 per cent efficient in the energy they consume were replaced by one-ton cars or better still by rapid transit, bicycles, or an occasional walk for city travel.

"We could achieve sizeable reductions in demand if all buildings were fully insulated so we would no longer heat the outdoors in winter and cool it in summer. And demand would taper off somewhat if promotional rates and government policies which subsidize and promote the use of energy were replaced and the price included all the social costs of production."

A rash of generator troubles, plus a heat wave caused a voltage cut in New York's Radio City

And Freeman concluded: "We live in the age of energy, and it is essential for almost everything we do. But that is all the more reason to practice conservation and to eliminate waste so that the essential uses can be met and so that the volumes of pollutants can be minimized. To implement these ideas would require a formidable undertaking. But can we really fail to make the effort if we are to do justice to future generations whose resources we are so lavishly using and wasting?"

To look at just one example of potential conservation, the automobile: It's been estimated that when both direct and indirect energy costs are included, the automobile accounts for 21 per cent of total U.S. energy consumption, according to the AAAS study. "Yet the standard American car gets only 12 miles per gallon of gasoline," the study said, "roughly half that of most European cars."

Looking at energy conservation in general, the AAAS study found this: "Although it seems unlikely that even extreme conservation measures can entirely halt the need for more energy, it is undeniably a poor idea to perpetuate waste and often ineffective uses of energy. The potential for reducing the demand for energy by means of more efficient use of energy resources appears to be enormous, amounting ultimately to perhaps 25 per cent of what would otherwise be consumed."

(The energy situation received major governmental attention later in the year when President Nixon urged states and cities to relax sulphur-content standards during the heating season so more high-sulphur fuel could be imported.

(The President also announced that he was determined to speed up the licensing of nuclear power plants and called for action on bills to de-regulate natural gas prices, to build deepwater tanker ports, set strip-mining standards and to authorize the Alaska pipeline.)

For the future, there was wide agreement on the need for more research and development with the aim of finding clean fuel sources for essential needs. These programs ranged from a new class of nuclear reactor, the breeder reactor, to removal of sulphur to allow the use of coal reserves, to the development of a fusion power reactor.

"New technology that will convert energy to usable form more efficiently and with less damage to the environment is really the key to obtaining an adequate supply of clean fuel for the future," said Freeman.

Another reason for developing new sources of fuel was to avoid dependence on foreign supplies, such as those in the volatile Middle East.

"The United States," President Nixon said, "would prefer to continue to import petroleum products from the Mideast, from Venezuela, Canada, from other countries. But also we are keenly aware of the fact that no nation, and particularly no industrialized nation, must be in the position of being at the mercy of any other nation by having its energy supply suddenly cut off."

But oil would continue to be the main source of energy in the United States for probably the remainder of the century. There were ample coal reserves in this country, but the methods of recovery and burning needed more research. So did the possible conversion of coal to synthetic gas. So did the possibility of removing sulphur from stack gas. There was the possibility of direct combusion of coal in MHD—magnetohydrodynamic—generators.

The Nixon Administration had declared that development of the breeder reactor had the highest priority in its energy program. But the AAAS study said that many nuclear energy experts believed the program should be expanded to include more than just one concept of breeder reactor.

The use of conventional nuclear power was growing slowly in mid-1973, still the target of environmentalists charging that the plants were inherently dangerous, their wastes a major hazard. The Atomic Industrial Forum, an industry organization, reported that 10 to 20 new plants were going into business during the year, making nuclear power about 5 per cent of the nation's total electric-generating capacity.

In some areas of the country, geothermal power plants could supplement other power supplies and interest in this possibility was picking up.

For the far future, the main possibilities were solar energy and fusion. The development of solar energy required technological advances only and a number of experimental studies were under way. To harness fusion power, the thermonuclear power of the sun and the hydrogen bomb, it must first be shown in the laboratory that it was scientifically feasible. Two main avenues of research were being explored, one using a laser beam to trigger the reaction and the other using magnetic confinement of the plasma or gas. If one or both worked—as most scientists expected—a clean and safe fusion power plant could be in operation by the year 2000, using as its fuel the virtually endless hydrogen in the earth's oceans.

From Sicily To The Alps Italy Is One Big Museum

Above, colonnades of the portico around the forum of Pompei. Right, view across Rome's ancient Forum

The nation is a treasure trove of monuments, ruins and artifacts

A S ANY GUIDE BOOK will tell you, Italy is one big museum. From Sicily to the Alps, the country is a treasure trove of monuments, ruins and artifacts of the Estruscan, Greek and Roman civilizations. Its museums and churches contain the finest Rennaissance works in the world. Romans say one cannot dig a hole in the city without finding some ancient ruins.

But in 1973, a combination of modern ills, neglect and plain old age was threatening this irreplacable patrimony as thieves working above and below the ground were carrying the treasures away. The S.O.S. was sounded, but it was questionable whether Italy's creaking bureaucracy could come to the rescue in time.

New views of the Rome Colosseum undergoing repairs because of faults caused by traffic vibrations and age

Rome and Venice, the queen of the Adriatic, were the two cities with the most to lose and feared just that. More than 30 monuments, museums, churches and palaces in Rome were considered by authorities in urgent need of repair. Rome's chief archaeologist recommended a $5 million facelift for the city's great monuments neglected for years by government indifference. Foremost among these was the Colosseum, emblem throughout the ages of Rome's eternity. When 44-pound chunks of masonry began falling from the jagged ruins of the

1,901-year-old amphitheater in late 1972, city officials ordered it closed to allow repair work. This was a great blow to tourism as the Collosseum is one of Rome's prime attractions for visitors. It was later reopened but with access restricted. Engineers blamed the condition on poor maintenance and on vibrations caused by heavy traffic. Its neighbor, the 1,658-year-old Arch of Constantine also went on the disabled list for the same reason.

Among other monuments and historical sights threatened by decay were the imperial palaces and temples on the Palatine Hill, the Appian Way, and the city's Roman aqueducts. It was a common sight in Rome to see one of the city's antiquities fenced off from traffic or encased in scaffolding, much like a man with his leg in a cast.

For years, superintendents for art had been complaining that they could not possibly cope with the enormous task of looking after even the most important of the the city's monuments. The government earmarks $340,000 a year to pay for the personnel and maintenance of the Colloseum, the forums, the Palatine, the Caracalla Baths, and the Appian Way. But as Parliament procrastinated in appropriating more funds, more monuments fell victim to neglect and the bill to repair them skyrocketed.

The sight of industrial workers in the Venice area wearing mandatory gas masks gave stark confirmation to the plight of the beautiful canal city on the Adriatic. Once Europe's mightiest city-state, Venice was having trouble keeping its head above water. It was sinking three millimeters a year or about an inch every 10 years. Tidal floods submerged the city, air pollution eroded its monuments and industrial wastes fouled its air. The 150 canals that inspired poetry and romance now churn with sewage and garbage.

The plight of Venice turns on a classic confrontation between conservationists and economists. Experts put much of the blame for the decline of Venice on the Marghera industrial complex, a mammoth port 2.5 miles from Venice. The 5,000-acre industrial area was built on drained "Barone," the mudflats that once absorbed the Adriatic's surging waters, saving Venice from flooding. Now the waters, deprived of any absorbant, rush back to Venice, flooding its famous squares an average of 200 times a year.

But if Venice offered museums, Marghera offered jobs. And the debate over which should get priority stalled Save Venice legislation in Parliament for years.

Finally, in 1973, the lawmakers adopted a plan to rescue the sinking city. They approved a $500 million proposal that was the backbone of an international effort, unprecedented in scale, to save Venice from the ravages of nature and the indifference of man.

The Italian plan called for the control of tidal floods, construction of sewers to cleanse the fetid waters of the canals, and the capping of the hundreds of wells which sucked up water from beneath the foundations of the city and caused it to sink.

"We intend to insure the rehabilitation of Venice," said a government official. "The city should once again resume its historic role as the center of the region and its chief economic dynamo."

Rome and Venice were not the only cities with a crumbling patrimony. Pisa was in danger of losing its famous Leaning Tower, an instantly recognizable symbol of Italy and perhaps the most unique monument in the world. Scientists said the 800-year-old tower could topple at any time because of the sinking of the subsoil, a condition that began centuries earlier.

The tower in mid-1973 was 14-feet off the perpendicular and the lean increases gradually each year.

The Italian government has sponsored an international competition to find a cure and has set aside $5.5 million for the work. In the meantime, a special commission proposed several emergency plans should the condition of the tower suddenly worsen before the competition was completed.

Milan's famed Gothic Cathedral also was on the sick list. Engineers determined that passing cars and trucks were threatening its stability and all traffic was barred from the Piazza Duomo.

With all the other troubles plaguing Italy's art patrimony, the country has also become a happy hunting ground for thieves. A newspaper described Italy as the country of "masterworks within a thief's reach." Known art thefts have risen from 168 for a total of 2,328 stolen items in 1968 to 342 thefts for 5,843 items in 1972. In just the first four months of 1973, 2,420 items were stolen from museums, churches and private collections.

Among the thieves' favorite targets were the countless churches in small Italian towns. Many are unguarded and lack even rudimentary alarm systems. Even in the big cities, such as

The Italian government has taken steps to preserve the statue of Emperor Marcus Aurelius on which, legend said, the world's future is hinged

Rome and Milan, authorities have had to close museums for lack of sufficient guards. Rome, one of the tourist capitals of the world, suffered the embarrassment of closing eight of its musuems in the summer of 1973 for lack of adequate security force. In addition to such above-ground thefts, police and art experts were concerned over the flourishing trade in stolen works dug up by bootleg excavators known as "Tombaroli."

The crumbling state of Italy's antiquities did yield one positive result in 1973. When the floor caved in as workers were repairing the 15th century church of St. Stephan the Rotund in Rome, it brought to light an underground pagan temple with frescoes and statues. The temple was one of the many underground ones in Rome for the Persian God Mithra, whose followers used to meet for secret rites.

SOUTH SEA ISLES A PARADISE FOR SOME

But many have found life no bed of blossoms in these Edens

THIRTEEN YEARS AGO, Don McCallum, Hugh Kelley and Jay Carlisle used to listen to Tahitian mandolins in Newport Beach, Calif., and dream of a South Seas paradise. Then the trio found their Eden and made more than a million dollars out of it.

The three fortyish bachelors opened their third Bali Hai Hotel on the French Polynesian isle of Moorea in 1973 and planned to build two more on nearby islands.

"I love it," said McCallum. "Every person who gets off the boat is worth at least $10, even day trippers. It's like Christmas every day."

"Actually we're not in this for money. We had to stay in Tahiti some way," said Kelley. Then, after a moment's reflection. "Yeah, you can say we're worth more than a million now."

The three had made out far better than many Americans who abandoned their office jobs to seek an idyllic existence in a Pacific retreat. On picturesque Fiji, the U.S. Embassy staff said it rarely got time to enjoy the local scenery. And on lovely Bali it was almost impossible to get the needed work permits and visas to stay.

Back in 1960, McCallum, Kelley and Carlisle set out for Tahiti with little idea of how they would support themselves.

"First we were going to plant vanilla," said Carlisle. "We had to write to find out if it was a bug or a potato. We didn't last long at that . . ."

In 1962, the trio scraped up enough money to buy a little hotel on the beautiful isle of Moorea. By 1973 they had two

138

Above left, youths beaching an outrigger canoe at Vila Island in the New Hebrides. Left, the cremation of the last of the Balinese kings, 87-year-old Radjah Anak Agung. Above, the native market place in Fiji

other hotels operating on the Tahiti outer islands of Huahine and Raiatea and all three were jammed.

It had all been fun but there was a lot of hard work too. McCallum often strolled through the dining room laughing it up with tourists. But he was up at dawn watering the lawn and usually kept working till 8 p.m.

Kelley liked to ride his motorcycle up Moorea's mountains, but much of the time he was busy hauling cement and drawing up plans for bungalows.

Carlisle liked to kid with the girl tourists but he spent long hours in a backroom counting deliveries from their egg ranch and poring over the latest exchange rates.

When time permitted the trio loaded up a jet with a dozen Tahitian lovelies, guitar players and drink pourers and flew back to California to watch old friends turn green with envy. For three guys who were broke on a beach in Tahiti little more than a decade ago, they were doing okay.

In contrast, take the embassy staff in Suva, Fiji. There three Americans covered four million square miles of the prettiest

water in the world. Their territory had more white beaches, coral reefs and palm trees than all others combined. But were they able to enjoy it?

"Let's see . . .," said William Todd Becker, the consul. "I last went swimming six months ago . . ."

Robert W. Skiff, the charge d'affaires, said he had a recent holiday at the beach. It was during a vacation and out of his region.

Just like embassies in colder climates, the staff in Fiji was kept busy stamping visas, repatriating destitute Americans, filling out forms in triplicate and shepherding vistors around.

In addition, Skiff and Becker flew more than 15,000 miles a year each to branch offices in palace backrooms and quonset huts in the Solomon Islands, New Hebrides, Tonga and the Gilbert and Ellice islands. They also kept watch on French Polynesia, Tahiti and New Caledonia.

By mid-1973 there were about 900 American businessmen, missionaries, beachcombers, Peace Corps volunteers and other types regularly living in the area. All presented certain problems. One yachtsman got seasick, shipped his boat on ahead and flew to meet it. Another died with no will and the embassy found itself in the used yacht business.

At times the tiny office underneath a hairdressing salon and over two duty free shops was almost impassable for all the crates of belongings left behind by Americans who died on island retreats, leaving no known heirs.

"It's pretty refreshing to be out in the unpolluted Pacific," said Skiff. "But it can get lonely. We miss the theater and things like that."

Skiff's London-born wife was more direct. Said she, "I loathe the sun, I hate bathing, and I only go into the water to cool off. But I adore the Fijians."

Below left, Charge d'affaires Robert Skiff and consul William "Todd" Becker at embassy doorway in Suva, Fiji. Below right, Jay Carlisle joined in the dancing at Bali Hai on a feast day in French Polynesia

The embassy staff got a pay differential. They said they needed it to offset the cost of throwing away shirts and records ruined by mildew. An air ticket from Fiji back home could wipe out a lot of savings.

But Skiff, Becker and the third staff member, Marilyn Miller, had some compensations. There were those handsome sunsets and an occasional island-style roasted pig.

Most every day on the isle of Bali in Indonesia some tourist, overcome with visions of Gaugin and low food prices, announced that he was staying on. But only a few outsiders have actually settled there.

"It's not easy to stay," said painter Han Snel, 47, who went to Bali in 1950 as a Dutch soldier and settled down. He married a beautiful Balinese and took up citizenship.

"Everyone wants to settle here," he said, "but they need a work permit, they need this and that. And I'm happy about it because otherwise we'd have a second Spain. Myself, I'm white but an Indonesian."

Work permits and long term-visas, if granted at all, required much effort, money, luck and usually a friend in Jakarta.

"Yes, we get a lot of people who want to retire in Bali," said the island's chief immigration official. "But that isn't the island's policy . . ."

There were various ways of getting a foothold in Bali, none of them easy.

Painter Antonio Blanco, born in the Phillippines to Spanish parents and now a naturalized American, was allowed in by the late President Sukarno who liked his paintings.

Tony Pogacnic, once a Yugoslav football star who coached Indonesia's 11, was granted a piece of land by grateful leaders.

But then there was the Australian millionaire who wanted to invest in a tourism project in Bali. He offered to underwrite a high-school education for every child on the island, but still was turned down.

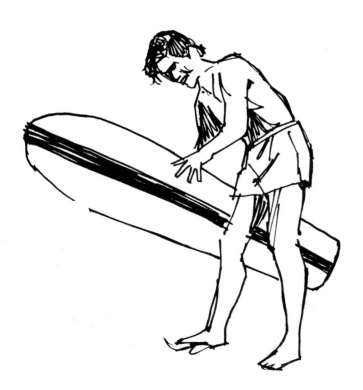

Some young travelers ignored the rules and hung around until the immigration officials deported them. One American told officials he no longer had a passport. He said he had burned it as an offering to the Hindu god Shiva.

A unique situation existed in the New Hebrides, a collection of 72 breath-taking islands reported to be the only region in the world run by two powers at once—Britain and France.

French gendarmes kept order on the islands, unless someone they arrested chose to be jailed by British constables and vice versa. The British and French each had immigration counters at the tiny airport in Vila.

This dual rule had distinct advantages for the outsider. Because both powers must agree on a tax code, there was hardly any tax in the New Hebrides. That, coupled with British company laws, made it possible for foreign companies to stash away profits made elsewhere. Learning that the islands are a tax haven, businessmen touched off a local real estate boom.

An American yachtsman discovered how immigration worked on the islands. When the British refused him a visa, he went to the French. With French approval, the British were constrained to add their endorsement, knowing that if they rejected a French-initiated request, they would not get approval for their next proposal.

"This will be the last colony in the world," said a retired French captain as he contentedly sipped a beer. "The British will never leave without the French, and the French will never leave."

Below, during World War II, one of the most pasted-up pinup photos in the barracks of American G.I.'s was that of a blond girl wearing a white bathing suit and displaying an inviting smile and most attractive legs. The girl was Betty Grable, the star of a score or more of Hollywood musicals in the 1940s and a sex symbol of the times. An actress and singer of admittedly modest talents, Miss Grable once remarked, "People like to hear me sing, see me dance and watch my legs. My legs made me." the actress, who retired from films in the 1950s, died of lung cancer July 2 at Santa Monica, Calif. She was 56.

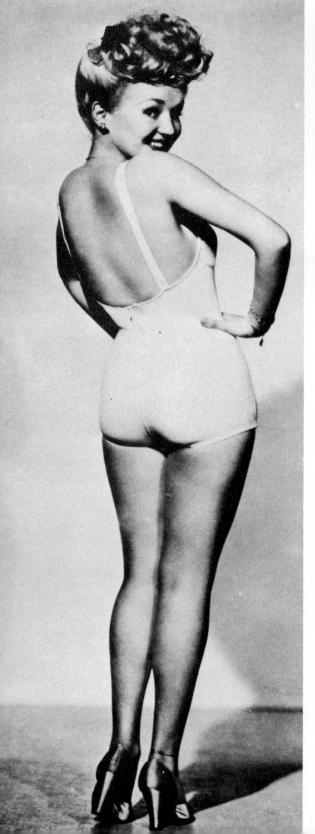

With her long blond hair falling over her right eye, Veronica Lake was one of Hollywood's most glamorous stars and a leading box office draw of the 1940s. The sultry star who stood 5 feet 2 inches and weighed 100 pounds appeared in 26 motion pictures before her career went into decline and she ended up working in summer stock and as a bar maid. But during her vogue, her peekaboo hair style set a fashion among American women and at one point during World War II a government agency asked her not to wear it long because many women imitators were catching their locks in factory machinery. Among her better known films were This Gun For Hire *and* I Married a Witch. *Miss Lake, 53, died July 7 at Burlington, Vt., where she had been hospitalized for treatment of acute hepatitis.*

UGANDA'S PRESIDENT IDI AMIN RUFFLED U.S. EAGLE'S FEATHERS

July was not a good month for Uganda-United States relations.

On July 4, Uganda's burly and unpredictable President Idi Amin, who in 1972 expelled some 40,000 Asians from his country in an effort to Africanize the economy *(The World in 1972, 223)*, sent a message to President Nixon in which he accused Nixon of murder in Cambodia and wished him a "speedy recovery" from the Watergate affair.

On July 7, a jet carrying 111 American Peace Corps volunteers landed at Entebbe, Uganda, to refuel. The plane was en route from London to Zaire, the former Congo. After refueling, the plane took off but was airborne momentarily when Amin ordered it to return. He threatened to have it shot down by his air force's Russian-built MIGs if it didn't. The plane returned, and the Americans got off.

Under armed guard, the Peace Corpsmen were held at the airport. One of them, Steve Sharp, recalled that "we spend the night lying on the ground or on benches in the air terminal but were later taken to a hotel where we were satisfactorily put up." Amin's reasons for holding the 44 women, 59 men and four married couples were that he suspected they might be mercenaries bent on "imperialist" or "Zionist" subversion in African countries. He said their arrival was "similiar to the situation" in the Congo civil war more than a decade earlier in which foreign mercenaries fought Africans.

The corpsmen were held 51 hours, then released and allowed to continue their journey after President Mobutu Sese Seko of Zaire vouched for them. After they had gone, Amin said his security forces had been ordered to closely watch all Americans in Uganda and that he had issued orders to be notified whenever Americans entered or flew over his country.

CAPT. EDDIE RICKENBACKER, WORLD WAR I FLYING ACE, DEAD AT 82

When the United States entered World War I in 1917, Edward Vernon Rickenbacker was earning $40,000 a year as a race car driver. Rickenbacker promptly gave up his lucrative career to enlist in the Army and almost as promptly was assigned as chauffeur to Gen. John Pershing, commander of the American Expeditionary Forces.

But Rickenbacker had developed a new love in addition to driving—flying. He suggested to Pershing that "I would make a good flier" and the general, who once commented that visiting the front lines "can't be any more dangerous than riding with Sgt. Rickenbacker," finally agreed, telling the aspiring flghter pilot, "If you're as dangerous to the Germans as you have been to me, you ought to be an ace within a week."

Taught to fly, and then commissioned a lieutenant, Rickenbacker was assigned to the 94th Aero Pursuit Squadron and on April 29, 1918, shot down his first enemy plane. In 30 days he had five kills to his credit and was an ace. He later rose to captain and was made commander of the squadron.

Captain Eddie, as he preferred to be called, downed a total of 22 German planes and four observation balloons during the war and much of his combat was against the "flying circus" of Baron Manfred von Richthofen, the "Red Baron."

After the war, Rickenbacker, who was born in Columbus, Ohio, and quit school at 12 to work at odd jobs to help his family, lent his name and talents to the Rickenbacker Motor Co., which produced the first car with four-wheel brakes in this country. The firm failed in 1927 and Ricken-

backer went to work for General Motors Corp. managing the firm's Eastern Air Transport Division. When GM was ordered by the government to sell its airlines, Rickenbacker raised the money to buy it and on March 2, 1938, he owned Eastern Air Lines. He guided the airline for 25 years, resigning as president in 1959 and then as director and chairman of the board on Dec. 31, 1963.

Rickenbacker, who died July 23, 1973, at 82 while visiting Switzerland, had two other brushes with death after his World War I aerial escapades. In February, 1941, he was a passenger on one of his own Eastern Air Lines planes when it crashed into a hill as it approached Atlanta, Ga. Although he was pinned to the body of a dead steward by the wreckage and was badly injured, Rickenbacker remained concious and took command of the plane, reassuring the survivors and sending some of the walking injured for help.

Just 16 months later, the First War "ace of aces" was making an inspection tour of World War II bases in the Pacific when the B17 on which he was riding crash landed in the ocean. When the plane sank, the eight passengers and crewmen took to rubber rafts, and Rickenbacker, although a civilian, again took command. For the next 22 days, as they drifted about the vast ocean, he distributed the little food and water available and constantly urged the others not to give up hope. When they were rescued, seven of the eight had survived.

Although he won a chest full of medals and was widely considered a hero, Rickenbacker never regarded his actions as heroic, saying once, "From hero to zero is about the average hero's fate. This hero business shouldn't be taken too seriously."

Eddie Rickenbacker shown standing next to one of the planes he piloted to become an ace in World War I

Some 9,000 panels covered the vast parabolic mirror of this solar furnace, world's largest, built in the Odiello Valley in France

PALACE COUP IN AFGHANISTAN
ENDED THE KING'S 40-YEAR RULE

When the Afghan Ariana Airlines plane winged out of London, its destination was Kabul, capital and largest city in Afghanistan. But instead of landing at Kabul as scheduled, the airliner put down at New Delhi. The pilot said that as he neared his original destination he was advised that Afghanistan's air space was closed. The reason: A palace coup.

The July 17 coup abruptly ended the monarchy and 40-year reign of King Mohammed Zahir Shah. While the 59-year-old king was off on the Italian island of Ischia for health treatments, his throne was taken from him by a group led by Lt. Gen. Sardar Mohammed Daud Khan, the king's brother-in-law.

Western sources said Daud Khan, who proclaimed the landlocked Central Asian nation a republic which would have genuine democracy in place of what he called "pseudodemocracy," apparently drew his main support from an armored division and a paratroop battalion while the coup itself was engineered by some 50 young officers loyal to him.

Zahir Shah became king of Afghanistan's more than 13 million people at the age of 19 after his father was assassinated in 1933. But from 1953 to 1963 he was little more than a figurehead ruler, barred from exerting any powers by his relatives. During that period, Daud Khan was the nation's prime minister. However, in 1963, the king deposed Daud Khan and took all powers for himself, promising the ancient, mountainous land which is bordered by the Soviet Union, China, Pakistan and Iran, a limited parliamentary democracy. To which Daud Khan remarked, after seizing power, "Instead of democracy, that is, people's government and constitutional monarchy, they got a despotic regime."

About a week after the take-over, Daud Khan, 64, said eight persons died in the coup, adding, "I can safely say that this was in every sense of the word a bloodless coup. It not only enjoyed the complete cooperation of all the branches of the Army but also the support of all the people of Afghanistan . . . We undertook this revolution solely to fulfill the wishes and aspirations of the people."

Afghanistan's King Mohammed Zahir Shah, vacationing in Naples, had no comment when told of the coup

Committee chairman Yuji Nagata, second from left, choked by opposition members of the Transportation Committee of the House of Councillors in Tokyo after Nagate broke off debate and forced a vote on a bill to raise railway fares

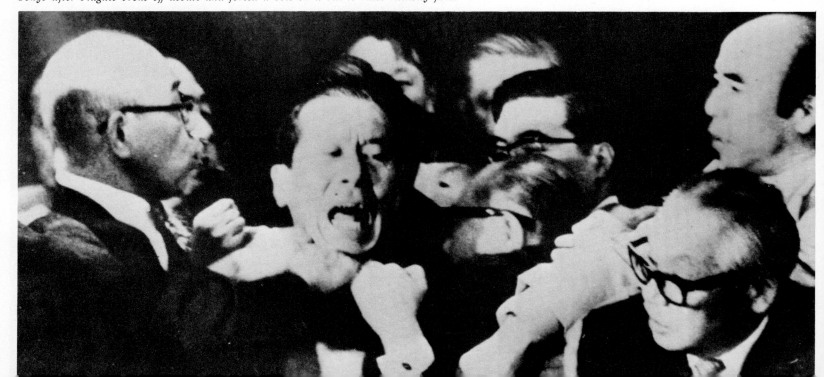

Rocking at the Glen

Top left, Allman Brothers Band played for some of the multitude that gathered for the rock festival outside Watkins Glen, N.Y. Top right, rock fans shinnied up a 30-foot pole to get a better view of the concert. Bottom left, a festival fan stood shivering atop a bus under a cold rain listening to the music. Bottom right, two townspeople walked through the debris left by the fans after the rock festival ended.

Miss Universe 1973, Margarita Moran of the Philippines, taking a bow in Athens theater

ATTEMPTED COUP IN IRAQ FAILED AND 36 MEN WERE EXECUTED

Since rising to power in a July 1968 coup, the Baath Socialist regime, headed by Ahmad Hassan al Bakr, had been charged with repressive police measures in Iraq, particularly against Jews in the capital of Baghdad.

In 1969, the regime ordered the execution of 14 Jews as spies, and then, in the following year, it had 42 Iraqis put to death on charges of attempting a coup backed by Iran.

There were other executions in the intervening years and the total of executions since the Baath party seized power rose to 130 in July 1973 when 36 men were executed after a coup led by Col. Nazim Kazzar, Iraqi security chief, failed.

Following Kazzar's failure to seize the government, a special tribunal was formed by the Iraqi Revolutionary Command Council.

The tribunal was given authority to try the defendants without reference to the Iraqi penal code and hand down sentences that, except for the death sentence, could not be appealed. Its decision: Death.

On July 7, Kazzar and 22 accomplices were executed by firing squad. The following day another 13 men were shot for plotting against the leftist government. Said the court which tried them, "The criminal clique which broke away from the will of the revolution, its leader, party revolutionary democratic traditions and the will of the people, has met the just punishment for its betrayal and crimes."

A few days after the executions, Iraq's constitution was amended to give President Bakr virtually unlimited authority. The amendment made Bakr "head of state, prime minister, and commander in chief," and gave him authority to directly supervise "the preservation of the country's independence and territorial integrity and the protection of internal and external security."

BAHAMAS WON STATEHOOD AFTER 300 YEARS OF BRITISH RULE

VIP's from the United States and 51 other nations watched as the Union Jack was lowered at 12:01 a.m., July 10, and replaced by the blue, gold and black banner of independence for the Bahamas, marking the end of 300 years of British rule.

The lights dimmed in Nassau's Clifford Park as the British colors came down for the last time to the playing of "God Save the Queen." Later that day, some 6,000 Bahamians assembled in the park again to watch Prime Minister Lynden O. Pindling receive from Britain's Prince Charles the constitutional instruments symbolizing freedom for the island chain.

"We are prepared to shoulder our responsibilities and, despite the ups and downs, we know that we are going to make it," Pindling told the cheering islanders. The prime minister, whose Progressive Liberal party had spearheaded the drive for independence also made clear that tourism would continue to be the prime goal of his government. The tourist trade earned the Bahamas $285 million in 1972 and accounted for 73 per cent of the islands' gross revenue.

The basis of Pindling's independence program had been to fill more white collar jobs with blacks who represented more than 80 per cent of the Bahamian population of 186,000. As a result, foreigners reportedly found it difficult to obtain working permits. White businessmen complained that they were having trouble finding qualified black trainees and that the work permit restrictions hampered their efforts to hire foreign help. The prime minister sought, however, to encourage national pride without too much stress on racial issues. Pindling made clear that he was anxious to continue trying to encourage outside capital in other ways besides tourism.

Tim B. Donaldson, selected by Pindling to run the central bank, said that government policy would be to continue to encourage international banking organizations. He noted that the Bahamas had only five foreign-owned banks in 1967 but that the number had soared to 120 by 1973. International banks set up offices in the Bahamas as a tax haven.

August

WATERGATE II:

*Scandal struck home
when Senate hearings
appeared on television*

RICHARD NIXON must have had a pretty good idea that he faced some rough political weather in the spring of 1973 when he publicly accepted responsibility for the spreading scandal known as Watergate. But when the storm struck, it did so with a fury that even the President, with his view from the eye of the tempest of the swirling wreckage of his Administration, could not have foreseen.

It came when a seven-member panel of senators, four Democrats and three Republicans, opened hearings May 17. The panel, formally titled the Senate Select Committee on Presidential Campaign Activities but known popularly as the Watergate Committee, had been established by unanimous Senate vote Feb. 7 and instructed to complete its findings by Feb. 28, 1974. Its chairman, Sen. Sam J. Ervin Jr., a courtly and colorful 76-year-old North Carolina Democrat, considered the Senate's leading constitutional scholar, called the hearings "the most important investigation ever entrusted to the Congress."

If that was political hyperbole there could be no denying they were among history's most fascinating. They were televised nationally without interruption and, for those who couldn't watch by day, rebroadcast on public service channels by night. They constituted a drama in real life which rivaled in incredulity the soap operas they replaced on daytime television. Continuing through June and July and into August, the hearings showed witness after witness telling of lies and bribes and offers of hush money, of burglars and bagmen and forgers and spies. They told of tapped phones and bugged rooms including—not even the Senate investigators were prepared for this—the Oval Office of the President. By the time the committee recessed for the summer the national audience, enthralled if not edified, had found the revelations, like Washington's summer heat, almost too much to bear.

By then Watergate, in its all-encompassing sense, had brought on eight civil suits, seven congressional inquiries, six grand jury investigations, three trials and numerous federal agency investigations, and it was far from over. The entire Watergate Affair, which had begun with a bumbled burglary in comic opera fashion, had come to resemble a medieval morality play acted out in 20th century terms on color television before an audience who couldn't be wholly sure who was good and who was evil. Conflicting testimony and a traditional respect for the office of the presidency had combined in the minds of many onlookers to make the exposers of the scandal almost as suspect as the perpetrators.

The Senate committee set out about doing its task in three stages. It would hear first the evidence that persons in both the White House and the President's re-election committee conspired to cover up the crime committed by the persons who plotted and burglarized the Democratic National Committee headquarters at the Watergate Hotel in 1972; next, evidence of political campaign espionage and sabotage—dirty tricks, as they came euphemistically to be called; finally, evidence concerning the ethics and legality of political fund-raising practices. At the mid-August recess the committee had not even quite finished the first phase.

Much of that evidence, recorded in 7,573 pages of transcript by 35 witnesses, simply filled in, under oath, the broad outlines of the scandal already dug out by reporters and pried out of reluctant trial witnesses by Judge John L. Sirica as the ugliness first surfaced. It did confirm that a criminal cover-up existed, but left in dispute the names and extent of participation of all those involved.

Here, subscandal by subscandal, is how the Watergate matter stood at the August recess:

The Liddy Plan. After joining the Committee to Re-elect the President, former White House assistant G. Gordon Liddy presented extravagant political intelligence-gathering plans to former Attorney General and Re-election Committee chairman John Mitchell, White House Counsel John Dean and Jeb Stuart Magruder, Mitchell's deputy at the Re-election Committee. The plans were twice rejected. When they were presented, scaled down, a third time by Magruder to Mitchell at a meeting in Key Biscayne, a Mitchell deputy, Fred LaRue, was present. The plan included wiretapping the Watergate, Democratic convention headquarters at Miami Beach and the headquarters of the eventual Democratic nominee.

Magruder testified that Mitchell approved the plan at this third meeting. Mitchell testified he vehemently rejected it. LaRue? He testified that Mitchell had done neither in his presence but had postponed a decision.

Magruder said he reported Mitchell's approval to presidential assistant H. R. Haldeman through Haldeman's aide, Gordon Strachan, and Strachan said he passed along the information in a memo to Haldeman but had destroyed the memo. He did so, he said, on what he construed to be an order from Haldeman to strip the files of embarrassing documents after the Watergate break-in. Haldeman said he could not recall reading any such memo. Dean said he also had reported the first two Liddy meetings to Haldeman, but Haldeman said he had no memory of that either.

Thus who finally approved a $250,000 intelligence-gathering plan, with the authority to approve such an expenditure, remained in dispute. Also, there was no direct evidence that the President had heard any of the details of the plan.

Destruction of Documents. In the hours following the arrest of the Watergate burglars, paper shredding machines at the CRP and the White House chewed up an impressive amount of paper. Liddy destroyed a stack of his papers described as a foot thick. Magruder ordered a sheaf destroyed which included wiretap intercepts at the Watergate. Strachan went through Haldeman's files. Herbert Porter, a CRP official, shredded expense vouchers given him by Liddy. LaRue and Herbert Kalmbach, the President's personal attorney, destroyed records on the amounts of money given to the Watergate burglars and their attorneys. Acting FBI Director L. Patrick Gray burned documents taken from Watergate burglar E. Howard Hunt's White House safe including a forged diplomatic cable manufactured to embarrass former President Kennedy. Although not necessarily in connection with the Watergate break-in, other documents, reports of campaign contributions made before a

John Dean III sat with his wife, Maureen, as he waited to testify

disclosure law went into effect, were destroyed by the CRP's finance chairman Maurice Stans, its treasurer Hugh Sloan Jr., and Kalmbach.

That the papers were destroyed was clear, but, again, who gave the orders? LaRue said that Mitchell told Magruder to have "a bonfire." Mitchell denied it. Gray said he burned the contents of the safe at the suggestion of presidential assistant John Ehrlichman, who said he merely gave Gray the papers for safekeeping. Haldeman could not remember directing Strachan to strip the files as Strachan claimed. Porter said he shredded at Liddy's insistence; Liddy refused to testify at all. The only thing that was clear was that the Watergate cover-up began in a blizzard of confetti.

Involvement of the CIA and FBI. Less than a week after the Watergate arrests, Haldeman and Ehrlichman met with top officials of the Central Intelligence Agency. They said they did so at the President's request to make sure that an FBI investigation in Mexico—where money found on the Watergate burglars had been traced—did not accidentally expose covert CIA operations in that country. Deputy CIA director Vernon Walters went immediately to FBI director Gray and told him of the meeting, although, Walters said, neither he nor CIA Director Richard M. Helms knew offhand of any CIA activities in Mexico at that time. After further checking and determining that the CIA was involved in no such activity, Walters said, he went back to Gray and the two determined that they were being "used" to impede the Watergate investigation. Whereupon, Gray phoned the President on July 6 and told him: "People on your staff are trying to mortally wound you." Gray said that President Nixon did not ask him whom he was talking about and merely told him to continue his investigation. Further, Dean testified that he had asked Walters whether the CIA might provide bail money for the Watergate burglars. Walters said he was profoundly disturbed at White House overtures which he interpreted as efforts to use the agency to take political heat off the White House and was prepared to resign if they persisted. For his part, the President said in a statement May 22 that he had no intention of impeding the Watergate investigation but was concerned only that the FBI might inadvertently interfere with matters of national security.

Money for the burglars. John Dean testified that he had helped arrange and direct payments to the arrested men to buy their silence. He said he had told the President of the money demands, and the President said it would be "no problem" to raise $1 million if it were needed. Haldeman said he had listened to a tape recording of the Nixon-Dean conversation—for the office was bugged—and that the President had added the phrase: "But it would be wrong."

What was uncontested was that large sums, totaling about $420,000, were taken mainly from campaign contributions and transmitted by Kalmbach and LaRue to the defendants and their attorneys through a former New York City policeman, Anthony T. Ulasewicz, using a bizarre system of code names and secret drops—cash left in a phone booth or storage locker, that sort of thing—so the recipients would never see them. Kalmbach testified that Ehrlichman had assured him the payoffs were proper, merely humanitarian gestures. Haldeman said he was aware of the payments but had not approved them and had made no judgments about their propriety. Ulasewicz did make such a judgment. "Something here is not kosher," he said.

Executive clemency. Only the President can grant executive clemency to a convicted felon. Testimony was clear that such an offer was made, thus risking implicating the President—but made by whom? Dean said that the President had told him at a meeting March 13, 1972, that he had discussed the matter with both Ehrlichman and White House assistant Charles W. Colson. All three denied it.

What is undisputed is that Dean, through Ulasewicz and another intermediary, John J. Caulfield, sent word to one of the convicted wiretappers, James McCord, that he could expect a pardon after maybe a year in prison if he kept silent about the involvement of others higher up. McCord was told that the suggestion was coming "from the very highest levels of the White House," although Caulfield said he had no knowledge of his own that the President had made the offer.

But Dean said he transmitted the message on the instruction of Mitchell. Mitchell denied it. Mitchell also denied making such a suggestion to Magruder. Magruder testified that when

Above, Sen. Howard H. Baker asking a question during the hearing. Center, John Mitchell testifying before the Senate Committee on Watergate. Right, Maurice Stans giving testimony

he had expressed concern about having perjured himself, both Dean and Mitchell told him that he could expect a pardon, plus support payments for his family, if convicted.

The White House intelligence plan. Undisputed testimony and documents showed that on July 23, 1970, President Nixon had approved, and had so notified the intelligence agencies involved, a plan for gathering information on antiwar demonstrators, campus radicals and others which included breaking and entering, opening personal mail and intercepting communications between United States residents and foreign points. One of the plan's originators, White House aide Tom Charles Huston, pointed out in a memo that the plan thus included activities that were "clearly illegal." The plan was sent to the heads of the FBI, CIA, National Security Agency and Defense Intelligence Agency.

In a statement May 22, President Nixon said he had rescinded the plan after five days because of the objections of FBI Director J. Edgar Hoover. Mitchell, who had been Attorney General at the time, and Dean, who had been White House counsel, said they had never seen a written directive rescinding the plan—but neither was there testimony that any illegal acts were carried out by the four intelligence agencies.

The Plumbers. The following year, in June 1971, the President created a White House group called the Special Investigations

Unit. It quickly earned a nickname, The Plumbers, because its job was to plug leaks of classified government information to newspapers, especially the Pentagon Papers.

Testimony revealed that Ehrlichman had over-all supervision of the group but that its director was Egil Krogh. Its members included Hunt and Liddy, two of the seven arrested at the Watergate. Its activities included tapping phones and other information-gathering schemes, and also burglarizing the office of a psychiatrist whose patient was Daniel Ellsberg, the man who leaked the Pentagon Papers to the press.

The Fielding burglary. The burglary of the psychiatrist's office, that of Dr. Lewis Fielding, happened in September 1971, three months after the Plumbers were formed. Ehrlichman denied authorizing the burglary but admitted approving a memo from Krogh proposing "a covert operation . . . to examine all the medical files still held by Ellsberg's psychiatrist." Ehrlichman said such data was needed to contribute to a "psychological profile" that the Plumbers had asked the CIA to compile. Dean testified that Krogh had told him the orders for the burglary had come "right out of the Oval Office" but there was no supporting evidence for the statement and Krogh did not testify.

The Judge Byrne incident. Ehrlichman testified that shortly before the trial of Daniel Ellsberg was expected to go to the jury the President had instructed him to find out whether Federal District Judge W. Matthew Byrne Jr., who was the presiding judge at the trial, might be interested in the job of FBI director if the President were to make such an offer. Ehrlichman met with the judge twice in California. Ehrlichman testified that neither he nor the President intended to influence the Ellsberg

case (which was eventually thrown out of court when the Fielding burglary was disclosed) and that since no offer was actually made the approach was proper.

In outline, then, those were the major findings—and controversies—produced by the Senate committee in the hearings that stretched over three months. Their dry recitation, however, does not nearly convey the drama.

The hearings were held in room 318 of the Old Senate Office Building, the Caucus Room, a high-ceilinged neoclassical chamber which in its 62-year history had been the scene of the beginning, and end, of many political careers.

And it was there, in the spring and summer of 1973, that for their political good or ill—such side effects of the hearings could not be ignored—the seven members of the Watergate Committee would receive more national exposure than ever before in their careers.

The seven senators included, besides Chairman Ervin, three Democrats: Herman E. Talmadge of Georgia, Daniel K. Inouye of Hawaii and Joseph Montoya of New Mexico; and three Republicans: Howard H. Baker Jr. of Tennessee, the committee vice chairman, Edward J. Gurney of Florida and Sen. Lowell P. Weicker Jr. of Connecticut. Their faces soon became familiar to millions. Ervin, with his dancing eyebrows, rustic philosophies and reverence for America's laws and traditions, became an overnight folk hero to many.

The hearings got off to a relatively slow start May 17, with witnesses describing the organization of the CRP and its 400 employes and with testimony by the Washington policemen who made the Watergate arrests. Next day, however, viewers

were treated to their first bit of drama with the appearance of convicted Watergate conspirator McCord. The stocky, balding veteran of 19 years with the CIA told of clandestine meetings with Caulfield—long drives in the countryside, usually—at which he received offers of executive clemency and financial aid if he would remain silent. He quoted Caulfield as telling him that "the President's ability to govern is at stake. Another Teapot Dome scandal is possible and the government may fall. Everybody else is on track but you. You are not following the game plan." When Caulfield testified a few days later he made it clear that the person at the White House who authorized him to make the clemency offers was not the President but counsel John Dean.

Caulfield was followed to the witness table by Ulasewicz, the former New York detective who enlivened the proceedings with some unintentional hilarity about the craft of electronic surveillance as done, in police parlance, by "wiremen." Under questioning by Sen. Baker he also commented on the bungled job done at the Watergate:

BAKER: You think your wiremen [in the police department] were better than McCord's wiremen?

ULASEWICZ: I will tell you, any old retired man in the New York City Police department who would become involved in a thing like that, he thought he had to for whatever reason it was, he would not have walked in with an army, that's for sure.

After a week-long Memorial Day layoff, the hearings resumed with testimony by Sloan, the former treasurer of the CRP, and Porter, the committee's scheduling director. Sloan

Sen. Edward J. Gurney accused chairman Sam Ervin of harassing Maurice Stans

described how he had been pressured to commit perjury but resisted. Porter, on nationwide television, confessed to having perjured himself at the trial of the Watergate conspirators and before a federal grand jury. He said that deputy CRP director Magruder had asked him to fabricate a story about what had happened to $100,000 in cash given to convicted Watergate conspirator Liddy. "Can you corroborate a story that the money was for something a bit more legal-sounding than dirty tricks?" he said Magruder had asked him. "I said, 'Yes, I guess I'd do that'," Porter replied. In a full day of testimony Magruder freely admitted his own complicity in the calculated planning to keep the facts from coming out.

Magruder's most damaging testimony, however, was his clear recollection that John Mitchell had given his approval to an over-all intelligence plan which included bugging the Watergate at a meeting in Key Biscayne on March 30, 1972. According to Magruder, Mitchell said, "O.K., let's give him (Liddy) $250,000." Sen. Baker asked Magruder if there were "any doubt" that Mitchell had approved the break-in.

"No, sir," Magruder said, adding that it was a "reluctant decision."

"Why reluctant?" asked Baker.

Magruder: "We knew it was illegal and nothing might come of it."

For weeks, Watergate-watchers had been anticipating the testimony of John Dean. Enough of what he might say had leaked, and his full account promised to be sensational. It was.

In a full week of testimony—beginning with a 245-page statement that took Dean six hours to read—the 34-year-old attorney, fired by Nixon April 30, presented the most comprehensive indictment thus far heard against the men who had been closest to the President. Dean accused Nixon himself of having known since September 1972 about attempts to suppress the scandal.

Accompanying his testimony were dozens of documents, which he turned over to the committee as supporting evidence. One set of papers opened up a new area of alleged administration political pressure: the use of tax audits to harass its opponents. He also released a document which came to be widely referred to as the "enemies list." It was a memorandum Dean had sent to Ehrlichman dated Aug. 16, 1971, and began:

"This memorandum addresses the matter of how we can maximize the fact of our incumbency in dealing with persons known to be active in their opposition to our Administration. Stated a bit more bluntly—how we can use the available federal machinery to screw our political enemies." The list contained 20 names.

Speaking calmly and deliberately, Dean said the Watergate affair "was an inevitable outgrowth of a climate of excessive concern over the political impact of demonstrations, excessive concern over leaks, an insatiable appetite for political intelligence, all coupled with a do-it-yourself White House staff, regardless of the law."

He testified that on Sept. 15, 1972, the day the seven men were indicted for the break-in, he received congratulations from the President that the case had reached no higher. Later, Dean said, on Feb. 27, 1973, he had met with the President again and repeated what he had told him in September, that he was not sure the cover-up could be maintained indefinitely. The next day, he said, he told the President that he, Dean, had been involved in the cover-up and a possible obstruction of justice. Nixon "reassured me not to worry, that I had no legal problems," Dean said. He said he had also met with the President March 13, and told him about the money demands of the conspirators, and that he went back on March 21 to report yet again to Nixon because "the President did not seem to understand the full implications of what was going on." At that meeting, he said, he told Nixon "there was a cancer growing on the presidency" and that if it was not removed "the President himself would be killed by it."

Dean said he met privately again with the President on April 15 and that Nixon began asking him "leading questions, which made me think that the conversation was being taped." Dean said Nixon told him he had been joking when he made the comment about how easy it would be to get a million dollars for Watergate hush money.

Later in the conversation, Dean said, "the most interesting thing happened." Nixon, he said, got out of his chair and walked to the corner of his office and, "in a barely audible tone," admitted he had been foolish to have discussed clemency with his aide Charles Colson.

It was heady stuff. In turn, the seven senators questioned him at length but Dean stuck by his version of what had happened. Asked finally how he would characterize the Watergate burglary, Dean replied: "The opening act of one of America's great tragedies."

John Mitchell followed Dean to the stand, denying flatly that he had approved the Watergate break-in but otherwise adding little to the growing volume of disclosures. He did, however, contribute a memorable phrase. Questioned by Sen. Talmadge about the reasons for not informing President Nixon of details of the Watergate matter, Mitchell replied:

"It was a question of not involving him at all so that he could go through his campaign without being involved in this type of activity, and I am talking about the White House horrors particularly." Inevitably, "White House horrors" became the definition of the Watergate scandal.

Despite all that had been revealed, the public still was not prepared for the bombshell dropped by an unexpected witness, Alexander P. Butterfield. Butterfield, the administrator of the Federal Aviation Administration, had been a White House aide. During his time there, he said, listening devices had been placed in all the Presidents offices and the phones in each office were tapped. Next day, the White House confirmed the report, saying the eavesdropping devices had been installed in the spring of 1971 for the purpose of preserving the President's conversations for posterity.

The Watergate committee wanted to get those tapes. So did the special Watergate prosecutor, Archibald Cox. The President, however, insisted that they fell within the realm of privileged material and refused to turn them over. The matter went before Judge Sirica, who ruled that the tapes should be given to him so that he could listen to them privately and determine whether executive privilege was involved. Both Cox and the White House appealed the ruling, and it appeared the case ultimately would go before the Supreme Court. President Nixon, for his part, said he would abide by a "definitive" Supreme Court ruling but would not say in advance what he would consider definitive.

Meanwhile the Watergate committee heard President Nixon's personal lawyer, Kalmbach, describe the cloak-and-dagger manner and the code names involved in distributing money to the Watergate defendants. He said he had told Ehrlichman that the secrecy of the operation bothered him and he wanted assurance that the payments were proper. Ehrlichman gave him such assurance, he said, and furthermore that it was inconceivable that Ehrlichman and Dean would involve him in any wrongdoing.

Ehrlichman, in his testimony, also saw nothing wrong in "support payments" for the defendants and rejected the suggestion that it was hush money. He also said he had approved a "covert operation" that resulted in the burglarizing of the office of Ellsberg's psychiatrist but that he did not have burglary in mind. He said he thought Ellsberg's records could be obtained perhaps through nurses' aides. In any event, he said, the break-in was "an important, vital national security matter well within the constitutional function of the President." This brought on a peppery exchange between Ehrlichman and Ervin. The chairman said he knew of no law authorizing the President to order an illegal act and that the constitution specifically forbade unreasonable searches and seizures. Further-

more, Ervin said, it was Ellsberg who was being investigated, not his psychiatrist.

As the hearings pressed on into August, it was plain to all that the committee members were tired and anxious to have done with it for a while. "The country needs a rest from Watergate," said Baker.

All the same there were more witnesses to hear, including former presidential assistant Haldeman. As Ehrlichman had done before him, Haldeman swore he had had no knowledge of a cover-up, but the biggest surprise in his testimony was that he said he had listened to some of the tape-recorded presidential conversations and they substantiated the President's position. The shocker was that he said he had taken the tape recording home with him overnight, listened to it alone and took notes from it in early July. This was after Dean's testimony and more than two months after Haldeman had left as White House chief of staff—that is to say, when he had the status of a private citizen. If a private citizen could listen to the tapes without doing harm to the principle of executive privilege, Ervin said, why couldn't the committee?

Haldeman also was asked about the so-called "enemies list." He said inclusion on the list meant simply that that person would not be given White House courtesies, such as invitations to functions.

Finally, on August 7 the committee heard its 35th witness and recessed for the summer. The result of the prolonged hearings was summed up in a speech before the American Bar Association by Supreme Court Justice Harry A. Blackmun, who had been appointed to the bench by President Nixon. The scandal, said the Justice, had created an atmosphere in which the "very glue of our ship of state seems about to become unstuck." He said grave damage had been done to the democratic process, and that "the pall of Watergate, with all its revelations of misplaced loyalties, of strange measures of the unethical, of unusual doings in high places, and by lawyer after lawyer after lawyer, is upon us." The pall had clearly descended upon the Nixon White House: a Haris poll taken on Aug. 6 showed that a majority of those questioned, 55 per cent, agreed with the statement: "President Nixon does not inspire confidence as a President should." Only 32 per cent disagreed. In a Gallup poll taken a week later, 57 per cent of those questioned said they disapproved of the way Nixon was handling his job and 31 per cent approved.

President Nixon responding to a question about Watergate during a news conference at the Western White House

Fires set by rioting convicts raged at the state penitentiary

Three Convicts Killed
And 53 Persons Injured
In Oklahoma Prison Riot

THE PRISON WAS OLD—ramshackle, some called it—and the cells were crowded with 500 more men than the rated capacity. There was bitter resentment at Oklahoma Gov. David Hall's stated policy of no parole for those convicted for crimes of violence or narcotics sales. Many prisoners existed on the drugs and liquor which found their way behind the high, white walls.

Throughout the muggy summer there had been rustlings of potential trouble. Prisoners and guards alike later told of hearing rumors that an uprising was planned for the annual prison rodeo at the end of August.

Near the end of July, the temperatures at McAlester in southeastern Oklahoma were nearly as hot as the rumors. For a week the mercury had hovered around 95 degrees, and on July 27 inched toward 98. Then, shortly after the mid-day meal, five prisoners who officials later would say were "doped up on something" attacked two guards, Capt. C. C. Smith and Lt. Thomas Payne. The spark had been struck, and within minutes the Oklahoma State Penitentiary was aflame. Before it ended nine days later, three convicts were dead at the hands of fellow inmates, at least 50 persons had been injured and a dozen prison buildings lay in ruins. The damage was estimated at more than $20 million, the highest monetary cost of any prison riot in American history.

"The Attica riot of 1971 resulted in a greater loss of life, but the McAlester riot unquestionably was the most destructive of

154

any riot that has ever taken place in American prisons," Lawrence A. Carpenter wrote after trudging through the rubble. Carpenter, a veteran of 30 years in the federal correctional system and a nationally recognized expert on penal affairs, termed the riot "one of the most disastrous events in American correctional history." In his report to the Oklahoma Crime Commission, Carpenter said the prison "was almost totally gutted—only the administration building and a few minor structures were spared." And, he added, only "timely negotiation" by Gov. Hall and officials of the Oklahoma Department of Corrections saved the lives of the 23 hostages the inmates had taken.

While the specific causes of the riot were not discovered, Carpenter wrote, the prison "has been ripe for a disorder of this kind for many years." Contributing causes, he said, were overcrowding, idleness and poorly paid guards, many of whom are "functionally illiterate or nearly so." Nearly everyone admitted the penitentiary was substandard. But most agreed with State Rep. John Miskelly, chairman of the House Appropriations Committee. He said conditions at the prison "were terrible" and the old buildings should have been torn down long ago. But, he said, the state just doesn't have the money to do the job in one year.

There had been signs of change, though. Heeding the cries for penal reform, the 1973 legislature appropriated a record $9.3 million for the corrections system, a 57 per cent increase over the previous year.

Through transfers of less dangerous prisoners to medium security honor farms and training facilities, Hall had reduced the prison's population from more than 2,300 inmates when he took office in 1971 to 1,636 when the riot erupted. But the prison was built to hold only 1,100 and much of the underlying unrest remained. When the spark was struck, the explosion followed.

As soon as the two guards were attacked in the dining hall, other prisoners raced through the cellblocks and the plants of the industrial area, grabbing hostages and setting fires. "We believe there are no more than 250 of them, but there could be as many as 1,000" involved, Deputy Warden Paul Graham said.

Some of the rioters commandeered the penitentiary's public address system and begged others to join. One group broke into the hospital, ripped open cabinets and fled with narcotics. Flames began licking through the chapel, the dining hall, the meat packing plant and other manufacturing units.

"It was something beyond description. It was something out of a nightmare," said Dr. Rafael Cott as he sat on the steps outside the prison's main gates, his pants stained with the blood of wounded convicts he had treated on the hospital floor before being forced to flee. "All I could see were burning buildings."

Inside, the convicts held 23 hostages. All were prison employes, including the deputy warden, Sam Johnston. They demanded that Hall come to negotiate with them. Hall said he would come, but not until all the hostages were released unharmed.

The fires burned and squadrons of state troopers and National Guardsmen went to the prison. Armored personnel carriers moved into position as helicopters flew reconnaissance flights above.

In the early hours of the rioting two convicts were stabbed to death by other inmates. Another would die Aug. 1 in a stabbing that revealed that more than 1,000 armed officers had yet to bring complete control.

Floodlights powered by portable generators kept the prison bathed in a garish glow throughout the night. Explosions punctuated the din as cans of paint and other combustibles went up. Flames leaped from building to building. And, throughout the state, wives and mothers waited and prayed.

"We never talked about it," said Mrs. Bill Hopkins, wife of a hostage. "We thought it would never happen. We've lived here for 25 years and never thought about anything like this happening before."

Hall remained in his office as the night wore on, a telephone line open to McAlester. The fires burned on, and suddenly two hostages walked out, released when their captors feared they might suffer heart attacks. Then several more came out.

As dawn broke the battle-ready Guardsmen and troopers, clad in flak jackets and peering through the plastic face shields attached to their helmets, marched to the main gate for a frontal assault. But by then the governor had made telephone contact with the convicts. Warden Park Anderson and Irvine Ungerman, chairman of the Oklahoma Board of Corrections, were negotiating in person. The troops were pulled back but told they might yet have to charge the prison.

Then the rioters sent out a list of four demands: total amnesty for the ringleaders; formation of a popularly elected inmate committee to deal with the administration; free access to U.S. Justice Department and American Civil Liberties Union lawyers, and suspension of a prison employe who, the prisoners said, hates convicts and "plays God."

Prison officials said many grievances voiced earlier by convicts had been reconciled before the riot erupted. Most of these dealt with medical problems, they said.

Eight more hostages were released and walked through the big gates. Expectations rose as more than 200 convicts approached the fence and asked to be removed, to be taken back into custody. "It looks like the rough stuff is over," said Oklahoma Adj. Gen. David Matthews. But one guard scoffed: "Hell, that's not half of them. There's 1,500 men in there."

The negotiation continued and almost 22 hours after the uprising began the last 11 hostages were released. "Order has been restored," the governor said as he prepared to fly to McAlester to meet with an inmate committee.

The first comments from the freed hostages touched only on the good treatment they had received. "They showed the highest respect for us," said Deputy Warden Johnston, the last hostage turned loose. "They conducted themselves very well."

But soon there were tales of personal heroism, of armed convicts barring the door to keep rampaging inmates, apparently either high on drugs or drunk, from harming the hostages. One guard reported that a convict stepped in front of a knife meant for him.

Hall emerged from the closed session with the nine inmate negotiators and said, "We have had an exchange. We're informed now as to what the consensus of the inmates is. Both interest groups have had a chance to compare their side of the question. A first step has been made." The governor said much of the inmate dissatisfaction apparently arose because the convicts were not aware of recent policy changes. He said the inmate negotiators admitted they had not read the communiques detailing these changes.

Throughout the riot there had been rumors of mass murders by the convicts, of inmates stabbed and tossed into the burning buildings or impaled on meat hooks in the cooler area. Authorities sifting through the ashes after order was restored found no bodies, and one guard who had been a hostage suggested one reason for the rumors.

155

Restless convicts roamed the prison yard as repair crews were dispatched to the damaged areas

"The hospital was one of the first things they took over, and that's where they keep the narcotics," the guard said. "They were hallucinating by 11 o'clock that night, and it takes less than 24 hours for them to draw off beer (in makeshift home-brew vats)."

By July 28 the officials said they had firm control. But after dark the inmates ran loose in the damaged cellblocks, venturing out from cells which couldn't be locked, and tossed more fire bombs. Three buildings were rekindled and guards moved 31 inmates from one section for their own protection.

Sporadic fires broke out throughout the weekend, but it appeared that peace, however tenuous, was returning. Then on July 31 about 700 convicts turned down the first hot meal since the riot began—meatloaf, green beans, corn, gravy, bread and coffee prepared in a field kitchen and served in the prison yard—and advanced on the Guardsmen chanting, "We want steak." The Guardsmen, their rifle bayonets glinting in the sunlight, drove the inmates into a cul de sac formed by the wall and a cellblock building. Early the next morning the third convict died, virtually under the eyes of the troopers and Guardsmen.

"We haven't got any way to keep them from killing each other," Ed Hardy, the governor's press secretary, said. "There are 750 inmates in there and we're not going to lose some highway patrolmen or National Guardsmen trying to save a couple of inmates. We'll help them if we can . . . It's too dangerous to go in there."

And then he revealed that several hundred other prisoners, instead of being locked in their cells, were building shanties in the industrial area, the manufacturing yard outside the walls but inside the steel fences.

It was another week before it was learned that seven convicts had escaped during the riot. Three fled from an honor farm where they had been transferred during the riot and one wounded inmate slipped out of McAlester General Hospital. The other three escaped from the penitentiary. They included one convict serving a life term who hid in a hole in the industrial area and cut through the fences with a bolt cutter after the guards relaxed their vigil.

Not until Aug. 4 were the last of the convicts herded back inside the cellblocks, stripped and searched, and then locked in the hastily repaired cells emptied of all the convict-accumulated comforts such as televisions, drapes and rugs. Padlocks and heavy chains substituted for the wrecked cell locks.

Makeshift repairs were started while state officials wrestled with the dilemma: rebuild at McAlester, saving what little wasn't destroyed, or move the prison elsewhere.

Carpenter, the prison consultant who had toured the ruins with a team from the Federal Law Enforcement Assistance Administration, said he could not recommend spending federal or state money to rebuild. "The buildings are not worth renovating," he wrote, "and the continuation of this facility in its present location would perpetuate many of the conditions that led to the riot."

He said the majority of the prisoners came from the state's three urban areas—Oklahoma City, Tulsa and Lawton—and were racially mixed "while the guards are almost entirely rural whites unacquainted with the problems of offenders from these urban areas. Under these circumstances, guard-convict misunderstandings and conflicts cannot be avoided."

Carpenter recommended that new maximum-minimum security institutions, each to hold no more than 400-500 inmates, should be built in the three urban areas where staff familiar with the problems of urban offenders could be hired.

He also said there should be sweeping changes in the pardon and parole system, including the review of all inmates, "with the exception of those actively involved in the riot," for possible paroles. "This includes not only those who have been denied parole in the past, but those whose (parole) consideration dates have not yet been reached, but who might be released without undue risk to the public."

Discovery of 27 Bodies Revealed Biggest Mass Murder Case in Modern U.S. History

IT FIRST APPEARED to have been a murder in self-defense; a tragic end to a paint-sniffing party for four.

But, after five days, the discovery of 27 bodies of youths ranging in age from 13 to 20 gave the nation its largest mass murder case in modern history.

The victims had been missing from six days to 34 months.

The fatal shooting of Dean Corll, 33, a bachelor electrician, on Aug. 8 had unveiled three years of homosexual rape, torture, and murder.

Many of the victims had disappeared from the once fashionable Heights area just northwest of downtown Houston.

The grim disclosures spread shock far beyond the Heights, where Corll had once operated a candy factory and had resided from time to time prior to moving to suburban Pasadena a month before he died.

At the local, state and federal level there were demands for stronger laws and stronger police authority to help curb the rising number of runaways and missing youngsters that in Houston alone totaled 5,200 in 1972.

Six weeks after Corll's death, investigators said the shooting that uncovered the mass murders was justifiable homicide. Only 18 of the 27 bodies had been identified but, by then, murder indictments were mounting against two junior high

school dropouts from the Heights, Elmer Wayne Henley, 17, and David Owen Brooks, 18.

Henley and Brooks were being held on $100,000 bond on each indictment. They named Corll as the homosexual mastermind who had paid them $5 to $10 for each boy they procured for him. Brooks had known Corll about three years, Henley about 2½ years.

Parents of a number of missing youths knew Corll or Henley or Brooks or all three.

"You fear the worst and hope for the best," said Mrs. Fred Hilligiest, whose son, David, then 13, disappeared with a friend, Gregory Malley Winkle, 16, on May 29, 1971, while the two were en route to a neighborhood swimming pool in the Heights.

David's playmates also included younger brothers of Henley, who resided just a block down the street.

David Hilligiest and Malley Winkle were last seen climbing into a white van similar to one that had become Corll's trademark in the Heights.

The Hilligiests' agony was compounded by an identification mix-up that caused the bodies of their son and the Winkle boy to be sent to Georgia for burial.

The mix-up was not discovered until Sept. 7 when it was de-

Right, Authorities removed one more body from a shallow grave. Below, Billy Ridinger, 20, who reportedly escaped from the homosexual torture ring wore a sack over his head as he entered the Harris County grand jury room

termined the county morgue still held the bodies of two brothers, Jerry Lynn, 13, and Donald Wayne Waldrop, 15, whose parents moved to Georgia after the boys disappeared in the Heights in January, 1971.

Without charge, a Houston funeral home arranged for the bodies of the Waldrop boys to be taken to Georgia and for the return of David Hilligiest and Malley Winkle to Houston for reburial.

The Hilligiests had paid a private detective $1,100 and offered a $1,000 reward in their long search for David while, at the same time, receiving sympathetic inquiries from Henley.

"There wasn't a week that I didn't meet him and he was always polite," Mrs. Hilligiest said. "He'd ask if there had been anything about my son and I'd ask if he had heard anything. He'd always answer 'No' but always said if there was anything he could do to just let him know."

At a nearby home, Henley's mother, Mary, was bewildered not only by the horrors her son and Brooks were unfolding but by what they were saying about the family friend, Corll.

"Dean loved to be around kids and prattle with them about cars and fishing," Mrs. Henley said. "I don't understand this man. He ate Easter dinner with us; he worked on my car; he loved to play with the kids. And Wayne loved him like a father. I know Dean must've done something terrible to Wayne to make Wayne shoot him. But Dean was such a nice, polite man who loved to be around kids. He sometimes piled 10 or 12 kids into his van and took them riding."

Mrs. Henley said her son told her early Aug. 8 he was spending the night with a friend.

"The next I heard from him he's calling me from the boat storage yard saying "Mama, I killed Dean," she said.

Elmer Henly, 17, led officers to grave sites

Later, Mrs. Henley quoted her son as having said in a telephone call from police headquarters that he had told police everything, including that he had murdered nine of the boys.

"Mama, be happy for me because now, at last, I can live," she quoted Henley as saying.

The Houston horror story began at 8:24 a.m. on Aug. 8 when Henley telephoned police in industrial Pasadena that he had killed Corll in self-defense.

When police arrived at Corll's home they found Henley, Timothy Cordell Kerley, 20, and Rhonda Louise Williams, 15, waiting on the porch. Corll's body, struck by at least four bullets, was found on a hallway floor.

Henley said the paint sniffing knocked him out and Corll awoke him while putting handcuffs on him. He said Kerley and the girl, stripped naked, were bound spread-eagled to a plywood board.

Henley said Corll, with a knife and a .22 caliber pistol, said he was going to kill all three "but first was going to have his fun." He quoted Corll as also saying he had killed others and had buried them in a boat stall.

"I started sweet talking him," Henley said. "I told him I would kill them if he would unhandcuff me."

Once free, Henley said he was ordered to sexually attack the girl while Corll attacked the youth. But an argument "over the chick's presence" developed.

Henley said Corll by then had put down the pistol and that he grabbed it and Corll came at him with the knife.

"I told him I would kill him if he came at me, and he came at me and I killed him," Henley said.

By nightfall, Henley had led investigators to a boat stall in southwest Houston and he sat on the ground and cried as he watched police and jail trusties dig for bodies.

"I knew Marty, and Marty's there," Henley said, nodding toward the stall. "And David. I grew up with him and he lived next door, and I went to school with Charles."

Before the digging operations halted for the night, the first eight bodies had been recovered.

Mrs. Julie Harriman, daughter of the owner of the 20-unit boat stall shed, said Corll was the last person she would have suspected of being involved in such a situation. "He was always very polite, quiet and well mannered," she said.

Corll had been renting the stall since 1970, and he did not own a boat.

Digging was to have resumed early the next morning at the stall but was delayed until early afternoon as investigators concentrated on two new developments.

Henley, still clinging to his self-defense claim in Corll's death, had abandoned a claim of ignorance of the mass slayings. And Brooks had appeared at police headquarters to make a witness statement.

In the early afternoon of Aug. 9, Houston Homicide Lt. Breck Porter told newsmen "25 to 30" boys had been killed and that the bodies not only had been buried at the boat stall but near Lake Sam Rayburn in the piney woods of East Texas and on a lonely stretch of beach near High Island on the Texas coast.

The final body count: 17 in the boat stall, four at Lake Sam Rayburn, and six near High Island.

And investigators were not certain all the victims had been found.

The boat stall digging ended late Aug. 9. At all three burial sites, most of the bodies were nude, had been covered with lime, and placed in plastic bags. Dental records became the best means for identification.

Henley accompanied officers to Lake Sam Rayburn, where two more bodies were found on Aug. 9 and two more the following day.

At Lake Sam Rayburn, Henley again chatted with newsmen.

"Here's some boys I helped get for Dean," he said. "He raped them and killed them and brought them out here to bury them."

"Billy's buried there," he said. When questioned, he gave the name of Billy Lawrence. William Ray Lawrence, 15, had been missing since June 11.

"I couldn't hold my sanity much longer," the mustachioed, long-haired Henley replied when asked why he had told police of the mass slayings.

"Dean was a nice easygoer, quiet, enjoyed himself. The man that did these killings was someone else. He had a lust for blood."

As Henley talked, Brooks gave police a long signed statement witnessed by his father.

And Corll's funeral services were being held in Pasadena.

"We must now deliver this man into God's judgment and also His mercy and grace," said the Rev. Robert D. Joiner of the Sunset United Methodist Church.

After signing his statement, Brooks was taken to High Island and Henley was moved there from Lake Sam Rayburn to help in the beach search.

Henley and Brooks helped locate the first two High Island bodies Aug. 10 but they were unable to pinpoint other grave sites.

Digging operations were terminated because of rain and high tides until Aug. 13 when heavy equipment was brought in and four more bodies were found. They were the last to be recovered.

Pasadena police refused to release Henley's statement on grounds it was pretrial evidence.

But newsmen obtained a copy of the statement Brooks made to Houston police and it contained names and places but no dates.

". . . I was present when most of the killings happened," Brooks said.

"I never actually killed anyone but I was in the room when they happened and was supposed to help if something went wrong."

"Wayne took part in getting the boys at first and then later he took an active part in the killings," Brooks said. "Wayne seemed to enjoy causing pain and he was especially sadistic at the Schuler address (in the Heights)."

"It was while we were living on Schuler that Wayne and Dean got me down and started to kill me," he said. "I begged Dean not to kill me and he finally let me go."

It also was on Schuler, Brooks said, that Henley and Corll let one boy go, Billy Ridinger.

"I took care of him while he was there and I believe the only reason he is alive now is that I begged them not to kill him," Brooks said.

Ridinger, now 20, testified Aug. 14 before the grand jury just minutes before the jury returned the first of the murder indictments against Brooks and Henley.

Ridinger entered the jury room with a grocery sack over his head and face.

"In all, I guess there were between 25 and 30 boys killed," Brooks said. "And they were buried in three different places. I was present and helped bury many of them but not all of them."

As the grand jury deliberations continued at the Harris

Skull lying in wheelbarrow was turned up as workers continued digging for victims

County Courthouse, Dist. Atty. Carol Vance said Henley and Brooks were the only suspects in the case.

"And we have no plans for immunity for anybody in this case," Vance said.

Vance and his staff quickly surprised defense attorneys by filing state motions for quick psychiatric examination of the two young defendants.

State District Court Judge William Hattan said the state's request was unusual, that the defense normally filed such motions. But Hattan approved the motions after Vance indicated he wanted any question of insanity settled quickly.

Henley's attorney, Charles Melder, objected, and on his advice, Henley refused to be examined both before and after the Hattan order.

Ted Musick, Brooks' attorney, offered no objection but he did object when the state-appointed psychiatrist wanted to postpone the Brooks examination after Henley had refused to cooperate. The psychiatrist changed his mind and examined Brooks.

Vance's chief prosecutor, Sam Robertson, wanted to reserve judgment but expressed doubt a new Texas death penalty law could be applied to the case. The law applies only to the specified felonies of kidnaping, burglary, forcible rape and arson.

Meanwhile, about 100 parents in the Hights organized a new 24-hours-a-day youth center and dedicated it to the 27 victims.

A dedication plaque with 18 names had space for nine more. But some of the 27 victims may never be identified.

"We have many bones and we don't know which go with which bodies," said Dr. Joseph Jachimczyk, chief county medical examiner.

A Tale of
Three Cities

Above, Philadelphia, Pa.: "What glorious sunsets have their birth in cities fouled by smoke"—William Henry Davies. Right, Cincinnati, Ohio: "The big city is like a mother's knee to many who have strayed far and found the roads rough beneath their uncertain feet. At dusk they come home and sit upon the door-step."—O. Henry. Below, New York City: "The City is of Night; perchance of Death, But certainly of Night."—James Thomson

Above, Russian high school girls pressed into service during the August harvest on a state farm in the Soviet Union's Azovsky region. Right, a dolphin named Speedy reached out to kiss bride Melanie Hunter in Durban South Africa where Melanie's parents owned a dolphinarium. Below, the baseball-playing Alou brothers of the Dominican Republic got together Aug. 10 when the Oakland Athletics played the Yankees in New York. Left to right: Felipe of the Yankees, Jesus of Oakland and Matty of the Yankees

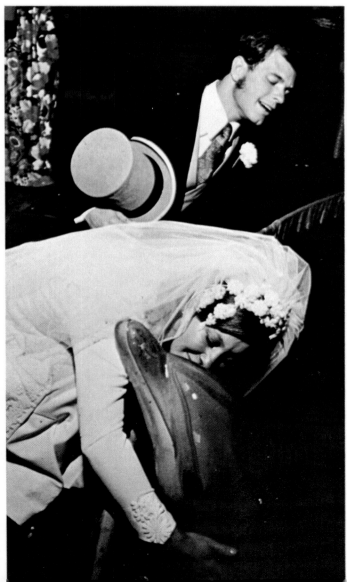

161

MEXICO HIT BY ITS WORST QUAKE IN MODERN TIMES

The first tremors rippled across Mexico shortly before 4 a.m. on Aug. 28, rousing people from their sleep. Within the next two minutes, the country was torn by its worst earthquake in modern times. The disaster left more than 600 known dead, an estimated 4,000 injured and thousands without homes.

Rumbling beneath the mountainous spine of Mexico, the quake did heavy damage in the states of Vera Cruz and Puebla.

The shocks caused widespread panic in Mexico City, where more than 50 had perished in a quake 16 years earlier, but there were no known deaths and little damage in the capital. But in the stricken area 120 to 220 miles south and east of Mexico City, some 50 towns were hit. So severe was the property damage that President Luis Echeverria ordered about 10,000 partially destroyed buildings razed.

A day after disaster struck, a mile-high cloud of dust hung over southeastern Puebla state. Cracks in the earth 100 yards across isolated at least four devasted towns near Ciudad Serdan.

Thousands of homeless trudged into Tehuacan and other cities in the devasted area, some carrying the bodies of their dead kin. In the cemetary at Tehuacan, lines of coffins awaited the bodies so that burial could be swift because of the steaming heat.

Santiago Martinez and his wife waited outside a Tehuacan cemetery for the body of their 30-year-old son, Jorge.

"It was dawn when the earthquake began, and then I thought it was going to be the end of the world," said Martinez. "So I ran out of my home with my wife and both of us knelt and started praying.

"But my son . . . I couldn't wake him up, and when I looked back at our home, the house had collapsed . . . Later me and friends pulled out his body."

Private cars made their way through rubble-piled streets in Tehuacan blaring appeals for blood, clothes and medicine over loudspeakers.

"We need your help to save the lives of our brothers in misfortune," said one voice.

It was much the same story elsewhere in the ravaged area. In the little village of Tlacotepec in southeastern Mexico, Diego Gonzalez Garcia described the quake.

Church altar survived almost undamaged by the devastating quake

"When it began, it sounded like a train slowly coming closer and then there was a roar," he said. "The house began to shake, little pieces began to fall and suddenly the whole place collapsed."

Gonzalez pointed to a bare wall; all that remained of his adobe home.

"Two of my sons were killed in there," he said. "I ran out before my room collapsed, but my sons never got out."

Electricity was out in most of the stricken sector and telephone links with the rest of the world were cut off. The quake was particularly disastrous because it came in the wake of a month of nationwide floods that had left 76 persons dead and 400,000 homeless.

SUBWAY COLLAPSE TRAPPED HUNDREDS IN BLISTERING HEAT

It had been a blistering hot day in New York City Aug. 28 and as thousands of workers left their offices for home that Tuesday evening the temperature stood at 96 degrees. It was even hotter for many sweltering commuters who had to go down into the subway tunnels to catch their trains.

One of the trains was moving along under 42nd Street near Grand Central Terminal when a piece of the tunnel's concrete ceiling broke loose and fell on the track, setting off an electrical fire. The 20-foot chunk of concrete crumpled the door of one subway car and trapped hundreds of passengers in 115-degree heat and smoke for 90 minutes.

One man, Robert Beyer, 35, was killed. Beyer, who had been standing near the battered door, died of chest injuries. Twenty-one other persons were hospitalized for treatment of smoke inhalation, heat exhaustion and other injuries. Summed up one of the rescued passengers; "It was pretty tough down there."

FIRE AT ENTERTAINMENT CENTER TOOK 51 LIVES ON ISLE OF MAN

During the summer months, vacationers flock by the thousands to relax and enjoy on the Isle of Man, conveniently located in the Irish Sea midway between Ireland and England.

Douglas is the main resort area on the island and one of the places there that attracted the tourists was the multimillion dollar Summerland hotel and recreation complex. The seven-story building, which had facilities for up to 5,000 people, included dance halls, bars and night clubs and was billed as the world's biggest indoor entertainment center.

The center was crowded with vacationers Aug. 2 when a fire broke out and, spreading rapidly, it soon engulfed the building. The fire, according to the manager of a nearby hotel, was followed by "an explosion—a hell of a bang." Many of those in the blazing building managed to escape. But, as fire and police officers went through the wreckage, they found the bodies of 51 persons who had not been able to flee. The toll made it one of the worst tragedies over to hit the pleasant vacation island.

SWEDISH POLICE USED "OPERATION SWISS CHEESE" TO FREE HOSTAGES

"We give up. We give up. Stop gassing us."

The words were shouted to police by a trapped gunman and ended a real life drama that had begun six days earlier when a prison escapee tried to rob the main office of the Kreditbanken in Stockholm, Sweden.

The attempt by Jan Erik Olsson, 32, to rob the bank was aborted by police Aug. 23. But Olsson managed to hold off the officers, wounding one with a submachinegun. He then seized four bank employes as hostages and a six-day siege began, a drama that was watched by millions of Swedes on national television from beginning to end.

With the gunman holding the hostages—three women and a man—the police were forced to negotiate and Olsson's first demands were met. One was that Clark Olofsson, a 26-year-old

life termer for murder, be freed from prison and allowed to join Olsson in the bank. A second was that $650,000 be delivered to Olsson.

The standoff continued, however, and the police did not make their next move until Aug. 25 when they crept into the bank and slammed shut the door of the 19-by-40 foot bank vault while the gunmen and their hostages were inside, leaving them trapped without food, water or sanitary facilities. The police then thought of pumping sleeping gas into the vault but that plan fell through when Olsson said he had placed ropes around the necks of his captives and tied them along the walls. "If you use gas, the hostages will strangle," he told offiicers through holes they drilled in the vault.

The police then lowered sandwiches, drinking water and sanitary facilities through the holes

they had drilled and planned their next move. It came Aug. 28 and was called "Operation Swiss Cheese." The police drilled a series of holes through the ceiling of the vault and placed sharpshooters at each of the holes. As each new hole was drilled it narrowed the space in which the two gunmen could safely maneuver. Then, other officers wearing gas masks and bullet proof vests began to pipe tear gas into the vault and gave Olsson and Olofsson a final ultimatum to surrender. The two men did. In minutes the gunmen were in handcuffs and the hostages were on their way to a hospital.

On Aug. 29, Olsson was booked on charges of abduction, unlawful threat, armed robbery, attempted murder and extortion. Olofsson was charged by authorities with abduction and unlawful threat.

Armed police with bullet proof vests stood ready to take cover behind piled sandbags in case the bandit started a shootout

COMMONWEALTH LEADERS DISCUSSED THEIR FUTURE

The presidents, prime ministers, military leaders and cabinet members who gathered in Ottawa Aug. 2 represented the 32 countries of the former British empire, a loosely-linked Commonwealth association which covers one quarter of the earth's peoples.

Although the empire had long been dissolved, Britain's Queen Elizabeth II made a point of being on hand in Canada's capital when Prime Minister Pierre Elliott Trudeau welcomed the assembled leaders.

Much of the nine-day conference dealt in generalizations, but there were some concrete results. In one move clearly aimed at France and China, the Commonwealth leaders called unanimously for a total world ban on nuclear weapons tests in the atmosphere, the seas and space. The French and Chinese were the only two nuclear powers that had not acceded to such a ban.

The parley was shaken up at one point when Uganda's president, Idi Amin, accused Britain of racism and political immorality. The maverick East African leader's onslaught was read to the startled members by Ugandan Foreign Minister Paul Etiang. Amin taunted Britain for having permitted Israel to take over Palestine, for permitting Prime Minister Ian Smith to consolidate his minority white regime in Rhodesia and for displaying support for what he called Portugal's "murderous regime" in Mozambique and Angola.

British Prime Minister Edward Heath rejected Amin's charges as untrue and contrary to the spirit of the meeting. He added that one of Amin's references to Uganda as "a truly black state" showed that Amin himself was a racist.

Southern Africa represented the hottest and most controversial subject on the conference agenda. And the leaders wound up their talks with an agreement to toughen their policy against the white minority regimes in southern Africa.

In an apparent switch of position, Britain joined its partners in a statement that said the heads of government "recognized the legitimacy of the struggle by non-whites to win full human rights and achieve freedom with justice." It seemed to be virtually the first time the British had identified themselves with African and Asian demands to help the independence-seeking black majorities in the apartheid state of South Africa, the rebel colony of Rhodesia and Portugal's African territories.

FOR THE RECORD

CONVICTED. Five young black men, for the slaying on St. Croix in the U.S. Virgin Islands of seven whites and one black person at the Fountain Valley Golf Club on Sept. 6, 1972 *(The World in 1972, 198.)* The five were given eight consecutive life terms each on Aug. 13.

Two zebras with but a single thought stared at a visitor at a game preserve in Stockbridge, Ga. The head belonged to the one on the left

Passengers rode a festively decorated cable car down a San Francisco street on Aug. 2 during a ceremony marking the 100th anniversary of the famed cars

After 18 Years of Exile, Juan Peron Returned to Power As President of Argentina

Walls in Buenos Aires were plastered with posters hailing Peron's return

Y<small>OU SIT</small> down to talk to Peron," said Juan J. Taccone, an Argentine labor union leader, "and in a few minutes he wins you into his world. The man feels what the people want . . . He has a charisma that must be rare in history."

Juan Domingo Peron's world was filled with violent contradictions in 1973. But 62 per cent of Argentina's voters elected him president anyway on Sept. 23. Most were won over by Peron's promise to reform Argentina "without hard and drastic revolution."

"I permit everyone in my movement," Peron said in a television interview shortly before his Oct. 12 inauguration. "We don't have prejudices and the movement has men of the extreme right and the extreme left."

The statement was an example of Peron's "pendulum politics." The phrase described the 78-year-old caudillo's [leader's] ability to swing from the left to the right, attracting both capitalists and Marxists to his giant movement.

"If I were Chinese, I would have been a follower of Mao," Peron said in February. The pendulum had swung to the right by October, when Peron donned a peacock-hued army general's uniform and once again took the oath of office.

"I am a Peronist and therefore I am not a Marxist," Peron told leaders of the Justicialist party, the political wing of Peronism. They were convened and told to rid the movement of "Marxist infiltrators."

That wasn't the approach which brought Peron back to the Argentine presidency after an 18-year period of exile and disgrace. During exile, Peron had nurtured the myth of a popular leader interested only in serving Argentina—and quite willing to correct the mistakes of his first presidency. Students, businessmen, union leaders, economists, landowners, athletes, theater people, writers, artists, even urban guerrillas, came to Peron's mansion in Madrid to talk for hours, to walk with him in the garden, to stay for dinner and to be won over.

Dr. Rolando Garcia, 54, a former university dean and a U.S.-trained meteorologist, was one of the converts. He headed a team of professionals assigned by Peron to develop socialist programs for possible adoption.

Garcia was among thousands of students who fought against Peronism during the caudillo's first presidency, from 1946 to 1955. Most young intellectuals hated Peron's paternalistic dictatorship, modeled on Mussolini's Italy.

"I was profoundly anti-Peronist and anti-fascist when Peron was president," Garcia said. "However, in 1968, when I was depressed about the political situation and saw no end to the military regime, Peron sent word he wanted to see me in Madrid. I went, mostly out of curiosity. I told Peron at the start of the conversation that I had been violently anti-Peronist during his government. He said, 'Yes, yes, I know all that, but let's talk.' He then stated flatly, with remarkable insight, that Peronism would return to power. I couldn't see how, but Peron said he wanted my help.

"He said he wanted to end the division between Peronism and intellectuals. He made me see that Peronism had awakened the laboring masses, given them rights, and for that reason had evolved into an irreversible popular movement heading toward socialism."

During those years in exile, Peron won thousands of young radicals to his movement, and many in Argentina's new middle class. He did it by promising "national socialism," a program of Marxist and non-Marxist reforms far more radical than the labor legislation of Peron's first presidency. He praised left-wing urban guerrilla organizations and said their violence was a natural reaction to the brutality of the military government which ruled Argentina from 1967 until May of 1973. He said young people were Argentina's hope and he named a 27-year-old lawyer, Juan Manuel Abal Medina, as one of his chief advisers in exile.

Peron owed a lot to the Peronist Youth. They staged countless demonstrations, rallies and acts of violence on his behalf. Their pressure was decisive in convincing the military regime to hold general elections for a civilian government. But the young people remained only a small fraction of Peronism, although the most vocal. The union-organized workers, more interested in better pay than ideology, "are the backbone which has kept our movement erect all these years," Peron declared.

Nevertheless, he did not greet these workers at rallies, as he had done so frequently 25 years earlier. Age made Peron less active. And Peronist functions sometimes were disrupted by young militants who chanted demands that Peron lead a Marxist revolution.

Once, when more than a thousand people came to Peron's three-story Tudor-style home in a Buenos Aires suburb, the aging politician slipped away unnoticed.

Security became a major problem. Leftist guerrillas ready to support Peron in January, turned against him in August, and warred with union leaders and other Peronists they labeled reactionaries. There were four political assassinations in the month preceding the Oct. 12 inauguration. That day, Peron and his pretty wife, Isabel, a 42-year-old former ballerina, appeared on a balcony at Casa Rosada, the pink presidential palace. But an almost opaque, bullet-proof glass shielded them.

"This government will continue the old Peronist custom so that each year I must present myself in this same spot to ask the people if they are satisfied with what we are doing," Peron declared, coming from behind the bullet-proof glass for a moment to acknowledge the cheers. His hair was dyed to the rich black color of 25 years ago, and his broad smile made him appear vigorous. But Peron's voice was hoarse and weak and he suffered from a prostate condition and other ailments.

In his heyday after World War II, Peron had appeared almost every month on that same second-story balcony at Casa Rosada. His blonde wife, Eva, who died of cancer in 1952 at the age of 33, shared the limelight and together they stretched their arms emotionally toward the cheering, chanting multitude. Peron spoke for hours into the night about the "new Argentina," in reality a paternalistic dictatorship.

Invariably, he would finish up declaring the following day "St. Peron's Day"—a holiday with pay for the entire audience.

These were the descamisados—the shirtless ones. Today most are skilled workers. Under Peron, the Argentine workingman achieved a sense of dignity he never had known before. Peronist legislation raised wages, instituted severance pay,

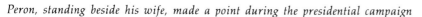

Peron, standing beside his wife, made a point during the presidential campaign

guaranteed vacations, extended social security, fixed the 40-hour week, and started the aguinaldo. This is a "13th month" salary which must be paid to all wage earners.

Eva was a great political asset to Peron and her death was a blow to his dictatorship. She institutionalized charity, distributing millions of dollars in food, clothing and gifts to the poor. Almost daily she received poor people in her office, listened to their problems and usually gave them money which she took from her desk.

Peron met Isabel less than a year after the armed forces deposed him in September, 1955 and chased him from the country aboard a Paraguayan gunboat. The ex-dictator was living in a hotel in Colon, a Panama port city. Isabel, a professional dancer, was appearing in a Panama night club and the two were introduced. Soon, the slightly-built brunette, then 25, was Peron's secretary, taking an interest in politics for the first time. They were married after moving to Madrid in 1960.

Isabel, daughter of rural bank manager, lacked Eva's fiery spirit. But she dressed with the same elegance as her predecessor, and she attempted to imitate Eva's fervor in public speeches. The Eva Peron Foundation which Eva had created to distribute charity throughout the country, was reorganized under Isabel, who toured shantytowns and hospitals as Eva had done. Isabel declared publicly that she was the custodian of Eva's spirit, and was filling the shoes of the woman still adored by many of Argentina's 24 million people.

Peron made his first return from exile Nov. 17, 1972, but stayed in Argentina only 28 days. It was long enough to organize a coalition for the March 11 general election; a coalition dominated by Peron's Justicialist party, but including other small parties. The military junta, headed by Lt. Gen. Alejandro Lanusse, decreed that Peron could not be the presidential candidate, so a surrogate was designated. He was Dr. Hector J. Campora, a 63-year-old dentist and former congressman. Campora had been serving as the exiled Peron's personal representative in Argentina and he campaigned in Peron's name while the aging caudillo watched from Madrid.

Campora was to win and to become president. But he ruled less than two months, then resigned in favor of Peron.

The Peronist campaign slogan was, "Campora to government, Peron to power." The genial Campora was dubbed "uncle" while Peron was the "father." Against eight other presidential candidates, Campora was expected to get 35 to 40 per cent of the vote on March 11, and then win in a run-off a month later. Instead, he received just over 49 per cent and a stunned military junta conceded victory to the Peronists without a run-off.

The conservative armed forces, which had dominated politics since Peron's downfall in 1955, finally were defeated. In the process, Peron's original labor union base had been expanded. It now included not only leftists, but thousands in the middle and upper classes who saw Peronism as an exciting popular movement; the best hope to solve Argentina's severe economic problems.

Peronism became fashionable. Actors, actresses and writers appeared on television talk shows to explain their conversions. A newspaper described the reaction of Horacio Rodriguez Larreta to Campora's election victory. Rodriguez Larreta, a wealthy jet-set friend of Marlon Brando and Jules Dassin, joined a victory parade, ripping off his shirt to salute workers. It was a gesture used by many young men to express spiritual solidarity with Peron's original "shirtless ones"—his poor supporters of the 40s.

After the election, Isabel Peron visited the People's Republic of China and strengthened her husband's image as a Marxist. He stayed in Europe, assuring French, Italian and German businessmen that Argentina needed their investment capital. U.S. businessmen received similar assurances in Buenos Aires. But this was done privately by Peron's aides. In public, Peron called America an imperialist nation.

In so heterogeneous a movement, there was conflict. Gunfire and clashes with police forced the authorities to cancel some of the ceremonies at Campora's May 25 inauguration, attended by Presidents Osvaldo Dorticos of Cuba and Salvador Allende of Chile. They appeared on nationwide television with Campora and stood beside him as he received the presidential sash. U.S. Secretary of State William P. Rogers, representing President Nixon, spent most of his visit at his hotel.

The crisis came June 20. That was the day Peron ended his exile and flew home from Europe. Encouraged by the government, more than one million people gathered in fields near Ezeiza International Airport to greet Peron and to hear him speak from a platform set up on a highway overpass.

Peron never saw the crowd. There was a gunfight which intensified as his plane neared Buenos Aires. The aircraft was diverted to a military airport, and the Perons went by helicopter to their home.

Many in the huge and festive crowd were caught in the cross fire. Police reported weeks later that 100 were killed. The combatants were from two Peronist camps. They fought for control of the speaker's platform and the spectator's area around the platform. Old Guard Peronists and tough security men from the union organizations occupied the platform and the surrounding area early in the day. They represented Peronism's conservative wing. Around noon, columns of young people, some carrying the banners of urban guerrilla groups, tried to occupy the area nearest the platform and the battle started. The shooting was still out of control when Peron's plane landed in late afternoon.

Thereafter, Peron moved steadily away from the leftists in his movement. Orders went out to arrest urban guerrillas, many of them recently freed from jail under a Peronist-sponsored amnesty. After Campora's resignation, two leftists—Esteban Righi, the interior minister, and Juan Carlos Puig, the foreign minister—were dropped from the cabinet. Other ministers continued to serve under interim president Raul Lastiri. Congress named Lastiri to serve until Peron could be elected Sept. 23 and installed in October along with his wife. Isabel became the western hemisphere's first woman vice president.

Peron was born in 1895 in Lobos, a rural town, and raised on a family farm. He entered a military academy at 15, shortly after he was sent to Buenos Aires to study. Some of Peron's ideas on economics and on Argentina's place in the world began to formulate while he was serving as a military attache in Mussolini's Italy at the outbreak of World War II. Since then Peronism has insisted that the United States and Russia are the two dominant imperialist powers. The submerged countries of Latin America are struggling to free themselves from this domination, Peronism holds, just as Western Europe has struggled since World War II.

"I believe completely in the inverse of what some affirm: that we cannot live without the United States," Peron has said. "I am convinced that the worst affliction of our peoples is precisely the economic, political and social intervention of the United States in Latin America. Either the North Americans modify this scheme of penetration, or we will have in a few years, multiplied by 100, the drama of Cuba versus the United States."

Demonstrations erupted in Santiago's streets

Bloody Revolution Ended Three Years of Marxist Government in Chile

Smoke billowing from the presidential palace and firemen removing the poncho-wrapped body of Salvador Allende stamped an end to Chile's tortured search for "The Road To Socialism."

Allende, a cocky, quotable, nonpracticing doctor, upset his traditional foes in elections Sept. 4, 1970, and became the western hemisphere's first freely-elected Marxist president.

Three years, eight days later on Sept. 12, 1973, he was dead, of self-inflicted bullet wounds according to police, and an anti-Communist military junta was in control.

Nearly a thousand persons were killed in shoot-outs that erupted after the early morning coup. Scores of prisoners were executed, either by military patrols or after drumhead courts-martial. Santiago's national soccer stadium became a prison for more than 7,000 suspected "extremists", and key leaders of the Allende years were sent to—windswept Dawson Island in the Straits of Magellan.

State-of-siege decrees, including an overnight curfew with shoot-to-kill orders, kept a lid on the capital and its three million residents.

The military took steps to swing Chile from the left to the right, severing relations with Cuba, the Soviet Union and other communist bloc countries while welcoming strong ties with the United States and Western Europe.

Allende's supporters went underground to try to build a guerrilla network as the junta pondered plans for a new constitution and eventual elections.

Allende, had dedicated most of his 65 years to the cause of Marxism and a quest for the presidency. He made the race three times and was soundly defeated until his Radical Socialist party and the communists put together a Popular Unity coalition that squeaked through to victory in 1970.

Allende received only 36.6 per cent of the popular vote, but this was a commanding plurality over the divided Christian Democrats and the National party. Congress formally elected him president in October. He was installed in office Nov. 3.

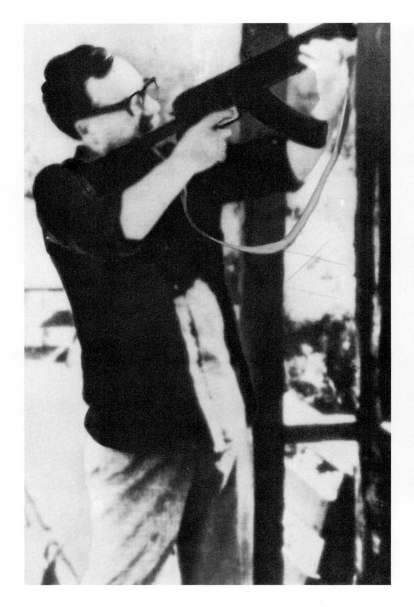

Left, the late President Salvador Allende indulged in target practice with a Russian-made submachine gun shortly before his death

In one of his first speeches, Allende vowed to take Chile "down the road to socialism," but within the framework of the constitution.

He acted quickly, nationalizing the immense holdings of three U.S. firms in mines that produced 80 per cent of the country's copper wealth. Private banks were taken over. Expropriation of large estates was acclerated with the land redistributed to peasants. When the process lagged, peasants seized property and the government tacitly acknowledged their squatters' "rights."

Allende's nationalization of the copper mines carried him to an early peak in popularity, with most of Chileans agreeing that the mineral was a national wealth which had been exploited too long by foreign interests.

A year later, Allende made a critical decision. He said no compensation would be paid to the U.S. copper companies, claiming they actually owed Chile $774 million for "excess profits" taken from the country since 1955.

The companies used international courts to hamper Chile's ore shipments and strained relations between the United States and Allende's government cut sharply into Chile's foreign credits.

Coupled with the copper dispute was a sharp decline in both agricultural and industrial production. Many supervisors appointed by the government to manage nationalized factories proved inefficient, absenteeism mounted and peasants who had

seized farms grew only enough food to feed themselves. Inflation went sky high.

Allende's pledge to introduce socialism caused a deadlock in Congress, where his Popular Unity coalition was outnumbered 93–57 in the House of Deputies and 38–18 in the Senate.

As positions hardened, with Chile's growing middle class providing the backbone of the opposition, Allende struggled to keep his floundering government afloat. In less than three years he was forced to make 24 cabinet changes.

With his government under fire, Allende sought help abroad. He traveled to Russia and its satellites, receiving pledges of aid and technical assistance.

In Havana, prime minister Fidel Castro gave Allende an inscribed, rapid-firing carbine. Thousands of arms, including anti-tank bazookas and machine guns, were shipped into Chile clandestinely from Cuba, Czechoslovakia and the Soviet Union, some crated in cartons listed as gifts of art.

By October 1972 the government was in deep trouble. A month-long general strike paralyzed the country and in desperation Allende named three military men to his cabinet to restore order. He managed a precarious balancing act for months, then on June 29, 1973, gunfire rang out at the presidential palace.

Some 100 members of the army's second armored regiment sought to oust Allende in a bloody attack masterminded by an extreme right-wing group, Fatherland and Liberty. Loyal units

Above, Army troops protected themselves from sniper fire. Right, Allende supporter held a machine gun on the balcony of Government House

crushed the revolt, but 22 persons were killed and 34 were wounded.

Fatherland and Liberty leaders fled into exile but an alarmed Allende told his followers there would be other efforts to remove him and he declared "I will only leave . . . (the palace) . . . in a pine box."

Allende was not the only worried person around. Opposition politicians claimed the president was developing a force of leftist militants, built around a cadre of foreign guerrillas from Uruguay, Brazil and other Latin American countries who gained asylum in Chile when it got too hot for them at home. They said 14,000 foreign extremists were welcomed into Chile by Allende and many were given government posts.

The tottering economy received a blow July 24 when 40,000 private truckers, fearing nationalization of their industry, went on strike.

Doctors and other professional groups staged brief strikes to support the truckers and the military became increasingly nervous as the economy began collapsing.

Allende began rejuggling his cabinet again. He named the chieftains of the army, navy, air force and national police to ministries in a bid for stability, but it didn't work.

After only nine days the air force commander who had been transport minister resigned because of the government's inability to settle the truckers' strike.

Allende, sensing his isolation from the traditionally neutral armed forces, appointed new commanders and placed lesser ranking military officers in his cabinet.

The Christian Democrats, Chile's largest single political group, had broken off talks with Allende's coalition in August, saying he refused to yield any ground. This didn't please the generals, who had hoped for a compromise.

Striking truckers agreed to 13 of 14 demands, but insisted that congress pass a law ordering Allende to honor his commitments.

By the first of September it was clear that the truckers and their allies had raised their sights—they would settle for nothing less than Allende's resignation half way through his six-year term.

With congress and the executive branch deadlocked, strike talks stalemated and the antagonists increasingly frustrated, the power play moved into the streets.

On Sept. 4, the anniversary of his election victory, more than 150,000 of Allende's supporters poured into the capital. They paraded past the palace on foot and in farm trucks and tractors.

Allende, in a brief speech, warned again of a pending coup and said "I will never resign."

The following day the youth movement of the Conservative National party called a rally in front of congress to demonstrate support of the striking truckers. Several thousand had gathered when shots were fired from nearby buildings and several young men fell wounded. Police moved in quickly, but the heart of the city was ravaged for hours by bands of teen-agers throwing debris at tear gas-firing police.

The next day, anti-Allende womens-groups called a demonstration in front of Catholic University and more than 100,000

Left, Chilean soldiers burned Marxist literature. Right, members of the junta attending a religious ceremony after their takeover

persons gathered, many marching in columns led by pot-pounding women with banners demanding the president resign.

Then thousands of youths, some wearing construction helmets and carrying clubs or chains, started marching on the palace 10 blocks away. Leftist militants who had gathered at the palace, set forth to meet them and a thin line of khaki-clad police was in the middle.

Water cannon trucks could not disperse the angry mobs and the police reverted to tear gas again.

Shops remained shuttered, high school and university students were in the streets instead of their classes, there was no heating oil and little gasoline or food in Santiago.

Officers of the conservative navy, who discovered a plot by militant leftist infiltrators to capture several ships, prepared to seize Valparaiso, Chile's second largest city and site of the navy's main base.

On Sept. 5, Gen. Augusto Pinochet, army commander, held secret talks with the air force and navy chieftains, Gen. Gustavo Leigh and Adm. Jose Toribio Merino, and the head of the national police, Gen. Cesar Mendoza. These men would become the new junta, ending 46 years of democratic rule in Chile.

"I don't think even my wife knew—of the planned coup," Pinochet was to tell newsmen later.

Allende, huddling with his advisers and surrounded by bodyguards, agreed to try and revive talks with the Christian Dem-

ocrats. Raul Cardinal Silva Henriquez offered his services as a mediator.

Gen. Leigh, at a news conference several days after the coup, said the commanders made their decision Sept. 9, to overthrow Allende.

"At that point it was irrevocable," he said, "The country was in chaos, subverted by foreign Marxist extremists. Peasants were not working, factories were closed, students did not go to school. It could not continue."

On Sept. 10, five warships left Valparaiso, ostensibly to join U.S. Navy vessels for joint training exercises. Shortly before midnight the Communist party warned its top officials of unusual military activity, and some began packing get-away bags.

Allende stayed up most of the night at his official residence studying urgent reports coming in from his lieutenants.

His fears were confirmed when a Cuban freighter, the Playa Larga, spotted the Chilean warships returning to Valparaiso at 1 a.m. on Sept. 11 and radioed the information to the Cuban embassy for relay to Allende. The report was intercepted by the navy vessels and jet fighters strafed the Cuban ship as it steamed for international waters.

Navy units seized Valparaiso, 90 miles northwest of Santiago. Police and troops sealed off the university section in Concepcion, 300 miles south of the capital. Concepcion was a center of radical activities and birthplace of the radical leftist movement (MIR) but the security patrols seized most of the wanted men without resistance.

Allende raced to the presidential palace, his limousine shielded by other cars carrying his Cuban-trained bodyguards. Palace police surrounded the building and parked half a dozen armored cars at the entrances.

The president broadcast a brief speech over a leftist-controlled radio network and told his listeners "I am now awaiting a decision from the army to defend the government."

The junta gave Allende until 11 a.m. to resign or face attack.

Allende again went on the air to make his last public declaration.

"I will not resign. I will not do it," he shouted. "I state my decision to resist with whatever means available, even at the cost of my life."

There were negotiations, with Army Gen. Ernesto Baeza representing the Junta and Allende's general secretary, Fernando Florez, speaking for his chief.

Air force jets would bomb the palace if Allende and an estimated 70 armed guards and government employes did not surrender, he was told. The police, informed that their command had joined the junta, retired from the palace.

Allende asked for a brief truce to permit about a dozen women to leave the palace. Sporadic sniping began from leftists in nearby government buildings—the mayor's headquarters, central bank, finance ministry and others.

At 11:05 a.m. the military carried out its threat. Jets wheeled in from the north and dropped several light bombs on the palace. They circled and returned a half dozen times.

Sniping increased and army tanks returned the fire. In the Carrera Sheraton hotel, guests who had ringside seats for the drama dove to the floor as their windows were shattered by the gunfire.

At noon the tanks started shelling the palace. A two-hour battle followed and then white cloths were waved from the building in surrender and troops charged into the building.

In a second-story salon they found the body of Allende, slumped on a red sofa, his face partially destroyed by bullet wounds. Invitations for a dinner celebrating Chile's anniversary of independence Sept. 18 were scattered across the floor.

The front section of the palace was ablaze and firemen wrapped the body in a poncho and carried it from the building to a waiting ambulance where it was taken to a military hospital for an autopsy.

The official report: Allende was armed with the carbine that Castro had given him. Gunpowder on his hands indicated he had been shooting at the troops. After giving his guards permission to surrender he entered the salon, placed the muzzle of his carbine at his chin and pulled the trigger, firing two quick rounds into his brain.

Jets also rocketed Allende's official residence when guards shot at approaching soldiers but Allende's wife escaped without injury and fled to asylum in the Mexican embassy, already crowded with nearly 500 political refugees. Later she was flown to Mexico City.

More than a thousand leftist government officials and politicians sought asylum in foreign embassies, but thousands of others were seized and held for questioning in the national stadium.

Summary executions were authorized for persons caught "in the act" of attacking army patrols or sabotage. In less than a month the toll of persons executed on the spot or after hurried courts-martial numbered 33.

Casualty lists indicated that nearly 500 persons were killed during the coup and fighting that raged for days afterward. At least 7,000 persons were arrested, according to government officials.

Police sources estimated that both number of dead and prisoners were higher than the government count.

Diplomatic relations were broken with Cuba in less than 24 hours after the coup. In following days the Soviet Union and its European satellites ended relations with Chile and recalled their diplomats.

Films shown over the junta-controlled television revealed huge arms caches uncovered in the presidential palace and official residence, including Soviet machine guns, antitank bazookas and hundreds of automatic rifles.

Government spokesmen said a "plan Z", found in a palace safe, set forth a scheme to assassinate the military commanders and opposition politicians on the eve of Armed Forces Day Sept. 12.

Gen. Leigh told newsmen that Allende had brought in 14,000 extremists from other Latin American countries and Cuban officers were giving them guerrilla training.

After making certain that the junta had full control, Britain, the United States and scores of other nations recognized the new government.

Government leaders said factories and farms illegally seized by workers would be returned to their owners and negotiations would resume with the U.S. companies over compensation for their copper mining losses. But they made it clear that the mines and many other industries nationalized by Allende would remain under government control.

Skylab 2's Astronauts Set a Record For Living in Space Despite Rocket Problems

THE SKYLAB 2 astronauts were just five days into their planned two-month mission when serious trouble struck. It was 5:40 a.m. Aug. 2, and the astronauts were still asleep.

Suddenly, a master alarm sounded, sending a shrill buzzing through the house-size, space station and jolted the astronauts awake. Navy Capt. Alan L. Bean, 41, scientist Dr. Owen K. Garriott, 42, and Marine Maj. Jack R. Lousma, 37, scrambled to a control panel in their attached Apollo ferry ship, where the alarm was buzzing.

Working with ground controllers, they located the trouble. Pressures and temperatures were falling rapidly in Quad Delta, one of four sets of steering rockets on Apollo's service module. A fuel line had sprung a leak. This was serious since Quad Bravo, one of the other steering rockets, had earlier developed a leak and had been disabled. That left only two rockets to guide the craft through critical re-entry maneuvers when it was time for the astronauts to return to earth. One was enough to do the job, but the flying task would be tricky.

Mission Control was concerned. Seventeen Apollo spaceships had flown in space, including nine to the vicinity of the moon, and there had never been a quad failure. Experts asked: What was causing the leaks? Was there a common cause that could spread to the other two quads and to the large main engine needed to brake the Apollo out of orbit? Fuel for all these engines came from the same source. Was this fuel contaminated?

For anxious hours, space agency officials debated the choices before them, including a quick return to earth by the astronauts. But this idea was discarded because the Skylab station itself was in good condition and could support the crew for several weeks until a rescue mission could be launched, if necessary.

Skylab director William C. Schneider ordered emergency preparation of a rescue rocket at Cape Kennedy, Fla., with more than 1,000 engineers and technicians working 12-hour shifts around the clock to get it ready for a launching as early as Sept. 5. Skylab backup astronauts Vance D. Brand and Don L. Lind began training to fly the rescue craft, an Apollo modified to carry five men.

Analysis determined there was no contamination in the batch of fuel at Cape Kennedy from which the Apollo drew its supply. And exhaustive study of radio data showed that the two quad failures were not connected.

Dr. Christopher C. Kraft, director of the Johnson Space Center at Houston, Tex., radioed the astronauts: "We feel fairly confident that we've got two quads for altitude control . . . We're proceeding here as if we're going to have a normal mission. We feel that's the proper way to go." As a precaution, he said, rescue preparations would continue.

"You said just the right words," replied Bean, the Skylab 2 commander. "We've been hoping you'd say that. We've been

On a tail of fire, the Skylab II rocket lifted off from Cape Kennedy

sort of concerned, and I think I speak for Jack and Owen and I know for myself, we're pretty happy with the way things are going at the moment.

"We feel we still have the capability to return home safely. We agree with you 100 per cent."

The problem developed just as Bean, Garriott and Lousma were recovering from bad cases of motion sickness that had plagued them since their arrival at the station July 28. Doctors blamed the illness on the fact that they had entered the station and began moving around in its cavernous interior soon after they linked up with it.

The Skylab 1 crew, which earlier had inhabited the laboratory for 28 days, remained in the smaller Apollo ship overnight and thus had a chance to adapt to the weightless world before entering the station. The Skylab 2 astronauts, especially Lousma, were barely able to perform routine housekeeping and experiment chores. Their first space walk was delayed several days. But once they recovered, there was no stopping them. They asked that the working day be extended; they gave up all eight of their scheduled days off and soon made up for lost time. By mission's end they had conducted 50 per cent more experiments than had been planned.

On the 10th day, Garriott and Lousma donned bulky white space suits and stepped outside the orbiting lab.

"Oh, what a view," Garriott exclaimed as he gazed down at earth. Looking out into space, Lousma commented: "There's nothing except a bit of light reflecting off the solar panels, a few stars and a half moon."

During the stroll, the astronauts worked four hours to erect a second sunshade over an area on the station where a protective heat shade had ripped away during the launch of the lab May 14. The Skylab 1 astronauts has raised one shade to cool down the Skylab, but it was beginning to deteriorate from constant bombardment by the sun's rays.

Lousma and Garriott also replaced film in their solar telescope array and set up a micrometeorite-measuring experiment. They were outside 6 hours and 31 minutes, nearly doubling the space walk endurance record set two months earlier by the first Skylab crew.

Two more shorter walks were conducted during the mission, one by Garriott and Lousma and one by Bean and Garriott. Both times the telescope film was changed, and on the second, a new set of gyroscopes was installed to help keep the station on an even keel. Otherwise, the astronauts busied themselves with earth resources, solar astronomy, metals processing and other experiments. They took weekly showers and generally seemed to enjoy themselves in their space home.

To keep their heart and other muscles from deconditioning too much because of lack of use in weightlessness, each exercised about an hour a day on a bicycle-like device.

Garriott, a solar physicist, had the time of his life observing the sun through the telescopes since it was very active for a period that was supposed to have been quiet. More than 100 flare eruptions were observed.

The flares spewed radiation into space and created magnetic storms in earth's atmosphere, causing brilliant aurora displays at both poles. "Because of all this activity we even saw in one day two auroras—both the northern lights and the southern light, which must be a record for anybody. It was fantastic," Garriott said.

The astronauts also had fun watching a couple of spiders, Arabella and Anita, in an experiment to determine if their web spinning was affected by weightlessness. After a few days of adaptation, each was able to weave a near-normal pattern.

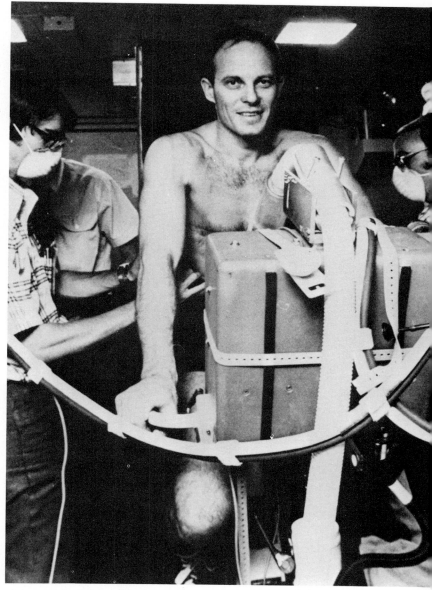

Astronaut Jack Lousma was tested to see how much work he could perform when returned to the gravity of earth

As the mission neared an end, Mission Control radioed procedures for flying the Apollo ferry ship with the two good steering rockets. Ground-based astronauts tested them in spacecraft simulators and informed Bean there would be no trouble. They were right. On Sept. 25, Bean, Garriott and Lousma finished deactivating the Skylab station and climbed through a connecting tunnel into the Apollo.

They cast off and flew a perfect re-entry, parachuting into the Pacific Ocean just six miles from the main recovery ship, the helicopter carrier USS New Orleans. The big ship came alongside and a crane hoisted the spaceship to the deck just 40 minutes after splashdown. Bean, Garriott and Lousma had been in space a record 59 days, 11 hours, 9 minutes.

A NASA flight surgeon climbed into the cabin to check the astronauts before they got out to make certain they had suffered no serious effects from their long exposure to weightlessness.

Then the spacemen walked out a little unsteadily, but waving and smiling at the hundreds of sailors on the deck. They quickly went to a medical facility for examination. Later, doctors reported none of the astronauts suffered from motion sickness and all three had normal blood pressures and heart

Scientist-Astronaut Owen K. Garriott performed extra-vehicular activity at the Apollo Telescope Mount of the space station

rates. There was some evidence of "vestibular disturbance," such as dizziness. But this was expected as part of the process of readapting to earth's gravity.

By the next day they were in excellent condition and flew to their homes in Houston for reunions with their families. Garriott told a welcoming crowd the mission had "days of adventure, days of hard work and there was even time for a little fun."

Experts, meanwhile began the long job of sorting out the 1,200 pounds of experiment data returned by the astronauts. Included were 77,600 photos of the sun and more than 12,000 pictures and 18 miles of computer tape gathered during earth resources surveys.

About the solar photos, Dr. Neil R. Sheeley of the Naval Research Laboratory said: "We've never had data of this superb quality. Now we've got the possibility of answering questions that we've only had clues to for years." He said such data

could help scientists better understand the sun and how it affected the entire solar system.

The astronauts conducted 39 earth resources passes, 13 more than planned. Most were over the United States, but at the request of other governments, four each were made over South America, Africa and Europe and one each over Australia, Japan and the Mediterranean.

Dr. James C. Fletcher, administrator of the National Aeronautics and Space Administration, said years might be required to completely evaluate all the data, but predicted it would prove man had a role to play in space.

"Space is a place, a very unique place and a new important resource that can be used for the benefit of people everywhere on earth," Fletcher said. "It provides us with a vantage point from which we can look outward toward the sun and stars and inward toward the earth to gather information impossible to collect on the ground."

LIBYAN DECREE CALLED FOR 51 PER CENT TAKEOVER OF OIL HOLDINGS

In oil-rich Libya, Sept. 1 was a special day: It marked the fourth anniversary of the revolution that toppled King Idris and installed a revolutionary military regime headed by Col. Moammar Khadafy.

Highlighting the commemoration in 1973 was the issuance of a decree. Signed by Premier Abdel Salam Jalloud and Oil Minister Ezzedin Marbrouk it called for a 51 per cent takeover of the holdings of all major oil companies which still operated independently in Libya.

It followed the June nationalization of the operations of Bunker-Hunt, a U.S. owned firm. Libya said that was a move against U.S. support for Israel, and Khadafy noted there was a need "to deal America a strong slap on its cool, arrogant face." After that several other oil firms—including Continental, Marathon, Amerada Hess and Occidental—bowed to Libyan pressure and sold out 51 per cent of their interests at bargain prices.

The remaining foreign oil firms caught by the September decree were Amoseas Oil Co.—jointly owned by Texaco and Standard Oil of California—Mobil Oil, the Esso Standard group—including Atlantic Richfield—and Royal Dutch Shell.

Libya told the firms they could continue to transport oil from the country provided ship papers indicated Libya's 51 per cent ownership.

EXPLOSION REPORTEDLY KILLED THREE AT LENIN'S MAUSOLEUM

The Lenin Mausoleum on Moscow's Red Square is the first thing most foreign tourists head for when they visit the Soviet Union. The mausoleum stands next to the red brick wall of the Kremlin and it holds the body of the founder of the Soviet state who died in 1924.

On Sept. 1, visitors were lined up waiting their turn to see the tomb when, according to usually reliable Soviet sources, a bomb exploded and killed three persons, although it did not greatly damage the tomb.

Soviet media kept silent about the blast, but the sources said the explosion was set off by a device carried by an unidentified man. They said the man was killed as were two women waiting in line. The man, they said, apparently was insane.

DENMARK HOTEL FIRE CLAIMED LIVES OF 35 FOREIGN TRAVELERS

"It was horrifying. Everywhere women and children screamed for help," a survivor recalled of the Sept. 1 fire which raced through the Hafnia, a 74-year-old popular family hotel and tourist landmark close to Town Hall Square in Copenhagen, Denmark.

Many of the 83 guests registered at the hotel were foreign tourists and of these 35 died in the flames. Nineteen of the dead were Americans and the rest other foreign tourists. It was the worst hotel fire in Denmark's history.

The flames turned the upper three stories of the plush five-story hotel into an inferno. Police said many of the dead died in their beds, overcome by smoke. Others fell to their deaths from window ledges and roofs and still others were buried under tons of debris as staircases and ceilings collapsed.

CHOLERA OUTBREAK IN ITALY TOOK 23 LIVES, SICKENED HUNDREDS

Mussels are called "cozze" in Italian, and they are especially popular in the southern part of that country where they are served raw with a splash of lemon. In Naples, the waterfront area was dotted with small stands that specialized in selling the tasty fish to passersby.

But the popularity of mussels—as well as that of many other kinds of fish—fell drastically in late August and early September as a cholera outbreak hit Italy and authorities blamed mussels as the source of the sickness.

In an effort to bring the outbreak under control, frogmen invaded the Bay of Naples and destroyed hundreds of tons of mussels, leaving 90 families without their only source of income. "Who else can give me a job at 60?" asked Cirillo De Crescenzio, one of the mussel growers. "I came to work here with my father when I was six. I cannot be happy anywhere else." Said another as he pointed to four drains letting the city's sewage out into the harbor where the mussel beds were, "The disease came from there. The sewage has been pouring out for years. Why are we suffering now for the city's failure to keep the sea clean?"

Despite the protests, mussel beds also were destroyed on the Adriatic coast near Bari, Italy's second worst stricken city. A nationwide ban on the shellfish was imposed and, as a side effect, consumption of all fish in Italy dropped sharply.

The outbreak began to recede near the end of September, but it left 23 dead and several hundred ill as well as bringing the lucrative tourist season to an abrupt end in most of peninsular Italy. As the cholera disappeared, so did thousands of jobs in tourism, fishing and commerce. The tourist business dropped an estimated 75 per cent, and the Association of Fish Traders estimated the industry lost over $17.6 million in the first two weeks alone of the outbreak.

Feeling the need for an outstanding tower, Kuwait has built three of them at a cost of $13 million. The towers, soaring nearly 600 feet skyward, were designed to include a revolving restaurant for 200 persons and a tourist center

Left, Heavyweight boxing champ George Foreman presented a trophy and a check for $100,000 to Billie Jean King after she defeated Bobby Riggs in their winner-take-all tennis match. Right, a tired Bobby Riggs walked off the court near the end of his third match with Billie Jean King

REQUIEM FOR A HUSTLER

There was a blare of trumpets, and the strains of "I Am Woman" rang through the huge, bustling arena. In came Billie Jean King, smiling and waving, borne over a golden carpet in a litter by four muscled young men. She could have been a modern day Cleopatra. Within moments from another portal appeared aging, bespectacled Bobby Riggs, teeth gleaming under the arc lights, riding a ricksha like a Kubla Khan. The ricksha was pulled by eight lovely ladies in red shorts. The band struck up, "Anything You Can Do I Can Do Better," from the stage play, "Annie Get Your Gun."

There was an exchange of gifts at court side. Bobby presented Billie Jean with a four-foot popsicle. Billie Jean responded by handing Bobby a small, brown pig in a Christmas-wrapped box.

It was the moment the world had waited for—the celebrated, ballyhooed tennis Battle of the Sexes, the ultimate hustle of a 55-year-old has-been who bounced from obscurity and conned the world by insulting the flower of our culture—womanhood.

"I'm fed up with women's lib," the veteran Riggs snapped one day. "They keep yelling for equal opportunity. I am an old man with one foot in the grave, but I can beat any woman tennis player in the world."

Then he added: "The way to treat women is to keep them barefoot and pregnant."

Women all over the world fumed. Billie Jean fumed most of all. But she turned down a challenge to play Riggs in a $10,000 winner-take-all match. The great Margaret Court of Australia took up the cudgel only to be humiliated 6–2, 6–1 on Mother's Day, May 13, 1973, in a remote development outside San Diego, California.

Billie Jean could stand it no longer. She had to shut Bobby Riggs' big mouth, she said. She called him a "creep," an "egotist" and a "male chauvinist pig" and took his dare for a match.

She was encouraged by a $100,000 offer from Jerry Perenchio, Los Angeles television producer and co-promoter of the $20 million Muhammad Ali-Joe Frazier heavyweight title fight in March, 1971. Perenchio recognized the match as more than a sports contest. He saw it as an event of deep social implication—the frustrated middle aged man against the militant woman libber. It would divide and excite the world—and it did just that.

Houston's Astrodome, the most famous sports arena in the world, was chosen as the site. The date: Sept. 20, 1973. Plans were made to fly in show business personalities from Los Angeles and Las Vegas and women libbers from the East. The American Broadcasting Company paid $750,000 for the TV rights.

The event was given a Hollywood buildup. Riggs began a sweep of the television talk shows. Newspaper stills of the bandy-legged little man with the thick glasses, hawk nose and shaggy hair in poses as Tarzan and Henry VIII.

He was presented as a middle-aged sex symbol. An entourage of lovely ladies followed him everywhere.

Bobby gulped pills—415 a day—, worked with his private professionals, talked all day and partied all night in preparation for the match. Billie Jean, 29, winner of five Wimbledons, went into hiding. She shunned public appearances and private interviews—and worked hard on her game.

The big night came. A crowd of 30,472—the largest ever to see a tennis match anywhere—poured into the domed, air-conditioned stadium. It paid more than $400,000, an Astrodome record. Seats were priced at $6 to $100. Champagne was served at ringside. It was part Hollywood, part circus, part heavyweight fight. The crowd was a bull-ring crowd. All over the country, people stopped and watched. The TV audience was put at 50 million.

The crowd roared when Billie Jean served the first ball and never stopped roaring. In exactly two hours and four minutes it was over. Billie Jean, after starting nervously, suddenly became a brilliant, incisive killer. Bobby was a tired old man, never in the match. He left his legs on the ballroom floor. Billie Jean won 6–4, 6–3, 6–3.

"Now I guess I'll have to keep my promise," said a weary Riggs. "I'll have to jump off Pasadena's Suicide Bridge."

"Take a parachute," Billie Jean responded charitably.

SUPER POWERS ASSAILED AT THIRD WORLD PARLEY

From the start it was plain that the meeting of 76 Third World nations was aimed primarily against big powers on both sides of the Iron Curtain and "imperialist exploitation" of poor countries by rich ones.

The fourth "Nonaligned Summit" opened in Algiers Sept. 3 in an atmosphere of suspicion that recent sharp changes in East-West relations might prompt the United States and the Soviet Union to collaborate at the expense of weaker states.

Algerian President Houari Boumedienne set the tone in his speech of welcome. "In the past," he said, "the world was divided into communist and capitalist blocs. Today it is divided into a rich world and a poor world. The whole problem is for us to find the means to defend our rights and interests against the immense interest groups and agreements among the big powers."

There were sharp differences between the so-called political neutrals. One boiled to the surface when Cuban Prime Minister Fidel Castro launched into an impassioned defense of Moscow, rejecting charges that it was guilty of imperialism.

Exiled Prince Norodom Sihanouk of Cambodia, who has had the support of Peking, interrupted the formal oratory to denounce Castro and the Soviet Union for backing the "clique of traitors" of President Lon Nol in Phnom Penh.

But as the four-day parley drew to a close, Third World leaders laid aside their differences and focused attention on their dislike for the remanants of the colonial system from which many had suffered. The declarations and resolutions were directed largely against "imperialist exploitation." Prodded by the Arab states, the members endorsed condemnation of Israel, but said nothing about the growing wave of Palestinian terrorism.

The United States bore the main brunt of the attacks, however. It was assailed for its Indochina policy, for its support of Israel, and for its economic domination in Latin America.

Several Latin American and black African nations which maintained good relations with Israel had no opportunity to air their views on the subject. Sweden, Austria and Finland were allowed only observer status at the parley. The majority apparently was anxious to screen out countries which despite political neutrality might express the views of Western Europe and the rich world.

Libyan President Moammar Khadafy of Libya sounded a pessimistic note when he told a plenary meeting, "Let us not fool ourselves into the belief that all this talk will lead anywhere."

DIVIDED LAOS MADE ANOTHER TRY AT GOVERNMENT BY COALITION

It seemed an unlikely alliance as leaders of the two Laotian factions which had been at war for 20 years gathered at a plush riverside villa and exchanged toasts in champagne.

On Sept. 14, the Vientiane government and the Pro-Communist Pathet Lao climaxed seven months of see-saw negotiations by signing an agreement making them partners in a coalition government. Inside the villa of Prince Souvanna Phouma, 72-year-old prime minister of both the old neutralist government and the new coalition,

Pope Paul VI and the Dalai Lama, exiled spiritual leader of Tibetan Buddhists, shook hands at a September meeting in Vatican City

the two sides exchanged handshakes. But ahead lay the long, risky job of trying to make the coalition work. Two previous ones in 1957 and 1962 had failed.

The 180,000 people of Vientiane took little notice of the signing. There were no banners or crowds in the streets.

The agreement set up three major governmental bodies to be divided equally between the Vientiane side and the Pathet Lao, headed, in name at least, by Souvanna's half brother, Prince Souphanouvong. The latter was named to serve in the new coalition as one of Souvanna's two deputy premiers.

But 80 per cent of Laos' 91,000 square miles and one third of its nearly three million people remained in territory controlled by the Pathet Lao.

The accord called for withdrawal of all foreign troops including about 200 Americans and several thousand Thai mercenaries, paid by the United States, within 60 days after formation of the coalition. At the time of the signing there also were about 40,000 North Vietnamese troops in Laos.

Some observers speculated that the agreement was based on the assumption that both sides

were tired of two decades of sporadic civil war and would rather make the coalition work than resume fighting.

Prince Souvanna reportedly believed that his half-brother Souphanouvong was not a Communist at heart and that they could get along once his 62-year-old sibling was away from North Vietnamese influence.

Unlike the first two coalitions, the 1973 version had the blessing of the United States which pledged cooperation, assistance and adherence to the peace agreement. Observers noted that the climate had changed since the earlier years. The strategic importance of Laos to either the United States or North Vietnam was now minimal, they said.

American officials acknowledged that many difficulties lay ahead, but they pinned their hopes for reconciliation on the loyalty of both sides to Laotian King Savang Vatthana and general respect for Souvanna, plus the appeal that expanded commerce and prospective new foreign aid programs would have for both sides.

"No one expects Laos to become a paradise with the stroke of a pen," said one diplomat, "and if the agreement results in paralysis, will anyone notice the difference?"

Chinese girls performing at a theater in Wusih, China's Kiangsu Province for local farmers on Aug. 23

Carol Lease watched as Columbus, Ohio, barber Wayne Bump lathered her leg in preparation for a shave. The cost of a leg shave was $2

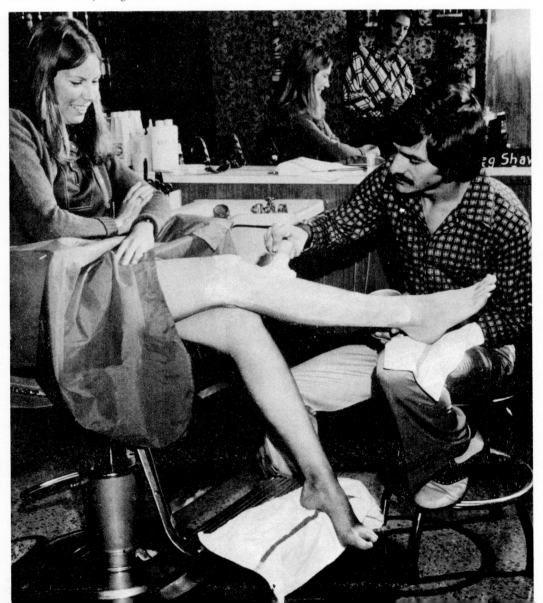

TWO GERMANYS WELCOMED INTO THE WORLD FAMILY

As the flags of East and West Germany were run up at the United Nations headquarters beside New York's East River, diplomats regarded it as a victory for one or the other or both.

Jubilant members of the Communist bloc hailed the event as a great triumph for East Germany's campaign for equal recognition with its western rival and for acceptance of its borders as permanent.

Delegates on the other side of the Iron Curtain viewed the entry of both Germanys as a crowning achievement for West German Chancellor Willy Brandt, who won a Nobel Peace Prize for his efforts to promote friendly relations between East and West.

Most everyone agreed the German entry was the fruit of reduced tensions among the Big Four World War II victors; the United States, France, Britain and the Soviet Union. It seemed to symbolize the start of a new chapter in the relations between the democratic and communist worlds.

The U.N. General Assembly's new president, Leopoldo Benites of Ecuador, declared the United Nations was embarking on a new era with the admission of the first of the world's divided states; leaving the two Koreas and the two Vietnams outside the door.

"The restrictive stage of the organization" is over and "the stage of true universality is beginning," Benites told representatives of the 135 member states gathered in the great blue and gold assembly hall.

Walter Scheel, the West German foreign minister, acknowledged that acceptance of U.N. membership on an equal footing with East Germany had been a difficult step for Bonn to take. "It is painful to face up to the political reality of the division of one's country," he said.

The East Germans made plain that as far as they were concerned the two Germanys would remain divided. Peter Florin, East German deputy foreign minister, told newsmen at U.N. headquarters that it was "useless" for West Germany to "spread illusions" about eventual unification.

Florin did say, however, that his government would work in "full cooperation" with West Germany in the United Nations when it came to areas of common interest.

FOR THE RECORD

ORDERED. International Business Machines Corp., to pay Telex Corp. $352.5 million in damages after being found guilty Sept. 17 in a federal court ruling at Tulsa, Okla., of monopolistic practices. U.S. District Court Judge A. Sherman Christensen also directed Telex to pay IBM $21.9 million for theft of trade secrets. Later Christensen said he had made "substantial" errors in fining IBM. He then reduced damages against IBM to $259.5 million.

ARRESTED. Herman Bell, 25, described as a "high echelon officer" of the Black Liberation Army. Bell was arrested Sept. 2 in New Orleans. He had been the object of a nationwide manhunt since Nov. 24, 1971, when he was indicted by a grand jury for the slayings of two New York City policemen in May of that year. He was the fifth man to be arrested in connection with the fatal shootings of patrolmen Waverly Jones and Joseph Piagentini.

October

Sixty-Five Fateful Days
Spelled Agnew's Downfall

Series of explosive developments
brought vice-president's resignation

FOR MORE THAN A YEAR the scandals known as Watergate had tarnished and eroded President Nixon's political family. But through it all, Spiro T. Agnew had stood unscathed. No hint of political scandal had touched the vice-president. No taint of corruption marred his reputation.

Agnew's political stock hit an all-time high, and it seemed inevitable that he would carry the GOP standard into the 1976 presidential race.

On Aug. 6, the final day of his grace, it seemed nothing could stop Spiro Agnew. Sixty-five days later, he had been destroyed politically.

On Oct. 10, in a series of explosive developments, Agnew resigned the vice-presidency, pleaded no contest to a federal felony charge that he evaded $13,551 in 1967 income tax, was convicted, fined $10,000 and placed on three years probation. Then he was confronted by an extraordinary document in which federal prosecutors portrayed him as a politician who cooperated with and encouraged a tradition of illegal shake-downs and bribes from Maryland contractors.

The plea, the sentence, the public humiliation were all part of a negotiated deal with federal prosecutors who felt they had the evidence to send the vice-president of the United States to jail.

And so the man from the law-and-order administration who had once warned of a threatening national crime crisis, stood ruined and disgraced.

Agnew in Singapore talked with foreign minister Rahim Ishak during the vice-president's Southeast Asian tour

The developments piled on a national psyche already shell-shocked by 16 months of the agony of Watergate.

"If somebody had written a novel like this, nobody would buy it because nobody would believe it," said one stunned citizen.

His resignation and conviction did not end the public life of Spiro Agnew, however. For more than two months, Agnew had steadfastly proclaimed his innocence and derided as liars those who bore witness against him. In his hour of defeat, he wanted the last word.

So five days after his court appearance, Agnew went on national television and, in a 17-minute valedictory said that his decision not to contest the felony charge of tax evasion "was the only way to quickly resolve the situation." He reasserted that he was innocent but offered a veiled acknowledgement that by some interpretations, his activities could have been deemed improper.

"Beyond the insinuation that I pocketed large sums of money, which has never been proven and which I emphatically deny, the intricate tangle of criminal charges leveled at me . . . boils down to the accusation that I permitted my fund raising activities and my contract-dispensing activities to overlap in an unethical and unlawful manner. Perhaps, judged by the new post-Watergate political morality, I did.

"But the prosecution's assertion that I was the initiator and the grey eminence in an unprecedented and complex scheme of extortion is just not realistic."

A sampling of public opinion taken several weeks later by Louis Harris, the pollster, showed that 15 per cent of the American public believed Agnew. More than 60 per cent said they did not believe him.

In his last public appearance, Agnew praised Nixon for his leadership and said the President had "borne a heavy burden in his attempt to be both fair to me and faithful to his oath of office. I want to pay tribute to the President for the restraint and the compassion which he has demonstrated in conversations about this difficult matter."

Although Agnew said publicly he wanted to avoid a paroxysm of bitterness, he was saying privately that Nixon had put him under tremendous pressure to step down and had, in fact, engineered the end of his political career. Nixon aides vehemently denied it. But Agnew aides were certain that Nixon and his associates encouraged the Agnew controversy to keep it prominently in the news and thereby gained a two-month respite from Watergate publicity. Again, the Nixon aides denied it.

The scandal began almost a year earlier at a rather innocuous luncheon between a Baltimore investigator for the Internal Revenue Service and the U.S. attorney in Baltimore, George Beall. The investigator mentioned casually that the income tax returns of several Maryland officials showed inexplicable discrepancies. Beall had been anxious for some time to look into rumored kickbacks by Maryland contractors and began checking out the IRS information.

By December, 1972, Beall was ready to request a special grand jury to hear evidence. In January, he subpoenaed thousands of documents related to contracts let by the state. By February, Agnew had received word of the probe—then the subject of lively gossip around Baltimore County—but the vice-president apparently was unworried. The investigation centered on N. Dale Anderson, the county's chief executive. Anderson had succeeded Agnew in that post when Agnew became Maryland governor in 1967.

But the chain of witnesses questioned by the prosecutors began to widen the scope of interest.

There was William E. Fornoff, Baltimore County administrative officer under Agnew and later under Anderson. He pleaded guilty to a minor tax charge and promised to cooperate with the prosecution.

It was reported that Fornoff implicated Jerome B. Wolff whom Agnew had appointed as chairman of the Maryland State Roads Commission, the predecessor of the Department of Transportation. The commission under Wolff chose the J. E. Greiner Co. as the engineers for the huge second span of the Chesapeake Bay Bridge. Wolff later became president of a Greiner subsidiary.

It was reported that Fornoff also implicated Lester Matz, another contractor who had had extensive dealings with Agnew county and state administrations.

By spring, reports said, both Wolff and Matz had warned Agnew that his name would be dragged into the probe unless it were stopped. Agnew hired an attorney, Judah Best, a partner of former White House special counsel Charles W. Colson.

Best went to Baltimore to see Beall in April.

"I explained to Beall that I represented the vice-president, that the vice-president had heard these stories that he'd better stop the investigation or they'd make charges about him and also that we'd heard rumors on the cocktail circuit about the dubious loyalties and lack of discretion of people on (Beall's) staff," Best recalled later.

Beall assured Best that the vice-president had no need to worry, that he had not been implicated. Beall said he realized the delicacy of the situation and would keep Best informed.

The two men spoke almost every week after that and Beall, each time, reiterated his assurances that the vice-president was in the clear—until July. Early that month one of Best's routine calls elicited the reply, "It would be beneficial if we didn't talk again." Best knew his client was in trouble.

Witnesses had begun to tell what they knew and the prosecutors were pressing hard. "The train is at the station," they warned witnesses. "Lots of people are getting on. Room is running out. Time is also running out. The train may leave at any moment."

On July 3, Beall and his three assistants reported what they knew and suspected to Atty. Gen. Elliot L. Richardson. Richardson expressed deep concern. Agnew was just a step away from the presidency. But Richardson told Beall to proceed.

On July 31, Beall called Best. "You'd better come down here tomorrow," Beall told Agnew's attorney. On Aug. 1, when Best appeared at Beall's office, Beall and his assistants were waiting. "Do you want to sit with your back to the wall?" Beall asked. Best replied: "I'd rather sit by the window."

Beall gave Best a letter notifying him that Agnew was under investigation for possible criminal violations of tax, conspiracy, bribery and extortion laws. Wordlessly, Best read the letter. He put it in his pocket and left.

Agnew at a Washington news conference Aug. 8 said "absolutely not" when asked if he planned to resign

When he returned to Washington, Best made arrangements to see Agnew the next day and then enlisted the aid of two New York lawyers, Jay H. Topkis and Martin London.

On Aug. 6, the three attorneys met with Agnew and Richardson. The attorney general outlined for them where the case stood and what the allegations were—basically that large engineering firms had funneled thousands of dollars to Agnew regularly in return for contracting favors. Agnew waited until the recitation ended, then hotly branded the allegations "a pack of lies."

That night, Richardson called on Henry E. Petersen to be liaison between him and Beall's office. Petersen, assistant attorney general in charge of the criminal division, was winding down from a heated defense before the Senate Watergate committee of his handling of the investigation of that case. Petersen knew nothing of the Agnew case. Richardson suspected Petersen would not be thrilled to be involved in it.

"You're going to be sorry you came back from vacation," Richardson told him.

Even later that night of Aug. 6, Agnew learned that a part of the story of the investigation was known and was about to be printed by the Wall Street Journal. From his office he issued a statement acknowledging the probe and declaring his innocence.

Two days later, on Aug. 8, Agnew held a televised new conference at which he branded the charges against him "damned lies" being advanced by persons in deep legal trouble who were trying to extricate themselves by implicating him.

Agnew also said he had no intention of resigning and began what would develop into an unprecedented attack on his own administration. He deplored the fact that information about the federal investigation was being leaked to the news media and added:

"Under normal circumstances, the traditional safeguard of secrecy under such (grand jury) proceedings would protect the subject. But apparently this protection is not to be extended to the vice-president of the United States. Well, I have no intention to be skewered in this fashion. And since I have no intention to be so skewered, I called this press conference to label as false and scurrilous and malicious these rumors, these assertions and accusations that are being circulated . . ."

The next day the federal investigators in Baltimore subpoenaed a carload of campaign and elective office records dating back to the beginning of Agnew's political career in 1962.

On Aug. 14, Agnew agreed to make available to the prosecutors all of his financial and tax records. The White House, making a rare comment on the Agnew probe, said Nixon wanted the prosecutors to take all appropriate steps in the investigation. But a spokesman said Nixon would not personally intervene.

By Aug. 21, the crescendo of allegations and news reports about the investigation had grown to the point that Agnew felt compelled to speak out publicly again. He denounced unnamed officials within the Justice Department and charged they were trying to indict him in the news media.

"I regret to say that it has become clear that the 'sources close to the investigation' so frequently quoted were indeed just that—persons involved in the investigatory process . . . This is a clear and outrageous effort to influence the outcome of possible grand jury deliberations . . ."

Then Agnew, long an adversary of the nation's news media, made a gesture of conciliation.

"I have not called you to this meeting for the purpose of criticizing the news media," he said. "I cannot fault you for publishing information given you by informants within the Department of Justice. The blame must rest with those who give this information to the press and who do so with an obvious motive of interfering with the independent investigative process of the grand jury."

Agnew asked for and got assurances from Richardson that the Justice Department would investigate the news leaks.

Meanwhile, Nixon was at San Clemente and on Aug. 22, held a news conference at which he made his first public comment on the Agnew affair. "I had confidence in the integrity of the vice-president when I selected him as vice-president," Nixon said. "My confidence in his integrity has not been shaken." Nixon's carefully worded statement of support was limited to Agnew's terms as vice-president. He did not include Agnew's political career in Maryland.

Nixon returned to Washington Sept. 1 for a two-hour personal meeting with Agnew. Some said Nixon wanted Agnew to step down but could not bring himself to personally ask Agnew to do so. Nixon later sent an intermediary, presidential counselor Bryce N. Harlow, to see Agnew and suggest he resign. Agnew discussed that possibility with his close friend and confidant, Sen. Barry Goldwater of Arizona. Goldwater told Agnew that if he were innocent as he professed, he should stand and fight.

Agnew said he would, but already he was considering striking a bargain with the prosecutors. By late September, the bargaining was well under way with White House Counsel J. Fred Buzhardt acting as go-between with Agnew's attorneys and the Justice Department. On Sept. 21, news of the plea bargaining leaked to the press and Agnew called it off.

Agnew went on national TV Oct. 15 after announcing resignation

Then the snowballing story became an avalanche of developments.

On Sept. 25, Agnew went to the House of Representatives and asked Speaker Carl Albert to give him a forum where the charges against him could be publicly and fairly explored. The same day Richardson announced he had given the Baltimore grand jury the green light to proceed with the Agnew case.

On Sept. 26, Albert turned down Agnew's request, later disclosing that he did so because Richardson had called him, summarized the evidence against the vice-president and said he expected an indictment.

On Sept. 27, the Agnew investigation actually went to the grand jury.

On Sept. 28, Agnew's lawyers filed a motion to stop the probe on the grounds that a sitting vice-president cannot be indicted and on grounds that news leaks had irreparably damaged the case.

On Sept. 29, in a rousing speech to a Republican women's group in Los Angeles, Agnew declared his innocence and vowed to stay in office even if he were indicted.

On Oct. 3, Judge Walter E. Hoffman, the federal judge from Norfolk, Va., assigned to supervise the Agnew investigation, gave the vice-president's lawyers unprecedented authority to subpoena Justice Department officials and reporters in an effort to find the news leaks.

A week later, Oct. 10, the question became moot. Agnew quit.

The key to the sudden turn of events was apparently Agnew's thundering speech in Los Angeles Sept. 29. Friends and associates reported that the response from the White House was very bad and the pressure on Agnew to resign was intense.

"The White House didn't like it," one Agnew associate said. "Especially his attack on the Justice Department for the news leaks and for trying to destroy him politically. Whatever favor he had left with Nixon probably was gone after that."

Although Agnew's press secretary, J. Marsh Thomson promised another rousing Agnew speech in Chicago Oct. 4, that address turned out to be a staunch defense of President Nixon. An associate said later the speech was an almost pitiful attempt by Agnew to get back in Nixon's good graces. It didn't work, and Agnew finally concluded he had to go.

The only question was how, and that was decided in an intense round of meetings among Agnew's lawyers, Buzhardt and Petersen. The Justice Department was willing to allow Agnew to plead to just one charge, but insisted that a summary of evidence against him be made public. Agnew's lawyers agreed as long as Agnew could see the document before it was released and as long as the charges were worded so Agnew could deny them.

Agnew's lawyers also insisted there be no jail term. The Justice Department was willing, but that was a matter that had to be determined by Judge Hoffman. On Oct. 8, Hoffman, Petersen, Beall and Agnew's lawyers met in a motel in suburban Alexandria, Va. Hoffman accepted all the terms of settlement except the lack of a jail sentence. He said he couldn't commit himself to that without a specific recommendation from the attorney general.

On Oct. 9, the negotiations resumed at the Justice Department with Richardson present. "It is my understanding that for you to give a guarantee you need an affirmative recommendation from me," Richardson said. "Judge, if it's a must, you've got it."

"If I've got it, okay, I will commit myself," Hoffman replied.

And so it was that on the next day, Oct. 10, Agnew sent his formal letter of resignation to Secretary of State Henry Kissinger. In a letter to Nixon, Agnew said he was resigning to spare the nation the long, debilitating struggle that would result if the issues surrounding him were dragged out in congressional or court procedures.

"It has been a privilege to serve with you," Agnew wrote. "May I express to the American people, through you, my deep gratitude for their confidence in twice electing me to be vice-president."

In a "Dear Ted" letter of reply, Nixon said he accepted Agnew's resignation "with a deep sense of personal loss."

"As vice president, you have addressed the great issues of our times with courage and candor," Nixon wrote. "Your strong patriotism and your profound dedication to the welfare of the nation have been an inspiration . . ."

With face drawn and hands trembling, Agnew stood in Hoffman's borrowed Baltimore courtroom and acknowledged that he received payments in 1967 which he failed to report as income although he knew the money was taxable. Then he entered his no contest plea. Hoffman said he considered it the equivalent of a guilty plea and fined Agnew $10,000 and sentenced him to three years unsupervised probation.

Outside the courtroom, private citizen Spiro Agnew promised an explanation to the public. It came in his televised address five days later.

Again he denied the truth of the allegations in the 40-page exposition of evidence against him. Again he said he had quit for the good of the nation. And he told the American people not to lose faith:

". . . the government in Washington does live. It lives in the pages of our Constitution and in the hearts of our citizens, and there it will always be safe. Thank you, good night and farewell."

Agnew left the television studio and slipped into his limousine. As the power windows slid closed, he was heard to say softly, "Good night, gentlemen."

Then Spiro T. Agnew drove off alone into the warm October night.

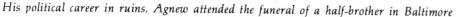

His political career in ruins, Agnew attended the funeral of a half-brother in Baltimore

Scores of Americans Caught with Drugs Abroad Faced Stiff Jail Terms

A MORE OR LESS accepted fact in the United States was that the last thing many of the young would do was listen to the establishment—especially the Washington establishment.

Too bad.

For there was one poster put out by the Department of Health Education and Welfare that hundreds, perhaps thousands either missed or ignored at their peril.

It reads: "When you're busted for drugs over there, you're in for the hassle of your life."

The scores of Americans caught in 1973 for smuggling, selling or using drugs and clapped into overseas jails brought the total Americans incarcerated on drug charges abroad to some 900. Many faced or were serving prison terms of 30 years or more.

Oddly some of the toughest terms, and worse jails, were in countries such as Turkey and Mexico which were at least way stations in wholesale smuggling of drugs into the United States.

The largest group of jailed Americans, some 260, languished in Mexican cells. Possession of drugs alone south of the border could lead to sentences of up to 10 years. Smuggling charges could cost 15 years of your life. Some of Mexico's prisons were considered among the most primitive in the world.

Americans busted abroad rarely could count on more than the most perfunctory help from U.S. embassies. For American diplomats to intercede would lay them open to charges of interfering with local justice and somehow assuming that Americans were outside the law of the countries they visited. Also, any interference would weaken U.S. credibility on the tough stance it urged foreign governments to take against drug traffic headed for America.

The HEW poster, surveys showed, did not overstate the case when it warned against the "hassle of your life." There was often no bail, trials might take months or even years to conclude and foreign court procedures could be a far cry from the standards expected in the United States.

William Hayes Jr., of Amityville, N.Y., was sentenced by a Turkish court to four years in prison for narcotics possession. He was told he would get 15 months off for good behavior, meaning that his sentence was to expire in July (1973). In Janu-

William Hayes of Amityville, N.Y. was sentenced to up to 30 years by Turkish authorities

ary, the public prosecutor, without explanation, decided to bring up the case again. The prosecutor's only comment at the time was that his action involved a "matter of public law," hardly something Hayes' lawyers could deal with directly. Later the charge was announced to be smuggling, which on conviction carried up to a 30-year sentence.

Sometimes in Turkey, those accompanying smugglers as mere hitch hikers could be jailed for many months while laborious investigations and court procedures wended their laborious way to some conclusion.

Drug arrests among Americans were increasing yearly. American diplomats said one of the biggest problems was that those arrested, almost all under 30, either did not believe foreign countries had jurisdiction over them or were confident that the local embassy would smooth things out. Some reasoned that if thousands of tons of marijuana were smuggled annually through Mexico, for instance, then how could the Mexican government be tough on "grass." The answer in many countries was that while some corrupt officials and international drug rings might escape prosecution for smuggling, the countries wanted none of the U.S. drug problems at home. Another factor seemed to be that the dress and life style of many American young distressed or angered local officials prompting them to crack down.

Embassies reported one of the most popular misconceptions among young drug users abroad was that the rest of the world was becoming more permissive on drugs. Hardly, U.S. diplomats said. In fact, many nations once tolerant of drug use had passed stringent antidrug laws.

Officials said relatively few of the foreign busts were for hard narcotics like heroin, and that for the most part it appeared that those arrested were planning to use their drugs themselves. This did not mean that the amount of narcotics involved was always small.

Many hoped to get packets of hash and the like back into the United States. A pound of Afghan black hash could be purchased in Kabul for about $100. In New York it would cost a user about $1,600 on the street. The temptation to stock up for a year or more was great. As great, say, as it was for the woman who bought furs and dresses in Paris and then switched American labels for the French ones. The penalties for those caught with drugs at U.S. ports of entry, however, were far more serious.

Again, many of the young were uninformed. Many believed a drug bust in U.S. customs simply meant confiscation of their contraband.

U.S. customs officers in New York said young smugglers often were duped and bought extremely low quality or drastically adulterated drugs making the risk no less but the gain, if any, far smaller than anticipated. In one case, a long-haired youth arriving from Morocco aroused officers' suspicions and his luggage was thoroughly searched. One agent found about 10 pounds of dark pungent smelling material wrapped in plastic, as hash often is to contain its telltale smell.

While the young man sadly considered the prospect of many years in an American jail, the inspectors examined the package more closely. One burst out laughing. The "hash" turned out to be camel dung.

Left, customs agents Edward F. Walsh and officer Anthony M. Simonelli went through a suitcase of marijuana at customs offices in New York. Below, a Lebanese customs officer looked through the bars of the customs prison at Beirut while inspectors checked a busload of hashish

The Mets Still "Be-leeved," But Athletics Were Victorious In Annual Baseball Classic

Athletics swarmed over each other after defeating Mets in the final game

T HERE IS A period of a week or more every October when Americans traditionally have been able to cast aside their troubles and woes and throw themselves wholeheartedly into what the purple prose pundits of another era labeled "the fall baseball classic," also known as the World Series.

The year 1973 was no exception, although the stresses of grave events at home and abroad were perhaps the heaviest since the series was inaugurated in 1903.

Yet interest appeared at an unprecedented peak when the Oakland Athletics, a team of mustachioed and bearded malcontents governed by a maverick owner named Charles O. Finley, took the field in Oakland's Coliseum Saturday, Oct. 13, against the implausible National League champions, the New York Mets, perpetrators of baseball miracles.

The Athletics, who beat the Baltimore Orioles in a five-game playoff for the American League title, were seeking to become the first team since the 1961–62 New York Yankees, to win consecutive World Series championships. They were a colorful, rollicking lot with their wild white, gold and green uni-

forms, their white shoes, orange warmup baseballs, long hair, 1890 mustaches and internal feuds. They were constantly barking at each other and berating their boss, Finley. They thrived on dissension. Yet they hit, threw and ran with wild abandon. They insisted they were driven by personal pride.

The Mets were cut from another bolt of cloth—always neatly trimmed, clean shaven and as square as the A's were mod. They were managed by a stoical, stocky little man named Yogi Berra; brunt of a thousand jokes. An expansion team born in 1962, they had astounded the baseball world by winning the National League pennant and beating Baltimore in 1969. That's when the once bumbling tail-enders changed their image almost overnight—as in some Cinderella fairy tale—and became the "Miracle Mets."

They weren't the "Miracle Mets," however, in the midst of the season when, crippled by recurring injuries to top players, they plummeted to last place in the National League East Division standings, at one stage 12½ games out of first. Berra, who had been fired after leading the Yankees to the American

League pennant in 1964, faced a second boot. Baseball buffs began making book on when he would get the gate. A New York newspaper polled fans on whether Yogi should be ousted (the result was a resounding "no"). Yogi stayed.

As the campaign moved into September, the Mets had cut their games-behind distance to the top in half but they still were in last place, needing to climb over five healthy clubs to get into first place. Impossible, every one agreed. But the skeptics hadn't calculated the magic of Yogi and his men. Injuries healed. Balls started bouncing the Mets' way. A wave of confidence swept through the team.

"God is a Met," read a sign in center field at Shea Stadium.

"You gotta be-leeve!" yelled Tug McGraw, the Mets' ace relief pitcher.

McGraw's rallying cry was picked up by other members of the team and their thousands of followers as the Mets swept through 20 of their last 29 games to take the division championship. Belief in Met miracles escalated when the New York team licked the strong Cincinnati Reds, winners in the West, for the National League title.

"How can you stop them?" even the most cynical of experts said as the Mets flew west to tackle the flamboyant A's in the World Series.

The A's produced a quick answer to that one in the first game. His name was Ken Holtzman. The stringbean left-handed pitcher, who hadn't had an official time at bat during the season, lashed a double to the left field corner and, with the aid of an error, scored the first run in a 2-1 Oakland victory.

Both of the A's runs came in the third inning and were unearned. After Holtzman's two-out double, the scoreboard in center field flashed "Go, Go, Go!" and the crowd of 46,021 screamed wildly. A's shortstop Bert Campaneris hit an easy hopper toward second and, before you knew it, the ball had squirted through Felix Millan's legs for an error, Holtzman scoring. The speedy Campaneris stole second and came home on a single by Joe Rudi.

That was enough. The run that the Mets collected in the fourth on a double by Cleon Jones and a single by John Milner

didn't count. Young Jon Matlack, who had been a stalwart through the Mets' September rush, had pitched eight hitless innings—all except the third—, given up only three hits and lost. Besides, the Mets obviously missed the bat of right fielder Rusty Staub, who hurt his shoulder in the playoffs.

Where had the Mets' magic gone?

"I just blew it," the sure-handed Millan moaned afterward. "The ball just went through my legs."

During the game, the A's made a public announcement that the Mets had refused an A's request to bring the Oakland roster up to a 25-man limit by adding Manny Trillo. The crowd booed. The A's owner was sharply reprimanded by Commissioner Bowie Kuhn for making the announcement which Kuhn said "embarrassed" the Mets.

Sunday's second game dripped with drama and tragedy.

The drama was provided by the 42-year-old Willie Mays who, playing the final hours of a brilliant career, delivered a key 12th inning single that set off a four-run rally for a 10-7 Mets victory. The tragedy fell upon Mike Andrews, a pickup infielder of the A's inserted late in the game. Andrews was guilty of two errors in that wild and woolly 12th, permitting three of the runs that swamped the dazed A's.

The game lasted four hours, 13 minutes—almost an hour longer than any other World Series game ever played—and it packaged all the elements of baseball excitement. Eleven pitchers in all strode to the mound. Cleon Jones and Wayne Garrett hit home runs for the Mets. The lead changed hands four times. Bud Harrelson of the Mets figured in a controversial play in the 10th, called out by the umpire at the plate on a tag that nobody—not even the television screens—saw.

"You gotta Be-leeve!" yelled Tug McGraw, who was credited with saving the game.

The series tied at one game each, the teams moved into chill, blustery New York for the next three games at Shea Stadium. Nobody suspected on the long overnight flight from the West Coast that these three games and much of the rest of the series would be clouded with controversy.

The Athletics noted after reaching cruising altitude in their chartered plane that Andrews, the goat of the second game,

Jon Matlack of the Mets pitched the first game in Oakland

was missing. His baggage was aboard but not the player. There were whispers and grumbles and finally suspicions which were confirmed when the team dressed at Shea Stadium for an off-day workout.

Andrews had been sacked because of his errors. Finley announced that, after Sunday's second game, he had ordered Andrews to undergo an examination by the team doctor. The examination had shown a back ailment, of which Andrews had a long history. Because of the ailment, Finley again asked that Manny Trillo be activated.

The act triggered a storm. From his home in Boston, Andrews told teammates that he had been encouraged to sign the doctor's report, saying he was hurt. The A's became furious. Some put on adhesive tape strips to form the number "17," Andrews number, and said they were wearing it out of mourning. Such stars as Sal Bando and Reggie Jackson told friends they wanted to be traded. Commissioner Kuhn acted swiftly. He advised Finley that Trillo could not be activated and that Andrews must be restored to his position on the team.

"We don't need 25 men," Finley retorted. "We can win with 23, or 20."

On Tuesday night, Oct. 16, when the series was resumed, a sign in Shea Stadium said: "The weather's as cold as Finley's heart."

But the chill in the air failed to get through to the marrow of Bert Campaneris, the A's wisp of a shortstop who lashed a two-out single in the 11th inning to score Ted Kubiak with the run that beat the Mets 3–2 and sent the A's into a 2–1 lead in the series.

It was a disappointment for a sellout crowd of 54,817 but it was the kind of game that kept them on their feet and scream-

ing. Manager Dick Williams used 18 of his 23 players. The Mets got off to a 2–0 lead off Jim "Catfish" Hunter, the A's ace, one of the runs an out-of-the-park blast by Wayne Garrett, and turned it over to Tom Seaver to hold it. But the A's inched back to pull even with runs in the sixth and eighth and then win in the 11th.

"I knew I was going to get a hit," Campaneris, who had three singles for the night, said.

"We proved what we can do despite the front office," said Sal Bando, the team's captain, in an obvious reference to the Andrews case.

Andrews rejoined his teammates for the fourth game Wednesday night but not before standing before news cameras in a formal press conference and accusing his boss, Finley, of "lying" about his injury. One might have expected the outspoken infielder to be relegated to the cobwebs, but such was not the case. He made his appearance at the plate in the seventh inning—called out as a pinch-hitter by Manager Williams—and received a standing ovation from the crowd of 54,817. He grounded out.

It was a big evening, however, for the Mets. Rusty Staub, playing with a shoulder so sore he could hardly raise his right arm above his head, drove in five of his team's runs with a home run and three other hits in a 4-for-4 performance and the Mets won 6–1.

Jon Matlack, hard luck loser of the opening game, pitched masterful three-hit ball for eight innings to get credit for the triumph. The series was now tied in games, 2–2.

The fever of loyal Mets fans took another jump and it almost busted the thermometer when the New Yorkers forged into the lead by taking the fifth game 2–0. Cleon Jones scored

Left, Mets' Jerry Grote out at home in the fourth game. Right, Oakland's controversial owner, Charles O. Finley.

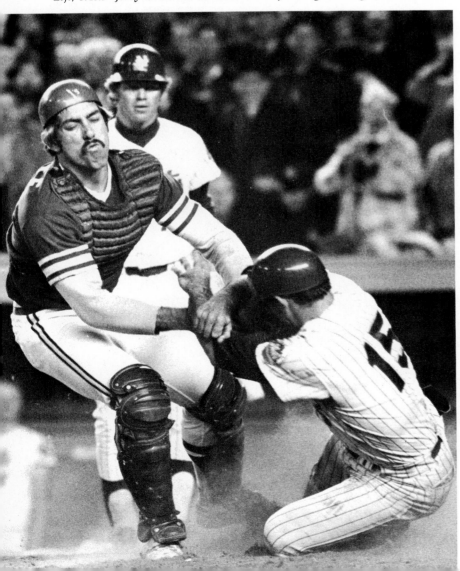

in the second inning after a double and a triple by Don Hahn knocked in the second run in the sixth. Meanwhile, Jerry Koosman shut out the A's for six innings before weakening and turning over the job to McGraw, the ultimate believer.

The boyish, 29-year-old McGraw weaved his way out of a bases-loaded situation in the seventh and got himself into a hole by walking two batters in the ninth. But he bore down and left home plate untouched.

"I don't intend it that way," the whooping, hip-slapping reliever said afterward, "but I just pitch better when I have pressure on me."

"I've got the best relief pitcher in baseball," bragged Manager Berra.

The Mets got a good night's sleep and took a mid-day plane the next day, Friday, for Oakland, certain that they would be heading home with the World Series title within 48 hours. They had reckoned without the Athletics' sleeping giant, Reggie Jackson.

The bearded Oakland center fielder had been a relatively unobtrusive character for the Mets through the first five games. In New York particularly his bat was about as potent as a tooth-pick, and observers, knowing his vast potential, were wondering when he might really bust loose.

It happened on a damp, hazy Saturday afternoon, Oct. 20, following an early morning rain.

The Mets' Mr. Terrific, Tom Seaver, had hardly worked up

Relief pitcher Tug McGraw shouting after he saved the fifth game for the Mets

a good sweat when—bam, bam—Jackson exploded doubles in the first and third innings, each accounting for a run, and it proved enough to win the sixth game. The final score was 3—1, with credit for the pitching victory going to "Catfish" Hunter.

Hunter simply overpowered the Mets for seven innings, holding them to three hits. In the eighth, after Ken Boswell of the Mets had hit a pinch-hit single, Hunter was yanked for Darold Knowles, who couldn't keep Boswell from scoring on singles by Garrett and Millan.

"It was nice to be home again," said Jackson.

The Athletics' sixth game victory brought the series down to a sudden-death climax, a Sunday finale played in bright sunshine with mountains looming in the distance.

Tension was increased when Williams, manager of the A's for three years with two more years to go on his contract, confirmed in the dugout before the game that he was handing in his resignation. He said he would have a formal announcement afterward—win or lose. This confirmed rumors that had been rampant throughout the series.

The game started. If it had been a fight, they probably would have stopped it. The explosion came in the fourth inning. For six games, the hard-hitting A's had been deprived of a home run by the Mets' sharp pitching staff. But in the fourth inning of the final game, Campaneris boomed one out of the park for two runs. Then Jackson came up with Joe Rudi on base and lashed the ball into the right center field stands.

The victim was Matlack, who had split in his previous two appearances in the series. It was disappointing for the youthful Met lefthander who had allowed only one earned run in the last 42 innings he had pitched.

The Mets scored single runs in the sixth and ninth and had the tying run at the plate. Knowles came in to put out the fire. The Oakland stands went wild. Fans poured out onto the field, mobbing the players. The huge scoreboard in center field began spitting fireworks like a Fourth of July celebration.

In the champagne cork-popping Oakland locker room, the mild-mannered Williams made official his intention to give up the reins of the best team in baseball.

"It's not because of Mr. Finley—he has been wonderful to me," Williams said. The Yankees later announced that he was headed for New York to succeed Ralph Houk as manager.

"I am doing this for family reasons," Williams added. "I want to be closer to my family on the East Coast." He lives in Florida.

In December, however, American League President Joe Cronin disapproved the contract and ruled that Williams remained the property of Oakland.

Over in the glum Mets' dressing room, spirits were low but the miracle makers accepted their fate.

"I'm proud of these men—very proud," said Manager Berra.

"I don't think we have anything to be ashamed of," said the veteran Willie Mays. "These kids developed a lot of togetherness."

"We've come a long way—it's been a tough summer," said McGraw, "and all of us still believe."

A week after the series, the other shoe dropped. Commissioner Kuhn fined Finley $7,000 for his conduct during the World Series, $5,000 of it assessed for Finley's action in the Andrews case.

"It's grossly unfair," complained Finley. "This is my ball club. This is my money. Nobody is going to tell me how to run my business. I'm going to appeal."

So the baseball season ended—the Athletics still fighting, the Mets still believing.

LE DUC THO REJECTED NOBEL PEACE PRIZE

The message sent to the president of the Nobel Prize Committee of the Norwegian Parliament in Oslo was a long one. But, in essence, it boiled down to the fact that Hanoi Politburo member Le Duc Tho would not accept the Nobel Peace Prize for 1973 because he felt "peace has not been really restored in South Vietnam."

Tho, who had been awarded the prize jointly with U.S. Secretary of State Henry A. Kissinger, said in his Oct. 23 message that "since the conclusion of the Paris agreement on Vietnam, the U.S. and the Saigon administration have continued to commit very serious violations of many essential provisions of the agreement. . . . "Under such circumstance I feel it impossible to accept the . . . peace prize that the committee has bestowed on me. When the Paris agreement on Vietnam is respected, guns are silenced, and peace is really restored in South Vietnam, I will consider the acceptance of this prize."

Left, Le Duc Tho refused the prize. Right, Henry Kissinger accepted the award.

IRATE CUBANS TRIED TO RUSH SPEAKER AT THE U.N.

The representative of Chile took a swipe at Cuban Prime Minister Fidel Castro in a speech before the U.N. General Assembly, and that touched it off.

Chile's Raul Bazan was just warming up Oct. 10, when fiery Cuban foreign minister Raul Roa jumped to his feet and headed for the rostrum flanked by several aides. Spectators said one Cuban opened his jacket showing a gun in a holster, and another shouted "be careful I am armed" as he neared the podium. As Roa and the others drew close to the speaker, U.N. guards and delegates intercepted them and a shouting match ensued.

Later, Roa told the assembly he had rushed toward Bazan "solely and exclusively to give him the slap that he required." Roa's wrath apparently was aroused when Bazan called Castro "an impotent leader with expansionist goals" and then termed Roa "a man who chews the cud of hatred and knows nothing of dignity." Bazan went on to say that Castro "used to watch executions and invited diplomats from other countries to watch."

It was at that point that Roa and his aides rushed toward the rostrum shouting obscenities in Spanish. The outbreak left veteran guards somewhat shaken. It moved the U.N. chief security officer, Lt. Col. Harold A. Trimble, to remark that the incident had been "potentially the most serious" moment in his five years at the United Nations.

When the dust had settled, assembly president Leopoldo Benites of Ecuador asked the delegates "to forgive this incident, which is unheard of in the history of the United Nations."

VIOLENCE FLARED IN THAILAND AS STUDENTS DEMONSTRATED

Normally quiet, the streets of Bangkok, capital of Thailand, suddenly flared with violence and saw blood run for two days in October.

As one witness put it: "It had an air of sur-realism. Peaceful Bangkok. Peaceful Thais. And suddenly the blood flowing. Some of the students were laughing while under fire. It must have been unreal to them."

Violence was new to the country's 400,000 university students, but confrontations between them and the military government had occurred several times since Prime Minister Thanom Kittikachorn and strong man Field Marshal Praphas Charusathien staged a November 1971 coup *(The World in 1971, 222)* to seize absolute power. The confrontation between the once docile students and the unpopular military regime came Oct. 14 and for two days there were bloody demonstrations against the military rule which claimed nearly 300 lives.

The situation calmed only after the nation's three most powerful military leaders—Thanom Kittikachorn, Praphas Charusathien and Col. Narong Kittikachorn, Thanom's son and Praphas' son-in-law—left the country.

Dr. Sanya Thammasak, the former rector of Thammasat University, was named by King Bhumibol Adulyadej to replace Thanom. He promised a new constitution within six months with general elections to follow soon after. A new constitution was one of the students' demands. Thailand had been without one since Thanom and Praphas placed the country under military rule.

Throughout the trouble, the students contended they had no intention of dismantling the basic structure of Thai government or society. During the uprising, they carried portraits of the king and chanted his praise. The king served as a unifying figure. One student was carrying the monarch's photograph above his head when he was shot and killed walking toward a line of government soldiers and police.

STRANGERS IN THE NIGHT?

For more than 20 years the U.S. Air Force investigated unidentified flying objects (UFOs) before it decided in late 1969 that its project Blue Book no longer was justified either for security or science. But closing the book had little, if any, effect on the UFOs. Sightings continued over the years, with a rash of them reported in October 1973.

The reports began to come in from around the country after two men went fishing at Pascagoula, Miss., and said they were briefly taken captive by reddish, wrinkled-skin creatures who emerged from a weird-looking spacecraft. After that there were tales of flying objects shaped like cars, cigars, basketballs and turnips and other alleged sightings of funny-looking beings such as the ones described in Pascagoula.

The reports centered largely on UFOs that flashed various colors at a distance too great to determine exactly what they were. The objects were explained by astronomers as probably either planes, stars, or balloons, or the planet Mars, their reflections made to look weird by atmospheric conditions. But that didn't explain the strange beings the two Pascagoula fishermen said they saw. Two scientists said they placed the men under hypnosis for four hours of questioning and were sure the two were telling the truth.

The modern UFO era in the United States began in 1947 when a businessman-pilot reported seeing nine strange moving objects over Mt. Rainier. A decade later there were a host of reports from Texas, New Mexico and Southern California. In 1965, there were worldwide sightings.

The Blue Book ascribed the bulk of sightings to aircraft, weather, sounding balloons, satellites, meteors, bright stars and planets, missiles, searchlights, clouds, birds, reflections, temperature inversion, mirages, electric wires sparking and swamp gas.

Despite this some sightings remained unexplained. Of the 1973 sightings, one astronomer said all of the cases should be thoroughly investigated by a special official agency. He said the report from Pascagoula supported the view "that a phenomenon exists which is as yet unexplained."

Jersey Turnpike became a jumble of wrecked vehicles

BLINDING FOG TURNED JERSEY TURNPIKE INTO A DEATH TRAP

Transit authorities had rated the 118-mile strip known as the New Jersey Turnpike as one of the safest highways in the nation and also the busiest. But fog could turn this superway into a super death trap.

It happened the first time in November 1969 when blinding, swirling mists closed in near the southern end of Exit 3, triggering a chain-reaction pile-up that claimed six lives.

Nearly four years later on Oct. 24, the fog crept in again blanketing a large stretch of the turnpike where it passes through the northern Meadowlands, reducing visibility to virtually zero.

Before the fog lifted, nine persons were killed and 40 injured in a series of collisions that sent 65 vehicles hurtling into each other.

To make matters worse, the region was swathed in a layer of stagnant air that trapped the fog and acrid smoke from a widespread meadow brush fire that had been burning for more than a week.

When the first rays of dawn finally pierced through the smoke and mist it revealed a scene of horror that stunned veteran highway police.

Along one stretch, trailer trucks, delivery vans, automobiles and buses lay tangled and smashed, their occupants sprawled in a bloody jumble.

"Nobody had a chance; nobody saw a thing," muttered a dazed survivor. Some victims perished in flames as colliding trucks spewed fuel and cargoes caught fire.

"You couldn't see the flames through the fog," said the driver of one truck who had survived after being hurled out of the cab of his truck when another van hit his vehicle.

RAMPAGING FIRE RAZED 401 BUILDINGS IN CHELSEA

The second major conflagration to strike Chelsea, Mass., in less than 70 years exploded at 4 p.m. on a warm and sunny—but very windy—fall afternoon, Sunday, Oct. 14. Within five hours, driven by winds gusting up to 50 miles an hour, the flames had destroyed 401 buildings over 30 blocks. Miraculously, no one was killed.

Nearly 2,000 firemen fought the blaze through the district of wooden tenements and rundown industry like an army in slow retreat. Fire Chief Herbert Fothergill said, "We would set up a line to fight the fires when suddenly a gust of wind put it right on top of us. The heat and flames would suddenly hit our line and we had to leave everything—hose, equipment, everything—and run for our lives."

The firemen stopped the flames at last-ditch defensive lines set up along a railroad track to the north and at a school on the south. "If we had lost that school," said a fireman, "it would have been all over. The fire could very well have swept through the entire business district."

The fire wiped out 56 businesses, 238 industrial buildings and 107 multifamily dwellings, mostly three-story wooden tenements. It left 600 persons homeless and 600 others without jobs. The total property damage was estimated at $100 million. The damage to human lives could only be guessed. "I have lost everything," said Henry Wogciechowski. "It's a crying shame. All the people who live in the stricken area are poor people. Just look at all these people standing around crying. They have no place to go from here."

One of Boston's finest suburbs at the turn of the century, Chelsea had been virtually destroyed by a fire in 1908 which flattened 1,000 buildings over 350 acres and left 12 dead. The city grew back as an industrial slum, full of oil and gas tanks, junk yards and dilapidated buildings. In February, 1973, the National Board of Fire Underwriters said the city had "the highest potential for conflagration of any city in the United States" because of the oil and gas tanks. None of the tanks were involved in the fire, however.

Flames billowed from a home in Chelsea

Crowds of local citizens and tourists pressed into the Munich Fair grounds for the opening of the annual Oktoberfest, the world's biggest beer bash

PABLO CASALS; A CAREER THAT SPANNED 75 YEARS

Pablo Casals was without dispute the foremost cellist of the 20th century, and some believed him to be the greatest of all time.

For the last 35 years of his life, Casals had used his enormous talent in protest against tyranny and to campaign for peace. But he would be remembered longest perhaps for his artistry as an instrumentalist and his complete mastery of the cello.

Casals was able with uncanny sensitivity to demonstrate what moving music could be drawn from the strings of a somewhat awkward instrument. For 75 years he held a unique place in the world of music, first as a cellist and later as a conductor, until death came on Oct. 22 at the age of 96 in Puerto Rico.

Success came early to Casals who was born in Vendrell, a fiercely independent part of Spain known as Catalonia. He played before Spanish royalty before he had reached the age of 15, and he was giving concerts while still a teenager.

In 1899, on the eve of his 23rd birthday, Casals made his debut in Paris and was an immediate sensation there. For the next 20 years he played in the principal cities of Europe and the Americas. In that period, Casals made close friends of such musical greats as Maurice Ravel, Sergei Rachmaninoff and Gregor Piatigorsky.

Casals was in Barcelona in January 1939 when Francisco Franco's forces entered the city. He fled to France vowing never to return while Franco was in power.

His only return to Spain was in 1955 when he accompanied the body of his third wife. Franco retitled the streets that had been named after Casals and had the plaque removed from his home in Catalonia, but in recent years the Spanish government indicated it would have welcomed the famed musician back.

Casals had also vowed that he would not play in any countries which recognized Franco Spain, but he relented in 1958 for a concert at United Nations headquarters. And in 1961 he appeared at the White House for President and Mrs. John F. Kennedy. In later years he performed frequently in both the United States and Europe.

Part of Casals' fame in the United States came late in life and rested largely on his talents as a conductor which he saw as his real mission. He became a source of inspiration to the musicians with whom he worked every summer at the Marlboro, Vt. music colony.

"Pablo Casals was one of the greatest musicians of all time and the greatest cellist," said Eugene Ormandy, the music director of the Philadelphia orchestra. "His love of people was probably the reason for his rich and long life."

In 1955, Casals moved to Puerto Rico. At the age of 80, he married his pupil, 20-year-old Martita Montanez who was at his bedside when he died 17 years later.

Until the end, his love for music seemed as fresh as ever.

"Sometimes I feel like a boy," he told an interviewer at the age of 88. "Music does that to me. I can never play the same piece twice in the same way. Each time it is new."

Pablo Casals playing the cello in 1971

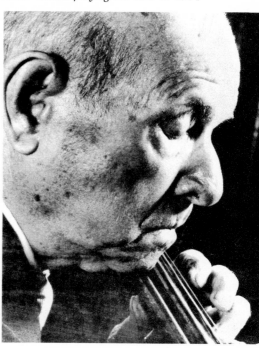

November

A Year of Promise Became a Nightmare For Richard Nixon

A RELAXED Richard Nixon, chatting in his Oval Office a few days before his second inaugural, told Saul Pett of The Associated Press about his zest for the challenges posed by his second term.

"I believe in the battle, whether it's the battle of a campaign or the battle of this office," the President declared.

For Nixon, fresh from a landslide election victory of stunning proportions, those were happy days. Welcomed were anticipated struggles to restrain federal spending, transfer more decision-making to state houses and city halls, and build on 1972's spectacular approaches to China and the Soviet Union.

The President had foreseen one pitfall but was convinced he had dealt with it effectively. Emerging briefly from seclusion at Camp David shortly after his re-election, Nixon had philosophized aloud to newsmen about his second-term thoughts and plans:

". . . the tendency is for an administration to run out of steam after the first four years, and then to coast, and usually coast downhill. This is particularly true when there is what you call a landslide victory . . ."

As he told the reporters in a helicopter hangar at his mountain retreat, "What I am trying to do is to change that historical pattern." He would do so, he said, by reorganizing his Cabinet and the entire federal bureaucracy so they would be more responsive to his commands.

Long before the end of 1973, Nixon's analysis of the problems of winning big had become a chilling prophecy. Almost as soon as his second-term team had taken the field, Nixon's game plan was destroyed by a wave of scandals.

In less than 12 months, an administration installed with overwhelming public support was riddled to the point where many questioned its capacity to provide effective leadership. For the first time, criminal conduct forced a vacancy in the vice-presidency. For the first time in a century, the Congress formally began to consider impeachment of the President himself.

The carnage of 1973 was mind-numbing. As the President and his men stumbled from crisis to crisis, in a downward spiral that seemed without end, there were three attorneys general, three directors of the FBI, three secretaries of defense, four Watergate prosecutors, and three directors of the Central Intelligence Agency.

No longer was the battle something to be sought and relished. Since the happy evening of dancing at the inaugural balls, the author of *Six Crises* had learned that past brushes with disaster were inconsequential when compared with the events of 1973. The challenge had become a fight for survival.

For Richard Nixon, little had gone well. Virtually all the good news had related to foreign affairs, the area that claimed his greatest interest and in which he was most sure-footed.

In late January, following controversial American bombing raids on Hanoi and Haiphong, a peace of sorts was achieved in Vietnam. White House image-makers huddled to ponder ways of inspiring an emotional public outburst of the sort that marked the end of World War II. The public, long tired of the "dirty little war" in Asia, saved its emotions for the homecoming of freed American prisoners.

By late June, the focus of public attention had shifted from POWS to the televised hearings of the Senate Watergate committee. Buffeted as one sensational disclosure followed another, Nixon had few close friends or associates, outside his immediate family, to whom he could turn for encouragement. His most frequent companions and confidantes were Florida banker Charles Gregory Rebozo and Press Secretary Ronald L. Ziegler, a youthful advertising man who had been in grade school when Nixon was elected vice-president in 1952. Gone were H. R. Haldeman and John D. Ehrlichman, early casualties.

Relief came in the unlikely, bulky figure of Leonid I. Brezhnev, first boss of the Soviet Communist Party to visit the United States since Nikita Khrushchev called on Dwight D. Eisenhower in 1959. The television lights in the big Senate Caucus Room were doused so Nixon could concentrate on summitry.

The respite was brief. A week later the nation was transfixed as boyish John W. Dean III, fired two months earlier as Nixon's chief attorney, voiced accusations that the President had been a party to obstruction of justice, to hiding the truth about Watergate. The President kept silent, relying on earlier denials of wrongdoing. But the pollsters said the public had found them unconvincing.

Watergate's stain spread until the term embraced allegations extending far beyond the June, 1972 burglary at the Democratic National Committee offices. There was a vigorously denied newspaper report that investigators were looking into Nixon's possible use of $1 million in unreported campaign funds to buy his San Clemente estate. New questions were raised about the settlement of an antitrust case involving ITT, about campaign contributions from milk producers, about illegal corporate donations to the Nixon campaign, about wiretapping and burglary by a secret White House police force, about federally-financed improvements at San Clemente and Key Biscayne.

A deeply troubled citizenry, its comprehension taxed by manifold allegations of misconduct, was perhaps almost as disturbed about an economy that seemingly had run out of control. Nixon, an avowed foe of formal wage-price restraints, had abandoned largely-successful Phase II controls in January, opting for a voluntary anti-inflation program. One result: the biggest inflationary binge in more than two decades.

Simultaneously, a new world money crisis erupted, forcing the second devaluation of the dollar in 14 months. The two-stage slash totaled 17.9 per cent and meant higher prices for imported cars, television sets and shoes. Householders were more concerned, however, about the soaring price of beef. There was a beef boycott and ultimately a temporary price freeze that, for a time, made red meat a vanishing commodity in supermarket freezers.

Nixon's Phase III economic game plan proved to be disastrous. At a White House briefing session at which an early return to stiffer controls was promised, Treasury Secretary George Shultz was asked if he agreed.

In the happy days after his landslide victory, the President and Mrs. Nixon paid a visit to Alice Roosevelt Longworth in Washington

"Oh, everybody thinks Phase III was a failure," he responded impatiently. "Let's move on."

Phase IV was unveiled in mid-summer and by year's end gave some promise of being at least moderately effective. More complex than any previous regulations, the Phase IV rules required corporations with annual sales of $100 million or more to notify the Cost of Living Council 30 days in advance of any price increases and justify them with proof of cost hikes. Firms with sales of $50 million to $100 million simply had to report all price boosts. Wage guidelines were continued and farmers were permitted to charge as much as the market was willing to pay. Food prices soared before retreating a bit from their peak in the autumn. By the end of 1973 the Cost of Living Council was moving steadily if warily toward decontrol and many Americans were wondering if inflation had become a way of life.

All but forgotten was Nixon's promise that 1973 would be the "Year of Europe." Addressing the annual Associated Press luncheon in April, Henry A. Kissinger called for a redefinition of the Atlantic partnership, saying, "The Atlantic nations must join in a fresh act of creation, equal to that undertaken by the postwar generation of leaders of Europe and America." A procession of European heads of government visited Washington and

Nixon, already on record as planning a "grand tour" of Europe in the fall, flew to Iceland in late May to meet French President Georges Pompidou on neutral ground. That was as close as he ever came to Europe. Consideration of a "new Atlantic Charter" slipped quietly off front pages as more pressing problems intervened.

At times Nixon had difficulty finding recruits for key administration positions. For most of 1973, there was no U.S. ambassador to the Soviet Union. Many other diplomatic posts were vacant as scandal put a brake on the time-honored practice of transforming campaign contributors into diplomats.

In August, however, the top diplomatic post of secretary of state, was placed in different hands. William P. Rogers went out and Nixon installed Kissinger, the spectacular White House foreign policy virtuoso. The nomination was widely regarded as formal recognition that Kissinger had been acting as Nixon's secretary of state since 1969.

The most startling personnel change came with the abrupt October resignation of Vice-President Spiro T. Agnew. Given a free hand, Nixon perhaps would have turned to Republican convert John B. Connally in nominating a successor to Agnew under the provisions of the 25th Constitutional Amendment. Faced with Republican opposition to Connally, Nixon went

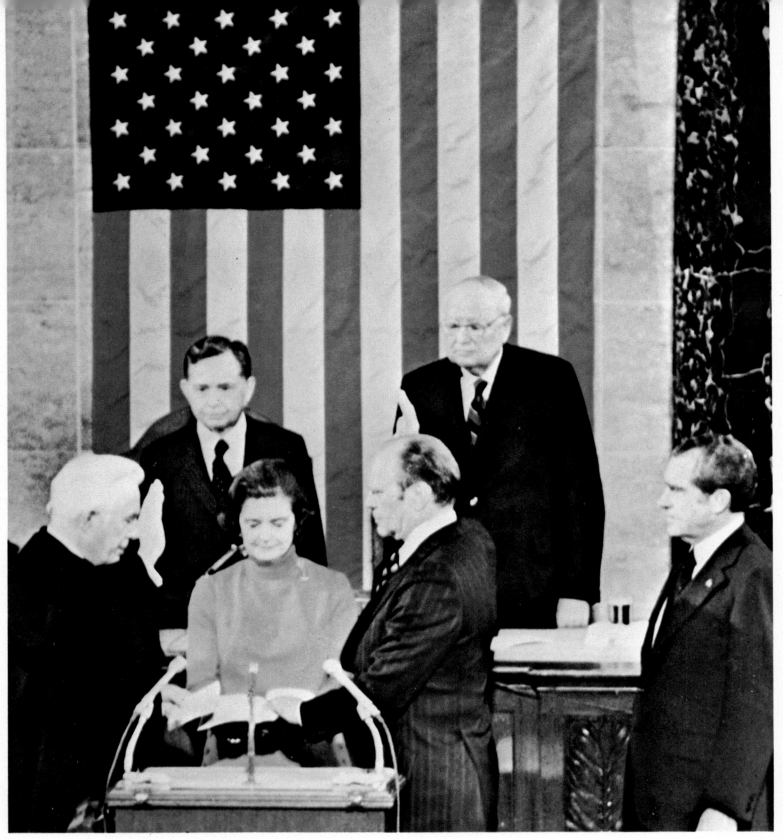

Gerald Ford was sworn in as the nation's 40th vice president after the resignation of Spiro T. Agnew

through the drill of soliciting opinion of GOP officeholders. Within 56 hours of Agnew's fall, he announced a seemingly safe and inoffensive nominee: Gerald R. Ford, the popular House Republican leader and Capitol Hill veteran. In light of the Agnew case, Congress gave careful consideration to Nixon's choice. Confirmation never was seriously in doubt, however, inasmuch as one of Ford's principal qualifications was a singular absence of enemies. Following his confirmation, Ford was sworn in on Dec. 6.

Nixon's dealings with the Democratic-controlled Congress were not always as smooth throughout the year. Presidential

pledges of cooperative partnership alternated with slashing attacks tinged with partisanship.

Given the climate of suspicion and controversy in which Nixon became enmeshed, relations between the White House and Congress actually were more productive than might have been expected.

Nixon had begun the year by throwing down a clear challenge in his budget message: He was determined to dismantle Lyndon Johnson's Great Society blueprint by abolishing or sharply cutting more than 100 federal grant programs. Sizeable chunks of appropriated funds would be impounded. The anti-poverty

Left, the President lashed out at critics of his Indochina policies. Above, the President looked haggard when he was hospitalized for pneumonia in July. Below, Nixon and France's President Georges Pompidou at their meeting in Reykjavik.

agency would be shut down. Spending bills deemed excessive would be vetoed.

Foes of impoundments won at least 30 court battles involving more than $1 billion. A federal judge ruled that the administration's effort to kill the Office of Economic Opportunity was illegal. Veto messages were plentiful and, eight times in succession, majority votes to override fell short of the required two-thirds margin.

Significant compromises were worked out, however. For the first time, highway funds were tapped for urban mass transit. A new farm program was enacted. Social Security benefits were raised. By the time Congress returned in September from a late-summer recess, Nixon had signed 25 major bills.

If scandal eroded Congressional support for Nixon's legislative initiatives, there were moments of partnership. With former Rep. Melvin R. Laird carrying the ball as a new Nixon aide, a notable compromise was arranged to legislate an August 15 end to U.S. bombing operations in Cambodia. The President also later won a signal victory in successfully defending his top-priority military procurement bill against concerted pressure for heavy reductions and a strong Congressional drive to force a cutback in troop strength overseas.

The President lost his biggest legislative battle as his personal popularity hit a new low in autumn. Congress, after eight straight failures, overrode a Nixon veto and placed on the law books new restrictions on presidential powers to wage war.

Just as there was an impromptu air about Nixon's dealings with Congress, his handling of a rapidly escalating energy crisis seemed makeshift at times. Initially his approach seemed tentative and lacking in clear direction. An April message to Congress on energy was followed by yet another in early summer and still a third in November. The President waited until the first frost, and a cutoff of Arab oil, before moving with a show of decisiveness and, even then, he was accused of being too late with too little.

With each new shock during the year, it seemed inevitable that the travail of Nixon and the nation must soon end. Surely the worst was over. But it never happened that way.

The White House miscalculations produced the October "massacre" at the Justice Department that brought Nixon to the brink of impeachment. The shakeup saw Attorney General Elliot L. Richardson resign rather than comply with an Administration order to fire Watergate special prosecutor Archibald Cox. It saw dismissal of Deputy Attorney General William D. Ruckelshaus for the same reason and the final ouster of Cox by Solicitor General Robert H. Bork who had been named acting attorney general. Some members of Nixon's own party began suggesting resignation as the best and quickest solution.

In other times, Nixon's apparently deft handling of detente's first major test, in the Middle East, might have produced sustained applause, but success abroad was overshadowed by the relentless erosion of the President's standing at home.

Presidential tapes were found to be nonexistent. A promised Nixon dictabelt could not be found. The day after Nixon personally assured Republican governors he knew of no more impending bombshells, his lawyer went into court to report that a taped conversation relating to Watergate had been obliterated.

In the whole mind-boggling year, perhaps two statements stood out simply because their authors felt compelled to make them:

—Spiro T. Agnew: "I have full confidence in the integrity of President Nixon . . ."

—Richard M. Nixon: "I am not a crook."

The presidential shoulders seemed to sag as troubles piled up

Tremendous Financial Pressures Were Felt by Higher Education

THE CONCEPT of providing low-cost education at public colleges and universities was based on a belief that higher education for all those who can benefit from it—whether rich or poor—was in the best interest of society. Taxpayer support of such institutions reflected ideals of equality of opportunity.

In 1973, however, a number of experts concerned by the tremendous financial pressures on higher education, particularly private colleges and universities, reassessed that concept. Perhaps, they said, the tuition subsidy was not an efficient way to channel aid to students with the greatest need. Some critics claimed that the low-tuition structure at public institutions really served to divert needed funds away from poor students because it subsidized middle-income and wealthy students who could pay more.

In separate studies, both the Carnegie Commission on Higher Education and the Committee for Economic Development concluded that students and parents should pay as large a part of college costs as they could afford. They recommended higher tuitions be imposed by public institutions, and that student aid programs be expanded. The idea was to channel much of the federal and some of the state funds traditionally allocated to institutions directly to students themselves in the form of grants and loans awarded on the basis of economic need. In this way, the tuition increase would not create undue burdens on students from lower-income families because the increased aid would offset the higher fees, they said. The financial pressure on middle-income students was expected to increase, though.

Revenues from higher tuition might also add extra income for the public institutions which despite their taxpayer base of support had found themselves in increasing financial difficulties because of rising operational costs due to inflation and greater demand to provide facilities and services for changing student populations. The Association of State Colleges and Universities reported that three-fourths of its 300 member institutions anticipated financial problems during the 1973–74 academic year.

Allan M. Cartter, professor at the graduate school of education, University of California, Los Angeles, said that while total public subsidy for higher education grew from $2.2 billion in 1959–60 to $13.2 billion in 1971–72, the percentage share of costs borne by the average parent actually declined from about two-thirds to just under one-third during the past generation.

Cartter, who served on the Carnegie Commission, said it was easier to defend a policy of low-tuition or no tuition several decades ago when the public institutions attracted students mainly from among those who could not afford to go to private colleges, but this was no longer true. Today, some three-fourths of some 8.4 million college students attend nearly 1,200 public universities, state colleges and community colleges. Some economists have estimated that as high as 77 per cent of those families with annual incomes of $15,000 or more who have children in college use the public institutions in preference to more costly private ones.

Raising the cost of attending public colleges and universities would also benefit private institutions, whose economic exigencies have been exacerbated by the tuition gap between the two types of institutions. The traditional base of financial support for private institutions has been voluntary giving, from alumni, corporations and foundations. But the campus disruptions a few years ago and the national economic recession seriously hurt fund-raising efforts of many colleges. A survey of private institutions by the Association of American Colleges showed that the "average" institution finished its 1968 fiscal year with a surplus of $39,000 but that by fiscal 1971 the average institution faced a $115,000 deficit.

Tuition rose by more than 25 per cent in the past five years at public as well as private institutions, but the charges at tax-supported schools were substantially lower to begin with. According to the National Association of State Universities and Land-Grant Colleges, the median charge for tuition and fees for 1973–74 at 115 member institutions was $520. The median tuition-fee charge at a private institution in 1972–73 exceeded $1,700. The Carnegie Commission said that in order to preserve the diversity provided by a system of both public and private institutions, the tuition gap had to be narrowed.

Officials of public institutions said that although the Carnegie Commission and the CED emphasized that student aid programs must be expanded to assist low-income students faced with higher costs, experience had taught them that aid programs usually were grossly underfinanced and dependent on shifting political priorities. Indeed, as classes began in the fall of 1973, a survey of more than 300 state colleges and universities showed that the most-pressing problem those institutions faced was lack of financial aid for students. Layton Olson, executive director of the National Student Lobby, said grants "never keep up with the rise in tuition even for low-income families, much less for middle-income families."

It would be the middle-income student who would be most seriously hurt by any significant increase in tuitions, according to Allan W. Ostar, executive director of the American Association of State Colleges and Universities. Ostar said the middle-income student, ineligible for much aid, would be forced to borrow large sums to attend college and would have to start life in debt, while wealthy students and certain poor students would graduate debt-free. The National Education Association called the higher tuition proposals a "direct blow" to the moderate income family, and the AFL-CIO saw them as roadblocks to the advancement of the children of working men and women.

Once Again, Guns Roared and Bombs Exploded in Troubled Northern Ireland

For Northern Ireland, 1973 began in violence and despair and ended in violence tinged with hope. From the carnage of five years of riot and guerrilla war emerged the beginnings of agreement between Protestant and Roman Catholic and with it the hope of a united front against the gunmen.

As the bells of Belfast rang in the New Year, so the first bombs erupted to signal the end of a brief Christmas truce. Day after day the bombers struck, both the Catholic-based guerrillas of the Irish Republican Army and, increasingly as the

year wore on, the revenge-seeking Protestants of the Ulster Volunteer Force. By December the year's death roll was approaching 250, a record of hate exceeded only by the 469 slain in 1972 (*The World in 1972, 241-245*).

Alongside the bombers worked fanatic killers, striking by night, often for no known motive other than bloodlust. Some of the killings bore the hallmark of IRA executions of renegades or informers, a hooded body found at dawn with a cardboard label bearing one word: "Tout." Others, like the stabbing

Left, fireman fought the results of an explosion caused by a bomb planted by terrorists in Belfast. Right, mourners carried the coffin of Michael Wilson, shot to death by terrorists.

of Sen. Paddy Wilson and a girl friend, were the work of the Ulster Freedom Fighters and the Red Hand, shadowy Protestant groups proscribed by law and feared on both sides of Belfast's religious divide.

The bombings long had been commonplace. Belfast, the capital, was like a city under siege with shopping streets gated and guarded by troops. Londonderry, the second city, was a wreck. Dozens of smaller towns had their main streets devastated.

What was it all about? The basic cause lay in the centuries old antipathy between native Irish Catholics and "Planters," the Scots and English Protestants who were settled in Ireland before America was colonized. This old antagonism had become overlain with 20th century issues, among them Ireland's division after World War I into what is now the Irish Republic and Northern Ireland, and complaints of a raw deal in jobs and politics from the Catholic minority in the Protestant-dominated North.

The most active of the underground armies was the "Provisional" IRA—the "Provos"—battling to detach Northern Ireland from the British crown and the United Kingdom. In July 1972 it had come close to success, and its leaders had flown under safe conduct to London for abortive truce talks. In 1973 despite a series of spectacular coups, its prospects seemed to wane.

As IRA prospects receded, countermilitancy erupted on the Protestant side with strikes and riots during February as a warning against any British concessions to the Catholic side.

Northern Ireland voted March 8 in a referendum on the British link. Catholic-based parties boycotted the poll, but the result was in any case a certainty. The vote was to stay British.

The IRA chose referendum day to spread its bombing campaign to London. In mid-morning, a detective spotted a car with a Northern Ireland registration near Scotland Yard, headquarters of London's Metropolitan Police. In it was a mobile bomb of the type used by the IRA in Northern Ireland. It was defused. But two others were not spotted in time. One went off outside The Old Bailey, Britain's No. 1 criminal court, and another in Whitehall, Britain's government precinct. One man died and more than 200 were injured. Ten of the bombing team were arrested at London Airport boarding a place for Dublin even before the bombs exploded. Their leaders were two girls, Dolours Price, 22, and her sister, Marion, 20, daughters of an IRA veteran in his 50s. In November they were jailed for life.

Again in March, a ship left Cyprus and headed for North Africa to take on arms and rendezvous with Joe Cahill, an IRA veteran. On March 21 she passed through the Straits of Gibraltar, shadowed by British aircraft and submarines. A week later she appeared off the coast of County Waterford in the Irish Republic and was seized. Cahill was jailed for three years.

Other arms shipments bound for the IRA were picked up in Dublin harbor and in Montreal. Still others got through. Neither Catholic nor Protestant bombers were short of materials. The IRA, however, was running short of men, particularly in Belfast.

More than 1,000 were in Belfast's Crumlin Road Jail or held without trial at an internment camp. The British claimed 200 Provos had been killed since the fighting started for real in February 1971. As the year wore on, the bombing switched increasingly from Belfast to smaller towns. The British felt able to reduce their troop commitment from 22,500 to 15,500 and more reductions were in sight. Their casualties were 200 dead and around 2,000 wounded. Their aim, they said, was to defeat organized terror by methods acceptable to western democracy. That aim underlay the complicated political process which gradually took shape throughout the year.

Britain had taken total power in the province in March 1972, abolishing the former provincial Parliament, and installing in its place William Whitelaw as administrator with virtually unlimited power. His orders were to sort out the mess.

Whitelaw, 55, set out to win the confidence of less extreme politicians from both the Protestant and Catholic sides and to a surprising degree succeeded. His proposed cure was power-sharing and a new form of government in which the Catholic minority would be guaranteed a share of top jobs. By June the security situation was stable enough to allow elections for a new provincial assembly to be vested with considerable domestic powers but not control of the police and military. The results, under the newly introduced proportional representation system, neatly fitted the power-sharing concept. The once monolithic Protestant vote split into four main factions. The largest was the more moderate rump of the old Unionist Party, led by former Prime Minister Brian Faulkner, with 22 seats in the 78-seat assembly. The Catholic vote united behind the Social Democratic and Labor Party to become the second largest group with 19 seats.

The vote was a defeat for extreme hardliners closely associated with the gunmen. Tommy Herron, vice chairman and most prominent spokesman for the Ulster Defense Association, lost his bid for a place in the new assembly. Three months later his body was dumped in a ditch near Belfast with a single bullet through the head. The killing was unexplained. Opinion generally blamed it on rivals within his own organization. On the other side, the IRA kidnaped Patrick Duffy, 37-year-old father of seven, from his home in Londonderry and later told his wife he had been executed as an informer.

Summer brought a spate of IRA letter bombs in London and one to the British Embassy in Washington. In October the IRA pulled its most spectacular success of the entire campaign. A young man with an American accent went to Dublin Airport and hired a helicopter. The copter was hijacked and the pilot forced to fly to Dublin's Mountjoy Jail. It landed in an exercise yard and lifted out three top IRA commanders—Seamus Twomey, Joe O'Hagan, and Kevin Mallon. They flew off and vanished. Twomey, 54, quickly reappeared to announce the IRA had retrained with new weapons and new methods, and promised "commando raids as they have never been possible before." Twice in the following weeks the IRA disrupted the North's entire road and rail network with bombs and suspected bombs planted in hijacked cars and trucks throughout the province.

The political jigsaw devised by Whitelaw nonetheless continued to fall into place. By November, Whitelaw has persuaded the Unionists and Social Democrats to share power in a Protestant-Catholic administration. That fragile agreement achieved, Whitelaw quit the post and returned to London. His successor, Francis Pym, presided at London talks intended to bring Belfast and Dublin together in a council of Ireland from which a united government might emerge.

Hardline Protestants, led by the Rev. Ian Paisley, were sworn to wreck any such scheme. Three times between July and December they threw the northern assembly into uproar and premature closure. Their demand was for return of their old Protestant-dominated Parliament or total integration with Britain and a full voice in the British House of Commons.

Early in December, Britain, the Irish Republic and the moderate Protestant and Catholic leadership of Northern Ireland agreed on proposals for the future of Ulster which cleared the way for a Protestant-Catholic coalition to take office in the North for the first time, probably early in 1974.

Below, view of a wall erected on a bridge by the British Army to prevent illicit vehicle traffic between Northern Ireland and the Irish Republic. Right, demonstrators burned an effigy of British Prime Minister Edward Heath in Dublin.

Above, a brief and fatal drama took place in Hollywood when Edward F. Fisher 39, held a knife to the throat of 22-year-old Ellen Sheldon whom police said he was trying to kidnap. Left, security guard George H. Derby, 32, aimed his gun at Fisher's head. Below, Derby pulled back his gun after fatally shooting Fisher.

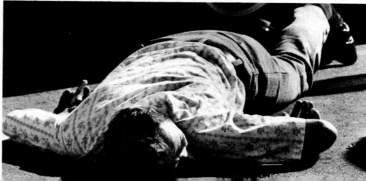

Princess Anne and bridegroom Mark Phillips waving from the balcony of Buckingham Palace

Trumpets blared, drums rolled and choirs sang in 900-year-old Westminster Abbey as Princess Anne, only daughter of Britain's Queen Elizabeth II, was wed to Mark Phillips, handsome cavalry captain and son of a sausage company executive.

It was the sort of celebration the British carry off with style. Among the 1,800 guests who jammed the ancient abbey Nov. 14 was a dazzling array of robes of many hues, plumed hats and medal-bedecked chests. The outside world watched the ceremony on television.

TV cameras flashed the scene around the globe as the couple gazed into each other's eyes and exchanged marital vows. Asked if she would love, honor and obey Phillips, the Princess, fourth in line to the British throne, said "I will."

Anne wore a white silk gown and diamond tiara. Mark wore a red dress uniform, spurs and sword. Anne honored bridal tradition and wore something new—her white silk wedding dress, along with something old, something borrowed and something blue. The something old was a sprig grown from the myrtle in Queen Victoria's wedding bouquet. The something borrowed was the diamond tiara belonging to her grandmother, Queen Mother Elizabeth. The something blue was Anne's secret.

Phillips had requested that he not be given a title. Anne would be known as "The Princess Anne, Mrs. Mark Phillips."

After the ceremony the couple feasted on lobster and partridge at Buckingham Palace, then departed for a wedding night hideaway.

The colorful ceremony and all the attendant pomp took Britons' minds briefly away from threatened oil shortages and a darkening economic crisis. It also gave London workers a brief respite from their jobs.

"It's a pity," said one young office worker as the glass Royal coach bearing the couple passed by on its way to Buckingham Palace, "that we don't have one of these each day."

EIGHT DIED IN CLEVELAND SUBURB: POLICEMAN WOUNDED

When Cyril Rovansek Sr. answered his telephone the sunlit Sunday morning of Nov. 4, he heard his son, Cyril Jr.

Everyone was down on him, he wanted to get the bosses off his back, the 31-year-old policeman told his father. He felt "like killing everyone." Then Rovansek heard his son say, "I'm going to get that s.o.b. upstairs," and he heard someone call his son's nickname, saying, "Sonny, don't shoot."

He heard a shot, then a click as his son hung up the phone. He called police. Sonny had killed eight persons at his duplex home, including himself, and wounded one policeman seriously, authorities said later.

"I saw my son lying on the bed," Rovansek said later. "He was dead. What can I do?" Also dead were the younger Rovansek's wife, Patricia, 32; their daughter, Kimberly, 7; and their son, Cyril III. Upstairs, in the other half of the residence, another family of four had been shot to death: Jerry DiLoreto, 46; his wife, Shirley, 29; their daughter, Linda, 7, and son, Michael, 5.

The younger Rovansek's boss, University Heights Safety Director Marshall Wien, knew the younger Rovansek as a model policeman during his nine years with the department in the Cleveland, Ohio, suburb. A friend knew him as

a quiet family man, "the last man I would have expected this from."

His father thought he might have feared an impending hernia operation. After 1971 appendix surgery the younger Rovansek was struck by peritonitis and pneumonia and "almost didn't make it," the father said. "Maybe he was afraid something like that might happen again."

But to his father the night before, when Sonny came visiting after work and stayed talking until 1 a.m., "there was nothing to see anything wrong." They had tea and cake together. They talked about vacations, the one they took together a year earlier, and the one they planned to take next year to Washington. "We shook hands on it," the elder Rovansek said, and the younger man "went out happy," heading home.

Sonny had wanted to be a policeman "since he was six years old," his father recalled. He also remembered his son as "always wanting to do other guys a favor" and "a good son."

"When he worked nights, he would call his mother, always wanting to know if she was all right," the elder Rovansek added.

The coroner's report said neither liquor nor drugs was involved in Sonny's last day. The coroner also said he found no anatomic or physiological cause for the violent outburst.

The Rev. Raymond E. Manak, who eulogized the younger Rovansek at services prior to burial, knew him as "a man who was troubled by all the evil in the world."

He said Sonny once told him, "I don't know if I want to take my family into this world" and that evil was "coming closer and closer . . . overwhelming him and overwhelming all the good in the world. He felt that, as a good man, he was not doing enough to fight evil."

The elder Rovansek's home is about 25 blocks from his son's duplex. Police arrived before the father did. One of them was Floyd Kidner. Police said Kidner opened the door and saw Mrs. Rovansek's body. They said shots followed and that Kidner's partner had dragged him from the door, wounded in stomach and leg. Then there was a final shot.

That was when the father arrived. He pleaded to the silent house for his son to give himself up. As police, unsure of what was going on inside, fired teargas canisters into the home, the elder Rovansek burst through the rear door. He saw the bodies of his son and his grandchildren. Then he ran back outside.

"I've lost my son, my daughter-in-law and my grandchildren," the elder Rovansek said. "I don't know what to do."

DETROIT VOTERS ELECTED THE CITY'S FIRST BLACK MAYOR

Detroiters, as did thousands of other Americans across the country, trooped to the polls in November, and when the ballots were counted the Motor City, the nation's fifth largest, had elected its first black mayor.

When Democratic State Sen. Coleman A. Young defeated former Police Chief John Nichols in a nonpartisan election, Detroit became the nation's third big city in 1973 to elect a black mayor, following Los Angeles and Atlanta. Los Angeles voters named Thomas Bradley to lead their city in May, and Atlanta elected a black mayor, Maynard Jackson, in October.

As mayor, Young, 55, faced problems of urban decay and crime as well as of trying to find ways to keep business from fleeing to the suburbs. But, he said, his victory was the first step in rejuvenating Detroit, adding, "We've got a long way to go."

In addition to Young, black mayors were elected for the first time in November in Raleigh, N.C., Dayton, Ohio, and Grand Rapids, Mich., while black mayors were re-elected in Chapel Hill, N.C., and East Orange, N.J.

By winning the Raleigh election, Clarence E. Lightner became the first black man elected mayor of a metropolitan Southern city with a white majority population. Lightner, 52, defeated a white candidate in the nonpartisan election.

PASSENGER SUCKED OUT OF PLANE THROUGH SHATTERED WINDOW

A National Airlines DC10 jetliner was flying westward over central New Mexico Nov. 3 when the cowling ripped loose from the right wing engine with an explosive noise and sent pieces of metal tearing into the side of the aircraft.

One of the pieces struck a window over the front edge of the wing, tearing the window and causing decompression in the aircraft that was flying at an altitude between 38,000 and 39,000 feet. In the seat beside that window was George Gardner, 45, a machinist from Beaumont, Tex., en route to Singapore for a job assignment with a steel company.

Sitting just in front of Gardner was Lou Spohn of Ukiah, Calif., who said he turned around after the explosion and saw another passenger struggling to hold the feet of a man in the window. Gardner was being sucked out through the 10 by 15-inch window.

"I reached around and was pushing the man down toward his seat, but I couldn't get a grip on him," Spohn said. "Before me or the other fellow could do much of anything, the man was gone, just completely gone."

Pilot William Brooke began taking the plane down to a lower altitude immediately because of the decompression situation. The jetliner, with its remaining 115 passengers and 12 crew members, landed in Albuquerque about 15 minutes later.

Searchers later found the window and pieces of the engine in a mountainous area 45 miles southwest of Magdalena in west-central New Mexico. No trace was found of Gardner and the search was called off.

AT LEAST 100 PERISHED IN BLAZING JAPANESE STORE

Waitress Kinuko Miyagawa was pouring tea for a customer in the restaurant of Japan's Taiyo Department Store when smoke began billowing into the room. For the next eight hours fire raged through the seven-story store in the southern provincial city of Kumamoto, killing at least 100 persons and injuring another 100.

The blaze, described by authorities as the worst of its type in Japan's history, broke out Nov. 29 on the third floor. Within minutes the flames had swirled up the stairs.

"It was like an inferno, full of cries of fleeing mothers and children," said Junko Nagai, another waitress. "I am lucky to be alive."

As the flames spread, shoppers and store employes headed for the windows. Some on the lower floors tried to escape by climbing down ropes. Some tried to leap to a nearby shop awning. Others jammed the stairs and escalators. Masatoshi Tsuruya, a university student, said he saw people tumbling down a stairway like an avalanche. Tsuruya managed to reach a window and escape by ladder.

Choking customers covered their faces with handkerchiefs and towels to try to keep the smoke out of their lungs. About 100 persons managed to reach the roof. Firemen raised ladders to rescue those on the roof but there were not enough fire trucks on hand to handle the job so helicopters were called in.

Firemen, soldiers and police wore oxygen masks, but they still had trouble entering the building because of fumes caused by building materials used to line the walls in remodeling the 20-year-old store.

The fire broke out on a day when the store would have normally been closed. It was open for the start of the year-end sales and the beginning of the Christmas period, a time of gift-giving even though only about 1 per cent of Japanese are Christians.

The sprinklers in the building were not working, officials said. They were under repair for fire prevention week.

London's famed Carnaby Street got a facelift when it was paved in a geometric design using, orange, white, yellow and black tiles

ALASKA PIPELINE BILL CALLED STEP TOWARD SELF-SUFFICIENCY

President Nixon hailed the bill as a first step toward making the United States wholly self-sufficient for its energy supplies by 1980.

The Chief Executive made the bright forecast as he signed the controversial measure authorizing a 789-mile pipeline from Alaska's North Slope to the Southern Alaskan port of Valdez.

Describing the $4.5 billion venture as "the largest single endeavor ever undertaken by private enterprise," the Chief Executive predicted that it would be completed by 1977.

Officials of Aleyska Pipeline Service Co., a consortium of seven oil companies that would build

the line, were less optimistic. They described the 1977 date not as a certainty but only a hope.

The pipeline faced possible snags. Two of the environmental organizations that had blocked the project through the courts at an earlier stage, issued a statement of disapproval. Hinting at the possibility of further court action, they said:

"The environmental issues that have been awaiting judicial determination should be left to the courts, in the absence of any adequate consideration of those issues in Congress."

Earlier the two organizations, the Wilderness Society and Friends of the Earth, had joined with

other plaintiffs in challenging the pipeline project on grounds it would have violated the right-of-way limitations in the Minerals Leasing Act of 1920. After the U.S. Court of Appeals for the District of Columbia had so held, the Administration called on Congress for special legislation. The bill that Nixon signed revised the right-of-way limitation and authorized the Secretary of the Interior to grant exceptions.

The 48-inch interior diameter of the pipe would give it a transmission capacity of 2 million barrels a day. It was not expected to funnel through more than 600,000 barrels daily at first, however.

A Nike missile site in Alaska was bathed in moonshine at sundown

CALIFORNIA'S MULTIPLE MURDERS

Walt Parkin worked hard running the only grocery store in Victor, Calif., and he managed to build his family a $60,000 home.

The new house amid the lush vineyards of the San Joaquin Valley was splattered with blood the morning of Nov. 7, 1973 when the bodies of Parkin, his wife and seven others were found.

Police called it a "professional-style" massacre, another bloody statistic on a rising roster of mass murders in Northern California.

On Nov. 8 in Santa Cruz, 80 miles south of San Francisco, Edmund Emil Kemper III was convicted in the mutilation slayings of his mother, her best friend and six hitchhiking coeds.

Mass murder made headlines in California two months earlier.

On Sept. 18, Herbert Mullin was sentenced to life imprisonment for slaughtering 10 persons in the Santa Cruz area.

On Nov. 8, the day that Kemper was found guilty and sane, two young men were captured in Sacramento and charged with the massacre

in Victor. Willie Steelman, 28, and Douglas Gretzler, 22, were said by police to be linked with a total of 17 murders in California and Arizona.

Steelman and Gretzler were drifters, one from California and the other from New York. They met in Denver, Colo. in October, 1973.

The night of Nov. 6, Walt Parkin and his wife went bowling. They left the neighbor's daughter to sit with their two small children.

Parkin, his wife and children, the baby sitter, her parents and brother and fiance all were shot in the head. Seven of the bodies were stacked in the closet in the master bedroom and two of the children were left sprawled across a bed.

Police linked the murder with the robbery of $3,000 from Parkin's grocery store.

Steelman surrendered in a Sacramento hotel and Gretzler was flushed out of his apartment hideaway with teargas.

Both had a history of drug use, according to police, and Steelman had been to jail for passing bad checks.

Herbert Mullin, 26, also had used drugs. "I didn't want to kill anyone, I didn't think it was right. I tried my whole life to do what was right," Mullin said during his August, 1973 trial for slaying 10 persons. On the witness stand he admitted three more killings.

On Friday Oct. 13, 1972, Mullin said, he clubbed his first victim to death. Within two weeks he felled another. On All Saints Day, Mullin, entered a confessional where he said he stabbed and kicked the priest to death. On Jan. 24, 1973, Mullin fatally shot a woman and her two small children.

The next day he went to the cabin of an old friend, James Gianera in Santa Cruz. Both had been honor students in high school, where Mullin also played varsity football and was voted "most likely to succeed."

Mullin said he blamed Gianera for involving him in drugs. He shot Gianera and his wife.

Less than three weeks later, Mullin said, he gunned down four teenage boys camping in the nearby mountains.

A few days later on Feb. 13, he fired a fatal bullet into a 72-year-old ex-prizefighter on a Santa Cruz street.

On Feb. 15 he was arrested. He was convicted Aug. 18 and sentenced to life imprisonment on Sept. 18.

Edmund Kemper's case went to Santa Cruz County Superior Court a month after Mullin's ended. It was his second trial. At the age of 15, Kemper had been convicted of killing his paternal grandparents and was sent to a state mental institution for five years. He was released in 1969.

The 6-foot-9, 280-pound Kemper had killed a total of six hitchhiking coeds by February 1973. He knew none of the young women.

Two days before Easter Sunday 1973, Kemper struck again. This time it was his mother.

"I certainly wanted for my mother a nice, quiet death like I guess everyone wants," he told police.

He struck her with a hammer and beheaded her while she slept, he related, and then strangled her best friend.

Kemper fled to Colorado where he was arrested April 24, 1973, after telephoning Santa Cruz police to confess. He was returned to California under heavy guard and helped police locate the bodies and parts of bodies of his eight victims.

He was sentenced to life imprisonment Nov. 8, 1973.

Jacqueline Onassis, widow of President John F. Kennedy, and her children, Caroline and John, attended services at St. Bridget Church in Peapack, N.J., on the 10th anniversary of his assassination Nov. 22

Left, Helen Stewart, winner of the International Woman of the Year Hat Award for 1973, modeled a new hat. Above, what looked like rows of marching stick figures actually were concrete piers for a highway being built in Kentucky. Below, Agatha Christie and her husband Sir Max Mallowan celebrated the 21st birthday of her thriller play "The Mousetrap"—longest running play in the history of British Theater.

December

War Flared in the Middle East After Months of Violence

But There Were Hopes for Peace as the Warring
Sides Sat Down to Peace Negotiations in Geneva

ARAB. Jew.
Cousins, both, of the Semitic peoples. Nations, both, whose Gods had decreed that the land should be theirs.

But whose?

The Arab's? Or the Jew's?

Only a family feud could be as bitter. Or, perhaps, religious strife. Arab and Jew have had both. But now, on Dec. 21, 1973, for the first time in a quarter century of bloodshed, Arab sons of Allah and Jewish sons of Jehovah sat down together for full-fledged negotiations—to decide the ancient question, perhaps, and to bring peace to the Promised Land.

The negotiations weren't easily arranged.

Guerrillas and commandos had been operating all year. There was a Palestinian attempt to bomb the Israeli ambassador's residence in Cyprus; the Israeli assassination of three Palestinian guerrilla leaders in downtown Beirut; the slaying of an Israeli military attache outside his suburban Washington, D.C., home; an attack on an El Al office in Athens by a Palestinian who was chased into a hotel where he held 17 hostages; the interception of an Iraqi airliner by Israeli jets, which forced it to land near Haifa, where the Israelis discovered the radical Palestinian leader they were looking for had decided not to take the flight. There were Palestinian shootouts at the airports in Athens and Rome, which killed 35 and wounded scores of others. And there were assorted hijackings—mostly of airliners, but one of a train carrying Jewish immigrants to Austria from the Soviet Union, which convinced Austria to close its transit facilities for Soviet Jews.

But a three-hour Syrian-Israeli dogfight Sept. 13 over the Mediteranean was portent of a larger bloodletting to come. It was the biggest air battle between Arabs and Jews since the six-day Middle East war in June of 1967 (The World in 1967, 110). Syria said it shot down five Israeli planes and lost eight of its own. Israel said it downed 13 Syrian jets and lost one of its own. Sporadic artillery fire was reported on the Syrian-Israeli border.

Oct. 6. The Jewish fast of Yom Kippur. The 10th day of the Islamic fast of Ramadan. A time for atonement.

At 2 p.m. Arab fighters shrieked across the Suez Canal from Egypt. They snarled over the rocky heights of Golan from Syria. Armored personnel carriers. Bulldozers. Tanks. T-34s, T-54s and T-55s. Missiles. SAMs, 2s, 3s and 6s. Artillery, breathing fire on the kibbutzim. Across the canal the Egyptians threw a bridge. Over the interlocking, reinforced plastic, treaded one tank, then another. The foothold became a staging area. By nightfall on two fronts, in the Sinai Desert and around Mt. Hermon, the Arab sons of Allah and the Jewish sons of Jehovah—at a time both had set aside to beg their Gods for forgiveness—were at all-out war. It was their fourth since Israeli independence.

At issue were the Sinai and the Golan Heights—stripped from the Arabs by the Israelis with lightning strikes in 1967—and pride: an end to the humiliation the Arabs suffered at that defeat. "Any kind of fighting," declared a Cairo resident, "is better than doing nothing."

The Arabs fought with a vengeance. They bridged the canal with more spans of plastic. Two. Five. Nine. Then eleven. Egyptian tanks by the hundreds crossed into the Israeli-held Sinai.

By the second day of fighting, the Egyptians said they had destroyed 57 Israeli planes, 92 tanks and a large number of halftracks—and spilled large amounts of Jewish blood onto the desert. Cairo television showed Egyptian soldiers hoisting the Egyptian flag on Israeli sand.

On the Golan Heights, the Syrians attacked with a thousand tanks. News correspondents were barred from most of the fighting. But an American reporter in Beirut learned the Syrians had penetrated Israeli defenses by several miles. And Arab broadcasts in Beirut said 100 Israeli planes had been shot down.

In Tel Aviv, the Israeli command said its forces had knocked out only nine of the 11 Egyptian bridges across the Suez. And the Israelis conceded: "Syrian forces succeeded in making a number of ground advances."

While Jordan, Iraq, Algeria, Tunisia, Morocco and Libya prepared to send aid to the Arab cause, President Nixon and Leonid I. Brezhnev, the Soviet Communist party leader, exchanged private messages. Administration officials said the United States, allied with Israel, and the Soviet Union, allied with the Arab nations, shared a desire to limit the conflict. But there was little immediate progress in efforts to end the war.

Egypt poured more tanks and infantry across the canal. The Cairo command reported holding the entire 100-mile length of the channel, from Port Faud in the north to the city of Suez in the south. Egyptian troops raided Israeli-occupied Egyptian oilfields at Balayim on the Gulf of Suez. And the Egyptians reported shooting down more Israeli Phantom and Skyhawk jets.

The Syrians massed their tanks on the Golan Heights and drove three wedges deeply into Israeli territory—some 10 miles behind Israeli lines at one point near the village of Hushniya.

On Oct. 8, Israel counterattacked.

Skyhawks and Phantoms reported knocking out all of the Egyptian bridges over the Suez canal and destroying 15 Egyptian warplanes in dogfights over the Sinai. In 30 hours of fighting, Tel Aviv said, most of the Egyptian armor and infantry on the east bank of the canal had been destroyed or driven back. The Israelis said remaining Egyptian units were cut off and surrounded.

Israeli fighter-bombers struck Syria's five major military airfields. They knocked down three fighter-bombers over eastern Galilee. On the ground, Israeli tanks and self-propelled ar-

Above, a Syrian villager and his donkey were victims of fighting on a road in the Golan Heights. Below, firemen of Trans-Arabian Pipeline Co. fought a blaze near the oil storage tanks at Zahrani, South Lebanon

Top left, Egyptian troops planting their flag on a former Israeli bunker on the Bar-Lev line taken by Egyptian troops Oct. 13. Bottom left, smoke billowed from a burning oil refinery at Homs, Syria. Above, an Israeli soldier leading blindfolded Egyptian war prisoners. Below, Israeli pontoon bridge across the Suez Canal

tillery concentrated on the three Syrian wedges. The fighting was intense. The Israelis reported surrounding and crushing two brigades in the Syrian spearhead.

By nightfall, said Lt. Gen. David Elazar, the Israeli chief of staff, "we managed to push almost all of them back to the (1967) cease-fire line." Elazar numbered the Syrian tanks destroyed in the "many hundreds."

But the Arab resistance was heavier than many Israeli commanders expected.

Under an umbrella of Soviet-built SAMs on the west bank of the canal, Egypt pumped fresh tanks and men across the Suez. They reported advancing nine miles into the Sinai, wiping out an entire Israeli unit—Armored Brigade 190—and capturing its commander, Col. Assaf Yagouri.

On the Golan Heights, Israeli columns pushed Syrian tanks back to the 1967 cease-fire line, and Israeli Phantoms attacked Damascus, killing and injuring 100 persons. But Maj. Gen. Aharon Yariv, special adviser to the Israeli chief of staff, conceded that the Israelis had failed to sweep the Golan clean. And Yariv conceded that Israel had abandoned its Bar-Lev line of blockhouses, dugouts and communication posts along the east bank of the Suez canal.

It was the Succoth. A silvery moon rose over the wailing wall in Jerusalem, marking the Feast of Tabernacles, one of the most joyous in the Jewish year. "My sons! My sons!" sobbed an Israeli woman, swaying and kissing one of the massive stones. "Oh, Lord, let them come back alive!"

In a religious holiday address, Premier Golda Meir said she had no doubt the war would end in an Israeli victory. "But," she said, "this may take more than six days."

Informed Israelis estimated the growing Egyptian invasion force at nearly 75,000 men. The Egyptians had crossed the canal with, in all, about 600 tanks, the Israelis said, and 300 to 400 of these still were operational. News correspondents, finally permitted by the Egyptians to venture into the Sinai, reported Egyptian forces 10 miles or more east of the canal. Amid signs of recent Israeli presence—peelings from Haifa oranges, Hebrew newspapers and a torn Israeli flag—they found Egyptian soldiers cutting yet another wedge into the east bank of the canal to accommodate still another bridge, this one made of loose boards and pontoons. Two young Egyptian soldiers danced on a truck to a hand-clapping rhythm. "Don't worry," yelled another, "God is with us!"

The Israeli high command made a decision. It would settle for containment of the Egyptians for the time being—and concentrate on defeating the Syrians first. Early Oct. 11, Israeli fighters flashed over the Golan Heights. Long columns of Israeli tanks, halftracks, armored personnel carriers and mobile heavy guns began rumbling into action. The tanks paused while the heavy guns pounded thousands of shells across a narrow no-man's land. Then the armor rolled again.

Israeli tanks, emblazoned the "Damascus Express," pushed to the top of a ridge, paused while their guns fired a final barrage, then crossed the old cease-fire line and swept into a broad Syrian valley opposite the Golan village of Birkat Ram. They left Syrian tanks in flaming wreckage on the gently rising slopes on the east side of the valley and pushed into the foothills as the afternoon light began to fade.

Israeli Defense Minister Moshe Dayan arrived by helicopter. He told correspondents: "The same road that leads from Damascus to Tel Aviv also leads from Tel Aviv to Damascus." By Oct. 13, the Israelis had struck to within 18 miles of the Syrian capital and consolidated their flanks around the Syrian village of Sassa, just 20 miles away.

In Washington, U.S. military specialists said the Soviet Union had begun to resupply Syria and Egypt with thousands of tons of equipment from supply centers in Hungary. The United States, in turn, began preparing to ship F-4 Phantoms to Israel to replace the 75 to 80 Phantoms and A-4 Skyhawks the Pentagon estimated the Israelis had lost so far.

Saudi Arabia warned that if the United States went through with its resupply plans, the Saudi Arabians would begin cutting their crude oil production. Of the 17 million barrels of crude oil the United States consumed each day, 1.1 million barrels came from the Arab states. And authorities said such cutbacks could cause even more severe dislocations in Japan and Western Europe.

Despite the warning, the United States began flying more planes and guns into the Middle East. The Soviets promised even more help for the Arabs. And the Arab nations began cutting their export of oil to what they considered unfriendly nations. Saudi Arabia cut back production by 10 per cent—and said it would cut off all oil to the United States if it continued sending Israel aid. Within days, Qatar, Kuwait, Bahrain, Dubai, Abu Dhabi and Libya embargoed all of their oil exports to the United States— and Libya doubled its prices for other importers.

Then, a surprise.

At 1 a.m., Oct. 16, Israeli tanks and troops in halftracks rammed through high earthen embankments near Deversoir on the east bank of the canal, just north of the Great Bitter Lake and at near midpoint on the channel. On self-propelled rafts and barges, they struck west into Egypt. Cairo said three tanks were destroyed and that the Egyptians were pursuing four others. The Egyptians said the Israeli bridgehead was knocked out.

But Egyptian Maj. Gen. Azzedin Mokhtar said the Israelis rebuilt it. The Egyptians knocked it out again, Mokhtar said, and the Israelis rebuilt it again—an untold number of times.

Through a wedge they had driven into the Egyptian positions on the east bank of the canal, the Israelis rolled more and more tanks over the channel. Reinforcements followed: halftracks and artillery. Israeli planes flew close support.

The next day, four Arab foreign ministers brought a general peace proposal to President Nixon—and Soviet Premier Alexei N. Kosygin met in Cairo with President Anwar el-Sadat. "This . . ." declared Secretary of State Henry Kissinger, "is a test of the . . . real meaning of detente."

East of the Suez canal, the Egyptians and Israelis assembled tank forces described by Israeli Maj. Gen. Haim Herzog as larger than the combined forces at El Alamein in World War II. The Israelis, estimated to number 20,000 by the Egyptians, pounded the Egyptians, estimated to number 70,000 to 80,000 by the Israelis and deployed the full length of the canal between three to five miles east of the channel. The Israelis said they trapped a number of the Egyptians in a classic "hammer and anvil."

At the same time, the Israeli bridgehead in Egypt was growing. Tel Aviv said scores of Israeli tanks, artillery units and foot soldiers had driven some 20 miles into Egypt. The Israeli invasion force increased to 10,000 men. Behind more than 200 tanks, they pushed north, west and south, attacking the SAM batteries providing umbrella protection for the Egyptians on the Israeli side of the canal.

As they cleared a 24-mile area west of the canal of artillery and missile emplacements, and more and more Egyptians east of the canal found themselves without air cover, the Israelis moved to sever the Egyptians' water, fuel and other resupply lines and cut off any attempt they might make to retreat.

The Israelis said they had cut Egypt's north-south road from Ismailia to Suez—and were within artillery distance of the main road from Ismailia to Cairo.

Casualties on both sides were heavy.

On Oct. 20, Kissinger flew to Moscow. Within little more than an hour after he landed, he began a round of talks with Communist leader Brezhnev that lasted two hours. The next day, Kissinger and Brezhnev met for four hours.

The war in the Middle East became a race by both sides to gain the best possible military position before the U.S.-Soviet efforts for a ceasefire bore fruit—one European ambassador called it "a race by both the Israelis and the Egyptians against Kissinger and Brezhnev."

The Israelis drove south on the Egyptian side of the canal to within 10 miles of the northern outskirts of the city of Suez. They drove north on the Ismailia-Cairo road to an area just southwest of Ismailia. Then they straddled the single rail line between Cairo and Suez, expanding the Israeli bridgehead into a dumbell-shaped enclave about 20 miles deep and 33 miles wide.

Grimly, the Egyptians held onto two strips of the Sinai on the Israeli side of the canal. One was about five miles wide from the southern end of the channel 30 miles north to the southern tip of the Great Bitter Lake. The other was a similarly narrow strip from above the Israeli wedge about 20 miles north to Qantara.

Right, Israeli soldiers raised the Star of David on a high point to mark Israel's cease-fire position after the second U.N. sponsored truce went into effect Oct. 24. Below, jubilant Egyptians cheered in Cairo's streets upon hearing of the cease-fire

Late Sunday, Oct. 21, the Soviet Union and the United States announced in Moscow and Washington they had agreed to submit to the United Nations a joint resolution to end the hostilities in the Middle East. Both requested an urgent session of the Security Council.

Diplomats converged at the U.N. in New York. The Security Council convened at 10 p.m.

"We believe this Council, in exercising its primary responsibility in the field of peace and security," U.S. Ambassador John Scali told the council members, "can make a major contribution to this end by adopting this resolution promptly." Declared Soviet Ambassador Yakov Malik: "The time will not wait."

Israeli tanks rumbled closer to subsidiary roads stretching toward Qantara in the north and rolled to within nine miles of the outskirts of Suez in the south, closing their trap on the thousands of Egyptians on the east bank of the canal.

Huang Hua, Chinese ambassador to the U.N., accused the two superpowers of "imposing their view on the Security Council." But at 12:49 a.m. Monday, Oct. 22, the council voted. Fourteen nations favored the cease-fire resolution. None opposed. China did not vote.

The resolution said: "All parties to the present fighting . . . (must) cease all firing and terminate all military activity immediately, no later than 12 hours after the moment of the adoption of this decision, in the positions they now occupy."

Premier Golda Meir met with her cabinet all night in Tel Aviv. She received a personal message from Nixon. In Cairo, President Sadat received "assurances" from Vladimir M. Vinogradov, the Soviet ambassador. The nature of the assurances remained secret.

But Mrs. Meir called Nixon's message "a personal appeal" to accept the truce. "At a time when Israel was more dependent than ever on the United States," she said, "we were hardly in a position to say no." At 7 a.m., Israel accepted the truce. At 2:30 p.m., Egypt did the same.

Syria—faced with Israeli occupation of 300 square miles of the Golan Heights within 20 miles of Damascus and outposts on Mt. Hermon and on other heights to the northeast—said it would consider.

At 6:52 p.m. (12:52 p.m. Monday, EST), as Israeli troops inched closer to Qantara and Suez, the commanders of the Egyptians and Israelis ordered their men to stop shooting.

"Dammit!" cursed an Israeli soldier in Egypt. "They're stopping it just as we have them on the run. We've run half the race, we're winning, and now they tell us to stop."

"It'll never work," said another.

The truce resolution had, indeed, left vast questions unanswered.

By Sadat's interpretation, it required Israelis to withdraw immediately from all Arab territories they had been holding since 1967. But the resolution itself did not speak about withdrawal. It referred, instead, to a Security Council resolution passed in 1967 instrumental in ending the six-day war. That resolution had called on Israel to withdraw—and declared the right of "every state in the area . . . to live in peace within secure and recognized boundaries." But for more than six years Israel had been refusing to withdraw, saying its occupied territory was necessary for it to maintain those "secure and recognized boundaries."

There was little argument, however, about provisions for peace talks. Arabs and Jews alike had suffered enormously. But

Israeli armor made use of protective sandpits in the desert which were dug by the Egyptian army west of the Suez Canal.

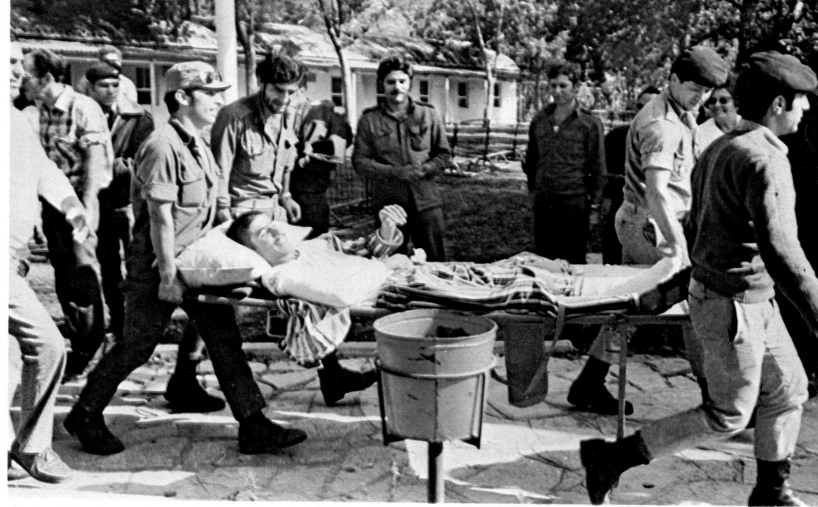

A returned Israeli war prisoner managed a weak gesture as soldiers carried him from an ambulance upon his arrival in Tel Aviv

how a "just and lasting peace" would be negotiated remained an open question.

So did exchange of prisoners.

Syria finally accepted the truce. But clashes were reported on the southern salient of the Israeli bridgehead in Egypt. Israel poured in supplies and fresh troops. The Soviet Union accused Israel of breaking the cease-fire and warned Tel Aviv of "grave consequences" unless the fighting stopped. But heavy artillery kept booming at El Firdan. And the Cairo command reported fighting with tanks, mechanized infantry and planes.

By dawn Oct. 24, the Israelis had closed their trap. They had driven all the way south to the city of Suez and beyond to the port of Adabiya, on the Gulf of Suez—isolating the Egyptian Third Army on the west bank of the canal. The 20,000 Egyptians, cut off from food and water and fuel for their 200 tanks, tried in vain to fight their way out.

At the behest of the United Nations, Israeli Defense Minister Moshe Dayan proposed a new cease-fire, to begin at 7 a.m. the next day. Egypt accepted.

President Sadat appealed to the Soviet Union and to the United States to send their armed forces into the Middle East to supervise the new cease-fire.

But the White House rejected the proposal, and added: "We hope other outside powers will not send troops to the Middle East."

As night fell, Brezhnev sent Nixon a note. Neither the Soviet Union nor the United States would reveal its contents. But Sen. Henry M. Jackson, D-Wash., characterized the note as "brutal, rough" in tone. And although the State Department denied it, Time magazine said the note "threatened the destruction of the State of Israel."

U.S. military officials said the Soviets had alerted their airborne troops and diverted air transports possibly for ferrying them into the Middle East. On Oct. 25, Nixon ordered a worldwide "precautionary alert" of U.S. forces.

Nations tensed.

The Security Council voted in mid-afternoon to establish a U.N. emergency force to supervise the cease-fire in the Middle East. It specifically excluded troops from the superpowers. Both the United States and the Soviet Union voted for it.

And the tension eased.

Nixon called it the worst crisis since the Cuban missile crisis in 1962. Because of it, he postponed a news conference he had scheduled to deal with a domestic crisis: Watergate.

Nixon said he had believed Moscow was planning to send "a very substantial force" into the Middle East. In his note, Brezhnev "was very firm," Nixon said, "and left very little to the imagination as to what he intended.

"And my response was also very firm and left little to the imagination of how we would react," Nixon said. "And it's because he and I know each other, and it's because we have had personal contact, that notes exchanged in that way result in a settlement rather than a confrontation . . ."

As the United Nations installed its peacekeepers between the Israelis and the Egyptians, the United States began removing its forces from their alert—carefully conditioning its actions on similar moves by the Soviet Union to take its airborne troops off their alert.

The world sighed with relief.

But, even in the presence of the U.N. peacekeepers, the Middle East truce was shaky.

The Egyptian Third Army tried again, in vain, to break out of its trap. The Israelis said they sent in blood plasma—but nothing else. Under what they described as compulsion from the United States, the Israelis finally permitted a U.N. truck convoy to reach the trapped soldiers with medical supplies, food and water.

In efforts to strengthen the cease-fire, first Egyptian Foreign Minister Ismail Fahmy, then Premier Meir conferred in Washington with Nixon.

Days later, in a whirlwind tour one official described as "diplomacy of the headlong rush," Kissinger visited five Arab nations: Morocco, Tunisia, Egypt, Jordan and Saudi Arabia. His assistant, Joseph Sisco, visited Tel Aviv.

They got agreements from both sides providing:

—Closer observance of the cease-fire;

—Mutual discussion of a return to positions held at the time of the first U.N. cease-fire and mutual disengagement and separation of forces;

—Food, water and medicine for the town of Suez and evacuation of all wounded civilians;

—Non-military supplies for the Egyptian Third Army;

—U.N. checkpoints on the Cairo-Suez road and the exchange of prisoners of war.

The prisoners numbered an estimated 241 Israelis in Egypt and 8,301 Egyptians in Israel. Total Arab casualties were said to number nearly 20,000. Israel counted 1,854 dead, 1,800 seriously wounded and thousands of others hurt.

As Arab nations tightened their oil boycott, contributing to an energy crisis in the United States and threatening economic disruption in France, West Germany, the Netherlands, Britain and Japan, Israeli Maj. Gen. Aharon Yariv and Egyptian Lt. Gen. Mohammed Abdel Ghany el Gamazy sealed agreements in a U.N. tent at Kilometer 101, an Israeli-held checkpoint on the Cairo-Suez road, spelling out the POW exchange and lifting the Israeli seige on Suez and on the Egyptian Third Army.

Syria, however, demanded the surrender of two strategic positions Israel had taken on the Golan Heights in return for its 127 Israeli prisoners of war. Israel rejected the Syrian demand.

Disengagement and separation negotiations between Gens. Yariv and Gamazy foundered in early December on Kilometer 101—because, Newsweek magazine said, Kissinger proposed making them the first items at the face-to-face Middle East peace negotiations in Geneva.

So it was that the Yom Kippur war left a mixed legacy.

Neither side scored a decisive victory. But Arab self-confidence

was restored. Resolute battle performances by the Egyptians and the Syrians had changed the image of the Arab soldier. Flushed with the success of their oil embargo and with their effectiveness on the battlefield, the Arab nations gave President Sadat a hearty endorsement at their December summit meeting in Algeria.

On the other hand, Israeli officials privately complained about a diplomatic setback. The United States, they said, had been able to force it to do things it hadn't really wanted to do—to halt its army while it was advancing and while Egyptian troops remained in the Sinai, for instance, and to permit resupply of the Egyptian Third Army. "It was a very big victory," said Maj. Gen. Shlomo Gazit, describing the end of the war for the Israelis, "which could have been bigger." Premier Meir's Labor Party lost ground during Israeli elections on the last day of the year. It weakened her hand at Geneva and confronted her with the prospect of having to form a new coalition government.

Both Israel and the United States were left questioning their intelligence capabilities. Despite several suspicious signals, including Soviet evacuation of dependents from Egypt and Syria, neither had seriously believed at the beginning of October that the Arabs were about to attack. There was talk in both countries about an "intelligence gap."

And the war caused a rift in NATO. For the first time since NATO was created in 1949, the United States openly criticized its allies for lack of cooperation. Britain had declined a U.S. request to sponsor a cease-fire resolution in the United Nations during the first week of the war. Other NATO allies had balked at U.S. demands to pressure the Soviet Union by chilling trade and political relations. Some NATO nations, apparently intimidated by the Arab oil boycott, had prohibited U.S. aircraft resupplying the Israelis from flying over their territories—and from re-fueling on the ground. In addition, the United States said, some of its NATO allies had been very flaccid in their response to the U.S. "precautionary alert."

The Yom Kippur war, however, had managed for the first time since the beginning of Arab-Israeli conflicts in 1948 to involve both the United States and the Soviet Union together in a search for peace in the Middle East.

As the Geneva negotiations went on, Kissinger cautioned delegates not to despair—even during times of deadlock.

"Remember," he said, "that this is the first real chance for peace the Middle East has had in three decades."

A cordon of blue-helmeted U.N. troops stood with fixed bayonets encircling a tent in which Israeli and Egyptian officers signed cease-fire accords

Sgt. Vincent R. Jacobucci grabbed a champagne bottle to celebrate leaving Vietnam

The Americans Came Home but the Fighting Went on in War-Weary Indochina

The shooting never stopped between the Vietnamese and strife increased in Cambodia

THE CEREMONY IN PARIS had been a solemn one, a proper mood for ending a great war that had cost perhaps two million lives. It had marked the end to negotiations begun in 1968 that had staggered, stalled, bogged down in propaganda

and hinged on the latest battlefield reports from Vietnam. It was peace at last, the negotiators including America's Henry Kissinger had told the world.

But privately diplomats voiced fearful reservations. The peace

South Vietnam's President Nguyen Van Thieu, with President Nixon at his side, expressed gratitude for the American contribution to the war effort

document and all its protocols hinged on one thing—goodwill. Unless a mood of give and take could be established, the elation in Paris that January day would be crushed by the realities of renewed fighting on the battlefield rather than peace conferences deciding the future for the war-weary Indochinese Peninsula.

Almost immediately it became apparent that there was in fact no spirit of give and take. The laboriously negotiated peace pact was virtually meaningless to the Vietnamese. It had, as diplomats suggested months before, only been a peace for the United States. America got back its prisoners of war and pulled out the last of its combat units from a force that once totaled more than a million men.

But between the Vietnamese themselves, the fighting never stopped. Mainly this was because neither side held a clear power edge over the other, and each side still felt force of arms would carry the day for it eventually.

As the tempo of fighting continued at a high level, the United States seemed to almost ignore Vietnam. It wasn't our fight anymore, the politicians said. President Nixon had negotiated a peace with honor, if not for the allied side at least for American

forces. Watergate and later the Middle East War and the energy crisis consumed public interest and occupied the nation's front pages.

But the killing went on in Vietnam at a level high enough one politician noted, "There is never a minute, never a moment when all the blood is dried." If the United States had stopped bombing, the void was filled by American bombs dropped by Vietnamese planes. There was no end to enemy attacks backed by Russian and Chinese communist-made rockets and mortar shells. Villages were still leveled or burned out. The fighting at times swirled dangerously close to Saigon and the ancient imperial capital of Hue. The war that was to have been ended had only reverted to its earlier status minus American military advisers. And much to the anger of the South Vietnamese, all the bombing and shelling and fighting was limited to their country. North Vietnam was again at peace within its own borders with the departure of American air power which had carried out history's most intensive air war against the north.

Kissinger and his Hanoi counterpart, Le Duc Tho; held two meetings in Paris during the year, the latest in December, in what Washington hoped would be sessions to make peace a reality. Both failed and the year closed with more North Vietnamese troops and tanks in South Vietnam than ever before. Saigon said all intelligence reports showed that the Communists planned a major offensive in 1974 and already had the military might to conduct high level battlefield operations with 200,000 men for a year. As Saigon's troops braced for the worst, it appeared that both sides still were angling for a clear battlefield decision that would leave one the victor and make the Jan. 27 peace accords interesting only to historians.

During the year, there were but few major battles such as those that regularly marked the war in the past. The Communists pushed into as much territory as possible and ominously pushed an all-weather road hundreds of miles southward from the North Vietnamese frontier. Much of the late year fighting seemed to involve Communist efforts to push the road farther south linking up with its major headquarters only two hours drive from Saigon.

Official South Vietnamese figures showed that during the first year of "peace," it had lost more than 11,000 dead, 52,000 wounded and 4,000 missing against 42,000 Communist soldiers killed. The Saigon command also said some 2,000 civilians were killed and 5,000 wounded in the fighting that created 600,000 new refuges, bringing the total homeless on the government side to 10 million, more than half South Vietnam's population.

More than anything, casualties showed the de-Americanization of the war. After more than a decade and some 45,000 dead, the United States lost only six men—three GIs and three civilians—during the year. All were involved in noncombat work such as seeking bodies of Americans who fell in fighting before the peace accords. One such incident, when an unarmed American officer was shot down by Communist troops as the American raised his arms in surrender, brought the closest thing to a crisis in American-North Vietnamese relations. But the North Vietnamese had powerful reasons for wanting to at least appear conciliatory toward the United States. They wanted promised U.S. aid dollars to begin flowing into Hanoi to help pay for reconstruction in the North. Kissinger apparently had made it clear that without genuine peace or at least major steps toward it, no dollars would be forthcoming. Although the Nixon Administration had promised such aid, it would have to be approved by Congress which was expected to prove balky even under the best of conditions. The argument at the Capitol was that there were too many unmet priorities inside the United States to allow for massive aid to a former enemy.

The peace-keeping machinery set up to defuse Indochina had proved a failure. The four-nation International Commission of Control and Supervision split as expected on ideological lines with Canada and Indonesia faced off against Poland and Hungry. Canada quit in disgust and was replaced by Iran.

Negotiations seeking to open the road to national reconciliation through political agreements between the Communists and the Saigon regime was equally ineffective. Both sides seemed content to carry out propaganda exercises rather than find meaningful accommodations. President Nguyen Van Thieu proved, as expected, to have no enthusiasm for political arrangements that would bring Communists into the government in any meaningful way. The Communists claimed, and U.S. diplo-

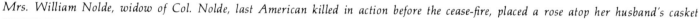

Mrs. William Nolde, widow of Col. Nolde, last American killed in action before the cease-fire, placed a rose atop her husband's casket

mats privately agreed, to have won the right on the battlefield to positions of power. By year's end the Communists controlled huge sections of the country although their hold was primarily not in densely populated regions. However, the land they do hold historically has been the launching pad for such giant offensives as the 1968 Tet push and the Easter offensive of 1972.

Thieu, despite promises in the peace accord, had kept his secret police busy intimidating or imprisoning government foes, even those who professed to be anti-Communist. His regime had lost none of its wartime oppressiveness and the government's mandate had been seriously eroded by an economic recession bordering on depression. Most of this was due to the vanishing, free spending Americans who poured perhaps a half billion dollars a year into the Vietnamese economy apart from the billions spent on the war and in direct economic aid. The sagging economy had hit the little men hardest, and it was among this group that Communist recruiters had always been the most successful. The mood in South Vietnam seemed one of apathy more than increased polarization at year's end. Increasing numbers of civilians, and some in the military as well, simply did not care which side won, as long as the war and its killing and destruction ended. Some diplomats said that Thieu, to maintain power, would have to make deals with the so-called third force, or his non-Communist opposition. American pressure in this direction repeatedly had failed in the past.

Although casualties during 1973 were roughly about half of those of 1972, military analysts said this did not mean that fighting in future months would remain at the lower level. They said after the massive casualties suffered on both sides during the Easter offensive of 1972, both armies had to spend most of their efforts rebuilding their combat forces before the expected climactic battles of the war could be fought. In the meantime, the Communists were proving reasonably successful in their nibbling campaign in the countryside.

The expected offensive could prove the first test of the Nixon doctrine, providing the means in terms of munitions and materials for a nation's self defense but no direct American support in terms of troops or aircraft. The original idea of injecting U.S. troops into Indochina was to give time to the badly battered Vietnamese troops to rebuild their shattered units following the 1965 spring offensive. Now, Washington had made clear, it was up to the Vietnamese to hack it, in President Nixon's words, or fail.

It was notable that during the previous two years the major powers in the region had made massive political swings in an effort to get on the right—or rather left-side of China which was expected to dominate the region with the withdrawal of American combat forces and the unlikelihood of their reintroduction. The other major competitor for power in Southeast Asia was the Soviet Union which wanted to build an alliance system in South and Southeast Asia that would isolate the Chinese, Moscow's current number one enemy.

The heaviest fighting during the year occurred in Cambodia, a nation that pretty much escaped the Indochina war until 1970 when American and Vietnamese troops poured over the frontier seeking out North Vietnamese supply depots in what had been sanctuaries. It also was revealed in 1973 that there had been a major clandestine bombing campaign in Cambodia years be-

A South Vietnamese sergeant kicked a soldier who had talked back to his commanders

Above, Government forces fired their howitzers a few miles from Phnom Penh, the beleaguered capital of Cambodia. Below, Viet Cong women prisoners of war transported in military trucks from the Mekong Delta

fore. The United States said the bombing was with the consent of then head of state, Prince Sihanouk. When the bombing became public in 1973 Sihanouk denied any complicity but observers recalled his comparative silence during the bombing.

During 1973, the ground war in Cambodia underwent massive changes. No longer were North Vietnamese troops the cutting edge for Communist offensives. To Phnom Penh's great embarrassment Khmer Rouge or Red Cambodian forces had grown to more than 45,000 troops from perhaps a couple of thousand when the war began in 1970. North Vietnamese troops provided heavy weapons support, but in the crunch of battle it was Cambodian against Cambodian.

These forces pushed during the year to within hand grenade distance of the capital which was routinely shelled and hit by sapper attacks. The offensive coincided with a congressionally mandated August cutoff of all American bombing in Cambodia and the worst fears, as it so often happens in Indochina, did not materialize once the skies were clear. The insurgent troops pulled back, easing the threat to the capital, although its vital road arteries were routinely cut.

The Cambodian army had fought for more than three years without a clearcut major victory, something that had weighed heavily on morale. Then came the battle for Kampong Cham, the nation's third largest city and an important military regional headquarters. Communist assault troops captured most of the town but reinforcements, sent partially at the urgent request of American specialists who stayed strictly in the background,

A Cambodian officer urging his men into battle

turned the tide of battle in perhaps the costliest single engagement of the war. The victory had electrifying effects on troops and civilians alike. And a major element in the battle was the lack of U.S. air support since the clash came after the Aug. 15 shutoff of U.S. aerial operations.

Perhaps the biggest problem in Cambodia was the declining influence and viability of its government. Marshal Lon Nol continued as head of the country although he suffered serious health problems. Cabinet reshuffles were sloughed off by the public as just so much more old wine in new bottles. The government enjoyed tremendous popularity after the 1970 coup which ousted Sihanouk, but the store of goodwill had eroded to virtually zero due to military reverses and runaway inflation coupled with shortages. At year's end, the Communists held 85 per cent of the countryside and about one-half of the population, placing the government in a far more precarious position than Vietnam had ever found itself in.

At year's end, Phnom Penh nervously awaited the coming of the dry season when traditionally military action is at its maximum. Little improvement in the quality of its forces had been made during the previous three years. The quality of leadership, crucial for Asian armies, remained low and that super enthusiasm noted among the troops at the beginning of the war had faded to a feeling of near depression as casualties mounted and government control shrank almost daily. The situation was serious enough that the Cambodian command was unable to launch one major offensive during the year, contenting itself in trying to meet the Communist initiatives when and where they appeared.

Those trying to find some reason for optimism in Indochina had to turn to Laos where not only peace was signed in February, but by and large all fighting stopped in the landlocked kingdom for the first time in nearly a quarter century. Unlike Vietnam, the warring parties in Laos did not only stop shooting. They held meaningful political talks that resulted in a coalition government, the third in 20 years but also one where real hope could be found. The Laotian Communists were given equal stature in the new government whereas in the past the coalition was divided between the right, the neutralists and the left. As usual, Prince Souvanna Phouma stayed on as premier since he was the one man acceptable to all parties. But at 73, the premier's role might be curtailed somewhat by his flagging strength. The new coalition was opposed by the rightists, and on Aug. 20, Air Force Gen. Thao Ma attempted a coup that failed within hours. The political realities in Laos were that no government could reasonably expect to survive without the backing of the U.S. Embassy which through its huge aid budget could make or break the power at the moment in Vientiane. This happened earlier when a right wing government refused to go along with an earlier peace deal and Washington cut off all aid to Vientiane.

There did not appear to be a final solution to the Laotian problem in the sense that both the Communists and the government were bent on exercising absolute control over the areas that were in their hands at the time of the peace accords. This gave the Communists roughly 85 per cent of the land, although nearly all of it was in the mountains, and roughly half of the population.

North Vietnam, which had called the tune for the Laotian Communists since the beginning, was expected to keep government forces and administrators out of Communist-held territory because this included the Ho Chi Minh trail so vital to supplying Hanoi's forces in South Vietnam and to a lesser extent, the Khmer Rouge in Cambodia.

Watergate III

1973 ended but it was clear the scandal wasn't over

URING THE DOG DAYS OF AUGUST, Supreme Court Justice Harry D. A. Blackmun had referred sadly to the "pall of Watergate" that covered the nation. By year's end the pall had by no means lifted. It had only grown heavier and the nation wearier.

For the first time in a century the House of Representatives had begun the formal processes to impeach a President. For the first time in its history the nation had found itself, at one traumatic point, with no vice president, no attorney general, no deputy attorney general, no independent official to probe the suspected sins of its government, and no early promise of sur-

cease. Faced with the many-tentacled scandal encompassed by the blanket term "Watergate," the President of the United States took to the political stump to try to restore his credibility. He had even resorted to the extraordinary declaration: "I am no crook."

The scandal unfolded in the spring, with allegations of perjury and payoffs and obstruction of justice and the dismissals and resignations of many in the highest echelons of the administration. Summertime brought the airing by a Senate Committee of much of the dirty presidential linen together with new dis-

About 200 demonstrators turned out in Boston to call for impeachment

Above, Special Prosecutor Archibald Cox was dismissed by the President for refusing to abandon his legal battle to obtain tape recordings of White House conversations between Nixon and his aides. Below, Attorney-General Elliot Richardson, whose resignation was accepted by the White House

closures of bugging and burglary done in the name of "national security." Through all this and the appointment of a special Watergate prosecutor, Nixon had avoided answering questions in public about the scandals, responding in formal speeches or letting others do his talking for him.

But with a Gallup Poll showing approval of his official conduct at its lowest ebb, and to fulfill a commitment that he would come out of seclusion following the first phase of the Senate Watergate hearings, the President on Aug. 22, called his first news conference in five months.

It was a remarkable session. Nixon conducted it on the lawn of his San Clemente estate and it ranked among the most grueling public interrogations of a President in memory. For 50 minutes he answered questions that at times bordered on the hostile. At one point he complained that all the questions dealt with Watergate rather than "the business of the people," implying that Watergate somehow did not fit that category. It was true that of 20 questions posed to Nixon 16 dealt with Watergate matters—and they were tough questions.

For example: Had the President not violated his oath of office by authorizing illegal wiretaps and burglaries, and therefore ought he not be impeached?

In his answers, Nixon was alternatively combative, defensive and angry. But he held his ground. No, he said, he had not violated his oath because the Supreme Court had granted presidents authority for surreptitious entries in the national defense. Furthermore, he said, "burglaries of this type" had been conducted under Presidents Kennedy and Johnson—an allegation hastily challenged.

(F.B.I. officials acknowledged that the agency had, over a period of 30 years, broken into various embassies to gather foreign intelligence and entered places frequented by organized crime figures to plant microphones. The practice was discontinued in 1966, agency spokesmen said, because F.B.I. Director J. Edgar Hoover did not consider it worth the risk. There was no indication that either Presidents Kennedy or Johnson knew it was going on. Former Attorneys General Nicholas DeB. Katzenbach and Ramsey Clark, who served both presidents, said even they did not know of such enterprises because, as the F.B.I. explained, information thus gathered had always been presented as deriving from "confidential informants.")

Responding to other questions, the President denied he had told John Dean that raising hush money for the Watergate defendants was all right, denied there was any particular significance in Acting F.B.I. Director L. Patrick Gray's warning that White House aides were trying to "mortally wound" him, denied that there was anything improper in his offering Judge Matthew Byrne the F.B.I. directorship. Nixon did acknowledge that his ability to govern had been impaired by Watergate, but he blamed collective enemies—politicians, the press, liberals—for keeping the case alive. Finally, he said with emphasis, "I shall not resign." Opinion surveys later showed that the President had benefitted from the confrontation, not so much because he had resolved any issues but simply because he had faced them in public.

Meanwhile the controversy over the presidential tape recordings continued. When it was disclosed that President Nixon had an elaborate system of voice-activated recorders to monitor not only phone calls but also conversations in his various offices, both the Senate Watergate Committee and Special Prosecutor Archibald Cox set out to get the tape recordings. Both issued subpoenas, which the President rejected. In a lengthy brief, Cox argued that the President did not have the right to withhold such information. On behalf of the President, Charles Alan Wright, a constitutional expert called in to bolster the Nixon legal team, argued for a privileged presidential status. Both submitted briefs to Chief Judge John J. Sirica of the Federal District Court in Washington. For its part, the Senate Committee sat back, as did the nation at large, to watch the legal battle unfold.

On Aug. 29, a week after the case had been argued, Sirica announced his decision. In a historic, 23-page opinion which threaded through a maze of legal and political precedents, Sirica ruled that the President must turn over the tapes to him. After examining them in private, Sirica said he would determine whether they contained evidence that should properly be submitted to a grand jury. He would, he said, excise any "privileged" portions, but he could not possibly rule on the claim of executive confidentiality without hearing the tapes himself. Thus, in principle, he supported Cox's contention that no man, not even a President, was immune from a grand jury's demand for evidence, because a grand jury derives its power not from the courts but from the people, the ultimate authority in a democracy.

The White House promptly announced that it would appeal the decision. The assumption was that it would ultimately be decided by the Supreme Court. Nixon himself said he would abide by a "definitive" Supreme Court decision, but he refused to clarify what he meant by "definitive."

In two months' time the tapes controversy would erupt into a full-blown constitutional crisis with the very tapestry of gov-

Trial lawyer Leon Jaworski was named to succeed prosecutor Cox

ernment seeming to unravel. Meanwhile, other developments kept the hydra-headed scandal before the public. Not the least of these was the disclosure that the President had once placed a wiretap on his own brother's phone. Donald Nixon's financial dealings with millionaire Howard Hughes had caused Richard Nixon embarrassment in the past. The White House, by way of explanation, said the taps were "related to the protective function of the Secret Service." As for its reason for tapping the phones of 17 government officials and newsmen—another disclosure which brought denunciations and lawsuits from some of those so spied upon—the official explanation was "national security."

One political satirist likened the almost daily developments of the Watergate scandal to a Japanese movie—"Just when you think it's over, there's another act." Thus, in Los Angeles on

Sept. 4, John D. Ehrlichman, the President's former chief domestic adviser, and three other White House aides, who were members of the "Plumbers" squad, were indicted for the burglary of the office of Dr. Lewis Fielding, [Daniel Ellsberg's psychiatrist]. Indicted with Ehrlichman were Egil Krogh, David Young and G. Gordon Liddy. Meanwhile, the Senate Watergate Committee reconvened to pursue the "dirty tricks" phase of its inquiry and the nation was treated to almost daily reports of political practices which would result, before the year was out, in the incarceration of one of the practitioners, Donald H. Segretti. As if Watergate weren't enough, the continuing troubles of Vice President Spiro T. Agnew, culminating in his resignation and refusal to contest a felony charge of tax evasion, added to the administration's woes and to the public's ever-growing skepticism.

But not even a nation surfeited with surprise and benumbed by a seemingly unending succession of shocks was prepared for the traumatic experience of a dizzying fortnight in October. The issue was the presidential tapes; Prosecutor Cox had sub-poenaed nine of them, along with other White House documents. On Oct. 12 the U.S. Court of Appeals for the District of Columbia, with minor alterations, sustained Sirica's ruling that he should examine the tapes in private. The court gave the President until midnight, Friday, Oct. 19, either to comply or appeal the decision to the Supreme Court. So confident was the President's own constitutional expert, Charles Alan Wright, that the course would be to appeal that he had gone to bed Thursday night, Oct. 18, secure in the knowledge that his petition to the Supreme Court had already been printed up and the $100 check for the filing fee written.

At 8:15 p.m. Friday, however, the President announced that he would neither comply nor appeal. He had, instead, a compromise.

He would, Nixon said, personally prepare a summary of the content of the tapes. This he would submit to Sen. John Stennis of Mississippi who would listen to the tapes and verify the accuracy of the summary. Stennis, 77, a former judge, was a Democrat with an unchallenged reputation for probity. It did

Ohio Sen. William Saxbe was named to succeed Elliot Richardson as attorney general

not escape notice, however, that Stennis also had a record of support for Nixon in his Watergate troubles; he once advised the President to "tough it out." There was also a towering caveat in the compromise: having accepted the summaries, Prosecutor Cox would then forswear any further attempts to get other presidential tapes or records.

In the behind-scenes discussions of the compromise, Cox had already made it clear he would not accept it. Atty.-Gen. Elliot Richardson, knowing that, also made it clear he would not support it. The White House went ahead with it anyhow. An hour after the announcement, Cox said: "For me to comply would violate my solemn pledge to the Senate and the country to invoke judicial process to challenge exaggerated claims of executive privilege. I shall not violate my promise. . . ."

At a news conference the next day, Saturday, Cox spelled out his objections. "It is simply not enough to make a compromise in which the real evidence is available only to two or three men operating in secrecy," he said.

Besides, he argued, it seemed most unlikely that a summary would be admissible in evidence when the "real evidence" was available.

Thus, he concluded that since the appeals court ruling had been neither obeyed nor appealed, he might have to ask that the President of the United States be judged in contempt of court.

"I have sort of a naive belief—forgive me for being corny— that right will prevail in the end," Cox said.

At 4:45 p.m. Saturday, Richardson went to the White House. He had been told that he must dismiss Cox for refusing to accept the compromise. His mission was to tell the President that he could not in conscience do so. He therefore must resign. Richardson argued that his own senatorial confirmation as Attorney General had been conditioned on a pledge that Cox would be unhindered in his investigation. Further, in guidelines written by himself and approved by Nixon, it had been agreed that Cox could be fired for no reason other than "extraordinary improprieties."

That done, Richardson returned at 5 p.m. to his office in the Justice Department. There, waiting, were the No. 2 and No. 3 men in line of authority, Deputy Atty.-Gen. William Ruckleshaus and Solicitor General Robert Bork. Richardson told them, "The deed is done."

In the next moment a secretary entered. Alexander Haig, the President's chief of staff, was on the telephone to speak with Ruckleshaus. Said Haig, now that Ruckleshaus was in charge it was his duty to fire Cox. Ruckleshaus demurred. "Your commander in chief has given you an order," said Haig, a former Army general, "You have no alternative."

"Other than to resign," Ruckleshaus replied.

Ruckleshaus passed the phone to Bork. Bork did not resign. He agreed to fire Cox.

At 8:30 p.m. the White House announced two resignations and a dismissal. And so ended Saturday, Oct. 20.

At 7 a.m. Sunday the President received on his Oval Office desk a 27-page document in a blue loose-leaf folder, his daily digest of Saturday's events as reported by the nation's press.

It was not comfortable reading. The digest reflected a national shock and anger that adminstration strategists clearly had not foreseen. A "miscalculation," one later called it.

"Impeachment" had suddenly grown from a whisper to a roar and the wind swirled across the country with a heat and fury that Nixon's chief of staff, Haig, could only liken to a "firestorm."

"A reckless act of desperation" . . . "Richard Nixon is a law-breaker" . . . "The administration is morally bankrupt" . . .

"His deeds are dishonorable" . . . "Impeachment at the earliest possible moment . . .". So ran the President's breakfast reading of comments in the news summary.

Outside the White House, out of the President's vision, pickets marched; inside, his ears could hardly have escaped an ongoing cacophony by passing motorists responding to a sign: "Honk for Impeachment."

Monday morning the firestorm burned hotter. The morning news digest delivered to Nixon carried more than 30 items of impeachment demands, mostly by members of Congress, and a statement by the head of the American Bar Association calling the President's actions "an assault of wholly unprecedented dimensions on the very heart of the administration of justice." At the Justice Department, another late development: Richardson's and Ruckleshaus's top assistants resigned, eight of them in all.

At noon on Tuesday, Oct. 23, the majority leader of the House of Representatives, Rep. Thomas P. O'Neill Jr., asked for recognition. He turned to the hushed chamber and said:

"Mr. Speaker, let us review the action of the President of the United States.

"No other president in the history of this nation has brought the highest office of the land into such low repute. His conduct must bring shame upon us all. . . .

"It is the responsibility of the House to examine its constitutional responsibilities in this matter."

Moments later the seed sown in the public consciousness during the early stages of Watergate ripened. Seven congressmen rose in turn to introduce resolutions to impeach Richard Nixon, cosoponsored by 29 Democrats and one Republican. The Speaker sent the resolutions to the Judiciary Committee for action.

Back in the Oval Office, an assistant relayed a blunt message to the President from Republican congressional leaders. They would not, they said, "go to the wall" with him, unless he made his tapes available to the courts. At about noon Richard Nixon made his decision. Wright was summoned and given instructions for his appearance before Judge Sirica, scheduled for 2 p.m., the first session of federal court since the Friday midnight deadline. At 2:07 p.m. Judge Sirica opened the hearing by reading his Aug. 29 order demanding the tapes and the ruling of the appellate court essentially upholding it. Was Wright, asked the judge, prepared to file "the response of the President?"

Wright moved to the lectern and said he was not. In the sudden hush of the packed courtroom all that could be heard was the scratching of reporters' pencils on notebooks.

"I am, however," Wright continued, "authorized to say that the President of the United States would comply in all respects with the order of August 29 as modified by the Court of Appeals."

Sirica appeared incredulous. "You will follow the decisions or statements delineated by me?"

"Will comply in all respects with what your honor has just read," Wright said.

All in the courtroom, including the judge, had expected Wright to propose the Nixon compromise. Judge Sirica smiled broadly. "Mr. Wright," he said, "the court is very happy the President has reached this decision." Across the nation the news of the abrupt capitulation was electric. "Thank God," said the junior senator from Arizona, Barry Goldwater.

On Wednesday, debate still sizzled in Washington over the matter of replacing the special prosecutor, who had been dismissed for demanding what the President ultimately yielded. At the Western Union office, circuits were clogged with more

Rose Mary Woods showed how she thought part of the tape erasure could have occurred

than 220,000 telegrams overwhelmingly unfavorable to Nixon, many demanding his impeachment. Senator Goldwater said the ratio of protests received at his office was 80 to 1 against the President.

On Thursday, a new crisis arose as American officials saw a possible threat of Russian intervention in the Arab-Israeli war. In the hours before dawn, President Nixon ordered a "precautionary alert" for all American military forces around the world.

However genuine the alert, it provided dismaying evidence of how deep suspicions of the President's actions had become. At a news conference, Secretary of State Henry Kissinger was obliged to answer three questions bearing on whether in effect the emergency had been contrived to draw attention from the President's Watergate and impeachment troubles.

Next day, at a tense and angry news conference of his own, the President announced that he would appoint a new Special Prosecutor, an action the Congress assuredly would take if he

didn't. The man finally picked was Leon Jaworski, an eminent Texas lawyer.

If the "Saturday Night Massacre," as the sackings of Oct. 23 became known in the press, hurt the President's credibility, it was destined to undergo another stern test a week later when the long-awaited moment arrived for the President to yield up the tape recordings he had so vigorously protected through three months of litigation. On Oct. 30 the President's special counsel on Watergate matters, J. Fred Buzhardt Jr., went before Sirica and exploded yet another bombshell. Two of the nine subpoenaed tapes, he said, were missing.

Which two? The two viewed as perhaps the most critical in getting at the truth of whether Nixon knew about or helped cover up the Watergate burglary. One was a record of a telephone conversation between Nixon and John N. Mitchell, his campaign manager, on June 20, 1972, three days after the burglary of Democratic headquarters. The other was the record of a meeting between the President and his counsel and chief accuser, John Dean, in the President's office April 15, 1973, during which Dean later alleged that Nixon had discussed clemency for the burglars. Ironically, it was Nixon's behavior at that meeting, Dean said, that led him to suspect their conversation was being recorded.

The White House offered two explanations for the missing tapes: the Mitchell conversation was made from a telephone extension not hooked into the recording system; the Dean conversation was not recorded because the tape had run out on the machine.

What Sirica found most puzzling, though, was why he had not been informed earlier. A White House aide, Stephen Bull, said he had told the President a full month beforehand that the two tapes were missing—three weeks before Cox had been fired for requesting them. And there were other mysteries. A White House archivist told Sirica that the official diary of Nixon's minute-by-minute whereabouts on April 15, the day of the Dean conversation, had been revised more than three months later, on July 26, the day the tapes were subpoenaed.

Buzhardt said he had ordered the revision because of conflicting statements about who had consumed the President's time that day. Also baffling was the fact that the carton in which an April 15 recording was kept had been labeled Part I, strongly suggesting there was a Part II. Bull said he had so labeled the box on the assumption that "there had to be another reel."

Perhaps most ominous for the President, more than the growing list of influential newspapers and magazines calling for his resignation or impeachment, was the erosion of support by some who had been among his most ardent backers. Conservative-Republican Sen. James L. Buckley of New York said of the disclosure of the missing tapes: "As of this moment, President Nixon has the clear burden of satisfying the American people that he has been speaking the truth." And Senator Goldwater of Arizona said Nixon's credibility "has reached an all-time low from which he may not be able to recover."

A survey by pollster Daniel Yankelovich showed that 55 per cent of Americans did not believe the President's story on the missing tapes and that less than half the public, 49 per cent, wanted him to stay in office. The Gallup Poll gave him a 27 per cent approval rating. Indeed the national debate seemed to reach a new level of discourse. It centered less on whether Nixon should remain in office than on which would be the less harmful means of his removal: resignation or impeachment.

At least one prominent Republican, Sen. Edward Brooke of Massachusetts, called publicly for resignation. Confronting the demands, the embattled President appeared on television Nov. 7, exactly a year after his sweeping election victory of 1972, to address the nation on the energy crisis. At the end of the speech he declared that he aimed to stay on the job so long as he was "physically able."

Meanwhile, almost as a sidelight to the central Watergate glare, Sirica gave the six original Watergate burglars and wiretappers sentences far lighter than the 35 to 40 years he had previously imposed on most of them. Apparently satisfied that they had told what they knew about the crimes, he imposed sentences ranging from one to 2½ years on five of the burglars; G. Gordon Liddy, who remained uncooperative with investigators, continued serving a minimum six-year, eight-month sentence.

To offset his low poll ratings the President, in mid-November, decided on a two-pronged strategy which the White House labeled "Operation Candor." For five days in succession he sat down with 280 Republican and 42 Democratic members of Congress to eat hot hors d'oeuvres and corned beef hash—and

to make his case before the one body of Americans who could do something about his tenure in office.

The second prong of his counterattack was to "go public." Standing before a gigantic electric replica of the United States flag he told a convention of enthusiastic realtors he was "not going to walk away" from his job until it was done.

Then, on Nov. 17, he took on the televised questions of news executives at the Associated Press Managing Editors convention in Florida.

He admitted that he had paid less than $1,000 in income taxes in both 1970 and 1971 because of deductions for the donation of his Vice Presidential papers to the government; declared that the burglary of Fielding's office was, in his personal view, "a stupid thing to do, apart from being an illegal thing to do"; said with some heat that "I have never profited from public service. . . . The people have got to know if their President is a crook. I'm not a crook."; and admitted that the Secret Service had tapped the telephone of his brother for "security" reasons he could not disclose.

Over in the Senate, the Watergate Committee began the third and final phase of its inquiry, a study of campaign financing practices, and once again the headlines that resulted added to the pall overhanging the administration. Executives from six out of seven companies that had admitted using corporate funds to help insure Nixon's re-election testified to the reasons for their illegal acts and how they concealed the donations.

One company paid phony bonuses to employes and had them donate the money. Five others channeled money through foreign subsidiaries or bank accounts. All six companies had earlier confessed to their part in raising an unprecedented $60 million for the 1972 Nixon campaign, and were fined.

Still pursuing his counteroffensive, President Nixon flew to Memphis and met behind closed doors with 16 Republican governors. At one point a governor asked him, "Are there any

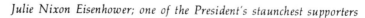

Julie Nixon Eisenhower; one of the President's staunchest supporters

other bombs waiting in the wings?" "If there are," replied the President, "I'm not aware of them."

The very next day counsel Buzhardt appeared before Judge Sirica—and dropped another fair-sized bomb.

Reading from a slip of paper, Buzhardt said that 18 minutes of conversation on one of the subpoenaed tapes had been mysteriously obscured by an unwavering "audible tone"—a hum. Under questioning, the lawyer conceded that the President had known about this before he talked to the governors.

The missing 18 minutes, Buzardt explained, "occurs during the course of the conversation, that is, not at the beginning or end." The conversation was one between the President and his former chief of staff, H. R. Haldeman, on July 20, 1972. The missing 18 minutes covered precisely the time the two spent talking about Watergate.

Obviously irritated, Judge Sirica ordered the remainder of the tapes handed over to him for safe-keeping, and recalled to court the President's personal secretary, Rose Mary Woods. Back on Nov. 8 Miss Woods had testified that she had spent 31 hours transcribing this very tape recording for the President. Why hadn't she told the judge at that time about the 18-minute gap? Contrite on the witness stand at her second court appearance, Miss Woods said that when she discovered it on Oct. 1 and told the President about it, he told her not to worry because it was not one of the subpoenaed tapes.

Miss Woods further testified that she might have caused four to six minutes of the erasure by accidentally pressing the "record" button, and simultaneously pressing a foot pedal, while she answered her telephone as she was transcribing the tape. But neither she, nor anyone else at the White House, could explain how the rest of the 18 minutes got lost. Sirica had the recording sent to technical experts for analysis.

As the year drew to a close it seemed the President was still plagued by scandal. He had tried silence, counterattack, small speeches of contrition, staff shake-ups, news conferences, written statements. None seemed to work. The latest matter he had to confront dealt with his own finances. For months he had been put upon to explain how he could sustain the burden of paying for and keeping up two large estates, in Key Biscayne and San Clemente, without some flow of cash in addition to his salary and his known borrowings from wealthy friends. Finally, in early December, Nixon released a massive dossier of documents, the most complete financial statement ever issued by an American president, even including his income tax returns. The documents showed him to have tripled his net worth during his years as President and to have become a millionaire.

The main question centered on the donation of his personal papers, with a resulting $235,000 tax windfall. The legality of the donation came under scrutiny. And there were other questions, such as why he paid no California income tax even though he voted in the state and claimed it as his legal residence, and why he paid no capital gains tax on the sale of a portion of his San Clemente property. It seemed that, once again, "disclosure" did not help the Nixon cause.

For another Watergate figure, however, disclosure reaped a dividend. In return for a plea of guilty, Special Prosecutor Jaworski dropped a perjury charge against Egil Krogh, the head of the "Plumbers" squad, who had been indicted in connection with the Fielding burglary. Krogh still faced a ten-year sentence and a $10,000 fine. As a part of his plea bargaining, Krogh agreed that after he was sentenced he would tell all he knew about the various activities of the plumbers. Earlier, Krogh, along with others, had claimed that the burglary was done on behalf of "national security." In entering his plea, he

Donald Segretti convicted of violating federal laws during the 1972 Presidential campaign entering a federal prison camp in Santa Barbara county, Calif. after being sentenced to six months imprisonment

discredited that rationale. "I now feel that I cannot in conscience assert national security as a defense," he said, adding that he now understood "the transcendent importance of the rule of law over the motivations of man."

Krogh thus became the twelfth person to plead guilty or to be convicted in the Watergate matter. In the same week, former presidential appointments secretary Dwight Chapin became the 18th person to be indicted. Chapin was accused of directing a clandestine guerrilla-warfare operation against Democrats during the 1972 campaign, the operation that involved convicted political saboteur Donald H. Segretti.

With the trials yet to come and the revelations yet to be made by Krogh and others who bargained for their freedom, it was clear as 1973 ended that the scandal known as Watergate was far from over.

Britain, Ireland and Denmark Became Common Market Members in 1973

On New Year's Day 1973, in a rare display of European unity, the flags of nine countries were hoisted at Common Market headquarters in Brussels. Britain, Ireland and Denmark had finally become members after knocking vainly at the gate for more than a decade.

Now they were joined with France, West Germany, Italy, Belgium, the Netherlands and Luxembourg in the world's most powerful trading bloc: officially known as the European Communities (EC) or more familiarly as just "the Community."

The Community was still a long way from becoming the United States of Europe, but it seemed to be on the road. Its leaders were seeing brave new visions. No longer would it spend most of its time and money supporting farm prices and manipulating customs duties. Sir Alec Douglas-Home, the British foreign secretary, said he did not expect to miss any sleep because of all night sessions over the tariff on fish.

Inside Europe there was to be a big new regional fund for raising the poor peasants of Sicily nearer to the affluence of big wheat farmers in the Ile de France, and unemployed dock workers in Scotland to the living standards of steelworkers in the Ruhr. In the outside world, western Europe was once again to become a force. Prime Minister Edward Heath and Douglas-Home were eager to restore it to the kind of influence that Britain, France, Germany and Italy lost after World War II. As a group, the Common Market countries would be the partner of the United States and, for some things, of Russia.

Before the year was out these ideas had landed in deep trouble, largely for fear of an energy shortage due to cuts in Arab oil production.

The Community's internal cohesion was threatened. The Arabs designated Britain, France and then Belgium as friends to whom full deliveries would be provided. But other Europeans were to suffer from production cuts and an embargo was declared against the Netherlands. The Dutch, if they were to be starved of power supplies, were thinking of a cut in the export of their own natural gas to their neighbors.

The nine countries held a summit meeting at Copenhagen in mid-December and called for a joint policy. But Douglas-Home stalled further action when the West Germans refused to help finance as big a regional aid fund as he wanted.

British Chancellor of the Exchequer Anthony Barber suggested that members make their currency reserves available during financial crises, but he got little support

The very end of the year brought a ray of hope with the Christmas Day decision by the Arabs to ease their production cutbacks. Fears of mass unemployment and business depression also eased somewhat in Western Europe, though there was still the problem of what the big oil price increase would do to the economy, already suffering from an inflation that neither the Community nor the individual governments could control.

Yet the crisis had brought western Europe a kind of identity, though not the kind many of its supporters were looking for. The nine countries acted together in the mid-East conflict by issuing a statement that came down on the Arab side, despite the fact that the United States—and probably a majority of Europeans—were for the Israelis.

"We deal with governments, not with public opinion," said Ahmed Zaki Yamani, the Saudi Arabian oil minister, at a news conference in Brussels.

Secretary of State Henry A. Kissinger's wry comment was that some Europeans appeared to see their identity in proportion to its distance from the United States.

There was a reason. Western Europe depended on the Arabs for about 80 percent of its oil, while the United States only got 10 to 15 per cent of its oil from the Arab countries.

So there had been a sharp and bitter clash between the United States and its European allies. The west Europeans for the most part refused to help the United States resupply Israel with arms. The United States gave the Europeans no warning when it decided to put its European bases on alert.

Defense Secretary James Schlesinger said angrily that the United States might have to reconsider its commitment to western Europe's defense. (Actually this had already begun a short time before. President Nixon signed a bill that provided for cuts in the 310,000-man U.S. force in Europe, to the extent that Europe failed to share the burden their stationing put on the U.S. balance of international payments.)

Nor was there any more cooperation on the energy problem.

When Kissinger proposed a joint attack on that by the United States, western Europe and Japan through an "Energy Action Group," the Common Market summit reacted only with vague muttering about further study.

In April, more than seven months earlier, Kissinger had proposed that the United States and western Europe join in a "new Atlantic charter," a broad statement of the principles that united the non-Communist world. Japan might also associate itself in some way, Kissinger thought. The hope was that Nixon would make a trip in the fall and the statement would be signed with a flourish at a transatlantic summit conference to crown his "year of Europe."

Things worked out differently. The Europeans did not want defense and economic matters linked in one statement: it might cost them money if a U.S. pledge to keep troops in Europe stood next to a statement about the cost of that operation to the United States. Nor were they enthusiastic about a link with Japan. They had their own problems about Japan. They wanted to avoid the influx of Japanese goods the United States had experienced, and when it came to defense Japan seemed a great distance off. Last year even the Mediterranean had seemed too far away. The West Germans balked at sending a destroyer to occasional joint maneuvers there, even before the Mid-east war.

Moreover some Europeans became convinced that the "year of Europe" was a public relations gimmick to distract attention from Nixon's troubles at home. They felt they were being used, and they disliked the feeling.

The Europeans insisted that there be two separate declarations: one on security to be drawn up by the North Atlantic Treaty Organization (NATO), which linked the United States and Canada with 13 European allies, and another on economic matters—to be negotiated between the United States and the nine Common Market countries.

Bargaining over these statements went slowly. The French, for example, objected to the word "partnership" on the ground that it would not translate into their language. More than five months of negotiations failed to bring an agreement on the size of the military-financial burden the United States wanted its allies to share.

This haggling, and the war in the Middle East, postponed Nixon's visit to Europe. At the end of the year it was hoped that there would be a presidential trip in April 1974, when NATO celebrated its 25th anniversary.

Meanwhile the Europeans kept working on internal unity.

In its usual low key fashion the Common Market had taken little notice of Britain's accession to membership. Few of its 10,000 employes were at work on the New Year's holiday. Largely because British reporters thought that something at least minimally photogenic ought to take place, a British diplomat brought over a couple of routine letters from Douglas-Home to the Executive Commission.

Britain was entering the Common Market "almost as a thief in the night," said the London Times. The ghost of President Charles de Gaulle's long opposition to British membership still haunted market corridors. A British poll reported 39 per cent of its sample unhappy with membership, only 38 per cent content and 23 per cent with no opinion.

Eight months later another poll showed only 31 per cent of the Britons queried as considering membership a good thing for their country, and 22 per cent a good thing for themselves personally.

Nevertheless things had begun moving, and in new directions.

Early in January Francois-Xavier Ortoli took over the presidency of the 13-man Executive Commission. He had been de Gaulle's finance minister when it was French policy to keep Britain out. At the same time Sir Christopher Soames became vice-president for external affairs. He had been a member of the first British government that tried to get in.

Not only were there three new member countries but an important group of west European governments had made free trade agreements with the Community: Norway, Sweden, Finland, Iceland, Switzerland, Austria and Portugal.

Negotiations were going forward with still another group in the Mediterranean area. A score of African countries—mostly former French colonies—already had the status of associate members.

Now another score from the British Commonwealth was starting talks. These included not only Africans but new nations from the Pacific and the Caribbean as well. These two ex-colonial groups made their first appearance together in Brussels in 1973.

A trade empire including all these countries would wield tremendous weight in world affairs if it could ever be consolidated. But the machinery for doing this was still weak. "Political integration" and "joint defense" were still embarrassing phrases. Nobody talked about electing an executive or composing an anthem.

Efforts toward unity concentrated on the nine core members.

After an all-night session, foreign ministers from the nine countries made an important agreement on international trade. They drafted a statement for the start of what some people called the "Nixon round" of talks on dismantling barriers to

Common Market members were in a jovial mood when they met in Copenhagen

the exchange of goods, farm produce as well as manufactured articles. Soames was named to deliver it on behalf of all.

But the actual horse-trading could not yet begin. Congress had not passed the trade bill that would give Nixon the authority he needed to negotiate with other countries. The Common Market itself was not yet in accord on its detailed bargaining position. The prospective negotiations were still clouded by an unsatisfied U.S. claim that its exporters should be compensated for a loss of business in Britain because of its joining the Common Market.

This was the situation on the traditional concern of the Community—trade.

When it came to breaking new ground, there was some talk of military cooperation among the nine countries—just enough for Moscow's Pravda to denounce it as "incompatible with the aspirations of the people for peace." But not enough to make any action seem imminent. The Common Market summit failed to take up the question, despite some expectations.

A "Eurogroup" operates within NATO, and NATO like the Common Market has its headquarters in Brussels. But there is no link between them. The French government, still placating de Gaulle's ghost, keeps apart from the military organization of the alliance, though retaining its membership.

Though the Community sought to tighten its economic bonds, it failed to do anything jointly about inflation—which was climbing faster and faster. Meetings of ministers passed joint resolutions, but the ministers then dispersed to their capitals and acted pretty much as their local voters and pressure groups dictated.

In the past most of the Community's attention had been spent on the farm problem. In 1973 almost all its terms suddenly appeared to change but it remained as big a puzzle as ever. The policy had been to pay high support prices for farm produce, higher than those prevailing in most other areas. To protect its farmers from foreign competition, the Community usually charged a "levy" to make up the difference. When surpluses appeared in Europe—most of the time, since prices were guaran-

teed and production virtually unlimited—the Community paid subsidies to ship them out of the area.

The United States and other outside countries complained steadily: they saw Community policy as unfair competition with their own production. European consumers grumbled, especially in Britain and West Germany, that they were paying out tax money to keep prices higher than need be.

In the spring, they found a good example of what they had been grumbling about. The high support price had built up a mountain of surplus butter at a cost to the European taxpayer of about a dollar a pound. With storage space growing short, the Common Market jumped at a chance to sell 200,000 tons to the Soviet Union at 19 cents a pound. Meanwhile housewives in western Europe had to go on paying $1.60 or more—because of the high support price.

About this time the Common Market began to feel the combined effect of events that had little to do with one another except that they all tended to raise food prices: the upsurge of demand from poorer countries; the failure of crops in the Soviet Union, China and central Africa; the disappearance of the huge anchovy runs off the Peruvian coast that had long provided big supplies of fish meal, an important ingredient in cattle feed.

Though the butter supply was not much affected, the surplus situation for other crops was reversed: surpluses turned into shortages. Market prices rose. Levies on imported grain were dropped, and so were subsidies on exports. A "negative levy" was imposed on the export of some products to keep supplies in Europe, while exports of rice and hard wheat were banned altogether lest Italians suffer a shortage of risotto and spaghetti. After a while, spaghetti exports were also banned.

The United States was no longer so concerned about European barriers to its farm exports—it was trying to conserve some supplies itself. Heavy restrictions were placed for a time on the exports of American soya beans, much to the indignation of farmers and governments in western Europe. Soya beans are an important ingredient in cattle feed, especially important in the absence of enough fish meal and essential to the production of all that butter—not to mention meat.

European farm planners had to consider whether shortages were likely to continue indefinitely or whether surpluses might appear once again. Meanwhile, what was to be done about French farm leaders threatening violence because they considered that wholesale prices for meat were too low, though consumers found retail prices considerably higher than in the United States? And about the thousands of poor peasants who looked to the weekly check they got from the dairy?

When Europeans looked at the broader economic picture, they found it to be the accepted wisdom that the way to European union—proclaimed as a goal for 1980—leads through economic and monetary union. A plan for all this had been laid down, to culminate in the creation of a single European currency. An area with a single currency would be well on the way toward unity on many other matters as well.

In 1973, six of the nine member countries agreed to keep their currencies tied together, barring all but slight fluctuations among them. Experts called this arrangement "the snake" because of the shape of the graph that illustrated its movement with relation to the U.S. dollar. Britain, Ireland and Italy did not join the snake, which was criticized by some experts and repeatedly seemed in danger of collapse.

A European Monetary Fund was set up but the amounts it was authorized to lend to a country in trouble were not enough to make much difference. The governments put off proposals to start pooling a significant proportion of their reserves.

Anthony Barber, Britain's chancellor of the exchequer, said that in an emergency all the member countries' reserves ought to be available to help any one of their currencies. He got little support.

The West Germans and the Dutch, who were not likely to need this kind of help themselves, were concerned that they would always be paying for what they considered the unwise policies of the weaker brethren. So they insisted on a deal: any increased aid they pledged to the weaker countries, they said, must be matched by increased cooperation—that is, by increased influence for themselves—on all economic policy in the nine countries.

This idea met great resistance for an old basic reason: the member governments were unwilling to give up sovereign rights. Enoch Powell, a maverick within Heath's Conservative Party, had gotten considerable political mileage out of the contention that the British Parliament had already given up too much of its sovereignty by even agreeing to join the Common Market. This view helped make the Community unpopular in Britain.

Yet in the Community's Council of Ministers, which made virtually all the important decisions, each member had a veto on anything it considered vital. The Executive Commission, pledged to look after the interests of the nine countries as a whole, had only the power to make proposals. If decisions were to be made on unified economic policies, overriding the particular interests of individual governments, somebody or some body would have to make them.

It seemed possible by the end of the year that the energy problem might speed the Community into some new joint decision-making process. The Arabs were distinguishing between some members as friends and others as enemies. The international oil companies, many of them under control of Americans, had taken over the responsibility of rationing out supplies to theoretically sovereign countries. Resentment could drive the west Europeans toward unity.

Britain's "Cod War" with Iceland arose over taking fish inside Iceland's 50-mile limit. Iceland linked the dispute with its membership in NATO. The Common Market stood behind Britain in the dispute.

Interior Secretary Rogers C.B. Morton announced plans to lease federal lands for commercial production of oil from shale

Shortages Plagued The U.S. Economy in 1973

Americans found themselves short of fuel, food and a lot of other things

THE MEANING OF THE WORD "shortage"—a word with which Americans had not had to deal in years—came home with a vengeance in 1973, a year in which they learned the nation no longer had things in abundance.

The shortages plaguing the economy ranged from fuel to food to basic materials. The most spectacular, perhaps, was the "energy crisis" brought on, in part, by the cutoff of oil exports to the United States by the oil-producing Arab nations.

Despite these problems, the economy perked along at a high rate of growth during the year and at times came close to overheating. If it hadn't been for the shortages of many basic materials, it might have expanded at a greater rate and shoved prices even higher than they were.

Inflation boomed, and a Gallup Poll, conducted near the year's end, showed that Americans were more concerned over inflation than they were over Watergate. A study by the Labor Depart-

Saudi Arabian Oil Minister Sheikh Ahmed Zaki Yamani at a conference in which he touched on planned Arab states oil production cuts

ment showed why: In the 12 months ended Oct. 31, the average hourly wage rose 6.7 per cent. But, subtract the effects of rising prices and Social Security taxes, and the real spendable earnings of an average married worker with three dependents declined by 3.3 per cent over the same period.

In January the Council of Economic Advisers predicted the rate of inflation would drop to 2.5 per cent by the end of the year, but by July, the forecast was abandoned. The council wasn't alone in its forecast. Many private economists had made similar optimistic predictions, although with not as low an inflation rate as the government predicted.

In his annual economic message to Congress, President Nixon saw potentially great things for the economy in 1973 if federal spending was controlled. The spending was held but inflation still soared.

Consumer prices surged ahead at an annual rate of eight per cent during the year, with food prices soaring at 20 per cent, the worst inflation since the Korean War.

It began with Phase 3, when, early in January, the Administration abandoned its Phase 2 mandatory system of wage-price controls. Phase 2 was replaced by a largely voluntary system in which business and labor were expected to keep their prices and wages in line with government guidelines. The government said that if any of these increases got out of step with its guidelines it would step in and order them rolled back.

The decision sent the stock market reeling while prices and wages soon began to explode. Overseas, a run began on the American dollar which couldn't take the pressure and formally was devalued Feb. 10. The agency charged with enforcing the wage-price controls, the Cost of Living Council, failed to move against many of the price hikes, blaming the upsurge in inflation on short food supplies and booming world commodity prices.

The U.S. economic situation was in such a state in March that even the freshly-devalued dollar couldn't stand up under pressure, so the United States and the other leading industrial nations finally quit trying to maintain fixed exchange rates for the world's major currencies.

With the dollar then slipping lower in value, U.S. goods became a bargain and foreign countries stepped up their purchases of agricultural products. This increased shortages in the United States and caused domestic prices to rise higher. The Soviet Union, for example, bought a lot more grain than U.S. officials had thought it would. The result was widespread shortages in America of grain for bread and for feeding animals.

President Nixon moved in mid-June to brake the speeding inflation by freezing prices for 60 days. Nixon said the freeze did not apply to wages since they had been moderate. They had hovered just a bit over the 5.5 per cent government standard.

The freeze was the second the President had imposed in an effort to gain time to create a more effective anti-inflation policy. But this time it did not get the same public support as had the first. Since the retail prices of all agricultural products were frozen, the producers discovered it wasn't profitable to market their beef and poultry so some drowned their baby chickens and others didn't send their beef to market.

In 1971 the United States had the largest laying flock in its history, over 307 million hens. But by August 1973, the flock had been cut to about 281 million, the smallest flock since 1961. Normally, the nation slaughtered 600,000 head of beef a week. But during the price freeze the number fell to 500,000.

Nixon released the food and health industries from the price freeze in mid-July, but kept it on beef prices and across the rest of the economy until mid-August. When the freeze ended, chicken and egg producers began rebuilding their flocks and beef poured to the market. Prices went down, at least somewhat. But only temporarily. Most experts said that as the market evened out, as short term oversupply cleared up, prices would go back up. The high cost of feed grain, they said, must send the price up again.

Nixon replaced the price freeze with a tough anti-inflation policy which, in some cases, squeezed the profits of industry by not allowing it to pass along on its costs. But Phase 4 still failed to curb inflation and the world prices of many commodities rose sharply.

In an effort to give the anti-inflation policy a boost, the Federal Reserve Board held on to a tight-money policy. This resulted in interest rates rising to record levels across the nation, and its impact immediately was felt in the housing industry, which had been expecting a good year.

Corporate profits were strong, particularly in the first half of the year, but the Dow Jones average of 30 industrials, a key indicator for blue chip stocks, which cracked the 1000 barrier in 1972 and opened 1973 at 1020.02 closed out the year at 850.86.

The troubled dollar got a boost near the end of the year because, surprisingly enough, of the fuel shortages. Analysts said that while the United States was in bad shape because of the shortages, the European nations and Japan were in worse shape.

And the monetary crises of early 1973 eased after most of the major nations agreed to abandon most fixed exchange rates for their currencies.

With things calmed down, the leading industrial nations postponed for another year the reform of the international monetary system.

James W. McLane was named director of the Cost of Living Council's special freeze group

David Ben-Gurion: To Many A 20th Century Moses

*Over the years, he became a symbol
of the rugged little state of Israel*

Romantics saw David Ben-Gurion as a reincarnation of Moses, leading a people out of slavery to a country of their own. Over the years Israelis came to regard him as a symbol of the rugged state he governed, a founding father who had transformed a dream into reality.

For nearly half a century, Ben-Gurion worked for creation of the state of Israel, a Jewish homeland amid a sea of hostile neighbors. He fought against the reluctance of the British and the enmity of the Arabs to bring Israel into being in 1948 and finally led it to stability.

The massive Ben-Gurion head with its fringe of unruly white hair became as familiar to millions as Winston Churchill's cigar. Millions mourned when Ben-Gurion died Dec. 1 at the age of 87.

Ben-Gurion became a dominant figure on the Jewish scene soon after he set foot in 1906 on the swampy lowlands and rocky mountains of a forsaken land called Palestine. He was the outstanding politician of Palestinian Jews under Turkish and British rule. And he served as premier, except for one brief interval, for the first 15 years of its statehood.

The prophetic architect of Israel was a tough politician with an adamant quality that helped him make decisions in times of adversity and also split governments and ruffled the feathers of his colleagues.

He guided Israel through a war of independence, an invasion of Egypt and a daily struggle for survival. Yet after he turned 86, Ben-Gurion commented that the Jewish state did not really exist, because—contrary to Biblical predictions—it had found no peace.

To world jewry, Ben-Gurion symbolized the rebirth of a people, risen from the ashes of Nazi crematoriums. He was viewed as the wise patriarch who embodied all the traditional virtues. But to many others, he was an abrasive figure. He alarmed the United Nations and became a target of Arab hatred by adopting a policy of not turning the other cheek when struck but striking back swiftly and ruthlessly in retaliation against Arab raids on Israeli soil.

Ben-Gurion also alienated many American Jews by insisting that all true Zionists should live in Israel. In 1957, he told a Zionist ideological conference in Jerusalem that a sound Jewish life was not possible outside of Israel.

"There seems to be a general agreement," he said, "that a Jew can live in America, speak and read English and bring up his children in America and still call himself a Zionist. If that is Zionism, I want no part of it."

Ben-Gurion was born in Plonsk, in Russian-occupied Poland on Oct. 16, 1886. His father, a lawyer, was devoted to Hibbat Zion, forerunner of the modern Zionist movement.

In 1906, Ben-Gurion who had had only a religious high school education, told his parents he was going to Palestine. The next nine years he spent working as a laborer on the tiny settlements that sprang up as other Jews migrated to the Middle East land.

Ben-Gurion was active in other ways. He organized the first Jewish Labor Union, later Histadrut. In 1910, he became editor of Unity and three years later went to Constantinople to study law.

By 1907, Ben-Gurion was already demanding that the Jews of Palestine arm themselves against marauding Arab tribes. Alarmed by his militance, the Turkish rulers of Palestine expelled Ben-Gurion in 1915 and told him "never to set foot again on Palestinian soil." Ben-Gurion went to the United States to muster support for the Jews of Palestine and to organize the American Jewish Legion to fight alongside the British in the Middle East campaigns that ended Turkish domination of Palestine.

After the war, the British took over control of Palestine under a League of Nations mandate and Ben-Gurion became leader of the Jewish community. In 1939 with the rise of Arab nationalism, the British sought to appease the Arabs by clamping

Ben-Gurion at the establishment of the Jewish State of Israel on midnight, May 15, 1948

Above, Ben-Gurion visited Israeli troops in 1957. Left, Premier Golda Meir at Ben-Gurion's grave

limitations on Jewish immigration to Palestine. As a result, thousands of Jews fleeing Nazi persecution found this sanctuary closed to them.

Ben-Gurion bitterly opposed the British White Paper barring immigration, but when World War II came, he backed the British and helped organize a Jewish brigade to fight for the allies.

But the White Paper had signaled the start of a nine-year Jewish guerrilla and terrorism campaign to oust the British from Palestine. A special United Nations commission set up at the request of Britain suggested in 1947 the partition of Palestine and establishment of an independent national state of Israel.

In 1948, Israel won independence and Ben-Gurion became the infant nation's first premier. It was a crucial point. For on May 14, 1948, the day Israel became a nation, Arab armies began their invasion of the state. Facing up to the challenge, Ben-Gurion donned battle dress and took over direction of military operations. Some of his decisions were questioned, but Ben-Gurion surrounded himself with able young officers like Moshe Dayan and Yigal Yadin. The fighting was finally ended with a U.N.-policed cease-fire and to Ben-Gurion fell most of the credit for victory.

Turning to internal problems, Ben-Gurion sought to unravel Israel's economic affairs and to absorb hordes of refugees from Europe. In 1953, Ben-Gurion resigned as premier, saying he was exhausted and retired to his cottage in the Negev desert to become a shepherd.

Within 18 months Ben-Gurion was back in harness. He was premier when Israel undertook a "punitive" war against Egypt. In October 1956, Israel invaded the Egyptian-held Sinai Peninsula and captured it in a 10-day campaign aided by British and French forces who landed in the Suez Canal zone, which had been nationalized by Egypt.

Later, crushed by ultimatums from the Soviet Union and the United States, Ben-Gurion had to tell his people that Israel was pulling back from the Sinai Desert and the Gaza Strip. It was one of the most unpopular decisions he had ever made. The collapse of the Sinai adventure was perhaps the darkest moment in Ben-Gurion's career.

Ben-Gurion resigned as premier in 1963 because of "personal needs." He retired to his home in Sde Boqer in the Negev Desert.

Quietly he switched from making history to writing it—11 volumes on Israel's early years.

The elderly statesman rarely emerged from the house in which a large portrait of his late wife and a map of Israel hung over worn furniture and a vase of roses.

In an interview on his 86th birthday, Ben-Gurion said that Israel would not really exist as a nation until there was peace with the Arabs, until Israel's population was tripled and its desert developed.

Military attendants surround the grave of Ben-Gurion

SUPREME COURT CRACKED
DOWN ON OBSCENITY

"Closed due to uncertainty of court decision. Open when situation more stable," read a sign on the door of an adult movie shop in Louisville, Ky.

At another shop the sign said: "Due to the most recent ruling by the Supreme Court, we are liquidating all stock—50 per cent off."

In New York City, three plainclothes policemen walked into one of the dozens of book stores that peddled sexually explicit magazines and films in Times Square. One picked up a colorful magazine with an unprintable name, leafed through it, then announced, "This looks obscene under the new Supreme Court decision."

The decision to which he referred came June 21 when a five-member majority of the High Court added new language to the obscenity issue. When the court first took on the issue in 1957, obscenity was ruled outside the protection of the First Amendment, and, with some detours along the way, the first decision set the base for the court's test for deciding just what was obscene: The material—taken as a whole—must appeal to the prurient interest as judged by contemporary community standards, and it must be utterly without redeeming social value.

In its 1973 ruling, the court dropped the requirement that the material be utterly without value, and substituted instead the question of whether the material constituted a serious work. It also held the standards should be those of the local community—they do not have to be national—and that juries needed no help from expert witnesses to make judgments.

In the majority opinion he wrote, Chief Justice Warren E. Burger said no one would be "subject to prosecution for the sale or exposure of obscene material, unless these materials describe patently offensive 'hard core' sexual conduct specifically defined by the regulating state law. . . ." But Justice William O. Douglas called the decision a "sharp and radical break with the traditions of a free society. He found that a word such as "offensive" could be subject to a wide range of interpretations, and said, "That test would make it possible to ban any paper or journal or magazine in some benighted place."

The obscenity decision was only one of many the Supreme Court made in 1973. Early in the year, on Jan. 22, it ruled 7 to 2 that the states couldn't materially interfere with a physician-performed abortion during the first six months of pregnancy.

Justice Harry A. Blackmun said that only in about the last three months—when the unborn child was developed enough to live outside the mother—could the state interfere with this "right of privacy."

Blackmun, speaking for the majority, rejected the idea that a pregnant woman had "an absolute constitutional right to an abortion on her demand." But, he said, the decision whether to end a pregnancy before the fetus became viable was best left to the woman and her doctor.

The decision followed two years of deliberations by the justices. It was based mainly on what Blackmun called a right of privacy. And, he said, the right was "broad enough to encompass a woman's decision whether or not to terminate her pregnancy."

In other 1973 decisions, the court:

—Struck down tax deductions for parents of nonpublic school students as violative of the First Amendment ban on establishment of religion.

—Ruled that federal and state governments could continue barring employes from engaging in partisan political campaigns.

—On the one man, one vote issue, it permitted Virginia to retain legislative districts which varied from absolute equality by more than 16 per cent. The majority said the state allowed the variations for the legitimate purpose of following existing political boundaries.

—Broadened the power of law officers to search persons without a warrant. The court held that persons taken into custody on minor charges then may be searched for evidence of more serious but unrelated crimes.

In other action, Justice Thurgood Marshall overturned on Aug. 4 a ban on U.S. bombing in Cambodia that had been issued just hours earlier by Justice Douglas. The Administration had ignored Douglas' order.

Marshall, who said he consulted with and won the agreement of seven other court members for his action, made clear that Douglas was a minority of one.

Douglas said he had not been ruling on the constitutionality of U.S. involvement in Cambodia. He said, however, the basic question was whether or not Congress had declared war on Cambodia. Douglas thought not.

"It has become popular," he wrote, "to think the President has that power to declare war. But there is not a word in the Constitution that grants that power to him. It runs only to Congress."

Workmen hauled books, magazines and devices out of a Cincinnati store after the Supreme Court ruling

Above, O. J. Simpson, center, and his teammates smiled as they were interviewed in the Buffalo Bill's dressing room at New York's Shea Stadium on Dec. 16 after Simpson ran up 200 more yards and set a new single-season rushing record of 2,003 yards. Right, remember the "Mad Bomber" who terrorized New Yorkers in the 1940s and 1950s? Now 70, George Metesky walked out of Manhattan's Supreme Court Building on Dec. 12 after 17 years' confinement.

Top left, ten persons were killed and more than 50 injured when the Paddington to Oxford express train crowded with Christmas shoppers was derailed near Ealing, West London. Bottom left, bell tower of Bethelehem's Armenian Church dominates this view of Manger Square used as a parking lot in the pre-Christmas season. Above, Soviet author Alexander Solzhenitsyn's long-hidden book about Soviet labor camps was published Dec. 28 in Paris causing a furor.

Left, atop the world's tallest building, the Sears tower in Chicago, John Rukavina worked on a boom 1,485 feet above the street. Right, view of excavation works under way at Sandgate on the French channel coast near Calais where work is going ahead for a tunnel under the English channel

SPAIN'S PREMIER SLAIN AFTER ATTENDING CHURCH

Spain's Premier Luis Carrero Blanco was a deeply religious man who looked on himself as a defender of Christian civilization.

Every morning before going to work, the premier would go to Mass in a church near his apartment home. On Dec. 20, Carrero Blanco attended Mass, then got into his car and set off for his office. The car had gone only a short distance before it was hurled into the air by a violent explosion. The blast killed the 70-year-old premier—who was named by Generalissimo Francisco Franco to the post in June 1973 in a move to lessen the load on the 81-year-old Franco—his driver and his bodyguard.

Police said the assassins had tunneled under a Madrid street to set off the explosion that blew up the car and hurled parts of it over the roof of the five-story church where Carrero Blanco had just attended Mass. It was the first known assassination of a high Spanish official since Franco took over the nation after the civil war in 1939.

The explosion happened about an hour before the start of a trial of 10 persons on charges of fomenting strikes. The Franco regime had been troubled by student unrest, labor strikes and an underground movement for autonomous rule for Spain's Basque provinces.

A communique issued in France said a Basque separatist movement was responsible for the assassination, but the head of the organization denied responsibility and said the communique was counterfeit.

FOR THE RECORD

RETURNED. J. Paul Getty III, grandson of the American oil billionaire, after disappearing from Rome July 9. Getty, 17, was found by police at a deserted service station in Italy's south Dec. 15. Getty, whose right ear was severed, told police, "my kidnapers cut my ear off." The kidnapers on Nov. 10 had sent a Rome newspaper a human ear and lock of hair they said belonged to young Getty. It was reported that $2.7 million in cash was paid to secure the boy's freedom. Police said they believed he had been held by gangsters with Mafia affiliations.

RESIGNED. Nelson A. Rockefeller as New York's governor, a post he had held since 1958. Sworn in Dec. 18 as the state's 50th governor was Malcolm Wilson, who had served for 1 years as lieutenant governor to Rockefeller. Rockefeller resigned to devote his time to national issues.

Year-End Headliners

(As this turbulent year came to an end, these major stories were still developing)

* * * * *

ENERGY CRISIS—

For a few hours on New Year's Eve, the lights in Times Square blazed brightly. At midnight, the ball of light dropped down to mark another year. Then, the lights of Times Square dimmed again.

During those Christmas and New Year's holidays in the United States in 1973, many of the traditional lights of celebration were dimmed. East of Times Square, in the small village of Northport on Long Island, a Christmas tree at the end of Main Street, on the edge of Long Island Sound, had in past years cheered the chill air with its lights flickering on the water. In 1973, the tree was dark.

The signals of summer—shuttered gasoline stations during vacations and warnings of worse to come—swiftly proved all too accurate. The great energy crisis came upon the American people, along with much of the rest of the world, with a surprising suddenness, triggered by an Arab oil embargo imposed in October.

At year's end, federal officials in the United States were scaling down somewhat their grimmest predictions of shortages, and there were hints of leaks in the Arab oil embargo, along with some easing of the embargo, but there was still plenty of trouble to go around.

In the United States, the shortage of gasoline affected millions of motorists, the stock market convulsed, thousands of workers were or were soon to be laid off, truck drivers protesting speed limits and fuel costs blocked highways, gas prices shot up, gas rationing loomed, home heating oil seemed in precarious supply, and the President of the United States took a commercial airliner from the nation's capitol to Los Angeles to, the White House said, demonstrate his concern for saving fuel—spokesmen said the trip saved some 10,000 gallons of jet fuel for his primary jet alone.

Mrs. Alfred Pauly stood next to her plastic clad house near Belle Plaine, Minn., which she hoped would keep out the cold winds and save fuel

Signs like this sprouted in front of gasoline stations across the country as the energy crisis became more acute

The fuel shortage also produced sweeping new petroleum allocation regulations, designed to spread the available oil around to where it might be most needed. Americans were to lower their thermostats six or ten degrees below the preceeding year's levels and they faced longer lines and higher prices for gasoline for their automobiles. Gasoline rationing remained a strong possibility, as rationing coupons, adorned with a portrait of George Washington, were being printed on a contingency basis. The government worked on a large research and development effort in energy, late perhaps but with the aim of energy self-sufficiency.

In England, the British government cut deeply into the nation's work week in hopes of avoiding a power breakdown. The three-day work week came in response to a host of headaches contributing to its energy crisis. Along with chilly homes and less television, the English could look forward to wider unemployment, perhaps up from 500,000 to 1 million persons. Europe was threatened by the general Arab-imposed oil shortages and Japan, almost totally dependent upon imported oil, was especially vulnerable.

Late in December, however, Arab oil ministers meeting in Kuwait announced an easing of their oil cutbacks to most countries, while maintaining the total embargo to the United States and the Netherlands. This surprise move in the Arab oil diplomacy was expected to most benefit Japan and Western Europe, but was not expected to have any effect on the doubling of crude oil prices announced a few days earlier by the major Persian Gulf exporting countries, a move that seemed sure to raise the cost of living sharply in most of the world's industrialized nations—and boost inflationary and recessionary pressures.

For all this, the new energy chief for the United States, William E. Simon, expressed optimism in a Christmas Eve interview, saying that the Arab embargo might end soon. Simon indicated that he had been encouraged by remarks earlier in the month from the powerful Saudi Arabian oil minister, Sheik Ahmed Zaki el-Yamani, but Simon did not go into detail.

And it was all this that left no doubt that the Arabs felt they had succeeded in their use of their vast reserves of "black gold" as a diplomatic instrument in their dispute with Israel and

in their efforts to manipulate other countries. They had shaken the world, and in their statement of easing their embargo, the ministers repeatedly indicated that they considered their oil a weapon they would continue to use.

Meanwhile, there were other pressures on the world's oil economy. Venezuela raised prices for crude oil and for refined products and Canada also raised prices.

So, the Middle East Arab-Israeli situation, on top of an existing fuel shortage in the United States, resulted in the strange sight of American motorists waiting in long lines at gasoline stations, while other stations across the street were closed, having run out of supplies.

But it came so suddenly that many Americans simply didn't believe there really was an energy crisis—some felt that the whole thing was a trick by the oil industry to take advantage of the situation to reap big profits. Others felt the Nixon Administration was taking advantage of the situation to distract the public from its other troubles.

The answers seemed more complex. The economics of the oil industry—its reliance on less

As fuel supplies continued to drop, Pat Rozycki of St. Cloud, Minn. tried out this old-fashioned coal stove

Reservoir was dug near a blazing oil well fire near Casper, Wyoming, in an effort to force mud and water into the well and stem the loss of oil feeding the flames

expensive Middle East oil, for example—seemed to have contributed to the general problem. But the industry, with an embarrassment of profits, argued in general that it must have adequate earnings to pay for its capital developments in a free enterprise society.

One major problem in discussing the oil industry in the energy crisis was the fact that the facts came only from the oil industry. From well-head to gas pump, the industry kept score. The same situation applied to natural gas. Oil and natural gas provided two-thirds of the energy consumed in the United States. There was no independent means of monitoring the performance of an industry long powerful in American economics and politics.

By controlling both the product and the facts about the product, critics said, the oil giants could understate their true reserves and then drive prices up, drive out independent competitors and, in general, have things their own way. The industry, for its part, had repeatedly denied all

such charges. Texaco Chairman Maurice Granville said this: "Those of us in the petroleum industry have been telling everyone for years that a serious energy shortage was developing."

The industry's profit position was difficult to defend in the midst of an energy crisis and in the background of widespread inconvenience and, in some cases, suffering.

A Chase Manhattan bank study said, however, that 1973 earnings looked healthier only in comparison to 1972, a year Chase described as one of low earnings proportions. "Clearly," Chase said, "in terms of the world's current and future needs for petroleum, the industry's earnings positively are not excessive—on the contrary, they are still subnormal." The long range results of this could only be guessed at.

The energy situation also commanded attention that had only shortly before been focused on the environmental situation. The rush of events seemed to some at first to have buried the environmentalists in, oddly enough, not an oil spill

but a shortage of oil. Because of the shortage, such environmental concerns as automobile emission standards would be put off. Power plants would be allowed to use high sulphur fuels. There were, indeed, setbacks.

But, as in physics, where for every force there is an equal and opposite force, the push against the environmental movement seemed most likely in the long run to produce a counter force, one the environmentalists wanted all along. No longer would Americans think they lived in a land of unlimited resources. We would no longer think that electricity was "free." No longer would many Americans think that a big station wagon, at eight or ten miles per gallon, was an unmitigated blessing. Perhaps in 1973, the energy crisis, the Arab oil embargo, all that, had finally made the point: There is no free lunch.

And the year of the energy crisis, 1973, ended with at least two symbols of that crisis: the locked gasoline pump and the dark Christmas tree.

GREECE—

Since World War II, Greece had endured five years of civil war, seven general elections in which 50 political parties took part, about a dozen governments, the fall of the monarchy, two referendums, occasional bloody political riots, and two successful coups.

The first coup came in 1967 (*The World in 1967, 150*) when a clique of obscure army officers, mostly colonels, moved and George Papadopoulos took over the government. The second came late in 1973 when Papadopoulos, who earlier in the year had abolished the monarchy and proclaimed himself the president of the new republic, was toppled by a group of army generals. The power behind them was believed to be Brig. Gen. Dimitrios Ioannides, chief of the military police.

"President Papadopoulos was so busy fighting off the left that he forgot to look to his right," said one Athenian.

A communique from the nation's new rulers said Papadopoulos was ousted because he was pushing Greece toward parliamentary rule too fast and straying from the goals of the 1967 coup that put him in power. Papadopoulos had crushed two previous coup attempts—one led by King Constantine who fled into exile in 1967 when the attempt failed and another in May 1973 by Navy officers.

A day after Papadopoulos had been sworn in as president Aug. 20, 1973, he lifted martial law for the first time since the 1967 coup. The nation's students, who had staged numerous protests earlier in the year but were silenced by arrests and drafting into the army, clashed with the police Nov. 4 and five demonstrators were arrested. To protest the arrests, the students later staged a massive sit-in at Athens Polytechnic Institute. The students first called for an end to political trials and for academic freedom. But these demands became mixed with calls for the ouster of Papadopoulos,

immediate elections and a withdrawal of North Atlantic Treaty Organization (NATO) forces from Greece.

To break up the demonstrations, soldiers, backed by tanks, and police moved in and ousted the students and martial law was reimposed. At least 13 persons died in the battles and more than a hundred were injured.

There was a brief lull, then, on Nov. 25, tanks moved slowly to the edge of Athens and Papadopoulos was removed from power. Gen. Phaedon Gizikis was picked to replace him.

Papadopoulos was not known for coddling leftists but his efforts to shed his image of a tyrant and promising elections in 1974 apparently was too much for the generals.

Said newly named Premier Adamantios Androutsopoulos, "We were being dragged into the humiliating adventure of rigged elections. Democracy cannot be imposed by law . . . When the country is ready it will be led to elections."

Greece's new president, Lt. Gen. Phaedon Gizikis

THE DOLLAR—

By year-end, the long troubled U.S. dollar was on the threshold of a spectacular recovery.

The U.S. currency, devalued in February for the second time in 14 months, had lost a further 15 to 20 per cent in value while floating down against European currencies during the spring and into the summer. Dealers attributed the dollar weakness partly to uncertainties over Watergate. The downward float amounted to a third devaluation. Then, in July, a turnaround started with the first signs that U.S. foreign trade figures were about to improve.

Devaluation had done its job, making U.S. goods cheaper in foreign markets, U.S. export

sales rose and the dollar began to improve.

In September, Treasury Secretary George P. Shultz told the International Monetary Fund meeting in Nairobi that the United States expected its basic balance of payments, its dealings with the rest of the world, to be in the black in 1974 for the first time in a decade. Shultz also made it clear that the dollar would have to be stronger before the United States would agree to reform of the International Monetary system. The IMF set a target date of July 1974 to try and reach agreement on the reforms.

By December, the dollar had recovered most of the ground lost floating down in Europe between February and July.

The improved U.S. trade and balance of pay-

ments figures were one factor behind the dollar's improvement. Oil was another. Arab oil cuts were expected to hurt Western Europe and Japan worse than the United States, to the relative benefit of the dollar. Leading European bankers began predicting by year-end that the dollar might have to be revalued upward in 1974.

As the dollar improved, pressures from the gold markets eased. The metal had soared to a record high of $127 an ounce on Europe's free markets in June when the dollar was weak. By December gold was back down to just above $100 an ounce, reflecting the dollar's recovery. The decision by U.S. and other governments to sell official reserves on the open market as needed, also helped depress the gold price.

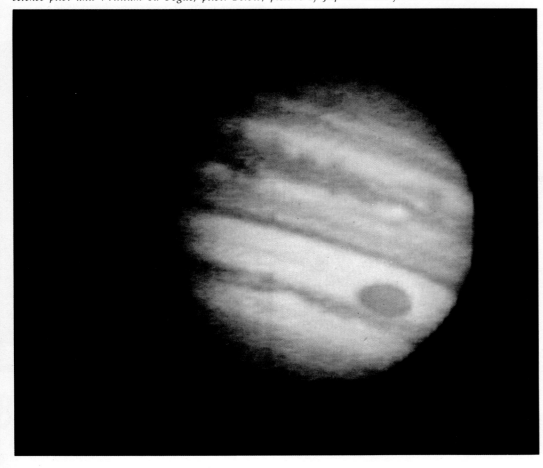

Left, Comet Kohoutek photographed from the McDonald Observatory in the Davis Mountains on Dec. 10. Above, Skylab III astronauts from left to right: Gerald P. Carr, commander, Edward G. Gibson, science pilot and William R. Pogue, pilot. Below, picture of Jupiter taken from Pioneer 10.

SKYLAB III—

On Dec. 28, the three Skylab astronauts soared past the halfway mark of their marathon mission, with flight controllers predicting they'd remain in orbit the planned 84 days.

Marine Lt. Col. Gerald P. Carr, 41, Air Force Lt. Col. William R. Pogue, 43, and Dr. Edward G. Gibson, 37, a solar physicist, were launched from Cape Canaveral, Fla., Nov. 16 on man's third and final visit to the 85-ton space station. They linked up with the station, 270 miles high, and quickly ran into problems with a heavy work schedule.

During the early portion of the mission, the astronauts fell behind schedule and made many minor mistakes trying to catch up. They complained often about the large work load and tight timetables.

Mission controllers determined the astronauts' working patterns were different from those of earlier Skylab crews and adjusted the schedule accordingly.

Carr, Pogue and Gibson then settled into a smooth and productive schedule of medical, solar astronomy, earth resources and other scientific experiments.

One of their major tasks was to chart the course of the comet Kohoutek as it sped in from deep space to loop around the sun in late December. They photographed and described the comet frequently as they gathered what scientists said should be the best data yet on the composition of a comet. On Christmas Day, Carr and Pogue took a record seven-hour, one-minute space walk to photograph Kohoutek with special cameras.

Knights of
the Road

Higher fuel costs and lower highway speeds provoked many of the nation's truckers to protest in December. Among them was Lloyd Wittman (left), known to his colleagues as "Monster Man," talking on the truckers' radio network about massive traffic tie-ups near Hebron, Ohio. Long-haul trucker Ted Bies, also known by his citizens band radio nickname of "Yogi Bear," relaxed during the protests with coffee and a sandwich (middle). At right, Andy Kenyon lounged at a cross-country truck stop. Near Lamar, Pa., lower left, truckers, reflected in a mirror, jammed the aisles of a rest stop. Lower right, rows and rows of tractor-trailers were parked around a Pennsylvania truck stop which served as a meeting place for drivers from across the nation.

Metastadt, a new modular building exhibited at the Hannover Fair in West Germany

Ethiopian children in the grounds of a mission orphanage in Wollo Province showed typical signs of the starvation that has been haunting many parts of the country

Above, The thousands of visitors who paid their respects to the Statue of Liberty in New York Harbor each year also had a chance to admire the city's famous skyline. Below, China's Mao Tse-Tung played host to royalty in Peking as he greeted Nepal's King Birenda Bir Bikram Shah Dev and Queen Aishwarya Rajya Maxmi Devi Shah

American Painter Norman Rockwell sat for his own portrait in his studio at Stockbridge, Mass. Rockwell, 80, is noted for his magazine covers depicting life in America

Project Supervisor: Keith Fuller

Editorial Director: Dan Perkes

Editor: Tom Hoge

Staff Writer: Phil Thomas

Color Photos: Helen Seebach

Photo Production: Stanley Kohler

Promotion and Distribution: Jack Elcik

Photographs
The illustrations in this volume
were selected for the most part
from the news photo reports of The
Associated Press and, except where
specifically credited, were taken
by staff photographers of The AP
and its member newspapers.

Feature Narratives:
Howard Benedict, Cocoa Beach, Fla.
  Skylab
Lee Byrd, Washington
  Presidential Inauguration
Mark Charney, New York
  Staten Island Blast
F. Richard Ciccone, Chicago
  Mississippi Floods
Frank Cormier, Washington
  The President's Year
Bill Crider, New Orleans
  New Orleans Sniper
Linda Deutsch, Los Angeles
  The Ellsberg Case
Philip Dopoulos, Athens
  Greek King Ousted
Colin Frost, London
  Northern Ireland
Will Grimsley, New York
  World Series
Carl Hartman, Brussels
  Common Market
Jean Heller, Washington
  Spiro Agnew
Tom Hoge, New York
  Meat Boycott
  Ben-Gurion
Holger Jensen, Beirut
  Mideast Terrorism
Bill Johnson, Oklahoma City
  Oklahoma Prison Riot

Garth Jones, Austin, Tex.
  President Johnson
David Lancashire, Tel Aviv
  Israel's Anniversary
Jules Loh, New York
  Watergate
Carole Martin, New York
  Education
Rick Meyer, New York
  Middle East War
Robert D. Ohman and William F.
  Nicholson, Santiago
  Chilean Revolution
Leonard Pratt, Taipei
  The Third China
William Ryan, New York
  Brezhnev Visit
Victor L. Simpson, Rome
  Italy's Antiquities
Max Skelton, Houston
  Texas Slayings
David Smyth, New York
  The Monetary Crisis
Brian Sullivan, New York
  The Energy Crisis
Kay Tateishi, Tokyo
  Japanese Art Buyers
Phil Thomas, New York
  Picasso
James Wilson, Minneapolis
  Wounded Knee

John Wheeler, New York
  Indochina
  Foreign Drug Arrests
Louis Uchitelle, New York
  Argentine Election

Contributing Reporters:
  Neil Bibler, Cleveland
  Fred Coleman, London
  Gordon Hanson, Des Moines
  Quane Kenyon, Grand Rapids, Mich.
  Linda Kramer, Los Angeles
  Paul Lloyd, Boston
  Lee Margulies, Los Angeles
  William Neikirk, Washington
  Ed Schuyler, New York
  Walter Stovall, New York
  Doug Willis, San Francisco
  Burt Wittrup, Albuquerque, N.M.
Indochina Staff:
  Tad Bartimus
  George Esper
  Matt Franjola
  Dennis Gray
  David Jenkins
  Dang Van Phuoc
  Carl Robinson
  Ly Phuc Thai
  Huynh Minh Trinh
  Neal Ulevich
  Huynh Cong Ut

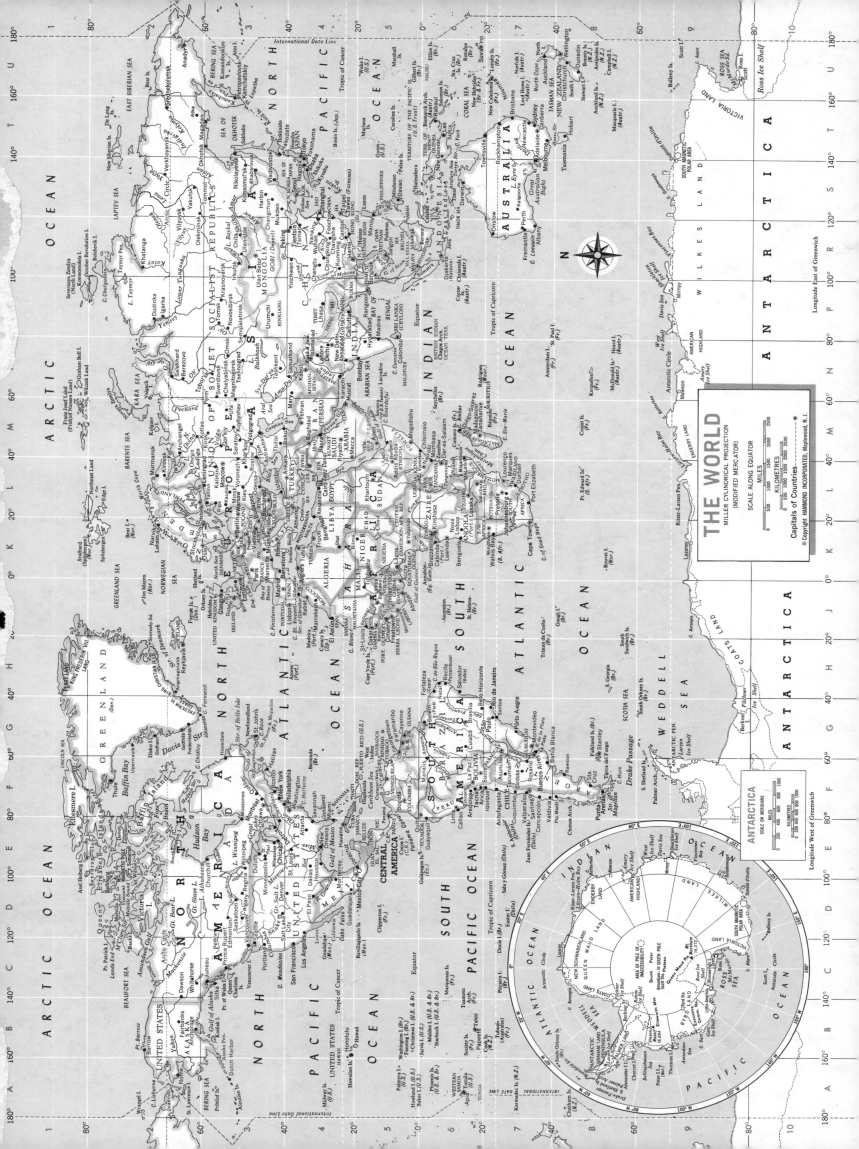

THE WORLD

MILLER CYLINDRICAL PROJECTION
(MODIFIED MERCATOR)

SCALE ALONG EQUATOR

MILES
0 500 1000 1500 2000 2500

KILOMETRES
0 500 1000 1500 2000 2500

⊛ Copyright HAMMOND INCORPORATED, Maplewood, N.J.

⊛ Capitals of Countries

NORTH AMERICA

LAMBERT AZIMUTHAL EQUAL-AREA PROJECTION

SCALE OF MILES
0 100 200   400   600   800

SCALE OF KILOMETRES
0   200   400   600   800

⭐ Capitals of Countries................
International Boundaries................
Other Boundaries................
Canals................

Copyright by C.S. HAMMOND & Co., N.Y.

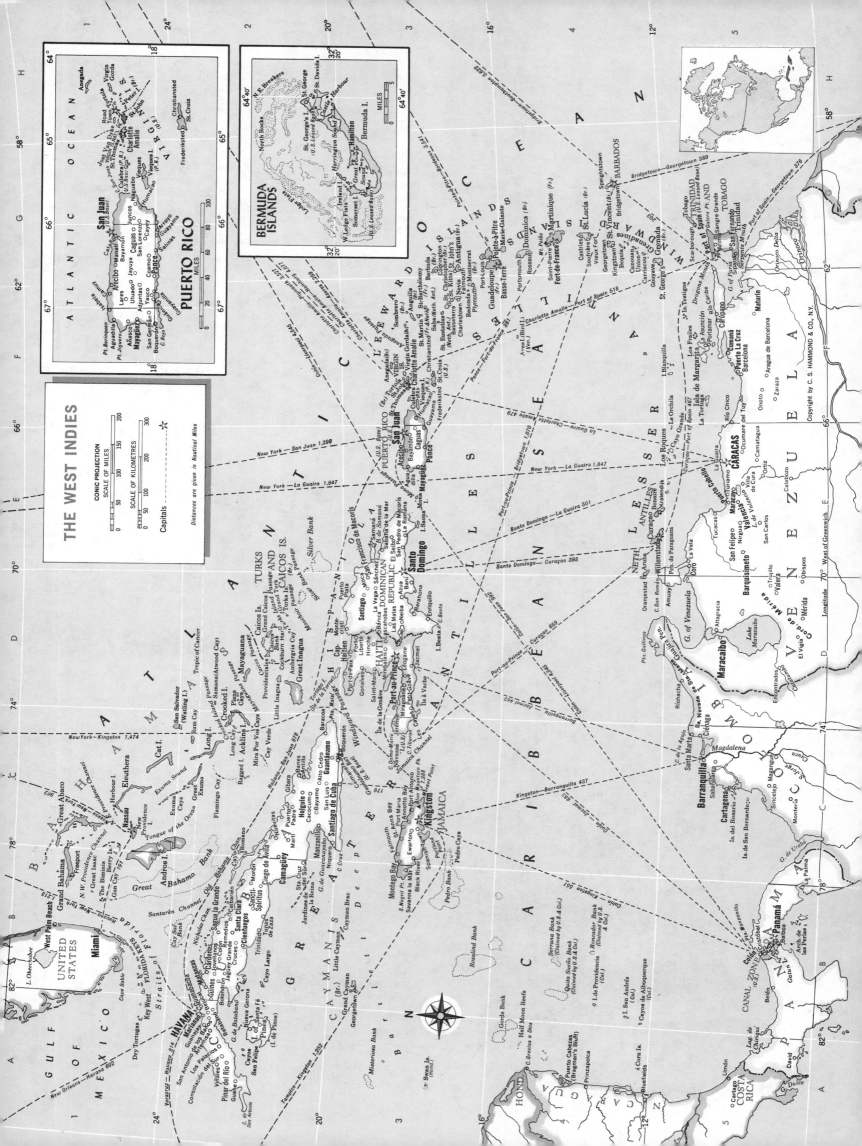

THE WEST INDIES

CONIC PROJECTION

SCALE OF MILES
0   50   100   150   200

SCALE OF KILOMETRES
0   50   100   200   300

Capitals .... ☆

Distances are given in Nautical Miles

PUERTO RICO

SCALE
MILES
0   20   40   60   80   100

San Juan

BERMUDA ISLANDS

MILES
0   5

Copyright by C. S. HAMMOND & CO., N.Y.

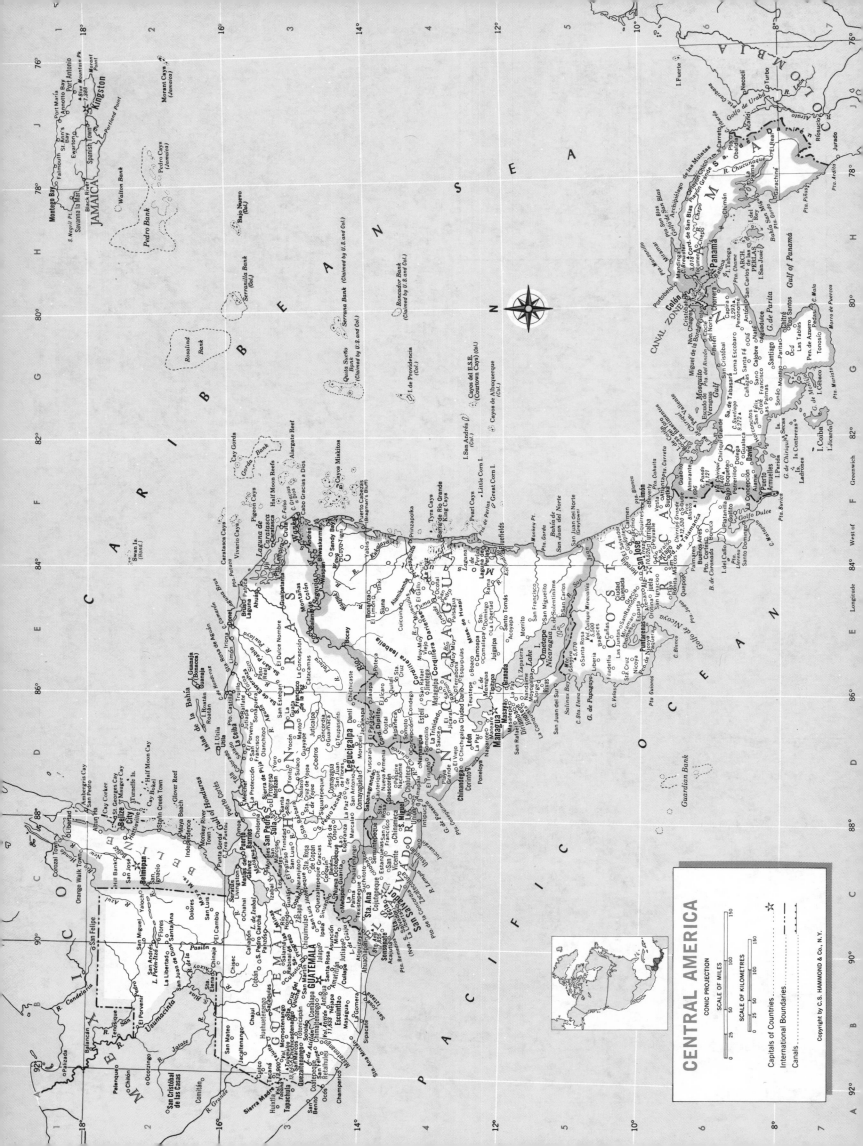

CENTRAL AMERICA

CONIC PROJECTION

SCALE OF MILES

SCALE OF KILOMETRES

Capitals of Countries..........★

International Boundaries..........

Canals..........

Copyright by C.S. HAMMOND & Co., N.Y.

SOUTH AMERICA

LAMBERT AZIMUTHAL EQUAL-AREA PROJECTION

SCALE OF MILES

0   100   200   400   600

SCALE OF KILOMETRES

0 100 200   400   600

Capitals of Countries .... ☆
International Boundaries .... ▬ ▪ ▬
Canals ....

GALÁPAGOS ISLANDS
(ARCHIPIÉLAGO DE COLÓN)
(To Ecuador)
SCALE OF MILES
0   50   100   150

Copyright by C.S. HAMMOND & CO., N.Y.

EUROPE

LAMBERT AZIMUTHAL EQUAL AREA PROJECTION

SCALE OF MILES

SCALE OF KILOMETRES

Capitals of Countries..........☆
International Boundaries........—·—
Canals.........................

Copyright by C.S. HAMMOND & Co., N.Y

The government of the United States has
not recognized the incorporation of Estonia,
Latvia and Lithuania into the Soviet Union,
nor does it recognize as final the de facto
western limit of Polish administration in
Germany (the Oder-Neisse line).

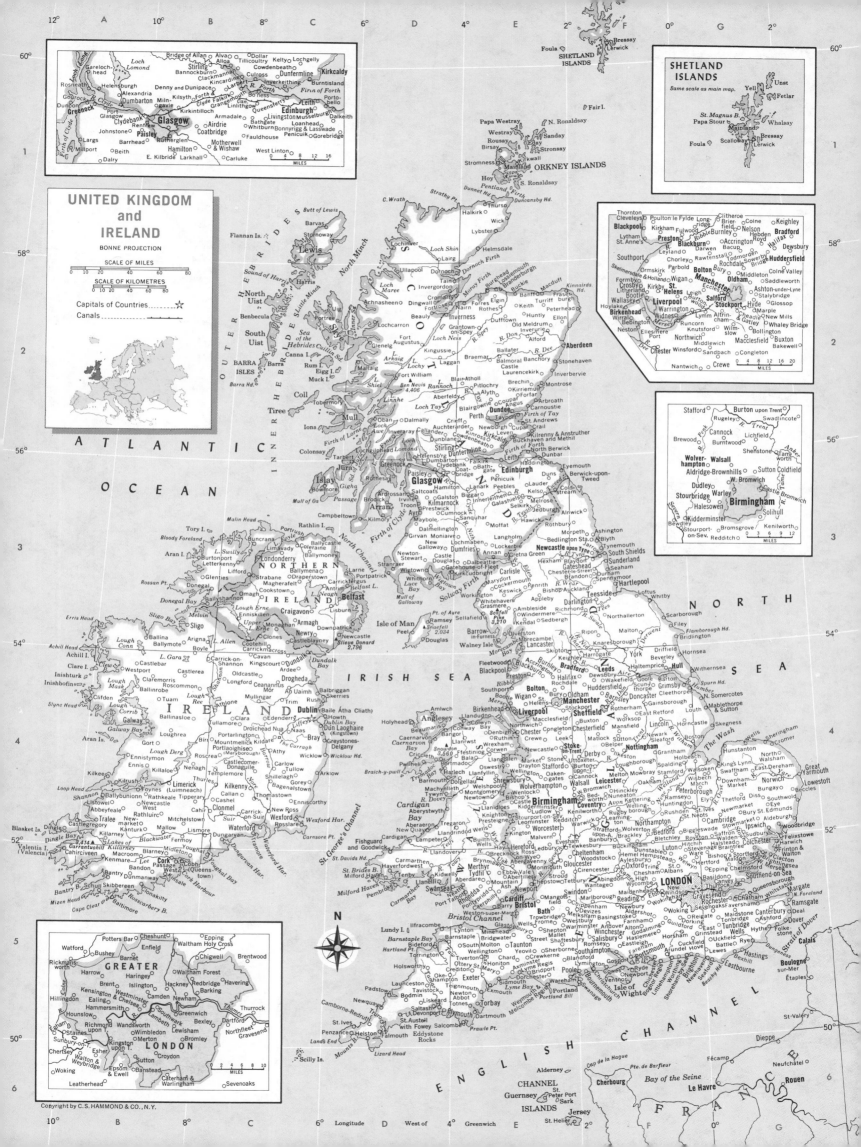

UNITED KINGDOM and IRELAND

BONNE PROJECTION

SCALE OF MILES

SCALE OF KILOMETRES

Capitals of Countries............⭐
Canals............

SHETLAND ISLANDS

SHETLAND ISLANDS
Same scale as main map.

GREATER LONDON

ATLANTIC OCEAN

NORTHERN IRELAND

IRELAND

IRISH SEA

NORTH SEA

ENGLISH CHANNEL

FRANCE

Copyright by C.S. HAMMOND & CO., N.Y.

ASIA

LAMBERT AZIMUTHAL EQUAL-AREA PROJECTION

SCALE OF MILES

0 150 300   600   900   1200

SCALE OF KILOMETRES

0   300   600   900   1200

Capitals of Countries .... ✪   Canals ....
International Boundaries ....

© Copyright HAMMOND INCORPORATED, Maplewood, N.J.

CHINA and MONGOLIA

CONIC PROJECTION

SCALE OF MILES

SCALE OF KILOMETRES

Capitals of Countries....☆
Provincial Capitals.......◉
Canals ....

International Boundaries ___
Provincial Boundaries ___
Walls ___

Copyright by C. S. Hammond & Co., N.Y.

*Wuhan municipality consists of
Hankow, Hanyang and Wuchang

BURMA, THAILAND,
INDOCHINA
and MALAYA

CONIC PROJECTION

SCALE OF MILES

SCALE OF KILOMETRES

International Boundaries
Provincial and State Boundaries
Capitals of Countries
Provincial and State Capitals

Longitude East 96° of Greenwich

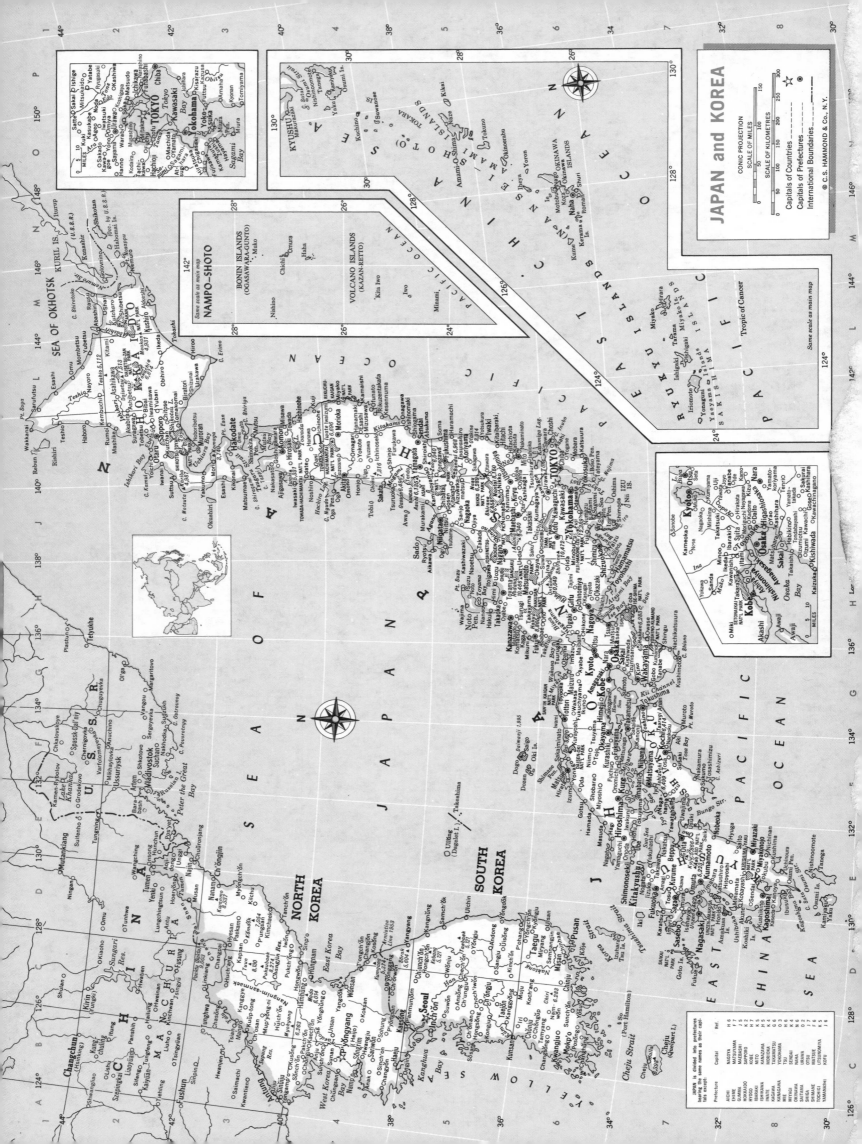

JAPAN and KOREA

CONIC PROJECTION

SCALE OF MILES

SCALE OF KILOMETRES

Capitals of Countries ☆
Capitals of Prefectures ◉
International Boundaries

© C.S. HAMMOND & Co., N.Y.

NAMPO-SHOTO

BONIN ISLANDS
(OGASAWARA-GUNTO)

VOLCANO ISLANDS
(KAZAN-RETTO)

Same scale as main map

SEA OF OKHOTSK

KURIL IS. (U.S.S.R.)

SEA OF JAPAN

PACIFIC OCEAN

EAST CHINA SEA

YELLOW SEA

NORTH KOREA

SOUTH KOREA

MANCHURIA

CHINA

U.S.S.R.

RYUKYU ISLANDS (NANSEI-SHOTO)

Tropic of Cancer

Prefecture	Capital	Ref.
AICHI	NAGOYA	H 6
EHIME	MATSUYAMA	F 7
HOKKAIDO	SAPPORO	J 5
HYOGO	KOBE	G 6
IBARAKI	MITO	K 5
ISHIKAWA	KANAZAWA	H 5
IWATE	MORIOKA	K 4
KAGAWA	TAKAMATSU	G 6
KANAGAWA	YOKOHAMA	O 3
MIE	TSU	H 6
MIYAGI	SENDAI	K 4
OKINAWA	NAHA	N 6
SAITAMA	URAWA	O 2
SHIGA	OTSU	J 7
SHIMANE	MATSUE	F 6
YAMANASHI	UTSUNOMIYA	J 6

JAPAN is divided into prefectures bearing the same names as their capitals except:

AP News Almanac

CHRONOLOGY—1973

JANUARY

1—The announcement that the United States and North Vietnam would resume private peace talks in Paris brought a cool reaction from supporters of South Vietnamese President Nguyen Van Thieu.

1—Britain's entry into the European Common Market was formally marked by a ceremony in London's Westminster Abbey. Thousands of workers took the day off unofficially to celebrate.

2—The United States and North Vietnam resumed their cease-fire talks in Paris with a four-hour session.

3—The 93rd Congress convened with an attack on the Nixon Administration by leaders of the Democratic majority.

5—President Nixon told a bipartisan group of Congressional leaders he was determined to do what he regarded as necessary to achieve "a proper kind of settlement" in Vietnam.

5—United States airlines began a routine search of every item carried aboard planes by passengers as well as scanning passengers with an electronic weapon detector.

7—Henry A. Kissinger arrived in Paris to resume talks on a Vietnam settlement that were broken off earlier amid accusations of obstructionist tactics from both the United States and North Vietnam.

7—Police killed a sniper atop a New Orleans motor lodge after six persons were slain and 12 wounded.

8—Henry A. Kissinger and Le Duc Tho resumed negotiations in Paris for a Vietnam cease-fire.

8—Israel and Syria fought extensive air and artillery battles.

9—New Orleans police identified the sniper atop the motor lodge as Mark Essex, 23.

11—President Nixon ended mandatory wage and price controls—except those involving food, health care and construction—and replaced them with a system relying largely on "voluntary cooperation."

11—E. Howard Hunt Jr., a former White House consultant, pleaded guilty to all six charges against him in connection with the break-in and alleged bugging of the Democratic national headquarters.

12—The Federal Reserve Board approved an increase in the discount rate from 4½ per cent to 5 per cent at all 12 Federal Reserve banks.

13—Henry A. Kissinger left Paris to report to President Nixon after six days of what he described as "useful" negotiations with Le Duc Tho, Hanoi's envoy.

14—President Nixon sent Gen. Alexander M. Haig Jr. to Saigon to consult with President Nguyen Van Thieu about cease-fire negotiations.

14—Premier Golda Meir of Israel arrived in Rome to confer with Pope Paul VI.

14—The Miami Dolphins beat the Washington Redskins 14-7 to win the Super Bowl.

15—President Nixon—citing "progress" made in the cease-fire negotiations—suspended bombing, mining, shelling and all other offensive action in North Vietnam.

15—Israeli Premier Golda Meir and Pope Paul VI discussed efforts to bring peace to the Middle East.

15—Four of the six remaining defendants in the Watergate trial pleaded guilty to all seven counts in the break-in at Democratic National Committee headquarters in Washington.

17—An informed source said South Vietnamese President Nguyen Van Thieu had raised several objections to aspects of a proposed peace settlement.

17—Philippines President Ferdinand E. Marcos proclaimed a new constitution, extending martial law indefinitely.

18—The United States and North Vietnam announced they would resume private peace talks in Paris Jan. 23 "for the purpose of completing the text of an agreement." Spokesmen said the agree-

ment had the "objective of stopping the fighting, ending the war and restoring the peace."

18—Juan V. Corona was found guilty of murdering 25 migrant farm workers whose bodies were found buried near Yuba City, Calif., in 1971.

18—Five children and two adults were murdered in a Washington house used by a Muslim sect.

20—President Nixon, in his inaugural address, opened his second term with an appeal to the nation and the world for greater self-reliance "as we stand on the threshold of a new era of peace."

21—A two-day battle by police and gunmen at a Brooklyn sporting goods store ended with a daring roof escape by nine hostages and the surrender a few hours later of the four black gunmen.

22—Lyndon Baines Johnson, 36th President of the United States, died at age 64 of coronary thrombosis following an attack suffered at his ranch in Johnson City, Tex.

22—The U.S. Supreme Court, by a 7-2 vote, overruled all state laws which prohibit or restrict a woman's right to get an abortion during her first three months of pregnancy.

22—General Motors Corp. recalled 3.7 million 1971 and 1972 cars, saying it would install a shield to keep gravel from bouncing into the steering mechanism.

22—A jetliner crashed at Kano (Nigeria) Airport, killing 176 persons. Officials said 33 persons survived.

23—President Nixon said Henry A. Kissinger and Le Duc Tho, North Vietnam's chief negotiator, had initialed an agreement "to end the war and bring peace with honor in Vietnam and Southeast Asia." The President said a Vietnam cease-fire would go into effect Jan. 27. He said under terms of the accord all American prisoners of war would be released and the remaining 23,700-man American force in South Vietnam would be withdrawn within 60 days.

23—A volcanic eruption opened a fissure in an island off Iceland's southern coast and forced evacuation of nearly all the 5,500 inhabitants.

24—Henry A. Kissinger said the United States had a "firm expectation" that the Vietnam cease-fire would extend to Cambodia and Laos.

26—Henry A. Kissinger told congressmen the Administration would consult them before making any firm commitments to North Vietnam on postwar aid programs.

26—The Nixon Administration confirmed it planned to abolish the Office of Economic Opportunity, an antipoverty agency established by President Johnson as one of the chief features of his Great Society.

27—The Vietnam accords were signed in Paris. The documents provided a settlement of the longest foreign war in America's history.

27—Secretary of Defense Melvin Laird announced the end of the military draft and said the armed forces would depend on volunteers.

28—A cease-fire went into effect throughout Vietnam at 8 a.m. although some fighting still was reported.

28—President Nixon disclosed plans for reductions in long-standing programs of aid to hospitals, schools and urban areas and appealed to the nation to put pressure on Congress to hold down federal spending.

28—Officials said about 100 American planes struck suspected Communist positions and supply lines in Laos after the Vietnam cease-fire went into effect.

29—South Vietnam said the Communists had committed hundreds of cease-fire violations during the first 22 hours since the truce agreement took effect, but indicated most of them were minor.

30—President Nixon presented Congress with a budget which estimated spending at $268.7 billion in the fiscal year beginning July 1. The budget contained a list of more than 100 cutbacks or terminations of government programs.

30—Leonid I. Brezhnev, the Soviet Leader, called the Vietnam settlement an important turning point in international affairs which would have "a positive effect" on Soviet-American relations.

30—Analysts said the level of fighting in Vietnam had declined substantially.

30—President Nixon's Economic Report to Congress disclosed the government wanted and expected economic expansion to slow after midyear.

30—G. Gordon Liddy and James W. McCord Jr. were found guilty in the Watergate trial of plotting to spy on the Democrats during the 1972 campaign.

30—Sen. John C. Stennis, D-Miss., was shot and wounded in an apparent robbery in front of his Washington home.

31—President Nixon said he was sending Henry A. Kissinger to Hanoi Feb. 10 to make the peace more secure and lay the groundwork for reconstruction of Southeast Asia.

FEBRUARY

1—Premier Chou En-lai hailed the Vietnam cease-fire agreement as a great victory for China's Vietnamese allies.

2—President Nixon sent Congress a State of the Union message that was firm in his intention to "draw the line" on spending.

2—Pope Paul VI nominated 30 new cardinals from all continents, including three Americans.

2—An explosion in Eagle Grove, Iowa, leveled three business firms, killed 12 persons and left a 13th missing and presumed dead.

2—A fire and explosion in a Miami Beach restaurant injured 139 persons.

3—The White House said Henry A. Kissinger would go to Peking Feb. 15 for five days of "concrete consultations" with Chinese leaders.

3—Fighting in South Vietnam reportedly came to a virtual halt, a week after a formal cease-fire went into effect.

3—Ten men were shot and wounded by bullets from a passing car as they walked along a street in a Roman Catholic area of Belfast.

5—The International Commission of Control and Supervision (ICC) dispatched seven regional teams around South Vietnam in the first major step toward monitoring the Vietnam cease-fire.

5—Sources said the Saigon government had released thousands of military and civilian prisoners, despite provisions of the Paris peace agreement.

5—Juan V. Corona was sentenced to 25 consecutive terms of life imprisonment after having been convicted earlier of murdering 25 itinerant farm workers.

6—The White House announced a further effort to achieve a cease-fire in Laos and plans for an international conference to try to solidify the Vietnam cease-fire agreement.

7—Widespread violence broke out in Northern Ireland after gunmen fired on Roman Catholic mourners at a funeral procession for three members of the Irish Republican Army killed by British troops.

8—Secretary of State William P. Rogers was told by some congressmen that plans to give economic aid to North Vietnam faced growing public opposition.

9—West German Chancellor Willy Brandt conferred by telephone with President Nixon, Prime Minister Heath of Britain and President Pompidou of France and asked their cooperation in a monetary crisis which by day's end had forced West Germany to buy up two billion more unwanted dollars.

9—The U.S. Court of Appeals blocked the issuance of government permits for building a trans-Alaska oil pipeline, reversing a Federal District Court decision.

9—The Alameda (Calif.) County coroner's office estimated no more than 15 or 16 residents of an apartment house in Alameda died when a Navy fighter-bomber crashed into it Feb. 7.

10—Henry A. Kissinger arrived in Hanoi to discuss postwar (U.S.) relations with North Vietnam.

10—Forty workmen were buried under tons of concrete and flaming debris in an explosion that ripped through the world's largest liquified gas storage tank on Staten Island, N.Y.

11—Most foreign exchange markets in Western Europe and Japan were ordered closed Feb. 12 as the major industrial powers entered bargaining over new patterns of currency values.

12—The repatriation of American prisoners of the Vietnam war began with the ceremonial turnover at Hanoi's Gia Lam Airport of the first planeload of men.

12—The United States announced a devaluation of the dollar of 10 per cent against nearly all of the world's major currencies. The action was taken in an effort to stop a currency crisis in which there had been a flight from the dollar in international monetary markets. It was the second devaluation of the dollar in 14 months.

13—President Nixon said the United States must have the power to raise trade barriers as well as lower them to gain a "fairer shake" for American business in world trade.

13—The newly devalued American dollar began moving downward against most other currencies.

13—The first two released war prisoners left Clark Air Base in the Philippines for the United States.

13—Federal District Court in Detroit fined Ford Motor Co. $7 million on charges some Ford employes tampered with engines to make them pass federal air pollution standards.

14—The United States and North Vietnam announced an agreement to establish a commission to channel American aid to North Vietnam.

14—Trading volume in dollars reached a near record daily level on the Tokyo foreign exchange market as the Japanese yen was allowed to float and rose as the dollar dropped in value.

14—President Nixon said he would soon propose a plan to assure adequate energy "at acceptable economic and environmental costs."

14—The first full planeload of returning prisoners of war flew from the Philippines to the United States.

15—The Laotian Government and the Pathet Lao failed to reach a predicted cease-fire agreement.

15—The Pentagon announced a significant increase in American air strikes against North Vietnamese and Pathet Lao troop and supply movements in Laos.

15—The United States and Cuba signed an agreement intended to stop hijacking. However, Secretary of State William P. Rogers said the United States would not ease its diplomatic and economic boycott of Cuba until "the policies and attitudes of the Cuban government" changed.

16—The murder conviction of First Lt. William L. Calley Jr. for his role in the My Lai killings was upheld by the U.S. Army Court of Military Review which also approved his sentence of 20 years confinement at hard labor.

17—The chiefs of the four-party Joint Military Commission appealed to the Communist and Saigon commands "to promptly issue orders" to halt any further fighting in South Vietnam.

17—The White House said Henry A. Kissinger and China's Mao Tse-tung met for nearly two hours in what were described as "frank and wide ranging conversations in an unrestrained atmosphere."

17—President Nixon nominated L. Patrick Gray III to be director of the Federal Bureau of Investigation.

18—Henry A. Kissinger conferred for five hours with Chinese Premier Chou En-lai on the fourth day of his visit to Peking.

20—Saigon military authorities said fighting in South Vietnam declined substantially during the previous 24 hours.

20—President Nixon asked for public understanding of the motives for and the potential benefits from the settlement in Vietnam.

20—Parts of New York City were without electricity for 2½ hours in a blackout affecting one million people.

21—The Laotian government and the Communist-led Pathet Lao signed a peace agreement that ended 20 years of war and established an interim coalition government.

21—Israeli Air Force jet fighters shot down a Libyan civilian jetliner over the Sinai Desert and 106 of the 113 persons aboard the airliner were killed.

22—The United States and China announced that each government would soon open a liasion office in the other's capital.

22—Israeli Defense Minister Moshe Dayan said the downing of a Libyan airliner Feb. 21 was a "tragedy," but accused the liner's pilot of ignoring repeated instructions to land.

22—The remains of Marshal Henri-Phillippe Petain, head of the French government that collaborated with the Germans in World War II, were found in Paris and returned to their grave on the Ile d'Yeu. The remains were taken from the island Feb. 19 by political kidnapers.

23—The Defense Department said American B52 bombers struck Communist troop positions in Laos less than 24 hours after a cease-fire had formally gone into effect. It said the raids were made at the request of the Royal Laotian government.

24—Israeli Defense Minister Moshe Dayan said Israel had made an "error of judgment" in shooting down a Libyan airliner Feb. 21.

24—President Nixon said his administration would underwrite social programs that would "give people the assistance they need without taking away their freedom or decreasing their self-reliance and their self-respect."

25—Secretary of State William P. Rogers began private talks in Paris with Foreign Minister Chi Peng-fei of China on settling each country's financial claims against the other.

25—Demonstrators threw rocks at the barracks of North Vietnamese members of the Four-Party Joint Military Commission in Da Nang and Hue, South Vietnam.

25—The Israeli government said it would make voluntary payments to the families of the victims of the Libyan airliner shot down over the Sinai Desert.

26—The international conference on Vietnam opened in Paris with a proposal by Canada for a forum that could act on any future breakdown of the cease-fire.

26—The Administration said it would retain 5.5 per cent as a standard for annual wage increases during Phase 3 of President Nixon's economic stabilization program.

27—A North Vietnamese spokesman said there would be no further release of American prisoners "until the United States stops concentrating their efforts on getting back prisoners while failing to correctly implement the Paris agreement."

27—The Administration accused Hanoi of violating major provisions of the Vietnam cease-fire agreement by delaying release of the American prisoners. President Nixon ordered Secretary of State William P. Rogers at the Vietnam peace conference in Paris "to demand clarification" from the North Vietnamese delegation "on the most urgent basis."

28—The White House said North Vietnam had given new assurances that the return of all American prisoners of war should be completed within the 60-day time limit agreed on in the Paris truce agreement.

28—Militant Indians, demanding government investigations into federal treatment of Indians, held at least 10 hostages and exchanged gunfire with federal officers at Wounded Knee, S.D.

MARCH

1—The Vietnam Conference in Paris completed its work as 12 foreign ministers initialed an agreement which provided that in the event of a breakdown in the cease-fire the conference can be reconvened by the United States and North Vietnam or any six of the other signers.

1—Ireland's Fiana Fail party, which had held power for 16 years, was defeated in the general elections by a coalition of the Fine Gael and the Labor party.

1—After meeting with militant Indians holding 11 hostages in Wounded Knee, S.D., Sens. George McGovern and James G. Abourez said they had been told the hostages were free to leave.

2—President Nixon said "there will not be another devaluation of the dollar." Nixon said "we believe the dollar is a sound currency," adding "we will survive" what he called an "attack by international speculators."

2—Government officials said shots fired from the seized hamlet of Wounded Knee, S.D., struck an FBI auto, part of the federal force that continued to surround the hamlet.

3—Federal officials said one of their armored personnel carriers took "20 rounds of fire" from the militant Indians entrenched at Wounded Knee, S.D.

4—Another 106 American POWS arrived at Clark Air Base in the Philippines after being released at Hanoi.

4—Eight Black September commandos ended their occupation of the Saudi Arabian embassy in Khartoum, the Sudan, nearly 60 hours after they had raided the embassy March 1 and had taken five hostages, three of whom they killed—two American diplomats and a Belgian diplomat.

4—President Nixon said the quality of life was on the upswing again in cities and towns and that "the hour of crisis has passed."

5—A North Vietnamese official said the Communists would boycott further meetings of the Joint Military Commission because of a dispute over the exchange of Vietnamese war prisoners.

5—The Sudanese foreign minister said the Black September commandos who killed three diplomats in Khartoum would have an early trial on murder charges.

5—Indians holding the hamlet of Wounded Knee, S.D., spurned a government peace offer, but negotiations continued.

5—Two Spanish jetliners bound for London collided over France during an air controllers strike. One plane crashed and killed all 68 aboard. The other made a safe landing.

6—The Nixon Administration imposed mandatory price controls on 23 of the country's biggest oil companies.

7—The White House denied that the Administration was considering price controls on raw agricultural products and meat "on the hoof." But authoritative sources reiterated that the Cost of Living Council was considering clamping price restrictions on farm prices.

7—Herbert W. Kalmbach, President Nixon's personal lawyer, told FBI agents that he had paid between $30,000 and $40,000 in Republican party funds to Donald H. Segretti, an attorney who reportedly ran a covert political sabotage operation during the 1972 presidential election campaign.

7—Richard Moore, a Black Panther, was convicted of attempting to kill two policemen who had been assigned to guard District Attorney Frank S. Hogan's apartment on Riverside Drive May 19, 1973.

8—The White House expressed "concern" at release of what it called "raw, unevaluated material" from the files of the Federal Bureau of Investigation that linked a former high aide of President Nixon to an alleged political sabotage operation.

8—Terrorists struck in London setting off two large explosions that killed one man and injured 243 persons. Officials expressed belief the IRA was responsible.

8—A cease-fire was reached between federal officials and militant Indians at Wounded Knee, S.D., but gunfire continued.

8—Archbishop Makarios, president of Cyprus,

was ordered unfrocked by three bishops of his church who charged he had violated church law by holding public office. But Makarios labeled the decision "of no value whatsoever."

9—President Nixon's re-election committee said it had returned $655,000 to three big contributors. They included $100,000 to Texas oilman Robert H. Allen who was the source of $89,000 that passed through a Mexican bank in an alleged political espionage operation against Democratic party headquarters in June 1972.

9—McGeorge Bundy, one of the architects of U.S. Vietnam war policy, said that disclosure of three of the documents in the Pentagon Papers case had not damaged the national defense. Bundy testified at the trial of Daniel Ellsberg.

10—President Nixon called on Congress to restore the death penalty for certain Federal crimes and to enact a new program of stringent minimum jail sentences for heroin pushers.

10—Sudanese authorities said one of the men accused of assassinating two American diplomats and a Belgian at the Saudi Arabian embassy in Khartoum had made a full confession.

11—France's Gaullist-led government won a renewed five-year mandate in legislative elections. The government coalition vote was stronger than expected.

11—A state of emergency was declared in Bermuda in the wake of the murder of Sir Richard Sharples, governor of the British colony and his aide de camp.

12—West Germany's finance minister, Helmut Schmidt, announced that the mark would be revalued upward by 3 per cent.

12—The military government of Argentina declared Dr. Hector J. Campora, the handpicked presidential candidate of Juan D. Peron, as the victor in national elections.

12—In a policy statement on the use of executive privilege, President Nixon said members and former members of his personal staff would decline to make any formal appearances before Congressional committees.

12—After more than 20 years as a prisoner in China, John Downey of the Central Intelligence Agency returned to the United States, following his release by Chinese authorities.

12—Police and FBI agents in Washington announced the arrest of three men in the Jan. 30 robbery and shooting of Sen. John Stennis of Mississippi.

13—John T. Downey, shot down over China in 1952 while on a mission for the CIA, told a news conference that the long imprisonment had cost him a great part of his life apparently for naught.

13—In a direct challenge to President Nixon, the Senate Judiciary Committee voted unanimously to call his chief legal counsel, John W. Dean as a witness at its hearings on the nomination of L. Patrick Gray for FBI chief.

14—John W. Dean, president Nixon's chief legal counsel, declined an invitation to appear before the Senate Judiciary Committee in connection with the nomination of L. Patrick Gray as FBI chief. Dean cited presidential policy against having members of Nixon's personal staff make such appearances.

14—The United States relaxed its total embargo on arms shipments to India and Pakistan, thus permitting the Pakistanis to receive about 300 armored personnel carriers.

14—Jordan's King Hussein announced he had commuted the death sentences passed against 17 Palestinian guerrillas.

15—President Nixon warned Hanoi not to move its military equipment toward South Vietnam and hinted it could lead to resumption of U.S. bombing.

15—President Nixon said he recalled Ambassador David K. E. Bruce from retirement to head a U.S. liaison office in Peking.

15—President Nixon flatly rejected the idea of putting controls on prices paid to farmers for their products, including meat.

16—South Vietnamese and U.S. officials said Communist-led forces were engaged in a major buildup of supplies and military equipment in the critical border province of Tay Ninh. In turn, the Viet Cong charged that the United States was shipping war materiel into South Vietnam bypassing the inspection required by the cease-fire agreement.

16—The United States and 13 other major trading nations agreed on a loosely formulated package of measures designed to ease the problem of excess dollars abroad and to assure the opening of official currency dealings under "orderly conditions."

17—A Cambodian Air Force captain stole a plane and bombed the presidential palace in what was reported to be an attempt to kill President Lon Nol.

17—U.S. intelligence officials said the Communist command had more war supplies in South Vietnam than it had before the big offensive in 1972, but that its combat units were far below fighting strength.

18—President Lon Nol of Cambodia ordered a series of stern measures after an apparent attempt to assassinate him in a bombing raid on the presidential palace. He suspended the nation's press and placed a number of members of the former royal family under house arrest.

19—The dollar was surprisingly strong in heavy trading on Tokyo Foreign Exchange Market, the first major market to reopen after the two-week suspension in trading during international monetary negotiations.

19—A House subcommittee made public documents purporting to show that at least six high-ranking officials of the Nixon Administration, including Vice President Spiro Agnew, were involved in a successful attempt to persuade the Justice Department to settle its antitrust suits against International Telephone and Telegraph Corp., on terms acceptable to the company.

19—Citing the "spirit" of a Cuban-American agreement against hijacking the United States refused to grant asylum to two Cuban fishermen who briefly seized control of their nine-man fishing boat at sea.

19—Soviet authorities waived emigration taxes for at least five educated Jews leaving for Israel. The move appeared to be the start of an effort to appease U.S. Congressional opposition to an easing of trade with the Soviet Union.

20—In a white paper, the British government announced a plan to insure a share of political power for Northern Ireland's Roman Catholic minority.

21—John A. McCone, former head of the Central Intelligence Agency and currently on the board of International Telephone and Telegraph Corp., denied the company had anything "surreptitious" in mind when it offered the government $1 million to help defeat Salvador Allende Gossens as president of Chile.

21—The Saigon military command said it had begun a major assault to break a Communist siege of an outpost near Saigon.

21—The Supreme Court ruled 5-4 that states could continue to finance public schools with local property taxes that provided more money for schools in wealthier districts.

21—Food prices rose 2.4 per cent in February, according to the government, which also said the increase led the over-all Consumer Price Index to its largest one month increase in 22 years.

22—Continental Illinois National Bank and Trust Co., one of seven banks that raised the prime rate March 19 by half a percentage point, said it was halving the increase to leave its prime rate at 6.5 per cent.

23—James W. McCord Jr., a key figure in the Watergate conspiracy, said in a letter read in court that he and others caught spying on the Democrats last year had been under "political pressure to plead guilty and remain silent." McCord, chief of security for President Nixon's political organization, throughout the espionage effort, wrote that "others" had escaped capture.

23—Twenty former directors of Penn Central Transportation Co., and the estates of two former directors agreed in principle to settle 18 lawsuits brought against them by scores of stockholders of the bankrupt railroad for alleged dereliction of duties.

23—Millions of dollars worth of equipment and property of Egyptian enterprises in the Sinai was looted by Israelis in the months after the June 1967 war, according to a confidential report by the Israeli State Controller.

24—A new attempt to break the deadlock over the release of the last American prisoners of war succeeded only in producing new Communist demands that the United States withdraw all marine guards and truce personnel.

25—President Nixon said he had ordered U.S. forces to remain in South Vietnam until all American prisoners of war had been released.

25—Democrats and Republicans on the Congressional Joint Economic Committee agreed unanimously with President Nixon that total government spending in the ensuing fiscal year should be held at $268 billion. But the Democrats said "Congress should make major allocations with the Administration's proposed expenditure total."

26—William J. Prater, a former organizer of the United Mine Workers, was convicted of first degree murder in the 1969 slayings of Joseph A. Yablonski, mine union official, his wife and daughter.

27—The White House said the United States would continue bombing in Cambodia until Communist-led forces in that country stopped their military operations and agreed to a cease-fire.

27—President Nixon vetoed a $2.6 billion vocational rehabilitation bill, describing it as part of a threatened "Congressional spending spree" that would dip into the "pocketbooks of millions of men and women."

28—AFL-CIO President George Meany called on Congress to "rock back prices to where they were last December" to assure Labor's cooperation in Phase 3 of the Administration's wage-price stabilization effort.

28—Defense Secretary Elliot L. Richardson maintained that President Nixon had clear constitutional authority to continue bombing in Cambodia to clean up a "lingering corner of the war."

29—President Nixon announced that the government was imposing price ceilings on beef, pork and lamb effective at once. As he spoke, a nationwide movement to boycott meat for a week got underway.

29—Former security official James W. McCord Jr., testified that his fellow conspirators in the Watergate affair gave him the impression they had cleared their clandestine operations with high ranking officials in the Nixon Administration.

29—The last American troops left South Vietnam as Hanoi freed the last American POW.

29—Former American prisoners of war began telling tales of mental and physical torture at the hands of the of the North Vietnamese captors.

30—Responding to mounting criticism, the White House indicated readiness to compromise with the Senate's investigation of the Watergate case on the issue of furnishing witnesses and information from President Nixon's personal staff.

31—North Vietnamese and Viet Cong members of the Four-Party Joint Military Commission left Saigon charging that the United States and South Vietnam had "systematically and very seriously sabotaged" major provisions of the Paris peace agreement.

31—Defense Secretary Elliot L. Richardson defended continuing American bombing of Cambodia as vital to keep the government of President Lon Nol alive.

APRIL

1—H. Rap Brown and three other defendants were found guilty of armed robbery and assault with a deadly weapon. But the jury deadlocked on charges that the robbers had attempted to murder three policemen in a running gun battle.

2—The Kremlin ordered a sweeping reorganization of the Soviet Union's industry as part of a continuing search for an efficient system of managing the vast government-run economy.

2—Supermarkets began to feel the impact of a meat boycott by consumers as shoppers shunned beef, pork and lamb to protest high prices.

2—The U.S. Supreme Court declined to review a decision by the U.S. Court of Appeals barring federal officials from authorizing construction of the Trans-Alaska pipeline.

2—Sen. Ervin, D-N.C., and the White House engaged in a spirited exchange over the Watergate case.

2—Presidents Nixon and Nguyen Van Thieu of South Vietnam opened a two-day conference at the Nixon home in San Clemente, Calif.

3—President Nguyen Van Thieu of South Vietnam ended his talks with President Nixon with a promise of continuing economic aid, but without a specific pledge of American military action if his country was imperiled.

3—The Senate voted to uphold President Nixon's veto of a bill to provide vocational aid to the handicapped.

4—The Pentagon said it foresaw no immediate collapse of the Cambodian government but added the United States might have to begin an airlift to the besieged capital of Phnom Penh.

5—The Senate voted to require President Nixon to get specific Congressional approval before giving foreign aid to North Vietnam.

5—South Vietnamese President Nguyen Van Thieu said he would "never, never" ask the United States to send troops back to Vietnam.

5—The rate of inflation for the first three months of 1973 was the highest since the Korean War on the basis of the wholesale price index, which rose at an annual rate of 21.5 per cent.

5—L. Patrick Gray III asked President Nixon to withdraw his disputed nomination as director of the FBI and White House officials said the President would grant the request.

5—Indian and government negotiators signed a formal agreement to end the 37-day occupation of Wounded Knee, S.D.

7—President Nixon sent Gen. Alexander M. Haig Jr., to Indochina to assess the military situation in the area.

7—A week-long nationwide meat boycott ended with its leaders calling for some form of continued consumer action in the fight against high meat prices.

8—Three tankers and two cargo ships from a convoy of 18 vessels reached the Cambodian capital of Phnom Penh with the first fuel the city had received in two weeks.

8—A Vietcong spokesman said six members of the two peace-keeping commissions, including two Vietcong officers, were killed when their helicopter was shot down by a Communist missile in South Vietnam. Three crewmen on the craft also died. The spokesman called the incident a "regrettable accident."

8—The Indian government took over the administration of the Himalayan monarchy of Sikkim which has been shaken by agitation for political reform.

9—A South Korean tanker carrying fuel to the beleaguered Cambodian capital of Phnom Penh was destroyed by rockets fired by Communist-led gunners. But no one was reported hurt and three other supply vessels managed to slip through the blockade along the Mekong River.

9—Washington's National Gallery purchased a major Cubist painting by the late Pablo Picasso reportedly for a record sum of $1.1 million.

9—U.N. Secretary-General Kurt Waldheim reportedly told the Viet Cong's Provisional Revolutionary Government that it could not open an office at the United Nations.

10—All flights by helicopters of the International Control Commission over Vietnam were suspended because of shooting incidents which resulted in the death of nine men, an ICC source said.

10—A band of Arab guerrillas using a powerful bomb blew out the entrance to the apartment building of the Israeli ambassador in Nicosia, Cyprus and then attacked an Israeli airliner in an apparent hijack attempt. None of the tenants of the apartment house was hurt.

10—Israeli commandos followed up the Cyprus incident with attacks on Arab guerilla bases in Beirut and Saida on the Lebanese coast. Three prominent leaders of the Palestinian Fatah guerrilla organization were killed in the attack on Beirut.

10—The United States began airlifting fuel into Phnom Penh, the besieged capital of Cambodia.

10—Premier Saeb Salam of Lebanon submitted his resignation following an Israeli commando raid in which three Palestinian guerilla leaders were killed.

10—President Nixon sent Congress a trade bill which would give him sweeping new authority to raise and lower United States tariffs and other trade barriers.

12—Occidental Petroleum Corp. and the Soviet Union signed a 20-year agreement to exchange American technology, equipment and chemicals for Soviet ammonia, urea and potash.

13—Sikkim's monarch, Chogyal Palden Thondup Namgyal, said he had reached a settlement with the Indian government for a drastic change in the political status of his kingdom.

14—An attack by armed men on an American owned oil terminal at Saida, Lebanon, produced conflicting claims that they were Palestinian guerillas, Lebanese revolutionaries, or Israeli raiders. Israel denied the attack as did the Palestinian revolutionary groups. However, a previously unknown group calling itself the Lebanese Revolutionary Guard took responsibility for the attack.

14—American officials said they believed the Communists secretly moved two truce commission helicopters they shot down in order to back their explanation of the incident.

14—President Nguyen Van Thieu of South Vietnam returned to Saigon after a two-week world tour and said his trip marked "the end of a difficult period and the beginning of a new era of peaceful reconstruction" for South Vietnam.

15—President Nixon said he planned to make "a grand tour" of Europe in the fall. It would be the first foreign trip of his second term.

16—Reports said South Vietnamese troops had pushed across the Cambodian border for the first time since a Vietnam cease-fire went into effect 2½ months earlier.

16—Pentagon officials said American bombers struck North Vietnamese positions in Laos for only the second time since the Laotian cease-fire.

16—The House rejected legislation sponsored by the Democratic leadership that would have placed ceilings on prices, rents and interest rates.

16—On the 71st day of his trial, Daniel Ellsberg told the jury for the first time that he had disclosed the Pentagon Papers to "give Congress the confidence to act" to end the Indochina War.

17—President Lon Nol of Cambodia announced the resignation of his cabinet and said he would nominate another premier to form a new government.

17—President Nixon said "major developments" had come to light in the Watergate case as a result of a new investigation conducted by himself.

18—Ten Chinese Communist officials arrived in Washington to prepare for the opening of Peking's "liaison office."

18—Sources said Atty. Gen. Richard G. Kleindienst disqualified himself from any further involvement in the Watergate investigation amid reports that at least three of his present and former colleagues in the Nixon Administration would be indicted.

19—The United States said it had suspended mine-clearing operations along the North Vietnamese coast. Officials said the move was aimed at halting North Vietnamese violations of the cease-fire agreement.

19—Former Atty. Gen. John N. Mitchell told friends he was aware of proposals to bug the Democratic opposition, but that he rejected the scheme each of the three times it was presented.

20—Officials said the United States had resumed military reconnaissance flights over North Vietnam despite the ban on such activity in the Vietnam cease-fire agreement.

20—Former Atty. Gen. John Mitchell testified before a federal grand jury in Washington. He said later that plans to spy on the Democrats repeatedly had been pressed on him in 1972 but that he "never approved any bugging plans during any period during the campaign."

21—The U.N. Security Council passed a resolution condemning Israel's military attacks in Lebanon.

22—A gunman shot and killed six persons in Los Angeles and wounded another nine in a shooting rampage before being shot and wounded himself by police.

23—Henry A. Kissinger, in a major policy address at the annual meeting of the Associated Press in New York, said the United States planned to build "a new Atlantic charter" with its European allies to overcome the economic, military and diplomatic strains that have developed in the alliance.

23—Thomas J. Mackell resigned as Queens, N.Y. district attorney 12 days after he had been indicted on charges of covering up a criminal investigation. Mackell repeated his assertion of innocence.

23—The Defense Department estimated that of 300,000 Army enlisted men who served in Vietnam between 1970 and 1972, fewer than 4,000 were civilian drug addicts.

24—Flooding along the Mississippi River system spread over thousands more acres and drove additional hundreds of families from their homes. About 50 persons were injured by tornadoes and savage winds in Mississippi, Arkansas, and Texas.

24—Cambodia's leadership became a four-man executive when a final agreement was reached under which President Lon Nol would share power equally with three political opponents in a new High Political Council.

24—The Japanese government rejected President Nixon's invitation to Emperor Hirohito to make a state visit to the United States.

24—Former Atty. Gen. John N. Mitchell testified before a federal jury in New York, apparently about a $200,000 cash contribution from Robert L. Vesco to President Nixon's 1972 election campaign.

25—The White House said Henry A. Kissinger would return to Paris in May for talks with Le Duc Tho, Hanoi's chief negotiator, aimed at achieving "strict implementation" of the cease-fire agreement.

25—The United States dropped nearly 39,000 tons of bombs on Cambodia during March, according to the Defense Department.

25—Vice President Spiro Agnew reaffirmed his faith in President Nixon, but conceded for the first time that some speculation on the Watergate affair might eventually be substantiated.

25—The swollen Mississippi River system continued to flood more farm and suburban areas.

26—Jeb Stuart Magruder, former White House and Nixon campaign official who reportedly accused former Atty. Gen. John N. Mitchell and chief White House counsel John W. Dean III of complicity in the Watergate affair, has resigned as an assistant secretary of commerce, according to his attorney.

26—The Mississippi River spread over more land and up to 10,000 persons were reported homeless while damage in seven Mississippi River states was estimated at more than $200 million.

27—The Soviet Union made its first major shake-up of the ruling Politburo since Nikita S. Khrushchev was ousted in 1964.

27—L. Patrick Gray III resigned in the intensifying Watergate case as acting director of the FBI and was replaced by William D. Ruckelshaus.

27—Insurgents holding Wounded Knee, S.D., said one of their number had been killed and another wounded in a gunfight with U.S. marshals.

28—Prince Norodom Sihanouk, Cambodia's exiled head of state, said his forces were positioned all around Phnom Penh, the Cambodian capital, but had no intention of assaulting and capturing it.

28—President Nixon was reported in "virtual

seclusion" to ponder his course of action amid the mounting Watergate bugging controversy.

28—A train loaded with munitions exploded in a railway yard at Roseville, Calif., injuring at least 48 persons.

30—President Nixon told the nation that he accepted the responsibility for what happened in the Watergate case even though he had had no knowledge of political espionage or attempts to cover it up.

30—Four top Nixon administration officials resigned as a consequence of Watergate. They were Attorney General Richard G. Kleindienst, H. R. Haldeman, White House chief of staff, John B. Erlichman, the President's chief advisor on domestic affairs, and White House counsel John W. Dean III. Defense Secretary Elliot L. Richardson was named to succeed Kleindienst.

30—The judge in the Pentagon Papers trial ordered four figures connected with the Watergate affair to produce affidavits concerning any link between that break-in and the trial in Los Angeles.

30—The Nixon Administration proposed changes in the tax laws and tax forms that would make it easier for millions of individuals to figure out their Federal income taxes.

MAY

1—Government and Senate investigators said they had evidence that high-ranking officials of the White House and the Committee for the Re-election of the President conspired after the Watergate break-in to arrange a cover story designed to obstruct a federal investigation.

1—Congress pressed for appointment of an independent prosecutor to take charge of the Watergate investigation.

1—John D. Ehrlichman told federal investigators a break-in at the office of Daniel Ellsberg's psychiatrist was a result of a secret White House investigation he ordered at President Nixon's request.

1—Defense Secretary Elliot L. Richardson was formally nominated as attorney general and began moving into over-all control of the Justice Department's investigation of the Watergate case.

1—North Vietnamese and United States negotiators left Paris for home with the Americans threatening resumption of military action in Vietnam if violations of the cease-fire continued.

2—Heavy fighting broke out between the Lebanese Army and Palestinian guerrillas in Beirut.

2—Former Texas Gov. John B. Connally, who served as President Nixon's secretary of the treasury, said he was switching from the Democratic to the Republican party.

3—The Lebanese armed forces attacked Palestinian guerillas in Beirut as heavy fighting in the capital continued for a second day despite a cease-fire agreement.

4—In a second truce, a cease-fire was arranged between the Lebanese Army and Palestinian guerrillas, ending more than two days of heavy fighting in and around Beirut.

4—Gen. Alexander M. Haig was named assistant to the President as President Nixon began to rebuild his White House staff.

4—Terrance G. Leonhardy, U.S. consul general in Guadalajara, Mexico, was kidnaped by the Armed Revolutionary Forces of the People.

6—The Mexican government met demands by the kidnapers of Terrance G. Leonhardy, U.S. consul general in Guadalajara, and released 30 prisoners and flew them to Cuba.

6—The defense in the Pentagon Papers trial said it planned to ask dismissal of the case on grounds the White House tried to compromise the trial judge.

6—Federal and Indian negotiators announced an agreement to end the 68-day occupation of Wounded Knee, S.D., by militant Indians. A previous agreement in April collapsed.

7—The White House proclaimed anew President Nixon's innocence in the Watergate break-in.

7—Charles W. Colson, President Nixon's former counsel, ordered the forgery of State Department cables to implicate President John F. Kennedy in the assassination of South Vietnam's President Ngo Dinh Diem, according to testimony by E. Howard Hunt Jr., a Watergate conspirator.

7—Terrance G. Leonhardy, U.S. consul general in Guadalajara was freed by left wing guerrillas in Mexico. He was released after 30 so-called "political prisoners" were flown to Havana.

8—New fighting erupted between Palestinian guerrillas and the Lebanese army and the Beirut government declared a state of emergency.

8—The Senate Watergate committee said it would start public hearings May 17 and that it would move to complete testimony by John W. Dean III, the deposed White House counsel.

8—A new cease-fire between Lebanese government forces and Palestinian guerrillas was announced after a day marked by heavy rocket attacks by government jets on guerrilla positions.

8—Seventy days after Wounded Knee, S.D., was seized by armed members of the American Indian Movement, the occupying militants surrendered to federal officials.

9—President Nixon assured Republican leaders his administration would "get to the bottom of this very deplorable" Watergate scandal and that the scandal would not paralyze the government.

9—Palestinian guerrillas invaded Lebanon from Syria and set up gun emplacements commanding a major highway.

10—Former Atty. Gen. John N. Mitchell and former Commerce Secretary Maurice H. Stans were indicted by a federal grand jury on charges growing out of a secret $200,000 contribution to President Nixon's 1972 campaign.

10—The House voted to block funds for the bombing of Cambodia.

11—The judge in the Pentagon Papers case, citing what he called "improper government conduct shielded so long from public view," dismissed all charges against Dr. Daniel Ellsberg and Anthony J. Russo Jr.

11—The White House said the United States would continue bombing in Cambodia despite the blocking of funds for such raids by the House.

12—The White House said Leonid I. Brezhnev, the Soviet Communist party leader, would visit the United States June 18–26 for talks with President Nixon.

14—William D. Ruckelshaus, acting FBI director, said records of 17 wiretaps placed on newsmen and government officials were discovered in a White House safe belonging to former Presidential assistant John D. Ehrlichman.

14—North Vietnam said U.S. planes struck Communist-held areas of South Vietnam and warned forthcoming talks with Henry A. Kissinger would be canceled if the raids continued.

14—The price of gold rose above $100 an ounce in Europe and the rate for the dollar weakened sharply against most major currencies.

14—Skylab, the nation's first space station, rocketed into orbit, but a failure in its solar-power wings forced a delay in the manned operations aboard the research spaceship.

15—President Nixon, responding to election reform demands in the wake of the Watergate case, told Congressional leaders serious consideration should be given to a single six-year term in the White House.

15—The Senate Appropriations Committee voted to cut off funds for further bombing of Cambodia.

15—The Skylab space station developed a new problem when temperatures aboard rose to 100 degrees Fahrenheit, reducing chances of astronauts boarding the ship.

16—G. Bradford Cook resigned as chairman of the Securities and Exchange Commission following allegations he had deleted a reference to Robert L. Vesco's secret $200,000 political contribution from an SEC complaint against the financier.

16—President Nixon said Congressional actions to stop American bombing in Cambodia "could severely undermine" chances of restoring peace in Indochina.

17—A special Senate investigating committee opened hearings on the Watergate affair.

17—The Lebanese government and Palestinian guerrillas said they had reached "identical viewpoints" on the settlement of their conflict which killed at least 250 people in the previous two weeks.

17—The launching of the Skylab 1 astronauts was postponed again until May 25, to give them time to train for the necessary repair job on the overheated space station.

18—James W. McCord told the Senate Watergate Committee that an Administration official who he said was acting with President Nixon's knowledge, had offered him executive clemency, financial aid and eventually a job to win his silence in the case.

18—The White House said President Nixon had no intention of resigning. White House secretary Ronald L. Ziegler said the President "has a lot to do" and "fully intends" to lead the country.

18—Elliot L. Richardson chose Archibald Cox, solicitor general in the Kennedy and Johnson administrations, as the special prosecutor in the Watergate investigation.

18—President Nixon accusing Congress of a "back door" assault on presidential authority, vetoed a bill that would require Senate confirmation of the director and deputy director of the Office of Management and Budget.

18—Glen W. Turner, a Florida businessman, and F. Lee Bailey, well-known criminal lawyer, were indicted by a Federal grand jury on charges of mail fraud and conspiracy in connection with sale of distributorships to three of Turner's companies, the Justice Department said.

19—Soviet Communist party leader Leonid I. Brezhnev and West Germany's Willy Brandt signed a 10-year agreement on economic development in Bonn.

19—President Nixon said Hanoi had "persisted in violations" of the Vietnam cease-fire agreement and had failed to provide adequate information about the fate of missing American servicemen.

20—President Nguyen Van Thieu announced a sweeping eight-year plan for reconstruction and economic development of South Vietnam.

20—A jury of five men and seven women found 17 members of the Camden 28 not guilty of breaking into a Federal building in Camden, N.J., in 1971 and destroying draft files, even though the defendants admitted having done so and the FBI caught them at it.

21—The second trial of four Black Panthers charged with the 1971 murder of a member of a rival faction ended in a Queens court when the defendants pleaded guilty to the reduced charge of attempted manslaughter in the second degree.

21—Renewed worries over the United States in light of the Watergate affair pushed up the price of gold in Europe by $6.50 an ounce to a new closing high of $112 an ounce.

22—President Nixon conceded in a 4,000-word statement that there had been "wide-ranging efforts" in the White House to conceal some aspects of the Watergate case, but he said those actions stemmed from his legitimate interest in protecting national security.

22—Prime Minister Edward Heath of Britain and President Georges Pompidou of France ended a meeting in Paris by virtually killing the idea of a summit conference of Atlantic leaders when President Nixon visits Europe in the fall.

23—Gerald Alch, former attorney for James W. McCord, sought in Senate testimony to undermine his ex-client's credibility and suggest that McCord had taken part in an anti-Administration vendetta.

23—The White House urged the FBI in 1970 to mount a massive counter-insurgency program, involving spying, wiretapping and burglaries against the Black Panthers, potential Arab saboteurs, antiwar radicals and Soviet espionage agents, well-placed sources said. President Nixon, briefly describing the program, said it had never been put into effect because of opposition by the late J. Edgar Hoover.

23—President Nixon won a victory in the House

which sustained his veto of a bill requiring Senate confirmation of the two top officials of the Office of Management and Budget.

23—The Ford Motor Company decided to meet terrorist demands to send $1 million worth of ambulances and donations to hospitals in Argentina to prevent further attacks on its employes and its subsidiary in Buenos Aires.

23—The Gallup poll showed that President Nixon's popularity had dropped to the lowest point since he had taken office. It showed his support at 45 per cent.

24—U.S. Attorney Harold H. Titus announced that Jeb Stuart Magruder, a key figure in the Watergate case, had agreed to plead guilty and serve as a prosecution witness at the trial.

24—President Nixon in a spirited address to about 610 cheering former prisoners of war, lashed out at those who threaten the secrecy of national security matters.

24—Rep. William O. Mills of Maryland, a Republican whose 1971 special election was aided by an unreported cash transfer of $25,000 from the Nixon campaign committee, was found shot to death near his home in Easton.

24—Britain's sex scandals widened with the resignation of Earl Jellicoe, leader of the House of Lords, who said he had engaged in "casual affairs" with prostitutes. Lord Lambton, under secretary for the Royal Air Force had resigned earlier because of his relationship with a prostitute.

25—The White House said the bulk of President Nixon's estate at San Clemente was controlled by an investment company formed by Robert H. Abplanalp, a multimillionaire businessman and close friend of the President.

25—Archibald Cox was sworn in as the special Watergate prosecutor in ceremonies at the Justice Department.

25—Dr. Hector J. Campora was inaugurated as president of Argentina, ending seven years of military rule.

25—The Skylab astronauts rode their Apollo spacecraft to a rendezvous with the 85-ton laboratory, docking after nine unsuccessful attempts.

26—The commander of the Greek Navy destroyer Velos and 31 officers and men who had joined in a mutiny against the military regime in Athens debarked in Italy and asked for political asylum.

26—An Icelandic gunboat shelled a British trawler off Iceland's northern coast and said the ship had sprung a leak but was not in danger of sinking.

26—The Skylab I astronauts boarded the space station and partially deployed a parasol over its roof in an effort to make the overheated vehicle habitable for a planned 28-day mission.

27—Temperatures in the parasol-shaded Skylab space station were dropping as the three astronauts checked out conditions aboard their orbital home.

27—The Fair Campaign Practices Committee said the Watergate affair was the low point in campaign tactics since it began monitoring campaign activities nearly 20 years ago.

28—The astronauts said Skylab was "in excellent shape" and that they expected to complete their planned 28-day mission in orbit.

29—The Canadian government, maintaining its cease-fire observers in Vietnam were not being allowed to do their job properly, said it would bring them home within 60 days.

29—The engagement of Britain's Princess Anne and Lt. Mark Phillips was announced.

29—Air Force Col. Theodore W. Guy charged five Army and three Marine Corps enlisted men with misconduct while they were all held as prisoners of war in a North Vietnamese prison camp.

30—President Nixon flew to Iceland for two days of talks with President Pompidou of France.

30—Thomas Bradley was elected the first black mayor of Los Angeles, defeating Sam Yorty.

30—Gordon Johnock won the Indianapolis 500 race.

31—The Senate voted 63-19 in favor of cutting off all funds for bombing in Cambodia.

31—H. R. Haldeman denied "categorically" that he had taken part in the Watergate cover-up.

31—Erskine Childers, an English-born Protestant, was elected president of the overwhelmingly Roman Catholic Republic of Ireland.

JUNE

1—The Greek government abolished the monarchy and proclaimed itself a republic, thus deposing King Constantine who had been living in exile since 1967.

1—President Nixon and President Pompidou of France ended their meeting in Iceland.

2—King Constantine II, deposed by the Greek government, said he was confident of returning to Greece as guardian of constitutional liberties.

2—Lt. Col. Lewis Hawkins, an American military adviser, was shot and killed by a terrorist outside his home in Tehran, Iran.

2—Eight men were dead and eight missing and presumed dead after an American cargo ship struck a Belgian tanker at anchor in New York Harbor.

2—After setting records for a plane hijacking in crisscrossing Latin America, two young gunmen disappeared in South America with $50,000 paid to them by a Colombian airline.

3—The Soviet Union's supersonic airliner exploded while making a demonstration flight at the international air show near Paris. The crew of six died and eight persons on the ground were killed.

4—Special Prosecutor Archibald Cox asked the Senate committee to delay its Watergate hearings, but Sen. Sam J. Ervin, committee chairman, denied the request.

5—The White House said it had left open the possibility that logs of President Nixon's conversations with John W. Dean III about the Watergate case would be made available to investigators.

6—President Nixon named former Secretary of Defense Melvin R. Laird as his chief domestic adviser and said Gen. Alexander M. Haig Jr. would reitre from active duty to continue as White House chief of staff.

7—The Saigon government said it would sign no new peace agreement growing out of United States talks with North Vietnam in Paris.

7—The House Foreign Affairs Committee approved a resolution aimed at limiting the President's war-making powers, but only after voting down a measure calling for the cutoff of all funds for the bombing in Cambodia.

7—The crew of Skyab 1 pulled off the first major repair job in space when, in a space walk, they managed to deploy a stuck solar power wing on their orbiting space station.

8—Generalissimo Francisco Franco, Spain's leader for more than 30 years, relinquished some of his power by naming Adm. Luis Carrero Blanco premier to run the government.

8—The Greek government announced plans to insure the continued rule of Provisional President Georges Papadopoulos for at least seven more years.

9—Fighting in South Vietnam reached its highest level since mid-February with both Saigon and the Communists appearing to be jockeying for more territory.

9—The State Department said it had asked Costa Rica to extradite Robert L. Vesco, who is facing charges in connection with his financial dealings.

10—Henry A. Kissinger and Le Duc Tho, Hanoi's chief negotiator, decided to break off their Paris talks for a few days when "it became clear" they could not quickly resolve the reservations raised by South Vietnam on strengthening the cease-fire.

11—Vice President Spiro Agnew said in a speech that the televised Senate Watergate hearings "can hardly hope to find the truth and can hardly fail to muddy the waters of justice beyond redemption."

12—Maurice H. Stans appeared before the Senate Watergate committee and denied any involvement in the affair.

12—John W. Dean III lost a two-month struggle for immunity and went before the Watergate criminal grand jury for the first time.

13—The United States, North Vietnam, the Saigon government and the Viet Cong signed an agreement in Paris calling for an end to all cease-fire violations.

13—President Nixon ordered a freeze of all retail prices, including those on food, for as long as 60 days.

14—Jeb Stuart Magruder, the former deputy director of President Nixon's 1972 re-election campaign, told how he and other high-ranking officials had plotted the bugging of the Democrats and then tried to cover it up. In testifying before the Senate Watergate committee, Magruder confessed his own guilt and implicated a number of former Administration officials—including John Mitchell, John W. Dean III, and H. R. Haldeman—but not the President.

14—The Senate voted to cut off funds for military operations in Indochina, including bombing in Cambodia, unless the actions were specifically authorized by Congress.

14—Prices of steel, copper, rubber tires and other major products were rolled back to early June levels in response to President Nixon's 60-day freeze.

16—Leonid I. Brezhnev, head of the Communist party Politburo, arrived in the United States for a nine-day visit intended to spur arms control talks and to promote cooperation and commerce between America and the Soviet Union.

17—President Nixon prepared for the start of talks with the Soviet's Leonid I. Brezhnev by conferring with Henry A. Kissinger.

17—A world space endurance record was set by the Skylab 1 astronauts as they began their 24th day of living and working in the space station.

17—Navy divers prepared to try to free a tiny research submarine trapped with its four-man crew under a scuttled destroyer's cables in the Atlantic Ocean off Key West, Fla.

18—President Nixon and the Soviet Union's Leonid Brezhnev met at the White House and pledged to strive together for peace.

18—Brazil's military leaders chose Gen. Ernesto Geisel as the nation's next president.

18—The Senate Watergate committee canceled its hearings for the week so they would not distract from the talks between President Nixon and Leonid Brezhnev.

19—Leonid Brezhnev presented his case for a major expansion in Soviet-American trade to leading members of Congress and urged them not to let quarrels about the emigration of Soviet Jews stand in the way of broad scale cooperation.

19—As Leonid Brezhnev and President Nixon looked on, Soviet and American officials signed four agreements involving cooperation in agricultural research, oceanography, transportation and a broadening of the current agreement on cultural exchanges.

19—Two crew members remaining locked aboard the sea research midget submarine were pronounced dead 24 hours after the craft was pulled from the ocean floor off Key West, Fla. Two other crew members survived the entrapment of their sub in the debris of a scuttled destroyer.

20—President Nixon's re-election committee was found guilty of concealing a $200,000 cash contribution from Robert L. Vesco and was fined $3,000.

20—Juan D. Peron returned to Argentina after 18 years of exile, and violence among the more than one million people gathered to welcome him left at least 20 dead and hundreds injured.

21—President Nixon and Leonid Brezhnev agreed to accelerate negotiations on a Soviet-American pact limiting offensive strategic weapons so that a permanent treaty could be achieved before 1975.

21—A Senate subcommittee said International Telephone & Telegraph Corp. "overstepped the line of acceptable corporate behavior" by seeking to get the help of the Central Intelligence Agency to prevent the election of Salvador Allende Gossens as president of Chile in 1970.

21—The Supreme Court handed down a new set

of guidelines on obscenity which would enable states to ban books, magazines, plays and motion pictures that were offensive to local standards, even if they were acceptable elsewhere.

22—President Nixon and Leonid Brezhnev signed an agreement to avert military confrontations that could lead the United States and the Soviet Union into a nuclear war with each other or with any other country.

22—The Skylab 1 astronauts, looking fit but a little shaky, returned to earth after a record 28 days aboard the nation's first orbiting space station.

22—A judge in Costa Rica refused a U.S. request that Robert L. Vesco be extradited in a fraud case connected with his secret donation of $200,000 to President Nixon's re-election campaign.

23—The United States and the Soviet Union announced agreement to increase air passenger service between the two countries.

24—President Nixon and Leonid Brezhnev wound up their U.S. summit with mutual declarations that their week of talks had moved not only the United States and the Soviet Union, but the entire world toward a durable, stable peace.

24—A flash fire raced through a second-story bar in the French Quarter of New Orleans killing 20 persons.

24—Ireland's Eamon De Valera, 90, the world's oldest chief of state, wound up a 57-year public career as he ended his second term as president.

25—John W. Dean III, dismissed White House counsel, told the Senate investigating committee that President Nixon had failed to heed a warning that the Watergate case was "a cancer growing on the Presidency". In his heralded appearance, Dean declared that Nixon had taken part in the Watergate cover-up for as long as eight months.

25—The House of Representatives, in its strongest antiwar action, voted to cut off all funds for U.S. bombing in Cambodia.

26—John W. Dean told the Senate investigating committee that President Nixon had misled the nation in his public statements on the Watergate case. The former White House counsel said the President had been "less than accurate" in a May 22 denial of involvement in the Watergate affair.

26—White House press secretary Gerald L. Warren said President Nixon stood by his May 22 statement on Watergate. Warren would not comment directly on John Dean's testimony.

26—The U.S. Department of Commerce said the nation's foreign trade had slipped back into deficit in May after showing an April surplus.

26—In its second antiwar action in two days, the House of Representatives voted to extend through Sept. 30 a proposed ban on the use of funds for U.S. bombing in Cambodia.

27—The White House in a counterattack against testimony by John W. Dean that President Nixon was enmeshed in the Watergate cover-up, declared that Dean was the cover-up "mastermind."

27—John W. Dean told the Senate Watergate committee that the White House lists of political enemies filled a file "several inches thick."

27—Frederick C. LaRue, special assistant to John N. Mitchell at the Committee for the Re-election of the President, pleaded guilty to charges of conspiracy to obstruct justice.

27—President Nixon vetoed a bill that would have cut off all funds for the bombing of Cambodia, declaring that a halt in U.S. air operations would undercut diplomatic efforts for a cease-fire there. The House failed to override the veto.

27—Uruguayan President Juan Maria Bordaberry, acting under military pressure, abolished the national congress, ending constitutional government for the first time in 40 years.

28—The Senate Watergate Committee publicly pressed President Nixon to make a formal reply—perhaps under oath—to the charges against the President by his former counsel, John W. Dean.

28—Spokesmen for President Nixon attempted to disassociate the President from any personal involvement in or approval of the statement charging that John W. Dean masterminded the cover-up. The statement was submitted to the Senate committee

by Fred Buzhardt, Jr. special counsel to Nixon on Watergate matters.

28—Sen. Lowell P. Weicker Jr. charged that supporters of President Nixon had tried to intimidate him since he became a member of the Senate Watergate Committee. The Connecticut Republican said he had reported these attempts to special Watergate prosecutor Archibald Cox, so that the latter could determine whether someone had violated the law.

28—The nation's trucking industry and the Teamsters Union agreed to a new 33-month master freight contract providing wage and benefit increases averaging 7 per cent a year to 400,000 truck drivers.

29—President Nixon assured Congress that U.S. military activity in Indochina would end by Aug. 15 and that he would seek Congressional approval if additional military action was needed after that date.

29—Armed forces loyal to Chile's Marxist government put down a revolt by part of an armored regiment after rebel troops had briefly taken control of the downtown area of Santiago, the capital.

29—West Germany increased the official value of the mark by 5.5 per cent against other European currencies in an effort to save European monetary unity and to end new turbulence in the foreign exchange markets.

29—John W. Dean completed his testimony before the Senate Watergate committee, unshaken from his central charge that President Nixon had been an active participant in the Watergate cover-up.

30—In one of the longest eclipses of modern times, the moon's shadow crossed the entire width of Africa.

JULY

1—Col. Yosef Alon, an Israeli military attache, was shot to death at his home in a Washington suburb.

1—Lt. Gen. Hammad Shihab, the defense minister of Iraq, was shot dead in Baghdad in what the state-controlled radio said was an assassination engineered by the chief of internal security, Col. Nazem Kazzar.

1—President Nixon said prices were being stabilized under the temporary freeze he ordered June 13 and that "we are determined that prices will continue to be held."

1—Charles W. Colson, a former White House special counsel, said President Nixon had complained to him of not being told the truth about the Watergate scandal even after John W. Dean III had supposedly disclosed all the facts to the President.

2—President Nixon, the White House said, will speak out on charges that have been made against him in the Watergate case after the Senate Watergate committee completes the current phase of its hearings.

3—The Conference on Security and Cooperation in Europe got under way in Helsinki with a proposal by the Soviet Union for a new charter of relations among all European states.

3—The Army and Navy dismissed charges against seven enlisted men accused by an Air Force colonel of misconduct and collaborating with the enemy while held as prisoners of war by North Vietnam.

4—White House officials said Henry Kissinger would go to Peking in late July or early August to confer with Premier Chou En-lai.

4—The Chase Manhattan Bank will act as a correspondent of the Bank of China in the United States, David Rockefeller, chairman of Chase Manhattan, said after a 10-day visit to China.

5—The United States has decided against sending a new ambassador to Uganda following a July 4 message to President Nixon from President Idi Amin in which the African leader wished Nixon "a speedy recovery from the Watergate affair." State Department spokesman Paul J. Hare said Amin's

message was "totally unacceptable in substance and tone."

6—Turmoil broke out on the foreign exchange markets as the dollar dropped to new lows for the ninth consecutive day. Officials said the United States had no plans for another dollar devaluation.

6—President Nixon conferred with Huang Chen, China's representative in the United States, in what appeared to be an effort to reassure Peking that the recent summit meeting with Leonid I. Brezhnev would not disturb the building of better relations with China.

6—American Airlines said it illegally contributed $55,000 in company funds to President Nixon's re-election campaign early last year.

7—Baghdad radio announced the execution of Col. Nazem Kazzar and 22 other alleged accomplices accused of an abortive attempt to overthrow Iraq's regime.

7—President Nixon told the Senate Watergate committee he would not appear personally before the committee under any circumstances to defend himself against charges he had participated in the cover-up of the Watergate affair. Nixon also said he would not grant the committee access to presidential files.

8—Sen. Edward J. Gurney, R-Fla., President Nixon's staunchest defender on the Senate Watergate committee, said he believed the presidential papers bearing on the investigation should be made available to the committee.

9—The U.S. General Accounting Office accused Agriculture Department officials of mismanagement of 1972 wheat sales to the Soviet Union and said that excessive export subsidies and high American food prices had resulted.

9—After almost two and a half days of detention in Uganda, 112 American Peace Corps volunteers were permitted to continue their journey to the neighboring Central African country of Zaire.

10—John N. Mitchell told the Senate Watergate Committee he had deliberately withheld information from President Nixon about the 1972 campaign conspiracy to prevent damage to the President's bid for re-election. Mitchell denied he had authorized the political intelligence-gathering scheme that led to the Watergate break-in.

10—Senate Majority Leader Mike Mansfield said it was "debatable" whether President Nixon could be impeached for not knowing of his staff's role in the Watergate affair, even if he had no personal knowledge of the break-in.

10—The Bahamas became an independent nation after three centuries of British colonial rule. The Bahamas, a subtropical chain of 700 islands, became the Commonwealth's 33rd independent member.

11—John N. Mitchell maintained in his second appearance before the Senate Watergate Committee that President Nixon had been shielded from any knowledge of the Watergate break-in or cover-up.

11—A Brazilian jetliner crashed just short of Orly Airport near Paris, killing 124 of the 136 persons aboard.

12—President Nixon consented to meet with Sen. Sam J. Ervin, chairman of the Senate Watergate Committee, to discuss Nixon's refusal to provide White House documents to the Congressional investigators.

12—Richard A. Moore, a special counsel to the President, contradicted charges made by John W. Dean III that President Nixon knew of efforts to cover up the Watergate affair as early as September 1972.

12—President Nixon was hospitalized for treatment of viral pneumonia. His doctor said he expected the President to be hospitalized about a week.

13—Richard A. Moore, a White House official, said President Nixon was deeply troubled in May that he had not recognized earlier the Watergate cover-up.

13—Argentina's Congress accepted the resignation of President Hector J. Campora, thus preparing for the election of Juan D. Peron.

15—Two Canadian officers of the International Commission of Control and Supervision in South Vietnam who had been held captive by the Vietcong for 17 days were freed and returned to Saigon.

16—Former White House aide Alexander P. Butterfield disclosed to the Senate committee that President Nixon had listening devices that would have automatically tape-recorded his conversations with key figures in the Watergate case and other visitors.

16—Presidential counsel J. Fred Buzhardt acknowledged that nearly all President Nixon's meetings were taped and added that the same system had been employed by President Lyndon B. Johnson. This brought quick denials from two of Johnson's closest advisors.

16—Herbert W. Kalmbach, attorney and political fund raiser for President Nixon, described to the Senate committee how during a series of clandestine meetings he had raised $220,000 for the seven Watergate defendants.

16—Secretary of Defense James R. Schlesinger acknowledged that U.S. Air Force B52 bombers were secretly attacking Cambodia in 1969 and 1970 while the United States was publicly professing its respect for that nation's neutrality in the Vietnam War. He said the raids were necessary for protection of U.S. servicemen.

17—President Nixon ordered the Secret Service to withhold from the Senate Watergate Committee all information about recordings that had been made of the President's White House conversations.

17—Herbert W. Kalmbach told the Senate Watergate Committee that under orders from the White House he provided $400,000 in cash in 1970 to men he had never seen before and whose names he still did not know.

17—The Kingdom of Afghanistan was proclaimed a republic in a coup led by a brother-in-law of King Mohammad Zahir Shah while the king was in Italy.

17—The Senate voted 77 to 20 to approve the Alaska oil pipeline bill after Vice President Spiro Agnew voted to support an amendment that would protect the project from further legal challenge by environmentalists.

18—President Nixon lifted the price freeze on health care and most food items as part of the Administration's latest program to fight inflation.

18—The Senate Watergate Committee heard two participants in the cover-up describe how they paid $450,000 in Nixon campaign funds to the seven original defendants and their lawyers.

19—Henry A. Kissinger said the White House "neither ordered nor was it aware" of any falsifications of Pentagon records to conceal the bombing of Cambodia ordered by President Nixon in 1969.

19—A White House official said President Nixon had decided not to release tapes of his talks with Watergate suspects.

19—A former Nixon campaign aide, Robert C. Mardian, told the Senate Watergate Committee that G. Gordon Liddy, a Watergate conspirator, had given him the "impression" that President Nixon had authorized the burglary of the office of Dr. Daniel Ellsberg's former psychiatrist.

20—The Senate approved legislation 71-to-18 that would limit the President's power to commit United States armed forces to future hostilities without Congressional approval.

20—Hijackers, who said they were fighting for the people of Palestine, seized a Japan Air Lines 747 jumbo jet with 137 passengers and crew members after it took off from Amsterdam and forced it to fly to the Persian Gulf state of Dubai.

20—The Labor Department said consumer prices in June continued to rise at the fastest pace since the Korean War.

20—President Nixon, recovered from viral pneumonia, left the hospital where he had been a patient for a week and went to the White House. Nixon denounced suggestions that he resign as "just plain poppycock."

21—France exploded the first nuclear device of a series at Mururoa, an atoll in the South Pacific, despite a world-wide protest movement.

23—President Nixon refused to release tape recordings of his conversations about the Watergate case. Both the special Watergate prosecutor, Archibald Cox, and the Senate Watergate Committee moved to subpoena the tapes.

23—A Japan Air Lines 747 jet, hijacked July 20 over the Netherlands, landed at Damascus, Syria, after a three-day layover in Dubai on the Arabian Peninsula.

24—A hijacked Japanese airliner flew from Damascus to Benghazi, Libya, where it was blown up at the airport. The place was blown up after the evacuation of all passengers. The four hijackers were arrested.

24—John D. Ehrlichman clashed with the Senate Watergate Committee as he sought to "refute every charge of illegal conduct on my part." The former Presidential assistant for domestic affairs said President Nixon had been thwarted in his "continued effort" to give the nation a "full, factual account" of the conspiracy. He also suggested that John W. Dean III, former Presidential counsel, misled the White House about the Watergate break-in and cover-up.

24—Secretary of State William P. Rogers, who participated in the original decision to begin secret bombing of Cambodia in 1969, repeatedly assured the Senate Foreign Relations Committee more than a year later that the United States was doing nothing to violate Cambodian neutrality, according to excerpts from his classified testimony.

24—The Shah of Iran arrived in the United States for a four-day state visit.

25—John D. Ehrlichman denied charges linking him to the Watergate cover-up and told the Senate investigating committee he never sought executive clemency for E. Howard Hunt Jr., one of the conspirators.

25—A federal judge in Brooklyn ruled the government must halt the bombing of Cambodia on the ground that it was unlawful and unauthorized.

26—President Nixon refused to comply with subpoenas requiring him to furnish tapes of his Watergate conversations to the Senate Committee and the special prosecutor.

26—John D. Ehrlichman said the special White House intelligence unit undertook in 1971 a mission so important to national security that it justified President Nixon's efforts to hide the group's existence.

26—Henry A. Kissinger postponed his trip to Peking for talks on Cambodia till after Aug. 15—the date that American bombing of Cambodia was slated to end, Administration officials said.

26—The United States vetoed a Security Council resolution that "strongly" deplored Israel's continuing occupation of Arab lands taken during the 1967 war.

27—John D. Ehrlichman, offering a detailed White House rationale for the Watergate cover-up, swore that President Nixon did not get a thorough briefing on the Watergate conspiracy until April 14, 1973.

27—Lending rates in Britain were lifted to the highest levels in history, while in West Germany a tight monetary squeeze was eased a bit in moves that helped halt the slide of the dollar and pound in international currency markets.

27—Rioting convicts seized control of Oklahoma's major prison at McAlester and began systematically to burn it.

28—Three American Astronauts embarked on man's longest planned journey into space. They linked-up with the nation's still-orbiting Skylab space station and planned to stay for 59 days.

28—Some 600,000 rock music fans gathered at Watkins Glen, N.Y., for a one-day festival that was twice as large as the Woodstock gathering four years earlier.

29—Greeks voted to endorse decisions already taken by their leaders to abolish the monarchy and install George Papadopoulos as the president of the new republic.

29—The leaders of the Senate Watergate Committee suggested, in a compromise move, that President Nixon allow a private hearing of the tape-recorded conversations related to Watergate. Sen. Sam J. Ervin Jr., committee chairman, and Sen. Howard H. Baker Jr., vice chairman, said such an arrangement in which they and Archibald Cox, the federal Watergate prosecuter would take part, would be "fine."

29—National Guardsmen drove rebellious convicts into an open compound and took tenuous control of the almost destroyed Oklahoma state prison at McAlester.

30—H. R. Haldeman said he and President Nixon were innocent of any involvement in the Watergate break-in or cover-up, but that they had been "badly misled" by John W. Dean III and others.

30—John D. Ehrlichman insisted that he and President Nixon were not involved in any aspects of the Watergate cover-up.

30—For the second time in less than two years, the Senate adopted reforms in the financing of election campaigns.

30—Gen. Earle G. Wheeler, retired chairman of the joint chiefs of staff, told a Senate committee President Nixon ordered the secret bombing of Cambodia to be conducted under the tightest security possible.

31—The Senate Watergate Committee challenged the testimony of H. R. Haldeman, former White House chief of staff, about the contents of the White House recordings of President Nixon's Watergate conversations. Sen. Sam Ervin, committee chairman, said Haldeman's testimony was part of a "planned action" by the White House to "leak" a favorable version of the taped conversations.

31—The White House said President Nixon, acting alone, would decide who would have access to the tapes of his conversations about the Watergate case.

31—President Nixon and visiting Premier Kakuei Tanaka of Japan agreed that Nixon would visit Japan within the next 18 months and that Emperor Hirohito would come to the United States in 1974.

31—Iran agreed to an American request to replace Canada on the four-nation cease-fire commission in South Vietnam.

31—A Delta Air Lines jet crashed and burned in a heavy fog at Boston, killing all but one of the 89 persons aboard.

AUGUST

1—The Senate Watergate Committee disclosed a 1972 White House memorandum warning of the existence of documents that could "directly involve the President" in the controversial settlement of antitrust actions against International Telephone & Telegraph Co.

1—Agriculture Secretary Earl Butz indicated support of beef industry demands for an early end to the price freeze, which has been blamed for shrinking meat supplies. Despite predictions that beef "will disappear" if the freeze was not lifted before Sept. 12, the Cost of Living Council denied any change was being considered.

2—The Nixon Administration said the United States would continue to give the Cambodian government all the help it could after the American bombing stops on Aug. 15.

2—Officials ordered emergency preparations for a rescue mission to retrieve the Skylab 2 astronauts who may be stranded in their space laboratory. The effort that could lead to the first space rescue was ordered after a set of steering rockets on the astronaut's ferry vehicle developed a serious leak which could prevent their return to earth.

2—Former CIA Director Richard Helms told the Senate Watergate Committee he had resisted White House efforts to involve the agency in the Watergate cover-up.

3—President Nixon said the bombing in Cambodia would end Aug. 15, but warned the cutoff imposed by Congress could have "dangerous potential consequences" in Indochina.

3—Three major banks raised the interest rate

they charge on loans to big corporations to 9 per cent—the highest prime rate on record.

3—Tests showed that Skylab 2's Apollo ferry vehicle should be able to return the astronauts safely to earth with only two of the four sets of steering rockets in operation.

3—L. Patrick Gray III changed his story and said he had examined files removed from the White House safe of E. Howard Hunt Jr., a Watergate conspirator, before burning them. Gray, former acting FBI director, told the Senate Watergate Committee the papers had not been "evidence in the case" and said his acceptance of the papers was a "grievous misjudgment."

3—The University Hotel in Manhattan, which as the Broadway Central was a landmark for about a century, collapsed. The bodies of two persons later were recovered and police said they believed at least four persons were missing.

4—Justice William O. Douglas of the Supreme Court ordered an immediate halt to the American bombing of Cambodia, but he was overruled by the higher court later in the day in an order issued by Justice Thurgood Marshall and supported by the seven other justices.

4—National Guardsmen and police swept into the yard of the riot-shattered Oklahoma State Penitentiary and moved the last of the inmates back into their cells.

4—The death toll in the Isle of Man amusement center fire climbed to 51 as an inquest began into the blaze that gutted the big holiday complex Aug. 2.

5—Secretary of State Rogers said Cambodian troops planned to give up exposed positions and move to more secure areas when American bombing stopped Aug. 15.

5—Two men identified as Black September guerrillas hurled grenades and fired machine guns, killing three persons and wounding 55, in the Athens airport.

5—Supreme Court Justice Harry A. Blackmun said the "very glue of our ship of state seems about to become unstuck" under the "pall" of the Watergate affair.

6—An American bomb strike on a Cambodian town killed an estimated 100 persons and wounded many more. It appeared to be the worst error bombing of the Indochina war.

6—For the first time in history, U.S. wheat passed the $4 a bushel level, closing at $4.04 on Midwest grain exchanges.

6—The Nixon administration said it had spent about $10 million for Presidential security at the Nixon homes.

6—Vice President Spiro Agnew said he had been told he was under investigation for possible violation of criminal statutes.

6—L. Patrick Gray told the Senate investigating committee that President Nixon apparently paid no heed to a warning in 1972 that White House aides were trying to "mortally wound" the President in the Watergate case.

7—Federal officials said indictments were expected within weeks in an investigation into bribery, extortion and tax fraud charges involving Vice President Agnew and some of his political and financial associates.

7—The Senate Watergate Committee completed the first phase of its inquiry and recessed until Sept. 10.

8—Three Vietnam War veterans told the Senate Armed Services Committee that they participated either in the designation of Viet-Cong and North Vietnamese hospitals as bombing targets or in their destruction.

8—Vice President Agnew called reports that he took kickbacks from government contractors in Maryland "damned lies." Agnew said he had "no expectation of being indicted" and no intention of resigning.

9—According to an official Pentagon memorandum released at a Senate Armed Services Committee hearing, Melvin R. Laird, as Secretary of Defense in 1969, approved a falsified reporting system to hide the secret bombing of Cambodia.

9—The Senate Watergate Committee filed a lawsuit to force President Nixon to produce White House tapes subpoenaed by the committee.

9—Houston, Tex., police said a 17-year-old youth had told them he and a 33-year-old man he later killed had been involved in more than 25 slayings.

10—Israel said her air force intercepted a Middle East Airlines jet airliner approaching Beirut and forced the plane to a military airfield in Israel. But military spokesmen said the wrong plane had been seized and after two hours it was allowed to fly to Iraq with its 74 passengers and crew of seven.

10—Melvin R. Laird, former Secretary of Defense, said he had authorized "a separate reporting procedure" for the Administration's secret B52 bombing raids in Cambodia in 1969 but insisted he had not sanctioned "the falsification of any Air Force, Navy or Defense Department records."

10—Federal investigators subpoenaed the records of the administration of Vice President Spiro Agnew during his two years as governor of Maryland. They also subpoenaed "any and all" financial records dealing with Agnew's campaign for governor.

10—Many of the nation's biggest banks raised their prime interest rate to 9¼ per cent from 9 per cent—a record.

10—The Administration said gasoline, heating oil and other petroleum products would remain under rigid price controls for an indefinite period.

10—Police unearthed four more bodies in Texas, bringing to 23 the number of victims allegedly sexually assaulted, tortured and slain over a three-year period by a 33-year-old Houston man and two teenage accomplices.

11—Lebanon charged Israel with air piracy for forcing a Lebanese commercial airliner with 81 aboard to land in Israel. Israeli Defense Minister Moshe Dayan said the airliner was diverted in hope of seizing the head of the Popular Front for the Liberation of Palestine.

13—The Arab states asked the U.N. Security Council to face up to the "arrogant challenge" of Israel and its "defiance of the United Nations and international law." Lebanon brought charges against Israel following that nation's interception of an Iraqi flight in Lebanese airspace.

13—Higher prices were announced for autos and the steel used to make a variety of consumer products as the Administration's 60-day price freeze gave way to Phase 4.

13—Archibald Cox, special Watergate prosecutor, said President Nixon could not be "a proper judge" of whether the public interest requires his making tape recordings of White House conversations available to a grand jury investigation.

13—Houston, Tex., police dug up four more victims in the biggest mass slaying in the country's history. The graves of 27 youths, mainly from the Houston area, were found by police.

13—All 85 persons aboard a Spanish airliner died when the plane exploded and crashed near La Coruna, Spain.

14—American bombing in Cambodia officially ended with the Nixon Administration still pledging to do everything possible within the law to support the government of President Lon Nol. The bombing stop, voted by Congress June 30, marked the official end to America's dozen years of combat activity in Southeast Asia.

14—John A. Scali, U.S. representative, told Israel in a meeting of the United Nations Security Council that while efforts to control terrorism must go forward they must do so "within and not outside the law." Scali said the United States deplored Israel's interception of an Iraqi airliner over Lebanese territory Aug. 10.

14—Vice President Agnew offered to answer questions personally and open his records to the U.S. Attorney in Baltimore who was investigating allegations of extortion, bribery, tax fraud and conspiracy that allegedly occurred when Agnew was governor of Maryland.

14—Two persons were missing and seven were injured in an explosion at a chemical company plant in Lodi, N.J.

15—President Nixon said "the time has come to

turn Watergate over to the courts" and "for the rest of us to get on with the urgent business of our nation" in a televised address. Nixon reasserted his own innocence, defended his refusal to disclose the White House tapes, and blamed civil disobedience in the 1960s for leading "a few over-zealous persons" into similar extremism.

15—President Nixon denounced Congress for forcing the end of American bombing in Cambodia and warned Hanoi not to take military advantage of the halt.

15—The United Nations Security Council voted unanimously to condemn Israel for intercepting a Lebanese commercial airliner Aug. 10 and forcing the plane to land in Israel.

16—The U.S. Defense Department said Saigon could legally use American-supplied military equipment to attack North Vietnamese sanctuaries in neighboring Cambodia that posed a direct threat to South Vietnam.

16—An apparently drunken Libyan hijacked a Lebanese airliner carrying 125 passengers and crew members and forced it to land at Israel's Lydda airport.

16—The Secret Service acknowledged that confidential information was passed to the White House from an agent guarding Sen. George McGovern in the 1972 presidential campaign.

17—Secretary of Defense James Schlesinger said the Soviet Union had successfully flight-tested missiles with multiple warheads that could be directed to separate targets. Schlesinger also told a news conference that the United States would support South Vietnam from the air in the event of "overt North Vietnamese aggression."

17—President Nixon's lawyers declared that the executive branch, not the courts or a grand jury, had the exclusive right to drop a criminal prosecution when "other governmental interests" outweighed its pursuit.

18—A federal appellate court upheld the beef price freeze, rejecting contentions of the meat industry that the Cost of Living Council was arbitrary and capricious and had exceeded its authority.

18—About 44 per cent of the people who watched President Nixon's Watergate address on television Aug. 15 found the speech "not at all" convincing while 27 per cent concluded it was "completely" or "quite a lot" convincing, according to a Gallup poll commissioned by the New York Times.

19—George Papadopoulos, who seized power in Greece six years ago and recently abolished the monarchy, took the oath as country's first president.

19—Sen. George McGovern warned that continued refusal by President Nixon to release tape recordings of conversations relating to the Watergate affair would lead to impeachment considerations by Congress.

20—President Nixon told war veterans in New Orleans that his order for secret bombing of Cambodia in 1969 was "absolutely necessary" to save lives and to move the war to the negotiating table.

20—The Secret Service announced that it had uncovered a "possible conspiracy to assassinate" President Nixon in New Orleans.

20—An exiled Laotian air force general, who had tried to overthrow the government of Laos, died after a small plane he was flying was shot down in Vientiane.

21—Several members of the rebel force who attempted a coup in Laos Aug. 20 were executed by the Laotian Army, and acting Defense Minister Prince Sisouk na Champassak said there would be "no trials" for the rest of the prisoners.

21—The Cambodian government appealed to Congress and the American people to abide by "the moral obligations" of the United States to help it remain alive in the face of growing insurgent pressure.

21—Street fighting flared for nearly five hours in Chile as supporters and opponents of the nation's Socialist government clashed.

21—Vice President Agnew said members of the Justice Department were trying "to indict me in the press" and called for an investigation to expose those responsible.

21—The Secret Service described a conspiracy to assassinate President Nixon during his visit to New Orleans Aug. 20 as "very serious, very large."

22—President Nixon said he would nominate Henry A. Kissinger to replace William P. Rogers as secretary of state.

22—President Nixon acknowledged at a news conference that the Watergate affair had hampered his ability to govern, but he said he had never considered resigning and would serve out this term with the full authority of a strong presidency.

22—President Nixon declared his confidence in Vice President Agnew and said he had ordered the attorney general to investigate the Justice Department and dismiss anyone found to be involved in leaking information about the investigation of Agnew.

23—The grand jury investigating a number of officials, including Vice President Agnew, returned a 39-count indictment against Baltimore County Executive N. D. Anderson, who succeeded Agnew in the position in 1966.

24—The United States announced an agreement with Thailand for the start of a phased withdrawal of American forces and aircraft from Thailand.

24—Some 5,000 right and left-wing militants clashed in Santiago, Chile, as another wave of strikes hit the nation.

25—Two men were injured when a letter bomb exploded in the Bank of England. Prime Minister Heath ordered an alert of all government departments because of the wave of bomb incidents, now officially blamed on elements of the Irish Republican Army.

25—Secretary of State Rogers criticized the White House sanctioned wiretapping of three high ranking foreign service officers under a program that President Nixon has defended as necessary "to find and stop serious national security leaks."

26—United Nations Secretary General Waldheim said in his annual message that the need for international cooperation "has never been so great or so urgent."

26—The Phnom Penh military command reported Communist-led forces had cut both the Cambodian capital's overland supply routes and that the lull following the cessation of American bombing of Cambodia Aug. 15 apparently had ended.

27—An exploding letter bomb blew off the hand of a secretary at the British Embassy in Washington, D.C. The bomb was described as similar to those sent in the London area a week earlier and attributed to Irish Republican Army terrorists.

27—Several banks raised the prime rate to 9¾ per cent from 9½ per cent.

28—India and Pakistan signed an agreement which opened the way for the release of most of the Pakistani prisoners held in India and the settlement of other problems arising from their war of December 1971.

28—More than 500 persons were killed and some 4,000 injured when an earthquake ripped through the central section of Mexico.

28—One man died and 1,000 passengers were trapped in 115 degree heat and heavy smoke when an archway in a subway tunnel under New York's East River collapsed on the first car of a subway train.

28—On the evening of the sixth day of their imprisonment in a bank vault, the four hostages of a gunman and his companion were freed without injury and their captors surrendered to police in Stockholm, Sweden.

29—President Nixon was ordered to make tape recordings of White House conversations involving the Watergate case available to a federal judge for his private examination, but aides said the President "will not comply with the order."

29—President Nixon's lawyers charged in papers filed in U.S. District Court in Washington that the Senate Watergate Committee had conducted a "criminal investigation and trial" that exceeded the authority granted to Congress by the Constitution.

30—The International Civil Aviation Organization voted to condemn Israel for intercepting a Lebanese airliner Aug. 10.

30—President Nixon said he would appeal a court ruling requiring him to yield secret tape recordings of conversations involving the Watergate case.

30—Three steel corporation—U.S. Steel, Bethlehem Steel and Armco Steel—were indicted on charges of price fixing and market sharing in the $40 million market for steel reinforcing bars.

31—Seven antiwar veterans and a supporter were acquitted in Gainesville, Fla., of charges that they plotted an assault with automatic weapons, slingshots and crossbows on the Republican National Convention in Miami in 1972.

SEPTEMBER

1—Twenty Americans were among 35 persons killed in a fire at a Copenhagen, Denmark, hotel.

1—Libya announced the nationalization of 51 per cent of the assets of all oil companies operating in the country.

1—Two Britons, trapped since Aug. 29 in a midget submarine 1,375 feet below the Atlantic off the coast of southern Ireland, were hauled to the surface and transferred safely to their mother ship.

1—President Nixon and Vice President Agnew met alone for two hours, discussing the federal investigations of allegations that Agnew received kickbacks from Maryland contractors.

2—United Nations Secretary—General Waldheim left Cairo for Amman, Jordan, after two days of talks with Egyptian officials, including President Anwar el Sadat.

2—The last of five alleged members of the Black Liberation Army indicted in connection with the murders of two New York City policemen in 1971 was arrested in New Orleans.

2—Inmates seized control of three cellblocks at the state prison at Michigan City, Ind., and took three officers hostage.

3—Reliable Soviet sources said three persons were killed by the explosion of a bomb in the Lenin mausoleum on Moscow's Red Square on Sept. 1.

4—A Los Angeles County grand jury returned secret indictments against unnamed defendants after the final day of testimony in the inquiry into the burglary of Dr. Daniel Ellsberg's psychiatrist's office.

5—A band of Palestinian commandos seized the Saudi Arabian Embassy in Paris and threatened to blow up the building and execute a number of hostages.

5—President Nixon said he would veto the minimum wage bill and challenged Congress to improve upon a "disappointing" record by enacting his "bipartisan" legislative proposals.

6—The occupation of the Saudi Arabian Embassy in Paris ended as five Palestinian commandos accompanied by four hostages bound hand and foot were put aboard a Syrian airliner for a negotiated escape.

6—W. A. Boyle, former head of the United Mine Workers of America, was arrested and charged with murder in connection with the 1969 slaying of Joseph A. Yablonski, who had sought Boyle's ouster.

7—Henry A. Kissinger was threatened with delay in his Senate confirmation as secretary of state unless the Justice Department turned over to the Senate Foreign Relations Committee a report on wiretaps carried out on 17 government officials and newsmen in 1969, 1970 and 1971.

7—Former White House adviser on domestic affairs John D. Ehrlichman pleaded not guilty in Los Angeles to charges of burglary, conspiracy and perjury in the 1971 break-in at the office of Dr. Daniel Ellsberg's former psychiatrist.

8—Five Palestinian guerrillas, who had been holding four Saudi Arabian hostages aboard an airliner at the Kuwait airport, surrendered their prisoners unharmed. The gunmen gave up after Kuwaiti officials refused to consider their demand for the release from prison of a guerrilla leader.

9—A cholera epidemic in Southern Italy has claimed at least 24 lives.

9—The world's nonaligned nations ended a five-day conference in Algiers with a warning to the big powers not to make decisions without consulting them.

9—President Nixon asked the American people to help him to resist the encroachments of Congress on the powers of the presidency.

10—The United States government authorized the steel industry to make a two-stage, $400 million-a-year increase in prices of sheet and strip steel.

10—President Nixon warned Congress in a State of the Union message that he would veto any legislation that would cut defense spending below his budget or raise the cost of domestic programs above it.

10—Atty. Gen. Elliot L. Richardson turned over to the Senate Foreign Relations Committee a memorandum on Henry A. Kissinger's role in the wire-tapping of 17 officials and newsmen from 1969 to 1971. But he failed to satisfy senators who have threatened to delay Kissinger's confirmation as Secretary of State.

10—The Defense Department acknowledged that U.S. fighter-bombers flew air strikes in support of the Cambodian government in 1970-71, with the attacks kept secret through a system of dual reports.

11—President Salvador Allende Gossens of Chile was deposed in a military coup, and the police said he had committed suicide rather than surrender to the attackers.

11—A postponement was granted in U.S. District Court for the trial of John N. Mitchell, former attorney general, and Maurice H. Stans, former secretary of commerce. The two were indicted on charges they obstructed a fraud investigation of financier Robert L. Vesco in exchange for a secret campaign contribution.

12—Chile's military rulers said a private funeral had been held for President Salvador Allende Gossens and warned that any of his supporters found armed would "be shot on the spot if taken prisoners."

12—Negotiators for the Vientiane government and the pro-Communist Pathet Lao initialed an accord providing for the first coalition government since the United States disengagement from Indochina.

12—The Senate Watergate Committee decided to limit its hearings into campaign financing and sabotage to three sessions a week.

13—Israel and Syria fought their biggest aerial battle since the 1967 war as Israel and Syrian jets clashed off the Syrian coast. Israel claimed 13 planes shot down with one Israeli loss, but Syria said "five enemy planes were shot down."

13—Chile's new military junta named an army general as president, formed a military-dominated cabinet, broke diplomatic relations with Cuba and temporarily lifted a round-the-clock curfew.

13—Representatives of the Vientiane government and the Communist-led Pathet Lao signed an agreement establishing a coalition government in Laos.

13—In a move aimed at avoiding a constitutional showdown over the issue of the White House tapes, the Court of Appeals in Washington unanimously urged an out-of-court compromise settlement.

14—Chile's new military junta said it overthrew the country's Marxist government because more than 10,000 "extremists" from other countries had entered Chile and threatened the "destiny of the country."

14—The United Auto Workers Union struck Chrysler Corp. when negotiators failed to reach agreement on a new contract.

15—The widow of President Salvador Allende Gossens of Chile confirmed army and police accounts that her husband took his own life.

16—The junta that took over Chile said armed civilians still were resisting military authorities and warned they would be killed unless they laid down their weapons.

18—Jordan's King Hussein declared an amnesty for political prisoners, including Palestinian guerrillas jailed since 1970, to further Arab reconciliation.

18—A three-year contract tentatively agreed to by the United Auto Workers and Chrysler Corp. was described within the auto industry as "liberal" and "a big, fat settlement."

20—President Nixon's lawyers and the Watergate prosecutor told the Court of Appeals in Washington they had not been able to reach a settlement of the issue of access to the White House tapes.

21—Chile's military junta said it had banned Marxist political parties and would soon announce a new constitution that would give the armed services a role in future legislative bodies.

21—Henry A. Kissinger was confirmed by the Senate as secretary of state—first naturalized citizen and the first Jew to hold the senior cabinet position.

21—The government said food prices recorded their biggest increase for a single month in 27 years in August.

23—Juan D. Peron was elected president of Argentina, 18 years after being ousted from power by a military coup. His wife, Isabel, was elected vice president.

24—Secretary of State Henry A. Kissinger told the U.N. General Assembly that the United States would never be satisfied "with a world of uneasy truces, of offsetting blocs, of accommodations of convenience."

24—Howard Hunt Jr. told the Senate Watergate Committee that Charles W. Colson, former White House special counsel, had been aware early in 1972 of the scheme that led to the Watergate break-in.

25—Vice President Agnew asked the House of Representatives to begin a full investigation of allegations that he accepted bribes as a state and local official in Maryland.

25—President Nixon asked the American people to give Vice President Agnew "the basic, decent consideration and presumption of innocence that are both his right and his due."

25—The marathon 59-day, 24 million mile flight of Skylab 2 ended with a safe splashdown in the Pacific Ocean.

25—W. A. Boyle, former president of the United Mine Workers Union, was reported near death after what officials said was an apparent suicide attempt on the eve of a court appearance on a murder charge.

26—Speaker Carl Albert refused to act "at this time" on Vice President Agnew's request for an investigation by the House of Representatives into allegations that he took kickbacks from state contractors in Maryland.

26—Patrick J. Buchanan, President Nixon's speech writer and political consultant, told the Senate Watergate Committee he had urged a White House strategy to undercut Sen. Edmund S. Muskie and "elevate" Sen. George McGovern in the 1972 Democratic presidential primaries.

27—The Soviet Union launched its first manned spacecraft in two years, an improved Soyuz carrying two astronauts.

28—Two Arab guerillas raided a Moscow-to-Vienna train, seized three Soviet Jews and an Austrian official and took them to the Vienna airport, where they demanded a plane to take them and the hostages to an Arab country. The hostages were later freed and the guerillas allowed to leave after the government promised to suspend the large scale transit of Soviet Jews through Austria on their way to Israel.

28—Lawyers for Vice President Agnew moved in federal court to block the Baltimore grand jury investigation of Agnew's activities.

28—A bomb demolished four rooms in the International Telephone and Telegraph Corp's New York City offices, apparently as a protest against the firm's activities in Chile. No one was injured.

29—The Austrian government's decision to close group transit facilities for Soviet Jews raised much controversy in the country.

29—A pair of Soviet astronauts returned safely to earth after a two-day test flight in a modified Soyuz spacecraft.

29—Vice President Agnew said he would not resign if indicted and denounced the Justice Department for what he called its "unprofessional and malicious and outrageous" handling of the investigation into charges that he got kickbacks while serving as governor of Maryland.

OCTOBER

1—The Senate approved a $20.9 billion military procurement bill after rejecting a last-minute proposal for an across the board $500 million cut in the defense budget.

2—Premier Golda Meir of Israel and Chancellor Bruno Kreisky of Austria met for nearly two hours in Vienna but were not able to agree on the issue of transit facilities for Soviet Jews emigrating through Austria to Israel.

2—Six persons were shot to death and two other persons wounded in Kentucky and police said two prison escapees were arrested in connection with the slayings.

3—President Nixon asked Chancellor Bruno Kreisky of Austria to reconsider his decision to close the transit camp for Soviet Jews emigrating to Israel.

3—President Nixon said it was "altogether proper" for Vice President Agnew to say he would not resign if indicted. Nixon added, however, the charges being assembled against Agnew were "serious and not frivolous." Meanwhile, Agnew's attorneys won federal court authority to investigate alleged news leaks on the investigation by the Justice Department.

5—The Justice Department argued that a sitting Vice President could be indicted and tried on criminal charges. But it said the House of Representatives could impeach Spiro T. Agnew before trial should he be indicted.

5—Lawyers for Vice President Spiro Agnew served at least eight subpoenas on news organizations and reporters in an unprecedented search for news leaks from the Justice Department.

5—The U.N. General Assembly voted to reject the credentials of South Africa but ruled that the delegation could take part in the work of the United Nations.

6—The heaviest fighting in the Middle East since the 1967 war erupted on Israel's front lines with Egypt along the Suez Canal and Syria in the Golan Heights.

6—The United States appealed to Israel and Egypt to stop fighting. Secretary of State Henry Kissinger called on the foreign ministers of Egypt and Israel to call off the new conflict, but it proved fruitless.

7—Israeli forces struck heavily in counter attacks at Egyptian and Syrian positions in the Sinai Peninsula and the Golan Heights and both sides claimed successes. A military spokesman in Jerusalem said Israeli forces had blocked the advance of the Egyptians and Syrians and cut off a force of about 400 Egyptian tanks on the eastern bank of the Suez Canal. In Cairo, the Egyptian command declared that Egyptian forces in large numbers were continuing to reach the eastern bank after an attempt by the Israelis to knock out Egyptian bridges.

8—Israel launched counterattacks on two broad fronts throwing the Syrian and Egyptian armies back to the cease-fire lines, a military spokesman said in Tel Aviv.

8—The Egyptian command said Egyptian troops raided the Israeli-occupied Egyptian oilfields at Balayim on the Gulf of Suez and touched off large fires.

8—The White House said President Nixon and Soviet leader Leonid I. Brezhnev had exchanged private messages indicating a common desire to limit the Middle East conflict.

8—The Justice Department branded as "frivolous" Vice President Spiro T. Agnew's allegation that it had engaged in a campaign of news leaks directed against him. It charged that subpoenas to newsmen to prove there was such a campaign were merely "fishing expeditions."

9—Cairo Radio said Egypt funneled armor and infantry across the Suez Canal for the fourth day.

9—Israeli jets attacked Damascus and Syrian sources said about 100 civilians had been killed or wounded. Israeli Ambassador Yosef Tekoah expressed condolences in the security council for civilian victims, and Soviet envoy Yakov A. Malik walked out in protest against the bombings.

10—Spiro T. Agnew resigned as vice president under an agreement with the Justice Department to admit evasion of federal income taxes and avoid imprisonment.

10—Evidence collected against Vice President Spiro T. Agnew by U.S. attorneys indicated that in three elective offices, including the vice presidency, he had asked for and accepted cash payments totaling more than $100,000.

10—U.S. Administration officials said they believed the Soviet Union was airlifting military equipment to resupply the forces of Egypt and Syria.

10—Western correspondents touring the Sinai Peninsula confirmed that Egyptian soldiers, tanks and equipment were continuing to pour across the Suez Canal.

10—Israel said the Syrian Army on the Golan Heights had been driven back to the 1967 Cease-Fire Line.

11—A large Israeli armored force pushed out of the Golan Heights in the direction of Damascus, smashing through Syrian defenses and leaving Syrian tanks in its wake.

11—Washington officials said the United States is supplying Israel with ammunition and missiles, but it is holding back on large-scale arms help.

11—A Federal grand jury indicted Egil Krogh Jr., the former Presidential aide who directed the White House "plumbers", on two counts of false declaration in a case growing out of the break-in at the office of Dr. Daniel Ellsberg's former psychiatrist.

12—Gerald R. Ford of Michigan, the 60-year-old minority leader of the House, was nominated by President Nixon as the 40th vice president of the United States.

12—Some Syrian Army units appeared to be in full retreat as Israeli forces advanced to within 18 miles of Damascus. Meanwhile, Egyptian military communiques said that country continued to pour men and heavy equipment across the Suez Canal to make the area secure against Israeli recapture.

12—The U.S. Court of Appeals ordered President Nixon to relinquish the White House tapes sought by the Watergate prosecutor.

13—Jordan said it had sent a detachment of its best troops to the Syrian defense against Israel.

14—Egypt said its forces had destroyed 150 Israeli tanks and shot down at least 44 Israeli aircraft in an all-day offensive along the Sinai front. Israel said its forces in Sinai repulsed an Egyptian offensive along the entire 100-mile front.

14—Sanya Thammasak, a university administrator, was named premier of Thailand after a series of violent clashes between troops and students.

15—The United States said it had begun resupplying Israel with military equipment to prevent what it termed "a massive airlift" to Egypt and Syria by the Soviet Union from upsetting the military balance in the Middle East. The Soviet, meanwhile, pledged "to assist in every way" the Arab effort to regain lands lost to Israel in 1967.

15—Thousands of Thai students and other demonstrators supported by the king completed the ouster of the military government when Thailand's former leaders left for exile abroad.

15—Former Vice President Spiro T. Agnew said he resigned in order to give President Nixon an opportunity to restore "unimpaired confidence and implicit trust" in the office he vacated.

15—More than 1,000 persons sought food, clothing and shelter as National Guardsmen patrolled the smoldering ruins of 18 blocks of Chelsea, Mass. An estimated 20 per cent of the city of 32,000 was burned over in a fire Oct. 14 that affected an estimated 900 buildings.

16—President Anwar el-Sadat of Egypt called for a cease-fire coupled with Israeli withdrawal from Egyptian territory seized in 1967. In Israel, Premier Golda Meir said the Middle East war would end "when we have succeeded in beating the enemy."

16—The Nobel Peace Prize was awarded to Secretary of State Henry Kissinger and Le Duc Tho for negotiating the Vietnam cease-fire agreement.

17—Diplomats in Cairo said the Soviet Union had begun high level efforts to persuade Egypt and Syria to move toward a diplomatic settlement of the Middle East conflict. Meanwhile, four Arab foreign ministers submitted a general peace proposal to President Nixon and asked the United States to help mediate the conflict.

17—Hundreds of Israeli and Egyptian tanks clashed at the Suez Canal in what appeared to be a battle for control of the canal's east bank.

17—The Arab oil states announced a program of successive five per cent monthly cuts in oil production with the burden of the reduction falling on the United States and other "unfriendly" countries.

17—American Airlines, Goodyear Tire & Rubber Co., and 3M Co. pleaded guilty to making illegal corporate contributions to President Nixon's 1972 re-election campaign.

17—Chief Judge John J. Sirica rejected a bid by the Senate Watergate Committee to force release of the White House tapes on the ground that the committee failed to establish the court's jurisdiction in the dispute.

18—Egypt said Soviet Premier Alexei N. Kosygin had held three meetings in Cairo with President Anwar el-Sadat, presumably to discuss a settlement of the Middle East War.

18—Five guerrillas seized a Bank of America office in Beirut and took a number of hostages. They demanded $10 million and the release of Palestinian guerrillas jailed in Lebanon.

19—The siege of the Bank of America in Beirut by guerrillas ended with police and army commandos fighting their way in to rescue 39 hostages. Before the battle ended, the guerrillas had killed an American hostage.

19—President Nixon refused to accept the order by the U.S. Court of Appeals to surrender the Watergate tapes, declined to take an appeal to the Supreme Court and ordered the special prosecutor, Archibald Cox to drop the case. But Cox declared that he would not accept the Presidential order that he stop trying to obtain the White House tapes through judicial action.

19—John W. Dean, former counsel to President Nixon pleaded guilty to plotting to cover up the truth about the Watergate break-in. He made his plea as part of a bargain with special Watergate prosecutor Archibald Cox under which Dean agreed to be a prosecution witness in future proceedings against alleged participants in the cover-up.

19—Israeli forces drove about 15 miles into Egypt knocking out artillery and missile batteries and expanding their bridgehead on the western side of the Suez Canal, a military spokesman in Tel Aviv said.

19—Egyptian officials said an Israeli tank column that crossed to the west bank of the Suez Canal Oct. 18 was no longer a serious threat.

19—Libya ordered a cutoff of all shipments of crude oil and petroleum products to the United States, and almost doubled prices for other importers.

20—President Nixon discharged special Watergate prosecutor Archibald Cox and Deputy Atty. Gen. William B. Ruckelhaus for refusing to obey his orders on handling of the Watergate tapes. Nixon also accepted the resignation of Atty. Gen. Elliot L. Richardson, who said he believed his pledge to provide Cox with full autonomy over the

Watergate probe had been violated by the President.

20—Sen. Sam J. Ervin, Jr. chairman of the Watergate committee, renounced and then accepted President Nixon's proposal to release an authentic summary of the Watergate tapes.

20—Israeli forces on the west bank of the Suez Canal pushed out in three directions, "enlarging and deepening" their foothold on Egyptian territory, a military spokesman in Tel Aviv said.

20—The Egyptian command said 85 Israeli tanks and 56 half-tracks were destroyed in fighting on the western bank of the Suez Canal and on the central front in the Sinai.

20—Secretary of State Henry Kissinger arrived in Moscow and began talks with Leonid I. Brezhnev, the Soviet Communist party leader, on the Middle East war.

21—The U.N. Security Council voted to call for a cease-fire in place in an attempt to end hostilities in the Middle East. The vote was 14-0 with China not participating in the balloting.

21—An Egyptian spokesman admitted that Israeli forces had established two positions on the west bank of the canal at Deversoir and Serapeum north of the Great Bitter Lake. He said Israeli tanks were "shooting out" from these bases in thrusts of about six miles.

21—U.S. Congressional leaders of both parties said Congress would have to begin looking at once into the question of impeaching President Nixon, but no one was willing to predict that the President would be removed from office.

21—The New York Mets lost the seventh and final game of the 70th world series to the Oakland A's 5-2.

22—A cease-fire in the Middle East war went into effect on the Egyptian front about 12 hours after the U.N. Security Council called for an end to hostilities. Egypt said it was accepting the cease-fire on condition that Israel pull back from the present front and from the Arab territories seized in the 1967 war. Damascus radio said Syria was considering the cease-fire but it also said Syrian forces were still battling the Israelis.

22—Democratic leaders of The House of Representatives agreed to have the House Judiciary Committee begin an inquiry into whether President Nixon has committed any offenses that could lead to impeachment.

23—In a stunning reversal of position, President Nixon abruptly agreed to turn over the Watergate tape recordings to Federal District Judge John J. Sirica. Aides said the President acted when he realized he was facing a "grave" nationwide crisis of confidence.

23—Israel announced that she and Egypt had agreed to a new cease-fire, the second in two days. Agreement came as heavy artillery boomed along the Suez Canal and Israel tightened her grip on captured Egyptian soil west of the canal.

23—U.N. Secretary-General Kurt Waldheim told the U.N. Security Council that Syria which had ignored the first cease-fire had said it would abide by the second one.

24—The Senate's top Republican leaders urged President Nixon to restore public confidence in the Watergate investigation by naming a new special prosecutor.

24—Democrats in control of the House Judiciary Committee decided to pursue as well as broaden their inquiry into the impeachment of President Nixon.

24—Acting Atty. Gen. Robert H. Bork made clear his intention to taken any steps needed, including judicial action, to obtain evidence from the White House if it was needed to prosecute the Watergate case.

24—Egyptian President Anwar el-Sadat appealed to the Soviet Union and the United States to send troops into the Middle East war area at once to supervise the cease-fire agreement they had inspired.

24—Parts of a 20,000-man Egyptian army cut off on the east bank of the Suez Canal, by Israeli

troops, have failed to fight their way out, an Israeli spokesman said.

24—President Nixon vetoed a bill which would limit the powers of the President to commit the armed forces to foreign hostilities.

25—The United States ordered its military forces on a worldwide "precautionary alert" citing concern that the Soviet Union was planning to introduce military forces into the Middle East.

25—The U.S. alert crisis abated when the U.N. Security Council voted to set up a U.N. emergency force to ensure a Middle East cease-fire using troops from smaller countries. Russia voted for the move.

26—President Nixon said the United States and the Soviet Union had agreed to "use our influence more than we have in the past" to put pressure on the Israelis and Arabs to reach a permanent settlement in the Middle East.

26—Leonid I. Brezhnev accused the United States of artificially fanning tensions over the Middle East with "fantastic rumors" of Soviet plans for unilateral military intervention.

26—President Nixon said at a nationally televised news conference that he would not be deterred by demands for his impeachment and that he had no intention of resigning. He also said a new Watergate special prosecutor would be named by Acting U.S. Atty. Gen. Robert H. Bork, and he pledged "total cooperation from the executive branch."

27—The State Department said Egypt and Israel had agreed to negotiate face-to-face on implementation of the cease-fire along the Suez Canal as a result of the "good offices" provided by Secretary of State Henry Kissinger.

27—The Soviet Union dismissed President Nixon's explanation of why American forces were put on alert Oct. 25 as "absurd." It called the tactics "an attempt to intimidate the Soviet Union."

27—The U.N. Security Council approved arrangements for a 7,000-man military force to serve as a buffer between Israel and Egypt's forces. Meanwhile, the first contingent of United Nations emergency forces reached the city of Suez.

28—Israel agreed to allow the encircled Egyptian III Corps to be resupplied by truck convoy. Sources said the agreement came after the Israeli government was told the Soviet Union had threatened to save the Egyptian force.

29—Israeli officials said continuation of the Middle East cease-fire was contingent on the early identification and release of Israeli soldiers captured by Egypt and Syria.

29—The first truck loads of supplies were ferried across the Suez Canal to the Egyptian III Corps trapped on the east bank.

30—Egypt offered to release Israeli prisoners of war on condition that Israel's troops withdraw to the cease-fire lines of Oct. 22.

30—The House Judiciary Committee began to consider possible impeachment proceedings against President Nixon.

31—President Anwar el-Sadat of Egypt warned that pressure from his army would force him to renew the Mideast War, if Israel did not withdraw to the Oct. 22 cease-fire line by the time the Secretary of State Henry Kissinger visited Cairo in a week.

31—President Nixon's lawyer told Chief Judge John J. Sirica that two presidential conversations considered important to the Watergate investigation had not been recorded, and the President could not comply with a court order to deliver the tapes.

NOVEMBER

1—Secret Service agents testified that more than 30 tape recordings of Presidential conversations had been removed from a safe by White House aides and their return had never been recorded. But special counsel J. Fred Buzardt Jr. said in Federal District Court that "all the tapes made on the White House system are still in existence in their entirety."

1—President Nixon said he would nominate Sen. William B. Saxbe (R-Ohio) attorney-general. It was also announced that Leon Jaworski, a conservative Texas Democrat, had been named to succeed Archibald Cox as special Watergate prosecutor.

2—Moham Z. Ismail, the Syrian Deputy Foreign Minister, flew to Washington to meet with Henry Kissinger.

2—President Nixon learned two Watergate conversations were missing from the White House tape recordings more than a month before his lawyers admitted the fact in court, according to Presidential aide Stephen Bull's testimony in U.S. District Court.

2—The White House said President Nixon "is not giving any thought to resigning."

3—The effort of Secretary of State Henry Kissinger to resolve the problems of the Middle East cease-fire apparently intensified as he shuttled between Egyptian Foreign Minister Ismail Fahmy and Israel Premier Golda Meir.

3—The U.N. Emergency Forces said they were easing tensions between Egyptian and Israeli troops.

3—A Gallup Poll showed that only about one person in four—27 per cent—approved of the way President Nixon was handling his duties.

4—Edward W. Brooke of Massachusetts became the first Republican senator to urge President Nixon to resign. Brooke said he had "reluctantly" concluded the President should resign "in the interest of this nation."

5—Secretary of State Henry Kissinger flew to the Middle East in an effort to overcome cease-fire problems and to promote the start of full-scale peace negotiations.

6—Israel said 1,854 of its soldiers died in the Middle East War. It did not give the total number of wounded but said that 1,800 wounded still were hospitalized.

6—American financier Robert L. Vesco was arrested in the Bahamas under a magistrate's warrant issued at the request of the United States for his extradition on a fraud charge.

6—Former Atty. Gen. Elliot Richardson said President Nixon should agree to drop all claims of executive privilege in the investigation of the Watergate case.

7—Congress overrode President Nixon's veto of a bill which limited a President's power to wage war without congressional approval.

7—The United States and Egypt said they would resume diplomatic relations and exchange ambassadors within two weeks.

7—President Nixon asked Congress to give him a variety of powers to deal with the worsening oil shortage.

7—President Nixon said he had "not violated the trust" of the American people and that he would not quit. He said, "I have no intention whatever of walking away from the job I was elected to do."

8—Aides to Secretary of State Henry Kissinger said Israel and Egypt had agreed on new arrangements opening the way to full-scale peace negotiations.

9—President Nixon told Republican congressional leaders he planned to make public the White House tape recordings and other Watergate documents after they were submitted to the Federal grand jury.

9—E. Howard Hunt Jr. former spy who was hired by the White House to carry out clandestine operations, was sentenced to two and a half to eight years in prison and fined $10,000 for his role in planning the Watergate break-in. The five men who carried out the plan only to be caught and arrested, were sentenced by Federal Judge John J. Sirica to lesser terms.

10—A Federal judge who had found the International Business Machines Corporation in violation of the Sherman Antitrust Act announced that he had reduced the amount of the damages to be assessed against the company from $352.5 million to $259.5 million.

11—Egypt and Israel signed the six-point cease-fire agreement sponsored by the United States and began direct discussions on carrying out the accord.

12—President Nixon offered to furnish Federal District Judge John J. Sirica with background information on two conversations sought by Watergate investigators that the secret White House recording system had failed to record.

12—The White House established what it hoped would be a policy voice independent of President Nixon. The 28-member Republican Coordinating Committee consisting of party elders, Congressional leaders, governors and other GOP officials assigned itself the role of seeing the party through the crisis of confidence in Mr. Nixon.

13—The United States and six European countries terminated a five-year-old agreement that barred them from transactions in gold in the free market.

13—Britain's worsening economic position forced the government to adopt a series of measures to try to bolster her balance of payments, curtail the money supply and cope with labor disputes that threaten to cause widespread power blackouts.

13—The U.S. Senate approved the Alaska pipeline bill by a vote of 80–5. The measure would lay a 48-inch pipeline across 789 miles of mountains, tundra and rivers between Alaska's North Slope oil fields and the Southern Alaskan port of Valdez.

14—Israeli and Egyptian negotiators broke a three-day deadlock on steps to carry out a cease-fire accord agreeing on the immediate exchange of all war prisoners.

14—Princess Anne, only daughter of Britain's Queen Elizabeth II, was wed to Capt. Mark Phillips, son of a commoner.

14—President Nixon warned Republican leaders in Congress against demands for his resignation, saying "if you cut off the legs of the President, America is going to lose."

14—A federal judge ruled that the dismissal of Archibald Cox as special Watergate prosecutor was illegal. But the decision did not order Cox reinstated.

14—Twymon Ford Myers, 23, a reputed member of the Black Liberation Army, was killed in New York City in a gun battle with agents of the Federal Bureau of Investigation and city police officers.

15—The first Israeli prisoners of war released by Egypt arrived in Tel Aviv. All were wounded. At about the same time, 44 wounded Egyptians who had been held by the Israelis, arrived in Cairo.

16—Greek troops using a tank crashed through the iron gates of Athens Polytechnic University to help the police dislodge some 2,000 students who had seized the campus and demanded the overthrow of the government of President George Papadopoulos.

16—President Nixon signed the Alaska pipeline bill and hailed it as a first step toward making the United States wholly self-sufficient for its energy supplies by 1980.

16—Three American astronauts were launched on the nation's last manned space flight for at least a year and a half, a planned 84-day mission aboard the Skylab space station.

16—Fire in a Los Angeles apartment house killed 24 persons in the worst residential fire in the city's history.

17—President George Papadopoulos of Greece imposed martial law after a night of street clashes in Athens between the police and student and worker demonstrators.

17—President Nixon defended himself against all charges of wrongdoing in a televised one-hour session with 400 members of The Associated Press Managing Editors Association at their convention in Disney World, Fla. Nixon said he had never "profited from public service." He added: "I've earned every cent. I'm not a crook."

18—Greek demonstrators defied the martial law and clashed with police in scattered fights throughout the Athens area.

19—A number of young persons who had gathered at the approaches to Athens University were taken into custody on charges of unlawful assembly, and four men were court-martialed on similar charges and sentenced to four years in prison.

20—President Nixon told the nation's Republican governors he would clear up public doubts with the release of detailed information about Watergate, his personal finances and other charges of scandal in the White House.

21—Secretary of State Kissinger said the United States wouldn't change its Middle East policies because of the Arab oil embargo. He warned that "countermeasures" would have to be considered if the embargo continued "unreasonably and indefinitely."

22—Egyptian and Israeli generals met to discuss the details of disengaging their troops under the cease-fire agreement.

22—Saudi Arabia threatened to cut oil production by 80 per cent if the United States, Europe or Japan tried to counter the current Arab oil embargoes.

22—The British government gave details of a compromise under which moderate Protestant and Roman Catholic parties agreed to share power in Northern Ireland.

22—John Swint, an American and general manager of an Argentine subsidiary of Ford Motor Co., and three bodyguards were killed by 15 gunmen in Argentina.

23—Israeli Defense Minister Moshe Dayan said he did not share the optimism generated by the Egyptian-Israeli talks on carrying out the six-point cease-fire agreement.

24—Israel officials said a major gap still separated Israel and Egypt on the question of disengaging their forces along the Suez Canal.

24—Egypt Foreign Minister Ismail Fahmy told an Arab foreign ministers' conference that the Arab countries should step up their use of the "oil weapon."

25—President George Papadopoulos of Greece was ousted in a military coup and replaced by Lt. Gen. Phaidon Gizikis.

25—Israel accepted a proposal to attend peace talks with Egypt, Syria and Jordan on Dec. 18.

25—President Nixon said he would take a variety of actions to reduce the consumption of energy, including a cutback in home heating oil deliveries and a reduction in gasoline production. The President said he would prohibit gas sales on Sundays and lower highway speed limits.

26—President Nixon's personal secretary, Miss Rose Mary Woods, said that by error she caused an 18-minute gap in one of the Watergate tapes.

26—A conference of Arab heads of state began in Algeria with spokesmen exulting over the Arab "oil weapon" but adding words of caution about its use.

27—President Nixon signed into law the Emergency Petroleum Allocation Act of 1973.

28—Arab leaders ended their summit conference in Algeria and announced an embargo on oil exports to Portugal, Rhodesia and South Africa and gave a conditional endorsement to Arab efforts for a Middle East peace settlement.

28—Three Palestinian gunmen surrendered a Dutch jumbo jet they hijacked over Iraq Nov. 25 and freed the last 11 hostages they were holding in return for safe-conduct guarantees.

29—The Egypt-Israel talks on troop disengagement broke down in disagreement.

29—More than 100 persons died when fire swept a Kumamoto department store in the worst such disaster in Japan's history.

29—The White House charged the staff of the special Watergate prosecutor had displayed an "ingrained suspicion and visceral dislike for this President and this Administration."

30—The commander of the United Nations emergency force made separate approaches to the highest-ranking military leaders of Egypt and Israel in an effort to get the suspended cease-fire talks started again.

30—Egil Krogh Jr. pleaded guilty to a civil rights charge growing out of the 1971 office burglary of Dr. Daniel Ellsberg's former psychiatrist.

30—Spurred by the energy crisis, Transportation Secretary Claude S. Brinegar said the Administration was moving toward a broader look at mass transit.

DECEMBER

1—David Ben-Gurion, a founder of modern Israel and its first premier, died at the age of 87.

1—Egypt asked the United States and the Soviet Union to break a Middle East deadlock by pressuring Israel to withdraw her forces to the cease-fire lines of Oct. 22.

2—Egyptian officials hinted Egypt might refuse to go to a proposed Middle East peace conference Dec. 18 if Israel didn't withdraw troops to the Oct. 22 cease-fire lines by that date.

3—An effort to force passage of a landmark measure financing Federal election campaigns with public funds collapsed in the Senate.

3—Pioneer 10 sped within 81,000 miles of Jupiter and sailed past the glowing giant ball for man's first close-up exploration of the lare planet.

3—John A. Love resigned as President Nixon's "energy czar" because he had been shunted aside in a shake-up of energy policy making.

4—William E. Simon, new head of the government's energy programs, said the Administration would have to decide by the end of December whether to ration gasoline.

5—The Egyptian government told the United Nations it had not decided whether to resume the suspended military talks with Israel.

5—Saudi Arabia's Minister of Petroleum said, after meeting with Secretary of State Henry Kissinger, that peace in the Middle East now was "more feasible than at any time in the past."

5—President Nixon and Romania's President Nicolae Ceausescu signed a statement pledging "continued development of friendly relations" between the two nations.

5—The Administration approved a two-cent a gallon increase in the price refiners charge for heating oil and ordered a penny a gallon reduction in the refiners' price for gasoline.

6—Secretary of State Henry Kissinger said the United States had told the Arab countries the oil embargo was "no longer appropriate" since the United States was seeking a Middle East settlement.

6—Gerald R. Ford was sworn in as the 40th vice president of the United States. Ford, who pledged "equal justice for all Americans," was sworn in shortly after the House completed Congressional confirmation of his nomination to replace Spiro T. Agnew.

7—Diplomats said Egypt had decided to attend a Dec. 18 Middle East peace conference even in the absence of a prior Israeli troop withdrawal from the Suez area.

7—The Senate passed a bill calling for a 10-year research and development program to make the United States self-sufficient in sources of energy.

8—Two Arab oil ministers indicated they believed the embargo on oil shipments to the United States would be lifted sometime in 1974.

8—President Nixon made public a voluminous amount of information, including income tax returns, which he said should end "false rumors" about his personal finances.

9—Proposals on the future of Ulster were agreed on by Britain, the Irish Republic, and the moderate Protestant and Roman Catholic leadership of Northern Ireland.

9—Arab oil ministers ordered a new cutback in oil production of about 750,000 barrels a day, starting Jan. 1.

10—The U.S. government abolished price and wage controls over the auto industry in exchange for promises by three manufacturers—American Motors, General Motors and Ford—that they would limit increases on 1974 models. Chrysler refused to go along with the agreement negotiated with the Cost of Living Council.

10—The North Atlantic Treaty Organization opened its annual two-day meeting in Brussels with a clash between the United States and France over whether improved relations between the United States and the Soviet Union enhanced or undermined the security of Western Europe.

11—The Supreme Court broadened the power of law officers to search without a warrant persons taken into custody on minor charges for evidence of other more serious but unrelated crimes.

12—Secretary of State Henry Kissinger suggested the United States, Canada, Europe and Japan join in an effort to meet the energy crisis challenge. He called for creation of an international energy action group.

13—Prime Minister Heath said the government would impose a three-day work week on most British industries beginning Jan. 1, 1974, because of the energy crisis.

13—As the Administration proposed new energy saving measures, President Nixon expressed the hope voluntary conservation would make gasoline rationing unnecessary.

13—Thousands of truck drivers stayed home or pulled off the road to protest the effects of the fuel shortage.

14—The first blackouts of Britain's energy crisis darkened large parts of London and the rest of the nation.

14—J. Paul Getty III, grandson of the American oil millionaire, was found by Italian police after having been kidnaped July 9.

16—Secretary of State Henry Kissinger met with Premier Golda Meir in an effort to ease Israel's concern about the projected Middle East peace conference.

17—Arab guerrillas attacked an American jetliner in Rome killing at least 29 persons aboard and gunning down two outside the plane.

17—The Senate Watergate Committee won statutory authority to seek help from the Federal courts in obtaining some of President Nixon's tape recordings and documents.

17—The Senate by a vote of 75-10 confirmed President Nixon's nomination of Sen. William B. Saxbe (R-Ohio) to be attorney general.

17—Faced with labor disruptions and an energy crisis, the British government announced the largest budget reduction in Britain's history.

18—Arab terrorists, who hijacked a West German airliner in Rome and left behind 31 dead in Rome and one in Athens, flew to Kuwait where they released the hostages aboard their commandeered jet.

18—Syria said she would not attend the Middle East peace conference in Geneva.

18—Malcolm Wilson was sworn in as New York's 50th governor, replacing Nelson A. Rockefeller, who resigned.

19—Kuwait said it had no plans "at the moment" to try the five Arab terrorists who hijacked a jet from Rome to Kuwait in a guerrilla operation that left 32 dead.

19—Chief Judge John J. Sirica ruled that nearly all of two of the subpoenaed White House tapes and part of a third wouldn't be turned over to the special Watergate prosecutor.

20—Premier Luis Carrero Blanco of Spain was assassinated in an explosion that blew his car five stories into the air as he was being driven from a Madrid church.

20—The commander of the United Nations forces in the Middle East protested to Israel and Egypt as outbreaks of heavy fire endangered Finnish troops stationed at the cease-fire line.

20—The Administration urged Americans to practice do-it-yourself gas rationing to avoid the necessity of mandatory allocations.

21—The first Arab-Israeli peace conference opened in Geneva. Both the United States and the Soviet Union urged a permanent settlement that would avert another Middle East war.

21—The Shah of Iran said any tightening of the Arab oil embargo would lead to an economic disaster. He urged the Persian Gulf nations to end the measure.

22—The Middle East peace conference ended its first round with agreement on moving toward talks on separating Israel and Egyptian forces entangled on both sides of the Suez Canal.

22—Congress adjourned after abandoning efforts to pass major legislation giving the President powers to impose gas rationing and take other emergency steps to conserve energy.

25—The Arab oil producers decided to increase the flow of oil to most countries while keeping a total embargo against the United States and the Netherlands.

25—The Skylab 3 astronauts made a record seven-hour space "walk" and focused their cameras on the comet Kohoutek.

26—Egypt and Israel resumed negotiations aimed at separating their forces on the Suez Canal front.

27—Secretary of State Henry Kissinger said improved American-Soviet Union relations were possible only as long as the Soviet maintained a "responsible course" in the Middle East.

27—William E. Simon, federal energy director, said his agency had developed a gas rationing system that could be in working order by March 1.

28—Nobel Prize winning author Aleksandr I. Solzhenitsyn published in Paris a documentary expose of the Soviet secret police, prison camp and terror system. The book was called "The Gulag Archipelago, 1918–1956."

28—Acting Atty. Gen. Robert H. Bork said the Justice Department would seek restraining orders against gasoline dealers found to be charging motorists excessive prices.

28—General Motors Corp. said it planned to lay off some 86,000 workers because of the drop in sales of its standard-size cars resulting from the energy crisis.

29—Generalissimo Francisco Franco of Spain named Carlos Arias Navarro as new premier and successor to the assassinated Adm. Luis Carrero Blanco.

THE TOP TEN STORIES OF 1973

(Selected by the news editors of Associated Press member newspapers and radio and television stations)

1. Watergate: The investigation, the resignations and firings, the indictments, the tapes and the related scandals.
2. The resignation of Spiro Agnew as vice-president.
3. The end of the Vietnam War and the return of the POWs.
4. The state of the economy.
5. The Mideast situation and Yom Kippur War.
6. The energy crisis.
7. The mass murders of teen-age boys in Texas.
8. The death of Lyndon B. Johnson.
9. The Skylab missions.
10. The Chilean revolution.

DEATHS–1973

JANUARY

J. Carrol Naish, 73, was a screen, stage and television actor whose mastery of dialects enabled him to appear in as many as 30 movies a year during the 1940s, playing Italians, Japanese, Arabs, Jews and Mexicans. Naish's acting career spanned some 30 years and during that time he played supporting roles to every major actor. Naish, who roamed Europe during his youth and picked up a command of eight languages, got into acting in his mid-20s and appeared in his first major film in 1932. The film was a romanticized version of San Francisco's "Tong Wars" and Naish played the part of an aging Chinese businessman. Although he made more than 250 films, Naish was best known for his radio comedy series, *Life With Luigi*, in which he played an Italian immigrant. At La Jolla, Calif., Jan. 24.

Edward (Kid) Ory, 86, was a noted Dixieland jazz trombonist who wrote *Muskrat Ramble* and gave Louis Armstrong one of his first jobs. Ory's jazz career began when he formed his own band at the age of 13 and continued almost uninterrupted until he was 80. A self-taught trombonist, Ory went to New Orleans when he was 21 and formed a band that was one of the best known in the city from 1910 to 1919. The band employed a number of musicians who later became famous, among them King Oliver, Sidney Bechet and Jimmie Noone. When Oliver left the band in 1917, Ory replaced him with Louis Armstrong. Trummy Young, a fellow trombonist, once said of Ory, "Dixieland trombone is punch. It's got to come out and it's got to build. I don't think anyone really knows it outside of Ory." At Honolulu, Jan. 23.

Edward G. Robinson, 79, appeared in more than 40 plays and 112 movies during his long acting career but it was his portrayal of a tough-talking mobster in the movie *Little Caesar* that made him a star. His portrayal came to be considered a classic and Robinson went on to play sinister gangster roles in some 10 other films. Although playing a tough guy made him famous, Robinson appeared in other memorable roles such as the patient scientist in *Dr. Erlich's Magic Bullet* and the hard-driving managing editor in *Five Star Final*. The stumpy, thick-lipped actor was born as Emanuel Goldenberg in Bucharest, Romania. He came to the United States at age 10 in 1903 and was educated in New York. He studied drama and in the late 1920s appeared in his first movie, a silent film called *The Bright Shawl*. He went to Hollywood in 1930 and appeared in such hits as *The Hatchet Man, Barbary Coast*, and *The Last Gangster*. He also was a noted art collector and his extensive collection was displayed in a gallery built on the badminton court of his Beverly Hills home. At Hollywood, Calif., Jan. 26.

FEBRUARY

Elizabeth Bowen, 73, was a novelist who, a British critic said, "moved out of the ranks of interesting minor writers to become a major modern novelist" with the publication in 1949 of her *The Heat of the Day*. Born in Ireland, Miss Bowen moved to London at 19 and began to write. She was to later recall, "I wrote my first short story when I was 20. From the moment my pen touched paper, I thought of nothing but writing, and since then I have thought of practically nothing else." Among her books were *The Hotel, The Little Girls, Eva Trout*, and *The Death of the Heart*, which many critics considered as one of her best books. In London, Feb. 22.

Wally Cox, 48, bespectacled comedian, was best known for his TV role of Mr. Peepers. The diffident actor once described himself as "a harmless, preoccupied guy in a constant state of reduced effect." He won fame for his portrayal of Robinson Peepers, the junior-high-school teacher in the television series "Mr. Peepers." He also attained note with his portrayal of a shy newspaper proofreader in "The Adventures of Hiram Holliday." Cox had been appearing since 1966 on the taped TV game show "Hollywood Squares" on the National Broadcasting Company network. On Feb. 15, at his home in Bel Air, Calif.

David Lawrence, 84, began his newspaper career while still in high school and went on to become a widely-read columnist and founder and editor of U.S. News & World Report magazine. While at Princeton, Lawrence was campus correspondent for The Associated Press and in 1910 he joined the wire service's Washington bureau. He left after six years to become Washington correspondent for The New York Evening Post, which permitted him to syndicate his own column. In 1947, he merged the magazines United States News and World Report into U.S. News & World Report. The weekly magazine featured his own regular signed editorial comment and eventually achieved a circulation of almost two million. He reported from Washington for more than 60 years and his views were aired in the magazine and in his syndicated column whch at one time appeared in some 300 newspapers. At Sarasota, Fla., Feb. 11.

Charles Stewart Mott, 97, helped guide the General Motors Corporation to its place as the world's largest industrial organization. A sharp businessman, he was once G.M.'s largest stockholder and amassed one of America's great personal fortunes. His huge G.M. holdings dated back to 1908 when he sold a 49 per cent interest in the Weston-Mott Company, an axle-maker to the newly-formed G.M. for $1,481,000 worth of its stock. In 1913, he turned over the remainder of the company for another block of stock. His favorite philanthropy, the Charles Stewart Mott Foundation was one of the chief beneficiaries of his G.M. stock. The foundation was begun in 1926 with 2,000 shares of the stock and it grew. In 1963, Mott gave his foundation 1,826,421 G.M. shares with a market value of $129 million. In 1969, Mott told a senate committee that his foundation had assets of $300 million and distributed an income of $16 million a year. In addition to G.M., Mott had many other business interests. He had been chairman of the board of the Untied States Sugar company, president of the Northern Illinois Water Company and owner of several department stores. He was a G.M. vice president from 1916 to 1937 and a director from 1913 to his death. On Feb. 18 in Flint, Mich.

Katina Paxinou, 72, was a native of Greece who studied drama and speech in Switzerland before making her first stage appearance in Athens in 1920 in an opera. She switched to acting in 1929, joining the Greek National Theater. When World War II broke out, she was in England and unable to return to her homeland. She went to the United States and acted on stage and in the movies, appearing in the 1943 film *For Whom the Bell Tolls* for which she won an Academy Award for her portrayal of Pilar. She returned to Greece in 1962 and worked with her actor husband, Alexis Minotis, in a variety of plays. In Athens, Feb. 22.

Winthrop Rockefeller, 60, a grandson of oilman John D. Rockefeller, moved to Arkansas in the 1960s and established a baronial cattle farm on a remote mountaintop. He then decided to seek public office, and in 1966 he became Arkansas' first Republican governor since Reconstruction. He won a second term in 1968 but lost when he ran again in 1970. While in office, Rockefeller claimed a number of legislative achievements, among them the state's first general minimum-wage law, reforms in the prison and parole laws, and a freedom of information law. He also was a philanthropist, with his gifts in Arkansas running into the millions of dollars. He was the brother of Gov. Nelson Rockefeller of New York. In Palm Springs, Calif., Feb. 22.

Joseph Szigeti, 80, was an internationally known violinist who began his concert career at the age of 13 and later played as soloist with major symphony orchestras around the world. The Hungarian-born artist made his American debut in 1925 and became a United States citizen in 1951. No conformist, Szigeti played duets with comedian Jack Benny. Many musicians considered Szigeti among the most distinguished of performers. His autobiography, *With Strings Attached,* was translated into several languages. At Lucerne, Switzerland, Feb. 20.

MARCH

William Benton, 73, was publisher of the *Encyclopedia Britannica* and onetime assistant secretary of state. Benton crammed at least five careers into his lifetime, serving at various times as an advertising executive, university vice president, public servant and senator and head of a vast publishing empire. Despite his talent for making money, Benton preferred to regard himself as a dedicated educator and statesman. As chairman of the company that published and sold the encyclopedia, Benton and his family made a great deal of money, much of it given to the William Benton Foundation. The company also enriched the University of Chicago, a contractual beneficiary, by more than $25 million in 25 years. In politics, Benton was a liberal Democrat whose record as senator was highlighted by his opposition to Sen. Joseph R. McCarthy, the Wisconsin Republican and anti-Communist crusader. As assistant secretary of state, a post he held from 1945-47, Benton organized the Voice of America and was active in the establishment of the United Nations Educational, Scientific and Cultural Organization. On March 18, in New York City.

Pearl S. Buck, 80, wrote more than 85 books and won the Nobel and Pulitzer prizes during her long literary career. At the time of her death she had just completed a children's book and was working on two novels. Mrs. Buck spent almost all of the first 40 years of her life in China and much of her writing dealt with Chinese subjects. In a tribute to her, President Nixon said she was "a human bridge between the civilizations of the East and West. It is fitting (she) lived to see two peoples she loved so much draw closer together during her last years . . . With simple eloquence she translated her personal love for the people and culture of China into a rich literary heritage, treasured by Asians and Westerners alike." Mrs. Buck published her first novel, *East Wind: West Wind* in 1930 when she was 38 and she continued to publish steadily after that. He second novel, *The Good Earth,* won the Pulitzer Prize in 1931 and she received the Nobel Prize in 1938. The daughter of Presbyterian missionary parents, she was three months old when her family left the United States and went to China. She returned to the United States at 16 to attend college and then went back to China where she married John Lossing Buck, an agricultural missionary. Divorced in 1935, she married publisher Richard J. Walsh. The family left China in 1927 when Communist revolutionary soldiers invaded Nanking. Other books she wrote included *Sons, A House Divided, The Exile, Fighting Angel,* and *The Townsman.* At Danby, Vt., March 6.

Eugene "Bull" Connor, 75, the police commissioner in Birmingham, Ala., used dogs and fire hoses to break up civil rights demonstrations in the early 1960s. For millions of Americans he symbolized the harsh segregationist police officer of the Deep South. Many liberal Alabamians felt Connor's reputation as a racist was undeserved, but some did feel he was to blame for Birmingham's slide from preeminence as the South's most influential city. Connor's influence was said to have gone beyond his elected position during much of his long term of service. As one of the city's three elected officials, he was conceded to be a major power in the city government. Connor's scorn for blacks who began to fight segregation following World War II was matched by his disdain for whites of a liberal tendency. For most of his career, Connor was firmly supported by the white community. After a mayor-council form of government replaced the commissioner form, Connor was elected to two terms as president of the Alabama Public Service Commision. But he was defeated last year. On March 10 in Birmingham.

Frankie Frisch, 74, the old Fordham Flash, went from the college campus to the Baseball Hall of Fame as one of the game's greatest second basemen. Frisch kept running fast from the time he stepped off the campus in 1919 and joined the New York Giants. For the next 19 years he was one of the most versatile and tempestuous performers in baseball. His talent for umpire baiting rivaled his skill as a player. As a manager, he once was ejected from a game for arguing and drew a five-day suspension the next day for arguing again. He was a daredevil base runner. Starting in 1921, the Giants won four straight National League pennants while Frisch batted .341, then .327, then .348 and .328. In 1926, he was traded to St. Louis and in 1933 became manager of the famed St. Louis Gas House Gang. But times changed. Lamented Frisch in 1954: "Rampaging, dictatorial managers have vanished with the bunny hug and the hip flask. Gone are the feuds, fines, profanity and fun. This is an era of love and kisses, of sciences and psychology." Leo Durocher once said that he loved to get Frisch riled. "He lets go with a full fireworks display. It's like the Fouth of July." On March 12 in Wilmington, Del.

Lauritz Melchior, 82, was recognized as the supreme Wagnerian tenor of his era. Not only did his bright, gleaming voice carry over the orchestra, Melchior also was regarded as a distinguished actor who played memorable roles in *Tannhauser, Lohengrin, Siegfried* and *Tristan and Isolde.* Melchoir sang more than 1,000 performances in Wagnerian operas, more than three times the total of any other singer in his time. Standing 6-feet-4-inches and tipping the scales at 270 pounds in his mid-years, Melchior was a big eater, convivial drinker, a big game hunter and a big party giver. In the 1940s he took up a Hollywood career which was said to have led to differences that prompted him to part company with the Metropolitan Opera management. He made his tenor debut in 1918 in *Tannhauser,* but it was not until several years later that he began to realize his potential. In 1924 he attained great success in *Die Walkure* and was invited to Bayreuth, the Wagner shrine in Germany where he sang the role of Parsifal. It was at Beyreuth that Arthur Bodanzky, the Met conductor, heard Melchior and promptly engaged his services. On March 18 in Santa Monica, Calif.

Edward Steichen, 93, a craftsman who transformed his medium into an art, became the nation's most celebrated and probably highest-priced photographer. Steichen not only interpreted man as he had never been interpreted before through his probing portraits, he gave the 20th century a new vision of flowers, trees, insects and cityscapes. Some of his photographs with their blurred softness resembled French Impressionist paintings. Others, with their use of light and shadow, seemed like Rembrandts. Said Steichen: "I don't think any medium is a work of art in itself. It is the person who creates the work of art." Steichen went to great pains in preparing for a picture. He once took more than 1,000 shots of a single cup and saucer as he experimented with the effects of various lighting arrangements. It was this infinite care critics said, that gave his pictures their special quality. Steichen also was famed as a picture editor. In 1942, during World War II, he set up the exhibition *Road to Victory* at the Museum of Modern Art in New York. He reportedly scrutinized 10,000 prints before selecting 150 he believed reflected the quality and spirit of the American people, their land, and their resources. Among the famous figures who posed for him over the years, were J. P. Morgan, the financier; comedian Charlie Chaplin; the Barrymore family, and Greta Garbo. During World War II, he was in charge of all Navy combat photography. After the war he became director of photography for the Museum of Modern Art. In 1952, he traveled to 11 countries to obtain material for the *Family of Man* exhibition which opened in 1955 and was seen by more than nine million people from 69 nations. At West Redding, Conn., March 25.

APRIL

Hamilton Fish Armstrong, 80, was one of the nation's leading nonofficial experts on foreign policy and for 44 years edited *Foreign Affairs* quarterly. The magazine, under his guidance, won high recognition and served as a forum for scholars and world figures such as Leon Trotsky and Indira Gandhi. Armstrong served as U.S. minister in London during 1944. He published a number of books, among them *Hitler's Reich—the First Phase* and *Europe Between Wars?* In New York City, April 24.

Jacques Maritain, 90, was a noted Roman Catholic philosopher who ranked in the forefront of the century's most influential intellectuals. A metaphysician, he was among the first to urge Christian involvement in secular affairs, molding a philosophy of Christian worldiness that was considered a major factor in creating the climate of opinion which led up to Ecumenical Council Vatican II. In Maritain's view, the Catholic dogma was eternally true but he felt it should focus on the world as it was and tried to close the gap between spiritual and worldly matters by stressing the role of reason and conscience. At Toulouse, France, April 28.

Willie (The Lion) Smith, 79, called himself the greatest pianist on earth and always played his jazz piano wearing a red vest, a derby tipped at a jaunty angle and clenching a big cigar in the side of his mouth. Taught to play piano by his mother, Smith started playing professionally as a teen-ager to launch a career that spanned half a century. He, along with Fats Waller and James P. Johnson, developed the stride style of piano playing. It drew heavily on ragtime and was called stride because the left hand shuttled between low notes and mid-range chords in an oompah pattern. Smith said it required "a two-fisted tickler" to make it roll. In New York City, April 18.

MAY

Jack E. Leonard, 62, was a nightclub comedian whose trademark was the one-line insult, such as the time he told Perry Como, "You have a very fine voice—too bad it's in Bing Crosby's throat." But, as Leonard was to explain, "An insult is only funny if it's really ridiculous, and it's ridiculous if it's aimed at some really big shot." Born Leonard Lebitsky, he broke into the business during vaudeville then moved on to nightclubs. In New York City, May 10.

Jacques Lipchitz, 81, was among the first to apply the principles of cubism to sculpture and was regarded as one of the foremost sculptors of the 20th century. A native of Lithuania, Lipchitz began to draw and model in clay and bread by the time he was 13. He later studied in Paris, fleeing France when the Germans invaded that country during World War II and settling in the United States. In Capri, Italy, May 26.

JUNE

Earl Browder, 82, had served as general secretary of the U.S. Communist party from 1930 to 1946 when he was expelled from the party in a bitter debate over his leadership. An accountant by profession, Browder became interested in leftist causes in his youth. At various times he belonged to the Socialist Party and the Syndicalist League which worked with the American Federation of Labor. Opposing entry of the United States into World War I, Browder was arrested for conspiring to defeat operation of the draft law and for non-registration. He spent a year in jail on the latter charge and rejoined the Socialist party when his term was up. In 1919 he was returned to jail on the conspiracy charge and spent 16 months behind bars. Browder became an honorary charter member of the U.S. Communist party at about that time and had his first direct contact with it in 1921. Embroiled in factional strife from the start, the American Communist party threw out its leader in 1929 and in 1930 named Browder chief. For a while Browder and his party backed the New Deal policies of President Franklin D. Roosevelt, but they split with the administration with the outbreak of World War II, following the signing of the Soviet-German pact in 1939. In 1941 Browder began serving a four-year sentence for unlawful use of his passport. With the Nazi invasion of the Soviet Union in June 1941, the Communist party abruptly shifted its policy and supported the U.S. war effort. A few months after Pearl Harbor, Roosevelt commuted Browder's sentence. In 1946 Browder was accused of being a right deviationist and thrown out of the party. Without a cause, Browder drifted into a bywater where he spent the last years of his life a virtually forgotten figure. At the home of his son in Princeton, N.J.

John Creasey, 64, began writing fulltime at the age of 27 and was so prolific that he turned out 560 mystery and detective novels. Creasey, whose books were translated into 23 languages and sold 60 million copies, wrote under 28 pen names, among them J. J. Marrie, Gordon Ashe and Jeremy York, and published at an average rate of 12 books a year. Before publishing his first novel, *Seven Times Seven* in 1932, he had received more than 700 rejection slips. Shortly before his death he said he had enough unpublished books on hand to bring out seven a year through 1975. At his home near Salisbury, Wiltshire, Britain, June 9.

William Inge, 60, became an instant success after his play *Come Back Little Sheba* opened on Broadway in 1950. His initial success was followed by others such as *Bus Stop, The Dark at the Top of the Stairs,* and *Picnic,* for which he won a Pulitzer Prize in 1953. Inge, whose work dealt with small town life, denied that laying bare social problems was the concern of his plays. He said his job was to create characters and allow them to live. "I think we have to accept the world as it is," he said. "We can't make an overnight change. We have to make so many acceptances in life, over and over again." At Hollywood Hills, Calif., June 10.

Frank Leahy, 64, served as head football coach at Boston College and Notre Dame for 13 years. In two seasons at Boston College, he directed the Eagles to 19 victories in 20 games. His Notre Dame teams won 87 games, lost 11 and tied nine, giving him a career coaching record of 106-12-9. Leahy, who in 1930 played on the last football team coached by the celebrated Knute Rockne, returned to Notre Dame 10 years after being graduated in 1931 and stayed as coach until 1954 when he resigned. His college coaching innovations included the double quarterback, having his teams run from an erect stance, and optional blocking assignments for linemen on the same running play. In 1970 he was elected to the National Football Foundation and Hall of Fame. At Portland, Ore., June 21.

Samuel Irving Rosenman, 77, was a State Supreme Court justice who became an influential advisor to Presidents Franklin D. Roosevelt and Harry S. Truman. He drafted nearly every speech made by FDR and coined the historic phrase New Deal and assembled the original "brain trust" of academic advisors. He began his 17-year association with Roosevelt in 1928 when FDR was running for governor of New York. When Roosevelt ran for President in 1932, Rosenman wrote the classic phrase of FDR's acceptance speech, pledging a "New Deal for the American people." Through the hectic days of the New Deal and the grim years of World War II, Rosenman enjoyed a special position among Roosevelt's advisors. There were few matters on which he was not consulted. In July 1944 he accompanied the President to Honolulu for a conference with Gen. Douglas MacArthur and Adm. Chester W. Nimitz. After Roosevelt's death, Rosenman agreed to stay on at the White House as counsel to President Truman, helping draft Truman's major speeches until Feb. 1, 1946 when he finally resigned as special counsel. He returned to private law practice but served on fact finding labor panels for both Presidents Truman and John F. Kennedy. On June 24 in New York City.

JULY

Joe E. Brown, 80, was an elastic-faced comedian who grew accustomed to having his mouth referred to as the Great Open Space, the Grand Canyon and the Mammoth Cave. But Brown shrugged off the cracks by saying, "I'll open my mouth until my stomach shows if people think it's funny." And the people did think it was funny because almost from the start of his movie career in 1928 until the 1940s his films were among the 10 biggest box office attractions. Brown ran away from home to join the circus when he was nine, learned to become an acrobat, then began a stage and movie career. Among the some 50 films he appeared in were *You Said A Mouthful, Chatterbox,* and *Hollywood Canteen.* At Brentwood, Calif., July 6.

Lon Chaney Jr., 67, was an actor most moviegoers thought of in terms of "monster" roles, but to the critics his most noted role was that of Lennie in *"Of Mice and Men."* The role was that of a stupid man who liked the feel of smooth things but he was so strong and clumsy he killed them, a bird, a mouse and finally a woman. Chaney, whose father played the title roles in *The Hunchback of Notre Dame* and *The Phantom of the Opera,* played many monsters, among them the Wolf Man, Count Dracula, Frankenstein's Monster, and the Mummy. He once said, "All the best of the monsters were played for sympathy. That goes for my father, Boris Karloff, myself and all the others. They all won the audience's sympathy. The Wolf Man didn't want to do all those things. He was forced into them." At San Clemente, Calif., July 12.

Jack Hawkins, 62, first appeared on the London stage at the age of 13 and went on to a career in which he took part in more than 60 plays and nearly as many films. Hawkins played a variety of roles but usually was cast as a solid, responsible British military man or policeman. In *The Bridge on the River Kwai* he played the leader of a group of commandoes sent to destroy the bridge and in *The Cruel Sea* he was the captain of a ship involved in the Battle of the Atlantic. In London, July 18.

Otto Klemperer, 88, an exacting conductor, was considered one of the century's great masters of the German musical repertory. Klemperer, who headed the Philharmonic Orchestra, conducted with strict observance to the text and always was in complete command of the orchestra. In addition to conducting, Klemperer also composed, creating several symphonies, a violin concerto, five operas, a mass and numerous songs. In Zurich, Switzerland, July 6.

Robert Ryan, 63, began drifting after graduating from college and worked as a ship's fireman and as a sandhog before turning to acting at the age of 28 out of boredom and went on to make more than 100 movies. Ryan, however, considered only four or five of his films any good and said his favorite was *The Set-Up,* in which he played an aging fighter. He also liked *Crossfire, Bad Day at Black Rock,* and *Lonelyhearts.* Ryan also appeared on the stage, but relatively infrequently. In New York City, of cancer, Jully 11.

AUGUST

Conrad Aiken, 84, was a poet, essayist and short story writer who received critical acclaim for his autobiography "Ushant" and won the Pulitzer Prize in 1930 for his "Selected Poems." Aiken was a prolific poet but his audience was a small one and one critic thought this partially due to the fact that Aiken was "too much the analyst for his own—and the reader's—good." His other literary efforts also were largely ignored by the public and of some 50 published books not one was a best seller. Despite this indifference, Aiken won a number of awards besides the Pulitzer. They included the National Book Award in 1954, the Bollingen Prize in 1956, and the National Medal for Literature in 1969. At Savannah, Ga., Aug. 17.

Fulgencio Batista, 72, the dictator Fidel Castro overthrew, was the predominant figure in Cuban politics for more than a quarter century until he fled into exile in 1959. In' the years between 1933 and 1959, whether in or out of power, he had remained a pivotal force, boosting himself to power by coups, stage-managing regimes ostensibly headed by others and then carrying out a return to center stage. An army non-commissioned officer, Batista and a group of other sergeants staged a coup in 1933, threw out the existing regime and installed Ramon Grau San Martin as provisional president. Later, Batista, who had elevated himself to colonel, threw out Grau and installed Col. Carlos Mendieta. In 1940, Batista, who had moved up to major general, resigned from the army and had himself elected president. In 1944, he fled from Cuba settled in exile in Florida but he was back in his homeland by 1948, and in March 1952 he staged another coup taking over power once again. Exiled again after Castro took over in 1959, Batista first went to the Dominican Republic, then to the Madeira Islands and finally to Estoril, outside Lisbon. On Aug. 6, at Guadalmina, Spain.

Eddie Condon, 67, taught himself to play the ukulele, banjo and fourstring guitar and then launched his long jazz career wth such groups as Hollis Peavey's Jazz Bandits and the Mound City Blue Blowers. He picked up his technique playing at lakeside bandstands in Iowa, Minnesota and Winconsin but most of all in Chicago. Condon moved east in 1928 and before he was 35 he played with many of the jazz greats, such as Gene Krupa, Jimmy McPartland, Bud Freeman, Bunny Berrigan, Pee Wee Russell, Bobby Hackett and Artie Shaw. In 1946 he opened his own place in New York City. His autobiography, *We Called it Music,* written with Thomas Sugrue, was published in 1947. In New York City, Aug. 3.

John Ford, 78, was considered by many critics as the greatest American director in the sound film era, as D. W. Griffith was acknowledged the master of the silent movie. Ford went to Hollywood in 1913, following an older brother who had become a movie actor, and found work as an assistant director at Universal Pictures. His first film as a director was *Lucille the Waitress* in 1914. His silent films were mostly action movies and it was not until *Arrowsmith,* a talkie, that he had his first film of distinction. He was established as a director of the first rank in 1935 with *The Informer,* which won him his first Oscar. He was to win three more for *Grapes of Wrath, How Green Was My Valley,* and *The Quiet Man.* Oddly, he failed to win one for *Stagecoach* in 1939 which many critics considered his greatest film. At Palm Desert, Calif., Aug. 31.

Paavo Nurmi, 76, was known as the Flying Finn of the athletic tracks between the two world wars. A star in all distances between 1,500 meters and the marathon, he set 28 world records and won seven gold medals in the Olympics in 1920, 1924, and 1928. He might have won more but on the eve of the 1932 games in Los Angeles, he was declared a professional and banned from Olympic competition. Nurmi then became a successful businessman and operated a construction company until his death. In Helsinki, Oct. 2.

Arthur William Radford, 77, had a Navy career that spanned three major wars and hit its peak when he served from 1953 to 1957 as chairman of the Joint Chiefs of Staff, the nation's highest military post. Radford served aboard a battleship during World War I after graduation from the U.S. Naval Academy. After the war he took pilot training, and when the Japanese bombed Pearl Harbor he was picked to expand the Navy's flight-training program. 'He rose to rear admiral rank during World War II and was awarded the Distinguished Service Medal as commander of a task force that fought the Japanese in a series of major amphibious landings, including Tarawa. In 1949, he was named an admiral and appointed Commander in Chief of the Pacific Fleet and High Commissioner of the Trust Territory of the Pacific Islands, posts he held through the Korean War. At Washington, D.C., Aug. 17.

Walter Ulbricht, 80, fled his native Germany when Hitler rose to power and spent most of the Nazi years in Moscow. He returned to his homeland at the end of World War II, wearing the uniform of a Soviet Army colonel and began laying the foundations of what he called "Germany's first peasants' and workers' state"—Communist East Germany. On Oct. 7, 1949, the German Democratic Republic was proclaimed in the Soviet sector of Berlin and Ulbricht, as First Secretary of the ruling Socialist Unity Party, was in charge. He held power for a quarter of a century but was ousted as party leader May 3, 1971, after falling out with both his own people and the Russians. In 1953, the East Germans revolted against Soviet rule but the Red Army put down the revolt and Ulbricht not only remained in power but was permitted to present himself the order of Hero of Labor. In the years that followed, many Germans fled his state for a new life in the West, and Ulbricht ordered the Berlin Wall built, a barbed wire barrier at first and then replaced with a concrete wall nine feet high. At the time of his death, the wall, called "the anti-Fascist protective wall" in the East, still stood. In Berlin, Aug. 1.

Dr. Selman A. Waksman, 85, was a Nobel prize winner and principal discoverer of streptomycin. In 1941, he created the word "antibiotic" to describe penicillin and other "wonder drugs" which were showing up in scientific journals. Shortly after creating the term, he searched through 10,000 chemicals produced by microbes to find streptomycin which was the first antibiotic to show potency in curing tuberculosis. Millions of dollars in royalties from streptomycin and other antibiotics built and helped operate the Rutgers University Institute of Microbiology founded in 1949 and headed by Waksman until his retirement in 1958. In 1952 he was awarded the Nobel prize in medicine. On Aug. 10 in Hyannis, Mass.

SEPTEMBER

W. H. Auden, 66, was a British-born poet who was regarded by many as one of the outstanding literary figures of the century. Auden, who became an American citizen in 1946, won the Pulitzer Prize in 1948 for his long poem, *The Age of Anxiety.* When he became an American citizen Auden lost his chance to be Britain's poet laureate, but so great was his fame that he was proposed for the title regardless. In addition to the Pulitzer, Auden was awarded the British King's Gold Medal for Poetry, the Merit Medal of the American Academy of Arts and Letters, the Bollingen Prize in Poetry, and the Gold Medal for Poetry of the National Institute of Arts and Letters. Auden was called the "greatest living poet in English" by one noted critic, but he also was renowned as an essayist, playwright, editor and professor. Auden's first book of poems was published in 1928. Of his work, he said, "I always have two things in my head—and I always have a theme and the form. The form looks for the theme, theme looks for the form, and when they come together you're able to write." In Vienna, Austria, Sept. 28.

S. N. Behrman, 80, was the author of more than 20 plays and of filmscripts for some of Hollywood's leading stars, such as Greta Garbo and Ronald Coleman. Behrman began his career as a playwright in 1927 with *The Second Man* and was one of the wittiest playwrights of Broadway's golden years before World War II. His plays included *No Time for Comedy, The Burning Glass, Meteor,* and *End of Summer.* Behrman was also a contributor to the New Yorker magazine and the author of several books, among them *Duveen,* the celebrated biography of an art dealer. In New York City, Sept. 9.

King Gustaf VI Adolf, 90, was king of Sweden and the world's oldest chief of state. The popular and scholarly king died after weathering four crises during a month-long illness. King Gustaf was Sweden's sixth ruler from the Bernadotte dynasty, founded by one of Napoleon's marshals in 1818. Members of the family have been long-lived, and Gustaf VI's longevity was exceeded only by that of his father, Gustaf V, who died at the age of 92. After an apprenticeship of 43 years as crown prince, Gustaf VI became king Oct. 29, 1950. Twice married to British women of royal blood, he was a British admiral, a Danish general, and the holder of more grand crosses of German orders than any living German. He spent 23 years on the throne, which passed to 27-year-old Crown Prince Carl Gustaf. At Helsingborg, Sept. 15.

Pablo Neruda, 68, a Chilean who was regarded as one of Latin America's greatest poets, won the Nobel Prize for Literature in 1971. Neruda printed his first poems when he was 13, was an established poet at 20, and at 45 he still had written only a small fraction of the collected writing which by 1962 filled 2,000 pages. He acknowledged that he regarded himself as a politically militant poet and in 1947 was elected as a Communist to the Chilean Senate. However, he accused the government of selling out to the United States and had to go into exile for a time. At Santiago, Chile, Sept. 23.

Marjorie Merriweather Post, 86, became the owner of Postum Cereal Co. after her father's death in 1914 and, through a series of mergers, built the firm into General Foods Corp. During the years that she served as a director of the corporation, she held the post until 1958, she was an early and important backer of frozen foods. Her business success made her one of the world's wealthiest women and at one time her personal fortune was valued at more than $250 million. She gave much money and time to a wide range of philanthropies. Her life style, with its many estates and servants, often resembled that of royalty. At Washington, Sept. 12.

J. R. R. Tolkien, 81, was a retiring scholar who became the unwilling object of a literary cult because of his trilogy-novel *Lord of the Rings.* Prof. Tolkien was a solitary scholar, an Oxford don, an authority on Norse legend and the author of works on Early English. In his own words, he was a "persnickety old academic," but to his youthful readers he was a literary superstar. His best-loved creations were the Hobbits, a funny little folk given to overeating, and it was their struggle against Sauron, lord of the magic rings, which made up his long tale. The Rings books were translated into 14 languages and the wide readership propelled Tolkien into the public arena, a situation he tried to avoid by fleeing to a country hideout known only to his family. At Bournemouth, Britain, Sept. 2.

OCTOBER

James S. Copley, 57, was chairman of the board of the Copley Press Inc.—a group of 15 daily and 34 weekly newspapers—and also chairman of Copley News Service. Copley was adopted at the age of four by Ira C. Copley after the boy's parents died in a flu epidemic. He inherited part of the communications empire with the death of the elder Copley in 1947 and took sole control of the Copley Press Inc. in 1959. President Nixon said, "The untimely death of James S. Copley takes from us a noble American whose distinguished career in journalism and public affairs placed him in the direct line of descent from the country's printer-patriots of the past, from Zenger to Pulitzer." At La Jolla, Calif., Oct. 6.

Norman Chandler, 74, former publisher of the Los Angeles Times, was a builder of one of the great American publishing empires. The third generation of his family to run the Times, Chandler built it into one of the nation's biggest and most influential newspapers. Under his leadership the Times Mirror Company of which he was chairman of the board and chief executive from 1961–68, became a publisher of encyclopedias, paperback books, Bibles, dictionaries, medical books and periodicals, legal treatises, charts and maps. Chandler became chairman of the executive committee of the Times Mirror Company in 1968. The company also acquired Newsday, the Dallas Times Herald and the Orange Coast Pilot. Chandler was a former first vice president of the Associated Press. He was also a trustee of the California Institute of Technology. He once described the operations of the Times Mirror Company as "the knowledge industry." He said, "In the world today we are witnessing education and publishing rivaling the population explosion in dramatic growth." Chandler retired as Times publisher in 1960 to be succeeded by his son, Otis, but continued to direct the expansion and diversification of the Times Mirror Company. On Oct. 20, in Los Angeles.

Angelo DeCarlo, 71, reputedly a onetime powerful Mafia leader, was granted executive clemency by President Nixon on Christmas day 1972 because he was suffering from terminal cancer. DeCarlo who had once headed farflung loan-shark and gambling operations in northern New Jersey and on Staten Island, had been fined $20,000 and sentenced to a Federal penitentiary in 1970 for extortion. He was freed after having served 3 months of a 12-month sentence. DeCarlo's trial in 1970 prompted the Federal government to make public the "DeCarlo tapes" which detailed gangland murders and payoffs to public officials for rackets protection and influence. On Oct. 20 at his home in Mountainside, N.J.

Walt Kelly, 60, wrote and drew the daily comic strip *Pogo*—which made the Okeefenokee swamp famous —for almost a quarter of a century. Kelly was an animator for Walt Disney, then worked as a political cartoonist for the New York Star. During that time he developed the cartoon strip which featured characters of the Florida swamp such as Churchy Lafemme—the Turtle—Albert Alligator, and the strip's opossum hero, Pogo. The strip, which won quick recognition for Kelly as one of the nation's great comic artists and satirists, was syndicated to 420 newspapers in this country and abroad. In Hollywood, Oct. 18.

Gene Krupa, 64, got his first professional drumming job in 1925 when he was called on to replace the drummer at a dime-a-dance hall near Chicago who had become ill. His parents tried to change his career by sending him to a seminary in Indiana but he quit after a year and went to Chicago to play drums. He moved on to New York in 1929 and played with Benny Goodman in the mid-thirties, then later formed his own jazz band and went on to become the king of the hot drummers. Noted for his hard-driving beat, Krupa said once, "People are supposed to like me best when I'm loud but I think I do some of my best things when I play soft . . . a lot of people they're not satisfied unless you have a heart attack up there." In Yonkers, N.Y., Oct. 16.

NOVEMBER

Laurence Harvey, 45, projected the image of the screen's perfect cad who could wither willowy debutantes with utter boredom. After appearing in about 30 European films, he attained fame with his role in *"Room at the Top"* in 1958. It won him an Academy Award nomination. He added to his fame in the United States with his role in *"Butterfield 8."* Offstage, Harvey was a connoisseur of antiques, food and wine. He once described himself as "a flamboyant character, an extrovert who doesn't want to reveal his feelings." On Nov. 25 at his home in London.

Elsa Schiaparelli, 83, was one of the brilliant figures of high fashion whose Paris workshops turned out thousands of dress and coat styles over three decades. She was best-known not for a style, however, but a color; shocking pink. It was the name she gave to her perfume and used to describe the rich, vivid hue that became her trademark. Schiaparelli also introduced ice blue, sun yellow, poppy red and other brilliant tones to a fashion world that in the 1920s had seemed to equate haute couture with stodgy hues. Schiaparelli arrived in Paris in the late 1920s and started designing gold jewelry while she waited for a chance to break into the world of high fashion. Her break came when she appeared at a luncheon, where the fashion-conscious set of Paris was assembled, wearing a sweater with a butterfly pattern. It caused a sensation. Soon she was deluged with orders for similar sweaters. Among her fashion innovations were halter necklines, sweaters for formal wear, jackets that matched cocktail or evening dresses and furs dyed in unusual colors. Her designs were elegant and her creations were often extremely expensive. On Nov. 13 at her home in Paris.

DECEMBER

Albert C. Fuller, 88, was founder and chairman of the Fuller Brush Co., a firm whose trademark came to be known as the door-to-door salesman. Fuller established the firm in 1906 while still a teenager. He started out by making brushes in the basement of his sister's home. Fuller started the company with $375 and over the years built it into a giant business with sales of more than $130 million yearly. He served as president of the firm until 1943, when he became chairman. At Hartford, Conn., Dec. 4.

Harold B. Lee, 74, was the leader of the world's 3.3 million Mormons, serving as their president from July 1972. Recognized by the Mormons as a prophet, he guided the church's rapid world growth and headed its widespread business interests and social programs. He was an educator, businessman and politician before becoming a church General Authority in 1941. President Nixon said he knew Lee "as a warm and generous friend whose counsel and prayers I have valued greatly. While we will miss his presence among us, the greatest tribute we can pay to his life will be to carry on his mission of concern and compassion for mankind." At Salt Lake City, Dec. 26.

PRIZES—AWARDS

PULITZER PRIZES

National Reporting—Robert Boyd and Clark Hoyt.

Commentary—David S. Broder.

Music—Elliott Carter.

General Nonfiction—Robert M. Coles and Frances FitzGerald.

Special Citation—James T. Flexner for "George Washington" a four volume biography.

International Reporting—Max Frankel.

Spot News Photography—Huynh Ut.

History—Michael Kammen.

Poetry—Maxine Winokur Kumin.

Feature Photography—Brian Lanker.

Editorial Writing—Roger Bourne Linscott.

Drama—Jason Miller.

Criticism—Ronald Powers.

Biography—William A. Swanberg.

Fiction—Eudora Welty.

Special Local Reporting—The Sun Newspapers of Omaha for offering proof that Boys Town, the home of orphans, had a net worth of at least $209 million.

General Local Reporting—The Chicago Tribune for uncovering violations of the law in a primary election.

OSCARS

Best Movie—"The Godfather."

Best Director—Robert Fosse for "Cabaret."

Best Actor—Marlon Brando in "The Godfather."

Best Actress—Liza Minelli in "Cabaret."

Best Supporting Performers—Joel Grey in "Cabaret" and Eileen Heckart in "Butterflies Are Free."

Best Original Script—Jeremy Larner for "The Candidate."

Best Documentary—"Marjoe."

Best Song—"The Morning After" from "The Poseidon Adventure."

Best Foreign Film—"Discreet Charm of the Bourgeoisie."

Best Screenplay Based on Material from Another Medium—"The Godfather."

Best Sound—"Cabaret."

Short Subjects Animated—"A Christmas Carol."

Short Subjects Live Action—"Norman Rockwell's World."

Best Editing—"Cabaret."

Best Costume Design—"Travels With My Aunt."

Best Documentary Short Subject—"This Tiny World."

Best Art Direction—"Cabaret."

Best Scoring, Adaptation and Original Song Score—"Cabaret."

Best Original Dramatic Score—"Limelight."

Best Cinematography—"Cabaret."

NATIONAL BOOK AWARDS

Arts and Letters—Arthur M. Wilson for "Diderot."

Biography—James Thomas Flexner for "George Washington: Anguish and Farewell (1793-1799)."

Children's Books—Ursula Le Guin for "The Farthest Shore."

Contemporary Affairs—Frances Fitzgerald for "Fire in the Lake: The Vietnamese and the Americans in Vietnam."

Fiction—John Barth for "Chimera" and John Williams for "Augustus."

History—Robert M. Myers for "The Children of Pride" and Isaiah Trunk for "Judenrat."

Philosophy and Religion—Sydney E. Ahlstrom for "A Religious History of the American People."

Poetry—A. R. Ammons for "Collected Poems: 1951-1971."

The Sciences—George B. Schaller for "The Serengeti Lion: A Study of Predator-Prey Relations."

Translation—Allen Mandelbaum for "The Aeneid of Virgil."

TONY AWARDS

Best Play: "That Championship Season."

Best Musical: "A Little Night Music."

Best Dramatic Actor: Alan Bates—"Butley."

Best Dramatic Actress: Julie Harris—"The Last of Mrs. Lincoln."

Best Supporting Actress in a Play: Leora Dana—"The Last of Mrs. Lincoln."

Best Actor in a Musical: Ben Vereen—"Pippin."

Best Actress in a Musical: Glynis Johns—"A Little Night Music."

Best Supporting Actress in a Musical: Patricia Elliott—"A Little Night Music."

Best Director of a Play: A. J. Antoon—"That Championship Season."

Best Musical Director and Best Choreographer: Bob Fosse—"Pippin."

Best Author: Hugh Wheeler—"A Little Night Music."

A new series of special awards was introduced under the annually renewable designation. "Theater Awards of '73." The first three went to Mayor Lindsay, The Actor's Fund of America and the Shubert Organization.

NOBEL PRIZES

Peace—U.S. Secretary of State Henry Kissinger and North Vietnam's Le Duc Tho for their efforts in negotiating a Vietnam cease-fire agreement.

Literature—Patrick White, Australia, for his epic portraits of Australian pioneer life.

Medicine—Karl Ritter von Frisch and Konrad Lorenz, both Austria, and Nikolaas Tinbergen, Holland, for their studies of animal and individual behavior patterns.

Physics—Leo Esaki and Ivar Giaever, both USA, and Brian Josephson, Britain, for their research on semiconductors.

Chemistry—Ernst Otto Fischer, Germany, and Geoffrey Wilkinson, Britain, for their independent work on the organic and metallic atoms.

Economics—Wassily Leontief, USA, for development of a technique of production analysis now in practical use around the world.

NATIONAL ACADEMY OF RECORDING ARTS & SCIENCES (GRAMMYS)

Record of the Year: (Grammys to the Artist and A & R Producer) "The First Time Ever I Saw Your Face"—Roberta Flack. A & R Producer; Joel Dorn (Atlantic).

Album of the Year: (Grammys to the Artist and A & R Producer) "The Concert For Bangla Desh"—George Harrison, Ravi Shankar, Bob Dylan, Leon Russell, Ringo Starr, Billy Preston, Eric Clapton, Klaus Voormann. A & R Producers: George Harrison, Phil Spector (Apple).

Song of the Year: (A Songwriter's Award) "The First Time Ever I Saw Your Face." Songwriter: Ewan MacColl (Atlantic).

Best New Artist of the Year: America (W.B.).

Best Instrumental Arrangement: (An Arranger's Award) "Theme From The French Connection"—Don Ellis. Arranger: Don Ellis (Columbia).

Best Arrangement Accompanying Vocalist(s): (An Arranger's Award) "What Are You Doing The Rest of Your Life"—Sarah Vaughn. Arranger: Michel Legrand (Mainstream).

Best Engineered Recording (Non-Classical): (An Engineer's Award) "Moods"—Neil Diamond. Engineer: Armin Steiner (Album) (UNI).

Best Album Cover: (Awards to the Art Director, Photographer and/or Graphic Artist) "The Siegel-Schwall Band"—The Siegel-Schwall Band. Art Director: Acy Lehman. Artist: Harvey Dinnerstein (Wooden Nickel).

Best Album Notes: (An Annotator's Award) "Tom T. Hall's Greatest Hits"—Tom T. Hall. Annotator: Tom T. Hall (Mercury).

Best Jazz Performance by a Soloist: "Alone At Last"—Gary Burton (Album) (Atlantic).

Best Jazz Performance by a Group: "First Light"—Freddie Hubbard (Album) (CTI).

Best Jazz Performance by a Big Band: "Togo Brava Suite"—Duke Ellington (Album) (U.A.).

Best Pop Vocal Performance, Female: "I Am Woman"—Helen Reddy (Single) (Capitol).

Best Pop Vocal Performance, Male: "Without You"—Nilsson (Single) (RCA).

Best Pop Vocal Performance by a Duo, Group or Chorus: "Where Is The Love"—Roberta Flack, Donny Hathaway (Single) (Atlantic).

Best Pop Instrumental Performance by an Instrumental Performer: "Outa-Space"—Billy Preston (Single) (A&M).

Best Pop Instrumental Performance by an Arranger, Composer, Orchestra and/or Choral Leader: "Black Moses"—Isaac Hayes (Album) (Enterprise).

Best Rhythm & Blues Vocal Performance, Female: "Young, Gifted & Black"—Aretha Franklin (Album) (Atlantic).

Best Rhythm & Blues Vocal Performance, Male: "Me & Mrs. Jones"—Billy Paul (Single) (Philadelphia-International).

Best Rhythm & Blues Vocal Performance by a Duo, Group or Chorus:

"Papa Was a Rolling Stone"—The Temptations (Vocal) (Single) (Gordy/Motown).

Best Rhythm & Blues Instrumental Performance: "Papa Was A Rolling Stone"—The Temptations (Single) (Gordy/Motown).

Best Rhythm & Blues Song: (A Songwriter's Award) "Papa Was a Rolling Stone." Songwriters: Barrett Strong, Norman Whitfield.

Best Soul Gospel Performance: "Amazing Grace"—Aretha Franklin (Album) (Atlantic).

Best Country Vocal Performance, Female: "Happiest Girl in the Whole USA"—Donna Fargo (Single) (Dot).

Best Country Vocal Performance, Male: "Charley Pride Sings Heart Songs"—Charley Pride (Album) (RCA).

Best Country Vocal Performance by a Duo or Group: "Class of '57"—The Statler Bros. (Single) (Mercury).

Best Country Instrumental Performance: "Charlie McCoy/The Real McCoy"—Charlie McCoy (Album) (Monument).

Best Country Song: (A Songwriter's Award) "Kiss An Angel Good Mornin'." Songwriter: Ben Peters.

Best Inspirational Performance (Non-Classical): "He Touched Me"—Elvis Presley (Album) (RCA).

Best Gospel Performance (Other Than Soul Gospel): "L-O-V-E"—Blackwood Bros. (Album) (RCA).

Best Ethnic or Traditional Recording (Including Traditional Blues): "The London Muddy Waters Session"—Muddy Waters (Album) (Chess).

Best Recording for Children: "The Electric Company"—Christopher Cerf, Project Director; Lee Chamberlin, Bill Cosby, Rita Moreno, Joe Raposo, Producer & Music Director (Album) (W.B.).

Best Comedy Recording: "FM & AM"—George Carlin (Album) (Little David).

Best Spoken Word Recording: "Lenny"—Bruce Botnick, Producer (Album) (Blue Thumb).

Best Instrumental Composition: (A Composer's Award) "Brian's Song." Composer: Michel Legrand (Bell).

Best Original Score Written for a Motion Picture or a Television Special: (A Composer's Award) "The Godfather." Composer: Nino Rota (Paramount).

Best Score from an Original Cast Show Album: (Grammys to the Composers and A & R Producer) "Don't Bother Me, I Can't Cope." Composer: Micki Grant. A & R Producer: Jerry Ragavoy (Polydor).

Album of the Year, Classical: (Grammys to the Artist and Producer) "Mahler: Symphony No. 8 in E Flat Major (Symphony of a Thousand)." Georg Solti Conducting Chicago Symphony Orchestra, Vienna Boys Choir, Vienna State Opera Chorus, Vienna Singverein Chorus & Soloists. Producer: David Harvey (London).

Best Classical Performance—Orchestra: (A Conductor's Award) "Mahler: Symphony No. 7 in E Minor." Georg Solti Conducting Chicago Symphony Orchestra (London).

Best Opera Recording: (Grammys

to the Conductor and Producer) "Berlioz: Benevenuto Cellini." Colin Davis Conducting BBC Symphony, Chorus of Covent Garden. Producer: Erik Smith (Philips).

Best Choral Performance, Classical (Other Than Opera): (Grammys to the Conductor and Choral Director) "Mahler: Symphony No. 8 in E Flat Major (Symphony of a Thousand)." Georg Solti Conducting Vienna State

Opera Chorus, Vienna Singverein Chorus, Vienna Boys Choir, Chicago Symphony Orchestra & Soloists.

Best Chamber Music Performance: "Julian & John." (Selections by Lawes, Carulli, Albeniz, Granados) Julian Bream, John Williams (RCA).

Best Classical Performance—Instrumental Soloist or Soloists (With Orchestra): "Brahms: Concerto No. 2 in B Flat Major for Piano." Artur Rubin-

stein (Ormandy Conducting Philadelphia Orchestra) (RCA).

Best Classical Performance—Instrumental Soloist or Soloists (Without Orchestra): "Horowitz Plays Chopin." Vladimir Horowitz (Columbia).

Best Classical Vocal Soloist Performance: "Brahms: Die Schone Magelone." Dietrich Fischer-Dieskau (Angel).

Best Album Notes (Classical): (An

Annotator's Award) "Vaughn Williams: Symphony No. 2 (A London Symphony)." Annotator: James Lyons (RCA).

Best Engineered Recording (Classical): (An Engineer's Award) "Mahler: Symphony No. 8 (Symphony of a Thousand)." Georg Solti Conducting Chicago Symphony Orchestra. Engineers: Gordon Parry, Kenneth Wilkinson (London).

UNITED STATES GOVERNMENT
EXECUTIVE DEPARTMENT

President: Richard M. Nixon
Vice President: Spiro T. Agnew resigned Oct. 10.
Gerald R. Ford R-Mich sworn in Dec. 6, 1973

WHITE HOUSE STAFF

Counsellor to the President
Anne L. Armstrong
Counsellor to the President
Bryce N. Harlow
Counsellor to the President for Domestic Affairs
Melvin R. Laird
Assistant to the President
Roy L. Ash
Assistant to the President
Peter M. Flanigan
Assistant to the President
General Alexander Meigs Haig, Jr., USA (Retired)
Assistant to the President
Dr. Henry A. Kissinger
Assistant to the President
John A. Love
Assistant to the President
George P. Shultz
Assistant to the President for Legislative Affairs
William E. Timmons
Assistant to the President and Press Secretary
Ronald L. Ziegler
Chairman, Council of Economic Advisers
Herbert Stein
Special Consultant to the President
Patrick J. Buchanan
Special Consultant to the President
J. Fred Buzhardt
Special Consultant to the President
Charles J. DiBona
Counsel to the President
Leonard Garment
Special Counsel to the President
Richard A. Moore
Special Consultant to the President
Raymond K. Price, Jr.
Military Assistant to the President
Brigadier General Richard L. Lawson, USA
Special Assistant to the President
William J. Baroody, Jr.
Deputy Assistant to the President
John Charles Bennett
Deputy Press Secretary
Ken W. Clawson
Deputy Press Secretary
Andrew T. Falkiewicz
Deputy Assistant to the President for Legislative Affairs
Max L. Friedersdor
Deputy Assistant to the President for Legislative Affairs
Tom C. Korologos

Deputy Assistant to the President
Brigadier General Brent Scowcroft, USAF
Deputy Press Secretary
Gerald L. Warren
Executive Assistant and Personal Secretary to the President
Miss Rose Mary Woods
Special Assistant to the President
Mrs. Virginia H. Knauer
Deputy Assistant to the President
Lawrence Mead Higby
Special Assistant to the President for Legislative Affairs
Wilburn Eugene Ainsworth, Jr.
Special Assistant to the President
Lyndon K. Allin
Special Assistant to the President
Stephen B. Bull
Special Assistant to the President
Roland L. Elliott
Special Assistant to the President
Michael J. Farrell
Deputy Counsel to the President
Fred F. Fielding
Special Assistant to the President
David R. Gergen
Special Assistant to the President
William Henkel, Jr.
Special Assistant to the President
W. Richard Howard
Special Assistant to the President
Lee W. Huebner
Special Assistant to the President
Jerry H. Jones
Special Assistant to the President
Bruce A. Kehrli
Special Assistant to the President for Legislative Affairs
Vernon C. Loen
Special Assistant to the President
John E. Nidecker
Special Assistant to the President
Patrick E. O'Donnell
Special Assistant to the President
David N. Parker
Special Assistant to the President
Stanley S. Scott
Special Assistant to the President for Legislative Affairs
Frederick L. Webbe
Social Secretary
Mrs. Lucy Alexander Winchester
Press Secretary for Mrs. Nixon
Mrs. Helen McCain Smith

Physician to the President
Major General Walter R. Tkach, USAF, MC
Chief Executive Clerk
Robert D. Linder
Chief Usher
Rex W. Scouten

CABINET

Department of State
SECRETARY
Dr. Henry A. Kissinger replaced William P. Rogers confirmed Sept. 21

DEPUTY SECRETARY
Kenneth Rush

MISSION TO THE UNITED NATIONS
John A. Scali, *ambassador*

AGENCY FOR INTERNATIONAL DEVELOPMENT
Dr. John A. Hannah resigned July 9
Daniel Parker nominated to replace him, *administrator*

Department of Treasury
SECRETARY
George P. Shultz

DEPUTY SECRETARY
William E. Simon

UNDERSECRETARY FOR MONETARY AFFAIRS
Paul A. Volcker

INTERNAL REVENUE SERVICE
Donald C. Alexander replaced Johnnie M. Walters, *commissioner*

BUREAU OF CUSTOMS
Vernon D. Acree, *commissioner*

SECRET SERVICE
James J. Rowley, *director*

TREASURER OF THE UNITED STATES
Romana Acosta Banuelos

Department of Defense
SECRETARY
James R. Schlesinger replaced Elliot L. Richardson

DEPUTY SECRETARY
William P. Clements, Jr.

JOINT CHIEFS OF STAFF
Adm. Thomas H. Moorer, *chairman*
Gen. Creighton W. Abrams, *chief of staff, U.S. Army*
Adm. Elmo R. Zumwalt, Jr., *chief of Naval Operations*
Gen. John D. Ryan, *chief of staff, U.S. Air Force*
Gen. Robert E. Cushman, Jr., *commandant of Marine Corps*

DEPARTMENT OF THE ARMY
Howard H. Callaway replaced Robert F. Froehlke, *secretary*

DEPARTMENT OF THE NAVY
John W. Warner, *secretary*

DEPARTMENT OF THE AIR FORCE
Dr. John L. McLucas replaced Dr. Robert C. Seamans, Jr., *secretary*

Department of Justice
ATTORNEY GENERAL
Elliot L. Richardson replaced Richard G. Kleindienst
Richardson resigned; Robert H. Bork named acting Atty. Gen. Oct. 20.

DEPUTY ATTORNEY GENERAL
William D. Ruckelshaus nominated to replace Joseph Sneed, resigned Oct. 20.

SOLICITOR GENERAL
Erwin N. Griswald

DRUG ENFORCEMENT ADMINISTRATION
John R. Bartels, Jr., *acting director*

FEDERAL BUREAU OF INVESTIGATION
Clarence M. Kelley replaced acting director L. Patrick Gray II, *director* Sept. 22.

Depart of the Interior
SECRETARY
Rogers C. B. Morton

UNDER SECRETARY
John C. Whitaker

Department of Agriculture
SECRETARY
Earl L. Butz

UNDER SECRETARY
J. Phil Campbell

Department of Commerce
SECRETARY
Frederick B. Dent

UNDER SECRETARY
John K. Tabor

BUREAU OF CENSUS
Vincent P. Barabba replaced acting director Joseph R. Wright, Jr., *director*

Department of Labor
SECRETARY
Peter J. Brennan

UNDER SECRETARY
Richard F. Schubert

Department of Health, Education and Welfare
SECRETARY
Caspar W. Weinberger

UNDER SECRETARY
Frank C. Carlucci

PUBLIC HEALTH SERVICE
Dr. S. Paul Ehrlich, Jr., *surgeon general*

SOCIAL SECURITY ADMINISTRATION
James B. Cardwell nominated to replace Robert M. Ball, *commissioner*

OFFICE OF EDUCATION
John R. Ottina, *commissioner*

FOOD AND DRUG ADMINISTRATION
Dr. Alexander M. Schmidt, *commissioner*

Department of Housing and Urban Affairs
SECRETARY
James T. Lynn

UNDER SECRETARY
Floyd H. Hyde

Department of Transportation
SECRETARY
Claude S. Brinegar

UNDER SECRETARY
John Barnum replaced Egil Krogh, Jr.

FEDERAL AVIATION ADMINISTRATION
Alexander P. Butterfield replaced John H. Shafer, *administrator*

NATIONAL TRANSPORTATION SAFETY BOARD
John H. Reed, *chairman*

UNITED STATES COAST GUARD
Adm. Chester R. Bender, *commandant*

MAJOR INDEPENDENT AGENCIES

ACTION
Michael P. Balzano, Jr., *director*

ATOMIC ENERGY COMMISSION
Dr. Dixy Lee Ray replaced James R. Schlesinger, *chairman*

CIVIL AERONAUTICS BOARD
Robert D. Timm, *chairman*

CIVIL SERVICE COMMISSION
Robert E. Hampton, *chairman*

ENVIRONMENTAL PROTECTION AGENCY
Russell R. Train replaced William D. Ruckelshaus, *administrator*

FEDERAL COMMUNICATIONS COMMISSION
Dean Burch, *chairman*

FEDERAL POWER COMMISSION
John R. Nassikas, *chairman*

FEDERAL RESERVE SYSTEM
Arthur F. Burns, *chairman*

FEDERAL TRADE COMMISSION
Lewis A. Engman, *chairman*

GENERAL SERVICES ADMINISTRATION
Arthur F. Sampson, *Administrator*

INTERSTATE COMMERCE COMMISSION
George M. Stafford, *chairman*

NATIONAL AERONAUTICS AND SPACE ADMINISTRATION
James C. Fletcher, *chairman*

NATIONAL LABOR RELATIONS BOARD
Edward B. Miller, *chairman*

POSTAL SERVICE
Elmer Theodore Klassen, *postmaster general*

SECURITIES AND EXCHANGE COMMISSION
Ray Garret replaced G. Bradford Cook, *chairman*

SELECTIVE SERVICE SYSTEM
Bryon V. Pepitone, *director*

SMALL BUSINESS ADMINISTRATION
Thomas S. Kleppe, *administrator*

UNITED STATES INFORMATION AGENCY
James Keogh, *director*

VETERANS ADMINISTRATION
Donald E. Johnson, *administrator*

LEGISLATIVE

93rd Congress
Second Session

SENATE

PRESIDENT PRO TEMPORE:
James O. Eastland (D.-Miss.)
MAJORITY LEADER: Mike Mansfield (D.-Mont.)
MAJORITY WHIP: Robert C. Byrd (D.-W.Va.)
MINORITY LEADER: Hugh Scott (R.-Pa.)
MINORITY WHIP: Robert P. Griffin (R.-Mich.)
CHAPLAIN: Rev. Edward L. R. Elson

HOUSE OF REPRESENTATIVES

SPEAKER: Carl Albert (D.-Okla.)
MAJORITY LEADER: Thomas P. O'Neill (D.-Mass.)
MAJORITY WHIP: John J. McFall (D.-Calif.)
MINORITY LEADER: Gerald R. Ford (R.-Mich.)
sworn in VP Dec. 6
John J. Rhodes (R.-Ariz.) elected Dec. 7, 1973
MINORITY WHIP: Leslie C. Arends (R.-Ill.)
CHAPLAIN: Rev. Edward Gardiner Latch

STATE DELEGATIONS

Number which precedes name of Representative designates congressional district.

ALABAMA

Senators

John J. Sparkman   D   James B. Allen   D

Representatives

1. Jack Edwards   R
2. William L. Dickinson   R
3. Bill Nichols   D
4. Tom Bevill   D
5. Robert E. Jones   D
6. John Buchanan   R
7. Walter Flowers   D

ALASKA

Senators

Ted Stevens   R   Mike Gravel   D

Representative

At large—Donald E. Young   R

ARIZONA

Senators

Paul J. Fannin   R   Barry Goldwater   R

Representatives

1. John J. Rhodes   R
2. Morris K. Udall   D
3. Sam Steiger   R
4. John B. Conlan   R

ARKANSAS

Senators

John L. McClellan   D   J. W. Fulbright   D

Representatives

1. Bill Alexander   D
2. Wilbur D. Mills   D
3. John P. Hammerschmidt   R
4. Ray Thornton   D

CALIFORNIA

Senators

Alan Cranston   D   John V. Tunney   D

Representatives

1. Don H. Clausen   R
2. Harold T. Johnson   D
3. John E. Moss   D
4. Robert L. Leggett   D
5. Phillip Burton   D
6. William S. Mailliard   R
7. Ronald V. Dellums   D
8. Fortney H. (Pete) Stark   D
9. Don Edwards   D
10. Charles S. Gubser   R
11. Leo J. Ryan   D
12. Burt L. Talcott   R
13. Charles M. Teague   R
14. Jerome R. Waldie   D
15. John J. McFall   D
16. B. F. Sisk   D
17. Paul N. (Pete) McCloskey, Jr.   R
18. Robert B. (Bob) Mathias   R
19. Chet Holifield   D
20. Carlos J. Moorhead   R
21. Augustus F. Hawkins   D
22. James C. Corman   D
23. Del Clawson   R
24. John H. Rousselot   R
25. Charles E. Wiggins   R
26. Thomas M. Rees   D
27. Barry Goldwater, Jr.   R
28. Alphonzo Bell   R
29. George E. Danielson   D
30. Edward R. Roybal   D
31. Charles H. Wilson   D
32. Craig Hosmer   R
33. Jerry L. Pettis   R
34. Richard T. Hanna   D
35. Glenn M. Anderson   D
36. William M. Ketchum   R
37. Yvonne B. Burke   D
38. George E. Brown, Jr.   D
39. Andrew J. Hinshaw   R
40. Bob Wilson   R
41. Lionel Van Deerlin   D
42. Clair W. Burgener   R
43. Victor V. Veysey   R

COLORADO

Senators

Peter H. Dominick   R   Floyd K. Haskell   D

Representatives

1. Patricia Schroeder   D
2. Donald G. Brotzman   R
3. Frank E. Evans   D
4. James P. (Jim) Johnson   R
5. William L. Armstrong   R

CONNECTICUT

Senators

Abraham A. Ribicoff   D   Lowell P. Weicker, Jr.   R

Representatives

1. William R. Cotter   D
2. Robert H. Steele   R
3. Robert N. Giaimo   D
4. Stewart B. McKinney   R
5. Ronald A. Sarasin   R
6. Ella T. Grasso   D

DELAWARE

Senators

William V. Roth, Jr.   R   Joseph R. Biden, Jr.   D

Representative

At large—Pierre S. du Pont 4th   R

FLORIDA

Senators

Edward J. Gurney   R   Lawton Chiles   D

Representatives

1. Robert L. F. Sikes   D
2. Don Fuqua   D
3. Charles E. Bennett   D
4. Bill Chappell, Jr.   D
5. Bill Gunter   D
6. C. W. Bill Young   R
7. Sam M. Gibbons   D
8. James A. Haley   D
9. Louis Frey, Jr.   R
10. L. A. (Skip) Bafalis   R
11. Paul G. Rogers   D
12. J. Herbert Burke   R
13. William Lehman   D
14. Claude D. Pepper   D
15. Dante B. Fascell   D

GEORGIA

Senators

Herman E. Talmadge   D   Sam Nunn   D

Representatives

1. Ronald Ginn   D
2. Dawson Mathis   D
3. Jack Brinkley   D
4. Ben B. Blackburn   R
5. Andrew Young   D
6. John J. Flynt, Jr.   D
7. John W. Davis   D
8. W. S. (Bill) Stuckey, Jr.   D
9. Phil M. Landrum   D
10. Robert G. Stephens, Jr.   D

HAWAII

Senators

Hiram L. Fong   R   Daniel K. Inouye   D

Representatives

1. Spark M. Matsunaga   D   2. Patsy T. Mink   D

IDAHO

Senators

Frank Church   D   James A. McClure   R

Representatives

1. Steven D. Symms   R   2. Orval Hansen   R

ILLINOIS

Senators

Charles H. Percy   R   Adlai E. Stevenson 3d   D

Representatives

1. Ralph H. Metcalfe   D
2. Morgan F. Murphy   D
3. Robert P. Hanrahan   R
4. Edward J. Derwinski   R
5. John C. Kluczynski   D
6. Harold R. Collier   R
7. Cardis Collins   D
8. Dan Rostenkowski   D
9. Sidney R. Yates   D
10. Samuel H. Young   R
11. Frank Annunzio   D
12. Philip M. Crane   R
13. Robert McClory   R
14. John N. Erlenborn   R
15. Leslie C. Arends   R
16. John B. Anderson   R
17. George M. O'Brien   R
18. Robert H. Michel   R
19. Thomas F. Railsback   R
20. Paul Findley   R
21. Edward R. Madigan   R
22. George E. Shipley   D
23. Melvin Price   D
24. Kenneth J. Gray   D

INDIANA

Senators

Vance Hartke   D   Birch Bayh   D

Representatives

1. Ray J. Madden   D
2. Earl F. Landgrebe   R
3. John Brademas   D
4. J. Edward Roush   D
5. Elwood Hillis   R

6. William G. Bray   R
7. John T. Myers   R
8. Roger H. Zion   R
9. Lee H. Hamilton   D
10. David W. Dennis   R
11. William H. Hudnut 3d   R

IOWA

Senators

Harold E. Hughes   D   Dick Clark   D

Representatives

1. Edward Mezvinsky   D
2. John C. Culver   D
3. H. R. Gross   R

4. Neal Smith   D
5. William J. Scherle   R
6. Wiley Mayne   R

KANSAS

Senators

James B. Pearson   R   Bob Dole   R

Representatives

1. Keith G. Sebelius   R
2. William R. Roy   D

3. Larry Winn, Jr.   R
4. Garner E. Shriver   R
5. Joe Skubitz   R

KENTUCKY

Senators

Marlow W. Cook   R   Walter (Dee) Huddleston   D

Representatives

1. Frank A. Stubblefield   D
2. William H. Natcher   D
3. Romano L. Mazzoli   D

4. M. G. (Gene) Snyder   R
5. Tim Lee Carter   R
6. John Breckinridge   D
7. Carl D. Perkins   D

LOUISIANA

Senators

Russell B. Long   D   J. Bennett Johnston, Jr.   D

Representatives

1. F. Edward Hébert   D
2. Lindy Boggs   D
3. David C. Treen   R
4. Joe D. Waggonner, Jr.   D

5. Otto E. Passman   D
6. John R. Rarick   D
7. John B. Breaux   D
8. Gillis W. Long   D

MAINE

Senators

Edmund S. Muskie   D   William D. Hathaway   D

Representatives

1. Peter N. Kyros   D   2. William S. Cohen   R

MARYLAND

Senators

Charles McC. Mathias, Jr.   R   J. Glenn Beall, Jr.   R

Representatives

1. Robert Bauman   R
2. Clarence D. Long   D
3. Paul S. Sarbanes   D
4. Marjorie S. Holt   R

5. Lawrence J. Hogan   R
6. Goodloe E. Byron   D
7. Parren J. Mitchell   D
8. Gilbert Gude   R

MASSACHUSETTS

Senators

Edward M. Kennedy   D   Edward W. Brooke   R

Representatives

1. Silvio O. Conte   R
2. Edward P. Boland   D
3. Harold D. Donohue   D
4. Robert F. Drinan   D
5. Paul W. Cronin   R
6. Michael J. Harrington   D

7. Torbert H. Macdonald   D
8. Thomas P. O'Neill, Jr.   D
9. John J. Moakley   D
10. Margaret M. Heckler   R
11. James A. Burke   D
12. Gerry E. Studds   D

MICHIGAN

Senators

Philip A. Hart   D   Robert P. Griffin   R

Representatives

1. John Conyers, Jr.   D
2. Marvin L. Esch   R
3. Garry E. Brown   R
4. Edward Hutchinson   R
5. Vacant
6. Charles E. Chamberlain   R
7. Donald W. Riegle, Jr.   R
8. James Harvey   R
9. Guy Vander Jagt   R

10. Elford A. Cederberg   R
11. Philip E. Ruppe   R
12. James G. O'Hara   D
13. Charles C. Diggs, Jr.   D
14. Lucien N. Nedzi   D
15. William D. Ford   D
16. John D. Dingell   D
17. Martha W. Griffiths   D
18. Robert J. Huber   R
19. William S. Broomfield   R

MINNESOTA

Senators

Walter F. Mondale   D   Hubert H. Humphrey   D

Representatives

1. Albert H. Quie   R
2. Ancher Nelsen   R
3. Bill Frenzel   R
4. Joseph E. Karth   D

5. Donald M. Fraser   D
6. John M. Zwach   R
7. Bob Bergland   D
8. John A. Blatnik   D

MISSISSIPPI

Senators

James O. Eastland   D   John C. Stennis   D

Representatives

1. Jamie L. Whitten   D
2. David R. Bowen   D
3. G. V. (Sonny) Montgomery   D

4. Thad Cochran   R
5. Trent Lott   R

MISSOURI

Senators

Stuart Symington   D   Thomas F. Eagleton   D

Representatives

1. William (Bill) Clay   D
2. James W. Symington   D
3. Leonor K. (Mrs. John B.) Sullivan   D
4. Wm. J. Randall   D

5. Richard Bolling   D
6. Jerry Litton   D
7. Gene Taylor   R
8. Richard H. Ichord   D
9. William L. Hungate   D
10. Bill D. Burlison   D

MONTANA

Senators

Mike Mansfield   D   Lee Metcalf   D

Representatives

1. Dick Shoup   R   2. John Melcher   D

NEBRASKA

Senators

Roman L. Hruska   R   Carl T. Curtis   R

Representatives

1. Charles Thone   R   2. John Y. McCollister   R
3. David T. Martin   R

NEVADA

Senators

Alan Bible   D   Howard W. Cannon   D

Representative

At large—David Towell   R

NEW HAMPSHIRE

Senators

Norris Cotton   R   Thomas J. McIntyre   D

Representatives

1. Louis C. Wyman   R   2. James C. Cleveland   R

NEW JERSEY

Senators

Clifford P. Case   R   Harrison A. Williams, Jr.   D

Representatives

1. John E. Hunt   R
2. Charles W. Sandman, Jr.   R
3. James J. Howard   D
4. Frank Thompson, Jr.   D
5. Peter H. B. Frelinghuysen   R
6. Edwin B. Forsythe   R
7. William B. Widnall   R
8. Robert A. Roe   D
9. Henry Helstoski   D
10. Peter W. Rodino, Jr.   D
11. Joseph G. Minish   D
12. Matthew J. Rinaldo   R
13. Joseph J. Maraziti   R
14. Dominick V. Daniels   D
15. Edward J. Patten   D

NEW MEXICO

Senators

Joseph M. Montoya   D   Peter V. Domenici   R

Representatives

1. Manuel Lujan, Jr.   R   2. Harold Runnels   D

NEW YORK

Senators

Jacob K. Javits   R   James L. Buckley   C-R

Representatives

1. Otis G. Pike   D
2. James R. Grover, Jr.   R
3. Angelo D. Roncallo   R
4. Norman F. Lent   R
5. John W. Wydler   R
6. Lester L. Wolff   D
7. Joseph P. Addabbo   D
8. Benjamin S. Rosenthal   D
9. James J. Delaney   D
10. Mario Biaggi   D
11. Frank J. Brasco   D
12. Shirley Chisholm   D
13. Bertram L. Podell   D
14. John J. Rooney   D
15. Hugh L. Carey   D
16. Elizabeth Holtzman   D
17. John M. Murphy   D
18. Edward I. Koch   D
19. Charles B. Rangel   D
20. Bella S. Abzug   D
21. Herman Badillo   D
22. Jonathan B. Bingham   D
23. Peter A. Peyser   R
24. Ogden R. Reid   D
25. Hamilton Fish, Jr.   R
26. Benjamin A. Gilman   R
27. Howard W. Robison   R
28. Samuel S. Stratton   D
29. Carleton J. King   R
30. Robert C. McEwen   R
31. Donald J. Mitchell   R
32. James M. Hanley   D
33. William F. Walsh   R
34. Frank Horton   R
35. Barber B. Conable, Jr.   R
36. Henry P. Smith 3d   R
37. Thaddeus J. Dulski   D
38. Jack Kemp   R
39. James F. Hastings   R

NORTH CAROLINA

Senators

Sam J. Ervin, Jr.   D   Jesse A. Helms   R

Representatives

1. Walter B. Jones   D
2. L. H. Fountain   D
3. David N. Henderson   D
4. Ike F. Andrews   D
5. Wilmer (Vinegar Bend) Mizell   R
6. Richardson Preyer   D
7. Charles Rose   D
8. Earl B. Ruth   R
9. James G. Martin   R
10. James T. Broyhill   R
11. Roy A. Taylor   D

NORTH DAKOTA

Senators

Milton R. Young   R   Quentin N. Burdick   D

Representative

At large—Mark Andrews   R

OHIO

Senators

William B. Saxbe   R   Robert Taft, Jr.   R

Representatives

1. William J. Keating   R
2. Donald D. Clancy   R
3. Charles W. Whalen, Jr.   R
4. Tennyson Guyer   R
5. Delbert L. Latta   R
6. William H. Harsha   R
7. Clarence J. Brown   R
8. Walter E. Powell   R
9. Thomas L. Ashley   D
10. Clarence E. Miller   R
11. J. William Stanton   R
12. Samuel L. Devine   R
13. Charles A. Mosher   R
14. John F. Seiberling   D
15. Chalmers P. Wylie   R
16. Ralph S. Regula   R
17. John M. Ashbrook   R
18. Wayne L. Hays   D
19. Charles J. Carney   D
20. James V. Stanton   D
21. Louis Stokes   D
22. Charles A. Vanik   D
23. William E. Minshall   R

OKLAHOMA

Senators

Henry L. Bellmon   R   Dewey F. Bartlett   R

Representatives

1. James R. Jones   D
2. Clem Rogers McSpadden   D
3. Carl Albert   D
4. Tom Steed   D
5. John Jarman   D
6. John N. Happy Camp   R

OREGON

Senators

Mark O. Hatfield   R   Bob Packwood   R

Representatives

1. Wendell Wyatt   R
2. Al Ullman   D
3. Edith Green   D
4. John Dellenback   R

PENNSYLVANIA

Senators

Hugh Scott   R   Richard S. Schweiker   R

Representatives

1. William A. Barrett   D
2. Robert N. C. Nix   D
3. William J. Green   D
4. Joshua Eilberg   D
5. John H. Ware 3d   R
6. Gus Yatron   D
7. Lawrence G. Williams   R
8. Edward G. Biester, Jr.   R
9. E. G. Shuster   R
10. Joseph M. McDade   R
11. Daniel J. Flood   D
12. Vacant
13. R. Lawrence Coughlin   R
14. William S. Moorhead   D
15. Fred B. Rooney   D
16. Edwin D. Eshleman   R
17. Herman T. Schneebeli   R
18. H. John Heinz 3d   R
19. George A. Goodling   R
20. Joseph M. Gaydos   D
21. John H. Dent   D
22. Thomas E. Morgan   D
23. Albert W. Johnson   R
24. Joseph P. Vigorito   D
25. Frank M. Clark   D

RHODE ISLAND

Senators

John O. Pastore   D   Claiborne Pell   D

Representatives

1. Fernand J. St Germain   D   2. Robert O. Tiernan   D

SOUTH CAROLINA

Senators

Strom Thurmond   R   Ernest F. Hollings   D

Representatives

1. Mendel J. Davis   D
2. Floyd Spence   R
3. Wm. J. Bryan Dorn   D
4. James R. Mann   D
5. Tom S. Gettys   D
6. Edward Young   R

SOUTH DAKOTA

Senators

George McGovern   D   James Abourezk   D

Representatives

1. Frank E. Denholm   D   2. James Abdnor   R

TENNESSEE

Senators

Howard H. Baker, Jr.   R   William E. Brock 3d   R

Representatives

1. James H. Quillen   R
2. John J. Duncan   R
3. LaMar Baker   R
4. Joe L. Evins   D

5. Richard H. Fulton   D
6. Robin L. Beard   R
7. Ed Jones   D
8. Dan H. Kuykendall   R

TEXAS

Senators

John G. Tower   R   Lloyd M. Bentsen   D

Representatives

1. Wright Patman   D
2. Charles Wilson   D
3. James M. Collins   R
4. Ray Roberts   D
5. Alan Steelman   R
6. Olin E. Teague   D
7. Bill Archer   R
8. Bob Eckhardt   D
9. Jack Brooks   D
10. J. J. (Jake) Pickle   D
11. W. R. Poage   D
12. James C. Wright, Jr.   D

13. Robert D. Price   R
14. John Young   D
15. E (Kika) de la Garza   D
16. Richard C. White   D
17. Omar Burleson   D
18. Barbara Jordan   D
19. George H. Mahon   D
20. Henry B. Gonzalez   D
21. O. C. Fisher   D
22. Bob Casey   D
23. Abraham Kazen, Jr.   D
24. Dale Milford   D

UTAH

Senators

Wallace F. Bennett   R   Frank E. Moss   D

Representatives

1. K. Gunn McKay   D   2. Wayne Owens   D

VERMONT

Senators

George D. Aiken   R   Robert T. Stafford   R

Representative
At large—Richard W. Mallary   R

VIRGINIA

Senators

Harry F. Byrd, Jr.   I   William Lloyd Scott   R

Representatives

1. Thomas N. Downing   D
2. G. William Whitehurst   R
3. David E. Satterfield 3d   D
4. Robert W. Daniel, Jr.   R
5. W. C. (Dan) Daniel   D

6. M. Caldwell Butler   R
7. J. Kenneth Robinson   R
8. Stanford E. Parris   R
9. William C. Wampler   R
10. Joel T. Broyhill   R

WASHINGTON

Senators

Warren G. Magnuson   D   Henry M. Jackson   D

Representatives

1. Joel Pritchard   R
2. Lloyd Meeds   D
3. Julia Butler Hansen   D
7. Brock Adams   D

4. Mike McCormack   D
5. Thomas S. Foley   D
6. Floyd V. Hicks   D

WEST VIRGINIA

Senators

Jennings Randolph   D   Robert C. Byrd   D

Representatives

1. Robert H. Mollohan   D
2. Harley O. Staggers   D

3. John Slack   D
4. Ken Hechler   D

WISCONSIN

Senators

William Proxmire   D   Gaylord Nelson   D

Representatives

1. Les Aspin   D
2. Robert W. Kastenmeier   D
3. Vernon W. Thomson   R
4. Clement J. Zablocki   D
9. Glenn R. Davis   R

5. Henry S. Reuss   D
6. William A. Steiger   R
7. David R. Obey   D
8. Harold V. Froehlich   R

WYOMING

Senators

Gale W. McGee   D   Clifford P. Hansen   R

Representative
At large—Teno Roncalio   D

DISTRICT OF COLUMBIA

Delegate
Walter E. Fauntroy   D

GUAM

Delegate
Antonio Borja Won Pat   D

PUERTO RICO

Resident Commissioner
Jaime Benitez   D

VIRGIN ISLANDS

Delegate
Ron de Lugo   D

CLASSIFICATION

Senate

Democrats 56
Republicans 42
Conservative-Republican 1
Independent 1
     Total 100

House

Democrats 243
Republicans 190
Vacant 2
     Total 435

JUDICIARY

SUPREME COURT

CHIEF JUSTICE OF THE UNITED STATES

	Home State	Date of Birth	Date took Court seat	Appointed By
Warren E. Burger	Minn.	Sept. 17, 1907	Oct. 6, 1969	Nixon

ASSOCIATE JUSTICES OF THE SUPREME COURT

	Home State	Date of Birth	Date took Court seat	Appointed By		Home State	Date of Birth	Date took Court seat	Appointed By
William O. Douglas	Wash.	Oct. 16, 1898	April 17, 1939	Roosevelt	Thurgood Marshall	Md.	July 2, 1908	Oct. 2, 1967	Johnson
William J. Brennan	N.J.	April 25, 1906	Oct. 16, 1956	Eisenhower	Harry A. Blackmun	Ill.	Nov. 12, 1908	June 9, 1970	Nixon
Potter Stewart	Ohio	Jan. 23, 1915	Oct. 14, 1958	Eisenhower	Lewis F. Powell, Jr.	Va.	Sept. 19, 1907	Jan. 7, 1972	Nixon
Byron R. White	Colo.	June 8, 1917	April 16, 1962	Kennedy	William Rehnquist	Ariz.	Oct. 1, 1924	Jan. 7, 1972	Nixon

UNITED NATIONS

THE SECRETARIAT

SECRETARY-GENERAL

Kurt Waldheim	Austria

UNDER-SECRETARIES-GENERAL

I. H. Abdel-Rahman	Egypt	Executive Director Industrial Development Organization.
Philippe de Seynes	France	Under-Secretary-General for Economic & Social Affairs.
Roberto E. Guyer	Argentina	Under-Secretary-General for Special Political Affairs.
Leonid N. Kutakov	U.S.S.R.	Under-Secretary-General for Political & Security Council Affairs.
Bohdan Lewandowski	Poland	Under-Secretary-General for Conference Services.
C. V. Narasimhan	India	Chef de-Cabinet.
George F. Davidson	Canada	Under-Secretary-General for Administration & Management.
Vittorio Winspeare-Guicciardi	Italy	Director-General, U.N. Office at Geneva, Switzerland.
Constantin A. Stavropoulos	Greece	Under-Secretary-General for General Assembly Affairs & Legal Counsel.
Issoufous S. Djermakoye	Niger	Under-Secretary-General, Special Advisor on African Questions.
Bradford Morse	U.S.A.	Under-Secretary-General for Political & General Assembly Affairs.
Tang Ming-chao	China	Under-Secretary-General for Political Affairs & Decolonization.

GENERAL ASSEMBLY

Country	Year of Admission	Permanent Representative
Afghanistan	1946	Abdur-Rahman Pazhwak
Albania	1955	Rako Naço
Algeria	1962	Abdellatif Rahal
Argentina	1945	Dr. Carlos Ortiz de Rozas
Australia	1945	Sir Laurence McIntrye
Austria	1955	Mr. Peter Jankowitsch
Bahamas	1973	Livingston Basil Johnson
Bahrain	1971	Dr. Salman Mahomed Al Saffar
Barbados	1966	Waldo E. Waldron-Ramsey
Belgium	1945	Edouard Longerstaey
Bhutan	1971	Sangye Penjor
Bolivia	1945	None
Botswana	1966	Thebe David Mogami
Brazil	1945	Sergio Armando Frazão
Bulgaria	1955	Guero Grozev
Burma	1948	U Lwin
Burundi	1962	Joseph Ndabaniwe
Byelorussian. S.S.R.	1945	Vitaly Stepanovich Smirnov
Cameroon	1960	Michel Njine
Canada	1945	Dr. Saul Rae
Central African Republic	1960	Michel Adama-Tamboux
Chad	1960	Vacant
Chile	1945	Dr. Humberto Diaz Casanueva
China	1971	Huang Hua
Colombia	1945	Dr. Augusto Espinosa
Congo	1960	Nicolas Mondjo
Costa Rica	1945	José Luis Molina
Cuba	1945	Ricardo Alarcon Quesada
Cyprus	1960	Zenon Rossides
Czechoslovakia	1945	Dr. Zdeněk Cernik
Dahomey	1960	Tiamiou Adjibade
Democratic Yemen	1967	Vacant
Denmark	1945	Otto R. Borch
Dominican Republic	1945	Dr. Porfirio Dominci
East Germany	1973	Peter Florin
Ecuador	1945	Lepoldo Benites
Egypt	1945	Dr. Ahmed Esmat Abdel Meguid
El Salvador	1945	Dr. Reynaldo Galindo Pohl
Equatorial Guinea	1968	Primo José Esono Mica
Ethiopia	1945	Dr. Zewede Garbre-Sellassie
Fiji	1970	Semesa K. Sikivou, CBE
Finland	1955	Aarno Karhilo
France	1945	Louis de Guiringaud
Gabon	1960	Alexis Obame
Gambia	1965	Vacant
Ghana	1957	Frank Edmund Boaten
Greece	1945	Constanantine P. Panayotacos
Guatemala	1945	Rafael E. Castillo-Valdés
Guinea	1958	Madame Jeanne Martin Cisse
Guyana	1966	Rashleigh Esmond Jackson
Haiti	1945	Raoul Siclait

Country	Year of Admission	Permanent Representative	Country	Year of Admission	Permanent Representative
Honduras	1945	Roberto Martinez Ordoñez	Luxembourg	1945	Jean Rettel
Hungary	1955	Károly Szarka	Madagascar	1960	Blaise Rabetafika
Iceland	1946	Haraldur Kroyer	Malawi	1964	Vacant
India	1945	Samar Sen	Malaysia	1957	H. M. A. Zakaria
Indonesia	1950	Chaidir Anwar Sani	Mali	1960	Seydou Traore
Iran	1945	Fereydoun Houeyda	Malta	1964	Joseph Attard Kingswell
Iraq	1945	Abdul Karim Al-Shaikhly	Mauritania	1961	Moulaye El Hassen
Ireland	1955	Cornelius C. Cremin	Mauritius	1968	Radha Krishna Ramphul
Israel	1949	Yosef Tekoah	Mexico	1945	Dr. Alfonso Garcia Robles
Italy	1955	Vacant	Mongolia	1961	Tsevegzhavyn Puntsagnorov
Ivory Coast	1960	Siméon Ake	Morocco	1956	Mehdi Mrani Zentar
Jamaica	1962	Donald O. Mills	Nepal	1955	Shailendra Kumar Upadhyay
Japan	1956	Toru Nakagawa	Netherlands	1945	Robbert Fack
Jordan	1955	Sherif Abdul Hamid Sharaf	New Zealand	1945	John Vivian Scott
Kenya	1963	Joseph Odero-Jowi	Nicaragua	1945	Dr. Guillermo Sevilla-Sacasa
Khmer Republic	1954	Truong Cang	Niger	1960	Abodoulaye Diallo
Kuwait	1963	Abdalla Yaccoub Bishara	Nigeria	1960	Edwin Ogebe Ogbu
Laos	1955	Vacant	Norway	1945	Ole Algard
Lebanon	1945	Edouard Ghorra	Oman	1971	Failsal Bin Ali Al-Said
Lesotho	1966	Mooki V. Molapo	Pakistan	1947	Iqbal Ahmad Akhund
Liberia	1945	Nathan Barnes	Panama	1945	Aquilino E. Boyd
Libyan Arab Republic	1955	Kamel Hassan Maghur	Paraguay	1945	Dr. Francisco M. Barreiro

ECONOMICS

EMPLOYMENT

Year	Civilian Labor Force	Un-employed	Percentage Unemployed
1929	49,180,000	1,550,000	3.2
1933	51,590,000	12,830,000	24.9
1940	55,640,000	8,120,000	14.6
1944	54,630,000	670,000	1.2
1960	70,612,000	3,931,000	5.6
1961	71,603,000	4,806,000	6.7
1962	71,854,000	4,007,000	5.6
1963	72,975,000	4,166,000	5.7
1964	74,233,000	3,876,000	5.2
1965	75,635,000	3,456,000	4.6
1966	75,770,000	2,875,000	3.8
1967	77,348,000	2,975,000	3.8
1968	78,737,000	2,816,000	3.6
1969	80,733,000	2,831,000	3.5
1970	82,715,000	4,088,000	4.9
1971	84,113,000	4,994,000	5.9
1972	83,542,000	4,840,000	5.6

1973 Employment—Seasonally adjusted

January	86,921,000	4,366,000	5.0
February	87,569,000	4,442,000	5.1
March	88,268,000	4,379,000	5.0
April	88,350,000	4,433,000	5.0
May	88,405,000	4,381,000	5.0
June	88,932,000	4,258,000	4.8
July	88,810,000	4,196,000	4.7
August	88,651,000	4,217,000	4.8
September	89,403,000	4,276,000	4.8
October	89,764,000	4,069,000	4.5
November	89,952,000	4,264,000	4.7

(Source: Bureau of Labor Statistics, Dept. of Labor)

GROSS NATIONAL PRODUCT

(The total output of goods and services in the United States measured in terms of expenditures by which they were acquired)

Year	GNP
1929	$103,100,000,000
1933	55,600,000,000
1940	99,700,000,000
1945	211,900,000,000
1950	284,800,000,000
1960	503,700,000,000
1961	520,100,000,000
1962	560,300,000,000
1963	590,500,000,000
1964	632,400,000,000
1965	683,900,000,000
1966	743,300,000,000
1967	789,663,000,000
1968	865,700,000,000
1969	931,400,000,000
1970	974,100,000,000
1971	1,050,400,000,000
1972	1,155,200,000,000
1973 (est)	1,288,000,000,000

(Source: Department of Commerce)

PER CAPITA PERSONAL INCOME

1950	$ 1,496	1968	3,421
1960	2,215	1969	3,687
1961	2,264	1970	3,921
1962	2,368	1971	4,156
1963	2,455	1972	4,492
1964	2,586	1973 (est)	4,916
1965	2,765		
1966	2,978		
1967	3,159	Source: Department of Commerce	

U.S. TOTAL GROSS PUBLIC DEBT

Year	Total	Per capita
1860	$65,000,000	$2
1900	1,263,000,000	17
1920	24,299,000,000	228
1930	16,185,000,000	132
1940	42,968,000,000	325
1945	258,682,000,000	1,849
1960	286,331,000,000	1,585
1961	288,971,000,000	1,573
1962	298,201,000,000	1,598
1963	305,860,000,000	1,615
1964	311,713,000,000	1,622
1965	317,274,000,000	1,631
1966	319,907,000,000	1,625
1967	326,221,000,000	1,638
1968	347,578,000,000	1,727
1969	353,720,000,000	1,741
1970	370,919,000,000	1,811
1971	398,129,000,000	1,922
1972	427,260,000,000	2,045
1973	458,142,000,000	2,177

(Source: Department of the Treasury)

STATES OF

State	Rank in Population*	Population*	Capital	Population of Capital*
Alabama	21	3,539,000	Montgomery	133,386
Alaska	50	330,000	Juneau	6,050
Arizona	33	2,058,000	Phoenix	581,562

Country	Year of Admission	Permanent Representative	Country	Year of Admission	Permanent Representative
Peru	1945	Javier Peréz de Cuellar	Tunisia	1956	Rachid Driss
Philippines	1945	Narciso G. Reyes	Turkey	1945	Osman Olcay
Poland	1945	Eugeniusz Kulaga	Uganda	1962	Grace S. Ibingira
Portugal	1955	Antonio A. de Medeiros Patricio	Ukrainian S.S.R.	1945	Mikhail Deonisovich Polyanichko
Qatar	1971	Jasim Yousif Jamal	Union of Soviet Socialist		
Romania	1955	Ion Datcu	Republics	1945	Yakov Aleksandrovich Malik
Rwanda	1962	Fidèle Nkundabagenzi	United Arab Emirates	1971	Dr. Ali Humaidan
Saudi Arabia	1945	Vacant	United Kingdom of		
Senegal	1960	Médoune Fall	Great Britain and		
Sierra Leone	1961	Ismael Byne Taylor-Kamara	Northern Ireland	1945	Sir Colin Crowe
Singapore	1965	Shunmugam Jayakumar	United Republic of Tanzania	1964	Salim Ahmed Salim
Somalia	1960	Hussein Nur Elmi	United States	1945	John Scali
South Africa	1945	Carl F. G. von Hirschberg	Upper Volta	1960	Telesphore Yaguibou
Spain	1955	Don Jaime Alba	Uruguay	1945	Dr. Carlos Giambruno
Sri Lanka (Ceylon)	1955	Hamilton Shirley Amerasinghe	Venezuela	1945	Dr. Marcel Alfredo Granier
Sudan	1956	Rahmatalla Abdulla			Doyeux
Swaziland	1968	N. M. Malinga	West Germany	1971	Walter Gehlhoff
Sweden	1946	Olof Rydbeck	Yemen	1947	Dr. Mohamed Said Al-Attar
Syrian Arab Republic	1945	Haissam Kelani	Yugoslavia	1945	Lazar Mojsov
Thailand	1946	Vacant	Zaire	1960	Ipoto Eyebu Bakand'Asi
Togo	1960	Anand Panyarachun	Zambia	1964	Paul J. F. Lusaka
Trinidad and Tobago	1962	Eustace E. Seignoret			

CONSUMER PRICE INDEX (Living Costs)

Year	All Items	Food	Apparel	Housing	Rent	Medical Care	Transportation
1913	34.5	33.6	33.8	--	55.7	--	--
1920	69.8	70.8	98.0	--	72.9	--	--
1929	59.7	55.6	56.2	--	85.4	--	--
1933	45.1	35.3	42.8	--	60.8	--	--
1940	48.8	40.5	49.6	--	63.2	--	--
1945	62.7	58.4	71.2	--	66.1	--	--
1950	83.8	85.8	91.5	83.2	79.1	73.4	79.0
1960	103.1	101.4	102.1	103.1	103.1	108.1	103.8
1961	104.2	102.6	102.8	103.9	104.4	111.3	105.0
1962	105.4	103.6	103.2	104.8	105.7	114.2	107.2
1963	106.7	105.1	104.2	106.0	106.8	117.0	107.8
1964	108.1	106.4	105.7	107.2	107.8	119.4	109.3
1965	109.9	108.8	106.8	108.5	109.8	122.3	111.6
1966	113.1	114.2	109.6	111.1	110.4	127.7	112.7
1967	116.3	115.2	114.0	114.3	112.4	136.7	115.9
1968	121.2	119.3	120.1	119.1	115.1	145.0	119.6
1969	127.7	125.5	127.1	126.7	118.8	155.0	124.2
1970	135.3	132.4	132.2	135.9	123.7	164.9	130.6
1971	121.3	118.4	119.8	124.3	115.2	128.4	118.6
1972	122.9	123.5	122.3	129.2	119.2	132.5	119.9

1973 by month	All Items	Food	Apparel	Housing	Rent	Medical Care	Transportation
January	127.7	128.6	123.0	131.5	121.8	134.9	121.0
February	128.6	131.1	123.6	132.6	122.3	135.3	121.1
March	129.8	134.5	124.4	132.4	122.8	135.8	121.5
April	130.7	136.5	125.8	132.8	123.2	136.2	122.6
May	131.5	137.9	126.7	133.3	123.7	136.6	123.5
June	132.4	139.8	126.8	133.9	124.0	137.0	124.6
July	132.7	140.9	125.8	134.2	124.4	137.3	124.8
August	135.1	149.4	126.5	135.2	125.0	137.6	124.5
September	135.5	148.3	128.3	136.6	125.4	138.3	123.9
October	136.6	148.4	129.6	138.1	125.9	140.6	125.0
November	137.6	150.0	130.5	139.4	126.3	140.9	125.8

Source: BLS—Dept. of Labor

THE UNION

Largest City	Population of Largest City*	Governor	Party	Term Expires
Birmingham	300,910	George C. Wallace	D	1975
Anchorage	48,029	William A. Egan	D	1974
Phoenix	581,562	John R. Williams	R	1975

State	Rank in Population*	Population*	Capital	Population of Capital*
Arkansas	32	2,037,000	Little Rock	132,483
California	1	20,601,000	Sacramento	257,105
Colorado	30	2,437,000	Denver	511,900
Connecticut	24	3,076,000	Hartford	158,017
Delaware	46	576,000	Dover	17,488
Florida	9	7,678,000	Tallahassee	72,624
Georgia	15	4,786,000	Atlanta	495,039
Hawaii	40	832,000	Honolulu	324,871
Idaho	42	770,000	Boise	74,990
Illinois	5	11,236,000	Springfield	91,753
Indiana	11	5,316,000	Indianapolis	746,428
Iowa	25	2,904,000	Des Moines	201,404
Kansas	28	2,279,000	Topeka	125,011
Kentucky	23	3,342,000	Frankfort	21,902
Louisiana	20	3,764,000	Baton Rouge	165,963
Maine	38	1,028,000	Augusta	21,945
Maryland	18	4,070,000	Annapolis	30,095
Massachusetts	10	5,818,000	Boston	641,071
Michigan	7	9,044,000	Lansing	131,546
Minnesota	19	3,897,000	St. Paul	309,980
Mississippi	29	2,281,000	Jackson	153,968
Missouri	13	4,757,000	Jefferson City	32,407
Montana	43	721,000	Helena	22,730
Nebraska	35	1,542,000	Lincoln	149,418
Nevada	47	548,000	Carson City	15,264
New Hampshire	41	791,000	Concord	30,022
New Jersey	8	7,361,000	Trenton	104,638
New Mexico	37	1,106,000	Santa Fe	41,167
New York	2	18,265,000	Albany	115,781
North Carolina	12	5,273,000	Raleigh	123,793
North Dakota	45	640,000	Bismarck	34,703
Ohio	6	10,731,000	Columbus	539,677
Oklahoma	27	2,663,000	Oklahoma City	368,164
Oregon	31	2,225,000	Salem	68,296
Pennsylvania	3	11,902,000	Harrisburg	68,061
Rhode Island	39	973,000	Providence	179,213
South Carolina	26	2,726,000	Columbia	113,542
South Dakota	40	685,000	Pierre	9,732
Tennessee	17	4,126,000	Nashville	447,877
Texas	4	11,794,000	Austin	251,808
Utah	36	1,157,000	Salt Lake City	175,885
Vermont	48	464,000	Montpelier	8,609
Virginia	14	4,811,000	Richmond	236,500
Washington	22	3,429,000	Olympia	23,296
West Virginia	30	1,794,000	Charleston	71,505
Wisconsin	16	4,569,000	Madison	171,769
Wyoming	49	353,000	Cheyenne	40,914
District Of Columbia		746,000		
Commonwealth Of Puerto Rico		2,712,033	San Juan	452,749

* Source of population totals: Estimate Bureau of the Census

SPORTS

BASEBALL

FINAL MAJOR LEAGUE STANDINGS

NATIONAL LEAGUE

EASTERN DIVISION

	W.	L.	Pct.	G.B.
New York	82	79	.509	—
St. Louis	81	81	.500	1½
Pittsburgh	80	82	.494	2½
Montreal	79	83	.488	3½
Chicago	77	84	.478	5
Philadelphia	71	91	.438	11½

WESTERN DIVISION

	W.	L.	Pct.	G.B.
Cincinnati	99	63	.611	—
Los Angeles	95	66	.590	3½
San Francisco	88	74	.543	11
Houston	82	80	.506	17
Atlanta	76	85	.472	22½
San Diego	60	102	.370	39

AMERICAN LEAGUE

EASTERN DIVISION

	W.	L.	Pct.	G.B.
Baltimore	97	65	.599	—
Boston	89	73	.549	8
Detroit	85	77	.525	12
New York	80	82	.494	17
Milwaukee	74	88	.457	23
Cleveland	71	91	.438	26

WESTERN DIVISION

	W.	L.	Pct.	G.B.
Oakland	94	68	.580	—
Kansas City	88	74	.543	6
Minnesota	81	81	.500	13
California	79	83	.488	15
Chicago	77	85	.475	17
Texas	57	105	.352	37

New York defeated Cincinnati 3 games to 2 to win National League Championship. Oakland defeated Baltimore 3 games to 2 to win American League Championship. Oakland defeated N.Y. 4 games to 3 to win World Series.

Largest City	Population of Largest City*	Governor	Party	Term Expires
Little Rock	132,483	Dale Bumpers	D	1975
Los Angeles	2,816,061	Ronald Reagan	R	1975
Denver	511,900	John D. Vanderhoof	R	1975
Hartford	158,017	Thomas J. Meskill	R	1975
Wilmington	80,386	Sherman W. Tribbitt	D	1977
Jacksonville	535,300	Reubin Askew	D	1975
Atlanta	495,039	Jimmy Carter	D	1975
Honolulu	324,871	John A. Burns	D	1974
Boise	74,990	Cecil D. Andrus	D	1975
Chicago	3,369,357	Daniel Walker	D	1977
Indianapolis	746,428	Otis R. Bowen	R	1977
Des Moines	201,404	Robert R. Day	R	1975
Wichita	276,554	Robert B. Docking	D	1975
Louisville	361,706	Wendell H. Ford	D	1975
New Orleans	589,000	Edwin W. Edwards	D	1976
Portland	65,116	Kenneth M. Curtis	D	1975
Baltimore	896,900	Marvin Mandel	D	1975
Boston	641,071	Francis W. Sargent	R	1975
Detroit	1,511,482	William G. Milliken	R	1975
Minneapolis	434,400	Wendell R. Anderson	D	1975
Jackson	153,968	William L. Waller	D	1976
St. Louis	586,400	Christopher S. Bond	R	1977
Billings	61,581	Thomas L. Judge	D	1977
Omaha	347,328	J. James Exon	D	1975
Las Vegas	125,787	D. N. O'Callaghan	D	1975
Manchester	87,754	Meldrim Thompson Jr.	R	1975
Newark	381,930	Brendan T. Byrne	R	1978
Albuquerque	243,751	Bruce King	D	1975
New York	7,847,100	Nelson A. Rockefeller	R	1975
Charlotte	241,178	James E. Holshouser Jr.	R	1977
Fargo	53,365	Arthur A. Link	D	1977
Cleveland	750,903	John J. Gilligan	D	1975
Oklahoma City	368,164	David Hall	D	1975
Portland	379,967	Tom McCall	R	1975
Philadelphia	1,916,000	Milton J. Shapp	D	1975
Providence	179,213	Phillip W. Noel	D	1975
Columbia	113,542	John C. West	D	1975
Sioux Falls	72,488	Richard F. Kneip	D	1975
Memphis	623,530	Winfield Dunn	R	1975
Houston	1,232,802	Dolph Briscoe	D	1975
Salt Lake City	175,885	Calvin L. Rampton	D	1977
Burlington	38,633	Thomas P. Salmon	D	1975
Norfolk	283,000	Mills E. Godwin Jr.	R	1978
Seattle	530,831	Daniel J. Evans	R	1977
Huntington	74,315	Arch A. Moore Jr.	R	1977
Milwaukee	717,099	Patrick J. Lucey	D	1975
Cheyenne	40,914	Stanley K. Hathaway	R	1975
San Juan	452,749	Rafael Hernandez Colon		1977

PRO FOOTBALL

Final Standings

NATIONAL CONFERENCE

Eastern Division
	W	L	T	Pct.
Dallas	10	4	0	.714
xWashington	10	4	0	.714
Philadelphia	5	8	1	.393
St. Louis	4	9	1	.321
N.Y. Giants	2	11	1	.179

Central Division
	W	L	T	Pct.
Minnesota	12	2	0	.857
Detroit	6	7	1	.464
Green Bay	5	7	2	.429
Chicago	3	11	0	.214

Western Division
	W	L	T	Pct.
Los Angeles	12	2	0	.857
Atlanta	9	5	0	.643
San Francisco	5	9	0	.357
New Orleans	5	9	0	.357

x—Gained Wild Card Berth.

AMERICAN CONFERENCE

Eastern Division
	W	L	T	Pct.
Miami	12	2	0	.857
Buffalo	9	5	0	.643
New England	5	9	0	.357
N.Y. Jets	4	10	0	.286
Baltimore	4	10	0	.286

Central Division
	W	L	T	Pct.
Cincinnati	10	4	0	.714
xPittsburgh	10	4	0	.714
Cleveland	7	5	2	.571
Houston	1	13	0	.071

Western Division
	W	L	T	Pct.
Oakland	9	4	1	.679
Denver	7	5	2	.571
Kansas City	7	5	2	.571
San Diego	2	11	1	.179

x—Gained Wild Card Berth.

N.F.L. Playoffs

Semifinal Round

Minnesota defeated Washington 27 to 20
Oakland defeated Pittsburgh 33 to 13

Dallas defeated Los Angeles 27 to 16
Miami defeated Cincinnati 34 to 16

Final

NFC—Minnesota defeated Dallas 27 to 10
AFC—Miami defeated Oakland 27 to 10

Minnesota wins NFC championship.
Miami wins AFC championship.

Minnesota and Miami
meet in the Super Bowl in
Houston, Jan. 13

COLLEGE FOOTBALL

Ratings

The top teams, with points figured on a 10-9-8-7-6-5-4-3-2-1 basis for first through 10th places (first-place votes in parentheses) and won-lost records:

	W.	L.	T.	Pts.
1—Alabama (34)	11	0	0	1,090
2—Oklahoma (16)	10	0	0	1,023
3—N. Dame (2)	10	0	0	810
4—Ohio State (2)	9	0	1	799
5—Michigan (1)	10	0	1	780
6—Penn State (3)	11	0	0	679
7—So. Calif.	9	1	1	528
8—Texas	8	2	0	412
9—UCLA	9	2	0	312
10—Arizona St.	10	1	0	293
11—Texas Tech	10	1	0	255
12—Nebraska	8	2	1	222
13—Louisiana St.	9	2	0	193
14—Houston	10	1	0	161
15—Miami, Ohio	10	0	0	85
16—No. Carolina St.	8	3	0	56
17—Tulane	9	2	0	44
18—Maryland	8	3	0	30
19—Kansas	7	3	1	27
20—Tennessee	8	3	0	16

ALL-AMERICANS

Offense

E—Andre Tillman, Texas Tech.
E—Lynn Swann, Southern California
T—Buddy Brown, Alabama
T—John Hicks, Ohio State
G—Tyler Lafauci, Louisiana State
G—Bill Yoest, North Carolina State
C—Bill Wyman, Texas
QB—David Jaynes, Kansas
RB—John Cappelletti, Penn State
RB—Tony Dorsett, Pittsburgh
RB—Roosevelt Leaks, Texas

Defense

E—Pat Donovan, Stanford
E—Randy White, Maryland
T—John Dutton, Nebraska
T—Dave Gallagher, Michigan
G—Lucious Selmon, Oklahoma
LB—Randy Gradishar, Ohio State
LB—Rod Shoate, Oklahoma
LB—Richard Wood, Southern California
DB—Jimmy Allen, UCLA
DB—Artimus Parker, Southern California
DB—Mike Townsend, Notre Dame

CONFERENCE STANDINGS

Ivy League—Dartmouth.
Southeastern—Alabama.
Atlantic Coast—N. Carolina St.
Southern—E. Carolina
Big Ten—Ohio St.
Pacific-8—U.S.C.
Southwest—Texas.
Missouri Valley—Tulsa.
Big Eight—Oklahoma.
Big Sky—Boise St.
Mid-Eastern—Miami.
Western Athletic—Arizona St.
Pacific Coast Athletic—San D'go St.
Ohio Valley—West. Ky.
Yankee—Conn.

BOWL GAMES

Sugar Bowl—Oklahoma 14, Penn St. 0.
Cotton Bowl—Texas 17, Alabama 13.
Orange Bowl—Nebraska 40, Notre Dame 6.
Rose Bowl—USC 42, Ohio State 17.

PRO BASKETBALL

NATIONAL BASKETBALL ASSOCIATION

Final Standings
Eastern Conference
Atlantic Division

	W	L	PCT.	GBfl
Boston	68	14	.829	—
New York	57	25	.695	11
Buffalo	21	61	.256	47
Philadelphia	9	73	.110	59

Central Division

	W	L	PCT.	GBfl
Baltimore	52	30	.634	—
Atlanta	46	36	.561	6
Houston	33	49	.402	19
Cleveland	32	50	.390	20

Western Conference
Midwest Division

	W	L	PCT.	GBfl
Milwaukee	60	22	.732	—
Chicago	51	31	.622	9
Detroit	40	42	.488	20
KC-Omaha	36	46	.439	24

Pacific Division

	W	L	PCT.	GBfl
L. Angeles	60	22	.732	—
Golden St.	47	35	.573	13
Phoenix	38	44	.463	22
Seattle	26	56	.317	34
Portland	21	61	.256	39

Playoffs

Eastern Division—Boston defeated Atlanta 4 games to 2.
N.Y. defeated Baltimore 4 games to 1.
N.Y. Defeated Boston 4 games to 3.
Western Division—Golden State defeated Milwaukee 4 games to 2.
Los Angeles defeated Chicago 4 games to 3.
Los Angeles defeated Golden State 4 games to 1.
Championship—N.Y. defeated Los Angeles 4 games to 1.

Final Scoring Leaders

	G.	F.	P.	Avg.
Archibald, K.C.-Omaha	1028	663	2719	34.0
Abdul-Jabbar, Mil.	982	328	2292	30.2
Haywood, Seattle	889	473	2251	29.2
Hudson, Atlanta	816	397	2029	27.1
Maravich, Atlanta	789	485	2063	26.1
Scott, Phoenix	806	436	2048	25.3
Petrie, Portland	836	298	1970	24.9
Goodrich, Los Angeles	750	314	1814	23.9
Wicks, Portland	761	384	1906	23.8
Lanier, Detroit	810	307	1927	23.8

MOST VALUABLE PLAYER
Kareem Abdul-Jabbar, Milwaukee

ROOKIE OF THE YEAR
Bob McAdoo, Buffalo

AMERICAN BASKETBALL ASSOCIATION

Final Standings
East

	W	L	Pct.	GB
Carolina	57	27	.679	—
Kentucky	56	28	.667	1
Virginia	42	42	.500	15
New York	30	54	.357	27
Memphis	24	60	.286	33

West

	W	L	Pct.	GB
Utah	55	29	.655	—
Indiana	51	33	.607	4
Denver	47	37	.560	8
San Diego	30	54	.357	25
Dallas	28	56	.333	27

ABA Playoffs

Eastern Division—Carolina defeated N.Y. 4 games to 1.
Kentucky defeated Virginia 4 games to 1.
Kentucky defeated Carolina 4 games to 3.
Western Division— Utah defeated San Diego 4 games to 0.
Indiana defeated Denver 4 games to 1.
Indiana defeated Utah 4 games to 2.
Championship—Indiana defeated Kentucky 4 games to 3.

Final Scoring Leaders

	F.G.	P.T.	Pts.	Avg.
Erving, Virginia	889	475	2268	31.9
McGinnis, Indiana	860	517	2261	27.6
Issel, Kentucky	899	485	2292	27.3
Cunningham, Carolina	757	472	2028	24.1
Simpson, Denver	727	421	1890	23.3
Jones, Dallas	521	324	1495	22.3
Johnson, San Diego	732	195	1770	22.1
Wise, Utah	669	476	1823	22.0
Thompson, Memphis	559	549	1727	21.6
Gilmore, Kentucky	686	368	1743	20.8

MOST VALUABLE PLAYER
Billy Cunningham, Carolina

ROOKIE OF THE YEAR
Brian Taylor, N.Y.

COLLEGE BASKETBALL

MAJOR CONFERENCE CHAMPIONS

Ivy League—Penn.
Middle Atlantic, East—St. Joseph's.
Middle Atlantic, West—Lafayette.
Yankee—Massachusetts.
Atlantic Coast—N.C. State.
Southeastern—Kentucky.
Southern—Davidson.
Ohio Valley—Austin Peay.
Big Ten—Indiana.
Mid-American—Miami, Ohio.
Ohio—Capital.
Indiana Collegiate—Butler.
Big Eight—Kansas State.
Missouri Valley—Memphis State.
Southland—SW Louisiana.
Southwest—Texas Tech.
Southwestern—Alcorn A&M.
Western Athletic—Arizona State.
Big Sky—Weber State.
Pacific-8—UCLA.
West Coast Athletic—San Francisco.
Pacific Coast Athletic—Long Beach State.
Far Western—Sonoma State.

NCAA CHAMPION—UCLA.
NIT CHAMPION—Virginia Tech.

Ratings

1—UCLA
2—N.C. St.
3—L. Beach St.
4—Providence
5—Marquette
6—Indiana
7—S.W. La.
8—Maryland
9—Kans. St.
10—Minn.

All-Americans

Bill Walton, junior, U.C.L.A.
Ed Ratleff, senior, Long Beach State.
David Thompson, sophomore, No. Carolina St.
Ernie DiGregorio, senior, Providence.
Kermit Washinton, senior, America U.

LEADING SCORERS

Player, College	G	FG	FT	Pts.	Avg.
Averitt—Pepperdine	25	352	144	848	33.9
Lewis—L.A. State	24	325	139	789	32.9
Biles—Tulsa	26	323	142	788	30.3
Stewart—Richmond	19	242	90	574	30.2
Williams—Austin Peay	29	360	134	854	29.4
Lamar—SW Louisiana	28	339	130	808	28.9
Edwards—Okla. City	27	332	103	767	28.4
Terry—Arkansas	26	264	207	735	28.3
Williamson—N.M. State	18	202	86	490	27.2
Collins—Illinois St.	25	269	112	650	26.0

HOCKEY

NHL STANDINGS

(East)

	W	L	T	Pts	GF	GA
Montreal	52	10	16	120	329	184
Boston	51	22	5	107	330	235
Rangers	47	23	8	102	297	208
Buffalo	37	27	14	88	257	219
Detroit	37	29	12	86	265	243
Toronto	27	41	10	64	247	279
Vancouver	22	47	9	53	233	339
Islanders	12	60	6	30	170	347

(West)

	W	L	T	Pts	GF	GA
Chicago	42	27	9	93	284	225
Philadelphia	37	30	11	85	296	256
Minnesota	37	30	11	85	254	230
St. Louis	32	34	12	76	233	251
Pittsburgh	32	37	9	73	257	265
Los Angeles	31	36	11	73	232	245
Atlanta	25	38	15	65	191	239
California	16	46	16	48	213	323

STANLEY CUP PLAYOFFS

East Preliminaries—
Montreal defeated Buffalo 4 games to 2. N.Y. defeated Boston 4 games to 1.

West Preliminaries—
Chicago defeated St. Louis 4 games to 1. Philadelphia defeated Minnesota 4 games to 2.

Semi-Finals—
Montreal defeated Philadelphia 4 games to 1. Chicago defeated N.Y. 4 games to 1.

Championship Final—
Montreal defeated Chicago 4 games to 2.

SCORING

	G	A	PTS
Esposito, Bos.	55	75	130
Clarke, Phil.	37	67	104
Orr, Bos.	29	72	101
MacLeish, Phil.	50	50	100
Lemaire, Mont.	44	51	95
Ratelle, Rangers	41	53	94
Redmond, Det.	52	41	93
Bucyk, Bos.	40	53	93
F. Mahovlich, Mont.	38	55	93
Pappin, Chi.	41	51	92

TROPHY WINNERS

Ross Trophy (Leading Scorer) Phil Esposito—Boston.

Norris Trophy (Best Defenseman) Bobby Orr—Boston.

Calder Trophy (Best Rookie) Steve Vickers—N.Y.

Hart Trophy (M.V.P.) Bobby Clark—Philadelphia.

Vezina Trophy (Leading Goalie) Ken Dryden—Montreal.

Lady Byng Trophy (Sportsmanship) Gil Perrault—Buffalo.

ALL STAR GAME
Jan. 31, N.Y.C., N.Y.
East 5, West 4

TENNIS

International Team Champions
Davis Cup—Australia.
Wightman Cup (Women) United States.
Federation Cup (Women) Australia.

Wimbledon Champions
Singles, Men—Jan Kodes.
Singles, Women—Billie Jean King.
Men's Doubles—Jimmy Connors & Ilie Nastase.
Women's Doubles—Billie Jean King & Rosemary Casals.

U.S. Open Champions
Singles, Men—John Newcombe.
Singles, Women—Margaret Court.
Men's Doubles—John Newcombe & Owen Davidson.
Women's Doubles—Virginia Wade & Margaret Court.

U.S. Indoor Champions
Men Singles—Jimmy Connors.
Women's Singles—Evonne Goolagong.
Men's Doubles—Juan Gisbert & Jurgen Fassbender.
Women's Doubles—Olga Morozova & Marina Kroskina.

U.S. Clay Court Champions
Men's Singles—Manuel Orantes.
Women's Singles—Chris Evert.
Men's Doubles—McMillian & Carmichaek.

TRACK & FIELD

NCAA CHAMPIONS
440 Yard Intermediate Hurdles—Robert Primeaux, Texas.
One Mile Run—Dave Wottle, Bowling Green.
880 Yard Run—Skip Kent, Wisconsin.
300 Meter Steeplechase—Doug Brown, Tennessee.
440 Yard Relay—Memphis State.
440 Yard Dash—Maurice Peoples, Arizona State.
220 Yard Dash—Marshall Dill, Michigan State.
Three Mile Run—Steve Prefontaine, Oregon.
One Mile Relay—UCLA.
Javelin Throw—Sam Colson, Kansas.
Pole Vault—Dave Roberts, Rice.
Triple Jump—Milan Tiff, UCLA.
Discus Throw—Mac Wilkins, Oregon.
High Jump—Reynaldo Brown, California Poly.
Team Champion—UCLA.

AAU CHAMPIONS
Three Mile Walk—John Knifton, New York A. C.
3,000 Meter Steeplechase—Doug Brown, Tennessee.
440 Yard Intermediate Hurdles—Jim Bolding, Pacific Coast Club.
220 Yard Dash—Steve Williams, San Diego T.C.
One Mile Run—Len Hilton, Pacific Coast Club.
440 Yard Dash—Maurice Peoples, D. C. Striders.
880 Yard Run—Rick Wohlhuter, U. of Chicago T. C.
Three Mile Run—Steve Prefontaine, Oregon T. C.
Javelin Throw—Cary Feldmann, Club Northwest.
Triple Jump—John Craft, Univ. of Chicago T. C.
Discus Throw—Mac Wilkins, Oregon T. C.
Pole Vault—Mike Cotton, Florida T. C.
High Jump—Dwight Stones, Pacific Coast Club.

GOLF

US OPEN—Johnny Miller.
PGA—Jack Nicklaus.
MASTERS—Tommy Aaron.
US AMATEUR—Craig Stadler.
BRITISH OPEN—Tom Weiskopf.
BRITISH AMATEUR—Dick Siderowf.
NCAA TEAM—Florida.
NCAA INDIVIDUAL—Ben Crenshaw.
WOMEN'S OPEN—Sue Berning.
WOMEN'S PGA—Mary Mills.
WOMEN'S AMATEUR—Carol Semple.
RYDER CUP—U.S.

BOXING

World Professional Champions
Heavyweight—George Foreman.
Light Heavyweight—Bob Foster.
Middleweight—Carlos Monzon.
Jr. Welterweight—Antonio Cervantes.
Lightweight—Roberto Duran.
Junior Lightweight—Kuniaki Shibata.
Featherweight—Vacant.
Bantamweight—Romero Anaya.
Flyweight—Venice Borkorsor.

HORSE RACING

Kentucky Derby
Churchill Downs, Ky.

$155,050
MARGIN 12½ Lengths

HORSE	JOCKEY
1—Secretariat	R. Turcotte
2—Sham	Pincay Jr.
3—Our Native	Brumfield

Preakness
Pimlico, Md.

$129,900
MARGIN 12½ Lengths

HORSE	JOCKEY
1—Secretariat	R. Turcotte
2—Sham	Pincay Jr.
3—Our Native	Brumfield

Awards
Horse of the Year—Secretariat.
Three-Year-Old Colt—Secretariat.
Grass Horse—Secretariat.
Two-Year-Old Colt—Protagonist.
Two-Year-Old Filly—Talking Picture.

Belmont Stakes
Belmont Park, N.Y.

$90,120
MARGIN 31 Lengths

HORSE	JOCKEY
1—Secretariat	R. Turcotte
2—Twice A Prince	Baeza
3—My Gallant	A. Cordero Jr.

Older Fillies—Susan's Girl.
Three-Year-Old Filly—Desert Vixen.
Sprinter—Shecky Green.
Steeplechase and Hurdle—Athenian Idol.

THE WORLD IN 1973 – INDEX